Sacred and
Mythological Animals

ALSO BY YOWANN BYGHAN

*Modern Druidism:
An Introduction* (McFarland, 2018)

Sacred and Mythological Animals
A Worldwide Taxonomy

YOWANN BYGHAN

McFarland & Company, Inc., Publishers
Jefferson, North Carolina

ISBN (print) 978-1-4766-7950-1
ISBN (ebook) 978-1-4766-3887-4

LIBRARY OF CONGRESS AND BRITISH LIBRARY
CATALOGUING DATA ARE AVAILABLE

Library of Congress Control Number 2020006966

© 2020 Yowann Byghan. All rights reserved

No part of this book may be reproduced or transmitted in any form or by any means, electronic or mechanical, including photocopying or recording, or by any information storage and retrieval system, without permission in writing from the publisher.

Front cover images © 2020 Shutterstock

Printed in the United States of America

*McFarland & Company, Inc., Publishers
Box 611, Jefferson, North Carolina 28640*
www.mcfarlandpub.com

To my daughter
Emmeline Isolde

Acknowledgments

My thanks are due to my good friend Margret Powell-Joss of Oban, Scotland, linguist, translator, interpreter and guide, for her reading of the initial manuscript and her helpful comments and suggestions; and to my wife Sharon Dolan-Powers, not only for proofreading the text and helping in many practical tasks, but also for suffering my daily bombardments of interesting snippets from every day's writing.

The editorial and administrative staff at McFarland, and particularly Layla Milholen, have, as always, been as kind and helpful as could be.

I am also particularly indebted to *Am Balloch Mòr* (Scottish Gaelic for the Big Boy), the second eldest of our four cats, who has faithfully sat either on my lap (or directly on the keyboard) every single day I have been working, and has therefore supervised the writing of this book from the feline point of view: other cat parents and writers will know exactly what I'm talking about. To all the gods, spirits and animals that have helped and guided me, I give very grateful thanks.

Table of Contents

Acknowledgments	vi
Preface	1

Sacred Animals and Animal Classification

1. Sacred Animal Traditions	4
2. Classification	9

Mammals (*Mammalia*)

3. Dogs (*Canidae*)	16
4. Wolves, Wild Dogs and Foxes (*Canidae*)	25
5. Cats and Wildcats (*Felidae*)	38
6. Big Cats, Hyenas and Mongooses (*Felidae* and *Viverroidea*)	46
7. Cattle (Oxen), Antelopes and Hippopotamuses (*Artiodactyla: Bovidae, Hippopotamidae*)	62
8. Sheep and Goats (*Caprinae*)	77
9. Deer, Elk and Moose (*Cervidae*)	85
10. Bears, Pandas and Raccoons (*Ursidae, Procyonidae*)	95
11. Horses and Rhinoceroses (*Perissodactyla: Equidae* and *Rhinocerotoidea*)	106
12. Camels and Giraffes (*Artiodactyla: Camelidae*)	120
13. Pigs and Hedgehogs (*Suidae, Erinaceidae*)	127
14. Elephants (*Proboscidia*)	135
15. Monkeys and Apes (*Primates*)	142
16. Hares and Rabbits (*Lagomorpha*)	151
17. Mice, Rats and Beavers (*Rodentia*)	156
18. Bats (*Chiroptera*) and Other Odd Animals	165
19. Weasels, Otters and Badgers (*Mustelidae*)	173
20. Seals and Walruses (*Pinnipedia*)	179
21. Whales, Dolphins, Porpoises and Sirens (*Cetartiodactyla, Delphiniodae, Sirenia*)	185

Birds (*Aves*)

22. General Birds and Crows (Several Orders and *Corvidae*)	198
23. Raptors (Several Orders and Families)	208
24. Freshwater Birds (Several Orders and Families)	220
25. Sea Birds (Several Orders and Families)	232
26. Chickens and Peafowl (*Galliformes*)	238
27. Perching Birds and Singing Birds (*Passeriformes*)	244
28. Cranes and Cuckoos (*Gruiformae, Otidimorphae*)	253
29. Hoopoes, Hummingbirds, Doves and Woodpeckers (Several Orders and Families)	259

Fish and Sea Animals (Several Orders and Families)

30. Sea Fish (Several Orders and Families)	268
31. Freshwater Fish (Several Orders and Families)	278
32. Crabs, Clams, Conches and Corals (*Crustacea, Mollusca, Cnidaria*)	285

Amphibians (*Amphibia*)

33. Frogs, Toads, Salamanders and Newts (Several Orders and Families)	294

Insects and Other Creepy-Crawlies
(*Insecta, Arachnidae* and *Gastropoda*)

34. Flying Insects (*Insecta*, Several Orders and Families)	302
35. Creeping, Crawling Animals (*Insecta, Arachnidae, Gastropoda*, Several Orders and Families)	312

Reptiles (*Reptilia*)

36. Snakes and Lizards (*Squamata*)	328
37. Crocodiles and Turtles (*Crocodylia, Testudines*)	344

Mythical Animals, Hybrids and Animal Gods

38. Dragons	352
39. Animal Hybrids and Monsters	357
40. Human-Animal Hybrids	364
41. Animals in the Sky	378
Glossary	391
Appendix: World Religions and Mythologies	401
Chapter Notes	409
Bibliography	419
Index	423

Preface

Humans have gathered, hunted and eaten animals for millennia, farmed them, made pets of them, used them for transport and other work, observed them, classified them, dissected them and experimented upon them. We have also worshiped them. The classical author Diodorus Siculus describes the classical Greek gods or Olympians being chased by their predecessors, the ancient giants or Titans, and transforming themselves into animal forms to hide, gods inside animals. Shamans, ancient and modern, have shape-shifted or transformed themselves into animals to achieve new vision and insight, or to take in spiritual strength and guidance from animal spirits. All the world's religions include animals somewhere in their mythologies or traditions. Even the three Abrahamic religions, Judaism, Christianity and Islam, which specifically deny that animals have souls and condemn animal worship or idolatry, make references to many different animals in their sacred literature, often as emblems or metaphors for divine attributes, and all refer to the abundance and glory of God's creation. Islamic tradition even admits ten animals into heaven, including the dog of Ashab-e-Kahaf, the ram of Hadhrat Ismail, the camel of Hadhrat Saleh and the donkey of Hadhrat Uzair.[1]

The diversity and complexity of life on our planet is a constant source of wonder, and our lives since we ourselves began as a separate species have been intricately interwoven with the lives of other animals. It is hardly surprising that in many religious and cultural traditions, animals are worshiped in their own right or as exemplars of God's, the Goddess's or the gods' beneficence and miraculous creativity.

The purpose of this book is to provide a convenient and accessible summary of the main sacred, mythological and folkloric traditions associated with various animals. It is, of course, impossible to include all animals or all religions, myths and folklore. There are perhaps 100 million species currently extant on our planet. (Nobody knows for certain, nor is there even universal agreement on what a species actually is—this point is explored further in Chapter 2.) It is estimated that there have been perhaps as many as five to ten billion species on the planet since life first appeared. In other words, a very large percentage of all the animals that have ever been in the world are now extinct, although there are many animals that are with us now which descended from the same ancestor or ancestors as the animals that are now extinct. A familiar example is the elephant (extant) and the mammoth (extinct). The family tree of extant animals with common ancestors is called a clade (see Chapter 2). Tragically, the rate at which species are disappearing has greatly accelerated, and the trend is very disturbing; several of the species included in this book may well have disappeared in 20 or 30 years' time.

There are countless animals which are fascinating, but which have little or no connection with religion or myths or folklore and are not generally considered sacred. For example, the armadillo is one of the most peculiar and interesting animals in the animal kingdom. It was known to the Aztecs and probably eaten by them. There are several distinct species, similar in shape but very different in size. The pink fairy armadillo is about 5–6 inches (13–15 centimeters) long, while the giant armadillo can grow to almost 6 feet (150 centimeters) in length and weigh 120 pounds (54 kilograms). All armadillos give simultaneous birth to four identical offspring from a single egg, so geneticists and other scientists love to use it for experiments where identical test subjects are needed. It is very prone to leprosy, mostly because of its unusually low body temperature, and humans have been known to contract leprosy from handling armadillos or eating armadillo meat. Its shell has been used for centuries to make the back of the *charango*, an Andean folk lute. However, despite all these fascinating facets of its character, the armadillo is not worshiped, considered sacred, or the subject of major religious or folkloric traditions, so it does not appear in this book, along with many other extraordinary and interesting creatures.

Sacred or mythological does not necessarily mean beloved, however. There are several animals that are feared, loathed and despised by many humans: spiders are a familiar example of the type. But these and other similar animals are considered to have supernatural qualities, or are included in religious mythologies or superstitions in folklore, so they *do* appear in this book. So also do the gods, spirits, dragons, monsters and legendary beasts that are not real animals, but are animal hybrids, or animal-human hybrids, or simply mythological creatures.

Despite these anomalies and necessary omissions, the author hopes that this summary will be informative, entertaining, and useful to those who wish to explore further the ways in which human spirituality has incorporated animal themes, images and associations in its diverse rituals, mythologies, literature and ceremonial practices. Whether the human animal is the only animal able to conceive of a divine being or beings would be the subject of a long and complex discussion. That animals have been included in human visions of divinity and supra-mundane reality is indisputable, and this book aims not to persuade or proselytize, but merely to describe the astonishingly numerous and diverse ways in which animals appear in religious, mythical and folkloric traditions.

I was inspired to write this book after reading and using Philip and Stephanie Carr-Gomm's *The Druid Animal Oracle*, which I recommend very highly; my book has a completely different approach and scope to theirs, but without their direct inspiration I would probably not have written it. I have also frequently referred to the work of Anthony Mercatante, particularly *World Mythology and Legend*, for sources. Mercatante (1940–1991) wrote several excellent books on mythology, myths and legends, covering Native American, African and Eastern cultures extensively, as well as the usually more accessible classical, Celtic and Norse traditions. I have also made extensive use of *The Greek Myths* by Robert Graves (1895–1985), surely the most comprehensive and accessible compendium of classical Greek legends. Stories and myths retold here without a source citation are from my own retellings. If I relied on a specific source for a retelling, that information is provided in a note.

Sacred Animals and
Animal Classification

1

Sacred Animal Traditions

Animals in Religion

The closely related Latin words *anima* (breath, physical life) and *animus* (soul, mind or sensibility), are derived from the Greek root ανμι, *anmi*, (literally that which breathes), which, of course, is also the root of the English word animal. Planet Earth is populated by an astonishingly large number of animal species, as yet not finally reckoned. Humans are animals too, and we have interacted with other species in a variety of ways for millennia. In some cultures, clans or tribes have associated themselves with particular animals, sometimes adopting the animal name as the tribal name. Groups and individuals have adopted certain animals as their totems, or simply kept animals as domestic pets. In Europe, familiar spirits (often simply called familiars) were spiritual guides who presented themselves in animal form, or in actual animals, to help practitioners, usually pagan, to engage with magical, philosophical and mystical activities; the witch's cat and the druid's crow or raven are well-known examples. In many religions, animals are sacred, or represent important spiritual attributes which the celebrant or acolyte should recognize and pursue.

The three Abrahamic religions, Judaism, Christianity and Islam, deny that any animal can ever be sacred: only humans have souls. Animals can, however, be symbols or emblems of the sacred—the Christian Lamb of God is an obvious example—but these religions tell us that animals themselves were created to feed, serve and please human beings, nothing more.

Having said that, it is worth noting that animals are not entirely ignored in the Abrahamic religions. Indeed, the Qur'an, in one of its earliest *surahs*, goes out of its way to explain that even the lowliest of animals, such as spiders, flies or other insects, may be used to illustrate God's truth: "Behold! Allah is not ashamed to propound the parable of a gnat, or even of something more lowly. On hearing these parables the believers know that it is the truth from their Lord."[1] But Moses, who figures prominently in all three religions, orders his people to slaughter a cow to prove that they are not infected with the error of animal worship, and gives precise instructions as to what nature of cow would be most suitable for the sacrifice when they appear reluctant to follow God's commandment:

> They said: "Pray to your Lord that He make clear to us what she is like." Moses answered: "He says, she is a cow, neither old nor immature, but of an age in between the two. Do, then, what you have been commanded." They said: "Pray to your Lord that He make clear to us of what color she is." Moses answered: "He says, she is a yellow cow, with a bright color which is pleasing to those who see!" They said: "Pray to your Lord that He make clear to us what cow she is. Cows seem much alike to us, and if Allah wills, we shall be guided." Moses answered: "Lo! He says, she is a cow unyoked to plough the earth or to water the tillage, one that has been kept secure, with no blemish upon her!" Thereupon they cried out: "Now you have come forth with the information that will direct us aright." And they slaughtered her although they scarcely seemed to do so.[2]

Other religions not only use animals as symbols or exemplars of sacred characteristics, they also include some animals into their pantheons of divine beings, or they represent their divine beings in animal form. The vast majority of animals that are sacred in human religions are either mammals or birds. In terms of species and diversity, the insects and other allegedly lower orders of animals vastly outnumber even the vast number of mammal and bird species, but they rarely figure in sacred traditions, for the obvious reason that we are more likely to imagine as sacred those species with which we most frequently knowingly and deliberately interact. In the course of history, humans have probably interacted (mostly unknowingly) with a greater number of microbial creatures, fleas and bedbugs and the like, than with horses, dogs, cats, parrots and crows, but it is the latter rather than the former which have become part of many of our religious traditions.

Oracular Animals

Birds figure commonly as oracular animals in many traditions, probably because most of them fly and can therefore be seen as moving between heaven and earth, or the Otherworld and this world. Bird song also presents us with a complex variety of sounds that suggest language. It is not surprising, then, that the flight of birds and bird song have been used in many religious traditions for the purposes of divination. The Greeks and Romans both placed great store in bird augury. There was a dove oracle in ancient Boeotia dedicated to Zeus. Parrots, perhaps the most talkative of birds, have been used to give astrological predictions in tropical regions, a practice which continues to this day with green parakeets in southern India. In the story of Noah in the Bible, it is the raven that first brings back the bad news that there is no land in sight after the Great Flood, but the dove that eventually brings news of land, carrying a small olive branch in its beak, becoming thereby a symbol of hope, peace and love.

Bird song among certain species can be as melodic and complex as human musical compositions—the French composer Olivier Messiaen was particularly influenced by bird song—so listening for news from the natural world (or from the Otherworld) in bird song is common in many traditions, particularly in Celtic Druidism. Notable oracular songbirds include the blackbird, robin, nightingale, and skylark. The swan, which does not normally sing, is reputed to sing once only, in anticipation of its own death, hence the expression "swan song." There are actually over 5,000 species of bird that are technically known as songbirds (*Oscines*, from the Latin *oscen*, songbird), although many of the songs may be repetitive and robotic, or even harsh to some ears (consider the cawing of crows and rooks).

Almost any animal can be a prophet. For example, in traditional Chinese mythology, the tortoise was an oracular animal. The shells were cut into "bones" or casting dice, which were thrown on the ground and read for prognostication, rather like rune stones in the Nordic tradition, or Tarot cards. Runes and other symbols were often carved in animal bones, horns or tusks, suggesting that many cultures have attributed foresight to different animals. Live animals can be seers too. There are countless folk tales of animals—sometimes a family pet—foretelling an imminent disaster and giving their humans a chance to escape. Birds have evacuated areas where tsunamis or earthquakes or devastating landslides have occurred some time after the birds have left. Crows, ravens, cats and hares have all been reputed to bring humans foreknowledge of future events.

Many animals have been and continue to be slaughtered following religious traditions.

Mostly the ritual protocols are to do with notions of cleanliness or uncleanliness and suitability for human consumption, as in the Jewish and Islamic traditions of *kosher* and *halal* food respectively. Some religious traditions have also used the nature of the animal's death, the disposition of its organs and entrails, and so on, for divinatory purposes. (Human victims have also been used for the same purpose, of course.)

Shamanism and Animals

A shaman is a human priest or celebrant, male or female, whose main function is to enter the world of spirits on behalf of individuals or the community. Shamanic traditions are very ancient, originating in Asia but now known and recognized in religions across the world. Typical shamanic activities include entering a trance state during ritual, practicing divination after visiting the spirit world, and healing, either individually or collectively.

In many traditions, the shaman identifies with a particular animal species. He or she may wear that animal's skin, or horns, or a mask representing the animal. He or she may "become" the animal during the trance state, the fundamental underlying belief being that animals are closer to the divine spirit than humans are able to be, because they are driven by instinct rather than by conscious intention. The obvious advantage of the wild or animal spirit being channeled through the shaman is that the oracular message can be delivered in human speech: it may be garbled or inchoate (particularly if the shaman has used drugs to induce the trance, which is a common practice), but it is still in human language.

The substances used in shamanism and elsewhere to generate religious awareness are called entheogens (from Greek, literally in + god + maker or creating the divine within). Traditional entheogens include fly agaric mushroom (*Amanita muscaria*), peyote, uncured tobacco, mescaline extracted from cacti, and alcohol brewed, fermented or distilled from a variety of sources. The shaman may often have extensive herbal and plant knowledge as well as animal knowledge. Drumming is common across many shamanic cultures, the hypnotic rhythms encouraging trance states. The shaman is not possessed or taken over by the animal spirit, as in demonic possession in Christianity or Judaism. Rather, the animal is a guide and companion on the shamanic journey. Often, several animals are invoked. Birds in particular (especially soaring birds like hawks and eagles) may lift the shaman into the spiritual realm.[3]

Shamanism is most common among indigenous peoples, where animism remains part of cultural belief. The Selkups, a Samoyedic people of northern Siberia, revere the sea duck (22 species in 10 genera, of the tribe *Mergini*) because it lives both in air (where human spirits go after death) and water (where animal spirits go after death). The Paora people of the Orinoco Basin in Venezuela depend on their shaman priests to tell them when certain animals may be hunted—the shaman acts as a kind of ecological protector, as well as guide and healer.

But shamanism, despite some neo-pagan revivals, is much less common now than it has been in the past. To some extent, this decline has been the result of Christian proselytizing, especially in Africa. Among the Inuit of North America, shamanism has declined rapidly as more modern cultural influences have become present. In general, shamanism has declined wherever small indigenous communities have also declined or disappeared, such as the Nganasan people of northern Siberia, whose last known shamanic ceremonies were filmed in the 1970s.[4]

1. Sacred Animal Traditions

Religious, Mythological and Folklore Traditions

Animism predates all organized religion. It is based on the simple idea that everything—every animal, every plant, every tree, every rock, every speck of dust—is charged with divine energy or spirit. This belief is still found to this day in various religious traditions, particularly in modern Druidism and in many ancient and indigenous traditions, such as that of the Maori of New Zealand or the Aborigines of Australia.

In early animistic religions, and even in the classical pantheons of Greece and Rome, divine beings were associated with specific animals, or became those animals in a similar way to the shaman becoming his or her totem animal. The ancient Celtic Druidic goddess Artio was a bear, and Epona was a horse. The Irish goddess the Morrígan (Great Queen) was associated with horses, wolves and crows, and could appear as any one of those animals, usually on the battlefield. Arduinna, who gave her name to the modern European forest area of the Ardennes, was a boar, an animal sacred to the early Celts for its courage and ferocity (as well as for providing what they considered the best of all animal meats). Animal gods appear all across the world and in almost every religious tradition apart from Judaism, Christianity and Islam. Cernunnos is an antlered Celtic forest god. Babi is the Egyptian baboon god. Kanaloa is the octopus god of ancient Hawaii, and Kamohoalii is a Hawaiian shark god. Ganesha is the elephant god of Hinduism. Ravgga is a fish god in Sami mythology. Urcuchillay is a llama god worshipped by the Incas. Amaguq is a trickster and wolf god worshipped by the Inuit.

For Westerners, the most familiar animal gods are usually human-shaped gods from the classical Greek and Roman pantheons who, for any number of different reasons, chose to appear as animals temporarily. Zeus, the king of the gods of Mount Olympus, seduced various goddesses and humans in animal and other forms: Europa as a bull; Antiope as a satyr, siring Amphion and Zethos; Leda, Queen of Lakedaimonia, as a swan, leading to her laying an egg from which twins were hatched; Pithia as a dove; Eurymedousa, a princess, as an ant, siring Myrmidon, whose name means Ant-Man (Greek μψρμεξ, *myrmex*, ant); Danaë, a princess of Argos, as a golden (urine) shower, siring the semi-divine hero Perseus.

There are six religious/mythological traditions in which animal-god connections are especially abundant and significant: the pantheon of ancient Egypt; the Hindu pantheon; the classical Greek and Roman pantheon; the Norse or Nordic pantheon; the Celtic Druidic pantheon; and Native American and other indigenous religions. (These are covered more fully in later chapters.) There are many similarities within these different traditions. The most common animals known to humans (e.g., dogs, cats, sheep, goats, foxes) appear in all six traditions.

In Hinduism, but also in Buddhism and Jainism, is found the doctrine of *ahimsa*, which put simply says that all life is sacred. It is related to the Buddhist and Hindu concept of *karma*, which—again put simply—says that every action or word is a cause, that every cause has an effect, and that every effect returns to the originator of the cause. Following *ahimsa*, many Hindus and Buddhists, and all Jains, are vegetarians or vegans. Jains are known for sweeping the ground where they are about to walk, so that not even the tiniest insect is killed. Jains may also wear face masks to prevent them from accidentally killing insects by breathing them in. In many Buddhist temples, priests are forbidden from traveling in the rainy season, for fear that they will inadvertently kill insects or very small animals in the muddy ground with their robes or sandals.

Human attitudes to other animal species are continually changing. In the increasingly secular and scientific communities of the West, the idea that animals are or might be sacred has mostly disappeared, but the many different cultures in which that idea developed are still changing slowly. Very few Westerners now worship horses or believe them to be sacred, but by the same token many Western cultures still do not accept the eating of horse flesh, or dog flesh or cat flesh, for that matter. I think there is a good argument to be made, in fact, for thinking that increased mechanization and the ending of traditional interdependent roles of animals for work and transport, for example, have released us to think more about the animals around us as sentient beings in their own right, not just as utilitarian supports for the human species.

Philip Carr-Gomm takes this idea of sympathetic connection further. He expresses very succinctly how a closer understanding of animals brings us closer to our own spiritual truths, our inner beings:

> Our Judeo-Christian culture has taught us to be afraid of animals—our own animal nature and the animals of the wild. In teaching us to "subdue the earth" it also taught us to "subdue" our own instinctual selves. In this creation of a division between spirit and matter, mind and body, our inner animals were caged, frightened and forgotten. They appeared only in our dreams—they became the beasts that lurked at the fringes of our civilized world—werewolves and dangerous predators that symbolized the "bestial" urges of men too "civilized" to acknowledge the sacredness of the body and the animal....
> But paradoxically, as long as we reject the animals within us, we can never be truly human. To regain our humanity we embrace them—loving and coming to know each of them that exists in our hearts and souls. Working with the sacred animals can help us to do this—at the same time introducing us to a treasure-house of traditional wisdom which we can now reclaim and use for our own benefit, and for the benefit of all living beings.[5]

2

Classification

> Please note that in this book I use Greek to mean Ancient Greek unless otherwise specified. Most scientific classification names for animals are explained whenever they first appear, but the main Greek- and Latin-derived names and part-names in the book are also explained in the Glossary.

The Classification System

A system of grouping is called a taxonomy, with each level called a taxon. The complete basic taxonomy of animals has eight taxons: Domain > Kingdom > Phylum > Class > Order > Family > Genus > Species. The modern scientific classification of animals includes 108 classes of animals within 34 phyla, with the total number of species estimated as between two million and 100 million.[1] (The very wide range of this guesstimate indicates how much we still have to learn.) Since every subject in this book belongs to the kingdom of *Animalia* or animals, each description here begins with the phylum.

The word phylum comes from Greek φυλον, *phylon*, meaning race or stock, so it covers a wide general area. In simple terms, it means that the animals are either similar in shape (morphological similarity) or similar in their ancestry (developmental similarity).

Class is below phylum, and creatures in the same class generally have some specific features in common. For example, almost all members of the class of mammals (*Mammalia*) give live birth and suckle their young on breast milk.

Order is below class and indicates an even closer level of similarity. A familiar word ending in orders is *-formes* or *-iformes*, from Latin, meaning "in the shape of." An example is *Feliformes*, which means animals that are cat-shaped.

By the time we get to the next lower taxon, family, the relationship is even closer and clearer. For example, hares and rabbits both belong to the family *Leporidae*. The first part of this family name is from Latin *lepus*, meaning hare. The ending *-idae* is the standard ending for zoological families, and could be said to mean "belonging to the animal family of...."

Next below family comes genus, from Latin *genus*, meaning type, group, or race. For example, the lion (*Panthera leo*) and the tiger (*Panthera tigris*) are different species, but both members of the same genus, *Panthera*.

The last and most basic taxon is species (*leo* and *tigris* in the examples just given). A common definition of species is that it means an animal that cannot reproduce sexually unless it is with another member of its own species, but there are problems with that definition, since some species can, in fact, reproduce with other species, some species do not reproduce sexually in the normal sense, and some species actually change gender during their life cycles. Nevertheless, most people understand the concept of species well enough:

a lion, a cougar and a tiger are all very similar, and they are all obviously some kind of cat, but they are different species.

To complicate this basic eight-taxon sequence, as scientists have discovered more and more about genetics and DNA, the placing and connecting of different animals in the zoological taxonomy has introduced some more sophisticated ways of describing the relationships and, therefore, some additional levels of connection and some additional terminology.

The word clade is used for animals that share a common ancestry. It literally means branch, from Greek κλαδος, *klados*. It is also known as a monophyletic group (also from Greek, meaning one clan). A cladogram is a diagram of all the branches of the family tree of related species. Nowadays, cladograms are informed by genetic analysis and DNA coding as well as by general observations. Determining these family lines or family trees can be difficult or controversial, especially when extinct animals are involved, as they often are. Here is an example of a very predictable and very simple cladogram, using observed characteristics rather than technical data, which shows—not surprisingly—that fur seals and sea lions are more closely related to walruses than foxes or dogs are, because they share more of the same characteristics:

Characteristic	Canid (e.g. dog, fox)	Bear	Seal	Fur Seal and Sea Lion	Walrus
Feeds young on milk	Yes	Yes	Yes	Yes	Yes
Short tail	No	Yes	Yes	Yes	Yes
Arms become flippers	No	No	Yes	Yes	Yes
Very flexible spine	No	No	Yes	Yes	Yes
Hind limbs under body	No	No	No	Yes	Yes
Has tusks	No	No	No	No	Yes[2]

The Latin prefixes *super-* and *sub-*, meaning above and below, respectively, are well known. In zoological taxonomy, there is an additional level between order and family called superfamily, and another between family and genus called subfamily. Above species (only in the sense of being more general, not of being superior) is the description type species, which means "the typical or most common version of this animal." Below species is subspecies, which may indicate a variant or less frequent version of the main species. There are subphyla and superorders and magnorders as well as grandorders, and suborders and infraorders. Within families there may be not only subfamilies but also tribes. Taxonomy can get very complicated very quickly.

There are still many disputes about the relationships between extant species of animals, and even more about the relationships between extant species and extinct species, for the obvious reason that living animals can be put together to see whether or not they can mate and produce offspring successfully, whereas extinct or fossil species cannot. However, animal classification continues to become more and more precise and informative, as well as more complicated, as our knowledge increases.

Naming Animals

Animals are generally known by their common names, rather than their scientific names, in ordinary parlance. The common names obviously vary from language to lan-

2. Classification

guage. The scientific name, however, usually does not change, is international, is almost always based on either Greek or Latin roots, and is used in all serious discussion. In a few cases, the English common name and the scientific name are the same. For example, the common name hippopotamus and the scientific name *Hippopotamus amphibius* are both derived from the Greek roots ἱππος, *hippos*, meaning horse, and ποταμος, *potámos*, meaning river, the whole therefore meaning river horse (even though the hippopotamus is not actually a horse and doesn't necessarily live in a river).

The accepted scientific way of naming animals is based on the binomial (two-names, genus and species) classification system originally devised over 250 years ago by the Swedish botanist and zoologist Linnaeus (Carl von Linné, 1707–1778). For example, all hedgehogs belong to the kingdom *Animalia* (animals), the phylum *Chordata* (having a spine), the class *Mammalia* (mammals), the order *Eulipotyphla* (truly fat and blind or short-sighted), the family *Erinaceidae* (shrew-like, with long snouts and short tails) and the subfamily *Erinaceinae* (spiny mammal). Within this subfamily there are several genera and 17 species of hedgehog. Each species is named in two names, the first being the genus name, which is always capitalized, the second being the species name, which is never capitalized. For example, most pet or domestic hedgehogs belong to or are hybridized from two species, *Atelerix albiventris* (white-bellied hedgehog) or *Atelerix algirus* (Algerian hedgehog). The long-eared hedgehog is *Hemiechinus auritus*, and the Indian long-eared hedgehog is *Hemiechinus collaris*. If the genus name and the species name are the same, the name is simply repeated. Thus, a fox is *Vulpes vulpes* and a lynx is *Lynx lynx*.

The beauty of the system is its simplicity. Even when there are many closely related species, the scientific name is always short, simple and precise (even though there may be disagreements about which name is more correct or accurate). Sometimes a third name may be added to identify a subspecies or as a further descriptor or distinguishing characteristic. For example, *Felis sylvestris* (literally cat of the woods) generally refers to wild cats whereas the domestic cat may be written as either *Felis catus* or *Felis sylvestris catus* or *Felis catus domestica* to make clear that it refers to the subspecies of domestic cats, not to wild or feral cats.

Simple and efficient as this system is, there are still many issues concerning classification of particular species, as already described. To take just one example, there are some obvious correspondences between rats, mice, hares and rabbits, but there are also some obvious differences: rats and mice certainly appear more closely related to each other, as do hares and rabbits to each other. That is because, although they are all furry and have comparatively big teeth, they belong to different orders, rats and mice to the order *Rodentia* (rodents) and hares and rabbits to the order *Lagomorpha* (lagomorphs, from Greek λαγος, *lagos*, hare, and μορφε, *morphé*, shape), which also includes the pika, a small mammal with round ears and no tail that looks like a cross between a rabbit and a mouse. But the orders *Rodentia* and *Lagomorpha* appear from fossil records to have a shared history, and therefore they are connected in the clade *Glires*, which (confusingly) is the Latin for dormice. To complete this particular taxonomic overview, rats and mice (*Rodentia*) and hares, rabbits and pikas (*Lagomorpha*) are all in the clade *Glires*; along with tree-shrews (*Scandentia*), they are all in the superorder *Euarchontoglires*, which also includes *Primatomorpha* such as flying lemurs (*Dermoptera*) and even a group of now extinct primates. All this complexity has developed considerably since the days when the Romans called both rats and mice by the same word *mus* (mouse), distinguishing them only by size. In other words, although the species nomenclature may be simple, the classification itself may have a long history and may now be very complicated and sometimes disputed.

Of the 34 phyla, many are groupings of animals with which we hardly ever knowingly interact, even though we may recognize (or occasionally use or even eat) some of them, such as *Acoelomorpha* (flatworms), *Annelida* (segmented worms), *Cnidaria* (jellyfish, corals and anemones), *Echinodermata* (starfish and sea urchins) and *Porifera* (sponges). For obvious reasons, these less-familiar animals rarely if ever appear in religious traditions.

Mammals

Mammals, the class within which most sacred animals are found, are any vertebrates within the class *Mammalia*, from the Latin *mamma*, meaning breast. They are distinguished from other classes by the possession of a neocortex (the part of the brain involved in higher functions like perception and language), hair or fur (as opposed to feathers or scales), three middle ear bones, and mammary glands or breasts, which females use to nurse their young. Mammals may live on land, in the sea, in trees, or underground. They may have two legs, four legs, or none. They may be huge (for example, whales, the largest animals on the planet) or tiny (for example the bumblebee bat, one of the smallest). Most mammals are placentals, i.e., having a placenta which feeds the fetus during gestation. Five species (including the famous duck-billed platypus, see Chapter 18) lay eggs, but the vast majority of mammals give birth to live young. Modern mammals emerged after the non-avian dinosaurs became extinct.

We humans are mammals, of course. We think of ourselves as superior to all other mammals because of our comparatively large brains, intelligence, use of tools, and ability to manipulate our environments, but in fact these characteristics are also found in quite a few other mammal species. Domesticated mammals, in particular dogs, cats, horses, cattle, sheep, goats, camels and elephants, played a huge part in the human transition from hunter-gatherer to farmer and crop grower. From earliest times, they have provided transport, power, food, hides and leather, milk and cheese, or wool. Domesticated mammals and hunted wild mammals figure very largely in human religious traditions.

Birds

Birds (*Aves*) also figure largely in myth and religious traditions. Birds are defined as a group of vertebrates with feathers and beaked jaws without teeth. They lay hard-shelled eggs (reptiles and egg-laying mammals lay soft-shelled, leathery eggs) and have a lightweight skeleton, which enables most of them to fly. They are descended from the avian dinosaurs, emerging some six million years ago. Like mammals, they can be very big (the ostrich stands about 9 feet, 8 inches, or 2.75 meters, tall) or very small (the bee hummingbird is about 1.8 inches, or 5 centimeters, long). The vast majority are passerines, which means that they perch on branches, usually having claws that extend forwards and backwards to wrap around the branch. Some species have been domesticated and farmed for their meat, eggs and feathers, but the birds that appear most frequently in sacred myths and legends, such as the swan, the owl and the eagle, are wild birds.

Insects

Insects or *Insecta* (from Latin *insectum*, which means "cut into sections") are classified within the arthropod phylum, which means that they are exoskeletal (have a shell-like skeleton on the outside rather than a bony skeleton on the inside) and have paired legs or appendages. Insects, spiders and crustaceans are all arthropods. Insects, the largest group, always have six legs (spiders and crustaceans have eight or ten). Their exoskeleton is made from a hard substance called chitin, similar to human nails, which is also frequently strengthened with calcium carbonate or chalk. They usually have a three-part body (head, thorax and abdomen). It is estimated that there may be between six and ten million different species of insect, and that they may make up about 90 percent of all animal species on Earth, but nobody knows for certain. Several species can fly, and some can literally walk on water. Some have been farmed by humans (silkworms and honeybees, for example), some are still regularly eaten by humans as food (particularly grubs and larvae), some are recognized as playing an essential role in pollination, but many are regarded simply as pests. Nevertheless, some insects, notably the bee, are counted among the sacred animals.

Arachnids

Spiders, like insects, are joint-legged invertebrates or arthropods, but they belong to the class *Arachnida*, and all arachnids have eight legs rather than six. Scorpions, ticks, and mites are also arachnids. The arachnids, especially the spider and the scorpion, feature in several myths and legends, and some sacred traditions.

Fish

There are about 30,000 species of fish, divided into several classes or types. Those with webs of skin stretched over radial bony spines are called *Actinopterygii*, or ray-finned fishes, which make up about 99 percent of all known fishes. Those with lobed fins are called *Sarcopterygii*. *Chondrichthyes* is the class that contains the cartilaginous fishes; sharks, rays, skates, and sawfish are in this class. Several fish appear in religious traditions, most notably the salmon.

Cephalopods

Cephalopods (the name is from the Greek κεφαλοποδα, *kephalópoda*, meaning head-feet) include squid, cuttlefish and octopus. They are known in many fishermen's traditions as inkfish because they squirt dark liquid as a defense mechanism. There are about 800 living species of cephalopods, but two fossil species are also well known: the *Ammonoidea* (ammonites) and *Belemnoidea* (belemnites). The monstrous Kraken of northern mythology and quite probably the Gorgon of Greek mythology are forms of the octopus, whose unusual intelligence for a marine animal has only recently been understood.

Crustaceans

There are six classes of crustaceans, of which *Malacostraca* is the largest. The name, coined by the French zoologist Pierre André Latreille in 1802, comes from Greek words meaning soft-shelled, which is misleading because the shells are usually only soft for the brief period when they are newly formed. The *Malacostraca* class contains about 40,000 living species, including crabs, lobsters, crayfish, shrimp, krill, woodlice and many others. They live in the sea, in fresh water, and on land. Crabs appear in religious traditions as far apart as Peru, Africa and China.

Amphibians

Amphibians belong to the class *Amphibia*, with all modern living amphibians in the sub-class *Lissamphibia*, which includes frogs, toads, salamanders, newts and caecilians. They live in a wide range of habitats, but they usually begin as larvae with gills living in water and then undergo a metamorphosis into air-breathing land animals. Frogs and toads appear in many religious and mythological traditions.

Reptiles

For many people, the word reptile usually just means snake, but the class actually includes a huge number and variety of animals. For some scientists, birds (*Aves*) should also be included in the class *Reptilia*, since they are descended from dinosaurs, but that is a minority view, since birds have been around for long enough and in sufficient numbers to warrant a class of their own. The *Reptilia* class also includes turtles, crocodiles and alligators, and lizards, as well as snakes. All of these animals feature in religious traditions.

Gastropods

The *Gastropoda* or gastropods, more commonly known as snails and slugs, form a very large class (somewhere between 65,000 and 80,000 species) within the phylum *Mollusca*. The class includes not only land snails and slugs but also many marine animals, including whelks, periwinkles, conches and others. Surprisingly for such humble animals, some of these appear in sacred traditions.

Mammals
(*Mammalia*)

3

Dogs (*Canidae*)

Dog (*Canis familiaris* or *Canis lupus familiaris*)

Phylum *Chordata*, Class *Mammalia*, Order *Carnivora*, Family *Canidae*, Genus *Canis*, Species *Canis familiaris* or *Canis lupus familiaris*, Sub-species *Canis lupus familiaris*

Name

The common name dog has a curious history. The original Old English name *hund* survives in modern English as hound. A late and rare Old English word *docga* was used for a particular breed, but seems to have then become the general name for the whole species, although why is not clear.[1] *Canis* is simply Latin for dog. *Lupus*, Latin for wolf, indicates the connection with wolves. *Familiaris* means familiar or common.

Description

The dog is the first animal ever domesticated by man. The earliest undisputed dog remains date from about 14,700 years ago, while other remains dating from over 36,000 years ago have also been proposed as being from a domesticated dog. The dog is closely related to the wolf (*Canis lupus*), both being members of the family *Canidae*. It is also the most abundant terrestrial carnivore, being found in every part of the world apart from a few isolated maritime regions, such as Tierra del Fuego and some islands or island groups in the Pacific. Known since ancient times and very abundant, it is the most familiar animal in the world. There are now about 340 recognized breeds, divided into 10 groups by general function: sheepdogs and cattle dogs; pinschers and schnauzers; terriers; dachshunds; spitzes; pointers and setters; retrievers, flushing dogs and water dogs; companion and toy dogs; sighthounds.[2]

The domestic dog appears to be descended from a wolf species that no longer exists in the wild. Tame dogs were almost certainly used by early hunters, but herding other animals and providing protection were probably the tasks which most strongly cemented the bond between humans and dogs in the earliest stages of the transition from nomadic hunting and gathering to farming and settled communities.

General Attributes

Domestic dogs have two characteristics that separate them from wild dogs. The first is that they readily form attachments with humans, showing affection, discipline and loyalty.

The second is that they are able to digest cereals and starchy foods in their diets, similar to omnivorous humans, and unlike wild dogs, which are essentially entirely carnivorous and unable to easily process foods other than meat.

In the West, we tend to think of dogs as family pets or working animals, but it has been estimated that about 75 percent of the world's dogs are wild, feral or live as village or community dogs with no particular owners. Dogs are eaten by humans in some countries, notably Korea, Vietnam and China, but not generally in Western society. The Yeruba of southwestern Nigeria in Africa sacrifice and eat dogs in honor of their god of iron and war, Ogun Onire.

Dogs are thought to have been in Europe as early as 18000 BCE, if not millennia earlier, and there is good archaeological evidence that they were used to herd reindeer at about that time (domesticated animals show skeletal changes). Hunting dogs may well have retained some of the ferocity of wolves, and the religious and mythological traditions associated with dogs show some ambivalence between their loyal, friendly, obedient nature and their capability for inflicting harm.

Dogs are best known in modern times as working dogs, mostly herders of sheep and other animals, and as loyal guardians and pets. In the West, dogs are now almost all either working dogs or family pets, so their general status within the animal kingdom is high—which is why they are so abundant and found in almost every part of the world.

The overriding religious, mythical and folkloric persona of dogs is as loyal companions and faithful servants to humans. As helpers in hunting, as herders of sheep and other animals, as guardians of families, homes and communities, dogs have been "man's best friend" for thousands of years, and the respect and affection that many humans feel for dogs are reflected in countless religious and folkloric stories. Having said that, it is also true that dogs are portrayed as worthless, or even evil, in some cultures—and, as we have seen above, they are just meat animals for some people.

The willingness of the domesticated dog to please and serve humans is attractive to most, but unimpressive or even contemptible to others. As a sacred or mythological animal, the dog gets generally favorable reviews, but a mixed press in some locations.

Marindi

In Australian Aboriginal mythology, Marindi was a dog whose blood stained rocks red and produced the pigment ochre, which is still widely used in Aboriginal art. Marindi was challenged to a fight by the tiny Adno-artina, a gecko lizard. Marindi was convinced that he would snap up the lizard in a trice, but Adno-artina had tied string around the root of his tail so that his courage could not leak out, and he clung on ferociously once he had leaped up and seized Marindi by the throat. Marindi's blood sprayed everywhere, producing red rocks and ochre.

The Stink Eye

When herds succumb to disease or accident, several societies believe that the herd has been bewitched by the Evil Eye, and that dogs as well as humans are capable of this magic. In mainland Italy, this is called the *Mallochio*, and in Sardinia the *Ocru Male*, sometimes called in English the Stink Eye. It is a commonplace of folk knowledge that in a staring contest dogs will always lower their gaze before humans do. However, if a dog persists in staring, it may be working the Stink Eye.

Chinese Zodiac and Mythology

A hunting dog is one of the twelve animals in the Chinese Zodiac (see Chapter 41). People born under the sign of the dog are supposed to share their qualities of loyalty, exuberance and playfulness.

Di Ku, a semi-historical Chinese emperor, had a pet dog named Panhu. Di Ku promised that whoever brought him the head of his enemy would be allowed to marry the imperial princess. The dog Panhu achieved the feat, and in order to marry the princess put himself beneath a magical bell for 280 days so that he could turn into a human. Di Ku had the bell lifted a day early, and Panhu emerged with a human body but a dog's head. Nevertheless, Di Ku kept his promise, Panhu married the princess, and they had many descendants who went on to found great dynasties. In honor of Panhu, several peoples in China, notably the Yao, She, Miao and Li, refuse to eat dog meat.[3]

The Chinese mythical hero Erlang, who is similar to the classical Herakles/Hercules, has an unnamed dog companion. (There are no articles or distinctions between nouns and proper nouns in Mandarin, so dog can also mean Dog, i.e., an animal with the personal name Dog.) Erlang's dog performs several heroic feats, including biting the head off an insect monster.

A myth from the ethnic Tibetan people in Sichuan credits another unnamed dog with bringing grain to humans. According to this rather earthy tale, the world was abundant with grains, but humans only used the grown plants to wipe themselves clean after defecating, and the God of Heaven, annoyed and disgusted, came down to Earth to repossess all the grains he had provided. The faithful dog bit into the God of Heaven's trouser leg as he was leaving, whining and pleading piteously on humankind's behalf, and the God of Heaven relented, leaving behind a few seeds of every grain known to humans, from which all current grains are descended.

Ch'en Nan was a legendary Chinese sage, reputed to have lived for 1,350 years. (His name is Chinnan in Japan, where he is also recognized.) According to the legend, he lived for so long because he ate sacred dogs' flesh and almost nothing else. In a terrible drought, he found a dragon hiding in caked mud and forced it out of its hiding place, which caused life-saving rain to fall. In most depictions of him, he is coaxing the dragon out of the mud, rather than chewing on a dog's leg.

Foo Dogs or Fu Dogs are lion-dogs. Both lion-like and dog-like, they are frequently represented in statues outside important buildings, including temples. The dog breed Chow Chow (or simply Chow) is said to be a real-life model of a Foo Dog. It has a sturdy body, thick fur, and a curly tail. One legend has it that Queen Victoria carried her beloved Chow Chow puppy everywhere with her, and that the teddy bear toy was modeled after her dog, although the better-known story is that the toy was named after American President Theodore (Teddy) Roosevelt.

In some Chinese legends, eclipses are caused by a celestial dog eating the Sun or the Moon, until other deities and human prayers frighten them away. Eclipses have supernatural explanations in many other mythologies.

Philippines

In the mythological traditions of the Tinguian Islands in the Philippines, Kimat (Lightning) is the hunting dog of the god Tadaklan or Kadaklan, who like the Norse Thor or the classical Zeus, creates storms and thunder. During storms, Tadaklan is said to be playing his drums to entertain himself. Kimat can also create thunder and lightning bolts, but he is said to avoid striking any house where another dog is present, so some people believe that having a pet dog in the house is a protection against lightning strikes.

India

Muthappan, a god from the North Malabar region of India who combines features of both Vishnu and Shiva, also has an inseparable unnamed hunting dog companion, and his worshippers bring bronze hunting dog figurines in offering at his temple shrines. The Muthappan Temple at Parassinikkiadavu has many live dogs and puppies roaming at large within the temple, and there is a story that, when the authorities some years ago tried to remove some of the animals because of overcrowding, the priests lost the power to speak or move and prayer activities came to a grinding halt, beginning again only when the dogs and puppies were returned to their temple home.

Ah Puch

Ah Puch, who is also called Yum Cimil (Lord of Death), is the god of death in Mayan mythology. He is associated with three animals of death: the dog, the Moan bird, and the owl.

Burkhan's Dog

In Siberian mythology, the god Burkhan created the first man, leaving him lifeless and covered in thick hair from head to toe. Burkhan left his dog to guard the as-yet lifeless body, but the dog was tempted with food by the devil Shulman, who licked much of the hair off the man's body while the dog was eating his tidbits. According to the Buryat people, humans would never have known sickness if it had not been for the foolishness and greed of Burkhan's dog.[4]

Torongoi and Edji

Also from Siberia comes a myth very similar to the Christian story of Adam and Eve but with a few interesting differences. Torongoi and Edji, the first man and woman, were created with thick fur on their bodies so that they would not get cold. They were told by God that they could eat fruit from branches that pointed towards the sunrise, but not from branches that pointed towards the sunset. To help them, God set a dog and a snake to bite the Devil if he should come by. The Devil did come by, of course. He crept inside the skin of the sleeping snake, and, in his disguised form, persuaded Edji to eat the forbidden fruit.

Edji in turn persuaded Torongoi. They became so anxious about what God would say to them that their fur fell off, and humans have had to cover their naked skin with clothes ever since. God returned, saw the couple in their nakedness, and asked them what had happened.

"It's not my fault. Edji made me eat the fruit," said Torongoi.

"It's not my fault. The snake made me eat it," said Edji.

"It's not my fault. The Devil was inside me," said the snake.

"I didn't see anything," said the dog.[5]

Adu Ogyinae's Dog

According to the creation legends of the Ashanti of Ghana in Africa, Adu Ogyinae was the first human being. He emerged from a huge worm hole in the ground, accompanied by seven other men and a small group of women, a leopard, and a dog. Adu Ogyinae was the only one who showed no fear of all the new and wonderful things they saw. Ironically, Adu was the first to die, when a tree fell on him. The others, still relatively helpless, sent the dog to find fire. When the dog returned with a blazing branch, they cooked some meat. However, they were still uncertain, so they gave the dog a little of the meat to try first. When the dog showed no signs of illness, they also ate it themselves.[6]

Argos

When Odysseus returns after an absence of twenty years in Homer's classical Greek epic poem *The Odyssey*, only his faithful (and now very old) dog Argos recognizes him. Odysseus has disguised himself as a beggar so that he can investigate the many suitors gathered around his wife Penelope. He finds Argos neglected, flea-bitten, and lying on a dung-heap. In a very moving passage, Argos whimpers and wags his tail to greet Odysseus, but he is too old and sick to stand. Odysseus walks by without acknowledging the dog in order to preserve his disguise. Argos, broken-hearted, dies.[7]

Kerberos/Cerberus

In classical mythology, Kerberos or Cerberus is the three-headed dog that guards the entrance to Hades, the Underworld. In various tales, he has one head, fifty heads or a hundred heads. He may also have a serpent tail, or several snakes attached to him. The twelfth and last labor of Herakles or Hercules is to capture Kerberos and bring him to King Eurystheus of Tiryns. In order to enter the Underworld and complete the task, Herakles is initiated into the Eleusinian Mysteries and guided by Hermes and Athena. He carries a lion-skin shield. He is not allowed to use iron or any other metal to subdue the dog, so, according to different variations of the legend, he uses a wooden club, a stone-tipped spear, or just his bare hands. He brings Kerberos to Eurystheus, then releases him. It was once thought that the Greek name κερβερος, *kerberos*, was derived from a Proto-Indo-European word meaning spotted one, and it would be amusing to think of the most terrifying mythological dog in the world being called Spot, but that theory is now discredited.[8]

Other Guard Dogs

In several early religious traditions, dogs were typically guardians. For example, the ancient Mesopotamian goddess Ninisina or Nintinugga, a goddess of healing, was frequently depicted as being attended by a seated dog, representing magical protection; she is reputed to have breathed life back into mankind after the Great Flood. Orthus is a two-headed guard dog, featured in Dante's *Divine Comedy*.

Similarly, a four-headed dog called Garm or Garmr guards Helheim (Niflheim in some versions) in Norse mythology. He is chained in a cave called Gnipahellir. At Ragnarök (the Day of Judgment, the end of the world) Garm will break his chains and kill the god Tyr, and in turn be killed by Tyr at the same stroke.

As well as multiple heads, sacred guard dogs sometimes had multiple eyes. In the Zoroastrian religion of ancient Persia, the Chinvat Bridge, which separates the world of the living from the world of the dead, is guarded by two four-eyed dogs, the four eyes presumably indicating exceptional visual perception, like that of the god Heimdal who guards Bifröst, the bridge to Asgard in Norse mythology. Yama, lord or master of death in Hinduism, also has two four-eyed dogs, which guard the gates of Naraka, the Hindu equivalent of Hell, where sinners are tormented after death.

The Zoroastrians of ancient Persia placed dead bodies to decompose and be eaten by birds on a special tower called a *dokhma*, but only after death had been confirmed by a dog approaching the corpse. The same rite, called *sag-did* (the glance of the dog) is still practiced by Parsees in India. In Persian mythology, Nasu is a corpse demon, the personification of bodily corruption, plague, decomposition, and impurity. He often appears in the form of flies surrounding the body, but is driven away by the glance of the dog in the *sag-did* rite.

The Dog and the Shadow

Æsop (c. 620–564 BCE) is famous as an Ancient Greek storyteller, even though none of his actual writings has survived, and there is no absolute proof that he even existed. Nevertheless, from classical times to the present day, his short stories, mostly fables about animals, have been immensely popular.[9]

One of the many fables attributed to Æsop tells of a dog stealing a piece of meat and running away with it. The dog crosses a footbridge over a stream. Seeing his reflection in the water, the dog believes he sees another dog with another piece of meat. He drops his own piece of meat and jumps into the stream where, of course, he finds nothing. The stream rapidly carries his original piece of meat away.

Moral: Grasp at the shadow and lose the substance.

See also **jackal**, Chapter 4.

Dogs in the Celtic Underworld

In *Pwyll Prince of Dyfed*, one of the tales from the Welsh mediaeval stories known collectively as the *Mabinogi* or *Mabinogion*, Pwyll (pronounced approximately *pwilth*) is hunting with his dogs in the forest when another pack of dogs approaches. We know that these dogs are from the Underworld because of their red and white coloring, red and white being the colors of death in early Celtic Druidism:

> Of all the hounds he had seen in the world, he had seen no dogs the same color as these. The color that was on them was a brilliant shining white, and their ears red; and as the exceeding whiteness of the dogs glittered, so glittered the exceeding redness of their ears.[10]

The hounds belong to Arawn Pen Annwn, the king of the Underworld. Pwyll drives them away from the stag they have caught and allows his own pack to finish off the stag, which Arawn not unreasonably takes as an insult. In recompense for the insult, Arawn asks Pwyll to look after the kingdom of Annwn for him for a year, since he has to go off and fight a battle with someone else and needs a caretaker king. Arawn shape-shifts Pwyll into his own likeness. Pwyll spends a year and a day ruling Annwn in Arawn's place, while Arawn, in the form of Pwyll, rules Pwyll's kingdom of Dyfed and brings fertility and prosperity to its people. Pwyll rises admirably to the challenge of ruling Annwn wisely, including having the decency to avoid making love to Arawn's queen despite spending every night for a year in the same bed with her. After the end of the year, when they have changed back into their own bodies and semblances, Pwyll takes on the honorific title of Pen Annwn (Chief of the Underworld), and returns to long and successful rule over Dyfed.

Ghost Dogs and Black Dogs

In Christian legends, ghost dogs (particularly black ghost dogs, sometimes called grims) guard churches and holy places, their fierceness discouraging impious and sacrilegious activities. In Western folklore, seeing a black dog is often said to presage death. By the 20th century, the capitalized Black Dog referred to a ghost dog or evil dog spirit of any color, of which there were many reported sightings. Most were identified by their locality, e.g., the Black Dog of Newgate or the Black Dog of Bungay. Many UK sightings have been reported, particularly in Lincolnshire, North Devon and Cornwall, all of which have ancient herding trackways where guard dogs may have accompanied packhorses and wheeled carriers. A ghost dog seen frequently running between Liskeard and Launceston in Cornwall is known locally as Carrier. Black Shuck, described as "an 'orrible shaped thing," was reported in the parish church of Bungay, Suffolk, England in 1577, leaving a heap of dead bodies in its wake.[11]

The Black Dog is a metaphor for depression in modern life—Winston Churchill often complained of being followed by "the Black Dog." It seems likely that this is a modern continuation and extension of the legend of the ghostly Black Dog or grim, the harbinger or companion of death.

In the Christian legend of Saint Andrew, a dead boy is brought to the saint. The boy's father begs the saint to revive him. When questioned by the saint, the father explains that the boy was killed by seven black dogs, which the saint recognizes as seven demons that have been plaguing the people of Nicea. Saint Andrew brings the boy back to life, but only on condition that thereafter he will serve as one of the saint's disciples.[12]

In the Bible, Jezebel, the epitome of the evil woman, is killed by being thrown out of a window, and her body is eaten by dogs. This fulfills the prophecy, "The dogs shall eat Jezebel by the wall of Jezreel."[13]

One of the few positive images of a dog in Christian legends is of the pet dog of Saint Quiracus of Ostia, the port of Rome. The saint was stabbed in the back and beheaded. The faithful dog (not named in the legend) retrieved the head and brought it back, placing it in the saint's hands. In mediaeval art, Quiracus is usually portrayed holding his own head, his dog by his side.

Nodens and Lydney Park

Nodens is an early British Celtic god, frequently depicted as a dog and sometimes simply called the Dog. A large healing sanctuary at Lydney Park in Gloucestershire, England was dedicated to him. His name is related to the Irish god Nuadu Argat Lámh (Nuada of the Silver Hand). The Lydney Park sanctuary, like many others across Europe, had a special isolated sleeping chamber or dormitory called an *abaton*, where supplicants would invite the god to visit and heal them while they slept. The word is Greek, literally meaning "do not tread," indicating any extremely wild or inaccessible place. The attributes of affectionate companionship and fierce protection are obvious for the domesticated dog, but the association of dogs with healing was also very common in early Celtic society, suggesting that there was a general belief that dogs could support or promote health and recovery. Frequent observation of dogs licking their own wounds would have tended to confirm that belief.

The Celtic word for dog, *cù* in Gaelic, plural *coin*, *ci* in Welsh, plural *cŵn*, appears in warrior names and historical royal names, as well as in the names of deities. A healing sanctuary at Nettleton Shrub in Wiltshire was dedicated to the god Apollo Cunomaglus (Apollo Dog Lord). There were British kings called Cunoglasus (Red-Brown Dog) and Cunobelinus or Cunobelinn (Dog of the god Beli, better known in the form used by Shakespeare, Cymbeline).

Cú Chúlainn and Fionn mac Cúmhaill

In early Irish mythology, Cúlann the Smith (smiths were frequently associated with magic and divine power) had a fierce guard dog. The warrior-hero Setanta, still only a two-year-old child, was in Cúlann's smithy when the huge, powerful dog attacked him. Setanta coolly grabbed the dog by the throat and smashed it against a pillar, killing it instantly. The Druid Cathbad was summoned to examine the child and give judgment. He decreed that henceforth the child must guard Cúlann's smithy in place of the dog, and that his name would no longer be Setanta but would be Cú Chúlainn (Cúlann's Hound.) After many miraculous adventures and feats, Cú Chúlainn died when three female druids fed him dog-meat roasted on spits made from the sacred rowan tree. By breaking the *geis* or taboo against eating the flesh of his totem animal, he lost his strength and was soon killed in battle.

Another Irish warrior-hero, Fionn mac Cúmhaill (White or Shining One, son of Cúmhall), is surrounded by dogs which were once humans: his aunt Turen, and his two nephews Bran and Sceolang. The dog symbolizes friendship, guardianship and loyalty in Celtic mythology. Many gods, goddesses and heroes have named dogs as companions. King Arthur's dog was Caball or Cavall, a sighthound, probably a greyhound.

The Wild Hunt

A European legend of unknown date appears in several countries and languages. It seems to be pre–Christian in origin. It is based on supposed sightings (or, more frequently, hearings) of a pack of hounds crossing the sky, in search of a quarry that varies from legend to legend. They make a hideous, thunderous noise, howling and barking until the whole sky echoes with the sound. The passing of the Wild Hunt is said to presage a time of terrible calamity. In Cornwall, the pack is led by the Devil, and the hounds are called the Devil's Dandy Dogs; in Devon, England, the pack is called the Wisht Hounds; in Wales, they are *Cwn Annwn*, the hounds of Annwn, the Underworld, or hounds led by Gwynn ap Nudd, a psychopomp (guide of the dead); in northern England, they are Gabriel's Hounds. In Europe, the hounds were said to be led variously by gods like Odin or Wotan, or even by historical figures like Theodoric the Great (454–526 CE) or Valdemar Atterdag (1320–1375), King of Denmark. The name Wild Hunt (originally German *Wilde Jagd*) was popularized by Jacob Grimm (1785–1863) in his *Deutsche Mythologie* (1835).[14]

Gelert and Beddgelert

A well-known Welsh legend tells the story of the faithful hound Gelert:

The wife of Llywelyn, Prince of Gwynedd, had died in childbirth, leaving him with a baby son. Whenever he went out hunting, he left his faithful hound Gelert at home to guard the baby. (In earlier versions of the story, the father was a humble woodsman who had to go into the forest to work every day.)

One day, Llywelyn returned home to be greeted as usual by Gelert, but the dog's muzzle and paws were covered in blood, and the baby's crib was overturned. Convinced that Gelert had killed and eaten his baby son, Llywelyn drew his sword and killed the dog with a single thrust.

Riven with grief, the prince finally brought himself to tidy the mess in the room. When he picked up the overturned crib, he discovered his baby son sleeping safe and sound on the floor, and behind him, previously hidden by the crib, the body of a large and savage wolf, obviously killed by faithful Gelert to protect the child.

Realizing his terrible mistake, Llywelyn picked up the dog's body and took it outside for burial. He placed an additional stone on the grave every day for the remainder of his life, and he never smiled again. The stone pile can still be seen in the small town named after the story, Beddgelert, which means Gelert's Grave.

4

Wolves, Wild Dogs and Foxes (*Canidae*)

Wolf (*Canis lupus*)

Phylum *Chordata*, Class *Mammalia*, Order *Carnivora*, Family *Canidae*, Genus *Canis*, Species *Canis lupus*

Name

The common English name is from Old English *wulf*, which in turn is said to derive from Proto-Germanic **wulfaz*. The Latin *lupus* was borrowed from the Sabine language. Both *wulf* and *lupus* are presumed to derive from a Proto-Indo-European root **wiqos* or **lukos*. A lycanthrope (from Greek λυκανθροπος, *lukanthropos*, wolf man) is another name for a werewolf (from Old English *wer-wulf*, man-wolf).

There is a curious connection between the name for a wolf and the name for a tailless dinner jacket. A sub-tribe of the Delaware Indians called themselves the Ptuksit, meaning "round foot" in allusion to the pads of the wolf, their sacred totem animal. White settlers heard the name Ptuksit and pronounced it *tuxedo*, the closest approximation they could make. In 1890, a small country club in what is now called Tuxedo Park, New York, about forty miles from Manhattan, named after the Ptuksit people, required a tailless dinner jacket for formal occasions, and the jacket subsequently became known as a tuxedo, often shortened to tux.[1]

Description

Known also by its most common subspecies names as the gray wolf (*Canis lupus*), Eurasian wolf (*Canis lupus lupus*), eastern American timber wolf (*Canis lupus lycaon*) and northern or northwestern American timber wolf (*Canis lupus occidentalis*), the wolf is the largest of the wild dogs.

The gray wolf is the only wolf species found in both the Old World and the New World. There are 37 extant species of wolf, although some designations are disputed. All four main subspecies are famed for their gregarious nature and the complexity of the social structure of the pack. Rudyard Kipling (1865–1936) presented an Indian wolf pack led by the male elder Akela as the exemplar of civilized animal society in his *Jungle Book* stories (1894). It used to be thought that wolves in the wild followed a strictly hierarchical order of social ranking below the alpha-male, beta-male, and so on, but it is now thought that the hierarchical structure was normal only for captive wolves who were unfamiliar with each other, and that in the wild the pack follows an older male-female pairing and their first offspring.[2]

Where natural prey is readily available, wolves do not usually predate on livestock. When they do, their most common targets are sheep in Europe, domestic reindeer in Scandinavia, goats in India, and cattle and turkeys in North America. Wolves do also attack humans, although far less frequently than depicted in fiction. Wolves can become rabid, and, if and when they do, they can be far more dangerous than rabid dogs because of their greater size and strength.

General Attributes

Wolves are feared for their ferocity, but admired for their strength, endurance, and social cohesion. The wolf pack represents loyalty. A lone wolf is considered an aberration from the normal social pattern. Wolves in Europe generally live in colder, northern areas, and are respected for their hardiness and tolerance of harsh conditions.

Wolf Names

Many humans have called themselves Wolf to convince others of their superior stature. The classical name Autolycus (well known as a charming rogue in Shakespeare's play *A Winter's Tale*) is from Greek, meaning the wolf (*lycus*) itself (*auto*). Æthelwulf (Noble-Wolf) was King of Wessex in England from 839 to 858. His father had defeated King Beornwulf (Bear-Wolf) of Mercia. Cynewulf (Kin-Wolf) was a great Old English poet of the ninth century. Another Cynewulf was King of Wessex from 757 to 786. Wolfgang, Mozart's first name, means Wolf-Walk. In ancient Rome, *lupa*, meaning she-wolf, was a nickname for a prostitute, not unlike the modern epithet foxy.

American Indians

The wolf is the totem animal of two American Indian nations, the Oneida and the Pawnee. The Oneida reservation lies to the west of the Green Bay metropolitan area. The Oneida were one of the five nations of the ancient Iroquois Confederacy, the others being the Mohawk, the Onondaga, the Cayuga and the Seneca nations. The Pawnee are a Plains Indian nation now based in Oklahoma, although historically they lived in Nebraska and Kansas. The Skidi or Skiri Federation of the Pawnee historically called themselves *Ckírihki Kuuruúriki* (Look Like Wolves People) and were therefore called *Loups* (Wolves) by the French and Wolf Pawnee by Americans.[3]

The Big Bad Wolf

The Big Bad Wolf of modern cartoons is based on a very ancient archetype. A very famous Æsop fable is the story of The Boy Who Cried Wolf, i.e., invented a fictitious marauding wolf to attract attention and sympathy, and was then ignored when a real wolf attacked the flock he was supposed to be guarding. Little Red Riding Hood was first portrayed by Charles Perrault in 1697—much earlier than many people may imagine—and the wolf who eats Grandma, then threatens the little girl using human speech, is the Big Bad Wolf incarnate. The tale of the Big Bad Wolf and the Three Little Pigs dates from the 19th century in printed form, but is probably much older.

Other Æsopic Wolf Tales

There are three other well-known Æsopic wolf tales.

The first is linked to the Biblical text, "Beware of false prophets, who come to you in sheep's clothing but inwardly are ravenous wolves,"[4] which was supposedly expanded into a fable by an Italian writer called Abstemius in the 15th century, although the tale itself is simple enough to have come from Æsop or some other similar early source:

> A wolf followed a herd of sheep for days, growing more hungry and desperate each day. Finally, it found a discarded sheepskin and wrapped itself in it. It managed to fool the shepherd, and was locked in with the rest of the flock for the night. However, before it could make itself a meal, the shepherd, thinking to make himself a supper, came to the fold and grabbed the first sheep that came to hand, which quite by chance happened to be the wolf in sheep's clothing. The shepherd killed the wolf on the spot.

Moral: Appearances can be deceiving.

The second tale probably originated in India, where a lion replaces the wolf, but the moral remains the same:

> A wolf got a bone stuck in its throat after eating. It was in agony, and begged all the other animals to remove the bone for him. The other animals, naturally cautious, refused to help. Finally, a crane, persuaded by the offer of a fine reward, put its long bill all the way down the wolf's throat and carefully removed the bone, to the wolf's huge relief. However, when the crane asked for its reward, the wolf grew offended and aggressive. He told the crane to fly away before it became the wolf's next dinner.

Moral: Those who live in expectation are sure to be disappointed.

The third tale appears all over the world, with the versions in India, Madagascar and Tibet featuring a panther rather than a wolf and a kid rather than a lamb:

> A wolf was drinking from a mountain stream. He looked up and noticed a small lamb also drinking a little further downstream. He thought the lamb looked like a tasty dinner, but he needed an excuse for attacking it.
> "How dare you foul my stream?" he howled.
> "But, sir," bleated the lamb in reply, "how can I be fouling your stream? I am downstream from you."
> "Don't argue," said the wolf. "I know you were telling terrible lies about me a year ago."
> "But, sir," bleated the lamb, "a year ago I wasn't yet born."
> "Well, then," roared the wolf, "it must have been your father," and with that he leaped upon the poor lamb and tore it to pieces.

Moral: For a tyrant, any excuse will serve.

Lycaon

Lukaon or Lycaon (Greek Λυκαων, *Lukaōn*, The Wolf) is the name given to several different personages in ancient Greek mythology. Lycaon son of Aezeius, a giant, was one of the first Peloponnesian kings. Lycaon son of Pelasgus was a king of Arcadia. Lycaon son of the god Ares was killed by Herakles. Lycaon or Lycus son of the god of the sea, Poseidon, was also royal. Another Lycaon was a prince of Troy, son of Priam and Laotho. Hardly surprisingly, it is very easy to confuse one Lycaon with another. What they all have in common is their status as divine or semi-divine warriors, embodying the qualities of ferocity, strength and courage associated with the wolf. The cult of Zeus Lycaeus (Zeus the Wolf-Man) allegedly promoted cannibalism, as described by Ovid in his *Metamorphoses* and Virgil in his *Georgics*. According to the legend as told by these authors, those who ate human flesh became wolves and wandered in the wilderness for ten years before they returned to human form.

Lupercalia, Romulus and Remus

The ancient Greek festival of the Arcadian *Lykaia* celebrated the wolf. Its Roman counterpart was the *Lupercalia*, which took place every February 15.

A *februum* meant any means of cleansing or purifying, including fire, and an alternative name for the *Lupercalia* was *Dies Februa* (the Day of Cleansings.) Over time, the whole month of February took its name from this origin. The *Lupercalia* involved many rituals of cleansing and purification for the city.

A specific legend and a specific wolf were celebrated in the festival. The Lupercal was the cave in which Romulus and Remus, the legendary founders of Rome, were suckled as babes by the she-wolf Luperca, who later became a goddess of the same name. Romulus and Remus were twins born of a vestal virgin, Rhea Silvia, who had been miraculously impregnated by the god Mars. Rhea Silvia's father was Numitor, former king of Alba Longa, who had been deposed by his brother Amulius.

Amulius ordered the baby twins to be exposed to die on the banks of the River Tiber. However, Tiberinus, the father-god of the river, rescued the boys and sent them to the Lupercal, where Luperca suckled and saved them. They were subsequently raised as shepherds, having no idea of their royal and semi-divine lineage. Eventually, they discovered their heritage, restored Numitor to the throne, and set out to build a new royal city.

They argued over which hill it should be built on, the Palatine or the Aventine, then agreed to settle the argument by bird augury. Remus saw six auspicious birds and claimed victory, but Romulus then saw twelve auspicious birds. In the aftermath of the argument, Romulus or one of his supporters killed Remus. Romulus went on to found Rome and became its first king.

Fenrir and Managarm

The monster wolf Fenrir plays a significant role in Norse mythology. At Ragnarök, the Day of Judgment, Fenrir will kill and eat Odin, father of the gods, and will then destroy the world by consuming it. Until Ragnarök, Fenrir remains chained with a sword propping his jaws open so that he cannot bite. The story of Fenrir is found in the 13th-century poem the *Poetic Edda*, poet unknown, and the 13th-century prose texts called the *Prose Edda* and *Heimskringla*, written by Snorri Sturluson (1179–1241).

Fenrir was born of the hideous giantess Angurboda (Bringer of Sorrow). Odin chose to raise Fenrir, even though, as the all-seeing *Alfadir* or Allfather, he was perfectly aware that Fenrir will eventually be the agent of his death and the destruction of the world.

As the wolf grew bigger, the Æsir tried different methods for binding him. Fenrir burst apart the first iron fetter, called Leyding, without any difficulty. The gods made a second fetter of huge chains, called Dromi, twice as strong as Leyding. Fenrir broke it with similar ease. The Æsir therefore sent messengers down to Svartálfaheimr (Black Dwarf Land) and the dwarfs sent back a magical fetter, thin and soft as a silk ribbon, called Gleipnir. Fenrir was rightly suspicious of the magical fetter.

To prove that he did not need to be fettered, Fenrir challenged any of the gods to put a hand in his mouth. The war-god Tyr accepted the challenge. The instant Tyr put his hand in Fenrir's mouth, Gleipnir tightened around Fenrir's body. Infuriated, Fenrir bit off Tyr's hand. The gods then took a cord hanging off Gleipnir and tied it to a great rock called Thviti. They also thrust a sword between Fenrir's jaws.

Fenrir remains fastened by Gleipnir to Thviti to this day, but when he escapes, then Ragnarök will come, Odin will be killed by Fenrir in battle and eaten, the world will end, Fenrir's sons Sköll and Hati will devour the Sun and Moon, Fenrir himself will be killed by Odin's son Víðarr, but the revenge will come too late to save the nine worlds.

Another wolf, called Managarm (the name means Moon's God), will also be present at Ragnarök, according to the *Prose Edda*. He is an evil giant, born of a giantess, who will devour the Moon (or whatever is left of it after Sköll and Hati have finished their work), and "stain the heavens and earth with blood."

Dingo (*Canis lupus dingo*)

Phylum *Chordata*, Class *Mammalia*, Order *Carnivora*, Family *Canidae*, Genus *Canis*, Species *Canis lupus*, Sub-species *Canis lupus dingo*

Name

The common name dingo comes from the Dharu language of the Australian Aborigines. There are many other indigenous names for both dogs and dingoes, the most common variants being *tingo* for a bitch and *worigal* for a large animal.

Description

Dingoes are native to Australia. Although they live in the wild, they are classed as feral since they are presumed to have descended from domesticated dogs.

They are medium-sized, leaner than wolves, and short-haired, usually tan, black and tan, or off-white in color. They are notoriously hardy and adaptable, living in the deserts of central Australia and the tropical wetlands of the north, as well as in temperate areas and the alpine regions of the eastern mountains. They hunt in packs like wolves, but they may also live and hunt as solitaries or breeding pairs, and sometimes attach themselves to human communities or even individuals. Unlike wolves, they respond to human cues, gestures and commands.

General Attributes

Dingoes are often perceived as nuisance animals in urban and suburban areas, but they are still respected by traditional aboriginal communities. They are generally more friendly than wolves and will respond to human contact, although not as immediately or as enthusiastically as domesticated dogs. They have been part of the indigenous landscape for thousands of years, and figure quite prominently in aboriginal mythology.

Dreamtime Ancestors

In Dreamtime mythology, dingoes were ancestors to humans. They feature in some aboriginal paintings, but not as frequently as the Tasmanian wolf, which is now extinct. Many of the dingo stories involve shape shifting, similar to myths in ancient Celtic Druidism. As is common in aboriginal religion, many features of the landscape are said to be dingoes or dingo-people turned to rock, or tell stories involving dingoes.

Bagadjimbiri

The aboriginal Karadjeri people of northwestern Australia include in their creation myth twin brothers, the Bagadjimbiri, who first appeared in the world as dingoes. The brothers created three things to help humankind: water holes in the desert; sexual organs for men and women; and the rite of circumcision. They were eventually killed when the sound of their laughter enraged the cat man Ngariman, who speared them to death. Their mother, the earth goddess Dilga, was so distressed that she caused milk to flow from her breasts, which drowned Ngariman and his followers and brought the Bagadjimbiri back to life. When the twins eventually tired of life among humans, they ascended to the sky, leaving their dingo bodies behind, which, as they decayed, transformed themselves into water snakes.[5]

Najara

Najara, an aboriginal tribesman of the Djauan region in Australia, went walkabout. A group of dingoes found him sitting under a palm tree and ripped his body to pieces, although he did nothing to provoke them. The moon god, Deert, angered at what the dingoes had done, buried Najara's remains. After three days, Najara rose from his grave, but he now lived as a bewitching spirit, not as a man. He went from community to community, summoning young men to him with a low whistle. Sometimes the young men returned, but they would not eat the tribe's food, nor speak the tribe's language. More often, the boys would never return. To this day, any young man who goes missing from a tribe is said to have been lured away by Najara, and dingoes are said to be Najara's agents.[6]

Coyote (*Canis latrans*)

Phylum *Chordata*, Class *Mammalia*, Order *Carnivora*, Family *Canidae*, Genus *Canis*, Species *Canis latrans*

Name

Coyote is a Spanish borrowing, made in 1780 by Francisco Javier Clavijero, of the Nahuatl or Aztec name *coyótl*. The name was variously spelled *cayjotte* and *cocyotie* until coyote became the standard spelling by the 1880s. Its alternative English names include prairie wolf, little wolf and American jackal. The *latrans* of the species name *Canis latrans* means barking, since the coyote is well known for its many different howls, barks, growls and other vocalizations.

Description

The coyote is native to North America. It is slightly smaller than the gray wolf, but similar in appearance, except that it has short fur around the face and neck. It is hardy and adaptable, and is abundant in numbers, found throughout all of North America and down into Mexico and Central America. A coyote was spotted in Panama in 2013. There are at least 19 subspecies of coyote. Coyotes sometimes interbreed with wolves, the hybrid being called a coy-wolf. They have even occasionally mated with dogs, the hybrid being called a coy-dog. Coyote pups are rough and aggressive in play, growing rapidly and reaching adult size and almost full adult weight by the age of eight months.

General Attributes

Coyotes are generally far less liked and respected by humans than wolves. In folklore, the coyote represents the trickster, the huckster, somebody mean and deceptive. Coyotes can change into human form, transact their con tricks or robberies, and then change back into coyote form to escape detection. In part, this tradition has arisen because coyotes are far bolder than wolves in entering human urban and suburban areas, so they are a comparatively familiar sight, raiding trash bins, lurking behind food outlets, hiding in parks and other public places. They may live in loosely formed packs, or in breeding pairs or small families, or as lone agents. They are portrayed as opportunists, good-humored but also sly and cunning, always looking for the main chance.

Native American Mythology

The Navajo call the coyote a skin-walker, meaning an evil being that can change into human form and carry death. In the Creation story of the Maidu people of northern California, it was Coyote who brought work, suffering and death into the world.

However, several nations—including the Pawnee, the Ute, the Chinook and the Tohono O'odham—have a more positive view of the coyote: they believe that Coyote helped the Creator make the world. In one legend, he plants some wooden figures that the creator god has made to turn into animals, but has left behind—the wooden figures grow into the first humans, each original intended animal becoming a separate tribe. In another, similar legend, it is feathers that Coyote plants.

In the Tohono O'odham story of the Great Flood, it is Coyote who rescues Montezuma, the emperor. In the ancient Aztec city of Teotuihacan, warriors wore coyote costumes as their uniform in honor of the animal. Coyote was known as Huehuecóyotl (Old Coyote) and was depicted as a man with a coyote's head, the lord of dance, music and merrymaking as well as trickery, deceit and death. The Chinook call the coyote Italapas, and credit him with helping the Creator, whom they call Ikanam, not only to shape the first humans but also to teach them various arts. Italapas pushed back the sea and so created the first prairies. He taught humans the laws of hunting. To these Indian nations, the coyote is not mischievous or evil—he is a collaborator and close friend of the Creator.

Jackal (*Canis aureus, Canis mesomelas, Canis adustus*)

Phylum *Chordata*, Class *Mammalia*, Order *Carnivora*, Family *Canidae*, Genus *Canis*, Species *Canis aureus, Canis mesomelas, Canis adustus*

Name

The common name has been in use since 1600, and is derived from the French *chacal*, which in turn was derived from Persian *shoghâl*. In the species names, *aureus* means golden, *mesomelas* means black-backed and *adustus* , literally burnt or scorched, indicates striped or side-striped.

Description

The jackal is the general Eurasian and African equivalent of the American coyote, which is also called the American jackal. There are many species, and there are some disputes about classification, but the three main species of Eurasian and African jackals are agreed: *Canis aureus* is the most widespread, found throughout southern Europe, the Middle East, and western and southern Asia; *Canis mesomelas*, the smallest, lightest and most aggressive species, is found in southern Africa, Kenya, Somalia and Ethiopia; and *Canis adustus*, the least aggressive of the jackals, is found in woodlands of central and southern Africa.

General Attributes

Jackals are widespread in Europe and Asia, and are not generally thought of as noble animals. They are indiscriminate feeders and will typically scavenge more than they hunt, anything from insects and small rodents to discarded human food scraps. The associations with Anubis, a major god in the Egyptian pantheon, and with Kali or Kalika, the great mother goddess of the Hindu pantheon, are exceptional. It seems that what connects them is an association with death.

Anubis

Anubis, the Egyptian god of death, mummification and resurrection, is depicted as a human with a jackal's head, sometimes referred to as an Egyptian golden wolf. His name is a Greek version (Ανουβις, *Anoubis*) of his original Egyptian name Anpu or Inpu. His main role is to escort the dead as a psychopomp to the afterworld to meet Osiris, the principal god of the afterlife. (See also Chapter 40.)

Kali

Kali or Kalika is a great Hindu goddess, called Mother of the Universe and the Divine Mother. She is frequently depicted standing on the prostrate god Lord Shiva, the Creator and Destroyer, symbolizing her role as the goddess of creation and destruction, of time (her name means Time) and power, to whom even the mighty Shiva is willingly subservient. She is the Shakti (divine universal spirit) and wife of Shiva. She is accompanied by snakes and by a jackal, both symbolizing her connection with death and resurrection. Kali is also known as Devi, Mahadeve, Mahakali, Parvati, Durga, and many other names and epithets. (See also Chapter 40.)

Indra the Jackal

In Hindu legend, there is a variant of the Æsopic tale of *The Dog and the Shadow* (see **dog**). An unfaithful wife is running away with her lover. They come to a stream, and the lover persuades the woman to take off all her clothes, which he will carry across so that they stay dry. The foolish, trusting woman agrees. The lover takes her clothes, crosses the stream, but then runs off, never to be seen again. The woman is left standing, naked, by the stream.

The god Indra sees the woman's plight. He changes himself into a jackal carrying a piece of meat, and comes down to the stream's edge. Seeing a huge fish in the water, Indra the jackal drops his piece of meat to chase the fish. The fish escapes and the meat is carried away by the stream.

The foolish woman mocks the god, for having lost both meat and fish. The god mocks the foolish woman, telling her that she now has no husband, no lover, and no clothes. He leaves her to her plight.

Bible Jackals

The jackal is mentioned or suggested fourteen times in the Bible. Examples include: "Even jackals offer their breasts to nurse their young, but my people have become heartless like ostriches in the desert"[7]; "By night I went out through the Valley Gate toward the Jackal Well and the Dung Gate, examining the walls of Jerusalem, which had been broken down, and its gates, which had been destroyed by fire"[8]; and "I have become a brother of jackals, a companion of owls."[9]

Cumulatively, the references portray jackals as sad, lonely creatures of the night, sneaking around trash piles and dung heaps, with minimal understanding of companionship. They symbolize the loneliness and desolation of being separated from God.

Fox (*Vulpes vulpes*)

Phylum *Chordata*, Class *Mammalia*, Order *Carnivora*, Family *Canidae*, Genus *Vulpes*, Species *Vulpes vulpes*

Name

The common name is from Old English *fox*, ultimately from Proto-Indo-European **púksos* (the tailed one). The scientific name is from *vulpes*, the Latin for fox. There are two expressions in Latin that tell us something about how Romans saw foxes. The first is *iungere vulpes*, literally "to yoke or harness a fox," which was used to describe any hopeless or futile exercise—"herding cats" might be the modern English equivalent. The second is a saying of Suetonius, *vulpes pilum mutat, non mores* ("A fox may change its fur, but not its behavior"), indicating that foxes are always cunning and untrustworthy.

Description

Although the many genera of fox all belong to the family *Canidae*, they are generally much smaller than dogs or wolves. The fennec foxes of northern Africa (*Vulpes zerda*, from Greek ξερος, *xeros*, dry place—the Xerox reprographic process is a dry process) are the smallest members of the canid family, with a body length of about 25–40 centimeters (10–15 in.). Foxes also have flatter skulls than dogs, and more pointed snouts (usually slightly upturned), upright triangular ears, and bushy tails. They live everywhere in the world except Antarctica. By far the most common species is the red fox, *Vulpes vulpes*, which has about 47 recognized subspecies.

General Attributes

Because they are known and recognized globally, foxes appear in the folklore of almost every culture. They are quick and elusive animals, will eat almost anything with (or sometimes without) meat in it (including what they might find in human trash), will forage in human settlements as easily as in the wild, and are very difficult to trap or contain. They are universally thought of as resourceful and cunning. Foxes also have a very broad vocal repertoire, which includes barking, yelping, whining, howling and an explosive, screaming call that defies description. The cry of a vixen (female fox) from a distant hill in the middle of the night is almost identical to the crying of a human baby, and can be very disturbing. The complexity of the many vocalizations increases the fox's reputation for intelligence and subtlety. (In Celtic mythology, there is a Welsh goddess of streams, whose blood-curdling shrieking foretells an imminent death. Her name is Cyhiraeth, which means Dog of Longing, and it may be the cry of a vixen that is being described.)

Because they are so universal, resourceful and industrious, as well as rather handsome with their bright eyes, alert ears and interesting coloring, foxes are often admired, even loved and kept as pets by a few humans, but they are also considered pests in many communities, particularly by farmers. Recreational fox hunting takes place in several countries, including the United States. Ironically, foxes have been employed successfully to control pests on fruit farms, where they eat the pests but leave the fruit alone.

The Fox and the Grapes

In Æsop's well-known fable, a hungry and thirsty fox longs for some grapes hanging on a vine. Unfortunately, no matter how hard he tries, he cannot jump high enough to reach them. Finally, he gives up in disgust and leaves, saying, "They're not ripe anyway. Who wants to eat sour grapes?" The expression "sour grapes" for ill-tempered resentment came into English from this well-known story. The process of rationalization also has a counterpart in modern psychology: it is called cognitive dissonance, which means changing the truth inside your head to fit your emotional needs rather than the perception of external reality. A Greek vase, dating from about 450 BCE, portrays Æsop listening to a speaking fox.[10]

The Fox and the Crow

In this fable attributed to Æsop, a fox sees a crow fly into the branches of a tree with a piece of cheese in its beak. The fox flatters the bird, praising every aspect of it, but reaching his finale in his passionate praise of the bird's beautiful song and begging the crow to sing just a few notes. The crow, used to hearing nothing but negative reactions to his harsh cry, foolishly opens his beak to sing. The cheese falls and the fox snaps it up before it even reaches the ground.

Moral: It is easy to be deceived by flattery.

The Fox and the Mosquitoes

In another story attributed to Æsop, a fox gets his brush tangled up in a thorn bush. Mosquitoes take advantage of his predicament and start biting his body all over. A friendly hedgehog comes along and asks the fox whether he would like him to chase the mosquitoes away. The fox thanks the hedgehog for the offer, but philosophically concludes that if the hedgehog drives away the mosquitoes that have by now almost drunk their fill, other mosquitoes with fresh appetites will simply take their place and eventually bleed him to death. The moral of the story is that sometimes putting up with present irritations and tribulations may be better than exposing yourself to a whole new set of irritations and tribulations. Apparently, several Roman emperors and their senior administrators used to repeat this story frequently to provincial officials, who were often plagued with minor conflicts and petty political infighting.

The Fox and the Sick Lion

Another Æsopic fable has two variants, each of them showing how the fox's cunning saves its skin:

> The lion was on his deathbed. He invited all of the animals of the forest to come and hear his last will and testament. The goat, the sheep and the calf all went in. The fox waited some distance from the cave entrance. After a while, the lion emerged, looking remarkably healthy.
>
> "Why do you not come in to pay your respects to me?" the lion asked of the fox.
>
> "I did not wish to crowd you, Your Majesty," replied the fox. "I have seen many of your subjects go into your cave, but none of them has yet come out. Until they do, I think I will wait out here in the fresh air."

Moral: Don't believe everything you see or hear.

Version Two:

> The lion was sick and on his deathbed. The other animals all visited him and offered themselves as a final dinner for him before he died. The lion chose the bull, and asked the wolf to do the carving. The wolf tried to be clever, and gave the lion the bull's entrails, saying they would be good for him in his weak condition. The lion responded by clipping the wolf about the head, removing some skin and one of his ears. The lion then asked the fox to take over from the wolf. The fox gave the whole body to the lion, and the hooves, horns and entrails to the rest of the animals.
> "Who taught you to carve so well, my dear?" the lion asked of the fox.
> "I studied the wolf's head and learned from it," replied the fox.

Moral: He who learns quickly lives longer.

Celtic Druidic Fox Attributes

The Celts admired the fox's cunning and inventiveness. The name Louernius (Son of Fox) is found in inscriptions in Gaul and in Britain. Ua Leochann, a Scottish king who died in 989, was known in Gàidhlig as *An Sionnach*, pronounced approximately *an-shin-ogh*, meaning The Fox. The same epithet is found in Ireland, where the aristocratic family of the O' Caharney or O' Kearney were also nicknamed *Sinnach*.[11]

Huathiacuri

In the mythology of the Huarochiri or Warachiri Indians of Peru, two foxes help Huathiacuri, son of the hero god Pariacaca:

> Huathiacuri learns of a rich man who has made a claim that he is a creator god, and goes to investigate. He discovers that the man's house is roofed with yellow and red bird feathers, and that he has bred llamas with wool of several different colors, so that it does not need to be dyed. Huathiacuri is impressed. But he also discovers that the rich man is lying close to death, suffering from a mysterious illness. Two foxes recognize Huathiacuri in the forest, and, without revealing themselves, have a loud question-and-answer conversation about why the man is sick: His wife has committed adultery.... Two magical serpents are hovering over his house, slowly eating his soul.... A two-headed toad, hidden under the grinding stone of the mill, is cursing the man.
> Having overheard every word of the conversation (just as the foxes intended), Huathicuri forces the adulterous wife to confess. He finds and destroys the malevolent monsters. The rich man recovers. Huathiacuri marries the rich man's daughter. And the foxes congratulate each other on a job well done.[12]

Mu-monto

In Siberian mythology, Mu-monto is a hero who visits the land of the dead to demand the return of a horse that he had sacrificed earlier. To find the land of the dead, he heads north and finds a rock, which he lifts, calling down into the space, "Come here." A black fox emerges and leads Mu-monto to the place he is seeking.[13]

The Nine-Tailed Fox in China and Japan

In Chinese mythology, the nine-tailed fox is a sacred animal. It will answer prayers, but it is still cunning, so the granting of the prayer may not be exactly what was expected—

the be-careful-what-you-wish-for motif. (See also *The Monkey's Paw*, Chapter 15.) The nine-tailed fox is also found in Japanese and Korean mythology.

Inari, the Japanese god of rice, tea, saké wine and fertility, is often depicted as a bearded old man seated on a sack of rice, with a fox seated on the ground on each side of him. The two foxes are his servants or messengers. Since Inari is also the god of prosperity and trade, seeing a fox is a lucky omen, foretelling imminent wealth.

Kitsune is a clever trickster character, who appears in many classical Japanese folktales, often whimsical or humorous in nature. He also features in several modern Japanese *animé* and *manga* cartoons. His name means Fox.

One series of Japanese legends concerns Abe no Seimei, a hero-magician, whose father Abe no Yasuna was a poet and whose mother was Kuzunoha, a nine-tailed white fox, a good witch. Kuzonoha is often portrayed as carrying a writing brush in her mouth, symbolizing her knowledge and articulacy. Because of his birth and his knowledge of nine-tailed foxes, Abe no Seimei is able to cure Emperor Toba of a terrible wasting sickness by recognizing that the Emperor's mistress, Tamamo no Maye, is a malevolent nine-tailed fox witch, who has been slowly poisoning Toba. Abe no Seimei is sometimes portrayed conjuring white mice from an empty box.[14]

The Japanese magical fox features in *The Forty-Seven Ronin*, a legend based on a genuine 18th-century historical event, but with a great deal of magic and mystery added afterwards, first written down by A.B. Mitford in *Tales of Old Japan* in 1871, and subsequently the subject of several films made in Japan, but better known in the West by the Keanu Reeves 2013 film, *47 Ronin*. The particular fox-witch of this story is evil, and transforms into a flying serpent at the climax of the film.

Cunning Foxes of the West

The oldest folkloric legend of the cunning fox in the West is the story of Reynard the Fox. Reynard has robbed just about all the other animals. Noble, the lion king, sends Bruin the bear to arrest the fox. Reynard easily outwits Bruin, and then Tybert the cat. Finally brought to trial, Reynard convinces Noble (who is the judge) that he has hidden treasure, and the lion is foolish enough to believe him, and sets him free. William Caxton published his translation of a Flemish version of the story in 1481, so the story of Reynard has been around for a long time.

Another very well-known literary cunning fox is the Br'er Fox of Joel Chandler Harris's bestseller of 1880, *Uncle Remus: His Songs and His Sayings*. Like Reynard, he is a sharp talker and a smooth operator, who always has some new trick or ruse up his sleeve.

The cunning fox is also well personified in the 1970 Roald Dahl children's novel *The Fantastic Mr. Fox*. The story was made into a very entertaining movie in 2009 directed by Wes Anderson and starring George Clooney, Meryl Streep, Bill Murray and others.

5

Cats and Wildcats (*Felidae*)

Cat (*Felis catus* or *Felis silvestris catus*)

Phylum *Chordata*, Class *Mammalia*, Order *Carnivora*, Suborder *Feliformia*, Family *Felidae*, Subfamily *Felinae*, Genus *Felis*, Species *Felis silvestris*, Subspecies *Felis catus* or *Felis silvestris catus*

Name

The common name is from Old English, which had two variants: *catt* for a male and *catte* for a female. These were assumed to be derived from Late Latin *cattus* or *catta*, but how those words came into Latin is still a matter of controversy and mystery. Middle English had *kitoun* or *kiton*, which became kitten. The shorter word kit is used for the young of several other animals, including the rabbit, rat, hedgehog, squirrel, fox, beaver and badger. The *felis* of the scientific name means cat, and *silvestris* is literally "of the woods." *Catus* is New Latin, back-formed from the English word.

Description

The *Felidae* family existed about 10 to 15 million years ago, and the genus *Felis* appeared some six to seven million years ago. The earliest known remains of a domesticated African wildcat were found in Cyprus, and appear to date from about 7500 to 7200 BCE, so cats both wild and domesticated have been around for a long time, and are very familiar across the whole world.

Domesticated cats have smaller canine teeth than wildcats or large cats, since their prey is smaller. All cats have large eye sockets and keen eyesight, especially at night. Their hearing is also highly sensitive. They also have an organ of smell that humans don't have, namely the vomeronasal or Jacobson's organ that allows them to respond to pheromones and certain plants, such as catnip and valerian. Cats move far more precisely than dogs, and are famed for their good balance, supposedly always landing on their feet from moderate heights—it even has an official scientific name, the cat righting reflex. Cats like to perch in moderately high places, presumably to feel safer from attack and to get a better view of potential prey. They excrete almost perfectly dry feces, and have very efficient kidneys, producing highly concentrated urine (which can be strong-smelling to humans).

Cats are found in every part of the world except Antarctica. The world population of domestic cats alone is well over 500 million.[1] Cats tolerate a very wide range of habitats, living conditions and diets, and make excellent pets.

General Attributes

The cat is sacred to the Goddess in several traditions, notably the Egyptian and Nordic pantheons, and Celtic Druidism. Cats are notoriously independent of mind, even when thoroughly domesticated—"A cat may look at a king." Witches are often described or portrayed as having a cat as a familiar, or guiding spirit. Domestic kittens (or cubs of larger species) are so universally adorable that they bring out the maternal instinct in humans (male as well as female). A crazy cat-lady (of whom there are many real examples) is a person who cannot resist the charms of cats and kittens and fills her house with them, often to the detriment of her and their health. I imagine there must be some male crazy cat-gentlemen somewhere, too.

Above all, the cat represents the Goddess or feminine spirit: independent, sometimes contradictory or capricious, sensitive, sensual, adaptable, often loving and tender, fiercely protective as a parent, indifferent to strangers but deeply affectionate with trusted friends—cat lovers will know that this list of attributes could go on much longer.

Bastet

Bastet (also Bast, Baast, Bsst, Oubaste and Pasht), one of the most important deities in the Egyptian pantheon, was a cat goddess. In Greek, she was called Αιλουρος, *Aïluros*, which simply means Cat. Since the Egyptian hieroglyph for an ointment jar was sounded *bs*, and the ending *-t* was a feminine ending, and the goddess was a goddess of healing often associated with curative unguents and ointments, Stephen Quirke suggests that her name meant She Who Provides Ointments.[2] Bastet was portrayed as a cat, or as a woman with the head of a cat, but originally as a lioness (see the comment on Sekhmet below). Her worship was widespread across all Egypt for literally thousands of years, but her spiritual center was the ancient city of Bubastis in the Delta of the Nile, which the Egyptians called *Per-Bast*, the Greeks βουβαστις, *Boubastis*, the Arabs *Tell-Basta*, and which may be the same as the Hebrew *py-byst* or *Pi-beseth* mentioned in the Bible in the Lamentation for Egypt: "The young men of On and of Pi-beseth shall fall by the sword"[3] (because they worshiped the pagan goddess). The city's ruins are in the suburbs of the modern city of Zagazig.

Bastet offered protection against all diseases, to men, women and children, but was especially the protector and healer of pregnant women. Long before the classical and Abrahamic religions, the Sun was often perceived as a female deity and the Moon as male, but that polarity was later reversed, certainly by classical Greek and Roman times. Bastet, however, is a goddess of the old order. She represents the warming, healing, procreative power of the sun. (Sekhmet, the Egyptian lion goddess, represents its destructive power.) It was in Bastet's name that cats were originally said to have nine lives, because they were so special to the gods and to Bastet herself that it was only the ninth death that would actually take them from the world.

Bastet's annual festival was perhaps the most popular in Egypt. Her cult was important as early as the Second Dynasty (beginning about 2890 BCE), when she was generally called Bast and depicted with the head of a lioness. After about 1070 BCE, she began to be depicted more frequently as the more friendly and approachable domestic cat, and another

-t feminine ending was added to her name, so that from Bast she became Bastet. Her cult was still widespread as pharaonic Egypt slowly declined (it lasted for three thousand years, about the same amount of time as the whole span of ancient Egyptian history, which technically didn't end until Egypt became a Roman province in 30 BCE) so it was very, very long lasting and obviously popular. The Greek historian Herodotus (484–425 BCE, often called "the father of history") describes her annual festival, which included decorated barges on the Nile, huge feasts, and much dancing and singing, presumably of celebratory hymns. According to Herodotus, women shouted abuse at men and even exposed their breasts or danced naked on the banks of the river. Some 700,000 or more followers of Bastet were said to have attended the festival at its peak, and to have consumed more wine than in all the rest of the year put together.

Because of Bastet's widespread influence, cats were considered sacred animals in ancient Egypt. They were honored, petted and pampered. Where owners could afford it, dead cats were carefully mummified before burial. When Bastet's temple in Bubatis was first excavated, some 300,000 mummified cats were found, many of them buried alongside their human owners. When a cat died in the family, legend says that all members of the family shaved off their eyebrows in mourning.

The Cat Maiden

A well-known legendary tale attributed to Æsop is that of the beautiful female cat who fell in love with a human young man:

> A female cat fell in love with a young man. The young man enjoyed the cat's affectionate attention, but obviously nothing further. The cat appealed to Venus, goddess of love, to help her. Venus obligingly turned her into a stunningly beautiful young woman. The young man instantly fell in love with her, and soon they were married.
>
> One evening, the couple were sitting in their home, enjoying each other's company. A mouse ran across the floor. The wife pounced on it, tossed it several times in the air, and then put it in her mouth to eat it. Her husband looked on, absolutely horrified. Venus took pity on both of them, and instantly changed the woman back into a cat.

Moral: What is bred in the bone will never be absent in the flesh.

Roasting Cats

Cats were routinely captured, tortured and burned to death in baskets by Christians in Britain and France in the Middle Ages, as part of the Church's general war against witchcraft. They were perceived as evil agents in the spirit world. The roasting of cats on spits is also reported in Scotland from the 15th to the 17th centuries, and even given a Gàidhlig name, *Taghairm nan Cath* (Choice of the Cat), but the reporters were Christian clerics who may have had reasons of their own for inventing or exaggerating such stories.

Guardian Cats

In Celtic mythological literature, there are guard cats as well as guard dogs. The goddess Brighid or Bride has a companion cat (who disappears from the stories as soon as Brighid transmogrifies into a Christian saint).

There are several stories in Irish called *immrama*, spiritual tales of voyages, often including amazing or symbolic events. In the best known of them, the *Voyage of Maelduin*, the hero and his companions sail to several different islands governed by animals. On the Island of the Cat, they discover a vast treasure, but when one of them attempts to steal a gold necklace, the cat that is guarding the horde lazily waves her paw and the would-be thief is instantly burned to a pile of ash.

Japanese and Chinese Cats

Cats in Japan are generally considered to bring good luck. Mi-ki, the tri-colored or tortoise-shell cat, is particularly favored by sailors, and one is often carried on board ship. A mechanical toy of a cat waving its left paw to bring good luck is sold widely in Japan, where it is called Maneki-Neko (Beckoning Cat). Its influence has spread to Chinese take-out restaurants in the West, where these small toys are sometimes up for sale. Ancient Chinese legend has it that cats are descended from lions and monkeys: lions because of their grace, agility and dignity, and monkeys because they are so adventuresome, curious, and entertaining.

Pussy Willows

The willow tree is said to be commonly called the pussy willow because it is in mourning for all the little unwanted kittens that are tied in a sack with a stone and thrown into the river or lake to drown. It is said to trail its branches into the water so that the kittens can climb up them to safety.

Muhammad and the Cat

According to Islamic folk tradition, Muhammad considered dogs to be unclean, but loved cats. Legend has it that he once cut the sleeve from his robe because a favorite cat had fallen asleep on his arm, and he didn't want to disturb it. The M-shaped marking that sometimes appears on the forehead of tabby cats is said to be the mark of the Prophet's hand making the initial M.

Freyja's Cats

In Norse mythology, Freyja is the goddess of youth, beauty and love. She was sometimes called a nanny goat because of her sexual promiscuity, but the animal with which she is most closely associated is the cat, both domestic and wild. She rides in a golden chariot drawn by two or more cats (or sometimes lynx). Her most famous possession is a magical necklace called Brising, which she reportedly extorted from the dwarfs who created it in return for sexual favors. (In a well-known legend, the thunder-god Thor steals the necklace to impersonate Freyja and trick the giants: the point of the bawdy story, in which the huge, hairy, muscular Thor minces coquettishly, is to show how dim-witted and easily deceived the giants are.) Freyja's cats are usually plain, common-or-garden domestic cats, not lions or panthers, which gives depictions of her great charm and human warmth—she is a stunningly beautiful and powerful goddess, but her chosen animal companions are just ordinary household pets.

Freyja is often confused with Frigg or Frigga, wife of Odin, who gave her name to the day Friday, or Frigg's Day. Freyja is the sister of Frey, the boar-god (see Chapter 13), and the wife of Óðr or Odur, which may account for some of the confusion, since Óðr is a possible source for the name Óðinn or Odin. The Old Norse word *óðr* has many meanings and connotations, including mind, spirit, song, inspiration, and possession. Frigg is the equivalent of the classical Hera and Juno, mother of all the gods, while Freyja is the Nordic equivalent of Aphrodite or Venus, the younger goddess of beauty and love.

Kilkenny Cats

The epithet "a Kilkenny cat" means a fighter so tenacious that he or she will fight to the death, indeed, to complete self-obliteration. It is based on a very old piece of Irish folklore, the true origin of which is unknown.

One suggestion is that the story derives from a cat monster called Banghaisgidheach (the name, pronounced approximately *ban-ghash-gyogh*, is Irish Gaelic for heroine), but there is no convincing evidence. Another is that the hated Oliver Cromwell set cats to fight each other in the cruel manner described in the legend. There are at least six or seven other explanations, any of which might be true. At all events, the legend supposes that two cats are tied tail to tail, then left to fight each other. Often, they are tied together and then placed over a line or wire so that they cannot escape. The essential event of the legend is given in a slightly extended limerick:

> There once were two cats of Kilkenny;
> Each thought there was one cat too many.
> So they fought and they fit
> And they scratched and they bit
> Till, (excepting their nails
> And the tips of their tails),
> Instead of two cats there weren't any![4]

Pangur Bán

Pangur Bán is the cat of a 9th-century Old Irish poet, who compares the cat's hunting to his own hunting for words. There have been many translations, but this is that of the Irish poet Seamus Heaney (1939–2013):

> Pangur Bán and I at work,
> Adepts, equals, cat and clerk:
> His whole instinct is to hunt,
> Mine to free the meaning pent.
>
> More than loud acclaim, I love
> Books, silence, thought, my alcove.
> Happy for me, Pangur Bán
> Child-plays round some mouse's den.
>
> Truth to tell, just being here,
> Housed alone, housed together,

Adds up to its own reward:
Concentration, stealthy art.

Next thing an unwary mouse
Bares his flank: Pangur pounces.
Next thing lines that held and held
Meaning back begin to yield.

All the while, his round bright eye
Fixes on the wall, while I
Focus my less piercing gaze
On the challenge of the page.

With his unsheathed, perfect nails
Pangur springs, exults and kills.
When the longed-for, difficult
Answers come, I too exult.

So it goes. To each his own.
No vying. No vexation.
Taking pleasure, taking pains,
Kindred spirits, veterans.

Day and night, soft purr, soft pad,
Pangur Bán has learned his trade.
Day and night, my own hard work
Solves the cruxes, makes a mark.[5]

The King of the Cats

In an old British story, *The King of the Cats*, first noted in 1553 but frequently re-told since then, a sexton digging a grave sees a group of nine black cats with white spots on their chests, carrying a cat-sized coffin with a crown resting on it. One of the cats tells the man, "Tell Tommy Tildrum that Timmy Toldrum is dead."

> The man returns home to his wife and tells her the news, while their housecat, Old Tom, keeps interrupting his story with frantic meows. The couple ignores the cat, and they continue discussing the strange occurrence, amidst the racket. Finally, at the end, the man asks his wife if she knows who Tommy Tildrum is, so he can tell Tommy that Timmy has died, whereupon the cat cries out in human words: "What? Old Tim dead? Then I'm the King of the Cats!"

At this, Old Tom scrambles up the chimney and is never seen again.

Cat Weather Forecasters and Other Folklore Beliefs

As anybody who owns a cat will have frequently observed, cats lick themselves all over to wash. They are fastidious about it. Because cats are very sensitive to prevailing atmospheric conditions, modern folklore has it that they can predict the weather. If the cat washes its body in the normal way, the weather will remain fine. It points its tail towards the fire, or if it spends an unusual amount of time cleaning its tail and the forehead space between its ears, then rain is on its way. If it stops washing and starts clawing the carpet or curtains, windy weather is on its way.

A common folklore belief persists that cats will climb into a baby's cot or crib and steal the baby's breath, i.e., smother it. In 1791, a jury in Plymouth, England, found a cat guilty of infanticide by smothering. In 1929, the Nebraska State Journal published the story of a doctor called when a baby had died reporting that he had seen a housecat "lying on the baby's breast, a paw on either side of the babe's mouth, the cat's lips pressing those of the child and the infant's face as pale as that of a corpse, its lips with the blueness of death."[6]

Certain cats are considered more propitious than others. In Buddhist tradition, a dark-colored cat promises gold, while a light-colored cat will bring silver. Another Buddhist belief is that cats sometimes hold the souls of dead humans while they are on transition to their next reincarnation—the Buddha is sometimes depicted with a sleeping cat at his feet, and Thai kings have gold-decorated cats present at their coronation ceremonies.

Black cats were widely condemned by early and medieval Christians as literally diabolical, including even the belief that they (and snakes) were responsible for spreading plagues, which led to the unfortunate mass killing of both cats and snakes, which in turn allowed rat populations to increase.

Polydactyl cats (cats with extra toes) were considered especially lucky by American sailors, which explains why there are larger than average populations of polydactyls in New England to this day.

Wildcat (*Felis silvestris, Felis lybica*)

Phylum *Chordata*, Class *Mammalia*, Order *Carnivora*, Suborder *Feliformia*, Family *Felidae*, Subfamily *Felinae*, Genus *Felis*, Species *Felis sylvestris, Felis lybica*

Name

The English name is obvious. The scientific classification loses the *catus* of the domesticated cat and remains simply *Felis silvestris*, "cat of the woods," indicating the European wildcat. There is a second species, the African wildcat, *Felis lybica* (of Lybia). There are 22 recognized subspecies of wildcat. It is important to distinguish between wildcats and feral cats (although it is sometimes very difficult to do that in practice). A wildcat has nothing but wildcat ancestry, whereas a feral cat is a domesticated cat that has become undomesticated or feral, or is living wild but is descended from domesticated cats.

Description

Both the European and the African wildcats are significantly stockier and stronger than a domesticated cat. The European wildcat is striped and has thick fur and a bushy, round-tipped tail. Its domain is Europe and the Caucasus. The African wildcat, *Felis lybica*, despite its name, is found in Africa, Asia, India and China. It is slightly smaller than *Felis silvestris*, a paler gray in color, the stripes are less prominent, and the tail is slimmer. The subspecies *Felis lybica ornata*, the Asiatic wildcat, is even slimmer and more sinuous, and has spots instead of stripes.

General Attributes

Wildcats, as the name suggests, are not at all friendly or familiar towards humans. They hiss and bare their teeth when approached, or run and hide. They are generally solitary animals, marking their territories with scent glands to keep other wildcats away. They are prolific hunters, catching rabbits, rats, weasels and stoats, quite large birds like ducks, even prey as large as deer fawns on occasion. They like to sleep in natural hollows, shallow caves, or clefts in rock, rather than climb trees. They were particularly venerated by the Celts, especially in Ireland, Scotland and northern Britain. (Cats were not domesticated in the British Isles until the Middle Ages, particularly after the 11th century when several cities had uncontrolled rat infestations.)

Cat Totems

Several Scottish clans have the wildcat as their totem animal, including Clan MacIntosh, Clan MacNeishe, Clan MacNicol, Clan MacBain, Clan Chattan (The Cat Clan) and Clan Sutherland. The Clan Sutherland chief is known as *Morair Chat* (Great Man of the Cats) and the clan shield shows a wildcat with the motto above in French, *Sans Peur* (Without Fear). The northern Scottish county of Caithness means Ness or Promontory of the Cats, and neighboring Sutherland is called *Cataibh* (Place of the Cat People) in Scottish Gaelic. The motto of Clan Chattan is "Touch not the catt bot (without) a glove." The Irish *Yellow Book of Lecan* describes warriors wearing cat-skin helmets with the cat's head still attached. One Irish king was called *Cairbar cinn Chait* (Carbar Cat Head).[7]

Jólakötturinn

The *Jólakötturinn* or Yule Cat is a monster in Icelandic folklore. It is a domestic cat, but is big enough to eat a human being in three or four bites. It preys particularly on people who have not received gifts of new clothes by Christmas Eve, which suggests that its origins lie with farmers wanting their wool processed in plenty of time for the Christmas sales.

The Troll Cat

A troll cat in Scandinavian folklore is a witch's familiar made from scraps of wool, human hair, wood shavings and other materials. It is also called a milk rabbit or a troll ball. It swallows milk from cow's udders and steals cream from human kitchens. It can be trained to regurgitate the stolen milk or cream so that the witch can drink it.

6

Big Cats, Hyenas and Mongooses (*Felidae* and *Viverroidea*)

Lion (*Panthera leo*)

Phylum *Chordata*, Class *Mammalia*, Order *Carnivora*, Suborder *Feliformia*, Family *Felidae*, Subfamily *Pantherinae*, Genus *Panthera*, Species *Panthera leo*

Name

The English name is derived from Latin *leo*, lion, which in turn is derived from Greek λεων, *léōn*. The genus name *Panthera* is also originally Greek, πανθερα, *panthéra*, probably originally indicating either panther or leopard, but it is difficult to be certain because classical animal descriptions were not scientific in the modern sense; *panthéra* originally meant whitish-yellow, suggesting an animal of that color.

Description

Lions are easily recognized by their distinctive, broad-chested, muscular bodies. Males (typically 150–250 kilograms or 330–550 pounds in weight) are usually considerably larger than females (120–180 kilograms or 265–390 pounds), and in maturity have a prominent mane surrounding the head. A group of lions (called a pride) in the wild usually consists of a few males, one of them dominant over the others, and several females, plus any cubs they may have. Females do most of the work in lion families: they do almost all the hunting, and all of the raising and training of the young. Male lions can often be aggressive towards cubs, and their mothers may have to protect and defend them. Lions will occasionally scavenge, but they are mainly game hunters, with the females usually working cooperatively. Lions live typically on grasslands and savannahs rather than in forests, and they tend to be diurnal (active during the day).

Cave paintings of lions in the Lascaux and Chauvet caves in France are estimated to be between 15,000 and 17,000 years old. Lions have been hunted for many thousands of years. An inscription of c. 1380 BCE says that the Egyptian pharaoh Amenhotep III killed 102 lions "with his own arrows" during the first ten years of his reign. The Romans frequently used lions in gladiatorial combats. Lions have also hunted humans: there have been many recorded incidents throughout history of lions killing and eating humans, most of them happening at twilight or at night, and almost all of them involving male lions—illness and dental decay have been suggested as aggravating factors.

General Attributes

The lion has been "King of the Jungle" for centuries, although its normal habitat is open grassland rather than forest or jungle. The more generic "King of the Beasts," which is common in many cultures, is a better title. Lions are seen as proud, majestic, royal, dignified and worthy. In Swahili, which is spoken in several African countries, the word for lion is *simba*, which also means king, strong, and aggressive.[1] Lions feature in the religion, mythology or folklore of every country in which they are found, but also in many countries where they are known only through zoos; they have been big money-earners for zoos all around the world since the 19th century.

Mafdet, Sekhmet and Tefnut

As we saw in the previous chapter, Bast or Bastet, the cat goddess, was worshiped widely in ancient Egypt. The first cat-headed goddess was Mafdet, who was popular during the First Dynasty, 2920–2770 BCE. As Bast became popular, Sekhmet also rose in popularity. Bast had occasionally been portrayed as a lioness, but Sekhmet took over that role. Both were solar deities, but Sekhmet became the goddess of the cruel, hard, burning sun. She was the daughter of Ra, the sun god. Before Sekhmet, there had also been Tefnut, who was one of the original Ennead or nine gods of Egypt. Tefnut was a woman with the head of a lioness. Thoth, the god of wisdom, criticized her for going off into the Nubian deserts and neglecting the people of Egypt, and she wept great tears when he condemned her. However, her tears turned to smoke and she reverted to her earlier bloodthirsty nature, her lioness face glowing like the burning sun of midday. Of the four main cat goddesses, Bast or Bastet, the goddess of the cat, was the most popular, followed by Sekhmet the lioness.

Anath

Anath was a Canaanite (Middle Eastern) war goddess. The lion was her totem animal. The god Baal helped her to conquer and possess the mountains of Lebanon. In return, she called Baal's enemies to a feast and then slaughtered them. Her cult became wild and ruthless, frequently involving human sacrifice. She is depicted in full battle armor with a lion or lioness standing beside her.[2]

Androcles and the Lion

The story of Androcles (or Androclus) and the lion is Roman in origin. It features in *Noctes Atticae* or Attic Nights by the Roman author Aulus Gellius (c. 125–180 CE), but it first became widespread in medieval Europe, where it rapidly became very popular. George Bernard Shaw's play *Androcles and the Lion* (1912) is very well known. The tale recounts the story of a slave, Androcles, who hides in a cave, where he meets a lion with a thorn in its paw, and is saved by the same lion some years later when he is thrown in amongst a pack of wild lions in a gladatorial combat.

Guardian Lions

There are guardian lions in many cultures. Karashishi (also Shishi and Shesa) are stone lions often found in front of Buddhist temples in Japan. Typical of guardian dogs and other animals, they are usually set either side of a pathway or gateway. The Chinese Imperial guardian lions are also called lion dogs or foo dogs (see Chapter 3). Often, one is male, with a ball under its right paw, and the other is female, with a cub. Although they were first used in the Chinese Imperial court, they have since spread all across the Far East. Stone lions are also found at the gateways to many European castles and fine houses.

Lions in the Bible

In Judaism and Christianity, Jacob calls his son Judah by the name Gur Aryeh, which means Young Lion.[3] In the Book of Daniel in the Old Testament, Nebuchadnezzar's captain is called Arioch, which means Like a Lion.[4] (The same name is used by Milton in *Paradise Lost* for one of the fallen angels.) In the Book of Isaiah, the holy city of Jerusalem is called Ariel, which means The Lion of God.[5] The epithet Lion or Lion of Judah therefore has strong positive associations, and later came to be used for Jesus, or for other prophets. It is one of the titles given to Haile Selassie the First, Emperor of Ethiopia between 1930 and 1974, who is revered in Rastafarianism.

Chapter 6 of the *Book of Daniel* tells the story of Daniel in the lions' den. Darius the Mede elevates Daniel to high office, but jealous plotters conspire to have Daniel condemned and sent for execution. Darius, praying that Daniel may be spared but unable to ignore or defy the plotters, has Daniel thrown into a pit or den filled with lions. The next morning, Darius finds Daniel safe and well, because, explains Daniel, God found him "blameless." Darius has the plotters thrown into the den after Daniel has been released.[6]

In the *Book of Revelation*, John has a vision of God's throne on which four creatures are seated: "Around the throne, and on each side of the throne, are four living creatures, full of eyes in front and behind: the first living creature like a lion, the second living creature like an ox, the third living creature with a face like a human face, and the fourth living creature like a flying eagle."[7] These have been interpreted as representing the four evangelists: Matthew is the man, representing Christ's incarnation in human form; Luke is the ox, representing Christ's sacrifice; John is the eagle, representing Christ's ascension and resurrection; and Mark is the lion, representing Christ's majesty and sovereignty. In the vision, each of the living creatures has six wings and they "are full of eyes all around and inside,"[8] similar to many depictions of Hindu deities.

Tiger (*Panthera tigris*)

Phylum *Chordata*, Class *Mammalia*, Order *Carnivora*, Suborder *Feliformia*, Family *Felidae*, Subfamily *Pantherinae*, Genus *Panthera*, Species *Panthera tigris*

6. Big Cats, Hyenas and Mongooses

Name

The English name was *tigre* in Middle English, borrowed from Old French, originally from Greek τιγρις, *tigris*, which was also the name of the River Tigris in Mesopotamia. The *Panthera* genus name is used for all the big cats.

Description

The tiger is the largest and most powerful of the big cats. It generally has dark vertical stripes on orange-reddish fur, with a lighter color on the underside. It is an apex predator, usually leading a solitary life and requiring a large territory to provide sufficient food for its large appetite. Tigers were once widespread throughout Asia, but since the beginning of the 20th century their territories have shrunk by about 93 percent, and they are now found in fragmented ranges between India and the temperate forests of Siberia. It has been listed as an endangered species since 1986.

General Attributes

The tiger is a very popular and charismatic animal, mostly because of its size, power and physical beauty. The English poet and visionary William Blake (1757–1827) famously described it as: "Tyger, tyger, burning bright / In the forests of the night." It is the national animal of India, Bangladesh, Malaysia and South Korea. It features in many Asian religions and mythologies.

Zhurong

In Chinese mythology, Zhurong (also Chu Jung and other variants) is the god of fire. He is also nicknamed Ch'ih Ti (also several variants), meaning Red Emperor. He is occasionally depicted riding a fire dragon (see Chapter 39), but more often riding a tiger. He may have a third eye in his forehead. He is surrounded by servants and fire implements or symbols. He also carries a notepad to write down the addresses of places he intends to burn. Believers pray to Zhurong both to cause fires in the places of their enemies, or to prevent fires in their own homes or important places.

White Tigers

A white tiger is a Bengal tiger of the subspecies *Panthera tigris tigris*, normally gold-orange with black stripes, in which the gold-orange is replaced by white or off-white, although the stripes remain, sometimes only faintly visible. They are found in several states in India. Scientifically, as with all albinism, the whiteness in white tigers is actually caused by an abnormality in pigmentation. Nevertheless, white tigers have achieved mythological status in several areas.

In Chinese astrology, there are four symbols for the constellations, and within each symbol seven mansions. The ancient Chinese belief was that a tiger's tail starts turning white only when it reaches the age of 500 years, so a pure white tiger was an extremely powerful and venerable beast indeed. In practice, real white tigers are not found in China, so there the beast can be called entirely mythical. The white tiger represents one of the four cardinal directions, and is called *Xī Fāng Bái Hǔ* (White Tiger of the West). The main stars of its seven mansions correspond to stars recognized in the West (see Chapter 41).

The well-known *wuxia* or martial heroes movie *Crouching Tiger, Hidden Dragon*, 2000, conceals in its title a paradox that has been understood for centuries in Chinese, Japanese and Korean martial arts, all of which have an underlying religious or spiritual element. The tiger represents physical reality, the observable or Aristotelian world, and a white tiger is its supreme representation or icon. The dragon represents spirituality or intellectualism, the universe of pure thought as opposed to impure matter. So, the master in martial arts controls both elements, both animals, at once: he crouches like a tiger, supremely attuned to the physical location and reality of every possible actual event, but at the same time he is also concealing his dragon, his detached intellectual and spiritual assessment, the fundamental wisdom that converts thought into action.

In Japanese Buddhist mythology, the *arhat* Hattara Aonja, one of the disciples of the Buddha who has achieved perfection, is often depicted with a white tiger at his feet, symbolizing his conquest of the material universe.

Harimau Kramat

Harimau is the Malayan word for tiger. The tigers of the Malayan Peninsula were accepted as a unique, separate species only recently (2004), and the chairman of the Malaysian Zoo Association asked, not unreasonably, that the subspecies should be called *Panthera tigris malayensis*, but the scientific community insisted on *Panthera tigris jacksoni* (for Peter Jackson, 1926–2016, a tiger expert from London), but allowed Malayan tiger as the common name.

Harimau Kramat (Ghost Tigers) were believed in legend to have been created when the Princess of Malacca was traveling in a boat with her husband, Nakhoda Ragam. She killed her husband (why is not clear) with a needle, and his blood filled the boat. When another boat passed close by, the master asked what the Princess had in her boat, and she lied, "Just spinach juice." When the boat landed, all that remained of Nakhoda Ragam was one thigh (the princess had thrown the rest of his body overboard), which she buried at the foot of Jurga Hill. She also took her two domestic cats ashore, and these turned into *Harimau Kramat*, the guardians of Nakhoda Ragam's shrine. If ever tigers mysteriously appear and then disappear in Malaysia, they are called *Harimau Kramat*.

Pulimau Harimau (Tiger Island) is an island in Johor in the south of the Malay Peninsula. The Malayan national tiger appears in the coat of arms of Malaysia, of Johor, and of Singapore. The Malayan nickname for the animal is *Pak Belang*, which means Uncle Stripes.

In Hinduism

In Hindu mythology, the tiger represents courage and strength. The god Shiva is frequently depicted seated on a tiger skin or rug, or wears a tiger skin as a cloak. The war goddess Durga rides a tiger (or occasionally lion) into battle. The god of growth, Ayyappan, son of Shiva, is also associated with the tiger.

In Folklore

There are many folklore stories in India and China about catching a tiger by the tail: the general moral seems to be—don't! In Korea, the tiger is a powerful guardian that brings good luck and prosperity. Koreans living in forest or mountain country call the tiger San Gun, meaning Mountain Lord. In Buddhism, the tiger is one of the Three Senseless Creatures: it represents anger (the monkey represents greed and the deer lovesickness). Just as there are werewolf stories in Europe, in India and Malaysia there are weretiger stories, with very similar motifs, including shape-shifting when exposed to the light of a full moon.

Leopard/Panther (*Panthera pardus*)

Phylum *Chordata*, Class *Mammalia*, Order *Carnivora*, Suborder *Feliformia*, Family *Felidae*, Subfamily *Pantherinae*, Genus *Panthera*, Species *Panthera pardus*

Name

The word leopard derives from Greek λεοπαρδος, *leópardos*, from λεων, *léōn*, lion, and παρδος, *párdos*, pard or male panther, which in turn may have come from an unattested ancient Persian or Egyptian word. The word panther usually refers to a leopard (occasionally also a cougar or jaguar) which is black in color.

Description

The leopard is found in Africa and some parts of Asia. It is thought that it now lives in only about 25 percent of its range a century ago. It is easily distinguished by its spots, technically better called rosettes, which are black on a background of sandy yellow or light orange. Melanistic (black-turning) leopards are black all over, and are often called panthers. It is an opportunistic hunter, relying on its powerful running (it can reach a speed of 36 miles per hour or 58 kilometers per hour). It also uses its great strength to drag killed prey up into the branches of a tree to keep it away from other predators or scavengers.

General Attributes

In contemporary folklore, leopard stories are now mostly limited to Africa, although they have also appeared in European tales in earlier ages. They are featured in European heraldry, usually in groups of three, but are easily confused with heraldic lions. In Africa generally, a leopard skin is a symbol of high status, and leopard-skin decorations and furnishings are common among many African royal and aristocratic families.

West Africa

The leopard is worshiped widely in West Africa. The Ashanti people of Ghana do not allow anyone to kill a leopard, nor to display a leopard skin, although a complete stuffed leopard may be acceptable as an object of worship. If someone does kill a leopard, they are made to follow its body around the town or village, smear themselves with dirt, and make leopard movements to appease the animal's spirit.

Tourism

India, Sri Lanka and South Africa all offer tourist safari programs to see leopards in their natural environments. Visitors often complain, however, because leopards are well camouflaged by their coats in savannah or safari-park terrains, and visitors frequently simply never see them, even though they may be there in some numbers.

Man-Eating Leopards

Leopards very rarely kill or eat humans, but, when they do, they apparently do it with considerable persistence. In India, the Leopard of Rudraprayag reputedly killed more than 125 people, while the Panar Leopard killed and ate more than 400. Big-game hunter Kenneth Anderson described leopards as far more dangerous than tigers:

> Although examples of such animals are comparatively rare, when they do occur they depict the panther [leopard] as an engine of destruction quite equal to his far larger cousin, the tiger. Because of his smaller size he can conceal himself in places impossible to a tiger, his need for water is far less, and in veritable demoniac cunning and daring, coupled with the uncanny sense of self-preservation and stealthy disappearance when danger threatens, he has no equal.[9]

Jaguar/Panther (*Panthera onca*)

Phylum *Chordata*, Class *Mammalia*, Order *Carnivora*, Suborder *Feliformia*, Family *Felidae*, Subfamily *Pantherinae*, Genus *Panthera*, Species *Panthera onca*

Name

The common name is thought to derive from *yaguara*, the name used by the Tupi peoples of South America, via early Portuguese *jaguar*. The scientific species name *onca* has a curious derivation. It was *onça* in Portuguese, and *l'once* in Old French. *L'once* and the Italian *l'onza* were thought to contain the definite article *l'*, equivalent to English "the," so the word came into English as "(the) ounce," which is also the alternative name for the closely related snow leopard. However, these words were derived from Latin *lyncea* (lynx), so it is a false etymology.

Description

The jaguar is found in the Southwestern United States, Mexico, Central America and South America as far south as Paraguay and parts of Argentina. The jaguar is very similar to the Asian and African leopard, but larger and stronger. It is the largest big cat in the Americas, and the third largest in the world after the tiger and lion. It is the only North American native big cat that roars. Like many of the big cats, it is a threatened species, with much of its typical preferred habitat of broad-leaf forest disappearing or being fragmented. It is a powerful swimmer and hunter, tending to lead a solitary life. Like the Asian and African leopard, it sometimes changes its spots for an all-black fur coat, and is then commonly also called a panther. In 2000, an international conservation effort was started, which designates selected territories as JCUs or Jaguar Conservation Units.[10]

General Attributes

The jaguar appears frequently in New World religion and mythology, especially in Mesoamerican cultures. It is a symbol of courage, power, strength and high social status.

Dajoji

In the mythology of the Iroquois nation of North American Indians, the cardinal winds are all gods. The god of the west wind is Dajoji, the jaguar/panther. When he snarls, even the sun hides its face.

Andean Cultures

Depictions of jaguars are found in the Chavin culture of Peru dating from 900–250 BCE. The later Moche culture of Peru (100–700 CE) depicted jaguars in ceramic sculptures. In Colombia, the pre-conquest Muisca Federation worshiped the jaguar, dressing in jaguar skins for rituals. The third ruler or *zipa* of Bacatá (modern Bogotá), Nemequene (ruled 1490–1514), took his name from native words *nymy* and *quyne* meaning Force of the Jaguar.[11]

Olmec, Maya and Aztec Cultures

The Olmec (c. 1500–400 BCE), who lived mostly in the tropical lowlands of Mexico, featured stylized jaguars or werejaguars (humans in jaguar form) in their sculptures. We know that shamans were very active in Olmec society, so it is reasonable to presume that shamans may have channeled jaguar spirits for conversations and journeys with spirits and gods.

In Mayan culture (c. 2000 BCE to the present day, with the last Mayan city colonized by the Spanish in 1697 CE), jaguars protected the royal household and communicated between the living and the dead. The Mayan word for jaguar was *b'alam*, and Balam is still a common Mayan surname.

The Aztecs (Central Mexico, c. 1300–1521 CE, colonial status 1521–1821 CE) saw the jaguar as a symbol of warriors and aristocrats. There was an elite group of guards who were called the Jaguar Knights. The jaguar was also the totem animal of the god of the night sky, Tezcatlipoca. Aztec culture was notoriously bloodthirsty, with regular and sometimes vast sacrificial ceremonies involving both animals and humans. At the same time, Aztec art was extremely diverse and sophisticated, and there are many fine examples of jaguar statues and figurines.

Cheetah (*Acinonyx jubatus*)

Phylum *Chordata*, Class *Mammalia*, Order *Carnivora*, Suborder *Feliformia*, Family *Felidae*, Subfamily *Pantherinae*, Genus *Acinonyx*, Species *Acinonyx jubatus*

Name

The English name derives from Hindi *cita*, which in turn is derived from Sanskrit *citrakayah*, which means variegated bodied. The genus name *Acinonyx* comes from Greek ακινετος, *akínetos*, motionless, and ονυξ, *onyx*, claw. (By comparison with other cats, the cheetah has only limited ability to retract its claws.) The cheetah is the only extant member of the genus *Acinonyx*. The species name *jubatus* is Latin for maned, because the cheetah has a small dorsal crest of fur.

Description

The cheetah is taller than the leopard, but much more lightly built, and is famed for its speed. It is the fastest land animal, able to run routinely at speeds up to 40 miles per hour (64 kilometers per hour) while hunting, but recorded as achieving an astonishing 70 miles per hour (112 kilometers per hour) while accelerating over short distances. It has a slim body with long legs, a grayish-tan coat covered with around 2,000 small black spots, black tear-drop markings on its face, and a long tail. It lives in various parts of Africa, apart from a single subspecies, *Acinonyx jubatus venaticus*, which lives in Iran, making it now the only Asian cheetah (although it is a critically endangered species there and may number fewer than 50 individuals). The cheetah's favored habitat is dry forest or grassland or savannah, but it has suffered considerable loss of habitat. By 2016, the world population of cheetahs was estimated to be only 7,100 individuals, most of them restricted to Southern Africa.[12]

General Attributes

Lions and cheetahs are the only big cats that travel and live regularly in groups, although cheetah females often go off by themselves. Males are very territorial, scent- and urine-marking defined territories. Females are not territorial. Cheetahs are very talkative, in the sense that they are very communicative with each other. They have a wide range of sophisticated vocalizations, and a number of physical social communication behaviors, such as sniffing each other's bodies, cheek rubbing or face licking, to maintain relationships. The cheetah has been tamed by human beings since antiquity. It was once widespread across Asia as well as Africa.

Cheetahs in Captivity

In ancient Egypt, during the reign of the pharaoh Hatshepsut (1507–1458 BCE), an expedition brought back two types of panthers to the royal palace: the first, called "panthers of the north," were leashed cheetahs, while the "panthers of the south" were leopards, which were much more aggressive. From the 16th to the 11th centuries BCE, cheetahs were common pets in royal and aristocratic homes. They were leashed and wore ornate collars. Their owners would bring them out into the desert or dry grassland, and let them loose to catch wild prey, like hunting dogs.

Cheetahs gradually spread widely across Asia as well as Africa. In the 3rd century CE, Roman authors described hunting with cheetahs in India, although Greek and Roman accounts are not entirely reliable because classical descriptions of big cats are notoriously imprecise. However, from the 7th century CE onwards, it is clear that cheetahs were well established in India and further eastwards. As late as the 19th century, royal households in western Asia still kept and displayed cheetahs as pets. Cheetahs were sold into China in return for gold, silver and silk.

Cougar/Puma/Mountain Lion (*Puma concolor*)

Phylum *Chordata*, Class *Mammalia*, Order *Carnivora*, Suborder *Feliformia*, Family *Felidae*, Subfamily *Pantherinae*, Genus *Puma*, Species *Puma concolor*

Name

The *Puma concolor* literally holds the world record for the number of different names it has, with over 40 in English alone. Cougar, probably the most common name in English, is derived from Portuguese *çuçuarana*, originally from a Tupi name. In 21 of the 23 North, Central and South American countries in which it is found, it is called a puma rather than a cougar. Puma is Spanish, picked up by the Conquistadors from the indigenous Quechua language in the 16th century: it means powerful. In addition to cougar and puma, the names mountain lion, *gato monte* or cat of the mountain and catamount (probably a corruption of *gato monte*) are commonly heard. There are dozens of Indian names, too. The genus name *Puma* is taken from the Spanish, and the species name *concolor* is Latin for "of the same color" (see description below).

Description

The cougar is not a little big cat; it is a big little cat. That seems like gobbledeygook, but the meaning is this: the cougar, large as it is, is more closely related to the domestic cat, *Felis sylvestris catus*, than any of the big cats, even the smaller big cats. The species name *concolor* is a clue: the cougar is an even color more or less all over (as are many domestic cats), usually a grayish-tan, rather than spotted or striped. It is the biggest cat in North America.

Although the cougar has largely disappeared from the Eastern United States, it is widely distributed across North, Central and South America; it is found everywhere from the Yukon in Canada to the southern Andes. It can survive in open areas, but its preferred habitat is rocky ground with canyons, escarpments, and bush or tree cover, since its favored hunting method is to approach prey stealthily and then leap upon it, preferably from a height.

General Attributes

Cougars have featured in several indigenous New World cultures. They are generally considered resourceful, powerful and beautiful animals. They do predate on livestock, and so, like wolves, are less popular with farmers. Although they can be physically intimidating, they rarely attack humans: the majority of human fatalities have been children, and there is evidence that a loud voice and determined counter-intimidation are often enough to drive away a potential attack.

In South and Central American Cultures

The Inca revered the cougar: their city Cusco or Cuzco in southeastern Peru was designed in the shape of a cougar. Several regions and tribal groups incorporated the cougar in their names. The Inca sky-god and creator deity Viracocha, also known as Con-Tici (the Kon-Tiki of Thor Heyerdahl's balsa raft) was associated with the cougar.

The Moche civilization, which flourished in northern Peru from about 100 to 700 CE, produced many ceramic statues and figurines of cougars. Moche art is distinctive, and the superbly finished cougar pieces suggest high status for the living animal.

In North American Indian Mythology

The cougar has a varied reputation among different Indian nations. For the Algonquins and the Ojibwe it is an evil animal, connected with the Underworld and death. The Apache and Walapai of Arizona also believe that the wailing, howling sound sometimes made by cougars is a harbinger of death. The Cherokee, however, deem the cougar sacred and celebrate it in song and ritual dance.

Lynx (*Lynx lynx*)

Phylum *Chordata*, Class *Mammalia*, Order *Carnivora*, Suborder *Feliformia*, Family *Felidae*, Subfamily *Felinae*, Genus *Lynx*, Species *Lynx lynx*

Name

The name *lynx*, found in Middle English and in Latin, is derived from Greek λυνξ, *lynx*, which is thought to have come from a Proto-Indo-European root **leuk-* meaning light or brightness, relating to the brightness of the animal's eyes. It is also called the bobcat, the bob- part meaning cut short, because it has a very short tail. Two other cats, the caracal and the jungle cat, are commonly called desert lynx and jungle lynx respectively, but are not actually in the *Lynx* genus.

Description

The lynx is larger than the domestic cat or wildcat, but considerably smaller than the big cats. There are four living species, the Eurasian lynx (*Lynx lynx*), the Canada lynx (*Lynx canadensis*), the Iberian lynx (*Lynx pardinus*) and the bobcat (*Lynx rufus*), of which the bobcat is the smallest and the Eurasian lynx is the largest, with considerable variations in size within each species depending on location. All lynx have distinctive tufted ears. Body color ranges from full brown to beige, sometimes with darker brown spots, and chest and belly fur is typically white. They are usually solitary animals, hunting a wide range of prey, from large deer to small voles.

General Attributes

Lynx are small but powerfully built, often elusive, and with a reputation for keen eyesight (in some cultures they are reputed to be able to see through solid objects) and clairvoyance (because of their preternaturally bright eyes). The Eurasian lynx is the national animal of North Macedonia and of Romania. The lynx features particularly in Greek, Norse and North American Indian mythologies.

The Lynx Stone

The Greek philosopher Theophrastus (c. 371–c. 287 BCE) claimed that lynx urine hardens into a stone with magical properties. This notion was carried forward in Roman mythology by Ovid and Pliny the Elder, and continued in medieval European folklore until it gradually died out in the 17th century. The stone was called *lapis lyncurius* (stone of the lynx) in Latin, which was believed to be the source of the Latin word for amber, *lyncurium*, although the region in which amber was mined in the greatest quantity in classical times was the northern Italian region of Liguria, a pre–Latin name, which may be a more plausible source.

Lyncus

One of the transformation stories in the Roman poet Ovid's *Metamorphoses* tells the legend of King Lyncus of Scythia:

> The goddess Demeter, who was also called Σιτω, Sitō, She of the Grain, was determined to spread knowledge of agriculture throughout the world. Her ambassador, Triptolemus (Three-times Ptolemy), traveled the world teaching agricultural knowledge and skills. Triptolemus came to the court of the Scythian king, Lyncus. The Scythians were a largely nomadic people, who cared very little for farming and were not interested in learning about it. Lyncus formally welcomed Triptolemus to his palace, but privately considered what advantage he could take from the visit. In the end, he decided that there was nothing that Triptolemus could offer him. While his guest was sleeping, Lyncus took out his sword and raised it above his head. To save Triptolemus, Demeter instantly transformed Lyncus into a lynx, and Triptolemus was saved.[13]

American Indian Lynx Gods

Lusifee, a spirit of the Wabanaki people, is a personification of malevolence and greed. It is thought that the name may be a corruption of the European name Lucifer (Bright Shining), an alternative for Satan or the Devil, or of the French-Canadian for lynx, *loup-cervier*.

The Great Lynx, sometimes called the Water Panther, Underwater Panther, Night Panther or Matchi-Manitou, is recognized by the Ojibwe, Algonquin, Ottawa, Menominee, Shawnee and Cree as a combination of lynx and water-dragon. It lives in deep water and sucks humans down into the depths to drown. The Real Lynx is a similar monster recognized by the Miami and the Illini. Its Indian name Aramipinchiwa means Underneath Lynx.[14]

Freya

In Norse mythology, Freya is the goddess equivalent of Greek Aphrodite or Roman Venus, i.e., the goddess of love, beauty and sex, but Freya is also a war goddess. Her chariot is normally drawn by two or more domestic cats, but in her war goddess aspect she may be drawn by lynx, which are simultaneously more powerful and more mysterious and elusive than ordinary cats.

Accademia dei Lincei

The Italian naturalist Federico Cesi (1585–1630 CE) founded the *Accademia dei Lincei* (Academy of the Lynx) in 1603.[15] One of its most famous members was the world-renowned physicist, astronomer and engineer Galileo Galilei (1564–1642 CE). Cesi and his colleagues chose the name of the academy after seeing a drawing of a lynx on the cover of *Magia Naturalis*, a book of popular science by Giambattista della Porta published in 1558. The preface to that book described the lynx as the emblem of clear-sightedness and courageous determination to see the truth clearly, characteristics which the fledgling Academy held dear. The well-known story of Galileo's recantation under pressure from the Catholic Church, but his determined belief in the truth that the earth does, indeed, revolve around the sun and not the other way round ("*Eppe si muove,*" "And yet, it does move") exemplifies this fundamental scientific concept.

Hyena (*Hyaena hyaena* and three other species)

Phylum *Chordata*, Class *Mammalia*, Order *Carnivora*, Suborder *Feliformia*, Infraorder *Viverroidea*, Family *Hyaenidae*, Genus *Hyaena*, Species *Hyaena hyaena* and three others

Name

There are four extant species of hyena, of which *Hyaena hyaena* is the most abundant. The common name and species name *Hyaena hyaena* are derived from ancient Greek ʽυαινα, *húaina*. This species is sometimes called the striped hyena. *Hyaena brunnea* simply means the brown hyena, which is its common name. *Crocuta crocuta* is the spotted hyena, also known as the laughing hyena, which diverged from the striped and brown hyenas about 10 million years ago. It was thought for a long time that the name *crocuta* was derived from Latin *crocus* (the flower), meaning saffron-colored, but it is now thought that the name derives from Greek κροκοττας, *krokóttas*, which originally signified the golden jackal. The fourth species is *Proteles cristata*, commonly called the *aardwolf*, which is Afrikaans and Dutch for earth-wolf. The genus or generic name comes from two Greek words, πρoτος, *protos*, and τελεος, *teleos*, collectively meaning "complete in front" (because it has five toes on each front paw and four on each hind paw), and Latin *cristata*, meaning crested, describing the animal's mane.

Description

The hyena is more dog-like than cat-like in appearance. It is not a big cat or member of the family *Felidae* at all, but it is included in this section because it does belong to the suborder *Feliformia* (animals shaped like cats) and some of its behaviors are similar to big-cat behaviors. Hyenas are dog-like in that they catch prey mainly with their teeth, and their claws do not retract. They are cat-like in that they have strong-smelling urine, use scent marking, and wash themselves by licking.

General Attributes

Hyenas have a reputation as cowardly scavengers, but the reputation is undeserved. The spotted hyena (*Crocuta crocuta*) is a pack-hunting animal and kills most of what it eats, while the striped hyena (*Hyaena hyaena*) is more of a scavenger. Medieval Christian symbolism saw the hyena as unclean, representing the Devil.

In Greek and Roman Folklore

The ancient Greeks and Romans believed that the hyena could change sex at will. Neither cat nor dog, it was also neither female nor male. As a result, hyena testicles were believed to have magical properties. The trick was to catch the animal while it was male and castrate it quickly, before it changed to a female. The testicles were crushed and left to dry into a powder, which was then deemed to have magical restorative properties.

In Medieval Christian Folklore

Medieval Christians believed that hyenas could imitate human voices, like parrots, and that they used this skill to entice humans to approach. They would then kill the humans and eat them. They also believed that hyenas mated with lions, producing an animal called the *crocote* with no teeth and gums, but a single curve of biting bone like a box lid. At the time, very few people knew that hyenas rarely if ever attack humans.

The modern Hebrew word for hyena is *tzavoa*, which is very similar to the word *tsavua*, meaning colored. This explains the variance between the Authorized King James Version translation of the Hebrew *ayit tsavua* (Jeremiah 12:9) as "speckled bird," while more modern versions have "hyena."

In Africa

In West Africa, hyenas have a similar reputation as in medieval Christianity. They are often considered malignant and unclean.

In East Africa, the Lungu people of the Congo, Tanzania and Zambia worship the hyena as a solar deity, although in Tanzania there is also a belief that witches ride hyenas, and that if a hyena cackles while a child is being born, the child will grow up to be a thief. The Kaguru of Tanzania and the Kujamaat of Senegal share the ancient Greek and Roman belief that hyenas are hermaphrodites.

In the Middle East

A Persian medical treatise of 1376 identifies human cannibals called *kaftars*, who were believed to be half-human and half-hyena, a kind of werehyena. Hyenas generally are considered evil and malevolent, like *jinns*. Arab folklore says that hyenas can hypnotize humans, and that the mere smell of them (we would say pheromones today) can lure women to their deaths.

Mongoose (several species)

Phylum *Chordata*, Class *Mammalia*, Order *Carnivora*, Suborder *Feliformia*, Infraorder *Viverroidea*, Family *Herpestidae*, Type genus *Herpestes*, Genus (14) Species (34)

Name

The common name appears to be derived from the Marathi language of western India, where the animal is called a *mungus*, which came first into Portuguese as *mangusto*. The -goose ending, first recorded in 1698, arose simply from English folk pronunciation and spelling. Historically, the common name quite often appears with the spelling mungoose. The name has nothing at all to do with geese, and the plural is mongooses.

The type genus name *Herpestes* is New Latin, coined from ancient Greek ʽερπεστες, *herpestes*, which means creeping.

Description

The mongoose is neither a cat, nor a dog, nor a goose, but it has to live somewhere in the classification matrix, and it is included in this section because, like the hyena, it belongs to the suborder *Feliformia* (cat-shaped animals). It is a member of the infraorder, *Viverroidea* (civets or genets, which have four or five toes on each foot and semi-retractile claws). The Viverrids include the civet, the genet, the binturong, the linsang and the oyan, most or all of which are relatively unfamiliar in the West. These animals, including the mongoose, all look more like weasels or stoats (mustelids) than cats. They have long faces and bodies, short rounded ears, short legs and long tails. They have long claws, used mainly for digging.

The mongoose is native to southern Eurasia and most regions of Africa. It is one of four animals in the world that are genetically programmed to be unharmed by snake bites: the other three are the honey-badger, hedgehog and pig. Mongooses don't particularly like snake meat, but they are famed in India for their ability to attack and kill venomous snakes, especially cobras. Their diet is very varied, and includes carrion and food waste.

Mongooses in the Middle East

The mongoose was sacred to the god Ninkillim in ancient Mesopotamia. Ninkillim was invoked for protection from snakes. A Babylonian folkloric tale has a mouse running away from a mongoose straight into a snake's hidey-hole and announcing, "Greetings from the snake charmer." The Roman historian Diodorus Siculus tells us that the ancient Egyptians venerated the mongoose because of its ability to kill snakes.

Mongooses in Hinduism and Buddhism

Kubera, the Hindu god of wealth, is frequently depicted holding a mongoose in his left hand, so the mongoose has become a symbol of prosperity. Similarly, the Tibetan Buddhist deity Vaishravana (a name also used for Kubera) holds a mongoose that spits out jewels, symbolizing generosity (the snake symbolizes greed).

Rikki-Tikki-Tavi

Probably the most famous mongoose in literature is Rikki-Tikki-Tavi, who appears in the *Jungle Book* stories of Rudyard Kipling (1865–1936). A British family living in India take him in as a pet and as a protector against harm from snakes. The other animals in the garden warn Rikki-Tikki-Tavi about Nag and Nagaina (names which mean Lord Snake and Lady Snake), two venomous cobras. Nag comes into the house to kill the family, but Rikki-Tikki-Tavi fights ferociously with him, until the paterfamilias comes in and dispatches Nag with his shotgun. Nagaina plots revenge, but Rikki-Tikki-Tavi destroys her eggs, and finally destroys her in her underground nest. The story became so popular after *The Jungle Book* was published in 1894 that it has since been frequently anthologized, and even published by itself as a short book for children.

7

Cattle (Oxen), Antelopes and Hippopotamuses (*Artiodactyla: Bovidae, Hippopotamidae*)

Ox, Cow, Bull (*Bos taurus*)

Phylum *Chordata*, Class *Mammalia*, Order *Artiodactyla*, Family *Bovidae*, Subfamily *Bovinae*, Genus *Bos*, Species *Bos taurus*

Name

Cows and bulls collectively are cattle, and all of them can also be called oxen. An ox is typically a castrated male adult used as a draft animal or occasionally as a riding animal, although cows (females) and bulls (intact males) may also be called and used as oxen in some areas. Cow is from Middle English *cou*, in turn from Old English *cu*. Bull is from Middle English *bole*, *bul* or *bule*, in turn from Old English *bula* and Old Norse *buli*. Cattle is from Old French *chattel* via Anglo-Norman French, which also gave us chattels for personal possessions. The species binomial is from Greek βους, *bous*, ox, and Latin *taurus*, bull.

Description

Cattle were first domesticated probably about ten thousand years ago, but there are now estimated to be about 1.5 billion domesticated cattle in the world. In many languages, words for cattle and words for wealth are related, indicating that in many cultures cattle have been and still are indicators of wealth and status. The word cattle itself is related to capital, both being derived from Latin *capitale*, and ultimately from *caput*, meaning head.

Cattle are large, quadripedal (four-legged) ungulates (hoofed animals) with cloven (split) hooves. They are ruminants (animals that have a specialized stomach to ferment and pre-digest plant foods with low food value, such as grass). They are found all over the world, apart from the Arctic and the Antarctic and other very cold regions. Modern farmed breeds are typically raised on range land or in grass pastures with plentiful fodder, but older breeds could survive in quite sparse environments.

General Attributes

The cow has been venerated in Hinduism for centuries. Cow's milk has been an important food source to so many human groups throughout history that several superstitions and ritual practices are associated with it. Cattle feature in the ancient Egyptian and Greek pantheons, and in Zoroastrianism. As one of the largest and most powerful mammals on the planet, it is hardly surprising that the bull has been a symbol of fertility, virility and superiority for millennia.

Gilgamesh, Enkidu and the Bull of Heaven

Perhaps the oldest written legend concerning a sacred bull is from the poem *The Epic of Gilgamesh,* which celebrates a real king who ruled the Sumerian city-state of Uruk in ancient Mesopotamia (parts of modern Iraq, Kuwait, Saudi Arabia, Turkey and Iran) sometime between 2800 and 2500 BCE. After his death, Gilgamesh was deified. The Bull of Heaven story runs as follows:

> Gilgamesh took his great strength for granted and was a cruel and despotic king, until he met Enkidu, who until that meeting had lived as a long-haired, semi-naked wild man amongst wild animals. Gilgamesh taught Enkidu the rules of civilization, and Enkidu taught Gilgamesh compassion, sensitivity and patience. Their friendship was deep and long lasting.
>
> The great goddess Ishtar invited Gilgamesh to make love to her, but he refused. In retaliation, Ishtar asked her father, the creation god Anu, to fashion a mighty bull, the Bull of Heaven. She sent the Bull of Heaven to kill Gilgamesh, but Gilgamesh destroyed the beast. Enkidu, who had the same superhuman strength as his friend, added insult to injury by throwing the dead body of the Bull of Heaven in Ishtar's face.
>
> Ishtar then punished Enkidu by casting a wasting sickness on him. For twelve days he suffered great torment, but then he fell into a deep sleep, from which he never recovered. Gilgamesh wept seven whole days and nights for his departed friend after his death, and for the first time felt intimations of his own inevitable death: "I'll also die and worms will feast on my flesh. I now fear death and have lost all my courage." Gilgamesh left Uruk and went in search of immortality, but never found it. When he finally returned to the city, he was warmly greeted by the ghost of Enkidu, and he resigned himself to his mortality.[1]

Apis

Apis is the Greek version of the older Egyptian name Hapi, the name of the sacred bull associated with the god Ptah of Memphis. When the Apis bull died, it was buried with great ceremony in the Serapeum, a vast cemetery of underground catacombs in the desert outside the city gates, as if it had been a pharaoh who had died.

Hathor and Other Cow Goddesses

Hathor is a major goddess of the Egyptian pantheon, frequently depicted as a cow or with the head of a cow. Her four legs are the pillars that hold up the sky. The hawk god Horus is both her husband and her son, because at every sunset he flies into her mouth and at every dawn he flies out again. Her Egyptian name, *hwt-hwr,* can be translated either as House of Horus or My House Is the Sky. She is the mother of all living things, but she can also be a destroyer. (In one legend, she so enjoyed killing humans that the other gods flooded the fields with beer dyed red to look like blood, to make her too drunk to carry on the slaughter.) At the same time, she is so beneficent and loving that she cares not only for the living, but also visits the underworld, Duat, to protect and care for the dead. In the same way that she brings the living sun, Horus or Ra, into the living world each day, so she assists the souls of the dead to emerge from the night of death into the bright day of the afterlife.

Shrines and temples were dedicated to Hathor throughout Egypt. She was most often depicted as a beautiful woman with cow horns containing a sun disk. Her colors were red, gold and turquoise. She first came to prominence during the Old Kingdom (c. 2686–2181 BCE) and rapidly gained superiority over the other deities, mostly because she was identified as the wife of the sun god Ra and goddess, protector, mother, wife or lover of every ruling pharaoh in succession. She was often depicted nursing the pharaoh at her breast.

But she was also worshiped at every level of society. She had more temples dedicated to her than any other Egyptian goddess. She had temples in other countries beyond Egypt, in Africa and in the Near East, particularly in Syria and Canaan. She was also a goddess of the home, and was invoked especially by women, particularly those seeking to become pregnant or about to give birth. (Egyptian women gave birth squatting over special sanctified bricks: the only surviving birth-brick from ancient Egypt is decorated with images of Hathor.) It was not until the period of the New Kingdom (c. 1550–1070 BCE) that the goddess Isis began to supersede Hathor, and even then Hathor remained a major deity right through to the end of ancient Egyptian religion during the first few centuries CE.

During the Late Period (664–323 BCE), the divine family or trinity of mother, father and holy child gained prominence, and Hathor was usually the mother. At Dendera (on the west bank of the Nile, north of Luxor), a major center of Hathor worship, Horus was the father and Ihy the sistrum-player was the child-god. A *sekhem* (the Egyptian name) or σειστρον, *seïstron* (the Greek name), now called a *sistrum* in West Africa, was a percussion instrument with a chiming or rattling sound, associated with celebration and joyous ritual. A sistrum or *menet* (rattling bead) necklace, representing Hathor, was a common piece of women's jewelry, and was shaken percussively during ceremonies. Hathor was associated with music, dance, merrymaking and unashamed sexual activity. From the early New Kingdom onwards, on the twentieth day of the month of Thoth, the first month of the Egyptian calendar (mid–September to mid–October in the modern western calendar), Hathor was celebrated in the Festival of Drunkenness, during which relatives would visit the tombs of deceased relatives, eat and drink to excess, dance and sing, flirt and make merry, and look for ecstatic connection with the great mother-goddess Hathor. Even when the more sedate and chaste goddesses Isis and Mut began to replace her as the dominant mother goddess, Hathor remained popular as the epitome of the beautiful, powerful, uninhibited woman. In one legend, the great sun god Ra is lying on his back, momentarily—and most unusually—doubting his power and unable to stir himself. To rouse him (literally) and restore him to his godly duties, Hathor stands over him and exposes her vagina, laughing coquettishly. Ra laughs too, gets up, and resumes his kingly tasks.

Greater even than the Festival of Drunkenness, however, was the Festival of the Beautiful Reunion, which lasted fourteen days during the month of Epiphi (modern June and July). A statue of Hathor was carried by boat from Dendera to several other temples, to visit their deities. The final destination was the Temple of Horus at Edfu. The images of Horus and Hathor were left to spend the night together, and nine months later the festival of their son, Ihy, was celebrated.

In the Zoroastrian mythology of ancient Persia, the cow goddess Gavaevodata shares many of Hathor's attributes. Created by the lord of light Ahura Mazda, she was, like Hathor, the mother of all living beings, and was essentially beneficent and caring. Kamadhenu (From Whom All That Is Desired Is Drawn) or Surabhi (The Fragrant One), a cow goddess in Hindu mythology, is also a universal mother, the mother of all cows (which are sacred in Hinduism), often depicted as a white cow with the head and breasts of a beautiful woman. She is not worshiped in temples, but in actual cows, each of which is a manifestation of the goddess.

Big Redcoat and Little Redcoat

The Jatakas or *Birth-Stories of the Former Lives of the Buddha* are a vast collection of Buddhist folktales. Here is an example:

> The Buddha was born as an ox called Big Redcoat. His disciple, Ananda, was born as his younger brother, Little Redcoat. They lived with a poor family in a small village. The daughter of the family was engaged to be married to the son of a neighboring family. That family had a pig, called Celery.
>
> Little Redcoat complained bitterly to Big Redcoat that they were forced to eat poor quality grass and hay, while the neighbor's fat pig was given rice porridge, scraps from the table, and all kinds of luxuries.
>
> "Don't worry," answered Big Redcoat (the Buddha incarnate). "They're fattening Celery up for the wedding. Wait a few more days, then you'll see him dragged out, killed, chopped up, and served to the wedding guests."
>
> And so it happened. Little Redcoat (Ananda) learned from Big Redcoat (the Buddha) that sometimes it is wise to be contented with our lot in life, and not to be jealous of the apparent good fortune of others.[2]

The Augean Stables

Augeas (Bright Ray) was a Greek god, a son of the Titan Helios. He owned thousands of sheep and cattle, among which were twelve pure white, sacred bulls, which he kept in a large stable. The bulls were extremely fertile, but because they were so strong and savage, Augeas handled them as little as possible, and the stable, large as it was, gradually filled with their dung and urine. The sixth of Herakles's impossible twelve labors was to clean the Augean stable. He achieved the task by diverting the rivers Alphaeus and Peneus, which washed all the filth away. When Augeas refused to pay, Herakles killed him and all of his sons apart from one.[3] To this day, an "Augean stable" means any filthy, cluttered place.

Achelous

In Greek mythology, Achelous was the oldest of the river gods. He could shape-shift into any form, his favorites being the serpent and the ox. He fought with Herakles and lost one horn. He was widely worshiped in Greece and in the Greek colonies, especially Rhodes, Italy and Sicily. The sacred oracle at Dodona ended every prophecy with an injunction to sacrifice to Achelous.[4]

Io

The goddess Io in Greek mythology was one of Hera's priestesses. As he did with so many other beautiful young women, humans and goddesses alike, Zeus seduced Io. To protect her from Hera's anger (or as a punishment by Hera) Zeus turned her into a heifer. Her father, Inachus, came looking for her, but found only the heifer. When the heifer scratched the name Ιω, Iō, meaning Moon, in the sand with her hoof, Inachus realized that it was his daughter. Io wandered to Egypt, where she was restored to human shape before giving birth to Epaphus, her son by Zeus. Epaphus (Touch, from the legend that he was conceived by the mere touch of Zeus' hand against Io's skin) became a king of Egypt.[5]

Io is the fourth-largest moon of the planet Jupiter. It is the driest and most geologically active object in the Solar System.

The Cattle of the Sun

In Homer's *Odyssey* (Book 12), Odysseus and his men pass the island of Thrinicia. The cattle living on the island were sacred to the sun god Apollo, and Odysseus warned his men not to eat any of them. But the men were hungry after being at sea for a long while, and they slaughtered some of the cattle and ate them. Apollo took his revenge by sinking their ship and drowning all of the men except for Odysseus himself.[6]

Astarte/Ishtar/Ashtoreth/Astaroth

Astarte, also called Ishtar, Ashtoreth, or Astaroth, was a Great Mother goddess worshiped widely throughout the ancient Near and Middle East. She was one of the most popular pagan goddesses of the ancient world, and she has neo-pagan Druidic and Wiccan followers to this day. She was often portrayed as a cow in Canaan and Phoenicia, or with the head of a cow or bull. In later art, she was given the head of a lion, and was called the Queen of Heaven. She has been worshiped for at least four thousand years. An early statue in Mesopotamia, dating from about 2000 BCE, depicts her as a naked woman with a horned headdress.

In the Old Testament, she is named as the rival of Yahweh, the Hebrew deity:

> Then the Israelites did what was evil in the sight of the LORD and worshipped the Baals: and they abandoned the LORD, the God of their ancestors, who had brought them out of the land of Egypt; they followed other gods, from among the gods of the people who were all around them, and bowed down to them, and provoked the LORD to anger. They abandoned the LORD and worshiped Baal and the Astartes.[7]

Even the wise King Solomon built a temple for her in one of the "high places" typically sacred to pagan deities:

> The king defiled the high places that were east of Jerusalem, to the south of the Mount of Destruction, which King Solomon of Israel had built for Astarte the abomination of the Sidonians....[8]

Sidon, the third-largest city in Lebanon with about 250,000 inhabitants, has been inhabited as a Mediterranean fishing center since prehistory, and is still very multicultural, with many different religions represented in the populace.

Milton describes Astarte as having "crescent horns" in *Paradise Lost* (Book 1), which make her both a cow goddess and a moon goddess. She has always been associated with prosperity, fertility and sexual energy. The Romans associated her with both female and male prostitution, Apuleius describing her male priests in *The Golden Ass* as having "their faces daubed with rouge and their eye sockets painted to bring out the brightness of their eyes."[9]

In the Middle Ages, Christians converted Astarte into a male demon named Astaroth, connecting her/him with the archdemon Asmodeus. In 1637, the most famous mistress of King Louis XIV of France, named Françoise-Athénaïs de Rochechouart, Marquise de Montespan (or, more simply, Madame de Montespan), reputedly sacrificed new-born infants to the demons Astaroth and Asmodeus in order to gain the king's favor. The remains of 2,500 slaughtered babies were said to have been found in the home of Madame de Montespan's witch accomplice. She was accused of crushing the bones and flesh of the babies and secretly adding them to the king's food over a period of thirteen years. Beautiful and clever as she was, she lost the king's favor and died in obscurity at the age of 68.

In Ancient Celtic Culture

Three of the four major ancient Celtic festivals relate to the husbandry of cattle: at Beltan or Beltane (Bel's fire, on or about 1 May), cattle were brought out of their winter shelter and driven between purifying fires before being set out to graze on open pasture. At Samhain (pronounced *sa-wen*, on or about 1 November), the fittest and best of the cattle were selected to over-winter in sheltered housing, while the rest would be slaughtered to provide dried and salted meat through the long winter months. At Oimelc or Imbolc (on or about 1 February), the time of lambing and calving, the new calves were blessed and cosseted, their mothers providing a new abundance of milk, cream, butter and cheese.

According to Irish legend, the first cows emerged from the sea at Baile Cronin. They were colored white (the Virgin Goddess), red or brown (the Mother Goddess) and black (the Crone Goddess), and all cattle have been some combination of those colors ever since.[10]

Celtic Milk Offerings

In rural Ireland, the first few drops of milk from any milking were allowed to squirt onto the ground as an offering to the *sídhe* (pronounced *shee-uh*, the fairy folk). Ancient cup and ring markings on standing stones in Scotland were filled with milk, and milk would be carried and poured on the ground on mountain tops in offering to the gods and the ancestors. In Brittany, standing stones (of which there are very many) were traditionally washed with fresh milk in offering to the many gods and spirits that frequented them.[11]

Flidais

Flidais, the wife of the mythical hero Fergus, is an ancient Irish Celtic goddess of the woods and wild places. She is associated with deer, but even more with cattle. She is reputed to have had a magical cow that could give enough milk every day for 300 warriors. She appears in an Ulster poem called *Táin Bó Flidhais* (The Raid on Flidais's Cattle) and in *The Táin Bó Cúailnge* (see below).

Biróg, Balor and the Magical Cow

A Celtic tale of a magical cow runs as follows:

Biróg was a *ban-drui* or female Druid of the *Tuatha Dé Danann*, the fairy folk. Balor, the one-eyed giant God of the Fomorians, had been given a prophecy that he would be killed by his own grandson, and was determined that the prophecy would not be fulfilled. He imprisoned his only daughter, Eithne (Little Fire), in a high tower on Tory Island, so that no man could find her. Balor later stole a magically productive cow from a man called Mac Cinnfhaelaidh (McKinley). Mac Cinnfhaelaidh seethed at Balor's dishonesty and bullying, and longed for the return of his magical cow.

Biróg helped Mac Cinnfhaelaidh gain his revenge by magically bringing him to Eithne in the high tower, where he seduced Balor's daughter and made her pregnant. Eithne subsequently gave birth to triplets (a common event in druidic legends). Balor ordered a servant to murder the three infants, but the servant, having drowned two of them, unwittingly dropped the third, still alive, in the harbor. Biróg rescued the baby and brought it back to Mac Cinnfhaelaidh, who, in turn, gave it to his brother, Gavida the smith, in fosterage. In due course, the baby grew into a man (the personification of the god Lugh) and killed Balor, to fulfill the prediction.[12]

The Táin Bó Cúailnge

The ancient Irish epic the *Táin Bó Cúailnge* (pronounced approximately *toyn-baw-kool-nyuh*, meaning Cattle Raid of Cooley) is set in the 1st century CE and forms part of the Ulster Cycle. There have been many translations into English, but the best, in my view, is that of Thomas Kinsella (*The Táin*, Oxford University Press, 1969). It tells the story of the Connacht goddess/queen Medb and her husband Ailill raiding Ulster to steal the magical stud bull Donn, which the divine hero Cú Chulainn is sworn to defend:

The two great magical bulls of Ireland were Findbennach (White Horns) of Connacht and Donn (Brown) of Cúailnge or Cooley in Ulster. They were originally poor, filthy swineherds who could not stop arguing about anything and everything under the sun. They shape-shifted in to ravens, then stags, then water-monsters, then back to humans, then demons, then finally eels—which were eaten up by cows and delivered as bull calves. The story ends with the two great bulls fighting to the death, with Donn of Ulster defeating Findbennach (Donn is a Celtic god of death).

Before the ultimate battle, however, there were many incidents involving Cú Chulainn that are filled with druidical themes, several of them involving animals. The great goddess, the Morrígan, visited him before one combat and offered him her love, but he turned her down. In spite, she became an eel and tripped him at a ford (a place of religious significance for druids, being both land, the world of humans, and water, the world of the dead). She became a wolf, and stampeded cattle across the ford to kill him, but he survived the stampede. Finally, she became a heifer at the head of the stampede, and tried to gore him to death. He escaped. In all three confrontations, Cú Chulainn wounded the goddess. She finally appeared as an old crone milking a cow. Cú Chullain accepted and drank three cups of milk from her, and as he drank each one, each of the Morrígan's three wounds was healed.[13]

The Tarbhfess

The *tarbhfess* (*tarv-fess*, meaning bull sleep) was an ancient Irish Druidic ritual described as taking place at Tara, where the High King of All Ireland was chosen by the druids.

It is highly likely that similar rituals also took place in Britain. When a new High King was to be chosen, a selected druid was given meat and broth from a bull that had been ritually slain. He was then wrapped in the slain animal's hide. While he slept, four druids chanted spells of truth over him. When he awoke, he named the rightful new king.

The Golden Calf

In the Bible, Aaron is consecrated High Priest by Moses. When Moses goes up onto Mount Sinai for forty days and forty nights to receive the Ten Commandments from God, the Israelites begin to fear that Moses has abandoned them. In response to their demands for "gods to go before them,"[14] Aaron gathers their gold and melts it down to form a golden calf for them to worship. The Israelites pay homage to the image. God tells Moses what the Israelites have done, and says that he will destroy them. Moses pleads on their behalf. When Moses returns, he destroys the image, crushes its remains to powder, dissolves the powder in water, and forces the Israelites to drink it. Only the tribe of Levi had not taken part in the calf worship. Moses calls the Levites to him, and says, "Thus saith the Lord, the God of Israel: Put ye every man his sword upon his thigh, and go to and fro from gate to gate throughout the camp, and slay every man his brother, and every man his companion, and every man his neighbor."[15] The Levites obey Moses, and kill about three thousand of the other Israelites.

Haitsi-aibed

In the mythology of the Khoikhoi people of southwestern Africa, Haitsi-aibed, a great hero and the patron of hunters, was born of a cow and the grass it had eaten. His most famous battle was against a monster called Gaunab. The monster would sit at the edge of a deep pit and challenge passers-by to throw a stone at him. The stone would always bounce off Gaunab, ricochet back on to the thrower, and knock the thrower to his death in the pit. Haitsi-aibed's trick was to hit Gaunab just below the ear, the only place from which the stone could not rebound. Thus Haitsi-aibed knocked Gaunab into the pit and the world was rid of an evil monster.[16]

Audhumla

In the Norse Creation myth, the first living being was a giant cow, Audhumla, who was formed out of the primeval mist. She fed her milk to the primeval giant Ymir. She lived by licking the salt from stones. On the first day, her licking produced human hair. On the second day, a human head appeared. On the third day, an entire man appeared. He was Bur, who fathered Bor, who married the female giant Besla, and these primeval giants were the parents of the first gods, Odin, Vili and Ve.[17]

Bicorn and Chichevache

A satirical and sexist folklore story from early medieval France was popular in Europe. Two animals (husband and wife in some versions) were known as Bicorn (Two Horns) and

Chichevache (Thin, Niggardly or Greedy Cow). Bicorn was fat, because he ate nothing but patient husbands (of which there are always plenty), but Chichevache was thin, because she lived on patient wives (of whom there are very few). Chaucer (1340–1400) mentions the fable in the Clerk's story in *The Canterbury Tales*:

O noble wyves, ful of heigh prudence,	*great care*
Lat noon humylitee youre tonge naille,	*nail your tongue*
Ne lat no clerk have cause or diligence	*cleric*
To write of yow a storie of swich mervaille	*such marvel*
As of Grisildis pacient and kynde,	*Griseldas (women like her)*
Lest Chichevache yow swelwe in hire entraille!	*swallow you in her belly*[18]

The Dun Cow

In British folklore, there are several tales about a dun (gray-brown) cow, all so similar that they look like the same legend, but set in different places. The best known of them is the Dun Cow of Dunsmore Heath in Warwickshire, England. The Dun Cow was a monstrous and savage beast (quite unlike the typical cow), said to belong to a giant, but her greatest asset was that her supply of milk was inexhaustible. One day, a particularly greedy old woman wanted to fill not only her milk pail, but her sieve as well. The cow broke her tether and escaped to Dunsmore Heath, where Guy of Warwick slew her. A narwhal tusk, said to be one of the giant cow's ribs, is still on display in Warwick Castle. *Brewer's Dictionary of Phrase and Fable* suggests that the name Dun Cow is a corruption of *Den Gau*, meaning region of the Danes, and that Guy of Warwick's victory was actually over a Danish settlement.

A similar whale bone is exhibited in the Church of St. Mary Redcliffe in Bristol, also once believed to be a rib of the Dun Cow. The legend of the founding of Durham Cathedral, much further north in England, has a party of monks being told by the ghost of Saint Cuthbert that his body must be buried at a place called Dun Holm. A milkmaid comes by, asking if the monks have seen her dun cow, which she had last seen at Dun Holm. They follow the maid, and lay the cathedral foundations at Dun Holm. (A variant has the still living Saint Cuthbert following a donkey to the holy place.)

Dun Cow Rib Farm in Whittingham, Lancashire, has a large rib bone embedded in an ancient wall, also said to be from the Dun Cow, which is supposed to have died of shock when an old witch asked it to fill her riddle (sieve) as well as her bucket. Experts believe the bone to be either from a whale, or possibly from a Bronze Age aurochs.[19]

Babe the Blue Ox

In modern American folklore, Babe the Blue Ox is the giant animal companion of the lumberjack giant, Paul Bunyan. Both appear to have been invented over campfires by American and Canadian loggers. It has been suggested that Bunyan is an adaptation of Québécois French *Bon Jean* (John the Good). Bunyan first appeared in print in a 1916 pamphlet for the Red River Lumber Company written by William B. Laughead (1882–1958). The tales all rely for comic effect on stupendous exaggeration. One of the best remembered images is the description of Bunyan's iron stove: it was so long that to grease it ready for breakfast he strapped a ham to each foot and skated the whole length of it, half a mile, then back again, by which time the hams had worn quite away.[20]

Buffalo/Bison (Several Genera and Species)

Phylum *Chordata*, Class *Mammalia*, Order *Artiodactyla*, Family *Bovidae*, Subfamily *Bovinae*, Genus (several), Species (several)

Name

The common name buffalo and the scientific name *Bubalus* both come from the same source, the ancient Greek word βουβαλος, *boúbalos*, meaning either antelope or wild ox. This became *bufalus* in Latin, then *bufalo* in Portuguese and Spanish, and finally English buffalo. The word does a lot of work apart from just describing a group of animals. A buffalo soldier was originally a nickname for African American U.S. soldiers, given to them by American Indians, presumably because of their wooly hair. Buffalo wings are chicken wings fried in a cayenne pepper hot sauce, supposedly invented in the city of Buffalo in New York State in the 1960s. (There are at least 25 towns or cities called Buffalo in the United States, and more in other countries.) There is a well-known, large, freshwater, carp-like fish, found extensively in Canada, the USA, Mexico and Guatemala, which is called the buffalo fish, or simply buffalo. In addition, there are several fish and insects and at least one frog that have *bubalus* as their species or subspecies name.

The American bison is commonly called a buffalo in America, even though it is not actually a buffalo. Old English *wesend* and Latin *bison* are related, both probably coming from a Proto-Indo-European root *wisan*, referring to the aurochs.

Description

There are several different species of cow-like animals called buffalo. They are all members of the subfamily *Bovinae*. *Syncerus caffer* is the African buffalo or Cape buffalo. *Bubalus arnee* is the wild water buffalo, while *Bubalus bubalis* is the domesticated water buffalo. *Bubalus mindorensis* is the dwarf buffalo of the Philippines. They are all bovids with long horns that tend to hang low or curve backwards. The American bison (*Bison bison*) is quite a different-looking animal, with a massive head and upright horns, and a shaggy coat. The American bison and the related European bison (*Bison bonasus*, common name wesent, which has a much smaller head than *Bison bison*) are the largest extant terrestrial animals in North America and Europe respectively, and are stronger, hardier and more able to cope with cold weather than buffalo generally.

General Attributes

Like cattle, buffalo are generally placid creatures that provide milk, meat and work-service to humans. Wild buffalo will group together and defend themselves with great determination against predators, but they are still basically non-aggressive animals.

Bison, being larger and stronger than buffalo, are much more formidable. The vast majority of buffalo mythology and folklore is actually about American bison. The bison was such an important source of food for the Plains Indians that almost all the legends emphasize the power and sacred strength of the animal: buffalo hides were symbols of chiefdom or other high status, and buffalo horns were traditionally worn either by chiefs or by medicine men.

Buffalo Jumps

A buffalo jump was a site used by Native Americans to drive bison over a cliff or other sheer fall, either to their deaths or at least to immobilizing injury, as a way of hunting them. One of the best known is Head-Smashed-In Buffalo Jump near Fort Macleod, Alberta, Canada, where the Rockies and the Great Plains meet. This site was used by the Blackfoot people. Its preservation and development were spearheaded by Joe Crowshoot, Sr. (Aapohsoy'yiis, Weasel Tail, 1903–1999), a ceremonial Elder of the Piikani Nation. It is now a UNESCO World Heritage site.[21]

Horses were introduced late to American Indian culture, so hunting large, swift animals on foot required careful planning. Plains Indians like the Blackfoot drove the bison over natural cliffs or rock ridges. Special runners, often dressed as wolves or coyotes, walked bison from pasture areas towards the jump. They had to time their advance so that the bison had reached an unstoppable mass and speed at exactly the right place. Even if the animals were not killed outright, their incapacity—usually from broken bones—would make it much easier to kill them. This hunting method was used by American Indians for over five thousand years; it may well have descended from hunting mammoths, which finally became extinct only about 4,000 years ago.

White Buffalo Calf Woman

The rare albino White Buffalo was (and still is) considered especially powerful and sacred. It represented the spirit of all buffalo. Among the Lakota Sioux, there is a legend that it was White Buffalo Calf Woman who first brought the sacred rituals and the peace pipe to humans.

"The arrival of the white buffalo is like the second coming of Christ," according to Floyd Hand Looks for Buffalo, an Oglala Medicine Man from Pine Ridge, South Dakota. "It will bring about purity of mind, body, and spirit and unify all nations—black, red, yellow, and white." He describes the birth of a white calf as an omen because these births happen in the most unexpected places and often among the poorest people in the nation. The birth of the sacred white buffalo provides those within the Native American community with a sense of hope and an indication that good times are to come.[22]

The Sun Dance

The sun dance is perhaps the third-best known Native American ceremonial ritual after the sweat lodge ceremony and the vision quest. It is famous (or infamous) because, by Western standards, it involves great cruelty. It achieved greater attention after it was featured in the 1970 movie *A Man Called Horse*, starring Richard Harris.

The Sioux were at one time one of the largest Native American nations. They were divided into three groups: the western or Teton group, who called themselves the Lakota; the central or Yankton group, who called themselves Nakota; and the eastern or Santee group, who called themselves Dakota. They all revered the omniscient and omnipotent sky god Wakan Tanka. As Plains Indians who depended on the buffalo (more strictly, bison) for survival, they also worshiped White Buffalo Calf Woman, Ptesánwin, as described above.

In addition to the *channúnpa*, the sacred peace pipe, the seven rituals that White Buffalo Calf Woman brought to the Sioux were: *Inipi*, the sweat lodge ceremony; *Wanagi Yuhapi*, the ceremony for the keeping of souls; *Hunkapi*, the ceremony for making relatives; *Ishnata Awicalowan*, the ceremony for initiating a girl into womanhood; *Tapa Wanka Yap*, the ceremony of throwing the ball; *Hanblecheyapi*, the ritual of the vision quest; and *Wiwanyag Wachipi*, the annual summer ceremony of the sun dance.[23]

Warriors who aspired to become chiefs or medicine-men were fastened to a pole and had to remain on their feet for 24 hours in high summer, dancing slowly around the pole and facing the hot sun. What made it a particularly grueling experience was that they were fastened by skewers through their own flesh, usually the pectoral muscles of the chest and the quadriceps of the legs. The cuts made for the insertion of the skewers were deliberately deep and jagged, intended to cause as much pain as possible. The loss of blood, the intense pain and the remorseless sun meant that only the most determined were able to complete the trial. Most fainted or collapsed, and several died.

(Thathanka Iyotake, known as Sitting Bull, was already a chief of the Hunkpapa-Lakota and a recognized medicine man when he underwent the sun dance ritual in June 1876, seeking advice from Wakan Tanka and Ptesánwin. He had a powerful vision of many white-skinned soldiers falling headfirst down from the sky. He therefore predicted a great Indian victory very soon. On June 26, the Lakota, Arapaho and Northern Cheyenne defeated the U.S. 7th Cavalry led by George Armstrong Custer at the Battle of the Little Bighorn, entirely wiping them out.)

Antelope (Several Species)

Phylum *Chordata*, Class *Mammalia*, Order *Artiodactyla*, Family *Bovidae*, Genus (30), Species (91)

Name

The common name derives ultimately from medieval Greek ανθολοψ, *anthólops*, first recorded in about 336 CE by Eustathius of Antioch and clearly referring to a mythical animal. The English word antelope did not appear until 1417.

Description

"Antelope" is what is called in classification jargon a "wastebasket taxon," i.e., a dumping ground for several species that don't have any other obvious place to reside. All antelope or antelopes (both words are used as the plural noun) are Old World artiodactyls and ungulates (even-toed and having hooves) within the family *Bovidae*, but they are defined almost as clearly by what they are not: cattle, sheep, buffalo, bison, or goats. They are found in Africa and Eurasia, most of the 91 species being African and often found in mixed woodland

and grassland savannahs. They are mostly deer-like in appearance, with horns of various shapes, sizes and complexity.

General Attributes

Antelope vary greatly in size. Like deer, they are herbivorous, but they generally live in hotter climates with more ferocious predators, so they tend to be less timid and more independent than deer. Their most obvious characteristic is their speed on the run. They are also associated with good eyesight. They feature in several religious and mythological cultures. In Egyptian mythology they are associated with Anubis, Set, Osiris and Horus. The Roman goddess Minerva has the antelope as one of her totem animals because of its keen vision. In Hinduism, the antelope is associated with Shiva, Soma and Chandra; in the Rig-Veda, they are ridden by the Maruts, the gods of the winds. In medieval Christian exegesis, the two horns of the antelope represent the Old Testament and the New Testament of the Bible.

Avalokiteshvara

In Buddhism, Avalokiteshvara is the Bodhisattva (compassionate seeker of Buddahood) who appears in human form to help people who are suffering or are in trouble. In India and generally, he is a male figure, but in China and Japan, she is often depicted as a female figure called Kuan Yin or Guan Yin. One well-known representation is the four-armed Bodhisattva of Infinite Compassion, whose first pair of hands are placed together in prayer or greeting, whose right hand holds a bead rosary, and whose left hand holds a lotus flower. The figure wears a cloak of antelope skin, symbolizing gentleness and comforting warmth. Avalokiteshvara is also the protector of horses and of farm animals generally. He is known in Japanese Buddhism as Bato Kanzeon (Kanzeon with the Horse's Head), or Kannon Bosatsu, whose image is often placed by roads (especially at crossroads) or at the beginning of mountain passes to bless those who travel by horse, mule or donkey, and travelers in general.[24]

In Heraldry

Antelopes first came into heraldry in the Middle Ages, when they were little known. As a result, early heraldic antelopes usually look nothing like real antelopes—they are sometimes given a tusk as well as horns, or a lion's tail. More modern heraldry uses a more naturalistic antelope, which are called specifically "natural antelopes."

Hippopotamus (*Hippopotamus amphibius*)

Phylum *Chordata*, Class *Mammalia*, Order *Artiodactyla*, Family *Hippopotamidae*, Genus *Hippopotamus*, Species *Hippopotamus amphibius*

Name

As described earlier, the name is derived from the Greek roots ‘ιππος, *hippos*, meaning horse, and ποταμος, *potámos*, meaning river. *Amphibius* means living both on land and in water.

Description

The hippopotamus is neither a cow nor an antelope. In fact, in terms of classification, its nearest relatives are whales, dolphins and porpoises. However, it is included in this chapter because it is an artiodactyl (has an even number of toes)—in fact, it is the largest artiodactyl in the world, often weighing in at over 1,500 kilograms (3,310 pounds).

General Attributes

The hippopotamus is generally seen as a comic, lazy, lumbering, entertaining beast by people who live in countries where it is not normally seen (they are very popular zoo animals), and, by contrast, as a deadly, lightning-fast killer in the countries where it lives. Hippopotamuses are more dangerous to humans than almost any other wild animal. They are extremely aggressive and unpredictable. A few years ago, a hippopotamus in Niger, Africa, overturned a boat and killed all 13 passengers, 12 of them children.[25]

In the Ancient World

Hippopotamus bones with human butchery marks on them have been found in Ethiopia, Africa, dating from 160,000 years ago. They are depicted in early African rock art, and in art from ancient Egypt. Egyptian mythology says that Horus, incarnated as Her-tchema (Horus the Piercer) attacked the god Set with a spear, after Set had shape-shifted into the form of a hippopotamus.

The Greek historian Herodotus described the hippopotamus in 440 BCE, and the Roman naturalist Pliny the Elder included the hippopotamus in his *Naturalis Historia* of about 77 CE. The Yoruba people of Niger/Congo described the animal, as did also the Zulus of Southern Africa.

It has been conjectured that the Behemoth of the Old Testament may have been a hippopotamus. The description is very apposite for the hippopotamus, that "eats grass," and lies "under the lotus plants" and "in the coverts of the marsh":

> Look at Behemoth,
> which I made just as I made you;
> it eats grass like an ox.
> Its strength is in its loins,
> and its power in the muscles of its belly.
> It makes its tail stiff like a cedar;
> the sinews of its thighs are knit together.
> Its bones are tubes of bronze,
> its limbs like bars of iron …
> …Under the lotus plant it lies,
> in the covert of the reeds and in the marsh.
> The lotus trees cover it for shade;
> the willows of the wadi surround it.
> Even if the river is turbulent, it is not frightened;
> it is confident though Jordan rushes against its mouth[26]

The San Contract

The San or Saan people of South Africa have a rather extraordinary myth about the hippo. When God was creating the world, the San were worried because the hippo had said that it wanted to live in the water, and the San were worried that such a huge animal would eat all the fish. They asked God to come up with a solution, and God did. God made the hippo a herbivore. What's more, God designed the hippo so that when he excreted, he did so by lifting his tail and spraying a huge jet of slurry across the ground, so that the San could check through it easily to confirm that there were no fish bones.[27]

Taurt/Taweret

Taurt or Taweret (Fat One), called Θουερις, *Thoueris*, in Greek, is a hippopotamus goddess in the Egyptian pantheon. She was a patron of childbirth and maternity, usually depicted as a pregnant hippopotamus, standing upright, with a round belly and prominent teats. Her image was often painted on Nile river boats as a protection against attack by hippopotamuses.[28]

8

Sheep and Goats (*Caprinae*)

Sheep, Ram (*Ovis aries*)

Phylum *Chordata*, Class *Mammalia*, Order *Artiodactyla*, Family *Bovidae*, Subfamily *Caprinae*, Genus *Ovis*, Species *Ovis aries*

Name

The common name was *sceap* in Old English and *schep* or *scheep* in Middle English. The genus name *Ovis* is Latin for sheep. There was a proverbial Latin expression or metaphor for betraying someone, which was *ovem lupo committere*, "to put a sheep in with a wolf." The species name *aries* is Latin for ram, from Greek εριφος, *ériphos*, domestic animal.

Description

Sheep are common and very familiar domesticated ruminants. They are raised for their fleeces, meat and milk. They are found in most countries of the world.

General Attributes

The sheep has been farmed for millennia on poor soils and rocky ground as well as richer pastures all across the world. The animals yield milk, wool and meat, and can adapt to many environments and climates. A legend among the ancient Celts was that sheep could speak to humans—sheep skins were used for drum-skins and for bagpipes. It was considered unlucky to burn sheep bones in the fire after roasting and eating the meat.

The ram is usually a feisty animal with an independent air. It head-butts other rams in mating, as do many other horned animals, but it seems more willing than most to also head-butt humans, other species, cars, fences—whatever has earned its mistrust or disapproval just by being there. Like surplus steers in cattle, rams not intended for breeding are useful only for meat, so there is a long tradition in many cultures of rams being used as sacrificial animals, since their virility and energy would make them pleasing to the gods. Traditional firedogs were often carved or cast with rams' horns or heads at each end.

Sheep and rams both represent stolidity, dependability, sacrifice and steady achievement. They will put up with many hardships, and still somehow manage to survive.

Ba-neb-jet and Khnum

In Egyptian mythology, Ba-neb-jet (also Ba-neb-tet, Ba-neb-Tatau) was a ram god, depicted with a ram's head with flattened horns and a *uraeus* (threatening cobra icon). A live ram was sacrificed during worship of the god. He was considered to be a combination of Ra, Osiris, Geb and Shu. The Ba- part of the name means soul.

Khnum (Shaper) was another Egyptian ram-headed god. He is depicted seated at a potter's wheel, where he shapes clay into humans and gods.

The Ram-Headed Serpent

A symbol unique to classical Celtic Druidism was the ram-headed snake or serpent. The most famous example is found on the Gundestrup cauldron, the largest and most complete piece of Iron Age silverwork ever found in Europe, which dates from the La Tène period of Celtic art, somewhere between 200 BCE and 300 CE. Gundestrup is in northern Denmark. On the cauldron, which is lavishly covered with symbolic designs, the antlered forest god Cernunnos is depicted, holding the ram-headed serpent in his left hand. Similar bronze and stone statues of Cernunnos have been found at various locations in France, along with Gaulish carvings that depict Cernunnos in the company of a goddess and a young man. An image found in Gloucestershire, England depicts the god with two ram-headed serpents in place of his legs. The combination of the serpent penis symbol with the ram's head is a doubled statement of virility, of masculine penetrative power.[1]

The Golden Fleece

A very well-known legend from classical times is that of the golden fleece. The god Hermes gave Atreus, King of Mycenae, a horned lamb with a golden fleece, which was to be sacrificed to the goddess Artemis. Instead, Atreus was so impressed by the lamb that he had it killed, stuffed and mounted, and announced that whoever possessed the fleece also possessed the right to the throne.

From that simple beginning, the legend expands into a series of gory murders, cannibalism and revenge killings that would put the Valentine's Day Massacre to shame—a long list of who killed whom, who ate whom, who raped whom and who killed, ate or raped whom in revenge, making a story too long and complex to re-tell here. Collectively, the House of Atreus stories inspired eight classical Greek dramas, as well as modern works by Eugene O'Neill, T.S. Eliot and many others.

Abigail

In the Old Testament , Abigail (Father's Joy) is the wife of Nabal (the Fool), who is a rich sheep owner. She gives David food and drink during his exile from King Saul, when

Nabal has refused him. When Nabal dies, David marries Abigail, his inheritance of the flocks of sheep being seen as a symbol of his spiritual leadership. The name Abigail became a synonym for faithful service, to the extent that by Elizabethan times it had become the common nickname for a lady's serving-maid.

The Lamb of God

In the New Testament, Jesus is called "the Lamb of God" by the prophet John: "The next day he saw Jesus coming towards him and declared, 'Here is the Lamb of God who takes away the sin of the world!'"[2] The same image is repeated four times in the Book of Revelation:

> After this I looked, and there was a great multitude that no one could count, from every nation, from all tribes and peoples and languages, standing before the throne and before the Lamb, robed in white, with palm branches in their hands. They cried out in a loud voice, saying, "Salvation belongs to our God who is seated on the throne, and to the Lamb...."
>
> "These are they who have come out of the great ordeal; they have washed their robes and made them white in the blood of the Lamb.... They will hunger no more, and thirst no more; the sun will not strike them, nor any scorching heat; for the Lamb at the center of the throne will be their shepherd, and he will guide them to springs of the water of life, and God will wipe away every tear from their eyes."[3]

The *Agnus Dei* (Latin for Lamb of God) is a standard component of the Latin Mass, and occurs throughout Christian liturgy. The standard visual image is of a lamb with one of its forelegs crooked to hold a small white flag bearing a red cross, sometimes called a *vexillum* after the similar small flag used by the Roman imperial army.

In the 11th century, Saint Anselm of Canterbury went to great lengths to separate the images of the lamb and the scapegoat. Whereas the latter represented a creature unwillingly or at best unwittingly taking on the sins of others, the Lamb of God knowingly and willingly gave himself in sacrifice.

Goat (*Capra aegagrus hircus*)

Phylum *Chordata*, Class *Mammalia*, Order *Artiodactyla*, Family *Bovidae*, Subfamily *Caprinae*, Genus *Capra*, Species *Capra aegagrus*, Subspecies *Capra aegagrus hircus*

Name

In Old English, the word *gat* meant a goat in general, or a female goat. Later, a male was called a *bucca* (from which buck is derived). (Bucca also means imp or ghost in Cornish and Welsh.) In the 12th century, *bucca* was replaced with *hegoot* or he goat. In the 19th century, the terms billy for a male and nanny for a female were introduced, and they are still in use. A young goat is a kid. *Capra aegagrus hircus* is Latin and means literally: *Capra* (she-goat or smell of the armpits) *aegagrus* (of Persia/Iran) *hircus* (smelly he-goat or filthy person) so the scientific name is not particularly flattering. Goats are notorious for their strong and distinctive body odor. The chemical element bromine (Br) takes its name from Greek βρομος, *brómos*, which means stink of a male goat.

Description

There are over 300 breeds of goat. The most common domesticated goat, *Capra aegagrus hircus*, is descended from wild goats in southeast Europe and southwest Asia. Goats have been kept for thousands of years by humans, both by nomadic peoples and by settled farmers. Like sheep, they provide abundant meat, milk, cheese and hides. Goat dung is often used as fuel by nomadic peoples, and goat-skin containers have been used for millennia to carry water and wine. Even more than sheep, goats can live in rocky, dry or otherwise hostile terrains, and are very hardy and adaptable. Like cats, if neglected or left to their own devices, they look after themselves and can become feral very quickly.

General Attributes

Goats appear in several religions, mythological tales and folklore. The Greek god Pan, adopted by the Romans as Pan or Silvanus (later Faunus), had goat legs and horns, and was widely revered as a nature god. The Greek nature spirits called satyrs were originally depicted as male humans with horse ears and a horse's tail (and a comically huge and permanent erection), but they gradually became more goat-like, and in later Roman and Renaissance depictions, more human and less grotesque. After the Roman god Faunus, they were sometimes called fauns, and they became gentler and more human. In C.S. Lewis's well-known children's book *The Lion, the Witch and the Wardrobe* (1950), the kindly character Tumnus is an example of a modern faun, far less intimidating than the original Pan or satyrs.

The Aegis and Aegisthus

The Greek word αιγις, *aigis*, spelled *aegis* by the Romans, means goatskin. As *The Aegis*, it described the magical shield forged by Hephaestus that had on it the Gorgon Medusa's head. When Zeus shook it, it made thunder. (The skin was later said to be that of the goat that had suckled Zeus when he was a baby. See *Amalthea* below.) Athena and Apollo also used the shield. It is mentioned by Ovid and Virgil, and in many poetical works. It was also represented as a cloak, rather than a shield, particularly for Athena and her Roman counterpart, Minerva. Robert Graves thought it was a skin pouch, used to hold magical tools, of the kind a druid might use. In English, the word has taken on a metaphorical as well as literal meaning: we speak of a particular event or person being "under the aegis of" so-and-so or such-and-such, and here the meaning is "under the protection or guidance of," or sometimes just "supervised by."

Aegisthus, whose name means goat strength (both *aegis* and Aegisthus ultimately derive from αιξ, *aïx*, a goat, although the word *aegis* can also mean a windstorm), was the lover of Clytemnestra and the murderer of Agamemnon, whose story is told in Aeschylus's great sequence of three dramas, the *Oresteia*. He was called Aegisthus because, like Zeus, he was nursed by a goat as a baby.

Like Aegyptus (meaning he-goat), another character in Greek mythology, these words and names derived from *aïx* led to the English name for the country of Egypt, via Latin *Aegyptus* and Middle French *Egypte*. However, Egyptians called their country Kumat or Kemet (the Black Land) in ancient Egyptian, and now call it Misr or Mesr in classical Arabic or Masr in Egyptian Arabic.[4]

Amalthea

In Greek mythology, Amalthea (Tender Goddess) was the goat which suckled Zeus as a baby. She was the daughter of the King of Crete. She and her sister Melissa (Honey Bee) fed Zeus on goat milk and honey, and in return Zeus gave her the cornucopia, the horn of plenty. She was later turned into the star Capella (Latin for Little Goat), the brightest star in the constellation Auriga, and the sixth-brightest star in the night sky (see Chapter 41).

Dionysian Rites

Dionysus was the son of Zeus and Semele, but was nicknamed "the twice-born" because of the unusual circumstances of his birth. Zeus had seduced Semele, a mortal priestess, but Hera, wife of Zeus and tired of his constant philandering, tried to sow doubt in Semele's mind as to whether Zeus was actually the father of her soon-to-be-born baby. When Semele was close to delivering Dionysus, she demanded to see Zeus in his full glory. But mortals cannot survive such a sight: Semele burst into flames, and died. As she was dying, Zeus snatched the baby Dionysus from inside her body, and sewed him inside his own thigh. Later, Dionysus was born from Zeus's thigh, hence "twice-born." Zeus later transformed Dionysus into a black goat, to hide him from the ever-jealous Hera.[5]

The sacred rites for Dionysus were savage. Followers would tear a live goat to pieces and eat its flesh raw. In the play *The Bacchae* by Euripides (480–406 BCE), the ecstatic rites are described in gory detail.

The Chinese Calendar and Zodiac

The goat is one of the animals in the Chinese calendar and zodiac. People born in the Year of the Goat are said to be shy, introverted, cautious perfectionists. (See Chapter 41.)

Agni

Agni, whose name means fire, is an important god in Hinduism. He is usually depicted as red-faced, with three legs and seven arms. He rides a ram, symbolic of his great power. He has many variant names, including Chagaratha, which means He Who Rides on a Ram.[6]

Daksha

In Hindu mythology, Daksha is one of the sons of the god Brahma—he sprang from his father's thumb. He and his wife Asikni tried to populate the world. Their first thousand sons lived, but did not produce any offspring of their own. They continued trying, and in all 5,000 boys were born to them, but they still could not produce any further offspring. It was only when Daksha and Asikni gave birth to 60 daughters, who then married and went on to have children of their own, that the world began to be populated. The god Shiva was Daksha's son-in-law. Shiva reacted to an insult from Daksha by changing his head into a goat's head, to show the world how foolish he was, and that is how Daksha is usually portrayed. Ironically, the name Daksha means able or intelligent.[7]

The Scapegoat

In the Old Testament, the ritual of the scapegoat is described:

> He [Aaron] shall take the two goats and set them before the LORD at the entrance of the tent of meeting: and Aaron shall cast lots on the two goats, one lot for the LORD and the other lot for Azazel. Aaron shall present the goat on which the lot fell for the LORD, and offer it as a sin-offering; but the goat on which the lot fell for Azazel shall be presented alive before the LORD to make atonement over it, so that it may be sent away into the wilderness to Azazel.[8]

Azazel was portrayed in Jewish and Christian folklore as one of the fallen angels, who came down to earth to have sex with women, and to teach humans witchcraft. In Islam, he is called Elbis, an alternative name for Satan.

The term scapegoat, originally specifically meaning a religious sacrifice to carry away the sins of the people, now means more generally any innocent person who is given the blame for a fault or difficulty.

Other Bible Goats

Exodus 25:4 tells us that goat hair was acceptable for the tent that contained the tabernacle. Goat meat is kosher in Judaic dietary laws. By contrast, Jesus uses goats to represent sinners and sheep to represent the faithful in his Parable of the Sheep and Goats :

> All the nations will be gathered before him, and he will separate people one from another as a shepherd separates the sheep from the goats, and he will put the sheep at his right hand and the goats at the left. Then the king will say to those at his right hand, "Come, you that are blessed by my Father, inherit the kingdom prepared for you from the foundation of the world."[9]

There may be little or no direct connection with Jesus' parable, but medieval Christian folklore began to portray Lucifer, Satan or the Devil as goat-like in appearance, with horns and a pointed goatee beard. The pentagram, or five-pointed star, turned upside down, is said to represent the Devil, with two horns at the top and a pointed beard below.

Egil's Goats

In Germanic mythology, the god Thor had befriended a human peasant called Egil. Whenever Thor visited Egil, he would bring his chariot, which was drawn by goats. One day, whilst visiting, Thor noticed that Egil had no food. He told Egil to slaughter the goats, but to make sure that he put the bones back inside the skins afterwards, when they had finished eating.

Loki, Thor's evil brother, persuaded Thialfi, Egil's son, to break one of the bones and suck out its marrow. When Thor returned to Egil's hut, he brought all the goats back to life, ready to be eaten all over again, but one of them was missing a leg. Thor naturally thought that Egil had disobeyed him. To appease the god's anger, he had to give his son, Thialfi, and his daughter, Roskova, to work as Thor's slaves in Asgard.[10]

Heidrun

In another Norse legend, Heidrun or Heithron is the sacred she-goat who provides the mead (rather than milk) for the death-hall of Valhalla. The *Prose Edda* says that she feeds on the leaves of a single tree called Laerath, and that she produces enough mead every day to fill a huge cauldron, enough to satisfy even the gargantuan thirsts of all the Norse warrior-heroes.[11]

Fainting Goats

So-called "fainting goats," originally bred in the American state of Tennessee and first described in 1904, have a genetically inherited condition called *myotonia congenita* that causes them to become absolutely rigid whenever they are startled. The attacks last for between five and twenty seconds, during which time the goat may fall to one side and remain completely immobilized, as if it were made of concrete. The goats recover quickly by themselves, and apparently suffer no long-term harm from these regular seizures.[12] There have been serious attempts by the U.S. military to weaponize the presumed psychic power that may trigger myotonic episodes, as recorded in the 2004 film, *The Men Who Stare at Goats*.

Ibex (Several Species)

Phylum *Chordata*, Class *Mammalia*, Order *Artiodactyla*, Family *Bovidae*, Subfamily *Caprinae*, Genus *Capra*, Species (several)

Name

The common name, which is also used as the species name, is from Latin, probably brought into the language during the Roman occupation of the Iberian territory.

Description

There are many species of wild goat. The ibex is well known because of the spectacularly long, curving horns of the male. The Alpine ibex (*Capra ibex*) is found in the European Alps, but has also been introduced to the USA, Canada and Argentina.

General Attributes

Alpine ibex are strikingly beautiful creatures, but they live in high, rocky places and generally do not interact with humans.

The Legend of Goldhorn

A folkloric legend from Slovenia tells the story of a rare white Alpine ibex which lived on Mount Triglav. The story was first recorded by Karel Dežman in 1868, and this is his summary:

Goldhorn's golden horns were the key to a treasure hidden in the mountains around Triglav. A young and brave hunter from the Trenta Valley fell in love with a beautiful girl and managed to win her heart by bringing her beautiful flowers. However, one day a rich merchant from Venice came by and tried to gain her attention by giving her golden jewelry and dancing with her. As the hunter approached the girl, she mocked him. The hunter was desperate and left. Persuaded by another hunter, called the Green Hunter, who was said to have brought about the fate of several honest boys, he decided to go that very night to find Goldhorn and claim his treasure.

In the morning, they found the animal, shot it and pursued it. The dying animal dragged itself onto a narrow, rocky ledge. Suddenly the boy saw on a dangerous trail the most beautiful and healing flowers. The Green Hunter forced him on to catch the Goldhorn before it ate the magic Triglav flowers that grew from its blood, but it was too late. The Goldhorn had already eaten one and the flower gave it tremendous life power. It ran towards the hunter, who being blinded by the bliss of its golden horns lost balance and fell from the mountain. The river Soča brought his corpse to the vale.[13]

9

Deer, Elk and Moose (*Cervidae*)

Red Deer (*Cervus elaphus*)

Phylum *Chordata*, Class *Mammalia*, Order *Artiodactyla*, Infraorder *Pecora*, Family *Cervidae*, Genus *Cervus*, Species *Cervus elaphus*

Name

The common name is from the animal's red-brown coloring, and from the Old English word *deor*, which until the 10th or 11th century CE meant any wild animal. Like the word dog, which originally meant only one particular kind of dog, *deor* was not originally the general word for deer. That was *heorot*, which survives as the modern English word hart, which is now a poetic alternative to deer. *Deor* became *deer* in Middle English, and the most widely used name, by the end of the 15th century.

Cervus is the Latin for deer. The Roman military nicknamed the forked defensive stakes they put in the ground to kill or slow down an advancing enemy *cervi*, or deer, obviously based on antlers. The species name *elaphus* is from Greek ελαφος, *élaphos*, which also means deer, so the binomial *Cervus elaphus* means deer deer. (Dear dear!)

Description

The red deer is comparatively large and very common (so common that it is considered an intrusive species in several areas). It is widespread in Europe, western Asia, and parts of America, but the distribution varies greatly. It has been a hunted animal for millennia, but it is now also farmed in several countries. In some places it is so numerous, and causes so much damage by foraging, that it is considered a pest, and its numbers are culled, whereas in others it is considered rare and endangered, although worldwide it is very numerous. The body is mostly plain brown or reddish-brown, which may become slightly gray in winter, with no spots or stripes. Only the males have antlers. Red deer interbreed with elk/wapiti and sika deer, producing fertile offspring. There are also many subspecies, each with slightly varying characteristics.

General Attributes

As a hunted animal for thousands of years, the red deer has acquired a considerable status as a spiritual and mythological totem. It is a gentle ruminant, apart from the rutting season, when males become very loud and aggressive. As a result, males and females have differing reputations and attributes. The female, called a hind (from Old English, the original derivation meaning without horns), is often symbolic of chastity, purity and gentleness, and the pursuit of the gentle, elusive hind in the wild forest is a metaphor for the spiritual hunt, the search for holiness. The variant white hind, in particular, is symbolic of purity. The male, on the other hand, particularly when fully grown and antlered, was a formidable adversary in the days of spears and knives, and represents the ultimate quarry for the hunt. Venison is still considered a royal or noble meat. Deer hide is unusually soft, supple and pliant: in one of the Irish tales, a charioteer wears "a skin-soft tunic of stitched deer's leather, light as a breath."[1] Both the loud stag and the timid hind appear in a single stanza of an Irish 14th-century poem:

> The clear voice of the red-backed deer
> Under the oak tree, high on the summit;
> Gentle hinds, and they so timid,
> Lying hidden in your well-wooded glade.[2]

In Art and Culture, Ancient and Modern

Depictions of red deer are found in cave art dating from 40,000 years ago. Edward Landseer's *Monarch of the Glen*, a portrait of a stag in full-antlered majesty painted in 1851, is recognized worldwide. In Scotland, wild red deer are sometimes called fairy cattle. Traditionally, there were three goddesses who cared for and protected them: Cailleach Mhòr nam Fiadh (Great Hag of the Deer) on the rugged Isle of Jura; Cailleach Mhòr Chlibric (Great Hag of Clibric), who protected deer from hunters; and Cailleach Beinn a' Bhric (Hag of the Wild Mountain), who herded and milked the deer.[3] The red deer was sacred to the ancient Greek goddess Artemis, to the Hindu goddess Saraswati, and to the Roman goddess of the hunt, Diana. In the Celtic Druidic tradition, the stag is the second of the five oldest animals in the world.

The Shape-Shifting/Disappearing Hind

In several legends, women become hinds, or hinds become women. The Irish story of how Lugaid became king begins with a druid telling King Daire that whichever of his sons is named Lugaid will succeed him as king. Daire therefore names each of his five sons Lugaid. The five princes hunt, kill and eat a young hind, but are then lost in a snowstorm. They stumble across a crude hut in the forest, where an ugly hag calls them in from the storm. She invites each of the brothers to sleep with her, but only Lugaid Laigde, the one who killed the hind, agrees. As he is making love to her, she shape-shifts into the most beautiful princess in the whole of Ireland. She marries him and becomes his queen.[4]

In a Scottish legend, a hunter's hound chases a white hind near Loch Ericht. The dog follows the hind into the waters of the loch, and neither dog nor deer are ever seen again.

In another Irish story, Fionn mac Cumhaill hunts a hind to the edge of a lake. As she reaches the water, she drops a ring into the shallow water. Fionn retrieves it, and instantly turns into an old man.

In yet another legend, the Fianna (war-band of Fionn, or Fenians) chase a fawn onto the slopes of Slieve nam Bán (Mountain of the Women) and the deer disappears into the ground as soon as its foot touches the mountainside.

The Song of Amergin

Amergin Glúingel (Amergin of the White Knees) was a great bard and druid of the Irish mythological cycles. He is famous for his mystical poem *The Song of Amergin*:

> I am a stag: *of seven tines,*
> I am a flood: *across a plain,*
> I am a wind: *on a deep lake,*
> I am a tear: *the Sun lets fall,*
> I am a hawk: *above the cliff,*
> I am a thorn: *beneath the nail,*
> I am a wonder: *among flowers,*
> I am a wizard: *who but I*
> *Sets the cool head aflame with smoke?*
> I am a spear: *that roars for blood,*
> I am a salmon: *in a pool,*
> I am a lure: *from paradise,*
> I am a hill: *where poets walk,*
> I am a boar: *ruthless and red,*
> I am a breaker: *threatening doom,*
> I am a tide: *that drags to death,*
> I am an infant: *who but I*
> *Peeps from the unhewn dolmen arch?*
>
> I am the womb: *of every holt,*
> I am the blaze: *on every hill,*
> I am the queen: *of every hive,*
> I am the shield: *for every head,*
> I am the tomb: *of every hope.*[5]

The poem, which was deliberately scrambled because it contained religious secrets too important to be easily discovered, is actually an explanation of the ancient Druidic tree-alphabet, or Beth-Luis-Nion, in which every letter is associated with a particular tree, and in turn with particular natural forces. The stag with the seven tines of antlers is the letter B, representing the birch tree, birth, and new beginnings. The whole alphabet (my version) runs as follows:

> I am B, *Beth*, birch, the proud stag with seven tines,
> I am L, *Luis*, rowan, a flash-flood on the plain,
> I am N, *Nion*, ash, a wild wind over the flood waters,
> I am F, *Fearn*, alder, a new-born glistening tear of the Sun,
> I am S, *Saille*, willow, the hawk nesting on the cliff,
> I am H, *Huath*, hawthorn, blossoming among flowers,
> I am D, *Duir*, oak, stinging your eyes with my sacred smoke,
> I am T, *Tinne*, holly, shaking my sacred spear in battle,
> I am C, *Coll*, hazel, the salmon who swims in the pool of wisdom,
> I am M, *Muin*, vine, a hill of wine-rich poetry,
> I am G, *Gort*, ivy, a deadly, ruthless, king-killing boar,
> I am Ng, *Ngetal*, reed, the terrifying roar of the wild ocean,
> I am R, *Ruis*, elder, the receding wave of the unconquerable sea.

Who but I knows the sacred sequence uncarved in ancient stone
of A, *Ailm*, silver fir, birth,
of O, *Onn*, gorse, growth,
of U, *Ura*, heather, age,
of E, *Eadha*, poplar, death,
of I, *Idho*, yew, resurrection?

Bharata

In Hindu mythology, Bharata was a king whose life was dedicated to worship of the god Vishnu. He even abdicated his throne in order to continue his devotions.

One day, after praying at his retreat in the forest, he went to bathe in the river. There he saw a lion menacing a heavily pregnant doe. The doe, in terror, gave birth to her fawn, which dropped into the water. While the doe and the lion ran off, Bharata swam across the river and rescued the fawn.

Bharata raised the fawn, and so doted on it that he forgot all about his prayers to Vishnu. Eventually, he died. As punishment for neglecting him, Vishnu caused Bharata to be re-born as a deer, but with full memory of his previous life as a human king. Rather than dwell in regret and self-pity, Bharata lived out his life as a deer with courage and equanimity. To reward him, Vishnu allowed him to be re-born again as a priest, albeit an ungainly and ugly one. Bharata lived this incarnation in full devotion to Vishnu, and was therefore spared any future re-births.[6]

Eikthyrnir

In Norse mythology, Eikthyrnir (The Oak-Thorned) is the holy stag that feeds on Yggdrasill, the sacred world tree. (Yggdrasill is an ash tree, so the combination of oak and ash signifies a sacred connection.) As he browses, drops fall from his antlers into the magical spring Hvergelmir (Bubbling Spring), which feeds all the streams and rivers of all the nine worlds.[7]

Fallow Deer (*Dama dama*)

Phylum *Chordata*, Class *Mammalia*, Order *Artiodactyla*, Infraorder *Pecora*, Family *Cervidae*, Subfamily *Cervinae*, Tribe *Cervini*, Genus *Dama*, Species *Dama dama*

Name

The fallow of the common name has nothing to do with untilled fields: it comes from a different root, *fealu* in Old English and *falwe* in Middle English, both meaning pale brown or dun. The *dama* of the scientific name is from Latin *damma* or *dama*, meaning both deer and venison.

Description

The fallow deer is generally smaller than the red deer. The most common coat color is chestnut to pale brown, with white mottles or large spots on the back. There are some variations in coat color, sometimes even within the same individual from summer to winter, when coats may darken. Males (bucks) have flat, spade-shaped, many-pointed antlers, while females (does) do not. Fallow deer were widespread before the last Ice Age, but are now mostly restricted to Europe, apart from some introduced herds in both North and South America. They were also introduced into New Zealand in 1860.

General Attributes

Like all deer, fallow deer are gentle, timid ruminants, although males become very aggressive when competing for females in the annual rutting season.

The Fallow Deer of Rhodes

The Crusaders are said to have brought fallow deer with them to Rhodes to combat infestations of snakes. They may actually have been there since the 6th century BCE. While deer never attack snakes, fallow deer antlers (which are thought to have many magical properties) are said to make snakes uncomfortable and drive them away.

Charlecote Park

There has been a substantial fallow deer herd at Charlecote Park for centuries. Charlecote lies on the banks of the River Avon, near Stratford-upon-Avon in England. Legend has it that a young William Shakespeare was caught poaching here and given a substantial fine. If so, he was lucky to get off so lightly, because venison poaching was still a capital offense in Elizabethan times.

Mouse Deer (Several Species)

Phylum *Chordata*, Class *Mammalia*, Order *Artiodactyla*, Family *Tragulidae*, Genera *Hyemoschus, Moschiola, Tragulus*, Species (several)

Name

Mouse deer are the smallest hoofed animals in the world. They are larger than a mouse, but not much larger than a domestic cat. The African mouse deer is also called a *chevrotain*, from the French for little goat. Asian mouse deer are also sometimes called *chevrotains*. There are also several different native names for the animal.

Description

Mouse deer are very small ruminants, either plain brown or reddish-brown in color, sometimes with spots or stripes, either white or black, on the upper body. They are solitary or live in pairs, rather than in herds like most other deer. They have neither antlers nor horns. In many respects, they appear closely related to several extinct similar species. They are found in South and Southeast Asia, and in the rainforests of Central and West Africa.

General Attributes

Mouse deer are even more timid and reclusive than most other deer species.

Hantu Pemburu

In Malaysian, the word *hantu* means ghost, spirit or demon. Hantu Ayer and Hantu Laut are water spirits or demons; Hantu B'rok is a monkey demon; Hantu Denej is the demon of wild beasts' tracks; Hantu Kubor is a grave-robbing demon; Hantu Orang Mati Di-Bunch is the ghost or spirit of any murdered person; Hantu Songkei steals wildfowl from traps laid by human hunters, has a penis where his nose should be, and has such wide eye sockets that he can see 360 degrees around him without moving his head. The most famous and feared ghost is Hantu Pemburu, the demon huntsman, who hunts every animal and eats the flesh and drinks the blood of humans. His wife demands the body of a pregnant male mouse deer (an impossibility of course) and the hunter destroys almost every living creature in the world during his ridiculous quest for it.

Elk/Wapiti (*Cervus canadensis*)

Phylum *Chordata*, Class *Mammalia*, Order *Artiodactyla*, Family *Cervidae*, Subfamily *Cervinae*, Genus *Cervus*, Species *Cervus canadensis*

Name

Early European explorers in America thought that moose and elk were the same (they are actually different animals), so they called the animal they saw an elk, which is derived from the Latin name *alces* (see **moose** below). The native Shawnee and Cree nations called the animal *waapiti*, meaning "white rump," and many authorities now prefer the name wapiti for *Cervus canadensis* because it avoids the earlier confusion about species. *Cervus* means deer, and *canadensis* means of Canada.

Description

By contrast with the mouse deer, the elk or wapiti is one of the largest species within the deer family. Only the moose, *Alces alces* (see below) is larger. Elk are native to North America and to Northeast Asia, but they have also been successfully introduced to many other countries, including Argentina and New Zealand. Mature males have large and impressive antlers, which are used during rutting to establish dominance over other males. The rutting call of the male elk (known as bugling) is loud and distinctive.

General Attributes

Several cultures revere the elk. In Asia, powdered elk antlers and antler velvet are used in traditional medicines.

Elk Teeth

When an elk dies in the forest, the last of its bodily remains are its bones and its teeth. The Lakota Sioux believe that elk teeth symbolize resurrection and eternal life. It is traditional to give a new-born Lakota baby an elk tooth as a talisman for a long and healthy life. The Lakota revere the elk not just as a powerful animal, but also as a guiding spirit, and young males in particular see it as a symbol of courage, sexual prowess and physical health and strength. Other Native American tribes that revere the elk include the Kootenai, Cree, Blackfeet, Ojibwa and Pawnee. Elk teeth and hides are used in costumes for ceremonial rites and dances.

The Hiisi Elk

In the 19th-century Finnish epic poem *The Kalevala* (runes 13–14), the Hisii create a magical elk. The Hiisi (literally Dreadful Place, referring to a grove used for sacrifices) describes either Juutas, the Finnish version of the Christian Judas, or a group of demons who bring harm and mischief to the world. The hero Lemminkainen has to defeat the Hisii Elk in order to win the Maiden of Pohjola as his wife. He uses ritual magic and prayers to defeat the elk, rather than brute force. Like Balder in Norse mythology, Lemminkainen is blinded by one of the gods. Like Osiris in ancient Egyptian mythology, he dies and goes to the Underworld; his mother follows him, gathers his clothes and all his body parts and stitches them all back together; he remains inert until a bee lets fall a drop of sacred honey into his mouth, and then he comes back to life.

The B.P.O.E.

The Benevolent and Protective Order of Elks or B.P.O.E. use the splendidly antlered head of an elk as their emblem. The order, often simply called the Elks, is a fraternal organization, which now has a worldwide membership. It was founded in New York in 1868 as a white men's social club, but now has a more inclusive membership and an international program of charitable and social support projects.

Moose (*Alces alces*)

Phylum *Chordata*, Class *Mammalia*, Order *Artiodactyla*, Family *Cervidae*, Subfamily *Capreolinae*, Genus *Alces*, Species *Alces alces*

Name

The name moose is first recorded in English in 1606. It is derived from Native American Algonquian languages. The Greek αλκε, *álke* and Latin *alces*, from which the English name elk is derived, may be early Germanic loanwords. In Britain and elsewhere in Europe, the moose is incorrectly called an elk.

Description

Moose are larger than elk: in fact, they are the largest of the deer family, reaching a height of 4.6–6.9 feet (1.4–2.1 meters) at the shoulder, which is about a foot taller than the elk. Males may weigh from 840 to 1,545 pounds (380 to 700 kilograms). The male's antlers, which are typically very large and heavy, are broad and palmate (flat) with many tines, quite distinctive from those of the elk. The widest antler spread recorded on a moose was 6 feet, 11 inches (210 centimeters) across.

Moose are found in Canada and the USA, mostly in the northern states or the Rocky Mountains. In Europe, the Eurasian elk (*Alces alces alces*, which is a moose) is found mostly in Finland, Sweden, Norway, Latvia and Estonia. Several species of moose are found in Russia, Siberia, Mongolia and China.

Moose are solitary diurnal herbivores. Since their land-based foods, such as roots and tree shoots, are low in sodium, moose eat a large amount of water plants, which contain more sodium. They also frequent natural salt licks to make up the deficiency.

General Attributes

Moose are massively impressive. When humans traveling in cars at high speed on Canadian roads hit a wandering moose, the humans are often the only fatalities, mostly because the moose is so tall that its weight comes down on the roof, and windscreen and seat belts and air bags have little or no effect. Finland, Norway and Sweden fence main highways to deter moose access. Moose are mostly killed by wolves, human hunters, trains and trucks, probably in that order of frequency.

In Pre-History

There are several depictions of moose in rock drawings and cave paintings. Excavations in Sweden found moose antlers in the remains of a wooden hut dating from about 6000 BCE, giving evidence of moose hunting from a very early date. Archaeological evidence shows that moose were trapped in pits from about 3700 BCE. This practice continued in Scandinavia at least until the 16th century CE.

In Classical Accounts

Descriptions of moose are found in two Roman authors. Julius Caesar (100–44 BCE), in his *Commentarii de Bello Gallico* or Commentary on the Gallic War, wrote:

> There are also [animals], which are called moose. The shape of these, and the varied color of their skins, is much like roes, but in size they surpass them a little and are destitute of horns, and have legs without joints and ligatures; nor do they lie down for the purpose of rest, nor, if they have been thrown down by any accident, can they raise or lift themselves up. Trees serve as beds to them; they lean themselves against them, and thus reclining only slightly, they take their rest; when the huntsmen have discovered from the footsteps of these animals whither they are accustomed to betake them-

selves, they either undermine all the trees at the roots, or cut into them so far that the upper part of the trees may appear to be left standing. When they have leant upon them, according to their habit, they knock down by their weight the unsupported trees, and fall down themselves along with them.[8]

The mention of lack of horns and description of legs without joints are obviously either mistakes or based on observations of females only. The description of no leg joints and knocking down trees by sleeping against them is also found in Pliny the Elder:

> There is, also, the moose, which strongly resembles our steers, except that it is distinguished by the length of the ears and of the neck. There is also the achlis [*alces*, or elk], which is produced in the land of Scandinavia; it has never been seen in this city, although we have had descriptions of it from many persons; it is not unlike the moose, but has no joints in the hind leg. Hence, it never lies down, but reclines against a tree while it sleeps; it can only be taken by previously cutting into the tree, and thus laying a trap for it, as otherwise, it would escape through its swiftness. Its upper lip is so extremely large, for which reason it is obliged to go backwards when grazing; otherwise, by moving onwards, the lip would get doubled up.[9]

Reindeer/Caribou (*Rangifer tarandus*)

Phylum *Chordata*, Class *Mammalia*, Order *Artiodactyla*, Family *Cervidae*, Subfamily *Capreolinae*, Tribe *Rangiferini*, Genus *Rangifer*, Species *Rangifer tarandus*

Name

The rein- in reindeer comes from a Norse word meaning pasturage. The same animal is called a caribou in North America, deriving from Canadian French, originally from the Indian Mi'kmaq name *qalipu*, which means snow shoveler, describing the reindeer's/caribou's habit of pawing down through snow to find food.

The genus name *Rangifer* and the species name *tarandus* (also found as *tarandrus*) are both Late Latin, both meaning reindeer. The Lapp or Saami name is *raingo*, which may be the root of *Rangifer*. *Taran* means thunder in many languages, but the origin of *tarandus* is unclear.

Description

Reindeer or caribou are found in Arctic, sub-Arctic, tundra and mountainous regions of Europe, Siberia and North America. The Taimur herd of Siberian tundra reindeer (*Rangifer tarandus sibiricus*) is the largest reindeer/caribou herd in the world, with an estimated population ranging from 400,000 to 1 million. Reindeer are domesticated by the Lapp or Saami (also spelled Sámi) people of northern Norway, Sweden, Finland and Russia. They use the animals for milk, meat, hides and as transport and pack animals. First Nation tribes of Canada have hunted caribou for centuries and have also domesticated or partly domesticated wild herds.

General Attributes

Reindeer are the hardiest of all deer species. They can tolerate very low temperatures and routinely forage through snow for food. They are revered as sacred animals by the Lapps and feature in the folklore of all Arctic peoples.

Madderakka and Sarakka

In Finno-Ugric mythology, Madderakka is the goddess of childbirth. She has three daughters, Sarakka, Juksakka and Uksakka. Madderakka forms the body of the child inside the womb. Juksakka determines whether the child is a boy or a girl, and teaches hunting lore and skills to the baby still inside the womb. Uksakka lives underground, and protects the child during its infancy, particularly when it takes its first steps—mothers will call on Uksakka to help their babies learn to walk. Sarakka helps reindeer with the birth of their calves, and is the goddess of menstruation. Lapp women who have difficult periods call on Sarakka to help ease their pains. Lapps believe that reindeer are sacred animals, and that they understand human speech.

Among Indigenous Peoples

A group of First Nation Inuit people were called Caribou Inuit because they followed the caribou herds throughout the Kivalliq region of Nanvut in northern Canada. The Caribou Clan in the Yukon territory acquired their name the same way. The Inupiat of Alaska, the Inuvialuit of Western Canada, the Han of Canada and Alaska, the Tutchone of Yukon, the Gwich'in of Alaska and the Duhalar of Mongolia are all indigenous peoples whose way of life revolves around the caribou.

Santa's Reindeer

Santa Claus rides in a magical sleigh to deliver Christmas presents to all the children of the world. The sleigh is drawn by flying reindeer, all of whom have acquired names and characters in modern folklore: Dasher, Dancer, Prancer, Vixen, Comet, Cupid, Donner, and Blitzen are the eight traditional reindeer. Rudolph is the ninth reindeer (made famous by the song about his red nose). All Santa's reindeer have traditionally been thought of as males, since they have antlers, but spoilsport zoologists have pointed out that male reindeer lose their antlers in winter and are generally enfeebled by their extensive mating activities, so, in zoological terms, all Santa's reindeer, including Rudolph, should be females, which keep their horns and their strength.

10

Bears, Pandas and Raccoons (*Ursidae, Procyonidae*)

Brown Bear (*Ursus arctos*)

Phylum *Chordata*, Class *Mammalia*, Order *Carnivora*, Family *Ursidae*, Genus *Ursus*, Species *Ursus arctos*

Name

The common name is derived from Old English *bera*. *Ursus* is Latin for bear, and *arctos* means of the north (which is what Arctic also means).

Description

The brown bear is found across northern America, Europe and Asia. The world population is estimated at 200,000, with the largest populations in Russia (120,000), the United States (32,500) and Canada (25,000), so it is fairly abundant, although several subspecies were hunted to extinction in the 18th and 19th centuries. Isolated populations are found in China and Korea, and the Japanese island of Hokkaido has a large brown bear population, estimated variously from 3,000 to over 10,000. The Ainu people, who live on several small Japanese islands, have traditionally worshiped bears, eaten bear meat, and worn bear-skin cloaks.

Brown bears vary greatly in size (and in color, despite the name), but the largest are among the largest carnivores on Earth, only slightly smaller on average than their close relative the polar bear (see below). In America, all brown bears are generally called grizzly bears, although grizzlies are technically a subspecies, *Ursus arctos horribilis* (terrifying), which is like other brown bears in almost every respect, but even larger. The largest brown bear subspecies is the Kodiak bear (*Ursus arctos middendorffi*, after the Baltic German zoologist Alexander von Middendorff, 1815–1894), which is found on the islands of the Kodiak Archipelago in Alaska. Kodiak bears eat essentially the same varied diet as other brown bears, but have been known to reach weights of 680 kilograms (1,500 pounds), twice as much as the average brown bear, and certainly large and powerful enough to be intimidating to every other animal, including the human animal.

Brown bears generally eat an enormously wide-ranging diet, about 90 percent of which is typically vegetable rather than animal. They are indifferent hunters, apart from their love of salmon and trout, which they catch by scooping them from the water with their huge paws, as has been well documented. Because they are willing to eat almost anything, particularly after hibernation, bears frequently stumble into conflict situations with humans if the humans have invaded their feeding territory. Bears will raid campgrounds, scavenge in trash containers, and even steal food from kitchens. Lone, older males and mothers with cubs are significantly more aggressive than young males and females, so a disproportionate number of bears killed in conflict situations are older, more mature individuals, creating the potential for spiraling levels of conflict as younger animals, who are less experienced at fending for themselves, tend to become even more dependent on human food.

General Attributes

Bears have been worshiped in many cultures, and there are many gods and goddesses associated with bears. First and foremost, they are exemplars of raw physical strength and power, and their psychic and spiritual energy has been invoked by warrior cultures for millennia. At the same time, they can be shy of human contact, which lends them an additional mystery. In particular, they hibernate, a behavior that has puzzled and fascinated humans for centuries. Hibernation is more than an ordinary sleep: it is a kind of small death, from which the hibernating animal emerges resurrected—hungry, potentially dangerous, but charged with an energy that humans cannot experience, perhaps from an unknown divine source.

Neanderthal and Stone-Age Bear Worship

The discovery of bear bones in several different caves near Drachenloch in Switzerland, which were inhabited by Neanderthals, has led some archaeologists to suggest that they were not only eaten, but also worshiped during the Paleolithic era, some 70,000 years ago. The evidence is not entirely convincing by itself, but the bear has been a sacred animal for such a long time, and in so many different parts of the world, that it is certainly possible that bear worship was part of Neanderthal culture.

A headless model of a bear, found in the Lascaux caves of France and dating to some 17,000 years ago, appears to have been used in religious rituals, probably with a real bear's head attached and a bear skin wrapped around it.[1]

Artemis, Ursa Major and Ursa Minor

The Greek goddess Artemis was associated with a bear cult. According to the legend, Artemis transformed a nymph, Callisto, into the constellation Ursa Major, which is Great Bear in Latin.[2] Ursa Minor means Little Bear, and is interpreted as the cub of Ursa Major (see Chapter 41). In the Artemis cult, virgins were not allowed to marry until they had participated in a ritual dance, wearing a sacred bear costume.

Atalanta

The ancient Greek goddess Atalanta of Arcadia was famed as a hunter, like Diana in the later Roman pantheon. According to legend, she was exposed to die on a mountain shortly after her birth (a common practice for girl babies in ancient Greece), but was found and suckled by a she-bear, until she eventually joined a band of hunters.[3] She became very skilled. She killed two centaurs who attempted to rape her. She also took part in the famous Calydonian boar hunt (see Chapter 13).

King Arthur

There was confusion even in classical times between the word *artus* and the word *arctus*. *Artus* meant fitted, joined together. It could also be used figuratively to mean narrow or dense. A Latin idiom was *dormitum artum*, literally a joined-together sleep, which we would call deep sleep in modern English. The alternative spelling *arctus* came about because the word was easily confused with αρκτικος, *arktikós*, the Greek word for "northern" and the Great Bear constellation, *arktikós* itself deriving from αρκτος, *arktós*, meaning bear. Eventually, a Roman name Arturus emerged, and it seems most likely to have been derived from Greek *arktós* rather than Latin *artus*. It was an aristocratic family name, and was very rare, until in 7th-century Britain it suddenly became the most popular male name of all, spelled variously Artur, Artor, Artos, Art, and other variants, and Arthur by the Middle Ages. The standard explanation is that the name was suddenly so popular because there had been a genuine historical Artur or King Arthur who had kept the advancing Germanic tribes of Angles, Saxons and Jutes at bay for a short golden age, sometime between the end of the 6th century and the middle of the 7th. So, although Arthur is not Arctur or Arcthur, there has been an association between the legendary King Arthur and the bear for centuries. In imaginary reconstructions, his battle flag is depicted as a dark or red bear's paw on a white background. In medieval Celtic culture, any great or unusually fierce warrior might be called *Art an neart*, the bear-man of power.[4]

Bear Gods and Festivals

Artio (also known as Dea Artio or Dea Artionis) was a Celtic bear goddess. She had a shrine complex and famous statue dedicated to her at Bern in Switzerland. (The name Bern also refers to bears.) Andarta was also a bear goddess, with several dedicatory inscriptions to her found across southern Europe. Her name has been interpreted as meaning either great bear (from *arctus*) or well-fixed, staying firm (from *artus*). Ardehe was a Celtic bear god, who gave his name to the village of St. Père d'Ardet near Lourdes in France.

Bears feature as totems of protective fatherhood in ancient Slavic culture.[5] In eastern Russia, the Nivkh people of Sakhalin Island still hold an annual bear festival at which a sacred bear, which has been raised with tender care, is sacrificed and eaten, similar to the rituals of the Ainu people in Japan.

In Korean mythology, the bear goddess Ungnyeo shape-shifted into human form to give birth to Dangun, who founded the first Korean kingdom, and bears still figure largely in Korean mythology.

There are various bear festivals in several towns and villages of the Pyrenees, in which the capturing and killing of the bear is a mock event (the bear and its victim both wearing masks and costumes), leading to much eating, drinking and merrymaking.

In Lapland, the bear god is called Leib-olmai. Any hunter who wants to hunt bear has to pray to Leib-olmai and ask his permission first.

Berserkers

A special type of Nordic warrior was called a *Berserkr* (plural *Berserkir*). Whether this means bear shirt (i.e., bear cloak or hide) or bare shirt (i.e., no chest covering at all) has been disputed, but the similar *Úlfheðnar* (wolf warrior) seems to suggest that a bear cult was involved. There were also warriors called *Hildisvíni* (battle swine) dedicated to the goddess Freyja. The Torslunda plates, four ancient cast-bronze dies found in Sweden in 1870, depict warriors wearing bear, wolf and boar helmets.

The Berserkers were famed for rushing into battle in an absolute frenzy, oblivious to danger, often foaming at the mouth and screaming incoherently. Whether alcohol or hallucinogenic drugs were used to excite the battle frenzy is unproven, but it certainly seems likely. A widespread belief in early Viking culture was that Berserkers actually shape-shifted into bears during their battle frenzy. Those that died in battle (and there were many of them, not surprisingly) were laid out on bearskins for their funeral rites. The traditional tall bearskin caps worn today by British royal guards at Buckingham Palace, and by similar guards in Denmark, are said to be a holdover from the ancient bear-warrior cult and tradition.[6]

Daniel and the Bear-Beast

In the Old Testament, Daniel has a dream (we would say nightmare) in which four terrible beasts appear before him: one is like a lion, but has eagle wings, and then stands up straight like a human; the second is like a bear, but with three tusks in its mouth; the third is like a leopard, but with four wings and four heads; and the fourth is like nothing on earth, but has iron teeth and devours all in its path. Christians take a later passage as an explanation that true believers will overcome the pagan enemies (the bear is said to represent the pagan gods of Persia, modern Iran) and "possess the kingdom" of eternal life:

> As for these four great beasts, four kings shall arise out of the earth. But the holy ones of the Most High shall receive the kingdom and possess the kingdom for ever—for ever and ever.[7]

Polar Bear (*Ursus maritimus*)

Phylum *Chordata*, Class *Mammalia*, Order *Carnivora*, Family *Ursidae*, Genus *Ursus*, Species *Ursus maritimus*

Name

The bear is polar because it lives mostly within the Arctic Circle, close to the North Pole. The species name *maritimus*, fairly obviously, means maritime.

Description

Polar bears are very large, generally about the same size as the average Kodiak brown bear. They are hypercarnivores, meaning that at least 70 percent of their diet consists of meat (mostly seal), and many of them eat almost nothing except meat. They live in what is called a "narrow ecological niche," i.e., within a very limited range of temperatures, habitats and geographical conditions. Although they are almost always born on land, they spend much of their lives traveling great distances walking over ice, which also frequently requires swimming in the very cold Arctic Ocean. Climate change has dramatically altered their environment for the worse, and polar bears are now considered an endangered species. Several pictures of weak, emaciated polar bears have been circulated on social media. Increasingly, they are entering or spending more time in human territory, looking for food in human garbage. To make matters worse, the large amounts of blubber in their diet contain many pollutants from human activity that are ingested by animals lower down the food chain, and these also affect polar bears adversely. Polar bears tainted by oil spills inevitably try to lick the oil from their fur and paws, which frequently leads to kidney failure and death. In general, human beings are not the polar bear's best friends.

General Attributes

The polar bear's immense physical strength and endurance have earned it enormous respect from northern peoples. Because, like brown bears, it can rise up to stand on its hind feet only, and because its skeletal structure is not that dissimilar to the human body, many myths and legends involve shape-shifting into human form. In fact, there is a general and widespread belief in Inuit and native Alaskan folklore that polar bears in their own homes are actually humans, and that they put on their fur "disguises" only to visit the outside world.

Siberian Rituals

The Chukchi and Yupik of eastern Siberia hunt and eat polar bears, but they treat the slain animals with unusual respect. The head is left attached to the skin until a ritual of thanksgiving for the meat is completed. The bear is addressed as if it were a human being: it is even offered a pipe to smoke. When the ritual has been completed, the head is severed and buried with great reverence close to the settlement, facing north.

The Nenets of Siberia remove the canine teeth of slain polar bears, believing them to be talismans of great power and protection. They sell them to other tribes further south, who sew them into their hats or into the hoods of their jackets as protection against attacks from brown bears: they believe that no brown bear would dare attack a human wearing polar bear teeth.

Asian Black Bear/Moon Bear (*Ursus thibetanus*)

Phylum *Chordata*, Class *Mammalia*, Order *Carnivora*, Family *Ursidae*, Genus *Ursus*, Species *Ursus thibetanus*

Name

Asian black bears live, not surprisingly, in Asia, and are black with a brown muzzle. They also have a distinctive white marking on the chest, which can look like a V or a crescent moon, hence the name Moon Bear. The species name *Ursus thibetanus* means Tibetan

Bear, but there was also an earlier classification name, *Selenarctos thibetanus*, meaning Tibetan Moon-Bear, from the Greek words σεℓενε, *selene* (moon) and αρκτος, *arktós* (bear).

Description

The Asian black bear is generally smaller and slighter than the brown bear. They have round, stick-out ears, like Mickey Mouse. They generally live in forest regions, and are excellent tree climbers. They also walk on just their hind legs more frequently than other bear species. They are agile and alert, but their hearing range is limited and they have notoriously poor eyesight. There are several subspecies. In several Asian countries, they are widely hunted for their body parts, in particular their paws, skin and gall bladders, since these are highly valued in Eastern medicine.

General Attributes

Asian black bears are generally shy and solitary creatures, but they have killed many humans and a great deal of livestock, and are therefore considered highly untrustworthy. In Yann Martel's 2001 novel *The Life of Pi* (subsequently released as a movie in 2012), Pi tells us that his zoo-owning father described the Asian black bear as one of the most dangerous of all animals because of its ferocity and unpredictability. Nevertheless, they are respected and revered animals in Hinduism and in Japanese folklore.

Jambavantha

In Hinduism, Jambavantha or Jambavat (he also has many other names in different languages) was the King of the Bears. He was formerly the King of the Himalayas, but agreed to be transformed into a black bear by Brahma in order to serve Lord Rama. He became an immortal, and Brahma was now his father. He helped Rama to discover the goddess Sita, who became Rama's wife. In return, Jambavantha was granted enormous physical strength ("the strength of ten million lions") and a very long life. He lived through two of the four great ages of humankind, and thus acquired wisdom as well as great strength. He was present at the "churning of the waters," when the Earth itself was being formed. In the epic *Mahabharata*, he fought with Lord Krishna for almost a whole month, until he grew tired and realized that even with his enormous strength he would never be able to defeat the god. He submitted to Krishna, who subsequently married Jambavantha's daughter Jambavati.[8]

Yamaotoko

The black bear features in the folklore of Japanese highland communities. He is called variously *yamaotoko* (mountain man), *yama no oyaji* (mountain father), and *yama no ossan* (mountain uncle). According to a legend from the district of Niigata, the mountain spirit (*yama no kami*) gave the bear a powerful magical amulet wrapped in silk, but when the bear returned the amulet, the silk left a distinctive white mark on its chest, shaped like the crescent moon.[9]

American Black Bear (*Ursus americanus*)

Phylum *Chordata*, Class *Mammalia*, Order *Carnivora*, Family *Ursidae*, Genus *Ursus*, Species *Ursus americanus*

Name

The common name and the classification name are both obvious.

Description

The American black bear is more closely related to the Asian black bear than to brown bears or polar bears. There are 16 subspecies. It is smaller than the brown bear, and much more abundant in numbers. It will eat almost anything, depending on where it lives. It prefers the quiet of the forest, but will enter human territory in search of food, and, like all bears (except the panda), can become habituated to human food very quickly. It bites and claws trees to leave messages for other bears, and these distinctive marks are useful indicators to hikers that black bears may be nearby.

American black bears are very strong for their size, and have three characteristics not found in Asian black bears: they have no moon blaze on their chests, and their color can range from dark black to almost white, with several other tawny shades in between; they are dexterous (they can open jam jars); and they have very good eyesight. They were historically hunted for their meat, which is still more highly prized than grizzly meat, and for their body fat, which was used in cosmetics, although conservation activists have largely ended that practice.

General Attributes

The American black bear is far more timid than either brown bears or the Asian black bear. It rarely attacks humans, and then usually only if habituated to human food sources. The black bear is seen as less ferocious and more friendly to humans than other bears.

Native American Legends

The Navajo believe that the sun god lives in a house protected on four sides, with the Big Black Bear guarding the north. Traditionally, they would pray to the spirit of the black bear for protection from marauding enemies.

Several nations believe that the black bear was created by the Good Spirit, while the brown bear or grizzly was created by the Evil Spirit. In the Indian legends of the Pacific Northwest, a black bear prince married a human princess, and that is why humans get on better with black bears.

Sleeping Bear Dunes National Lakeshore in Michigan is named after a Native American legend. A female bear and her cub swam all the way across Lake Michigan (118 miles or 190 km). Exhausted, they fell asleep on the eastern shore. They slept for years, and then centuries, and they are still asleep there to this day under the great sand dunes, which rose up over them to make a blanket for them.

Modern Black Bear Icons

A.A. Milne's famous creation Winnie-the-Pooh was named after Winnipeg, a black bear that lived at London Zoo from 1915 until 1934. The toy teddy bear, first made in 1902 by Morris Michtom, was supposedly so named after Michtom saw a cartoon of President Theodore (Teddy) Roosevelt refusing to shoot a black bear cub that had been tied to a tree. Smokey Bear, the cartoon mascot of the United States Forestry Service, was originally a real black bear, which was rescued from a forest fire in 1950.

Panda (*Ailuropoda melanoleuca*)

Phylum *Chordata*, Class *Mammalia*, Order *Carnivora*, Family *Ursidae*, Genus *Ailuropoda*, Species *Ailuropoda melanoleuca*

Name

Nobody is certain about the original derivation of the common name. It came into English from French, but is almost certainly Asian in origin, since pandas live in the wild only in China—the Tibetan language has been suggested. The family name is *Ursidae*, which means bears, but the genus name is not *Ursus*, bear, but *Ailuropoda*, which means "cat-footed animal," from Greek αιλουρος, *aïlouros*, domestic cat, and ποδα, *poda*, foot. The species name *melanoleuca* is New Latin for black and white.

Description

The giant panda (or simply panda, see below) is known worldwide, not least because its image has been adopted by the World Wildlife Fund as its symbol. The panda began to be called the giant panda to distinguish it from the red panda, or little panda, but it's now known that those two species are only distantly related, so the names giant panda and panda actually both now refer to exactly the same animal.

Beginning with Chi Chi at London Zoo in the 1960s, pandas have attracted huge numbers of visitors to zoos. They cost five times as much to maintain as the next most expensive zoo animal, the elephant, but zoo managers are still willing to pay enormous sums of money to rent them from other zoos, because they bring in so many eager customers. A private zoo on the island of Taiwan once notoriously painted a sun bear black and white to try to cash in on panda fever.

The Qinling panda (*Ailuropoda melanoleuca qinlingensis*), which lives only in the Qinling Mountains of Shaanxi Province in China, is colored light brown and dark brown rather than white and black. The red panda (*Ailurus fulgens*, cat-like shining) which, as mentioned above, is only distantly related to the black-and-white panda, lives in Nepal, whereas pandas live exclusively in China (unless they're in a zoo).

Pandas are peculiar animals. They are technically carnivores (in particular, their teeth and jaws are typical of carnivores), but they live almost exclusively on vegetable food. Pandas in the wild in China eat a diet of 99 percent bamboo shoots (as much as 9 to 14 kilograms or 20 to 30 pounds per day). They have even developed a thumb-like appendage to help hold the shoots while they eat them. They have such round faces because they need massive musculature to keep their powerful jaws cutting through the tough bamboo. They have to acquire gut bacteria to digest the bamboo, and in the first instance they get this as babies from eating their mother's droppings. Even when food is plentiful, bamboo delivers so little energy and protein that their nutrition is poor and they are sedentary animals with very little surplus energy.

General Attributes

Pandas are rare and peculiar creatures in the mythological sense, too. The few references all come from China. Because of their quiet and seemingly passive nature, pandas were considered to be emblems of peace in ancient China (although males can be very aggressive in the wild when competing for females).

Folk Medicine

In Sichuan Province, panda urine was reputedly used to dissolve metal objects that had been accidentally swallowed, such as needles, but there are no records of how effective it was. Panda fur was cut into strips for women to use as sanitary pads during menstruation. The Ming dynasty herbalist Li Shizhen suggested applying oil of panda (presumably panda fat) on the affected area of the body as a remedy for tumors.

How the Panda Acquired Its Black Markings

There are several versions of the legend that pandas were once white all over, but acquired black spots as they engaged with humans, i.e., lost their animal innocence. One is that the first panda in the world was befriended by four kind shepherdesses, but all four were killed. The distraught panda followed the local funeral custom of rubbing dirt on its arms, then rubbed more dirt into its eyes as it cried. After the funeral, the panda decided to keep its black stains as a perpetual reminder of its loss. It cast the spirits of the shepherdesses onto the horizon, where they formed the four-peak mountain range now called Siguniang, or Four Sisters' Mountain. A variant of the story is that there was only one shepherdess and a panda cub, and the shepherdess was killed by a leopard.

The Empress Dowager Bo

The Empress Dowager Bo, who died in 155 BCE, began life as a lowly concubine, but she survived and thrived in the complex politics of the imperial court. Eventually her son, Liu Heng, became Emperor Wen of Han. Bo was buried in her own temple, with a panda skull beside her, symbolizing her high status.

Raccoon (*Procyon lotor/Ursus lotor*)

Phylum *Chordata*, Class *Mammalia*, Order *Carnivora*, Family *Procyonidae*, Genus *Procyon*, Species *Procyon lotor / Ursus lotor*

Name

The common name is from the American indigenous Powhatan Nation's name *ärähkuněm*, which means literally "he scratches with his hands." Spanish colonists borrowed the Aztec name *mapachtli*, which had the similar meaning "the one who takes everything into his hands," so the Spanish word for raccoon is *mapache*. The genus name *Procyon* is a New Latin coining from Greek προ, *pró*, in place of, and κυων, *kuōn*, dog. The only other members of the *Procyonidae* family are the comparatively little-known coatis, kinkajous, olingos, olinguitos, ringtails, and cacomistles. The species name *lotor* is New Latin for a laundryman or "one who washes things," because of the frequently observed habit of raccoons apparently washing their food before they eat it (see below).

Description

The raccoon is not a bear, but it was thought for a long time that raccoons and pandas were closely related, so the species name *Ursus lotor* (washing bear) has been used as well as *Procyon lotor*. In Germany, where raccoons were introduced in the 1930s, the raccoon is called *Waschbär* (also washing bear). (Raccoons have been introduced to several other countries, including Japan.) The raccoon is noted for its expressive face, its extremely dexterous front paws (often called "hands") and its long ringed tail, and all three of these features are prominent in Native American folk tales. It is omnivorous, and particularly likes hunting for fish, frogs, crayfish, or anything else to be found in shallow water at the edge of a river or lake, which is where the hand washing myth comes from. The action, which is also observed in captivity, has been called "dousing," but "dabbling" for food would probably be more accurate. An amusing video that has been circulated widely on social media shows a pet raccoon playing with a garden watering fixture in such a way that it looks as though the animal is playing what looks like a harp of water spray. They seem to enjoy having their paws in water.

Although raccoons are quite often kept as pets because of their great entertainment value, they are not responsive to human control and they can inflict a powerful bite. Raccoons are susceptible to rabies, and the public are often warned to keep well away from animals that look ill or are behaving aggressively.

General Attributes

The raccoon is a lovable rascal, a trickster. It is an extremely active and curious animal. The Aztecs attributed supernatural powers to raccoons, having observed how quick and inventive the females are when protecting their young. There are rock carvings of raccoon tracks at Native American sites in Texas, Kentucky, New Mexico and California.

Native American Legends

The Lakota Sioux believe the raccoon has magical powers, associating its facial markings with their ceremonial face-paint patterns used during rituals to connect with ancestral spirits. The Tuscarora of the Great Lakes region have a number of folk tales that describe raccoons devising ingenious methods for capturing prey, particularly close to the water's edge, and it seems very likely that these tales were based on real observation. The Abenaki have a series of legends about a named raccoon, Azeban, who is a trickster (he also talks).

In Literature, Television and Film

There have been scores of fictional raccoons, all of them essentially the same lovable rascal. There are at least a dozen American children's books or book series with a raccoon as one of the main characters. There are even more American and Japanese comic books or series featuring raccoons. Rocket Raccoon, who first appeared in Marvel comic books, also stars in the *Guardians of the Galaxy* movies (2014 and 2017). Other well-known literary and cinematic raccoons include Ranger Rick (National Wildlife Federation), Rackety Coon Chile (the Pogo comic strip), Bright Heart (Care Bears), and Meeko (Walt Disney's *Pocahontas*).

11

Horses and Rhinoceroses (*Perissodactyla: Equidae* and *Rhinocerotoidea*)

Horse (*Equus ferus caballus*)

Phylum *Chordata*, Class *Mammalia*, Order *Perissodactyla*, Family *Equidae*, Genus *Equus*, Species *Equus ferus*, Subspecies *Equus ferus caballus*

Name

The name horse is Germanic in origin, deriving from a Proto-Indo-European word root **kers-*, meaning to run, which also gave us car, course, current, courier and many other words.

The order name *Perissodactyla* means "having an odd number of toes," from Greek περισσος, *perissós*, uneven, and δακτυλος, *dáktulos*, finger or toe. It is the opposite of *Artiodactyla*, which means "having an even number of toes." In members of the horse family, the middle toe has developed into a single hoof, which is not cloven like the hooves of some other animals.

Equus is Latin for horse, *ferus* means feral or wild, and *caballus*, also meaning horse, is Latin derived from Greek καβαλλες, *kaballes*. By the time the word *caballus* was fully established in Latin, it meant not all horses in general, but specifically a tired, old horse, a nag or a hack. A Latin proverb runs *optat arare caballus*, which means literally "An old nag chooses to plough," or figuratively "A hack (e.g. a hack writer) will always take the safe and easy option." The English word cavalry, the French *cheval* and the Spanish *cabal* are all derived from *caballus*.

Description

The horse has taken about 50 million years to evolve from a small, many-toed mammal about the size of a dog to the generally large and very familiar animal we know today. The domestication of horses is believed to have begun in about 4000 BCE. Today, horses are found in almost every part of the world. There are many breeds, often quite different in size, color and general appearance.

General Attributes

The horse is one of the most widely revered animals in human history. There are over 60 million horses in the world,[1] so it is a familiar as well as widely respected and revered animal. Although the stallion (intact male) has an iconography all of its own, horse deities are almost always female, and represent the Goddess in her most helpful (utilitarian) and loving (loyal, affectionate) aspects, whilst still maintaining an aura of mystery. The horse is depicted in cave paintings dating back thousands of years. In several mythologies, the horse represents the sun.

White Horses

The white horse is especially venerated and appears in almost every world religion and mythology. Some examples follow.

Sometime during the Bronze Age (c. 3200–600 BCE), the people of Britain carved huge, stylized white horses on the sides of hills. The images were made by cutting away the turf and topsoil to reveal the white chalk lying beneath. The most famous, and probably the earliest, of these figures is the White Horse of Uffington, in Oxfordshire, which is 360 feet (110 meters) from nose to tail and can be seen from miles away. It was built (or carved) into the hillside, probably after 1400 BCE, but the date is uncertain. From time immemorial, the chalk lines have been scoured or scraped clean approximately every seven years: without such attention, the chalk becomes overgrown and the image fades. There are modern copies of the Uffington Horse in Australia and Georgia, USA. There are several other similar white horses in Britain, carved at various times.

In Greek history and mythology, white horses were venerated. The Greek historian Herodotus (484–425 BCE) reports that white horses were worshiped as sacred animals in the court of Xerxes the Great (519–465 BCE). The famed winged horse Pegasus (see below) was white.

In Celtic mythology, the goddess Rhiannon rides a pale or white horse. Epona (see below) is often depicted as a white or pale gray horse.

In the ancient Zoroastrianism of Persia, Tishtrya, the personification of the star Sirius, is a white stallion (see below). Aredvi Sura Anahita, goddess of the winds and weather, has chariots drawn by white horses.

In Hinduism, the sacrifice of a sacred white or gray horse was an essential feature of kingship rituals (see *Ashvamedha* below). (White horse sacrifice rituals are also found in Celtic and Norse traditions.) Uchchaihshravas was a seven-headed white horse that appeared during the "churning of the waters" in which the world was formed (see below). The great god Indra rides a white horse in several legends. The sun god Surya crosses the sky in a chariot drawn by seven horses, alternately described as white or as all the colors of the rainbow (which seems to anticipate Newton's discovery that white light is really light of every color put together). Kalki, who will be the tenth and final incarnation of Vishnu, is predicted to appear as a white horse at the end of the world, to save believers.

In Buddhism, a white horse called Kanthaka was the most beloved animal of Prince Siddharta before he became the Buddha. When Buddha renounced the world, Kanthaka died of grief.

In the Bible, the four horsemen of the Apocalypse ride horses: a "pale horse" carries Death and a white horse carries Pestilence.[2] In the Book of Revelation, Christ (or perhaps the Holy Spirit) rides a white horse out of heaven to judge the world:

> Then I saw heaven opened, and there was a white horse! Its rider is called Faithful and True, and in righteousness he judges and makes war. His eyes are like a flame of fire, and on his head are many diadems; and he has a name inscribed that no one knows but himself. He is clothed in a robe dipped in blood, and his name is called the Word of God. And the armies of heaven, wearing fine linen, white and pure, were following him on white horses.[3]

In Islamic tradition, Muhammad rode a white, winged horse called Al-Buraq (Lightning) from Mecca to Jerusalem. He also rode Al-Buraq to heaven and back.

The sacred white horse also appears in many legends of the Far East, and in the mythologies of many indigenous peoples. The Blackfoot Indians of America have a snow god called Aisoyimstan who wears white clothing and rides a white horse.

Ashvamedha

Ashvamedha was a horse-sacrifice ritual performed during the Vedic period (c. 1700–500 BCE) of ancient Hinduism. According to the epic poem *The Mahabharata*, the ritual had to be performed by an anointed king. The priests selected a horse of a pre-determined color (white was the usual preference), which they then set free to wander at will for a year. The king and his army followed the horse wherever it went. If it entered a foreign territory, the foreign king was required to either submit to the invading king, or wage war against him. A king who conquered many territories would return in triumph and finally sacrifice the horse at a great victory feast. Exceptionally, the horse might be sacrificed only symbolically, and then allowed to go to pasture to live out the rest of its days.[4]

Uchchaihshravas

In Hindu mythology, Uchchaihshravas (Loud Neighing) was the seven-headed flying white horse of the storm-god, Indra. In some tales, he is also the mount of the sun-god, Surya, but also of Bali, the king of the demons. Uchchaihshravas was created from the *samudra manthana* or "churning of the milk ocean" at the beginning of the world. He has a brother-sister relationship with the great goddess Lakshmi, consort of the god Vishnu, because Lakshmi was also born of the *samudra manthana*. The former Beatle, George Harrison, who was greatly interested in Indian music and culture, used a stylized image of Uchchaihshravas for the logo of his music label Dark Horse Records.[5]

The Ashwin Twins

Also from ancient Hinduism, the Ashwins (or Aswins) were twin-brother gods, whose job was to clear the sky each morning ready for the god of dawn, Ushas, to appear. The Ashwins rode in a golden chariot, drawn by either horses or birds. The name Ashwin means horseman. According to the legend, their mother Saranyu (Fast Runner) took the form of a mare to be mated by her husband Vivaswat in the form of a stallion. In their haste, Vivaswat spilled his semen onto the ground, but merely smelling it was sufficient for Saranyu to become pregnant with the twins.[6]

Tishtrya

In Zoroastrianism, Tishtrya was the rain god. In the desert land of Persia, he was a very welcome visitor. His enemy was Apaosha, who was a demon of drought. Apaosha brought drought and destruction wherever he could. One day, Tishtrya decided to wage battle against Apaosha. He transformed himself into a white stallion. Apaosha came to the battle as a black stallion. The two fought for three days and nights, until they were both exhausted. Apaosha looked as though he was going to defeat Tishtrya. But the rain god prayed to the god of goodness, Ahura Mazda, to come to his aid. Ahura Mazda, whose goodness never fails, gave strength to Tishtrya, who finally defeated Apaosha and sent him back into the desert, where he belonged. Tishtrya was able to bring enough rain to the world to create lakes, rivers and seas. In the Persian zodiac (the ancient Persians were keen astronomers), Tishtrya is identified with the brightest star in the sky, Sirius (see Chapter 41).[7]

Abderus

The classical Greek hero Herakles had a semi-divine male lover, Abderus, son of Opus and the god Hermes. Herakles sent Abderus to secure and guard the man-eating mares owned by the Bistonian king, Diomedes. The mares were too strong for Abderus, and devoured him. In his memory, Herakles built the city of Abdera, which still stands on the coast of Thrace, in Greece.[8]

Pegasus

Pegasus was a winged horse in Greek mythology. He was the mount of the hero Bellerophon ("he who appears in the clouds"), who refused the advances of Antaea, wife of King Proteus, because he was a man of honor and would not have an affair with another man's wife. Antaea was furious, and eventually saw to it that Bellerophon was sent out to slay the Chimaera, a fire-breathing monster (see Chapter 39). Bellerophon slew the monster, and then flew on to several other epic adventures on Pegasus.

By legend, Pegasus was fathered by the sea-god Poseidon from drops of blood falling into the ocean from the severed head of the Gorgon Medusa, carried by the hero Perseus. After his birth, Pegasus was sent by Zeus to Mount Olympus, to bring back thunder and lightning. He created the fountain called Hippocrene (Horse Fountain) on Mount Helicon, and became a favorite of the Muses. To this day, the metaphor "to drink of Hippocrene" means to be inspired as a poet.

Bellerophon later tried to fly Pegasus up to heaven, but Zeus sent a gadfly to plague the horse, and Bellerophon fell from the sky and died. Zeus then transformed Pegasus into the constellation that still bears his name (see Chapter 41).[9]

Malayan mythology has a flying horse, similar to Pegasus. His name is Koeda or Kuda Sembrani, and he can fly or swim underwater as well as in air.

Arne or Melanippe

The Greek mythological figure Arne, also called Melanippe (Black Horse), was the daughter of King Aeolus of Magnesia and Thea (also sometimes called Melanippe), who was a daughter of Chiron the centaur (half man, half horse—see Chapter 40). Arne, who had been born in the form of a black foal (because of her centaur grandfather) but later took human form, was raped by the sea-god Poseidon in the form of a bull. Arne's keeper, Desmontes, blinded and imprisoned her when it became known that she was pregnant. Arne bore two sons, Aeolus and Boeotus. Her sons later released her from imprisonment, and Poseidon restored her sight. Through Boeotus, she became the legendary founder of the central Greek region of Boeotia and its capital city, Thebes.[10]

Bucephalus

Bucephalus (from Greek βους, *bous*, ox, and κεφαλε, *kephále*, head) was the mount of Alexander the Great (356–323 BCE). According to Plutarch, the strong, bull-headed horse was given to Alexander by his father, Philip of Macedon, because nobody but Alexander could tame him. When Bucephalus died after the Battle of Hydaspes in 326 BCE, he was buried with full military honors.[11] (The name Philip, in passing, is from Greek φιλ-, *phil*-, lover or loving, and ῾ιππος, *hippos*, horse, the whole therefore meaning "lover of horses.")

Hippolyte and Hippolytus

Hippolyte or Hippolyta ("of the stampeding horses") was the Queen of the Amazons in Greek mythology, the tribe of women warriors who came originally, by some accounts, from the deserts of Libya in Africa. They were beautiful but brutal women, notoriously savage and implacable as fighters. The ninth labor of Herakles was to seize the girdle or belt from the waist of Hippolyte, their queen. In one account, Hippolyte fell in love with Herakles and willingly gave him her girdle, but the other Amazons, believing that their queen was being abducted, fired arrows at Herakles, and he killed Hippolyte before escaping. In another version of the story, Herakles gave Hippolyte to Theseus to marry.[12]

Hippolytus (also "of the stampeding horses") was the son of that marriage. He was dedicated to chastity and worshiped Artemis. He refused the advances of his stepmother, Phaedra, and was flung from his chariot and dragged to his death by his own horses when Theseus asked Poseidon to arrange his death. In the later Roman version, Diana (Artemis) restores Hippolytus to life.[13]

Saint Hippolytus (same name, different person) was originally one of the jailers of Saint Lawrence in the 3rd century CE, but Saint Lawrence converted him to Christianity. Hippolytus helped to hide Lawrence's body after his death. His punishment was to be tied to wild horses, which dragged him to his death, like the earlier Hippolytus. The 3rd-century Hippolytus is the Christian patron saint of horses.[14]

Dharmapala

In Mahayana Buddhism, there are eight Dharmapala (Protectors of Dharma). *Dharma* cannot be translated in a single English word. It is used by many eastern Buddhists to refer to Buddhism itself, but it actually signifies truth, doctrine, or cosmic law and order, or the teachings of the Buddha. Of the eight Dharmapala, sometimes called the Eight Terrible Ones, who are essentially warriors against demons and other enemies of Buddhism, four have some kind of horse association: Lha-Mo, a goddess, rides a mule and carries a sword and a mace; the god Ts'angs-pa Dkar-po rides a white horse and carries a sword and a flag; Beg-Tse, god of war and protector of horses, carries a sword and wears Mongolian boots; and the god Hayagriva, borrowed from Hindu mythology, carries an ax and has a horse-shaped neck.[15]

Celtic Horse Goddesses

In Ireland, Etain and Macha were horse goddesses. Rhiannon in the Welsh tradition was also frequently depicted as riding a white mare, or as a white mare herself. A white mare was supposed to represent the spirit of royal sovereignty, and there was a coronation ritual in which the newly chosen king mated with a white mare, then ate of her flesh and bathed in her blood, before assuming the metaphorical crown (Celtic tribal kings did not wear actual crowns).

The most universally worshiped Celtic horse goddess was Epona (the word pony is supposedly derived from her name), who probably originated in Gaul, but whose worship spread not only to Britain and all across Europe, but also to imperial Rome, where the feast day of December 18 was dedicated to her. She was even included in the imperial rituals, dedicated to the Emperor between the 1st and 3rd centuries CE in the names Epona Augusta (the Venerable) and Epona Regina (the Queen).[16]

Like most horse-goddesses, Epona was also a goddess of fertility and prosperity. She holds a *patera* (large bowl for dispensing libations) or a *cornucopia* (horn-shaped container of food) in several sculptures. The Mari Lwyd (Gray Mare) ritual in Wales, the Padstow 'Obby 'Oss in Cornwall, and even the comic pantomime horse, are all said to have connections with ancient Epona worship, the widespread distribution of which was probably accelerated by the adoption by the Roman cavalry of the goddess as their emblem and protector.

Kelpies

A kelpie is a Scottish water-horse, a creature to be avoided wherever possible, a literal nightmare. The creature, usually white or pale gray in color, emerges from the water (usually a loch rather than a river or stream) in the form of a beautiful mare, especially in the gloaming, which is what the Scots call twilight or dusk. She approaches gently, with head lowered, inviting the onlooker to fondle her muzzle or mane, or to climb on her back to ride. However, the instant any part of your body touches the kelpie's skin, it is as if you have grasped the strongest glue ever made: you cannot let go, no matter how hard you try. The kelpie, its eyes now blazing like coals on a fire, drags you screaming into the water, and you are pulled down to drown in her royal domain.[17]

Hengist and Horsa

In the historical legends of the British Isles, King Arthur's father was Uther Pendragon (Chief or Head Dragon). Uther took over after the previous king, Vortigern, died some time towards the end of the 5th century—or was burned alive in a tower by his angry subjects, according to some versions.

Vortigern's name is actually a title—as Guorthigern in Old Welsh, it meant the same as the Latin *superbus tyrannus* or supreme leader. Vortigern had trouble coming at him from several different directions, his most urgent concerns being the Irish who raided from the west and the Picts in Scotland who raided from the north. Desperate for help, he invited Germanic tribes—Angles, Saxons and Jutes—to cross the English Channel and fight on his side as *confederati*, military allies. What he got for his trouble—and why he ended up being removed from the throne and possibly burned to death in a tower—was a small army of supposed auxiliary troops who soon became a large army of raiders and settlers themselves. They established a highly defensible territory in the south-east of England once occupied by the *Canti* tribe, now called Kent. As the years went by, more and more of them kept coming, until eventually a huge portion of the land that had been called *Britannia* by the Romans after the Celtic name *Prydain* now became instead *Angle-land*, eventually *England*.

According to legend, the supposed leaders of these Germanic invaders were two brothers called Hengist and Hors or Horsa. However, these names mean, respectively, Stallion and Horse (*Hengst* is the modern German word for stallion), so there has been much speculation about who or what the historical Hengist and Horsa really were—or even if they actually existed at all. They are said to have landed at Ebbsfleet in Kent and served as Vortigern's mercenaries for a while. Hengist (presumably the elder brother) was reputedly the first Jutish king of Kent.

The question whether Hengist and Horsa were legendary or historical has never been resolved, and is likely to remain unresolved. The meaning of their names is clear—perhaps they were even horse gods, or leaders who named themselves after such gods.[18] The irony is that, during the wars that the legendary or historical Arthur led for the Celtic British against the invading English (and Arthur's historical existence is still similarly unresolved), the Anglish, Saxon and Jutish armies were essentially infantry armies, with very few horses, while Arthur's astonishing success probably depended on rapid deployment of small cavalry units.

Bayard

In the legends of Charlemagne (also called the Carolingian Cycle or the Matter of France, whereas the Matter of Britain is the cycle of Arthurian legends), the Emperor had a magical horse called Bayard (Red-Haired). He gave it as a gift to the four sons of Duke Aymon of Dordone, namely Renaud, Guichard, Alard and Richard, who are the heroes of *Les Quatre Fils Aymon* or *The Four Sons of Aymon*.

Bayard's magical quality was a kind of shape-shifting. Whenever any of the brothers sat on him, he was a big, powerful but otherwise ordinary horse. However, if another son joined the first, Bayard's back stretched to accommodate the additional rider, and if all four brothers chose to ride him at the same time, he could stretch his spine out until all four were seated spaciously and comfortably.[19]

Saint Eloy

In Christian legend, Saint Eloy of Noyon (588–659 CE) is the patron saint of horses and farriers, as well as goldsmiths and general metal workers.

Eloy was a goldsmith in Limoges. He made a throne of gold and jewels for King Clotaire II of France. There was much gold and many jewels left over, which Eloy could very easily have stolen. Instead, he made the king a second throne, and was rewarded for his honesty by being brought into the king's service in Paris. Clotaire's successor, King Dagobert, made Eloy Master of the Royal Mint.

Eloy traveled widely in northern Europe. One day, so the legend goes, the Devil brought him a horse to be shod, meaning to trick and humiliate him. No shoe could ever be made to fit the horse. Eloy surreptitiously cut off the horse's leg and fitted a new shoe to it. Then he made the sign of the cross over the horse, and the leg with the new shoe instantly re-attached itself, perfectly healed.[20]

The Lud Ritual

In Finno-Ugric ritual, each extended family has a secret and sacred grove where important rituals take place. This grove is called a *lud*. The presiding spirit of the grove demands a blood sacrifice, which is usually a foal. To show whether the animal is willing to be sacrificed, cold water is poured over its back. If it shivers, it is willing. Women and children are not allowed to attend *lud* rituals.[21]

Solobong Yubin

In the mythology of the Buriat people of Siberia, Solobong Yubin (also Uhaa Solbon and Uuden Tenger) is the god of horses. The Mongolian names, respectively, mean Star of the Morning and Evening (i.e., Venus), Shepherd of Heaven and Keeper of the Gate. He rides through the sky with a lasso in his hand. He has three wives, one of whom he abducted from a wedding feast.

In one legend, Solobong Yubin left his horses in the care of his groom, Dogedoi, but Dogedoi left the horses unattended for three days and went hunting with his dog. When Solobong Yubin returned, he found that wolves had scattered the horses and eaten some of them. The god punished the groom severely.

The Buriat still keep some horses separate as sacrifices to Solobong Yubin. The horses are not ridden or used for any work. Prior to being sacrificed, they have their manes and tails cut. At the sacrificial feast, the Buriat throw wine into the air and burn food for the god's consumption.[22]

Skinfaxi and Hrímfaxi

In Norse mythology, Skinfaxi (Shining Mane) is the magical horse of Dagr (Day). He gallops across the sky, bringing light to the world and the heavens. Hrímfaxi (Frost Mane) is the mount of Nótt (Night), who brings the moon and stars. J.R.R. Tolkien (1892–1973) used the Nordic *-fax* ending for Gandalf's horse Shadowfax in *The Lord of the Rings* (1954).

Ass/Donkey, Onager (*Equus africanus asinus*, *Equus hemionus*)

Phylum *Chordata*, Class *Mammalia*, Order *Perissodactyla*, Family *Equidae*, Genus *Equus*, Species *Equus africanus*, *Equus hemionus*, Subspecies *Equus africanus asinus*

Name

All donkeys are asses, but not all asses are donkeys. The older name, ass, derives from Latin *asinus*, which is also the species name for the donkey, so the whole scientific name, *Equus africanus asinus*, means literally "African ass horse."

The origin of the word donkey is obscure. It first appeared in the 18th century as an English slang name, so it is much more recent than the word ass. One suggestion is that it comes from the word dun, meaning pale brown, but donkeys are often gray, so the fit is not perfect. Another suggestion is that it is a corruption of the Scottish name Duncan, but there is no confirming evidence.

An onager (*Equus hemionus*) is a wild ass, from Greek ονος, *ónos*, ass, and αγριος, *ágrios*, wild. The *hemionus* of the scientific name is Latin for "part burden-bearing," i.e., not fully tamed as a pack animal. (A mule—the offspring of a male or jack donkey with a female horse or mare—was called *hemicillus*: it was a common Roman insult for somebody stupid or stubborn.)

Description

The ancestor of the ass or donkey is the African wild ass, *Equus africanus*. The domesticated ass or donkey is a subspecies, *Equus africanus asinus*, as noted above. Donkeys have been domesticated for over 5,000 years, probably originally in Egypt and Mesopotamia. They are smaller than horses, but are used as pack animals across the world, and are typically strong and hardy. They have long ears and make a loud, braying sound or hee-haw.

General Attributes

The attributes of the ass are mostly negative. It is noted for its stupidity and obstinate nature. It was the mount or pack animal of the poor man—a rich man would use a horse. Its speech is a loud, repetitive braying or a piercing *hee-haw, hee-haw*. Jesus's riding of an ass or donkey into Jerusalem, celebrated on Palm Sunday, is highly symbolic: he deliberately chose the mount of the common or poor man, the mount of ridicule and shame, making it for a short while a mount of glory. (It was also an ass that Joseph and Mary rode into Bethlehem for Jesus's birth.) There are several moving Christian poems about Jesus and the donkey, but the best known is that by G.K. Chesterton (1874–1936), which frequently appears in anthologies:

> When fishes flew and forests walked
> And figs grew upon thorn,

11. Horses and Rhinoceroses

> Some moment when the moon was blood
> Then surely I was born;
>
> With monstrous head and sickening cry
> And ears like errant wings,
> The devil's walking parody
> On all four-footed things.
>
> The tattered outlaw of the earth,
> Of ancient crooked will;
> Starve, scourge, deride me:
> I am dumb, I keep my secret still.
>
> Fools! For I also had my hour;
> One far fierce hour and sweet:
> There was a shout about my ears,
> And palms before my feet.[23]

The "tattered outlaw" is associated with important figures in other religions and mythologies, too. It was a totem of the evil aspect of the god Set in Egyptian mythology. In Greek mythology, it is associated with the Titan of time, Cronos, with Dionysus (revelry and drunkenness), with Typhon (a serpentine giant, enemy of Zeus), and with the god of lewdness, procreation and the phallus, Priapus.

Balaam and the Talking Ass

In the Old Testament of the Bible, Balaam (who is reviled as a "wicked man" in both the Judaic Torah and the Christian New Testament) is riding a donkey, accompanied by two servants, when an angel appears before him, blocking the road:

> God's anger was kindled because he [Balaam] was going, and the angel of the LORD took his stand in the road as his adversary. Now he was riding on the donkey, and his two servants were with him. The donkey saw the angel of the LORD standing in the road, with a drawn sword in his hand; so the donkey turned off the road, and went in to the field; and Balaam struck the donkey, to turn it back on to the road.
>
> Then the angel of the LORD stood in a narrow path between the vineyards, with a wall on either side. When the donkey saw the angel of the LORD, it scraped against the wall, and scraped Balaam's foot against the wall; so he struck it again.
>
> Then the angel of the LORD went ahead, and stood in a narrow place, where there was no way to turn either to the right or to the left. When the donkey saw the angel of the LORD, it lay down under Balaam; and Balaam's anger was kindled, and he struck the donkey with his staff.
>
> Then the LORD opened the mouth of the donkey, and it said to Balaam, "What have I done to you, that you have struck me these three times?"
>
> Balaam said to the donkey, "Because you have made a fool of me! I wish I had a sword in my hand! I would kill you right now!"
>
> But the donkey said to Balaam, "Am I not your donkey which you have ridden all your life to this day? Have I been in the habit of treating you this way?"
>
> And he said, "No."
>
> Then the LORD opened the eyes of Balaam, and he saw the angel of the LORD standing in the road, with his drawn sword in his hand; and he bowed down, falling on his face.
>
> The angel of the LORD said to him, "Why have you struck your donkey these three times? I have come out as an adversary, because your way is perverse before me. The donkey saw me, and turned away from me these three times. If it had not turned away from me, surely by now I would have killed you and let it live."
>
> Then Balaam said to the angel of the LORD, "I have sinned, for I did not know that you were standing in the road to oppose me. Now therefore, if it is displeasing to you, I will return home."[24]

In the later Jewish legends, an angel slays the donkey to make sure that the Hebrews would not be tempted to worship it, as they had the golden calf. The ancient Romans accused the Jews of worshiping an ass-headed god, and 17th-century Jesuits accused Freemasons of doing the same.[25]

A medieval Christian belief was that the ass that Jesus rode into Jerusalem was a direct descendant of Balaam's ass. There was also much comparison of the ass seeing the angel while Balaam could not with the apostles seeing Jesus after his resurrection while Thomas saw Jesus but doubted what he saw.

The Feast of Fools, held on 1 January, was a medieval Christian parody festival, based on similar festivals in ancient Rome, such as the *Festa Stultorum* (Feast of Fools) and the fun and games of the *Saturnalia* (Festival of Saturn). Nominally celebrating the ass that carried Jesus into Jerusalem, the Feast of Fools was an opportunity to indulge in travesty versions of the holy rites. Prayers were ended with loud braying instead of "Amen." Men would dress as women and *vice versa*. So-called Fools were mock ordained as priests for a day. Puddings and sausages were eaten at the altar instead of the Eucharist. The practice died out by the end of the 16th century.

Æsop's Ass Fables

There are two well-known fables relating to the ass that are attributed to Æsop. The first is very similar to one of the *Jatakas*, the birth legends of the Buddha:

> An ass found a lion's skin and put it on. Wearing the skin, he frightened all the other silly animals. He strutted about, enjoying being king of the animals and frightening them all. When a fox came along, the ass strutted before him too.
>
> But the cunning fox said, "If you really want to frighten me, you need to disguise your bray."

Moral: Clothes may disguise a fool, but his voice will give him away.

The second also features a lion and fox, along with the ass:

> A fox and a lion went hunting together. They invited the ass to join them, and the humble, foolish ass accepted the invitation, flattered to be in the company of such aristocratic animals. But as soon as he turned up at the appointed meeting place, the lion pounced on him and began to devour him.
>
> After eating heartily for a while, the lion said to the fox, "This will be my dinner and supper for today. I'm off for a nap. Woe betide you if you dare to touch my supper before I return."
>
> While the lion was away sleeping, the fox ate the brains of the ass, and thought they were delicious.
>
> When the lion returned, he roared, "What have you done with the brains? Did you dare to eat them?"
>
> The fox replied, "Of course not, your Majesty! The ass never had any brains. If it had, it would never have fallen into your simple trap."

Moral: True wit always has an answer ready.

The same tale appears in *The Panchatantra* story collection in the Hindu tradition, and in a Jewish rabbinical commentary on the book of Exodus. In the Indian version, and in the Greek original, it is the ass's heart that is eaten, because the heart, rather than the brain, was considered the seat of intelligence.[26]

Dhenuka the Ass

In Hindu mythology, the god Vishnu took hairs from his head, one black and one fair. The black hair became Krishna and the fair hair became Balarama (Strong-Armed Rama).

As boys, Krishna and Balarama were picking fruit from an orchard belonging to the demon Dhenuka. Dhenuka shape-shifted himself into an ass, and began kicking Balarama. To the demon's astonishment, Balarama seized him by the heels, whirled him around until he was dead, then flung his body high up into a palm tree. Several other demons flew down to revenge Dhenuka, all of them changing themselves into asses, but Balarama killed them all "until the trees were laden with dead asses."[27]

Chang Kuo-lao's Mule

As noted above, a mule is the offspring of a male donkey, or jack, and a female horse, or mare. It is larger and stronger than a donkey. (The offspring of a female donkey, or jenny, and a male horse, or stallion, is called a hinny, and is much more difficult to breed successfully than a mule.) In Chinese Taoism, Chang Kuo-lao (called Chokaro in Japan) was one of the eight Pa-Hsien, or Immortals. He was a great magician, who could make himself invisible whenever he chose. He rode a magic mule. When the mule was not needed, Chang folded it up and put it in his wallet. To bring it back to life and full size, he poured a little water on it, and the mule sprang to full-sized life, ready to carry its master again.

Palden Lhamo

Palden Lhamo is a horrific goddess of death in Tibetan Buddhism. She has three eyes and great fangs. She rides a chestnut-colored mule, but the mule's girth and cropper are made of living snakes. Palden Lhamo's own belt is made from the skin of a recently flayed man. The mule tramples the mangled remains of a human body while the goddess drinks fresh blood from a human skull.

Rhinoceros (Several Species)

Phylum *Chordata*, Class *Mammalia*, Order *Perissodactyla*, Superfamily *Rhinocorotoidea*, Family *Rhinocerotidae*, Genus (4), Species (5)

Name

Rhinoceros, which is both the common name and one of the genera names, is from Greek ῥινο-, *hrino-*, nose, and κερας, *kéras*, horn.

Description

The rhinoceros (commonly shortened to rhino) is not a horse, nor even much like a horse, but it is included in this section because it is a perissodactylic ungulate, or odd-toed hoofed animal, as horses are. The rhino is a heavy, formidable-looking creature, frequently weighing more than a metric ton or approximately 2,200 pounds. Its skin is thick and tough, and it has a horn (single or double) on its nose (hence the name).

The horn is the main source of all the rhino's grief (see below). Rhinos eat leafy vegetable matter, and have a fermenting hindgut that allows them to cope with quite fibrous plants. It plucks leaves with its strong prehensile lips, rather than front teeth. There are five extant species, of which two are found in Africa and three in southern Asia. The African southern white rhinoceros (*Ceratotherium simum simum*) has two horns, and is a massive animal: females typically weigh 4,000 pounds (1,600 kilograms) and males 5,000 pounds (2,400 kilograms) or even more.

General Attributes

Unless attacked or provoked, rhinos are generally quite placid animals, happily munching through the huge amounts of vegetable matter they have to get through each day, but they can become aggressive very suddenly and charge without warning, their huge mass making them very dangerous. They have small brains for their body weight and size, and seem to prefer a simple, uncomplicated life. The folklore surrounding them is almost entirely to do with the supposed properties of their horns.

Rhinoceros Horns

The rhinoceros's horn is made of keratin, the same substance that makes human hair and nails. Biologically, there is nothing special or unusual about it. However, in terms of mythology and folklore, rhino horn is reputed to have magical properties, and the animal has been poached for centuries just for its horn, to the extent that at least one species is now severely endangered. Rhinos drink a lot of water as well as eating a lot of food, and it is very easy to kill them while they are making their daily visit to a watering hole. Several conservation measures are in place in different countries since international trade in rhino horns was made illegal in 1977, but there is unfortunately no sign of the illegal trade in rhino-horn diminishing. The largest market is Vietnam, where a single horn can fetch $250,000 to $300,000 on the black market. Zimbabwe in Africa also has a reputation for relatively uncontrolled trade and smuggling of rhino horn.

Powdered rhino horn is believed to cure everything from impotence to hangovers and cancer. Although it has been described scientifically as about as efficacious as drinking fingernails dissolved in water, it has been used in traditional medicine in the Far East for centuries. China subscribed to the Convention on International Trade in Endangered Species of Wild Fauna and Flora (CITES) agreement of 1993 and removed it from its pharmacopeia. Vietnam has made claims that it has reduced rhino horn sales, but there is little evidence of that.[28]

Tapir (Several Species)

Phylum *Chordata*, Class *Mammalia*, Order *Perissodactyla*, Family *Tapiridae*, Genus *Tapirus*, Species (5)

Name

The name tapir comes from *tapiir* in the indigenous Old Tupi language of Brazil.

Description

The tapir, like the horse and the rhinoceros, is also a perissodactylic ungulate. It is much smaller than either a rhinoceros or a horse, looking something like a slim pig with a short, somewhat moose-like prehensile snout and a long upper lip, like the rhino's. It is found in Central and South America, and in Southeast Asia. There are five extant species, all in the genus *Tapirus*.

General Attributes

Tapirs spend a lot of time underwater, or close to water. They are herbivores, eating mostly fruit, leaves and water plants. They are crepuscular (active at twilight) or nocturnal, so they are considered elusive and somewhat mysterious. They are shy and usually gentle, but they have a powerful bite and have occasionally inflicted severe wounds on humans, notably zookeepers. In 2013, a child was badly mauled by a tapir at Dublin Zoo.[29] There is really only one tapir legend or folklore story, but it is widespread throughout the Far East.

The Dream Eater

The legend is that tapirs eat human dreams, particularly nightmares. In China, the mythological dream-eating beast (as well as the regular tapir) is called *mò* in Mandarin and *mahk* in Cantonese. The Korean name is *maek*, and the Japanese name is *baku*. If someone experiences a disturbing nightmare, they visualize or imagine a tapir by their side, and they metaphorically feed the nightmare and all the feelings of discomfort it has created to the tapir. The folklore belief is that the tapir will take the dream away, keeping it underwater where its power is ineffective, and will metaphorically eat it along with its water chestnuts, water bamboo and other tapir salad-stuff. Like the rhinoceros, the tapir can cope with very tough or fibrous vegetable matter, and the hope is that the tapir will grind the nightmare away to nothing.

12

Camels and Giraffes (*Artiodactyla: Camelidae*)

Camel (*Camelus bactrianus, Camelus dromedarius, Camelus ferus*)

Phylum *Chordata*, Class *Mammalia*, Order *Artiodactyla*, Family *Camelidae*, Tribe *Camelini*, Genus *Camelus*, Species *Camelus bactrianus, Camelus dromedarius, Camelus ferus*

Name

The name is derived from Latin *camelus* and Greek καμελος, *kámelos*. There is an interesting correspondence between two nicknames. The camel is often nicknamed "the ship of the desert," because of its ability to survive in very arid surroundings. There is also a term used in shipping slang: when a ship is about to take a very heavy cargo, or is already severely overloaded, two empty ships may be fastened to it, one on each side, to help the middle ship sustain its load. These empty ships are known as "camels" in nautical slang.

The species name dromedary is from Greek δρομας καμελος, *dromas kámelos*, meaning running camel. The species name Bactrian comes from the historical region Bactria, which covered modern Afghanistan and parts of northern Pakistan.

Description

It is hardly surprising that the best known of the Camelids is the camel, which gave its name to the family, tribe and genus. The camel is an artiodactylic (even-toed) ungulate (hoofed animal) with distinctive humps on its back. Contrary to some popular beliefs, these humps store fat, not water. Camels are perfectly adapted to deserts and arid terrain, and have been domesticated for centuries. They provide milk, meat and hides, but they are also essential desert transport and pack animals.

The three extant camel species are: the dromedary, *Camelus dromedarius*, also called the Arabian camel, which has one hump and is found in the Middle East and the Horn of Africa, and which is easily the most abundant of the camel species; the Bactrian, *Camelus bactrianus*, which has two humps, which lives in Central Asia, and which makes up only about 6 percent of the world camel population; and *Camelus ferus*, the wild camel or wild Bactrian, which is now a critically endangered species. The mnemonic for remembering which camel has one hump and which has two is to visualize the capital letters D and B: D (one curve) stands for dromedary (one hump) and B (two curves) stands for Bactrian (two humps).

General Attributes

Camels can be spiteful, even aggressive (spitting at humans is well attested), but they are so useful and reliable in desert cultures that they are highly valued. In the same way that cattle have represented wealth in many countries, camels represent wealth in desert lands, and are greatly respected.

In Judaism

Camel meat and milk are not kosher, because the animal does not have a cloven hoof. The Talmud (central text of Rabbinic Judaism) talks about an elephant passing through the eye of a needle, which becomes a camel in the Bible (see below).

In Christianity

The most famous camel saying in Christianity is found in the New Testament: "Then Jesus said to his disciples, 'Truly I tell you, it will be hard for a rich person to enter the kingdom of heaven. Again I tell you, it is easier for a camel to go through the eye of a needle than for someone who is rich to enter the kingdom of God.'"[1] The metaphor has always seemed a little odd, and there have been two possible explanations suggested. The first is that "the eye of the needle" was a nickname for a special narrow gate into the city of Jerusalem, which was used only at night when the main gates were closed. A camel could pass through it, but only if all its baggage was removed and it stooped. That explanation has been around since the 15th century, and is very charming, but there is no evidence that such a gate ever existed. The second explanation is that the Greek word *kamelos*, camel, was accidentally written where *kamilos*, rope or cable, was intended. That is a more plausible explanation, but again there is no firm evidence.

In Islam

In Islam, camel meat is *halal*, or permitted, although some authorities add special observances or restrictions. According to Islamic legend, when Muhammad migrated from Mecca to Medina, he allowed his favorite she-camel to wander at will, and the place where she finally came to rest in Medina was where he had his house built.

Saleh

According to the Qur'an and Baha'i texts, the prophet Saleh (The Pious One), who lived before the time of Muhammad, was sent by God to the people of the Thamud in present-day Saudi Arabia to demonstrate to them his credentials as a true prophet. The Thamud community had acquired other gods and frequently indulged in idolatry. According to the Qur'an, God gave the people a blessed she-camel to show his beneficence.

Islamic folklore subsequently added significant color and invention to this basic story, as follows: Saleh struck a mountain rock, and the camel appeared miraculously; the camel drank the people's water every other day, but gave the people endless milk in return; God warned Saleh that a child would be born to the tribe who would hamstring the sacred camel; the child was born and did indeed perform the sacrilegious act; the camel's calf cried out three times, indicating that the people had only three days to live; a great earthquake came, and the people's faces turned yellow, then red, then black, and they died on the third day, as predicted; Saleh escaped.

Bahá'u'lláh (1817–1892), founder of the Baha'i faith, included mention of the She-Camel of God legend in the sacred text the *Kitáb-i-Íqán* (The Book of Certitude, often simply called *The Íqán*).

Rabi'a al-'Adawiya

Also in Islamic folklore, Rabi'a al-'Adawiya (714–801 CE) was a saint and mystic. She was born in poverty and sold into slavery while still a child. She lived a poor and simple life all her days, but attracted a strong following for the wisdom of her sayings. She once fed a large crowd on almost nothing, similar to Christ feeding the multitude on two loaves and five fishes. On another occasion, she raised a camel (or donkey—versions differ) from the dead in the desert after it had died during a holy pilgrimage.[2] Again like Christ, she appeared to a handful of her followers after her death, and said that she had already spoken with two of God's angels, contributing to the late Islamic belief that angels speak with the dead immediately after death in order to help prepare them for the judgment still ahead of them at the end of the world.

Llama (*Lama glama*)

Phylum *Chordata*, Class *Mammalia*, Order *Artiodactyla*, Family *Camelidae*, Genus *Lama*, Species *Lama glama*

Name

The name llama was picked up by the Spanish colonists from the Quechua language of the Peruvian Andes. It is pronounced in two different ways, either as *lama* or as *yama*. It has been written as *llama*, *lama*, *gama* and *glama*. The species name *Lama glama* (sometimes seen as *Lama gama*) is simply two of these spellings. (A *lama* is also the name of a Tibetan monk, but comes from a completely different source.)

Description

The llama is a camelid, but smaller than a camel. It has been domesticated in the Peruvian Andes for thousands of years. It is a very strong and hardy pack animal, gives good meat, and its wool is highly prized. It originated in the North American Plains, then became extinct there and survived in South America. It has since been re-introduced to North America.

General Attributes

The mythology and folklore associated with the llama have been determined by their precise geographical location: it consists mostly of pre–Incan and Incan myths. The closely related alpaca (*Vicugna pacos*) and vicuña (*Vicugna vicugna*) also feature in Incan mythology and in current Andean folklore.

Pre-Incan Mythology

The Moche or Mochica culture of Peru flourished from about 100 to about 700 CE. There is evidence that llama meat was buried with important personages, presumably as food for the journey to the afterlife. Moche culture produced very sophisticated ceramics, and the llama is a frequent subject: a typical pose is with its head slightly cocked in curiosity—llamas are very social and curious animals.

In Inca Myths

The Inca Empire began in the mountainous region of Peru some time during the early 13th century CE. It was at its height from 1438 to 1533 CE, but the arrival of Spanish colonists in the 16th century brought it to an abrupt end.

For the Inca, the llama was their only pack animal. There were many other ways in which the isolated Inca Empire was different to many other civilizations in history. They had no wheeled transport, no iron or steel, and no system of writing. They did have huge stone monuments, very fine textiles, stone-built roads that extended the full length of the territory, efficient agriculture, and a highly organized and stable system of government. The llama was so highly valued, that individual animals were buried with humans of high status.

The Inca related the movements of planets and constellations to their agricultural cycle. They considered their capital city, Cuzco, to be the center of the earth. Although they had no writing, they used a system of knotted cords, called *quipus*, to record information, and these became very sophisticated. Although debate about *quipus* continues to this day, it is agreed that the numerical basis is a fully articulated decimal system. A *quipu* could consist of a few simple threads, or a complex of hundreds of cords all tied together. *Quipus* were made either of cotton or of spun llama wool.

The Inca had a full pantheon of gods and goddesses. Among them was Urcuchillay, who was a god of herders and flocks, represented as a llama.[3] After colonization, the Spanish initially continued to use llamas in their thousands as pack animals to carry tools, materials and ore to and from the mines, but they gradually introduced donkeys, mules and horses to do the same work, as well as sheep as food and wool animals. Largely as a result of Catholic missionary work, Inca religious mythology rapidly declined or disappeared.

Giraffe (*Giraffa camelopardalis*)

Phylum *Chordata*, Class *Mammalia*, Order *Artiodactyla*, Family *Giraffidae*, Genus *Giraffa*, Species *Giraffa camelopardis*

Name

The ancient Persian name *zurnapa* came into Arabic as *xirāpha* or *zarāfa* (fast walker), and from there into French and then English as *giraffe*. The *camelopardalis* of the species name is, like the medieval English name camelopard, a combination of camel (for its general anatomical characteristics) and leopard (for its coloring), based on original Greek and Latin names.

Description

The giraffe is an immensely tall animal, having an extremely long neck and long legs. Males are typically 14.1–18.7 feet (4.3–5.7 meters) tall; females are shorter. The greatest recorded weight for a male giraffe is 4,250 pounds or 1,930 kilograms. Giraffes are found in several African countries, but there is concern that their numbers are rapidly declining.

The taxonomy of giraffes is disputed. Officially, *Giraffa camelopardalis* is the single type species, with nine subspecies, but since 2001 there has been an ongoing debate about whether various of these should be recognized as species in their own right.

General Attributes

Giraffes have been popular in many cultures. Because of their immense size and strength, they are free from predation, apart from occasional attacks by lions. They are obviously exotic and extraordinary animals, but they are also both beautiful and graceful. Giraffes are always popular exhibits in zoos.

Egyptian Pets

Rich ancient Egyptians kept giraffes as household pets. They traded them all around the Mediterranean. (Shipping them must have been an interesting engineering problem.)

Elsewhere in Africa

The Kiffian culture (c. 8000–3000 BCE) in what is now the Sahara produced a life-sized rock carving of two giraffes, suggesting that they may have been objects of worship. The carving has been described as "the world's largest rock art petroglyph."[4] There are many folk tales across Africa describing how giraffes came to be so tall.

In Ancient Rome

Giraffes were known to the ancient Romans. Julius Caesar brought a giraffe to Rome for public exhibit in 46 BCE. It was walked around the Circus Maximus, to great public astonishment and acclaim, and did much to confirm Caesar's political status.

A recent study suggested that giraffe meat may have been eaten in Pompeii. Pompeii was an ancient Roman city near modern-day Naples in Italy, which was wiped out and buried under six meters of ash and pumice following the eruption of Mount Vesuvius in 79 CE. Steven Ellis, a University of Cincinnati associate professor of classics, spent more than a decade excavating about 20 shop fronts near one of the busiest gates of Pompeii, known as the Portia Stabia, and discovered the jointed leg-bone of a giraffe:

> The latrines and cesspits behind the food sellers revealed charred food waste from the kitchens, as well as human waste that dated as far back as the fourth century B.C., when Pompeii was still in an early stage of development.... More upscale restaurants could be distinguished by the wider array of delicacies they served.... This is thought to be the only giraffe bone ever recorded from an archaeological excavation in Roman Italy.... How part of the animal, butchered, came to be a kitchen scrap in a seemingly standard Pompeian restaurant not only speaks to long-distance trade in exotic and wild animals, but also something of the richness, variety and range of a non-elite diet.[5]

How the Giraffe Really Got Its Long Neck

Most of the African folkloric legends about how the giraffe got its long neck are based on physical explanations that are amusing but completely implausible. A typical tale might run something like this:

> When he was young, Giraffe was a fussy eater. He liked the very softest, tastiest leaves at the top of the acacia tree. One day he stretched up for some succulent leaves, but he got his head caught between two branches. His friends gathered to help him. They pulled on his legs (or put rocks on him), and pulled and pulled again with all their might. Finally, the upper branches broke with a great crash and Giraffe came free—but his neck and front legs were stretched beyond all recognition, and he could never make them short again.

However, the question has also been one of genuine scientific interest for a long time, and it is still not fully resolved.

Okapi (*Okapia johnstoni*)

Phylum *Chordata*, Class *Mammalia*, Order *Artiodactyla*, Family *Giraffidae*, Genus *Okapia*, Species *Okapia johnstoni*

Name

The name is from the Mvuba language of Uganda and northeastern Congo in Africa. The *johnstoni* of the species name is for the African explorer Henry Hamilton Johnston, 1858–1927 (see below). It is also known as the forest giraffe, the Congolese giraffe, and the zebra giraffe.

Description

The okapi is a beautiful animal, quite distinctive in appearance. It is a camelid, but looks more like a small giraffe. It stands about 4.9 feet (1.5 meters) tall at the shoulder. Its face, which is usually a grayish-white in color, is similar to a giraffe's. Its upper body is usually a deep, chocolate brown in color. Its legs and the lower part of its body are striped with vividly contrasted black and white stripes, similar to those of a zebra, except that the okapi's run horizontally rather than vertically. It looks somewhat like an animal designed by a committee, but the overall effect is pleasing. It is found naturally only in the Democratic Republic of the Congo in Africa.

General Attributes

The okapi's mythological status is determined entirely by the fact that it was unknown to Europe and the West until the 20th century. For centuries, there was a rumor of a strangely beautiful, unusually marked animal in the Congolese forests, but nobody had ever seen one.

Henry Morton Stanley (1841–1904), the Welsh-American explorer who famously introduced himself by saying, "Doctor Livingstone, I presume?" when he finally found the presumed lost explorer David Livingstone in Tanzania in 1871, was exploring the Congo in 1887. He heard rumors from the Pygmy people of a kind of horse or donkey called an *atti* (he had misheard the word okapi). He recorded the encounter in his journal.

Years later, the British commissioner in Uganda, Sir Henry Hamilton (Harry) Johnston read about Stanley's discovery. The Pygmies showed him okapi tracks, and gave him a scrap of skin and a skull from an okapi, which Johnston ordered to be sent back to Britain. Although Johnston continued to search for the animal in vain, never actually seeing one, it was named *Equus johnstoni* in his honor in 1901. When it later became clear from examination of the skin and skull that the animal was a giraffid (in fact, the last and only remaining extant direct relative to the giraffe), and not a horse at all, it was renamed *Okapia johnstoni* from the Mvuba name *o'api*.[6]

13

Pigs and Hedgehogs
(*Suidae, Erinaceidae*)

Boar (*Sus scrofa*)

Phylum *Chordata*, Class *Mammalia*, Order *Artiodactyla*, Family *Suidae*, Subfamily *Suinae*, Genus *Sus*, Species *Sus scrofa*

Name

The true wild boar died out in Britain before the development of Modern English, so some of the English terms for wild pigs or boars have become mixed up with terms used for domesticated pigs. The word boar was *bar* in Old English, and seems to be Germanic in origin. It is used in modern English to refer both to wild pigs in general, and to male domesticated pigs, especially intact male pigs used for breeding. The word sow, now meaning female domesticated pig, is also Germanic, and comes from the same ancient root as Greek 'υς, *hys,* and Latin *sus*, both meaning swine, which gives the genus name *Sus* (and is probably the source of the pig call, "Soo-ee!"). In Old English, it was *sugu*. *Suidae* and *suinae*, the family and subfamily names, are from the same root. The species name, *scrofa*, is Latin for sow.

The derivation of the common name pig is less clear. It seems to have been *picg* in Old English. There may be a connection to the Latin *porcus*. The difference between pig and pork is worthy of brief explanation. When William the Conqueror successfully invaded Britain in 1066, Norman French became the language of the new aristocracy, and Saxon English remained the language of peasants. So, peasant Saxon farmers looking after farm animals called them by their Saxon names: pig, sheep, and cow. But the Norman-French overlords who ate them as meat called the animals by the Norman-French names familiar to them: *porc, mouton* and *boeuf,* which is why the animals and the meats have different names—pork, mutton, and beef –to this day.

Hog, which can be used more or less interchangeably with pig in modern English (particularly American English), originally meant a castrated male only. In Old English, it was *hogg* or *hocg*. It appears to be derived from a Proto-Indo-European root *kowə- meaning cut, related to hew and hewn, and to the name for a castrated lamb or young sheep, a hoggett.

Description

Wild boar are, unsurprisingly, generally hardier than domesticated pigs. They have longer, thicker hair, and males generally have small tusks. Originally native to Europe, Asia and North Africa, wild boar are now spread across many countries and regions. In some areas they are considered intrusive. In the wild, pig society is usually matriarchal, and boars are mostly solitary. In Australia, Canada, the United States and some South American countries, boar-pig hybrids (boars re-hybridized with feral pigs) have become a significant menace in some areas.

General Attributes

Pigs are clever animals. In confined farm conditions, they can be dirty and smelly, but wild pigs are no dirtier than any other wild animal. In mythology and folklore, which of course includes the mythology of hunting, they have high status. The wild boar is noted for its courage and ferocity.

Culhwch and Olwen

All of the spiritual, magical and symbolic attributes of the boar are to be found in the story of *Culhwch and Olwen* in the medieval collection of Welsh folk tales called the *Mabinogi* or (incorrectly, but commonly) *Mabinogion*. The story features two boars. The hero Culhwch (literally Pig Run) has to pull a tusk from the Chief Boar, Ysgithyrwyn, and use it as a razor to shave the giant Ysbaddaden Pencawr. From another great boar, Twrch Trwyth, he must pluck the comb and scissors resting between the boar's ears, and use them to cut the giant's hair.

These seemingly odd tasks are charged with religious and ritual significance. For the ancient Celts, the hair was the single most important designator of lineage, character, rank, social status, wealth and physical beauty. Men and women both wore their hair long, frequently plaiting it into elaborate patterns. Men shaved their cheeks and chin, but left a thick moustache on the upper lip that drooped down at either side of the mouth, a fashion that has been repeated several times in subsequent ages. Warriors washed their hair in diluted lime, and then brushed it backwards so that it stood erect in hard, white-tipped spikes. Members of the aristocracy dyed their hair, typically in three or more different colors.

Boars were depicted in ancient Celtic art with both combs and mirrors. The presence of the combs and mirrors clearly indicates the Great Goddess, so the boar represents the epitome of the Celtic male, a fierce, courageous, tireless warrior, but subservient to the epitome of the female, the goddess who combs her divine tresses and checks her beauty in the magical mirror.

Culhwch completes the dangerous tasks, kills Ysbaddaden, and marries the giant's daughter, Olwen (White or Fair Track). As Philip Carr-Gomm points out, the story's preoccupation with hunting the boar reflects a deeper spiritual meaning:

> The Hunt became the symbol or metaphor for the journey of the Spirit—in which both life and death play their part, and in which healing is found through the process of hunting. Hunting and healing seem unrelated activities, but the archaeological finds at the healing sanctuaries at Lydney in Gloucestershire and Nettleton Shrub in Wiltshire show that the Celts linked the two concepts. The perception that the death of one animal gave life to another led the Celts to connect the shedding of blood with ideas of rebirth, healing, and renewal.[1]

Calydonian Boar Hunt

The story of the Calydonian boar hunt is a typically complex ancient Greek myth, involving many characters. Ovid tells the tale in his *Metamorphoses* (books 8 and 10), but there are many variants, and it appears in later literature, including Algernon Charles Swinburne's well-known poetic drama *Atalanta in Calydon* (1865).

> King Oeneus of Kalydon or Calydon, a city in ancient Aetolia, had offended the goddess Artemis by not offering prayers to her. She sent a powerful boar to ravage his kingdom. Oeneus sent heralds all across Greece, inviting heroes to hunt the boar and kill it. Many great and famous heroes answered the challenge, including Castor and Polydeuces from Sparta, Theseus of Athens, Jason and his cousin Admetus, Peleus, father of Achilles, and Telamon, father of Ajax. From the royal family of Arcadia came Atalanta, the only woman to take part in the hunt.
>
> After nine days of feasting, the hunt began. Atalanta distinguished herself by wounding the boar, but it was Meleager, King Oeneus's son, who delivered the final death blow.
>
> Then followed an unseemly battle over the boar's skin. Meleager graciously gave the treasured prize to Atalanta, but his mother, Althea, disapproved—she felt the trophy should remain in Calydon. Her brothers fought with Meleager, but Meleager killed them. When Meleager had been born, the Fates had predicted that he would die when a stick from a fire burning at the hour of his birth was finally consumed. Althea had kept this stick hidden, but now, grief stricken at the loss of her brothers, she brought the stick out and had it burned. Meleager died in agony shortly afterwards. Artemis changed him into a guineafowl.[2]

The Erymanthian Boar

Another well-known boar in classical Greek mythology was the monstrous giant boar that lived on Mount Erymanthus in Arcadia. The fourth labor of Herakles was to kill this boar. The centaur Chiron (see **centaur**, Chapter 40) had suggested that Herakles drive the boar into deep snow to slow it down, and this stratagem proved successful. Herakles captured the boar alive, hog-tied it, and carried it on his shoulders back to the palace of Eurystheus, the king who had ordered Herakles to perform the impossible labors. As soon as Eurystheus saw the beast on Herakles' shoulders, he cowered down behind a *pithos*, a large storage container. This scene was very popular with painters and sculptors, and is well known. Eventually, Herakles threw the giant boar into the sea, through which it swam to Italy, its huge tusks eventually being displayed in the Temple of Apollo.[3]

The Killing of Pentheus

The Bacchae by Euripides (c. 480–c. 406 BCE) is rightly celebrated as one of the finest and most profound plays ever written. It is a violent, bloodthirsty tragedy, in which two human values are directly opposed to each other: order, justice, self-control and discipline, as represented by King Pentheus of Thebes; and passion, emotion, joy and sorrow, ecstasy and spiritual experience, as represented by the god of wine and joy Dionysus (also called Bacchus) and his followers the Bacchae or Bacchantes.

Dionysus arrives in Thebes to reclaim his divinity. He was sired by Zeus, he claims. King Pentheus declares Dionysus to be merely human, and orders his arrest. In the frenzy that follows, Dionysus persuades the Bacchae that Pentheus is a dangerous boar, which must be hunted and killed. Pentheus' own mother, Agave, and his two sisters, Ino and Autonoe, lead the hunt in a state of passionate devotion akin to intoxication and literally tear

Pentheus apart with their bare hands.[4] (The name Pentheus derives from πενθος, *penthós*, meaning sorrow.) The play leaves unresolved the question of how humans should live: in order and calm, but without passion, or in passion and vivid emotional experience, but without order. It goes without saying that those issues remain very much part of the human experience and never lose their significance. The boar of the legend of *The Bacchae* is like the pig's head in William Golding's *Lord of the Flies*: it represents the wild, dangerous blood-lust of the human hunter, the savage who lives only a very short distance beneath the veneer of civilization and human decency.

Arduinna

The boar-goddess Arduinna gave her name to the Ardennes, the forested region in modern France, Belgium and Luxembourg. The Ard- element of the name is an ancient Celtic prefix meaning high place. The Latin *Arduenna Silva* (Wooded Heights or Hills) was a common place-name in ancient Gaul, now France.

The worship of Arduinna was condemned by early Christians. In 585 CE, Saint Wulfilaich or Wolfroy preached at Villiers-devant-Orval in the Ardennes and persuaded his congregation to pull down the statue of Arduinna (or Diana, as some called her). They destroyed the statue with hammers.

Frey

In Norse mythology, Frey is a god of fertility, peace and wealth. He has a magical horse called Blodighofi (Bloody Hoof), but he usually rides in a chariot pulled by a golden boar, Gullinbursti. Traditionally, a boar was sacrificed to Frey on Yule Eve, in a ritual called *Sonargöltr* (Boar Atonement). A poem in the Poetic Edda called *Helgakviða Hjörvarðssonar* (Song of Helgi Hjörvarðsson) contains a description of the ritual: "That evening the great vows were taken; the sacred boar was brought in, the men laid their hands thereon, and took their vows at the king's toast."[5] The tradition still survives in the Swedish custom of baking pig-shaped biscuits at Christmas.

Saehrimnir

Also found in Norse mythology is the magical boar Saehrimnir (Blackened One). Every day in Valhalla, Saehrimnir is killed and cooked for that evening's feasting by the gods and heroes. In Norse culture, as with the ancient Celts, freshly killed boar flesh was considered the best of all meats. Saehrimnir was prepared and cooked by Andhrimnir (Sooty Faced), who boiled it in the magic cauldron, Eldhrimir. At the end of the feast, all the bones and scraps were returned to the cauldron, and next morning Saehrimnir sprang out of the cauldron, ready to be killed and eaten all over again.[6]

Pig (*Sus scrofa domesticus*)

Phylum *Chordata*, Class *Mammalia*, Order *Artiodactyla*, Family *Suidae*, Subfamily *Suinae*, Genus *Sus*, Species *Sus scrofa*, Subspecies *Sus scrofa domesticus*

Name

The name elements are all the same as for boar, the only difference being the addition of the subspecies name *domesticus*, which of course means domesticated.

Description

Pigs and humans share many anatomical features, which is why pig body parts (e.g., heart valves) are sometimes used in human surgery, and why pigs are often used in medical research. Pigs are omnivores, and farmed pigs were traditionally fed swill, human food waste, which might contain almost anything. They can also eat/drink excess cow's milk and whey from cheese and butter processing. Today, farmed pigs are more likely to be fed corn, soybean pellets and more controlled and predictable diets.

There are perhaps a billion domesticated pigs in the world. Of necessity, that means that many are raised in cramped conditions. One of the effects of overcrowding is that sows frequently damage their own offspring: it is estimated that up to 50 percent of young piglet deaths are caused by the mothers either accidentally crushing or deliberately attacking their own young, usually through stress. Sows will sometimes eat their young, too. Pigs are harder work than, say, sheep or goats: they are more sensitive to weather changes (they get sunburn very easily), they need more protection against the cold in winter, and they can be temperamental. In return, they deliver excellent meat, and pigskin makes a workable soft leather.

General Attributes

Since ancient times, pigs have been considered unclean, and their meat prohibited as human food, most notably in Judaism and Islam, but also more recently by Seventh-Day Adventists in Christianity. In other cultures, pigs are highly valued for their meat and frequently used as sacrificial animals. In the Celtic Druidic tradition, the sow symbolizes the Great Goddess, and is associated with fertility, fecundity and divine magic. The Celtic swine god Moccus is associated with Mercury in the Roman pantheon.

Vajravarahi

In the Mahayana Buddhism of Tibet, Vajravarahi (Diamond Sow) is a goddess of light. She is a double of the Tantric goddess Vajrayogini. According to one legend, a Mongol warrior came to a monastery to demand that the abbess show him the famous sow-shaped growth she had behind her right ear. However, when the Mongols broke into the monastery, they found only pigs and sows, with one sow much larger than the rest. Puzzled, they left, leaving the swine untouched. As soon as they had gone, the pigs and sows all turned back into monks and nuns.

Celtic Burials

The tougher and darker meat of the wild boar was the most highly prized meat among the ancient Celts, but farmed pork came a very close second, as the very frequent discovery of pig bones attests. Pig bones have been found in abundance at the Iron Age shrine on Hayling Island in Hampshire, at South Cadbury in Somerset, in the remains of the Romano-Celtic temple at Hockwold in Norfolk, and at Skeleton Green in Hertfordshire, where the bodies of men were surrounded by pig bones and the bodies of women by bird skeletons.[7]

Cerridwen

Ceridwen or Cerridwen (Crooked Fair One or Crooked Blessed One) is a Celtic goddess often depicted as a sow, whose tale of shape-shifting is very well known:

> Cerridwen bore a son, Morfran (Great Crow) or Afagddu (Black Face), who was hideously ugly. To compensate for that, she brewed a potion in her magic cauldron that would bring him poetic inspiration and knowledge of all things. The potion had to boil for a year and a day. She set her young servant, Gwion Bach, to tend the broth for a while. The magical brew splashed onto the boy, who sucked his thumb and was instantly filled with wisdom and poetic inspiration. (Sucking a thumb is a traditional Druidic method of concentration.)
> Furious, Cerridwen chased Gwion, intending to punish him. Gwion shape-shifted into a hare, so Cerridwen shape-shifted into a greyhound. He changed into a fish, so she became an otter. He changed into a bird, so she became a hawk. Finally, he transformed himself into a single grain of corn. She changed herself into a hen and pecked him up. (Some perceive this series of transformations as representing a druid or priestess instructing a student in the art of shape-shifting.) Nine months later, Cerridwen gave birth to a child, who was the god Gwion transformed into the renowned mystical poet Taliesin (Radiant Brow).

See also **Finnegas and Fionn mac Cumhaill**, Chapter 30.

Sido

Sido (also Hido and Iko) is a trickster god in Melanesian mythology. He fell in love with a beautiful woman, Sagaru, but she was in love with another, more powerful magician god, who killed Sido. His spirit now wandered aimlessly. He tried to get into Adiri, the land of the dead, but he was refused admission. He planted a garden in Adiri to feed the dead with pleasant fruits and vegetables, but that was not enough. Eventually, he changed himself into a pig and cut out his own backbone to make the roof of a house for the dead, and he was then admitted to Adiri. To this day, the Kiwaians of New Guinea put pig bones in the rafters of their houses to show reverence for Sido and to placate the spirits of the dead.[8]

Demons into Swine

In the Bible, Christ uses swine as vehicles or receptacles for demons, which he casts out from a man:

> Then they arrived at the country of the Ger'asenes, which is opposite Galilee.
> And as he stepped out on land, there met him a man from the city who had demons; for a long time he had worn no clothes, and he lived not in a house but among the tombs.
> When he saw Jesus, he cried out and fell down before him, and said with a loud voice, "What have you to do with me, Jesus, Son of the Most High God? I beseech you, do not torment me."
> For he had commanded the unclean spirit to come out of the man. (For many a time it had seized

him; he was kept under guard, and bound with chains and fetters, but he broke the bonds and was driven by the demon into the desert.)

Jesus then asked him, "What is your name?" And he said, "Legion"; for many demons had entered him.

And they begged him not to command them to depart into the abyss.

Now a large herd of swine was feeding there on the hillside; and they begged him to let them enter these. So he gave them leave.

Then the demons came out of the man and entered the swine, and the herd rushed down the steep bank into the lake and were drowned.

When the herdsmen saw what had happened, they fled, and told it in the city and in the country.[9]

Hedgehog (Several Species)

Phylum *Chordata*, Class *Mammalia*, Order *Eulipotyphla*, Family *Erinaceidae*, Subfamily *Erinaceinae*, Genus (5), Species (17)

Name

A hedgehog means a hog (see **boar** above) that lives in hedges. In Middle English, it was spelled *heyghoge*. It is also called an urchin, a hedgepig, and a furze-pig.

Description

A hedgehog is not really a pig at all, of course. It just has a snout that is slightly pig-like. It is a small, spiny mammal found in parts of Europe, Asia, Africa and introduced in New Zealand. It is not found in the Americas or Australia, although some have been introduced as pets. (Several U.S. states do not allow hedgehog importation. Hedgehogs notoriously carry fleas, many human diseases, and they can devastate bird populations in restricted areas, such as small islands.)

Its spines are stiff, hollow hairs, made of keratin, the stuff that makes human hair and nails. The hedgehog's only defense mechanism is to roll itself into a ball, about twice the size of a baseball for an adult. While a tight ball of spines may keep a cat or even a dog at bay, it is of little defensive use against a car or an 18-wheeler truck, so for many people, almost all the hedgehogs they ever see are flattened hedgehogs on the highway.

General Attributes

For such a humble, innocuous and generally inoffensive creature, the hedgehog has a small but interesting mythological and folkloric profile.

Hedgehogs were eaten in ancient Egypt and in medieval England. The itinerant Romani or Romany people of Europe still eat hedgehog meat to this day. I have had some Romany hedgehog stew myself (many years ago): well-seasoned with sage, it tastes like roast pork.

In the Middle East, and especially among the Bedouins, hedgehog meat is considered efficacious against arthritis and rheumatism.[10] Other diseases which may be remedied by hedgehog treatments of one kind or another include: fever, urinary tract infections, male impotence and tuberculosis.

The classical Zoroastrians of ancient Persia held the little hedgehog to be sacred to the good god Ahura Mazda, because it destroys so many agricultural pests, such as slugs. The Greek poet Αρκηιλοκος, *Arkhilokos* or Archilocus (c. 680–c. 645 BCE), presumably referring to the rolling-into-a-ball maneuver, said of the humble hedgehog, "The fox knows many tricks, the hedgehog, one good one."[11]

14

Elephants (*Proboscidia*)

Elephant (*Loxodonta africana, Loxodonta cyclotis, Elephas maximus*)

Phylum *Chordata*, Class *Mammalia*, Superorder *Afrotheria*, Order *Proboscidia*, Family *Elephantidae*, Genus *Loxodonta, Elephas*, Species *Loxodonta africana, Loxodonta cyclotis, Elephas maximus*

Name

The common name comes from Greek ελεφας, *elephas* (genitive *elephantos*) and Latin *elephas*, which are thought to have been derived from an earlier Phoenician name. The *Loxodonta* of the classification name means sloped or oblique-sided (*Loxo-*) teeth (*donta*), obviously describing tusks.

Description

Elephants have several extinct relatives, including the mastodon and the mammoth, but they are the only surviving family of the order *Proboscidea*. There are three extant species: *Loxodonta africana*, the African bush elephant, and *Loxodonta cyclotis* (round-eared), the African forest elephant, both of which have large ears to help cool the blood; and *Elephas maximus*, the Indian elephant, which, despite its epithet *maximus*, is smaller than the African elephant and also has smaller ears.

The elephant's most distinguishing feature is its trunk, which was originally a nose, but which evolved to become a very useful multi-tasking appendage. Elephants use their trunks not only for breathing, but also for sucking up water to drink or bathe, for drawing food down into their mouths, and for general investigation and manipulation of objects.

General Attributes

Elephants can live up to 70 years in the wild, and have highly developed social interactions. Once they have reached maturity, bulls usually live alone or in small groups with other males, apart from when they are mating. Bulls can become very aggressive during *musth*, the pre-mating season. Females and their young travel and feed as a family, but there is also a great deal of cooperative interaction and social cohesion between family groups. Elephant mothers are role-model parents. Females will foster young or stand in for other females who are sick or otherwise incapacitated.

According to folk legends, an elephant never forgets. The biological reality behind the legend appears to be that elephants are exceptionally intelligent and sensitive animals. They have been sacred in many African and Asian cultures for millennia.

Ganesh

Ganesh or Ganesha, the Hindu elephant-god, is perhaps the most popular and revered deity in modern Hinduism, and certainly the best known elephant god in the world. He also features in Jainism and Buddhism, and is actively worshiped today in India, Bangladesh, Nepal, Sri Lanka, Thailand and Bali.

Ganesh is portrayed either as an elephant, or as a human with an elephant's head. In Hindu images, he is sometimes light blue, a sacred color also used to depict other gods and avatars, but he is generally bright red. The color, the fat belly, and the elephant head make him instantly recognizable. He has anything from two to twenty-four or more arms, but four is common. One of his tusks is broken (he used it to write the vast epic poem *The Mahabharata* according to one legend, and he broke it off and threw it at the Moon when the Moon laughed at his fat belly, according to another), and he typically holds the broken tusk in the lower right hand. Among the other objects seen in his various other hands, the most frequently depicted are a conch shell, a disc or discus, a club, and a lotus flower.

The name Ganesh or Ganesha comes from two Sanskrit words, *gana*, meaning a group or multitude, and *isha*, meaning lord or master, so that he is sometimes called by the Biblical-sounding term Lord of Hosts. He has many other names as well. He is also Viniyaka, and for those who worship him as the supreme deity, Ganapati. He is called Dvaimatura (Two Mothers), Lambodara (Hanging Belly), Vighneshvara (Lord of Obstacles) and Ekadanta (One Tusk). In Tamil he is called Pillai (Child) or Pillaiyar (Noble Child). In Burma he is Maha Peinne (Great Bliss), in Thailand Phra Phikanet or Phra Phikanesuan (derived from Vighneshvara), and in Sri Lanka he is Gana Deviyo (God of Hosts).

Ganesh has probably been worshiped since the 2nd century CE, perhaps even earlier, but he came into prominence in the 4th and 5th centuries. Like most other Hindu deities, he began with both negative and positive aspects, but he rapidly became popular as almost entirely beneficent, helpful and propitious for all humankind. In particular, he became the deity of new beginnings, and then the patron of trade and commerce, so the practice of invoking Ganesha's support at the beginning of any new venture helped to spread his popularity. It also meant that he was (and still is) revered across a very wide range of religions, sects, castes, nations, regions, traditions and languages. He is non-sectarian, and is worshiped by Hindus of all denominations, as well as by Jains, Buddhists, and others.

His other roles are: Lord of Obstacles—he removes obstacles for good and devout people, and puts them in place for evil-doers; Lord of Knowledge—one of his epithets is Buddhipriya, literally Lover of Wisdom, which includes letters and learning; the personification of the primal universal sound, Om or Aum, as in the well-known Sanskrit mantra *om mani padme hum*—he is described as *oṃkārasvarūpa* ("Om is his form"); and the spirit or inhabitant of the first *chakra* (Tantric focal point) in every human body, who therefore governs all the other energies that propel the wheel of life—he is the Muladhara (First Base or Foundation).

There are several versions of Ganesh's origins, but he is generally deemed to be the son of Shiva and Pavati. One legend says that Shiva gave Ganesh his elephant head and pot belly because he thought the boy too handsome and he resented how Pavati doted on him. Another says that Pavati was so proud of her gorgeous boy that she asked Sani (the Hindu equivalent of Saturn) to look at him, and when Sani did so, the boy's head instantly burst into flame and was reduced to ash—Pavati had to find the nearest head to prevent him from dying, and that just happened to be an elephant's head. There are also different versions of his marital status, depending on geography and tradition. For some, he is a merry bachelor. For others, he has three wives: Buddhi (Intellect or Wisdom), Siddhi (Spirit) and Riddhi (Prosperity). The wealth and well-being motif continues in his two sons: Kshema (Wealth) and Labha (Profit).

Whilst being an animal-god himself, Ganesh is also associated with several other animals, and the symbolism of each of them is not always clear. He sometimes wears the *naga-raja* or king-snake Vasuki around his neck like a scarf, or as a belt, or around his feet. He rides on a mouse, shrew or rat—which could be interpreted as laziness (he is also very fond of candy and sweet cakes), or that he keeps such pests under control—the Lord of Obstacles subduing demons.[1] He is also depicted riding, or associated with, a horse, a lion, a tortoise, a ram and a peacock.

Akshobhya's Elephants

In Mahayana Buddhism, the Dhyani-Buddha Akshobhya carries a thunderbolt and rides an elephant. *Mayahana* is a Sanskrit word meaning "great vehicle," and indicates the search for enlightenment. A *dhyani-Buddha* is one of five emanations of the original Buddha called the five *Tathāgatas* or *pañcatathāgata* of wisdom. Akshobhya is known widely across the Far East, including India, China and Japan, and is depicted either riding an elephant or accompanied by two elephants.[2]

Indra

Several Hindu gods also ride elephants. Indra is the storm god, who determines the weather. His thunderbolt is called Vajra or Svastika. In ancient Hindu symbolism, the *svastika* or swastika was a sacred symbol of wealth and prosperity, derived from Sanskrit words meaning "conducive to wellbeing" or "auspicious." The Nazis appropriated this beautiful symbol in the 1930s, and it has been poisoned ever since: it now represents Aryan supremacy, racism and anti–Semitism, and will never be restored to its original power and beauty.

Indra has eyes all over his body, and therefore is called Sahasraksha (The Thousand-Eyed One). He is also Vajra-pani (Of the Thunderbolt), Megha-Vahana (Carried by Clouds) and Marutwan (Lord of the Winds).[3]

The Diggajas

In Hindu mythology, the world is supported by eight elephants, which in turn are standing on the back of the world turtle or tortoise. Each of the eight is male, and accompanied by his mate, but the females are not named. The named elephants are: Airavata,

Pundarika, Vana, Kumuda, Anjana, Pushapadanta, Sarvabhauma and Supratika. They are also known collectively as the Dikpala (Lords of the Directions).[4]

Maya and the Buddha

In Buddhist legend, and probably historically, Queen Maya of Sakya was the birth mother of Gautama Buddha. After living a pure life, Maya had a dream in which a white elephant entered her right side. This image is frequently depicted in Buddhist art. Maya is also often depicted giving birth to Gautama, standing under a sacred tree and holding on to one of its branches for support; the historical event is believed to have taken place in Lumbini in modern Madhesh in Nepal, c. 563 or 480 BCE (the exact date is disputed). Maya died seven days after giving birth to her son, who was raised by his aunt, Mahapajapati Gotami. Maya went to heaven, but would return on several occasions to give advice to her son.[5]

African Elephant Legends

There are many African folklore stories about elephants. In the Zulu language, the name for the elephant, *indlovu,* means "the unstoppable one"—it comes from the verb *dlovu,* which means "to crash through." King Shaka or Shaka kaSenzangakhona, also called Shaka Zulu (c. 1787–1828), perhaps the most renowned Zulu warrior and leader ever, was addressed as Wena Indlovu or Great Elephant.[6]

The elephant is revered for its huge strength, but it is also revered for its intelligence, integrity and sensitivity. It is widely believed among several African peoples that an elephant will only charge a human being if it knows that that person is an adulterer, blasphemer or otherwise worthless person.

If an elephant is observed with its trunk wrapped about its head, it is believed to be in deep mourning, as a human with their arms over their face and head would be. The Shona of South Africa call elephant tusks "wisdom sticks." They originated the legend of the elephant graveyard, the secret place where elephants go to die when they are approaching the end of their lives.

In a legend of the Wachaga people of Tanzania, the elephant was originally a human being who wandered into the forest and was ennobled by the gods. The price he had to pay was that he must lose all his human limbs, but after some bargaining he was allowed to keep his right arm, which became his elephant trunk. The Ashanti of Ghana believe that elephants carry the spirits of royal chiefs. If they find a dead elephant in the forest, they bury it with regal ceremonies.

The Story of the Blind Men and the Elephant

A parable about a group of blind men and an elephant comes from an Indian Buddhist text dating from about 500 BCE, but may be even older than that. John Godfrey Saxe (1816–1887) reshaped the ancient philosophical legend into a popular poem:

> It was six men of Indostan,
> To learning much inclined,
> Who went to see the Elephant

14. Elephants

(Though all of them were blind),
That each by observation
Might satisfy his mind.

The *First* approach'd the Elephant,
And happening to fall
Against his broad and sturdy side,
At once began to bawl:
"God bless me! but the Elephant
Is very like a wall!"

The *Second*, feeling of the tusk,
Cried,—"Ho! what have we here
So very round and smooth and sharp?
To me 'tis mighty clear,
This wonder of an Elephant
Is very like a spear!"

The *Third* approach'd the animal,
And happening to take
The squirming trunk within his hands,
Thus boldly up and spake:
"I see,"—quoth he—"the Elephant
Is very like a snake!"

The *Fourth* reached out an eager hand,
And felt about the knee:
"What most this wondrous beast is like
Is mighty plain,"—quoth he,—
"'Tis clear enough the Elephant
Is very like a tree!"

The *Fifth*, who chanced to touch the ear,
Said—"E'en the blindest man
Can tell what this resembles most;
Deny the fact who can,
This marvel of an Elephant
Is very like a fan!"

The *Sixth* no sooner had begun
About the beast to grope,
Then, seizing on the swinging tail
That fell within his scope,
"I see,"—quoth he,—"the Elephant
Is very like a rope!"

And so these men of Indostan
Disputed loud and long,
Each in his own opinion
Exceeding stiff and strong,
Though each was partly in the right,
And all were in the wrong!

MORAL: So, oft in theologic wars
The disputants, I ween,
Rail on in utter ignorance
Of what each other mean;
And prate about an Elephant
Not one of them has seen![7]

The Cyclops

Ancient legends tell of the Cyclops, a one-eyed monster. The name, from Greek Κυκλωψ, *Kyklōps*, means "circle-eyed." They are described by Hesiod, Homer and Euripides as having one huge eye in the middle of their foreheads. It is now thought that the legendary monster was based on the pre-historic skulls of dwarf elephants found in Crete and Sicily, which were about twice the size of a human skull and had a large central nasal cavity, where the trunk had been.[8]

In Islamic Tradition

The year 500 CE is believed to be the year in which the prophet Muhammad was born. It is known in Islamic tradition as the Year of the Elephant. The Qur'an (surah 105) describes how Abraha, King of Yemen, tried to destroy Mecca:

Seest thou not how thy Lord dealt with the Companions of the Elephant?
Did He not make their treacherous plan go astray?
And He sent against them Flights of Birds,
Striking them with stones of baked clay.
Then did He make them like an empty field of stalks and straw, (of which the corn) has been eaten up.[9]

Embellished by legend, the story says that Abraha led his army of 40,000 warriors on a white elephant named Mahmud. However, Mahmud refused to cross the boundary of the holy city, even when whipped. The incident discouraged Abraha's troops, and the invasion failed. The army and the war elephants were stoned to death by an extraordinary flock of swallows sent from heaven dropping billions of small stones upon them, crushing them to dust.

White Elephants

In the modern idiom, a white elephant is a useless object, something that costs more time and trouble to keep than it would cost to dispose of. More recently, it has been applied to expensive building or military projects with little real value or use. The idiom is based on an ancient belief about the special, sacred nature of white elephants.

In Buddhist folklore, Siddharta Gautama, the future Buddha—who, as we have seen, was probably from a royal family—gave away his father's white elephant to a nearby country that was suffering from drought. White elephants were associated with white clouds, and their presence was said to bring rain. The king's subjects were so annoyed to have their holy white elephant taken away from them that they demanded the prince be sent into exile, and he was. The loss of the white elephant was particularly hard to bear because, before the Buddha was born, his mother, Queen Maya, had dreamed about a white elephant entering her body, as we saw above. Her soothsayers had told her that it meant she was going to give birth to a son who would either rule the world or save it.

As a result of the legend, white elephants were often given as gifts to kings in India, Burma, Thailand, Laos and Cambodia. The gift was sometimes as much a curse as a blessing. The animals could not be refused or given away, because that would cause offence, they could not be worked, because they were sacred, but they still cost a fortune to feed and house—and they could easily live 75 years in captivity. Hence the unwelcome white elephant. According to one story, P.T. Barnum was promised a sacred white elephant for his circus in the 19th century, but it turned out to be dusty gray with a few pink spots, and it never earned its expensive keep.

15

Monkeys and Apes (*Primates*)

Monkey (Several Species)

Phylum *Chordata*, Class *Mammalia*, Order *Primates*, Suborder *Haplorhini*, Infraorder *Simiiformes*, Main groups *Cercopithecoidea* (Old World monkeys), *Platyrrhini* (New World monkeys) and *Hominoidea* (apes)

Name

Old French has *monequin*, Middle Dutch has *monekijn*, and Middle Low German has *moneke*, so the English name monkey is clearly in good European company, although the origin may have been Turkish *maymun*, which is also the Arabic word for baboon.

Simiiformes means monkey-shaped, from Latin, *simia*, monkey. *Cercopithecoidea* means tailed monkeys, from Greek κερκος, *kérkos*, tail + πιθεκος, *pithekos*, monkey. *Platyrrhini* means flat nosed, from Greek πλατυς, *platus*, flat + ῥινος, *hrinos*, nose. *Hominoidea* means human shaped, i.e., without a tail, from Latin, *homo*, man or mankind.

Description

Monkeys come in many shapes and sizes. Monkeys include apes (and, therefore, humans), but many humans, despite Darwin, still object strongly to being identified with monkeys. Three characteristics separate monkeys from the small number of other primates which are not monkeys: they have only two nipples, and these are high on the chest; males have a pendulous penis hanging downwards from the body; they do not have sensory whiskers. Again, these features are not reassuring to some humans, who see human identity as different entirely to monkey identity. (See any of the *Planet of the Apes* movies for further details.)

General Attributes

As everyone knows, monkeys and apes are relatively very close to humans—too close for the Abrahamic religions. In other traditions, they are seen as clever, resourceful, and even helpful. In ancient Egypt, an ape with a dog's head was one of the god Thoth's assistants in funerary rites, helping the god to weigh the soul of the dead person on the scales. Sacred baboons were kept in Egyptian temples. Some apes and monkeys were even mummified. Hanuman is a Hindu god of great beneficence, who helps Lord Rama (see below). A whole series of tales about monkeys grew up in China around the adventures of a Buddhist monk who traveled from China to India with a faithful and wise monkey as his companion. One of the great Shinto gods in Japan is depicted as a monkey (see below).

Jewish tradition, however, maintains that seeing a monkey means bad luck. One Jewish legend says that God punished some of the men who built the Tower of Babel by turning them into apes. An Islamic legend says that God turned some of the Jews who lived anciently in Elath on the Red Sea into apes, because they had gone fishing on the Sabbath. A 12th-century Christian bestiary describes monkeys as "disgraceful, yet their bottoms really are excessively disgraceful and horrible."[1]

Hanuman

Possibly the oldest and certainly the best-known monkey god is the Hindu god Hanuman. He is personified in the gray langurs of India, also called sacred langurs, Indian langurs and Hanuman langurs. They all belong to the genus *Semnopithecus* (revered ape, from Greek σεμνος, *semnos*, dignified or revered, and πιθεκος, *pithekos*, ape or monkey).

As in many of the Hindu legends, Hanuman's story is long and complex, and there are many variants of every tale. He has three main characteristics: he is immensely strong, wise and powerful; he is completely chaste and pure; he is a devoted follower of his personal favorite god, Rama, and of Rama's wife Sita. He appears in both of the classic Indian epic poems, the *Mahabharata* (probably originally from the 9th or 8th century BCE, but written down mostly between the 4th century BCE and the 4th century CE) and the *Ramayana* (written between the 7th and 3rd centuries BCE).

There are different accounts of Hanuman's birth, but one is that he was the son of Vayu, the wind god, and a monkey mother, Vanar. He is immensely strong and athletic (in *The Ramayana*, he jumps from India to Sri Lanka in one leap). He is described as being as tall as a mountain, with a face that glows like beaten gold and is as red as a ruby. He roars like thunder and can fly at great speed through the sky, as the son of Vayu.

As the god Rama gained importance in the Hindu pantheon, so did Hanuman, the god's faithful follower. He was seen as the perfect combination of *shakti* (cosmic primordial energy) and *bhakti* (devotion, fidelity, piety).[2] He became a patron and exemplar for martial artists and warriors.

One story says that when Hanuman was still young he woke up hungry one morning. Thinking that the early morning sun was a ripe fruit hanging close by, Hanuman leaped into the sky to grab it. The powerful god Indra saw Hanuman and was offended by his youthful insolence: he launched a thunderbolt which smashed Hanuman's jaw. (One legend suggests that his name comes from Sanskrit *hanu*, jaw, and *mant*, prominent or sticking out.) Another version of the same legend sees Hanuman burned to ash and bones by the thunderbolt. The gods gather the ashes and bone fragments and Surya (the sun) puts him back together, but a piece of his jawbone is missing, so he has a permanently disfigured jaw.

His most popular legendary feat followed the wounding of Lakshmana, Rama's brother, in battle. Lakshmana looked close to death, and Rama begged someone to fetch a healing herb from a mountain in the Himalayas. Hanuman was the only one swift enough to reach the mountain and come back in time to save Lakshmana. However, he was uncertain that he could identify the healing herb with absolute certainty, so he grew to immense size and brought the whole mountain back, allowing the herb to be found and administered to Rama's brother, saving his life.

In another legend which follows on from the one just described, Rama gives gifts to all who have supported him in battle. Surprisingly, Hanuman throws his gift away. When challenged to explain why, he says that he needs no gift—he has Rama's and Sita's name engraved on his heart. When challenged to prove that, he literally tears his own chest open, and all can see that the names Rama and Sita are indeed written on his heart. Deeply moved, Rama grants Hanuman immortality. Again, Hanuman refuses the gift, but Rama insists, and Hanuman joins the immortal gods for his exceptional sincerity and devotion.

Worship of Hanuman spread to China, Japan, Thailand, Cambodia and Indonesia. Jains and Buddhists also incorporated him into their legends in many regions. Sikhs adopted him as the exemplar of the faithful warrior, an important symbolic figure in Sikhism. Some Sikh regiments brought images of Hanuman to the battleground.

Hanuman also became an important political symbol during the long struggle for Indian independence, which was not achieved until 1949. For many Hindus, Hanuman was not just a god, nor just an exemplar of devotion and piety, he also symbolized India the nation, finally independent of the British Raj.

Sarutahiko

The name of the Japanese Shinto god Sarutahiko is often followed by the honorific title Ōkami, which means Great God. Sarutahiko is the leader of the earthly *kami* (deities, divinities, spirits or spirit ancestors, spirits of place). He is also the patron of all martial arts, especially Japanese *aikido*. He is usually depicted as a huge, bearded man with ruddy cheeks and a long nose.

The origin of his name is obscure, but *-hiko* means prince. *Saruta-* is generally translated as monkey-field, from *saru*, monkey. The anthropologist Emiko Ohnuki-Tierney lists three factors that identify Sarutahiko as a monkey deity: *saru* means monkey, his features "include red buttocks, which are a prominent characteristic of Japanese macaques," and as macaques gather shellfish at low tide, the *Kojiki* says his hand got caught in a shell while fishing and "a monkey with one hand caught in a shell is a frequent theme of Japanese folktales."[3]

The Three Wise Monkeys

The three wise monkeys are well known in Western culture, but they originated in the Far East. They are depicted in a Japanese panel of the 18th century CE, but it is thought that they may have come to Japan from Chinese Confucianism at a much earlier date.

The monkeys actually represent a pun or word play in Japanese. The first, Mizaru, holds his paws over his eyes, and represents "See no evil." The second, Kikazaru, has his paws over his ears, and represents "Hear no evil." The third, Iwazaru, has his paws over his mouth, and represents "Speak no evil." However, the original Japanese text makes no reference to evil. *Mizaru, kikazaru, iwazaru* means simply "See not, hear not, speak not." But the pun in Japanese is that *zaru* has two meanings: it is a negative ("not"), but *saru* (which becomes *zaru* in compound words) also means "monkey" (specifically the macaque monkey), so the whole phrase can also be taken to mean "Monkey see, monkey hear, monkey speak." In some later depictions, a fourth monkey is added, pictured either with his hands folded in his lap, or his arms crossed: this is Shizaru, "Do no evil," or "Monkey do." (The original Confucian saying had all four themes.)[4]

The Monkey's Paw

The Monkey's Paw was originally a short horror story written by W.W. Jacobs (1863–1943), published in England in 1902. From this small beginning, it became the source of countless similar macabre tales, and of many movies either of the story itself or developed along similar lines. It is now one of the most famous short stories in the world. It earns its place here because it represents a belief in the magical power of an animal—or even a part of a dead animal—to influence and change events in human life. In the story, Mr. and Mrs. White wish on a sacred monkey's paw for their dead son to come back to them. Only at the last moment does Mr. White realize that if their son comes to them, he will be a disfigured zombie, a wretched, terrifying and horrific apparition. Ignoring Mrs. White's longing and distress, Mr. White uses their third and last wish to send their son back to his grave before he even reaches their home.[5]

Orangutan (*Pongo pygmaeus, Pongo abelii, Pongo tapanuliensis*)

Phylum *Chordata*, Class *Mammalia*, Order *Primates*, Suborder *Haplorhini*, Infraorder *Simiiformes*, Family *Hominidae*, Subfamily *Ponginae*, Genus *Pongo*, Type species *Pongo borneo*, Species *Pongo pygmaeus, Pongo abelii, Pongo tapanuliensis*

Name

Orangutan (also written as orang-utan and orang utan) comes from Malay and Indonesian words *orang* (person) and *hutan* (forest), so the name means person of the forest. The genus name *Pongo* was first used in the 16th century by a captive English sailor in a Portuguese prison in Angola. Pongo was the name of a large ape (now believed to have been a gorilla), and the name somehow stuck for the orangutan genus. The type species name *borneo* is obvious: of Borneo. The three extant species names *Pongo pygmaeus* (the Bornean orangutan, which has three subspecies), *Pongo abelii* (the Sumatran orangutan), and *Pongo tapanuliensis* (the Tapanuli orangutan) mean respectively "pygmy," "named after zoologist Othenio Abel (1875–1946)" and "from South Tapanuli (on the island of Sumatra)."

Description

Orangutans are large apes with several human-like attributes and behaviors, particularly the structure of the hand and opposable thumb, and gestures and facial expressions. They live only in Borneo and Sumatra, and are a critically endangered species, mostly because of palm-oil forestry, which destroys their natural habitat.

General Attributes

Orangutans are gentle, passive animals. They forage for food in the mornings, rest at midday, and then travel to a fresh nest site in the evening, which they build in just over five minutes, choosing their branches and arranging them with great skill. Their main predators are tigers, leopards, wild dogs and crocodiles. They have a very wide range of vocalizations, including the ability to blow a raspberry, just like humans, when they are unimpressed. They are highly intelligent: experiments at Atlanta Zoo and Leipzig Zoo (2008) have involved orangutans playing computer games and keeping track of long sequences of gift giving and exchange. In the 1970s, the zoologist Gary L. Shapiro taught a female orangutan over forty sign words or phrases.

In Folklore

Male orangutans reach physical maturity by about 15 years of age, but may not copulate with a female for several more years. Older mature males have fatty flanges of dark skin on their faces, and females almost always prefer to mate with flanged males. The younger, unflanged males may copulate forcibly with reluctant females.

These behaviors have created some folkloric traditions in Borneo. It is said to be bad luck for anyone to look an orangutan directly in the face, and especially unlucky for a woman to do so. Male orangutans are suspected of making aggressive sexual advances towards human women. Birutè Galdikas (b. 1946), who is probably the world authority on orangutans, reported that her cook had been sexually assaulted by a male orangutan, but that animal had been raised in captivity. Galdikas, a Lithuanian Canadian anthropologist and primatologist, has lived and worked among orangutans for over thirty years.[6]

Gorilla (*Gorilla gorilla*)

Phylum *Chordata*, Class *Mammalia*, Order *Primates*, Suborder *Haplorhini*, Infraorder *Simiiformes*, Family *Hominidae*, Subfamily *Homininae*, Genus *Gorilla*, Species *Gorilla gorilla*

Name

When the Carthaginian explorer Hanno the Navigator (c. 500 BCE) was sailing the west African coast by what is now called Sierra Leone, he encountered some unfamiliar creatures which he called, in Ancient Greek, Γορίλλαι, or *Górillai*, which literally means "hairy women." Nobody knows whether what Hanno saw was gorillas, other apes, or actually just a group of unusually hairy women, but the name persisted for the animal we now call gorilla. The family and subfamily names *Hominidae* and *Homininae*, or hominids ("like humans"), refers to the four great ape genera: orangutans, gorillas, chimpanzees, and humans.

Description

Gorillas are the largest living primates, with wild males typically weighing between 300 and 430 pounds (135 and 195 kilograms). They are knuckle-walkers, i.e., they use the knuckles of their front limbs for walking. They live in the tropical and sub-tropical forests of central Africa. The two species, western gorillas and eastern gorillas, live either side of the Congo River. Both species are now critically endangered, mostly because of habitat destruction and poaching. Individual gorillas have slightly differently shaped noses, to the extent that to an experienced eye they can be recognized by their individual noseprints, supposedly with the same certainty as humans are by fingerprints.

(Much of our knowledge about gorillas comes from the work of the primatologist Dian Fossey, 1932–1985, who lived with and studied mountain gorillas in Rwanda until she was murdered in 1985, probably because of her anti-poaching conservation efforts. Her book *Gorillas in the Mist* was subsequently made into a film.[7] "The Trimates" is a nickname given to three women who worked with primates in recent times: Fossey with gorillas, Birutè Galdikas with orangutans—as described under **orangutan** above—and Jane Goodall, born in 1934, with chimpanzees.)

General Attributes

Gorillas are the third closest animal relatives to humans, after chimpanzees and bonobos. Despite their immense size and strength, they are mostly gentle vegetarians and lead complex social and family lives. It has been suggested that they not only have emotional feelings, just as humans do, but that they may also have some kind of spiritual sensibility.

King Kong

King Kong is a very well-known film character, mostly from three films named *King Kong* shown in 1933, 1976 and 2005, and *Kong: Skull Island* (2017). The character is based on African folkloric legends of male gorillas making aggressively sexual advances against human women. There are similar legends about orangutans (see **orangutan**). Since silverbacks (fully mature male gorillas) are so large, in legend they are sometimes represented as giant monsters, and King Kong is one such. In reality, gorilla males beat their chests, roar loudly, and will defend their families and territories very aggressively when required, but they are otherwise very calm, gentle and affectionate animals, and there are no records of them ever having sexually attacked human women.

The Bili Ape

In Malawi, there have been legends for decades of a mysterious primate, part gorilla, part giant chimpanzee, called Ufiti, or "the Ghost Ape." It has also been called "the Bondo Mystery Ape." Large chimpanzee-like skulls were found in 1908 in the Congo village of Bili, but the animal, now called "the Bili Ape," still remained elusive and a continuing mystery for many decades subsequently. Civil war in the Congo in the 1970s restricted further exploration. The Bili Ape has since been observed, although there is much still to learn about it. It is a large chimpanzee, but it behaves in many ways like a gorilla. In particular, it builds nests on the ground as well as sleeping in trees. The tree-sleepers are easily killed with poison arrows, so there have actually been some bodies to examine. The Bili Ape is now officially recognized and classified as a subspecies of the chimpanzee.[8]

Chimpanzee (*Pan troglodytes, Pan paniscus*)

Phylum *Chordata*, Class *Mammalia*, Order *Primates*, Suborder *Haplorhini*, Infraorder *Simiiformes*, Family *Hominidae*, Subfamily *Homininae*, Tribe *Hominini*, Subtribe *Panina*, Genus *Pan*, Species *Pan troglodytes, Pan paniscus*

Name

The common name was first recorded in 1738. It is derived from African languages, either the Vili *ci-mpenze*, or the Tshiluba *chimpenze*.[9] The colloquial version chimp was first used in the 1870s. The classification name was originally *Simia troglodytes* ("cave-dwelling monkey"), but the name *Pan* for the genus, from the Greek god Pan, was introduced in 1816 by the German naturalist, Lorenz Oken (1779–1851). The other species name, *paniscus*, is from a Latin named used by Cicero, meaning "a little Pan."[10]

Description

The chimpanzee is the most closely related species to humans. Unlike gorillas, it is an omnivore (eats all foods, including meat). It is a highly intelligent animal with a complex pattern of social interaction. It is far more aggressive than gorillas or orangutans. The very closely related bonobo is sometimes called the pygmy chimpanzee. The chimpanzee lives in the forests and savannahs of West and Central Africa. It is an endangered species, mostly because of poaching, loss of habitat, and susceptibility to disease (which is true of all the great apes).

Chimpanzees live in what is sometimes called a fission-fusion social pattern: groups coalesce and then dissolve, as occasion demands. They may travel as individuals, in small family groups, or in gatherings ranging in size from 20 to 150 individuals, depending on circumstances. Males stay with their birth groups, whereas females leave when they reach maturity, so in any grouping the males are usually more closely related to each other.

General Attributes

Chimpanzees do not appear in any mythology, and only very rarely in African folklore, probably because they are too close to humans for comfort.

In African Folklore

The Gio people of Liberia and the Hembe people of the Congo make chimpanzee masks, which are used at funerals and to intimidate people (usually children) who are considered to have misbehaved.[11]

In Western Culture

Chimpanzees have often been dressed as humans in the West, and used for advertising, entertainment and amusement. As modern science and journalism have revealed how aggressive and powerful they can be, chimpanzees have been used less frequently for frivolous purposes. They have been kept as pets (that happens quite often in Africa, too), but there have been several occasions when pet chimps have attacked and severely wounded their owners. There have been at least six documented occasions when chimps have kidnapped human babies and eaten them.[12]

There have also been many projects to teach chimps human language, and it was initially thought that individuals like Nim Chimpsky (a parody of the linguist Noam Chomsky) were showing evidence of linguistic ability close to that of humans. However, subsequent research has suggested that the chimpanzee's use of sign language is based mostly on rote learning and imitation, and that it does not have a human's underlying and innate (according to Chomsky) framework of syntax and meaning.

Chimps have also been widely used for many decades in medical and drug research, greatly to the concern of animal rights' activists. It has been demonstrated that the HIV-1 and HIV-2 viruses, which are responsible for human Auto-Immune Deficiency Syndrome or AIDS, originated in chimpanzees in Cameroon and elsewhere, and then crossed species to humans.

Gibbon (Several Species)

Phylum *Chordata*, Class *Mammalia*, Order *Primates*, Suborder *Haplorhini*, Infraorder *Simiiformes*, Parvorder *Catarrhini*, Superfamily *Hominidia*, Subfamily *Hylobatidae*, Type genus *Hylobates*, Genus (4 extant), Species (18)

Name

The common name was first recorded in English in 1774. It was borrowed from Indian French, but the original Indian word is now lost. The type genus name *Hylobates* is from Greek ὑλος, *hylos*, matter or creature, and βατος, *batos*, bush. There are three other genera and 18 extant species.

Description

Gibbons are small and very monkey-like in appearance, but they are apes. They have no tails. They live in several Asian countries.

General Attributes

The mythology of gibbons all comes from China, even though the vast majority of gibbons in China had died out by the 14th century CE through habitat destruction.

In Chinese Taoism and Folklore

Taoists believed that gibbons were magicians. They lived for several centuries, and finally turned into humans of great wisdom and compassion. Most gibbons have at least one fracture in their history (they are brachiators, which means that they swing through trees faster and more frequently than almost all other animals), so they may often look like humans who have lived a long and adventurous life.

Early Chinese writers called gibbons the *junzi* or gentlemen of the forest. There are several Chinese paintings of gibbons from the early Yuan dynasty of Kublai Khan, notably those by Yì Yuánjí (c. 1000–1064 CE) and Mùqī Facháng (1210–1269). The Mandarin word *yuán*, which now means ape in general, originally meant gibbon.

An image of a gibbon reaching for the reflection of the moon in water, which illustrates a Zen Buddhist theme about perception, spread from China to Japan, where it is the motif of many paintings, although gibbons have never naturally lived in Japan.

Howler Monkey (Several Species)

Phylum *Chordata*, Class *Mammalia*, Order *Primates*, Suborder *Haplorhini*, Infraorder *Simiiformes*, Family *Atelidae*, Subfamily *Alouattinae*, Genus *Alouatta*, Type species *Simia belzebul*, Species (15)

Name

Howler monkeys, as the name suggests, are famous for their loud shriek, which can be heard from up to three miles away in dense rainforest. The genus name *alouatta* was devised in New Latin in 1830 from the French name, *alouate*. The type species name, *Simia belzebul*, means Beelzebub monkey. (Beelzebub was a Philistine god, and is a major demon in Judaism, Christianity and Islam.)

Description

Howler monkeys are large monkeys, usually chocolate-brown in color, with long prehensile tails. They live in South and Central America.

General Attributes

Howler monkeys are not usually aggressive towards humans, but can appear surly or sulky. Their howls are so loud that they can cause an urgent sense of alarm and danger.

In Mayan Culture

Howler monkeys were worshiped as gods by some tribes in the Mayan civilization, which flourished from c. 2000 BCE until c. 900 CE, the last Mayan city being destroyed by the colonizing Spanish in 1697. Howler monkeys are still present in considerable numbers, acting, it is believed, as guardian spirits, at the ruins of the Mayan city of Copán in western Honduras, near the Guatemalan border.

16

Hares and Rabbits (*Lagomorpha*)

Hare (*Lepus timidus*)

Phylum *Chordata*, Class *Mammalia*, Order *Lagomorpha*, Family *Leporidae*, Genus *Lepus*, Type species *Lepus timidus*

Name

The name hare is *hara* in Old English, originally from Proto-Germanic **haswaz*, meaning gray or pale. The order name *Lagomorpha* is New Latin coined from two Greek words, and simply means shaped like a hare. The species name *Lepus timidus* means timid hare. There is a constellation called Lepus (see Chapter 41). The Romans used the word *lepus* as a term of endearment, as we might use "honeybun." The term "jackass rabbit" for a hare was coined by Mark Twain; it later became shortened to jackrabbit, and is often used in America to refer to a hare. A young hare is called a leveret.

Description

Hares are generally about the same size as rabbits or slightly larger, but with longer ears and more prominent eyes. They are very fast runners: the European hare (*Lepus europaeus*) can reach 35 m.p.h., and the five species of American jackrabbit found in central and western North America are even faster, reaching 40 m.p.h.

Unlike rabbits, hares tend to live as solitaries or couples rather than in a large group. When competing for mates in spring, hares of both sexes often square up to each other and hit each other like sparring boxers, and their lively antics have generated the simile "as mad as a March hare." Hare young or leverets are born fully sighted and ready to run, unlike rabbits.

General Attributes

The hare is inextricably linked to the Moon, to the Great Goddess and to shape shifting in Celtic Druidic iconography. It was associated with Aphrodite and Eros in the classical pantheon. In Mexico, China and Japan, the figure of "the Moon Hare" has traditionally been seen in the pattern of the dark craters, in the same way that Westerners talk of "the Man in the Moon." By contrast, the hare is a symbol of the Sun in Native American mythology (see *Michabo* below).

Hare meat was taboo in many Celtic tribes and remains taboo to many neopagans. Hares were thought to be able to penetrate the veil into the Otherworld even more easily than birds, and a hare in a hurry was perceived as conveying a message from or to the gods or the ancestors.

In medieval Christianity, the hare was considered a symbol of lust and promiscuity. It was also considered able to change its sex. The female (jill or doe) was said to be able to become a male (jack or buck) at will, and even to conceive without the aid of a male. The hare thus became, perversely, a symbol both of lust and of virginity. "The Hare" was a derogatory nickname for Queen Elizabeth 1st of England (1533–1603), who, because she remained unmarried, was also called "the Virgin Queen."

The Hare and the Tortoise

Perhaps the best known of all the Æsop fables is the story of the hare and the tortoise. The hare is expected to win because he is obviously so much faster than the tortoise, but the tortoise wins because he sticks to the task while the hare is arrogantly over-confident and stops to take a nap part way through the race.

Michabo

The principal deity of the Native American Algonquin nations is Michabo, the Great Hare. The name includes the element *wab*, which also means light or day. We have become accustomed in the West to the image of the hare as either timid and a little crazy, or a bold trickster, still a little crazy, like Bugs Bunny. But Michabo is a very serious deity indeed. He created the first island from a single grain of sand, and so vast was it that a young wolf attempting to walk across it died of old age before he reached the other side. He created the Meda, a society of medicine-men among the Algonquin tribes. He watched Spider and created the first fishing nets. He was the spirit of the east, of dawn, of light against darkness, of goodness against evil.[1]

The Midewiwin

In the creation myth of the Potawatomi, an Algonquian tribe of the Great Plains and western Great Lakes, Manabozho was a creator god, and his story shares some elements with that of Michabo. He has various names in different tribes, including Nanabozho or Nanabush (Ojibwe), Chikapash (Cree), Tshakapesh (Innu) and Tcikapec (Atikamekw).

Manabozho had three brothers, of whom the youngest, Flint, killed his mother at his birth. Manabozho and the second brother had human form (although Manabozho also sometimes appears as a skunk or porcupine), but the third brother was a white hare. Manabozho killed Flint for having killed their mother, but the gods were angry and killed the second brother. Manabozho then went to war against the gods, but the white hare eventually brought peace between them. The gods made the dead second brother the god of the dead. To Manabozho they taught the arts and science of magic, including healing, and they inducted him as the first member of the Midewiwin, or sacred medicine society. Every tribal medicine man is a member of this society, and calls on Manabozho and the spirit of the white hare for guidance.[2]

Wenenut

Unlikely as it may sound, one of the most ferocious of the ancient Egyptian goddesses was Wenen or Wenenut, who had the body of a woman and the head of a hare or rabbit, complete with floppy ears. She carried a knife in each hand, like the lion-goddess Sekhet, and she avenged crimes or insults. She had a more beneficent side to her, as is shown by depictions of her with an *ankh*, the symbol of eternal life, in one hand. Her consort was the hare god Wenenu or Wonenu, who was considered an incarnation or avatar of Osiris.[3]

Boudicca

The story of Queen Boudicca (also called Boadicea, or Buddug in Welsh) of the Iceni, an ancient British Celtic tribe, is well known. Recapitulated briefly, the beginning of the story runs as follows:

> Boudicca's husband, Prasutagus, made a weak and foolish alliance with the occupying Romans. In his will, he bequeathed all his wealth equally to his wife and daughters on the one hand and to the Roman Empire on the other. Upon his death in 59 CE, the Romans ignored the will and simply annexed the Iceni lands and treasures. When Boudicca protested, her daughters were raped and beaten while she was forced to watch. In reprisal, Boudicca led a revolt against the occupying forces. According to the Roman author Dion, after her first battle Boudicca released a hare from her cloak. The hare ran in the auspicious direction, and Boudicca gave thanks to the war goddess Andraste and prayed for further victories.

A statue of Boudicca and her daughters in a war chariot stands on the Thames Embankment in London, not far from the Houses of Parliament.

Oestre

Hares, unlike rabbits, sleep above ground on nests (called *forms*) of flattened grass. To the untrained eye, these appear identical to lapwings' nests. Since the birds' nests were often observed to hold eggs, the myth began to circulate that hares also laid eggs. The hare thus became the original inspiration for the Easter Bunny, the name Easter deriving from the Saxon fertility goddess Oestre, who also gives her name to the primary female sex hormone, estrogen.

Aino's Hare

In the Finnish epic poem the *Kalevala*, a Lapp maiden called Aino (Without Equal) was betrothed to the hero Vainamoinen, who was an old man. Her parents were very happy with the match because Vainamoinen was famous and powerful, but Aino was uncertain.

Aino agreed to meet Vainamoinen in the forest, but disliked him instantly. Her mother, however, bribed her with many gifts and insisted on the marriage going ahead. Aino, in full wedding costume, started out trying to obey her parents' wishes, but ended up on a lonely riverbank. She took off all her wedding clothes, threw herself in the icy water, and drowned. The animals of the forest, who had watched as Aino drowned herself, lamented her sad death and sent the hare, the messenger of death, to Aino's mother. The mother listened to the hare carefully, and acknowledged her own fault in having tried to persuade Aino to marry against her will. Later, Vainamoinen trawled the river, looking for Aino's body. He caught a fish, and realized that it was Aino, shape-shifted. He asked her again to marry him, she still said no, and so he put her back into the cold water.[4]

Rabbit (Several Species)

Phylum *Chordata*, Class *Mammalia*, Order *Lagomorpha*, Family *Leporidae*, Genus (8), Species (305 domestic, 13 wild)

Name

The word rabbit has a curious history. Rabbits used to be called coneys, but the Norman French introduced the dialect term *rabotte*, which they had borrowed from the word *robète* used by Walloons in what is now Belgium. This word was Dutch in origin (in Dutch, *rob* means both rabbit and seal).

The family is *Leporidae*, the same as hares (see above), and there are eight extant genera, with *Silvilagus* ("forest dwelling") representing the 13 species of wild rabbits. There are over 300 breeds of domesticated rabbits. The name for the European rabbit, from which domesticated rabbits are descended, is *Oryctolagus cuniculus*. *Oryct-* is Greek for "digging up" and *lagos* is Greek for "hare," so the New Latin coining *Oryctolagus* means "hare-like digging animal." The species name *cuniculus* means "burrow" or "small conduit."

Description

The European rabbit, *Oryctolagus cuniculus*, is a wild rabbit native to southern Europe and northern Africa, but it has been introduced to every part of the world except Antarctica, and is considered a disastrous pest in many places.

General Attributes

The rabbit is noted for its fertility ("breeding like rabbits" is a common saying) and for its speed ("Run, rabbit! Run, rabbit! Run, run, run! / Here comes the farmer with his gun, gun, gun!" is a well-known song). A common belief is that carrying a rabbit's foot brings good luck. The rabbit, like the hare, is associated with the Moon in many cultures. In Africa, the rabbit is often a trickster god or spirit, and this tradition transferred to America in the stories of Br'er Rabbit (see below).

Chang'e

In Chinese mythology, Chang'e (formerly Heng-e) is the goddess of the Moon. She was the wife of the divine archer, Yi or Houyi.

The best known of her legends is of the time when there were ten suns in the sky, and the world suffered from terrible heat. Yi shot nine of them down with his arrows, leaving just the one, which was much more acceptable. The gods rewarded him with a viol of the elixir of eternal life. Yi left the viol with Chang'e, intending that they should both drink it together.

However, while Yi was away hunting, his apprentice Fengmeng broke into Yi's house to steal the elixir. In desperation, not knowing how to prevent Fengmeng from stealing it, Chang'e drank it herself. She then flew up into the heavens, choosing the Moon as her home. According to different versions of the legend, she became a frog or toad, she rode a three-legged frog into the night sky, or—the most popular version—she became a rabbit (or perhaps a hare).

The legend of Chang'e was mentioned in a conversation between Houston CAPCOM and the *Apollo 11* crew just before the first Moon landing in 1969:

> **RONALD EVANS (CC):** Among the large headlines concerning Apollo this morning is one asking that you watch for a lovely girl with a big rabbit. An ancient legend says a beautiful Chinese girl called Chang-O has been living there for 4,000 years. It seems she was banished to the Moon because she stole the pill of immortality from her husband. You might also look for her companion, a large Chinese rabbit, who is easy to spot since he is always standing on his hind feet in the shade of a cinnamon tree. The name of the rabbit is not reported.
> **MICHAEL COLLINS (CMP):** Okay. We'll keep a close eye out for the bunny girl.[5]

In January 2019, the Chinese successfully landed a space vehicle on the far side of the Moon, the first nation to do so. The robotic rover is called *Yutu* (Jade Rabbit) and the name of the Chinese lunar space program is *Chang'e*, after the moon goddess.

Br'er Rabbit

In Joel Chandler Harris's *Uncle Remus: His Songs and His Sayings* (1880), Bre'er Rabbit is even smarter and sharper than Br'er Fox, which is saying something. The most famous tale sees Br'er Rabbit hopping merrily along his way when he finds his path blocked by a baby. He doesn't know that Br'er Fox has fashioned this life-sized creature out of sticky, black tar in order to trap Br'er Rabbit. Br'er Rabbit politely asks the tar baby to step aside, but of course receives no response. Finally, he makes to swipe the tar baby to one side, but his paw sticks to the tar. As he struggles to break free, Br'er Fox leaps out of hiding and seizes him.

> Br'er Rabbit, thinking quickly, yells, "Oh, please don't throw me in the briar patch! Not the briar patch! Oh, please, not the briar patch!"
> Br'er Fox, for once driven more by cruelty than cunning, tosses Br'er Rabbit straight into the briar patch.
> "Thanks!" laughs Br'er Rabbit. "I was born and raised in the briar patch!"
> And he runs off to freedom.[6]

17

Mice, Rats and Beavers (*Rodentia*)

House Mouse (*Mus musculus domesticus*)

Phylum *Chordata*, Class *Mammalia*, Order *Rodentia*, Family *Muridae*, Genus *Mus*, Subgenus *Mus*, Species *Mus musculus*, Subspecies *Mus musculus domesticus*

Name

The word mouse derives from Old English *mus*, which was also the Latin word—although it meant both mouse and rat, since the Romans assumed they were the same animals, just different in size. If they were talking about a small, domestic mouse, the Romans often used the diminutive *musculus*, little mouse, which is also the species name. The words muscle and mussel (the seashell) are both derived from *musculus*. In the modern age, "mouse" also refers to the device that guides the screen pointer on a computer, and the English word has been borrowed wholesale by many other languages for that specific meaning.

Description

Mice live in at least four different kinds of relationships with humans: truly wild mice, such as field mice, hardly interact with humans at all; semi-tame mice live in close proximity to humans, often literally in the same buildings or dwellings, but are considered intruders and are not domesticated (the technical term for species living close together in this way is commensalism); pet mice are deliberately kept as companion animals; and research mice are bred and kept in great numbers for scientific experimentation.

Mice probably came from northern India originally, but they spread to the eastern Mediterranean around 13000 BCE. It was not until about 1000 BCE that they spread across the rest of Europe, largely because they depend on human settlements of a certain size to live as semi-tame cohabitants (or pests). They are now common all across the globe. Mice breed very rapidly and have many biological similarities with humans, so they have become the most common laboratory research animals in the world.

General Attributes

Mice feature in a number of folk legends, partly because they are such common and easily recognized animals. They appeared in ancient Egyptian folklore and have since featured in many European folktales.

Belling the Cat

A well-known folktale, attributed to Æsop but probably Indian in origin, tells of a group of mice meeting to solve a problem:

> The mice in a large house were in disarray. The owner of the house had bought a large, fierce cat to rid the house of mice and other vermin, and every day the cat did its job efficiently, killing several mice. The other mice held a meeting to discuss the issue.
> "What can we do?" asked one old mouse. "The cat is too big, too strong and too quick for us. He's going to kill us all! Oh dear! What can we do?"
> The other mice nodded their heads in agreement. Nobody seemed able to suggest a solution. Finally, above the general muttering, a young mouse spoke up:
> "I know what we can do!" he said enthusiastically. "Let us tie a bell to the cat. That way, we'll hear him coming long before he gets to us. No matter how fast he is, with that warning we'll be able to run to the nearest mouse hole and find a safe place to hide."
> "Brilliant!" shouted the others. "What a marvelous idea! We're saved! We're saved!"
> When the cheering and clapping had died down, the old mouse spoke up again. "I have just one question," he said quietly. "Who is going to put the bell on the cat?"
> The other mice fell silent. They had no answer.

Moral: It is easier to propose than to deliver.

Archibald Douglas, the Scottish fifth earl of Angus, who died in 1514, was nicknamed Archibald Bell-the-Cat. King James the Third held a council of nobles in Lauder, bringing several of his young favorites with him. The elder nobles despised the king and his sycophantic new earls. "Who will bell the cat?" asked Lord Gray. "That will I," replied Archibald, drawing his sword. He then killed all the young men, with the king present and powerless to intervene.[1]

The Town Mouse and the Country Mouse

Another well-known Æsopic tale describes the experiences of a town mouse and a country mouse. The country mouse liked new adventures and went to visit his cousin, the town mouse. But the town mouse disparaged the country mouse for his pusillanimity when they were barked at by the town house dogs. The country mouse did not enjoy the experience at all, and concluded that a quiet country life, while it may be less exciting than town house living, is far safer and more comfortable.

The tale is found in the *Satires* of the Roman poet Horace, 65–8 BCE, and—with rats instead of mice—in the fables of Jean de la Fontaine, 1621–1695 CE.

Field Mouse (Several Species)

Phylum *Chordata*, Class *Mammalia*, Order *Rodentia*, Family *Muridae*, Subfamily *Murinae*, Genus *Apodemus*, Species (about 20)

Name

Field means wild here, i.e., neither domesticated nor closely dependent on human settlements.

Description

There are at least 20 species of field mice, and about 155 species of voles, which are much like field mice, but tend to be stouter. They vary in color and size.

General Attributes

In folklore, field mice are generally more independent and adventuresome than semi-tame urban mice. (They are the country mouse of the Æsopic fable, rather than the town mouse.)

The Lion and the Mouse

The Æsopic tale of the lion and the mouse is perhaps one of the best known, and certainly one of the oldest. The Greek version came into Egyptian literature in about 200 CE, but there is an Indian version (the same story, but with an elephant instead of a lion), which is centuries older.

> A lion was asleep in his den. Inadvertently, a little mouse ran across the lion's paw, over his chin, and up into his nose. The lion gave a great sneeze, and the mouse tumbled down to the floor between the lion's paws.
> "Please," squealed the little mouse, "please, Your Majesty, don't kill me. I didn't mean to wake you up. If you let me go, perhaps I will be able to return the favor one day and do you a service. Who knows?"
> The lion, amused by the little mouse quivering and shaking beneath his paw, let him go, chuckling at the thought that such a tiny creature could ever be of use to him.
> Not long afterwards, the lion was out hunting when some trappers caught him in a net. The lion roared and roared. The roar echoed throughout the forest, and even the little mouse heard it. He hurried to the scene.
> He saw immediately what the problem was. With his sharp little teeth, he worried away at the intricate net until he had opened it enough for the lion to escape. The lion thanked the mouse handsomely for his help.

Moral: No act of kindness, no matter how small, is ever wasted.

Mayauel and the Mouse

In Aztec mythology, Mayauel was the wife of a farmer. One day, she chased a mouse away from the agave cactus plants in the garden. She noticed that the mouse was staggering, and she realized that it was hopelessly drunk. She drained a small amount of agave syrup from one of the plants and left it to ferment in a clay jar while she and her husband went to work in the fields. When they came back, tired and thirsty, they drank the liquid in the clay jar. Within minutes, they too were staggering drunk, all their stiffness and pain vanished. Thus, the first *pulque* was discovered.[2]

Rat (*Rattus rattus, Rattus norvegicus*)

Phylum *Chordata*, Class *Mammalia*, Order *Rodentia*, Genus mostly *Rattus*, Species *Rattus rattus, rattus norvegicus*

Name

Rat is a Germanic word. In Old English it was spelled *ræt*. The genus and species name *rattus* is a New Latin coining from the English word. (In classical Latin, the word for rat was *mus*, or "mouse"—see **mouse** above.) The species name *norvegicus* means Norwegian.

Description

Rats are larger than mice, sometimes much larger, and usually have long tails. The two best known species are the black rat (*Rattus rattus*) and the brown rat (*Rattus norvegicus*).

Brown rats (which can be brown, white, or shades in between) are sometimes kept as domestic pets, usually quite successfully: they are intelligent, easily trained, and no more unclean or harmful to health than a dog or a cat.

Wild rats can wreak havoc on bird populations, particularly on isolated islands, and several countries and states have eliminated or almost eliminated rat populations on islands to protect sea-bird species, including South Georgia in the Falklands, Hawadax Island in Alaska, and Breaksea Island in New Zealand.[3]

Rats are frequently used in laboratory experimentation, particularly in cardiology (rats' hearts have many similarities to human hearts) and in psychological and behavioral science.

General Attributes

For centuries, rats (and their fleas) have been blamed for spreading Bubonic Plage among humans, but this claim has been questioned more recently. Nevertheless, rats can communicate several other diseases to humans, and they are generally considered as dirty pests. They are also very abundant, particularly in urban areas, where they are thought to congregate and breed in the safety of underground sewage systems. There is an urban legend that every city-dwelling human in the world is never further than approximately 4 meters or 12 feet away from a hidden rat.

In folklore, rats are usually villains, pests, or at best tricksters. They are rarely heroes.

Archbishop Hatto

A German legend tells the story of Archbishop Hatto, who was a historical rather than mythological figure. He was exceedingly ambitious, and advanced himself from a humble abbot in the year 888 CE to a personal friend of the King and Regent of the Empire by 899. At the height of his wealth and power, the people came to beg Archbishop Hatto, as he now was, to let them have some of the tons of grain he had stored in his many granaries. His response was to seal them in an empty granary and burn them all to death.

The next morning, a servant told him that rats had gnawed part of one his paintings away. As the days passed, rats came in their tens of thousands, ate all of Hatto's grain, and finally drove him into hiding in the highest part of the Mouse Tower, where they finally swarmed over him and ate him alive.[4]

(The Mouse Tower is a red herring, to mix animal metaphors briefly. It was actually built by Bishop Siegfried some 200 years after Hatto's death, but it is still associated with the legend in local folklore, and it does add a little extra dramatic color to the story.)

The Pied Piper of Hamelin

The story of the Pied Piper of Hamelin is one of the best-known pieces of folklore in Europe. In 1284, the town of Hamelin in Germany was plagued by rats. The Pied Piper turned up in his distinctive multi-colored (pied) clothing, and offered to rid the town of its rats for a set fee. The town worthies agreed, and the Pied Piper began playing his pipe. The rats came swarming out of their holes to follow the music. The piper led them to the River Weser, where they all drowned. The piper asked the town elders for his fee, which they foolishly refused to pay. So the piper began playing again, and this time all the children of the town followed him up to the summit of Koppenberg Hill, where they all vanished, never to be seen again.[5]

Pikoi

Hawaii has a folkloric rat-catcher, too. His name was Pikoi, and he was an archer. He was said to have caught 40 rats with one arrow, which pinned each of them by the whiskers.[6]

Squirrel (Several Species)

Phylum *Chordata*, Class *Mammalia*, Order *Rodentia*, Suborder *Sciuromorpha*, Family *Sciuridae*, Subfamilies (5), Genera (about 58), Species (about 285)

Name

The Old English name for this animal was *acweorna*, acorn eater, but it was replaced in Middle English by a name with a longer history. Ancient Greek σκιουρος, *skíouros*, shadow-tail, became *sciurus*, squirrel, in Latin, with a diminutive, *sciurulus*, little squirrel, added later. This became *escurel* in Old French and *squyrelle* in Middle English. The suborder name *Sciuromorpha* means squirrel-shaped.

Description

Squirrels are rodents, like mice and rats, but they come in a wide variety of shapes and sizes, many of them having long, bushy, upright tails. The *Sciuridae* family includes ground squirrels, tree squirrels, flying squirrels, marmots, woodchucks, chipmunks, and prairie dogs. Most squirrels cache their food in autumn to see them through the winter.

General Attributes

Squirrels and their variants are generally noted for their inquisitiveness and persistence. In urban gardens, they are notorious for stealing food from bird feeders. Like all rodents, their incisor teeth continue growing all the time, and so they gnaw at things incessantly. Squirrels gnawing through electrical cables have started many fires in buildings.

Squirrels have appeared in different religious traditions and mythologies. Because they have large eyes and move very quickly, they are often associated with intelligence and communication.

Rama and the Palm Squirrel

The Indian palm squirrel (*Funambulus palmarum*, "rope-dancer of the palms") has three white stripes on its back. According to the ancient epic *The Ramayana*, it was a squirrel that helped build a bridge from India to Sri Lanka, which allowed Rama to rescue his wife, Sita. Rama was so grateful that he ran three fingers down the palm squirrel's back to stroke it affectionately, and all palm squirrels now bear the mark of Rama's touch.

Medb's Squirrel

In Irish mythology, the mother-goddess Medb (pronounced approximately *mayv*) has two messenger totem animals on her shoulders. The first is a crow, raven or blackbird, all of which are associated with flight between the worlds and delivering sacred or oracular messages, and the second is a squirrel, which, like the hare, runs with messages between this world and the next. Squirrels are also known for their loud, warning screech when danger is near, and Medb's squirrel also acts as her guard.

Ratatoskr

In Norse mythology, the world tree is the ash Yggdrasill. At its roots, far beneath the human world, lies curled the great dragon Níðhöggr (see Chapter 39) while at its top, far above the human world, perches Odin's eagle. The squirrel Ratatoskr (Drill Tooth) scurries up and down the tree, carrying messages. Since both the dragon and the eagle are querulous, haughty beasts, the messages are often insults and complaints, which Ratatoskr delivers nonchalantly, no matter how foul or abusive the language. Odin is often amused by Ratatoskr's reports. Odin's magical ravens, Huginn and Muginn, also bring him news every day (see Chapter 22).

Marmot/Groundhog/Woodchuck (*Marmota monax*)

Phylum *Chordata*, Class *Mammalia*, Order *Rodentia*, Family *Sciuridae*, Genus *Marmota*, Species *Marmota monax*

Name

The name marmot came into English from Old French *marmotaine* or *marmontaine*, which seems to be from Latin *mus monti*, mountain rat. Groundhog and whistle pig are self-explanatory. The name woodchuck comes from Cree Indian *wejuk* or *otchek*, which was borrowed from Ojibwe *ojiig*, meaning fisher. The species name *monax*, which looks Greek, is actually from the Algonquian Indian name *móonack*, meaning digger.

Description

The marmot, a large squirrel, is found widely distributed across Europe, Asia and North America. The species *Marmota monax*, commonly known by the names groundhog, woodchuck and whistle pig, is found all across North America. Not many people know that the groundhog is used extensively as a laboratory research animal for human diseases, particularly for hepatitis B-induced liver cancer.

General Attributes

The groundhog cleans its face with its small paws and washes its body with its tongue, like a cat, so some people see the animal as cute and cuddly. Most people, however, think of it as an almighty pest. Its favorite food is any vegetable planted and grown by somebody else, and it seems to take delight in digging its burrows wherever they will cause the greatest harm and inconvenience to humans (cf. the well-known Bill Murray film *Caddyshack*, 1980).

Groundhog Day

Several places in the USA celebrate Groundhog Day on February 2 each year. The most famous oracular groundhog is Punxsutawney Phil from the town of Punxsutawney in Pennsylvania. Phil is given a temporary home on Gobbler's Knob, a hill about two miles out of town. People gather well before dawn to watch him emerge. If he sees his shadow and goes back into his burrow, winter weather can be expected for at least another month and a half. If he sees no shadow, and is content to roam, then an early spring is on its way.

Beaver (*Castor fiber, Castor canadensis*)

Phylum *Chordata*, Class *Mammalia*, Order *Rodentia*, Family *Castoridae*, Subfamily *Castorinae*, Genus *Castor*, Species *Castor fiber, Castor canadensis*

Name

The English name was spelled *beofor* in Old English, and is found in very similar forms in many languages, e.g., *bever* in Dutch, *bièvre* in French and *Biber* in German. The genus name *Castor* is from Greek καστωρ, *kástor* and Latin *castor*, both meaning beaver. *Fiber* is an alternative Latin name, so *Castor fiber* means beaver beaver, and *Castor canadensis* fairly obviously means Canadian beaver.

Description

Beavers are large semi-aquatic rodents, famous for their flat tails and for gnawing down trees, and building dams and large, complex homes called lodges, which are accessed via an underwater entrance. The two extant species are the North American beaver (*Castor canadensis*) and the Eurasian beaver (*Castor fiber*).

General Attributes

Beavers are noted for their industriousness and perseverance. Their presence is very easily observed in the wild, because they make such an impact on their immediate environment, usually for the better. (Beaver ponds and wetlands help to remove sediments and pollutants from watercourses.) Beavers feature in many North American Indian tales and legends. The name Beverley or Beverly, which is a common place name, first name (male or female) and surname in English, is derived from Old English *beofor* (beaver) and *leah* (lea, meadow or clearing).

Hunted Beavers

Beavers have been hunted for millennia. Their fur is thick and water-resistant, and makes excellent protective human clothing for harsh climates. Beaver pelts have often been more valuable than precious metals or currency cash in remote communities. Beaver testicles (which remain inside the body and can be removed only by killing the animal) are reputed to have powerful medicinal qualities, both in North America and in traditional Asian medicine.

An oily, yellowish substance called castoreum is secreted by both male and female beavers to mark their territories, and it, too, is recognized for its medical properties. It was used for centuries to treat hysteria, inflammation and fever. It is thought that castoreum is so effective because beavers eat a great deal of willow timber, which contains salicylic acid, the essential ingredient of aspirin. Castoreum is still used as a perfume and as a food additive, but its use has diminished greatly because it is now rare and expensive.

Beaver Medicine

A myth of the Algonquin Native American tribes connects the beaver to the medicine, the sacred knowledge that allows magic and magical healing to take place. The story has many variants, but the essence is that an Algonquin warrior called Akaiyan was abandoned on a remote island, where he learned medicine from the animals. He was rescued by a family of beavers, who invited him to live with them in their lodge for a year. The grizzled old father beaver taught Akaiyan everything he knew about the medicine, about the power of tobacco, about the gods and spirits, and he showed him all the medicine dances and taught him all the sacred songs. When Akaiyan returned to his own people, he brought all this knowledge and power to them.[7]

Porcupine (Several Species)

Phylum *Chordata*, Class *Mammalia*, Order *Rodentia*, Suborder *Hystricomorpha*, Infraorder *Hystricognathi*, Family *Hystricidae* (Old World porcupines), *Erethizontidae* (New World porcupines), Species (58)

Name

The name porcupine came into Middle English from Middle Italian via Middle French. It is derived from Latin *porcus* (pig) and *spina* (quill or spike). (In parts of America, a porcupine is called a quill pig.)

Description

There are two families of porcupines, *Hystricidae* (Old World porcupines, from Greek ʻυστριξ, *hystrix*, porcupine) and *Erethizontidae* (New World porcupines, from Greek ερεθιζειν, *erethizéin*, irritating, referring to the quills). Both are notable for their barbed quills or spines, which cover their bodies as a defense mechanism.

General Attributes

In the Far East, especially in Vietnam, porcupine flesh is highly valued as a delicacy. Porcupines are fairly easy to catch with a net or blanket, and in certain parts of the Far East they are now endangered, because they have been hunted so assiduously.

In North American Indian cultures, porcupine quills and guard-hairs have been used for centuries to make ritual headdresses. They feature prominently to this day at pow-wows, especially among the Mohawk, Pawnee, Mohegan and Lenape. The common modern name for this kind of headdress is a roach, which is also sometimes used for the Mohawk hair-cut, which shaves both sides of the head clean but leaves a strip of long or spiky hair in the middle.

18

Bats (*Chiroptera*) and Other Odd Animals

Bat (Several Species)

Phylum *Chordata*, Class *Mammalia*, Clade *Scrotifera*, Order *Chiroptera*, Suborders *Megachiroptera, Microchiroptera, Yinpterochiroptera, Yangchiroptera*, Species (more than 1,200 extant)

Name

The bat used to be called a flittermouse in English, because of its fluttering wing-like skin extensions. The old name is very similar to the German *Fledermaus*. The name bat appears to have come into the language from Middle English *bakke*, but the etymology before that is uncertain. The order name *Chiroptera* ("hand wings") is from Greek ξειρ, *xeir*, hand, and πτερον, *pterón*, wing.

Description

Bats are the only mammals capable of true, sustained flight. Their forelimbs have evolved to function as wings, with a thin membrane of skin, called a *patagium*, stretched across their elongated bones.

Bats comes in many different sizes and types. The smallest, which is also probably the world's smallest extant mammal, is Kitti's hog-nosed bat, which is only about 1¼ inches (30 mm) long. The largest, the flying fox, can weigh 4 pounds (1.6 kilograms) and have a wingspan of 5 feet, 7 inches (1.7 meters).

General Attributes

In ancient China and Japan, bats were considered symbols of good fortune and prosperity. The Chinese (who eat many things not eaten in the West) eat bats because they bring five blessings: wealth, health, old age, love of virtuous behavior, and a peaceful, natural death.

In the West, however, the bat is widely featured in horror films and associated with dirt and disease, and sometimes reputed to contain the soul of a dead person. A typical terror scenario is for a beautiful, screaming woman to have a frantic, struggling bat trapped by its claws in her long hair. The bat is listed in the Old Testament as an unclean animal. We are informed that when God pronounces judgment on the rich and the arrogant, "On that day people will throw away to the moles and to the bats their idols of silver and their idols of gold, which they made for themselves to worship."[1]

Camazotz

In the mythology of the Quiché Maya of Guatemala, Camazotz or Camalotz is a god of death. He is portrayed as a vampire bat (*Desmodus rotundus*), but with human hands. He holds his victim in one hand, and the sacrificial knife of death in the other. His evil character is founded on a genuine fear and disgust with real vampire bats, which attack animals, including farm animals, and suck their blood.[2]

There are two other vampire bat species: *Diphylla ecaudata* is the hairy-legged vampire bat, and *Diaemus youngi* is the white-winged vampire bat. All three species live in South and Central America, ranging from Argentina in the south to Mexico in the north, and all three live exclusively on blood. They have a number of adaptive traits not found in other bats, including very strong, sharp teeth for piercing animal hides and flesh, and the ability to run, hop and jump along the ground, as well as fly. They hunt and feed exclusively at night.

Hunahpú and Xbalanqúe

In another Mayan legend from Guatemala, the twin hero gods Hunahpú and Xbalanqúe have a typically strange birth. Their father, Hun-Hunahpú, was playing a ball game with his brothers. Unwittingly, they came close to the entrance to Xibalba, the Mayan underworld. The lords of the underworld challenged Hun-Hunahpú to a ball game, defeated them by trickery, and then slaughtered them all.

They left Hun-Hunahpú's severed head hanging in a tree. The tree immediately bore fruit. A maiden, Xquic (Little Blood), daughter of Lord Cuchumaquic, reached up to pluck some fruit from the tree. As she did so, some spittle from the skull fell onto her hand, and the tree spoke, saying, "In my saliva I have given you my descendants." She subsequently gave birth to Hunahpú and Xbalanqúe.

As did their father before them, Hunahpú and Xbalanqúe came across the lords of Xibalba. In the various chambers of the underworld they met many different creatures and apparitions, and in the House of Bats met Camazotz (see above). They made themselves very small and hid inside the hollowed-out tube of a blowgun. All night long, vampire bats flew all around them, but they remained safe.

Finally, however, Camazotz captured Hunahpú and bit off his head, hanging the skull in a tree, just as had happened to his father before. Hunahpú was restored to life, however, and the twins began a cunning campaign. They killed each other in turn, restoring each other to life after every killing. The lords of Xibalba watched all these rebirths with astonishment, and eventually asked if they, too, could be killed and brought back to life. The twins agreed readily, and killed all the lords of the underworld, but did not bring them back to life, so they were forced to remain in Xibalba and no longer walk the earth.[3]

Dracula

The legend of Count Dracula is partially founded on the historical figure of Vlad the Impaler (c. 1431–1476), Prince of Wallachia in Romania. He was called Vlad Dracula, the second son of his father, Prince Vlad Dracul. Stories spread of his unusual cruelty during his lifetime. He was called the Impaler because he impaled many victims on sharpened wooden stakes, making them die a slow and agonizing death. According to a contemporary witness, in 1463 Vlad had two Christian monks impaled, and, while they were still dying, also impaled their donkey, because its piteous braying was annoying him. According to contemporary German reports, he impaled mothers and their babies on the same stake. He also enjoyed watching victims being slowly boiled to death. He was said to have killed over 100,000 victims, the majority of them Ottoman Turks, most of them by impaling.[4]

When Irish author Bram Stoker wrote his novel *Dracula* (1897), he borrowed the name Dracul or Dracula (Son of the Dragon) from the historical Vlad Dracula, but apart from the name, there is little evidence of any other connection. By the end of the 19th century, vampire bats (see *Camazotz* above) and their habits were known. Among all the other details of vampire literature conventions, e.g., sleeping in a coffin, being unable to tolerate sunlight, etc., the convention of Dracula being able to shape-shift into a flying vampire bat came into being. It was a natural connection to make, and the association of vampires with bats has become more and more solid ever since.

Aardvark (*Orycteropus afer*)

Phylum *Chordata*, Class *Mammalia*, Order *Tubulidentata*, Family *Orycteropodidae*, Genus *Orycteropus*, Species *Orycteropus afer*

Name

The order name *Tubulidentata* means having tubular teeth—the aardvark is the only surviving member of this order. The genus name *Orycteropus* means burrowing-footed. The species name *afer* means African.

Description

The aardvark is a burrowing, nocturnal animal common to the southern two-thirds of the African continent. It has long, rabbit-like ears. It feeds on ants and termites, using its powerful claws to dig into the nests and its long, pig-like snout to root out the insects. It looks somewhat similar to the South American anteater, and it eats ants, but it is from a completely different order and family. (Anteaters belong to the order *Pilosa*, Latin for hairy, and the suborder *Vermilingua*, which means worm-tongued.)

General Attributes

The aardvark is generally admired in African cultures because of its persistence. It also stands up for itself. When confronted by an overwhelming adversary, it will rapidly dig itself an escape hole in the ground and wait patiently until it can crawl out backwards to safety.

Hausa Mythology

The Hausa people, who are concentrated mainly in Nigeria and Niger, worship the aardvark for its diligence and perseverance in seeking food and for its bravery in ignoring bites from powerful soldier ants. Hausa priests make a protective charm from aardvark body parts, which are ground together, wrapped in a leaf, and then worn as a necklace. The charm is supposed to allow the wearer to pass through walls and roofs, and is used in folk tales by robbers and secret midnight lovers. The peculiarly shaped tubular aardvark teeth are also used to make protective bracelets.

Pangolin (Several Species)

Phylum *Chordata*, Class *Mammalia*, Clade *Scrotifera*, Clade *Fereuungulata*, Order *Pholidota*, Family *Manidae*, Genus (3 extant), Species (8)

Name

The name pangolin sounds more like a musical instrument than an animal. It is derived from the Malay word *pengguling*, which means literally "one who rolls up." The order name *Pholidota* comes from Greek φολισ, *pholís*, which means hairy scale.

Description

Pangolins are found in Africa and Asia. They are the only mammals with large keratin scales all over their bodies, which makes them look reptilian. They have long snouts and tongues to pry out their main food, ants and termites. When threatened, they roll themselves into a tight ball, presenting their hard keratin scales towards the attacker. They are hunted for their meat and their scales. Of the eight extant species, four are vulnerable, two are endangered, and two are critically endangered.

General Attributes

Pangolins are nocturnal, solitary and very strange-looking, so they seem mysterious. On the other hand, they are the most trafficked animal in the world.[5] Their strangeness makes them vulnerable: the mysterious scales are deemed to have magical healing properties.

Asian Trafficking

Pangolin scales, like rhinoceros horns, are made merely from keratin, the same stuff that makes nails and hair. Nevertheless, the ground-up, powdered scales are widely believed to cure many diseases in China and Vietnam, especially asthma and various cancers, including lung cancer. An estimated 100,000 animals are illegally traded to China and Vietnam each year.[6] The Chinese film actor Jackie Chan has contributed generously to the worldwide effort to save the pangolin from extinction.

Echidna (Several Species)

Phylum *Chordata*, Class *Mammalia*, Order *Monotremata*, Suborder *Tachyglossa*, Family *Tachyglossidae*, Genus (4 extant), Species (4)

Name

Echidna was a monster in Greek mythology, half-woman and half-snake. She gave birth to several other monsters. The family name *Tachyglossa* is New Latin, from Greek ταξυς, *tachys*, quick, and γλωσσα, *glōssa*, tongue.

Description

The four extant species of echidna or spiny anteater and the platypus (see below) are the only mammals that lay eggs. Echidnas evolved from a platypus-like animal somewhere between 20 million and 50 million years ago. They eat ants and termites, like the true anteaters of the Americas, but they are not actually closely related. They are black or brown in color, covered with spines and coarse hairs. They have powerful digging claws. They have long, narrow snouts and long tongues to seek out their insect prey. Like the platypus, they have an unusually low body temperature for a mammal, normally about 33 degrees C (about 91 degrees Fahrenheit). They live for about 15 years in the wild, but, because of their low metabolism, have survived for 50 years in captivity.

General Attributes

Echidnas are solitary, very timid animals. They burrow into undergrowth in the forest, or take shelter in hollows and caves during bad weather. Their appearance and behavior make them exotic and mysterious.

An Australian Emblem

Three of the extant species, of the genus *Zaglossus*, live in New Guinea. The fourth, *Tachyglossus aculeatus* (quick-tongued barbed), or short-beaked echidna, is found across the whole of Australia, wherever ants and termites can be found for food, including urban areas. They can be picked up easily: like hedgehogs, they roll themselves into a defensive ball and can be held comfortably in two hands. Aboriginal Australians regard the echidna as a food delicacy. The echidna is depicted on the reverse of the Australian five-cent coin.

Platypus (*Ornithorhynchus anatinus*)

Phylum *Chordata*, Class *Mammalia*, Order *Monotremata*, Family *Ornithorhynchidae*, Genus *Ornithorhynchus*, Species *Ornithorhynchus anatinus*

Name

The common name platypus means broad footed, from Greek πλατυς, *platús*, broad or flat, and πους, *pous*, foot. The genus name *Platypus* was already in use for a type of beetle, so in 1800 Johann Blumenbach (1752–1840) named the animal *Ornithorhynchus anatinus*, meaning duck-like bird snout.

Description

The platypus, also called the duck-billed platypus, is found in Australia. When the first specimen (a drawing and a skin) was brought back to Europe, it was thought to be a practical joke: the animal was so peculiar as to be impossible. It is a mammal but lays eggs, it has a beaver's tail, it has webbed feet like an otter, and it has a poison spur that can inflict severe pain to humans. It uses a system called electroreception or electrolocation to locate prey: it can detect the electric fields created by muscle contractions in other animals.

General Attributes

The platypus is one of the most peculiar animals in the world. It is indigenous to eastern Australia and Tasmania. It features in the coat of arms of New South Wales and on the reverse of the Australian 20-cent coin.

Djanbun

In Australian Aboriginal mythology, Djanbun was going walkabout in the mountains and was carrying a fire stick (a smoldering branch taken from a previous fire to kindle a new fire). He blew and blew, but he could not get the glowing end to burst into full flame. Some sparks fell off the end and turned into gold nuggets when they hit the ground, but Djanbun had no use for gold—what he wanted was fire to cook his food. Djanbun blew and blew again. He felt his lips begin to grow larger and hotter. Fearing that he had set his own mouth alight, he threw himself into a nearby stream. Immediately, he turned into a platypus. To this day, natives blow on fire sticks very gently, for fear of turning into a platypus.[7]

Kangaroo/Wallaroo/Wallaby (Several Species)

Phylum *Chordata*, Class *Mammalia*, Infraclass *Marsupialia*, Order *Diprotodontia*, Family *Macropodidae*, Genus *Macropus*, Subgenus *Macropus, Osphranter*, Species (4)

Name

The name kangaroo is from the aboriginal Guugu Yumithirr word *gangurru*, which was first recorded in 1770 CE as *kangaru* by the English naturalist Sir Joseph Banks (1743–1820). There is a legend that when the colonizing British pointed at the animals and asked the Guugu Yumithirr natives what the animal was called, their reply, "Gangurru," actually meant, "I do not understand." However, the legend has subsequently been disproved, and the word did in fact refer to the animal. The genus name *Macropus* is from Greek, and means large foot.

Description

The kangaroo is a marsupial, which means that it has a pouch in which to carry its young. Other marsupials include koalas, opossums, wombats and Tasmanian devils. Kangaroos are indigenous to Australia. Small kangaroos are called wallabies and intermediate-sized kangaroos are called wallaroos. Kangaroos metaphorically have five legs, since the large, strong tail is used significantly in locomotion. The two back legs are large and very powerful, enabling the animal to reach speeds of up to 43 miles per hour (70 kilometers per hour) over short distances. The front limbs are very small by comparison. Kangaroos are the only large animals to use hopping as their main means of locomotion.

General Attributes

Kangaroos have been sacred to Australian Aboriginal peoples for millennia. They are valued for their meat, hide and bones. They are connected to the universal Dreamtime mythology, and feature in many aspects of aboriginal culture, including dance and art. As a symbol of the nation of Australia, the kangaroo is very familiar. It appears with the emu on the Australian Coat of Arms.

The First Kangaroo

The peoples of South-East Australia say that the first kangaroo appeared when a great wind came to the land.

> His back legs stretched longer and longer as he tried to gain a footing on the ground, but no sooner did he touch it than the wind swept him up into the air again. If his hind legs and tail had not grown as long and strong as they did, he would never have alighted except in the sea, where he would have been drowned. The people hunted the first kangaroo. The meat was superb, the hide was beautiful, the bones were large and strong, and the tendons could be used for many useful purposes. The Great Spirit had answered their prayers.[8]

How the Kangaroo Got Her Pouch

According to one legend, a kangaroo baby (a joey) became so hot and bothered one day that he was desperate for shade, but there was none to be found. So he launched himself at his mother's belly and stretched her belly until it formed a pouch for him to take shelter in. He jumped in, and from that day onward, all kangaroo mothers have pouches for their joeys.[9]

Thoorkook and Byama

In *Some Myths and Legends of the Australian Aborigines* (1923), W.J. Thomas tells the story of how the hero Byama and his younger brother took their revenge on the monster Thoorkook for having killed their families:

> Byama and his brother changed themselves into giant kangaroos, and set out to kill Thoorkook and his brutal dogs. The dogs chased them, but one by one the brothers killed them.
> Then they changed themselves back into men and went to Thoorkook's camp. Thorkook picked up his spears and shield, and the great fight between Byama and Thorkook began. They hurled spears at each other until they were both almost exhausted. Finally, Byama threw a spear with such ferocity that it shattered Thorkook's shield and pierced him in the throat.
> The brothers rejoiced. They turned Thorkook's body into a mopoke, a dismal night bird with a very harsh cry. When they returned to their camp, the brothers found the mothers still weeping for their lost children, so they turned them into curlews, and their cries are still mournful to this day.[10]

19

Weasels, Otters and Badgers (*Mustelidae*)

Weasel/Stoat/Ermine (Several Species)

Phylum *Chordata*, Class *Mammalia*, Order *Carnivora*, Family *Mustelidae*, Subfamily *Mustelinae*, Genus *Mustela*, Type species *Mustela erminea*, Species (17 extant)

Name

Weasel is a Germanic word. It was *weosule*, meaning cunning, in Old English. The name stoat appears in Middle English as *stote*, but the original derivation is unclear. Ermine, the name given to a stoat in its white winter coat, is from Old French *hermine*, and may be derived from Medieval Latin *Mus armenius*, Armenian mouse. The genus name *Mustela* is from Latin *mustella*, weasel.

Description

In Britain, the name weasel usually refers to the small animal (about 7 inches or 180 millimeters), *Mustela nivalis*, but in America and the rest of the world, weasel is a generic term for several different animals, including minks, ferrets, stoats and polecats, which are generally larger, sometimes much larger, in size. (The family *Mustelidae* also includes badgers and otters—see below.) Weasels are generally long-bodied and short-legged, brown or reddish-brown and white in color, with some species becoming all white in winter.

General Attributes

In Greek legends, weasels usually were bad omens, often foretelling death. (In Macedonian myths, however, they were considered lucky.) In some American Indian cultures, to see a weasel cross your path was an omen of imminent death. Weasels of every kind have generally been considered cunning and untrustworthy.

Galanthis

Book 9 of Ovid's *Metamorphoses* tells the story of Galanthis (Weasel) who helped bring the hero Herakles into the world:

> Galanthis was a maid to Alcmena, wife of Amphitryon. Alcmena was close to delivering her son Herakles. Unknown to Alcmena, Zeus's wife Hera was determined that Herakles should not be born, and had instructed Eilithyia, goddess of childbirth, to obstruct the birth. Eilithyia did this by lying down with her legs crossed and her hands clasped together. Quick-witted and sensitive, Galanthis guessed that some powerful magic might be at work. Suddenly, she began clapping her hands and praising her mistress for the successful delivery of her child. Alcmena, still in agony, could not understand why Galanthis was telling such a wicked lie.
>
> However, Eilithyia also heard Galanthis. Believing that Herakles had already been born despite her spells, she unclasped her hands and uncrossed her legs. Immediately, Alcmena gave birth, and Herakles was safely delivered.
>
> When Eilithyia discovered how Galanthis had tricked her, she transformed the maid into a weasel as punishment, and that is how weasels came to be common pets in ancient Greek households.[1]

In Japanese Folklore

In Japan, weasels are deemed to be the cause of strange events, usually unpleasant or unwanted events. They are often accused of starting fires. They are said to shapeshift into human form, like the *kitsune* or fox. They are believed to live for centuries, sometimes turning into badgers when they are old enough.

Ferret/Polecat (*Mustela putorius furo*)

Phylum *Chordata*, Class *Mammalia*, Order *Carnivora*, Family *Mustelidae*, Subfamily *Mustelinae*, Genus *Mustela*, Species *Mustela putorius*, Subspecies *Mustela putorius furo*

Name

The etymology of the name ferret is interesting. Ancient Greek φωρ, *phōr*, meant thief. It came into Latin as *fur*, meaning thief, knave or villain, and was a common insult used against slaves or common people of low status. The Late Latin *furo* came into Old French as *fuiron*. The Anglo-Normans made this *fuiret*, which in turn became English ferret. The pole- part of polecat is from French *poule* or *pole*, chicken—so, a cat-like animal that steals chickens. *Putorius* is Latin for stinking, so the species name *Mustela putorius furo* means the not very complimentary "little stinking thief mouse-like animal."

Description

Ferrets are about 20 inches (51 centimeters) long, usually brown, black and white. They have been domesticated as hunting animals (usually to hunt rabbits) for over 2,500 years, but in modern times they are frequently kept just as pets. There are estimated to be about 800,000 pet ferrets in the United States alone. They are also used extensively as laboratory animals in biomedical research. They are related and very similar in appearance to polecats, with which they frequently hybridize.

General Attributes

Ferrets are lively, curious animals. They show affection quite readily towards humans, but they can also inflict a nasty bite if angered or threatened. In Britain, there is a strange folk tradition of ferret owners stuffing the animals inside their pants to show how brave they are, risking very painful and potentially damaging bites to their most tender and susceptible parts.

Bajang

In Malaysian mythology, the polecat god Bajang visits households to foretell disaster. It mews like a frustrated cat, and may remain invisible, or appear and then disappear. Children wear black silk threads called *bajang* bracelets to protect themselves from the evil god, which carries disease as well as bad news. The *bajang* can be tamed and kept as a familiar, fed regularly on eggs and milk. Its master can send it out to bring sickness to any chosen victim, and only magical healing will get rid of the disease. But if the master ever neglects the *bajang*, it will turn on its owner and infect him instead.[2]

Otter (Several Species)

Phylum *Chordata*, Class *Mammalia*, Order *Carnivora*, Family *Mustelidae*, Subfamily *Lutrinae*, Type genus *Lutra*, Genus (8 extant), Species (13 extant)

Name

Otter was *otor* or *oter* in Old English. It comes from the same Proto-Indo-European root that gave us the word water. The Latin type genus name *Lutra* comes from the same root, but the additional L at the beginning of the word is unexplained.

Description

There are 13 extant species of otter, all of them living in or near freshwater or sea coasts, and living almost entirely on fish, shellfish, frogs and invertebrates. They have powerful, webbed front feet, they can hold their breath for long periods, and they are extremely fast and athletic swimmers. Their fur, which has been highly prized by humans for centuries, is double-layered to keep them warm in cold water. Their feces, which are called spraints, often have a powerful smell, something like wet hay mixed with rotting fish.

General Attributes

Otters are renowned for their delight in play. The cubs stay with their parents for longer than many other young animals, and otter mating bonds are very strong, so they have come to symbolize happy family life. They transition easily between two of the Celtic three worlds—land (where humans live) and water (where the dead live), so they are seen in Druidism as emissaries between the living and the ancestors.

Otter Skin

Otter skin was held to be magical by the Celts. Wearing an otter skin would make a warrior invincible. Otter skins were nailed to the inside of shields for protection. The skin could also be worn tied about the wrist as a charm against drowning, since no otter could ever drown—it swims faster and more athletically than most fish.

The magical properties of otter skin (particularly against drowning) are also recalled in the extraordinary life of a historical but also semi-legendary North American Indian known by his Mohawk epithet Skennenrahawi, which means Great Peacemaker. His personal name was Dekanawida or Deganawidah, which means Two River Currents Flowing Together. Sometime during the 15th century, he and two other famous Indian leaders, Jigonshasee and Hiawatha, formed the Haudenosaunee or Iroquois Confederacy. (See *Hiawatha and Atotarho*, Chapter 36.) This was a very early example of Indian nations working together to strengthen and protect themselves by mutual cooperation. The existence and strength of the confederacy greatly influenced the American struggle for independence and, indeed, the American Constitution itself. Benjamin Franklin said that "six nations of ignorant savages" had achieved a strong and long-lasting political unity that would be beyond the capabilities of the American colonies as they then stood.

Dekanawida was said to have been born of a virgin. His mother had been warned in a vision that her son would bring tragedy to the Hurons, so three times she drowned him in a river and left his body to float away, but each morning following the drownings the baby reappeared by her side. Needing to demonstrate his powers of prophecy when the Mohawk challenged the confederacy, he climbed to the top of a tall tree and ordered the tree to be chopped down. He was thrown into the turbulent, icy waters of the Mohawk River and was presumed dead, but he returned the next day, as he had promised he would. The Seneca nation were the last to join the confederacy, and when violence broke out during their discussions, Dekanawida waved his hand and the sun became dark, ending the fighting. (Some scholars argue that the legend is based on a recorded solar eclipse in 1451 CE). When Dekanawida left his mother's home, he nailed an otter skin to the wall. He predicted to his mother that if he died a violent death the otter skin would vomit blood.[3]

The Bahá'í Faith predicts the periodic emergence of a new Prophet. For many American Indian (and some non-native) Bahá'ís, Dekanawida was such a Prophet, and was a Manifestation of God, or the Divine Spirit.

Andvari and Otter

In Norse mythology, Andvari is a dwarf who is tricked into losing his riches by the mischievous god Loki. The story features Andvari's powerful magic ring, which Loki steals. Loki also kills an otter, which turns out to be the son of the king of the dwarfs. Andvari curses the lost ring, and a series of tragic events follows.[4]

The legend formed the basis for Wagner's huge cycle of four operas *Der Ring des Ni-*

belungen, often just called *The Ring*, where Andvardi is called Alberich, meaning Elf Rule. Wagner's story is vastly more complex than the Andvardi legend, but begins with the notion of the magical ring of great power. J.R.R. Tolkien's *Lord of the Rings* probably owes something to both Aldvardi and Wagner, and there is something otter-like about the original discovery of the ring by Déagol in a riverbed and the theft of the ring by Déagol's brother Sméagol (who becomes Gollum, a slick and slithery creature who eats raw fish and stays close to water, like an otter).

Saint Cuthbert

A rare but charming Christian legend concerning the otter is that of Saint Cuthbert (died 687 CE) living on the holy island of Lindisfarne in Northumberland, England. One night, after a day of fasting and penance, Cuthbert lay on the freezing cold pebbles next to the sea, exhausted and frozen almost to the point of death. Two otters emerged from the sea and licked his feet and hands earnestly, until he finally revived and was able to stagger back into the monastery.[5]

Badger (Several Species)

Phylum *Chordata*, Class *Mammalia*, Order *Carnivora*, Suborder *Caniformia*, Superfamily *Musteloidea*, Family *Mustelidae*, Subfamily (3), Genus (5 extant), Species (11 extant)

Name

The name badger comes from a 16th-century word *bageard*, meaning badge, which presumably refers to the distinctive white stripe on the head of the European badger. The older nickname Brock is borrowed from ancient Celtic *brogh*.

Description

Badgers are strong, stoutish members of the Mustelid family, European badgers being the largest and the ferret badger the smallest. They have strong front claws for digging, and unusually powerful jaws. They live in a burrowed chamber called a sett, which may have several tunnels and entrances.

General Attributes

European badgers have been hunted with terriers or baited (held captive and tortured by larger dogs, usually ending in the badger's death) for centuries, although in many countries the practice is now illegal. Badgers were either fought in their setts, or even extracted and placed in boxes, and then had dogs set on them. They would defend themselves furiously, often killing several dogs before they were killed themselves, thus providing plenty of bloody entertainment and betting opportunities for the onlookers. The German dachshund (badger hound) was bred for badger baiting.

Dzoavits and Badger

Dzoavits is an evil, cannibalistic monster in the mythology of the North American Indian Shoshone nation. He stole the Sun, and kidnapped children to eat them.

In one of his legends, he stole two of Dove's children. Eagle came to Dove's aid, and rescued the children. However, Dzoavits continued to plague Dove and try to seize her young ones. Badger dug two holes, and hid Dove and her family in one of them. When Dzoavits next appeared and asked where Dove and her children were, Badger pointed to the second hole. Dzoavits went into the hole, and Badger immediately threw in hot rocks and sealed Dzoavits inside. Devil's Hole, a large cave in Nye County, Nevada, is reputed to be the second hole dug by Badger.[6]

Tanuki Bozo

In Japanese folklore, the badger Tanuki Bozo disguises himself as a Buddhist monk. He brings good luck and prosperity, but he can also be a trickster and waylay or deceive foolish or naive people.

Badger-Hair Brushes

Badger hairs hold a lot of water. For this reason, badger hairs have been used to make brushes for centuries. The traditional soap-and-water shaving brush is made from badger hair. Painting brushes have also traditionally been made of badger hair. Nowadays, most badger hair comes from farmed animals in China.

20

Seals and Walruses (*Pinnipedia*)

Seal (Several Genera and Species)

Phylum *Chordata*, Class *Mammalia*, Order *Carnivora*, Clade *Pinnipedia*, Superfamily *Phocoidea*, Family *Phocidae*, Genus (14)

Name

Seal is a Germanic name, written in Old English as *seolh*. Middle Dutch *seel*, Old High German *selah*, Middle Low German *sale* and modern Danish *sæl* are all very similar. The clade name *Pinnipedia* is New Latin, coined from Greek words meaning fin-footed. The Pinnipeds were not identified as separate taxonomically until 1842. The family name *Phocidae* simply means seals, from Latin *phoca*, a seal.

Description

Pinnipeds include seals, sea lions and walruses. Perhaps surprisingly, their nearest relatives are bears and mustelids, like weasels, skunks, raccoons and red pandas. Pinnipeds have obviously evolved with front limbs shaped like flippers and rear limbs tucked under to form part of a tail-like rear of the body to facilitate swimming. There are 33 extant species of pinniped, and they spend most of their time in the cold seas of the Arctic and the Antarctic, or more generally of the temperate and cooler northern and southern regions.

General Attributes

In the Celtic tradition of the Three Worlds, the sea is the world of the dead, and the sea is where the seal lives. Although they are not human in size or shape, their large eyes and round faces are very expressive, and there are many legends that either turn seals into people or people into seals. Several of these stories are about loss and longing, or about mistaken identity, so there is often a vein of sadness or tragedy running through the narrative.

Seals are vital food animals for many peoples of the Arctic and sub-Arctic regions. They therefore also figure largely in Northern European and Northern American mythology and folklore.

Seal Families

In the Celtic Druidic tradition, whole clans and families are reputed to have descended from the union of humans and seals. They include: Clan MacCodrum (Of the Seals—see *Selkies* below) from North Uist in the Outer Hebrides; the Coneelys, Cregans and Hennessys from Ireland; the O'Sullivans of County Kerry; and the MacNamaras, whose name means Sons of the Sea-Hound (i.e., seal).[1]

Selkies

The name selkie derives from the Scottish word *selch*, which refers to the common gray seal (*Halichoerus grypus*). There are many variant spellings, including silkie, selchie and saelkie. The Scottish Gaelic name for a selkie is *maighdeann-ròin*, literally seal maiden, but in written tales the similar term *maighdeann-mhara* or sea maiden is more commonly found. The many selkie tales often involve a female seal leaving her skin so that she can appear as a woman in the human world, but then having her seal skin stolen and hidden by a man, who thus maintains a coercive power relationship over her. The tales are found in Scotland, Ireland, Orkney, Shetland and Iceland. Often the women end up having human children (frequently against their will) and then have to face the dilemma of whether to live out their lives in the human world, which is alien to them, or return to their ocean homes and abandon their human families.

Sometimes the genders are reversed, and the selkie is a male who comes to land to seek a female human as a wife or lover. Male selkies, according to folklore, are overpoweringly handsome and seductive. They deliberately seek out restless or unsatisfied women (such as fishermen's wives, tired of their husbands being away at sea for so long). The handsome selkie's advances are said to be irresistible, even for the most devoutly faithful women.

Children of mixed selkie-human marriages or relationships are easily recognized. They have webbed hands or feet, or failing that, prominent arcs of skin between their fingers and toes. Or they may simply show an extraordinary interest in swimming in the sea, or catching and eating fish. The MacCodrum clan of the Outer Hebrides had a genetic condition called syndactyly, in which webs of skins formed between their fingers, and were always called in full "the MacCodrums of the Seals."

Selkie legends abound in the various islands and archipelagoes to the north and west of Scotland, notably Orkney, Shetland, Iceland and the Faroes. In one Icelandic tale, first recorded by Jón Guðmundsson the Learned in 1641, a man comes across a group of selkies or sea elves (*marmennlar*) dancing and carousing in a sea cave:

> The cave was lined with the seal skins of the dancing elves. As soon as the elves took notice of the man, they rushed to don their skins and dive back into the ocean. However, the man was able to steal the smallest of the skins, sliding it underneath his clothes. The owner of the skin tried to retrieve her skin from the man but he quickly took hold of the young elf and took her to his home to be his wife. The man and the elf were together for two years, producing two children, a boy and a girl, but the elf harbored no love for the man. During this time, the former elf woman's elf husband swam along the shore by the couple's home, calling her name piteously and begging her to return to her home. One day, the elf woman found her skin, and ran away, never to be seen again.[2]

A charming and sad song, *Peter Kagan and the Wind*, by American folk-singer Gordon Bok (b. 1939) tells the tale of the fisherman Peter Kagan, who marries a selkie. The couple enjoy a very happy life together. However, one day, despite his wife's warnings, Kagan sails out in rough weather and is trapped in his sinking boat. His wife rescues him and carries him back to the shore, but, having changed back into her form as a seal, she can never become human again, so they must live apart for ever.

Several films have been made about selkie legends, the two most notable being *The Secret of Roan Inish* (1994), filmed in the west of Ireland, and *Song of the Sea* (2014), a heart-breaking Irish animation about a young boy whose selkie mother disappears.

Sea Lion (Several Genera and Species)

Phylum *Chordata*, Class *Mammalia*, Order *Carnivora*, Clade *Pinnipedia*, Family *Otariidae*, Subfamily *Otariinae*, Genus (5)

Name

The common name is obvious. The subfamily name *Otariinae* comes from Greek ὠτάριον, *hótarion*, which means little ears (see *Description*).

Description

The sea lion is distinguishable from seals by several features: small external ears or ear flaps; long fore-flippers; short, thick fur; a big chest and belly; and the ability to walk on all fours, albeit rather clumsily. They are found mainly in South America, on the west coast of North America, notably California, and in Australia and New Zealand.

General Attributes

Sea lions are popular entertainers in captivity: they can be trained to perform many amusing antics. In the wild, however, they are far less popular, mostly because they are more aggressive and temperamental than seals. They eat larger prey, often exactly the same fish that fishermen take in great numbers, so there is a natural tension and spirit of competition there. Sea lions have attacked and mauled several people, notably close to the shoreline between San Diego and San Francisco. In 2007, a sea lion leapt out of the sea in western Australia and seriously mauled a 13-year-old girl who was water-skiing.[3]

In Native American Indian traditions, by contrast, sea lions are associated with wealth and prosperity, and have high status, particularly among the tribes of the Pacific Northwest.

Potlatch Traditions and Regalia

A *potlatch* (from the Chinook and Nootka languages) is a traditional ceremony, generally amongst Indian tribes of the Pacific Northwest, in which gifts are exchanged and personal property sometimes destroyed to demonstrate wealth, power and generosity. It is similar to (and related to) the English word potluck, which means a communal meal where participants all bring food items to be shared out between everybody. Sea lion images are often used in potlatch decorations, because they symbolize wealth and strength. Sea lion whiskers are sewn into headdresses. Sea lion heads or faces are often carved into totem poles. Some tribes, including the Tlingit and the Haida, use the sea lion as their clan or tribal totem.[4]

Natsilane and the First Killer Whale

Natsilane is the hero of a sea lion myth of the Tlingits. In a similar way to the Algonquin hero Akaiyan, who lived with beavers and learned magic and medicine from them (see Chapter Seventeen), Natsilane was rescued by sea lions, lived among them, and learned from them. Using the magic skills and knowledge he had acquired, he later took a piece of cedar wood and carved it into a huge, black and white fish—the first orca or killer whale (see Chapter Twenty-One).[5]

Walrus (*Odobenus rosmarus*)

Phylum *Chordata*, Class *Mammalia*, Order *Carnivora*, Clade *Pinnipedia*, Family *Odobenidae*, Genus *Odobenus*, Species *Odobenus rosmarus*

Name

The etymology of the common name is uncertain. It seems to be Germanic. The wal- part, like Dutch *walvis*, could mean whale. The -rus part may be cognate with the *hross* in Old Norse *hrossvalr*, literally horse-whale. So walrus may be **walhross*, "whale-horse."

The genus name *Odobenus*, coined by Mathurin Brisson in 1762, is interesting. Οδους, *odous* is Greek for tooth, and βαινω, *bainō*, is Greek for walk, so the combination means "tooth walk"—which must have been based on the observation that walruses often pull themselves out of the sea by sinking their tusks into the ice first and them hauling themselves up literally by the skin of their teeth. The species name *rosmarus* is Scandinavian (*rosmhvalr* in Iceland, *rostungr* in Greenland), and means horse of the sea.

Description

The walrus is the only surviving member of the family *Odobenidae* and the genus *Odobenus*. It is seal-like in shape, but much larger. Only elephant seals are bigger. Adult bull walruses in the Pacific can weigh more than 2,000 kilograms (4,400 pounds). They can move on land or ice, as well as in water, but with that bulk the best they can manage on land is a shuffle—but even that can be quite fast when bulls are fighting each other to secure a female mate. Males have prominent tusks and whiskers. They are highly social animals, living in large groups within two species, *Odobenus rosmarus*, which lives in shallow waters or on sea ice in the Atlantic Ocean, and *Odobenus divergens* (turning apart, describing the tusks) in the Pacific Ocean.

General Attributes

Walruses used to be hunted as extensively as whales. As with whales, every part of the animal had some useful purpose: the meat was often stored overwinter, and walrus flippers were considered a great delicacy; the bones were used as tools; the tough hide made all sorts of tarpaulins and other coverings; the guts were used to make waterproof jackets, boots and parkas; the oil was used for heating and lighting; and the tusks were often used for ornamental carvings. (The famous Lewis Chessmen from the Isle of Lewis in Scotland's Outer Hebrides are carved from walrus tusks.) Today, only the Chukchi, Yupik and Inuit peoples are allowed to hunt walrus, and they have to stick to quotas. Walruses figure prominently in the religions and mythologies of many far northern peoples.

The Woman at the Bottom of the Sea

The principal sea deity for the Inuit/Eskimo people is Sedna (see **fulmar**, Chapter 25). Her counterpart in Chukchi mythology is the old woman with the head of a walrus who lives at the bottom of the sea. She has many names and nicknames, because—like Sedna—she is also the goddess of the dead.

According to the Inuit legend, Raven placed the Sun and Moon in the sky. When an evil magician stole them, Raven seduced the magician's daughter in order to get them back and replace them on high. In fury, the magician threw his daughter from a high cliff, and as she fell she shape-shifted into a walrus, becoming Sedna, the goddess of the sea and of the dead.

The Walrus and the Carpenter

In December 1871, Lewis Carroll's *Through the Looking-Glass* appeared, and in it was the famous poem about the walrus and the carpenter eating a meal of oysters. Although walruses do eat oysters, they eat many other things besides, and the many complex and sophisticated interpretations of the poem's symbolism are probably as useless and empty as shucked oyster shells. The poem ends:

> "A loaf of bread," the Walrus said,
> "Is what we chiefly need:
> Pepper and vinegar besides
> Are very good indeed—
> Now if you are ready, Oysters dear,
> We can begin to feed!"
>
> "But not on us!" the Oysters cried,
> Turning a little blue.
> "After such kindness, that would be
> A dismal thing to do!"
> "The night is fine," the Walrus said.
> "Do you admire the view?"
>
> "It was so kind of you to come!
> And you are very nice!"
> The Carpenter said nothing but
> "Cut us another slice:

I wish you were not quite so deaf—
I've had to ask you twice!"

"It seems a shame," the Walrus said,
"To play them such a trick,
After we've brought them out so far,
And made them trot so quick!"
The Carpenter said nothing but
"The butter's spread too thick!"

"I weep for you," the Walrus said.
"I deeply sympathize!"
With sobs and tears he sorted out
Those of the largest size,
Holding his pocket-handkerchief
Before his streaming eyes.

"O Oysters," said the Carpenter,
"You've had a pleasant run!
Shall we be trotting home again?"
But answer came there none—
And this was scarcely odd, because
They'd eaten every one.[6]

21

Whales, Dolphins, Porpoises and Sirens (*Cetartiodactyla, Delphiniodae, Sirenia*)

Whale (Several Species)

Phylum *Chordata*, Class *Mammalia*, Order *Cetartiodactyla*, Clade *Cetancodontamorpha*, Suborder *Whippomorpha*, Infraorder *Cetacea*, Parvorder *Mysticeti* (baleen whales), *Odontoceti* (toothed whales), Family (8 extant)

Name

Whale is a Germanic word. In Old English it was written *hwæl*. It comes from a Proto-Indo-European source related to Greek ασπαλος, *áspalos* and Latin *squalus*, both meaning great fish. The infraorder name *Cetacea* comes from Greek κετος, *ketos*, also meaning great fish, which became *cetus* in Latin.

Description

The *Cetacea* are divided into two parvorders (part or small orders): the 70 or so species of *Odontoceti*, or toothed whales, include dolphins, orca, porpoises, beluga whales, narwhals, sperm whales and beaked whales; the *Mysticeti* or baleen whales (from Latin *balæna*) use a filter-feeding system rather than teeth, and consist of 15 species including right whales, bowhead whales and gray whales.

The blue whale (*Balaenoptera musculus*, muscular baleen-feeder) is the largest animal ever known to have existed, the largest measuring almost 100 feet (30 meters) in length and weighing up to 190 tons (173 tonnes). They were hunted almost to extinction until 1966 CE, when the first international protections began.

General Attributes

Whales have been hunted since the Stone Age. As huge creatures willing to give themselves to humans for food, fuel and many other productive uses, they have always been revered in seafaring communities.

Whales feature in many religious and mythological traditions. Their stupendous size and largely unknown nature meant that in many early mythologies they were indiscriminately categorized as terrifying sea monsters. As we have learned more about them, and in particular after modern recording techniques have made the general public more aware of their complex vocalizations and interactions, they have become less terrifying but perhaps even more mysterious: we now know that they regularly undertake huge sea journeys, that they have complex social relationships, and that they communicate extensively with each other, but there is still much more for us to learn about them.

Jonah

The best-known whale in the Bible is the one that swallowed Jonah. The tale itself is told very perfunctorily, in one of the shortest books in the Bible. God commands Jonah to go to Nineveh to preach the gospel. Jonah runs away to sea, but a great storm arises. The sailors cast lots to see who is responsible, and it becomes clear that the fault lies with Jonah. (In British naval slang of the 18th and 19th centuries, a Jonah was anybody who brought bad luck or bad weather to a voyage.) Jonah asks the sailors to throw him overboard. In its entirety, the story runs:

> So they picked Jonah up and threw him into the sea; and the sea ceased from its raging [Jonah 1:15] … But the LORD provided a large fish to swallow up Jonah; and Jonah was in the belly of the fish for three days and three nights [Jonah 1:17] … [Jonah prays] … Then the lord spoke to the fish, and it spewed Jonah out upon the dry land.[1]

The same story occurs in the Qur'an, 37:139–148. The Biblical story is hardly much longer than the five-line verse from the song *It Ain't Necessarily So* in George Gershwin's *Porgy and Bess* (1935).

Nor is it certain, of course, that Jonah's fish was actually a whale, although it's difficult to think what else it might have been. Jonah's three days and three nights seem to foreshadow Christ's time in the tomb, a comparison that Christ himself makes explicit in the New Testament:

> Then some of the scribes and Pharisees said to him [Jesus], "Teacher, we wish to see a sign from you." But he answered them, "An evil and adulterous generation asks for a sign, but no sign will be given to it except the sign of the prophet Jonah. For just as Jonah was for three days and three nights in the belly of the sea-monster, so for three days and three nights the Son of Man shall be in the heart of the earth."[2]

Paikea

In the Maori mythology of New Zealand, Uenuku is the god of rainbows. He is revered especially by the Ngai Tahu *iwi* (people or tribe) of the southern region, and by the Tainui confederation of the western and central regions of North Island.

Ruatapu was Uenuku's eldest son. However, Uenuku raised Ruatapu's elder half-brother, Kahutia-te-rangi, to most preferred status, and Ruatapu was consumed by jealousy. He suffered in silence, until one day he borrowed Kahutia-te-rangi's comb and the god rebuked Ruatapu for daring to use the comb of one high-born, when he himself was of low birth and status (his mother was a slave-wife or concubine). Ruatapu was furious, and vowed to himself that he would bring down Kahutia-te-rangi.

Ruatapu built a great canoe or *waka*. He invited Kahutia-te-rangi and several other sons of Uenuku to join him on the *waka*'s maiden voyage. They paddled out into the ocean in high spirits. What his guests didn't know was that Ruatapu had deliberately cut a hole in the floor of the *waka*, which he covered with his heel while they sped out into deep water.

When they were far out at sea, Ruatapu lifted his heel. The boat rapidly filled with seawater, and Ruatapu went to each son in turn, holding his head under the rising sea to drown him. He knew that he would drown himself too, but in his fury and jealousy he didn't care.

But Kahutia-te-rangi threw himself into the ocean, and then sang a prayer to the right whale, asking for his help. A pod of right whales came to him as he trod water patiently. The *waka* had vanished beneath the waves and all the others had already drowned. The whales lifted Kahutia-te-rangi on their backs in turn, and brought him back safely all the way to shore. In honor of their assistance, Kahutia-te-rangi changed his name to Paikea, and Paikea has been the Maori name for the right whale ever since.[3]

This legend is the basis of the 2002 film *Whale Rider*, which stars Keisha Castle-Hughes as Kahu Paikea Apirana, a 12-year-old girl whose ambition is to become chief of her tribe despite the opposition of her grandfather, Koro Apirana, who believes that only males can be eligible to become chief. The movie was filmed in Whangara, where the original novel by Witi Ihimaera was set. Whangara is a *tapu* or *tabu* (sacred, origin of the English taboo) place to the Ngati Porou *iwi* of North Island.

Native American Whale Gods and Spirits

Glooskap (Liar) is a benevolent trickster god and culture hero sacred to the Abenaki, Penobscot, Maliseet, Passamaquoddy and Micmac peoples. He is a giant, so whenever he travels by sea he rides on the back of Bootup the whale. In payment for his journeys, Glooskap lends Bootup his sacred peace pipe: what humans see as the whale's spout or blowhole is, in fact, Bootup smoking Glooskap's pipe.[4]

Among the Wampanoag, Mohegan and Pequot, the giant and culture hero Moshup or Maushop also sometimes appears as a whale. According to one legend, Moshup loved to eat whale meat, and shared his food generously with the nearby Indian tribes. In return, they gave him vast stocks of tobacco, which he smoked in a great pipe. One day, he knocked the ashes out of his pipe into the ocean, and that's how the island of Nantucket was formed. Moshup warned the tribes that pale-skinned strangers were headed towards their lands, and that they must not let these strangers come ashore, or the tribes would disappear. The tribes ignored his warnings, and Moshup slipped quietly into the ocean to become a whale again, and has never been seen on land since then.[5]

Raven and the Whale

An Athabaskan Indian legend tells how Raven tricked the whale. Raven approached the whale and said that they were cousins. The whale asked for proof, and Raven said that their throats were very similar, if only Whale would be kind enough to open up and let him see inside. Whale foolishly agreed, and Raven spent several days feasting on Whale from the inside, eventually coming out again when Whale's body came to shore and the local fishermen cut him open.[6]

In 1896, an article in *The Pall Mall Gazette* popularized a practice of alternative medicine that probably began in the whaling town of Eden, Australia two or three years earlier. It was believed that climbing inside a whale carcass and remaining there for a few hours would relieve symptoms of rheumatism.[7]

Dolphin (Several Species)

Phylum *Chordata*, Class *Mammalia*, Order *Cetartiodactyla*, Clade *Cetancodontamorpha*, Suborder *Whippomorpha*, Infraorder *Cetacea*, Family (4 extant)

Name

The common name is derived from the Greek name for the animal, δελφις, *delphís*, which is closely related to the word δελφυς, *delphús*, which means womb. Dolphins are *Cetaceans*, like whales. The Medieval Latin name *delfinus* became *daulphin* in Old French. The heir to the throne of France was historically called the Dauphin, because the full title was Dauphin de Viennois, based on the use of the dolphin on the associated coat of arms. The title was used by heirs apparent to the French throne from 1350 to 1791, and again briefly from 1824 to 1830.

Description

There is a great deal of confusion in common parlance between whale, dolphin and porpoise. In scientific taxonomy, the name dolphin refers to those aquatic mammals in the parvorder *Odontoceti* (toothed whales) which belong to either the family of ocean dolphins, *Delphinidae*, or to one of the four families of river dolphins: *Iniidae* (Amazon, South America), *Pontoporiidae* (La Plata, Argentina), *Lipotidae* (Yangtze, China, last observed 2006, possibly now extinct) or *Platanistidae* (Ganges, India). Dolphins have conical teeth, whereas porpoises have more spade-shaped teeth. Dolphins are found in oceans and rivers all over the world, but most species live in warm to hot zones, like the Mediterranean or tropical oceans. There are 40 extant species of dolphin, and there have been several occurrences of hybridization between species.

General Attributes

Dolphins are extraordinary, complex animals. They are believed by some people to be as intelligent as humans, if not more so, and there has probably been more scientific research into dolphin intelligence than into the intelligence of almost every other species—certainly of any aquatic species. Dolphins have been used as active, trained military agents by both the American and the Russian Navy, and they are still used by the USA to this day, although the government denies that they have ever been used in combat. (At the time of writing, 2019, a beluga whale wearing a harness marked with Russian cyrillic script has been observed off the coast of Norway, and has been presumed to be a service animal trained by the Russian Navy.) We know that dolphins have a complicated pattern of vocalizations, so complex that it is often referred to as speech, and attempts to translate

Dolphinese have been ongoing for some years. They also use echo-location in hunting, and perhaps in general communication, too. Dolphins live in groups called pods, sometimes combining into hunting superpods of over 1,000 members, but we still have much to learn about the complexities of their social organization. Female dolphins have been observed teaching tool-using skills to their young. (The tools include small sponges for protection and sticks for digging, and the teaching always takes place between mothers and daughters: fathers and sons are excluded.) Dolphins (including orcas, or killer whales) are kept in captivity and taught acrobatic tricks for public entertainment. There continues to be great controversy about how ethical this practice is, in view of the intelligence and social complexity these animals clearly demonstrate.

With all these complexities, dolphins have acquired sacred or mythical status in many traditions, since ancient times. They have frequently been observed helping their own in sickness or in danger—lifting a calf to the surface to breathe, for example. They have even been seen giving assistance to other species: in New Zealand, a dolphin named Moko was seen to guide a female pygmy sperm whale and her calf safely out of shallow water, where they had been stranded many times.[8] Dolphins are generally depicted as unusually intelligent, sympathetic and helpful animals.

In Greek Myths

Dolphins were revered by the Minoans on Crete. The palace ruins at Knossos contain several depictions of dolphins swimming. Several ancient Greek coins have been found which depict a boy, man or god riding on a dolphin's back. In particular, Eros (later Cupid or Amor), god of love, appears riding a dolphin. Dolphins were sacred to Aphrodite and Apollo.

Dolphins swimming before, beside or behind a boat were always considered a good omen, as they generally still are to this day. They came to be associated with Poseidon, god of the ocean, and their presence always meant that Poseidon was in a favorable mood and would not bring on any sudden, unexpected storms. If sailors saw dolphins, they would pray to Poseidon and give thanks for his bounty.

Dionysus and the Pirates

One legend has the god Dionysus (or Bacchus) being captured by Etruscan pirates. They did not recognize the god, thinking instead that he was a rich noble who could be held for ransom. Dionysus soon disabused them: he turned the masts and spars of the boat into writhing branches and vines, and the oars into slithering snakes. He threw all the pirates overboard by merely flicking his hand, but relented just as they fell into the ocean and turned them instead into dolphins, so that they could be of some service to others to atone for their misdeeds.[9]

Saved by Dolphins

There are two well-known classical Greek legends in which dolphins save humans: The first concerns Arion, who was a *kitharode*, a singer and poet who played the κιθαρα, *kithara* or *cithara* (related to the modern word guitar), meaning lyre. According to the Greek historian Herodotus, Arion was returning by boat from Sicily, where he had won many rich prizes for his singing and playing of the *kithara*. Pirates got news of Arion's journey, and seized his ship. They offered him the choice of committing suicide on board, and they would later bury him on land, or suicide by throwing himself into the water. Arion begged to be given the opportunity to sing one last song. The pirates agreed. Arion improvised a magnificent hymn of praise to Apollo, which attracted several dolphins alongside the ship. At the end of the song, Arion threw himself overboard. One of the dolphins swam beneath him and carried him safely all the way to the sanctuary of Poseidon on the Greek coast.[10] Apollo later placed Arion in the sky as the constellation Delphinus, which means Dolphin (see Chapter 41).

The second, very similar story concerns Telemachus (Τελεμαξος, *Telémaxos*, Far-Fighter), son of the hero Odysseus, who spends years sailing the seas in search of his father. Telemachus also faces death by drowning, and is also rescued by a dolphin and carried safely to shore.

In Hindu Mythology

The river dolphin of the Ganges, *Platanista gangetica*, is sacred to Ganga, the eponymous goddess of the river. The dolphin was one of the animals that announced the descent of Ganga from the heavens. The goddess—like most other Hindu deities—is frequently depicted riding on a specific animal, which for Ganga is sometimes a half-terrestrial, half-aquatic hybrid called the Makara, and sometimes a dolphin.

Pelorus Jack

A 19th-century tale from New Zealand, based on many factual observations, is that of Pelorus Jack, a Risso's dolphin (*Grampus griseus*), which guided ships through the dangerous Cook Strait between Nelson and Wellington. Jack first appeared in 1888, when he appeared in front of a schooner called *Brindle* just as she entered the narrow and very dangerous French Pass between D'Urville Island and the South Island. The crew wanted to kill the dolphin, but the captain's wife talked them out of it. To their joint amazement, Jack guided the schooner safely through the channel. From then until 1912, he continued to guide every other ship that came the same way, until he was such a familiar sight that ships often waited for him to show up before attempting the narrow passageway. He was called Pelorus Jack after nearby Pelorus Sound.

Jack was about 13 feet (4 meters) long and white or pale gray in color. Although he was called Jack, the gender of the dolphin was never clearly determined. Risso's dolphins are very rare in that part of the world, or anywhere for that matter: they are the only extant species of the genus *Grampus*. For a period of about 24 years, from 1888 to 1912, the unmistakable Jack continued his/her service as pilot.

In 1904, a drunken passenger aboard the SS *Penguin* took a shot at Jack. The shot missed, but Jack never came to pilot the SS *Penguin* again, and the ship finally shipwrecked in Cook's Strait in 1909. The New Zealand government introduced legislation to protect him/her—the first time any individual sea-creature was protected by human law anywhere in the world. Jack himself/herself was last seen in April of 1912. Many feared that s/he had been harpooned by a whaler, but it seems more likely that s/he just died of old age, since his/her very pale coloring suggested s/he was old to begin with.[11]

Orca/Killer Whale (*Orcinus orca*)

Phylum *Chordata,* Class *Mammalia,* Order *Artiodactyla,* Infraorder *Cetacea,* Family *Delphinidae,* Genus *Orcinus,* Species *Orcinus orca*

Name

The orca is a dolphin, despite the whale of the common name "killer whale." Orca and the genus name *Orcinus* come from Orcus, a Roman god of the underworld and the dead. The taxonomy is disputed, with four types identified temporarily as A, B, C and D, any or all of which may later come to be designated as different species.

Description

Orca are the largest dolphins, measuring 20 to 26 feet (6 to 8 meters) in length and weighing in excess of 6.6 tons. They are apex predators (are not themselves preyed upon), some eating only fish, others also hunting marine mammals such as seals and sea lions, and even other dolphins.

Orcas, like dolphins generally, have complex social relationships: only humans, other primates, and elephants have similarly extended patterns of interaction. Orcas can live up to 60 years in the wild, and there is evidence of a great deal of cultural activity, including the teaching of the young found in other dolphins. (Campaigners against performing orcas and dolphins being held in captivity argue that the animal equivalent of human rights is being denied to these animals, because their isolation in captivity prevents them from having the full social life they would enjoy in the wild.)

General Attributes

The Roman writer Pliny the Elder first described the orca in about 70 CE, so they have been known even in middle and southern Europe for many centuries, but the vast majority of religious and mythological orca stories come from the north, either from Siberia, or from the northeast states and provinces of the USA and Canada, or from the Pacific Northwest. In all of them, the orca is a figure of power, grace and majesty.

Siberia

The Yupik people of Siberia believe that wolves and orcas are the same animal: they are wolves in winter and orcas in summer. They also believe that when they are hunting walrus, the orcas help them by driving the walrus out of the sea and onto land where they can be killed. Wolves do the same in winter with reindeer. The Yupik regularly drop small packages of tobacco into the sea by way of thanks to the orcas. Most Yupik men wear a small, carved wooden orca on their belts.

In the Pacific Northwest

The Native American peoples of the Pacific Northwest have worshiped the orca for centuries. There is a common belief that humans drowned at sea become orcas. We know this because orcas, mighty and ferocious as they are, do not attack human beings. When a pod of orcas come close to a boat, they are seeking reconnection with human relatives and families. The Tlingit have never hunted orcas, although they are highly skilled hunters of whales generally. The Kwakiutl believe that land hunters turn into wolves when they die and sea hunters turn into orcas. The Tlingit, Tsimshian and Kwakiutl all use the orca as a clan emblem: orcas are frequently carved on totem poles. A common legend is that Orca or Killer Whale was born of the union of Whale and Osprey.[12]

Porpoise (Several Species)

Phylum *Chordata*, Class *Mammalia*, Order *Artiodactyla*, Infraorder *Cetacea*, Parvorder *Odontoceti*, Superfamily *Delphinoidea*, Family *Phocoenidae*, Species (7 extant)

Name

The Anglo-Normans brought the word *pourpois* into early Middle English. It derives ultimately from Latin *porcus*, pig and *piscis*, fish, the whole name therefore meaning "pig-fish." The German cognate is *Meerschwein*, literally "sea pig."

Description

There are seven extant species of porpoise, all very closely related to the dolphin. They are distinguished by shorter beaks and flattish, spade-shaped teeth, whereas dolphin teeth are conical in shape. They reverse the sexual dimorphism found in dolphins: dolphin males are typically larger than females, but in the porpoise species, females are generally larger than males. Porpoises also have different social structures: whereas dolphins may congregate in pods of almost any size, porpoises rarely form a group larger than ten individuals, almost certainly all related to each other. To put it another way, dolphins often travel in clans or tribes, but porpoises travel in small families.

General Attributes

Just like dolphins and orcas, porpoises are highly intelligent animals with complex social relationships. They tend to stay close to coasts, particularly in the Arctic, so they are frequently observed by indigenous fishers and hunters.

Pawang Pukat

The story of Pawang Pukat comes from Malaysian mythology:

Pawang Pukat was a medicine man (*pawang* means medicine man, magician or wizard). He was unfortunate in everything he did, and he resolved to use magic to mend his fortunes, no matter what the cost. One day, after weeks of catching nothing at all in his fishing nets, he asked his friends to help him load his boat with mangrove leaves. He sailed out to the fishing grounds and threw the leaves into the water with the last few handfuls of rice he owned, saying magical prayers over them.

The next day, when he went out to the fishing grounds again, there were so many fish that he could barely find room in his boat for them all. He brought his stupendous catch back to the village, and ordered that the fish be distributed to his family and to all those people to whom he owed money. With his debts all settled and his family provided for, he plunged into the sea, where he became a porpoise. He waved his head from side to side to say goodbye, then swam off to a new and happier life.[13]

Narwhal (*Monodon monoceros*)

Phylum *Chordata*, Class *Mammalia*, Order *Artiodactyla*, Infraorder *Cetacea*, Family *Monodontidae*, Genus *Monodon*, Species *Monodon monoceros*

Name

The English name narwhal or narwhale comes from Old Norse *nár*, corpse, and *hvalr*, whale. Narwhals are a mottled blue-gray or purple-gray in color, like the body of a drowned human, which explains the corpse reference. *Monodon monoceros* is from Greek and means literally "one tooth one horn."

Description

The narwhal is similar to the other toothed whales in many respects, but its single most obviously distinctive feature is its long, thin tusk, formed from the left canine tooth, which may grow to over 10 feet (3 meters). Very occasionally, a male narwhal may grow a second tusk from the right canine tooth, but one tusk is the norm. Female tusks are generally much shorter than male tusks. Males often rub tusks against each other. For a long time, it was thought that this tusking was merely competitive mating season behavior, but closer observation has shown that it is usually accompanied by clicks, whistles and other vocalizations, suggesting that the tusk rubbing is part of a complex package of information sharing.

The narwhal is found only in Arctic waters, so it was a little-known animal for many centuries. Narwhals are medium-sized whales, considerably larger than most dolphins or porpoises.

General Attributes

Until modern times, the narwhal was known only to the indigenous peoples of the Arctic. When narwhal tusks first appeared in Europe, they were assumed to be from unicorns. The Inuit have a legend about the origin of the narwhal. A woman harpooned a narwhal, with the harpoon rope tied about her waist. The whale dragged her into the sea, where she became a whale. Her long hair dragged itself into a thin spiral, and became a long, thin, twisted horn. She was the first narwhal.

Queen Elizabeth I of England (1533–1603 CE) is said to have received a gift of a narwhal tusk from the explorer Sir Humphrey Gilbert. It was carved, gilded, and encrusted with diamonds, and described by Gilbert as coming from a "sea-unicorne." Its estimated value at the time was £10,000 ($13,000), which would be about £2.5 million ($3 million) in today's money.

Dugong (*Dugong dugon*)

Phylum *Chordata*, Class *Mammalia*, Order *Sirenia*, Family *Dugongidae*, Genus *Dugong*, Species *Dugong dugon*

Manatee (Several Species)

Phylum *Chordata*, Class *Mammalia*, Order *Sirenia*, Family *Trichechidae*, Genus *Trichechus*, Species (4)

Name

The dugong and the manatee are Sirens, of the order *Sirenia*. In ancient Greek mythology, a Σειρεν, *Seirén*, was a seductive nymph who lured mariners to their deaths on dangerous rocks. The name dugong comes from the Cebuano languages of the Philippines. The name manatee comes from the Cariban languages of South America (not to be confused with Caribbean). The manatee genus name *Trichechus* is a synonym for *Odobenus*, meaning "tooth walk" (see **walrus**, Chapter 20).

Description

The dugong is the only marine mammal that is completely herbivorous. Like most herbivores, it is a gentle, placid creature. It lives in the vast seagrass meadows of the West Pacific Ocean, Australasia and Malaysia. It has a dolphin-like tail.

Manatees are larger than dugongs, reaching up to 9.8 feet (3 meters) in length, and weighing up to 3,910 pounds (1,775 kilograms). They are often called sea cows. Manatees are almost entirely herbivorous. The three species live in widely separated areas: the West Indian manatee (*Trichechus manatus*) in the Caribbean and the Gulf of Mexico; the Amazonian manatee (*Trichechus inunguis*) in the Amazon Basin; and the West African manatee (*Trichechus senegalensis*) in the coastal areas and rivers of West Africa.

General Attributes

Both the dugong and the manatee are thought to have contributed greatly to the belief in mermaids (see Chapter 40). Seen from a ship, both can look remarkably like a physically well-endowed woman bobbing on the waves, or swimming underwater.

21. Whales, Dolphins, Porpoises and Sirens

The dugong has been hunted for millennia—a wall painting of a dugong in Tambun Cave, Ipon, Malaysia is thought to date from about 3000 BCE. Some Australian Aborigine tribes worship the dugong as creatures of the Dreamtime, made before the world began. They have also been revered in Japan and Southern China; gugong ribs were often used in Japan to make sacred carvings. There is a legend that the covering of the Tabernacle, the portable temple structure described in Judaic tradition and the Christian Old Testament, was made of dugong hides.

Native Americans hunted the slow-moving, gentle manatee by trailing bait alongside a canoe and then clubbing the creature to death. It was easy prey. The manatee was considered very good meat, but the bones were even more highly valued. Crushed into powder, they were said to be powerful medicine against asthma, earache, and inflammation. By contrast, many West African tribes considered the manatee to be a drowned human, and its meat was therefore taboo.

In his novel *Moby Dick*, Herman Melville (1819–1891) described manatees as unworthy of the serious consideration deserved by whales:

> But as these pig-fish are a noisy, contemptible set, mostly lurking in the mouths of rivers, and feeding on wet hay, and especially as they do not spout, I deny their credentials as whales; and have presented them with their passports to quit the Kingdom of Cetology.[14]

Birds
(*Aves*)

22

General Birds and Crows (Several Orders and *Corvidae*)

Birds (Several Species)

Birds of all kinds feature in many religions and mythologies. They are messengers between this world and the next. Gods often appear in bird form, or with bird heads. Birds represent a very wide range of attributes, from wise to foolish, evil to good, helpless to powerful, peaceful to aggressive.

Nobody knows the exact number of birds in the world, but it is estimated that there are 10,500 species, 21,000 subspecies, and perhaps somewhere between 400 billion and 600 billion individuals. They appear in myths, legends and folklore across the whole planet.

Karshipta

In Zoroastrianism, Karshipta was a sacred bird. After the first winter, in which the Earth was almost destroyed, the creator god Ahura Mazda put Yima, the first man, and all the other humans and animals into a deep cavern until it was safe for them to come out into the world again. Ahura Mazda sent down Karshipta to speak to them, to reassure them that all would be well. Kashipta recited the sacred *Avesta* in his own language, the language of birds, but all the humans and animals understood because at that time they all spoke the same language.[1]

Iduna

In Norse mythology, Iduna was the goddess who guarded the apples of eternal youth. The evil god Loki was sent by the giant Thjassi to trick her into giving up the apples. Loki promised Iduna that he knew where better apples could be found. She followed him into the forest, where Thjassi swooped down as an eagle and stole the sacred apples from the goddess. The gods of the Æsir began aging immediately. They told Loki to bring Iduna back. Loki found the goddess and changed her into a sparrow, and himself into a falcon. The three birds, Iduna the sparrow, Loki the falcon, and Thjassi the eagle, flew back towards Asgard. The gods lit a fire, which Iduna and Loki flew across, but Thjassi's tail feathers caught fire. He fell, and the Aesir killed him, regained the sacred apples, and thus restored eternal youth to Asgard.[2]

Crow/Raven (Several Species)

Phylum *Chordata*, Class *Aves*, Order *Passeriformes*, Superfamily *Corvoidea*, Family *Corvidae*, Genus *Corvus*, Species (more than 120)

Name

In scientific classification, there is no difference between crows and ravens. Crow was *crawe* in Old English. Raven is also a Germanic word: it was written *hræfn* in Old English. *Corvus* is Latin for crow. A Latin proverb was *in cruce corvos pascere*, literally "feed crows on a cross," i.e., don't feed them at all, nail them up instead.

Description

The term crow covers many different birds, including the raven, rook, jackdaw, magpie, chough, carrion crow, hooded crow, Indian jungle crow, collared crow, and several other species. Most crows are black, but with so many species there are also many variations in size and coloring. Crows are intelligent birds, most of them scavengers as well as hunters, and they can adapt to a wide variety of environments.

General Attributes

Crows and ravens are universally depicted as evil in Christian tradition, whereas in Celtic Druidism and other traditions they are animals of great intelligence, wisdom, spiritual significance and magical power. They are harbingers of death, but also symbols of rebirth into the afterlife. They are oracular birds: the druid-poet Taliesin says, "I have fled in the shape of a raven of prophetic speech." They are quick of mind and temper, not to be trifled with. The Welsh *Triads* (mystical poems) say, "Very black is the raven, quick the arrow from the bow."[3] The crow or raven is often the familiar of witches, wizards or druids. Huginn (Thought) and Muninn (Memory) are the two ravens in Norse mythology that perch on Odin's shoulders and act as his messengers (see below). In Japanese mythology, Karasu Tengu (Crow Tengu) is a trickster spirit, clever but mischievous. In the mythology of the Unalit Indians of the Bering Strait, Tu-lu'kau-guk is a raven god, the father of all things.

As Partisan Warriors

A classical Roman legend tells of the hero Marcus Valerius fighting in hand-to-hand combat against a Celtic warrior in Gaul. A raven swooped down between them and pecked out the eyes of the Gallic warrior, allowing Marcus Valerius to kill his opponent. The propaganda value of the legend lay in the fact that crows and ravens were revered by the Celts, so the attack by the raven signified that their gods were deserting them, and the legend was widely circulated and enjoyed by the populace of Rome.

A very similar tale appears in later Islamic legend. A Berber folk hero called Djokhrane was fighting against a Roman soldier. He was losing the fight badly, but suddenly a jay flew down and pecked out the Roman soldier's eyes, allowing Djokhrane to recover and win the fight. He told his children never to eat the jay, and if someone offered them a jay for food, to buy the bird and set it free. Again, the legend had propaganda value, this time against Rome, and may have originated during the Punic Wars between Carthage and Rome.

Brân the Blessed and the Tower of London

One of the best known of the Celtic Druidic tales is the wondrous journey of Brân the Blessed. Classical Druidism included belief in a life beyond this mortal life, although the Celtic versions of the afterlife and the Otherworld differ in many ways from both the classical visions of Hades, the River Styx, the Elysian Fields and so on, and the later Christian and Islamic visions of Heaven and Paradise.

The Celtic vernacular legend of *The Assembly of the Wondrous Head* tells the tale of the Welsh giant, king and god, Brân, also called Bendigeidfrân or Brân Fendigaidd, literally Blessed Crow or Blessed Raven. Mortally wounded in battle (gods can die in Celtic mythology), he orders his men to strike off his head. Reluctantly, they obey his command and are astonished to discover that the head remains alive and alert. The head commands them that under no circumstance may any of them look towards Cornwall. For seven years (which appears to them to be a blissful eternity) they travel with Brân's head, enjoying the god's company, until one of them forgets the order and inadvertently turns his gaze towards Cornwall. The god's head immediately begins to decay. He orders his followers to carry him swiftly to London and to bury the head on the White Hill where the Tower of London now stands, since Britain can never be successfully invaded while Brân remains on guard there, which explains why there have been and will always be ravens (and official raven keepers, called Raven Masters) at the Tower of London, and why their presence is so significant.

Raven Gods, Heroes and the Morrígan

The raven is associated with the Celtic god Lugh (also Ludd, Hu or Hugh), who gave his name to London (Caer Llundain in Welsh) and to Lyons in France (Lugudunum in Latin). Ravens warned Lugh of the advance of the Fomorians before the second battle of Magh Tuiredh. In the Old English epic poem *Beowulf*, ravens help the hero to victory in his battle against the monster Grendel. According to legend, King Arthur shape-shifted into a raven (or chough—see below) after his death.

The Morrígan (the name means Great Queen) is most frequently depicted as a raven. She paddles in the blood of the dead and dying on the battlefield, and is feared as much as she is loved and respected. The ability of druids to see beyond death was often called the "raven knowledge."[4] Paradoxically, the raven was also associated with healing: several of the Celtic healing sanctuaries have raven carvings. Dead ravens were often placed at the bottom of burial pits or shafts with their wings outspread, symbolizing the flight out of death into the afterlife.

Huginn and Muninn

In Norse mythology, Huginn (Thought) and Muninn (Memory) are the sacred ravens that perch on the shoulders of Odin Allfather. They are his messengers and ambassadors, and fly all over this world as well as the other worlds. They first appear by name in the *Poetic Edda* of the 13th century, but were almost certainly known well before that in myth and folk legend. They are depicted in many Germanic and Nordic art works.

Several writers have suggested that Huginn and Muninn are so named because they are connected to shamanic practices, where thought and memory connect to inspiration and visualization to accelerate the symbiotic experience. In a 9th-century Saxon adaptation of the Christian New Testament, the dove that appears above Christ when God says, "This is my Son, in whom I am well pleased,"[5] is described as perching on Christ's shoulder, which appears to be a deliberate reference to Huginn and Muninn, perhaps in an attempt to make him more accessible to heathen converts.

Chiminigagua's Ravens

In the mythology of the Chibcha Indians of Colombia, the creator god Chiminigagua was filled with light, but covered the only mountain of the world with giant ravens, so that all was darkness. While Chiminigagua stayed behind the mountain, the ravens flew up into the sky, and light from Chiminigagua spilled over the mountain-top and into the world for the first time.[6]

The Summer Molt

Most crows molt around midsummer, and during that time they will tend to stay away from their usual haunts and territories. During the Middle Ages, the folklore legend emerged in Christian communities that at and around midsummer crows visited the Devil, who was their lord and master, and gave him their own feathers in payment for his continuing protection.

Rook (*Corvus frugilegus*)

Phylum *Chordata*, Class *Aves*, Order *Passeriformes*, Superfamily *Corvoidea*, Family *Corvidae*, Genus *Corvus*, Species *Corvus frugilegus*

Name

Rook is derived from Old English *hroc* and Old Norse *hrókr*. *Frugilegus* is Latin, meaning "grain-gathering," although rooks are omnivorous.

Description

Rooks are middle-sized to large crows. They have prominent beaks and a small patch of bare skin around the base of the beak. By comparison with ordinary crows, the feathers on their legs tend to stick out a little more, giving them the appearance of wearing shaggy pants. They like to live in large groups, building their ramshackle nests in adjoining trees, close to each other, making a rookery. They have little or no compunction about stealing twigs and nesting material from other birds' nests, so squawky arguments are common.

General Attributes

To those who dislike them, rooks are noisy birds of little consequence. To most country-dwellers, who see rooks leaving *en masse* to gather food for the day and then returning together as twilight gathers to roost in their closely knit communities, the rook is a comforting and familiar sight, and a harbinger of the weather and other future events.

Weather Forecasters and More

Country folk in Britain and Ireland watch rooks closely to foretell the weather. If the birds fly far away from the rookery, the weather will be fine all day. If the rooks stay close by, or return to the rookery early, bad weather is on the way. In Yorkshire, England, they take note of whether the rooks are perching mostly on dead branches or live branches as they gather: dead branches mean heavy rain before nightfall.

Rooks are also believed to foretell death. If a rook or group of rooks abandons the rookery and flies off to live elsewhere, someone in the family will die soon.

In Christian Folklore

Rooks gather and socialize in large groups, so their collective excrement can be a nuisance. There are two directly opposite pieces of folklore relating to rook poop: the first says that if you are going to church in your Sunday best, a rook dropping its poop on you from on high is a lucky sign, a mark of approval; the second says exactly the opposite, i.e., that if a rook poops on you it's a sign that you haven't tried hard enough and you need to go home and find some better clothing for church.

In Shropshire, England, local folklore has it that rooks never work, hunt or tidy their nests on Sundays or Ascension Day, i.e., they abide by the Sabbath as a day of rest.[7] Washington Irving (1783–1859), the author of the famous American ghost story *Legend of Sleepy Hollow*, stayed at Newstead Abbey, Nottinghamshire, England, in the 1800s. He noted with interest that each morning the abbey rooks would fly away, *en masse*, to sweep the countryside for food. They would return in a similar manner in the evening, where their discussion of the day's events would echo around the estate. Irving was told that the rooks observed the Sabbath; they set out every day except Sunday, when they stayed in the abbey grounds. He didn't believe this until he saw it for himself. Indeed, it appeared that the rooks visited their neighbors and friends, devoting Sunday to their nearest and dearest, but didn't leave the estate. Irving tells us that the local tradition had it that the rooks at Newstead were the souls of the Black Monks reborn as birds, still occupying their old abbey. Indeed, so strongly was this belief held that, contrary to common country practice, the Newstead rooks were not shot, and were generally left unhindered.[8]

Jackdaw (*Coloeus monedula*)

Phylum *Chordata*, Class *Aves*, Order *Passeriformes*, Superfamily *Corvoidea*, Family *Corvidae*, Genus *Coloeus*, Species *Coloeus monedula*

Name

The jackdaw's call is a metallic *chyak-chyak*, and some people have suggested that as the origin of its name. The *-daw* part of the name is the original name for the bird, and it is more likely that the *jack-* part is just a diminutive, so a jackdaw is a "little daw." Linnaeus originally called it *Corvus monedula*, the *monedula* deriving from Latin *moneta* (money), because of the bird's reputation as a thief of shiny things, much like the magpie. (In fact, neither jackdaws nor magpies are particularly attracted to shiny things: they are just attracted to small things in general, and will happily steal and hide them.) Later, the jackdaw's taxonomy was disputed, and the genus name *Corvus* was replaced by *Coloeus*, reinstated by the eminent American ornithologist Pamela Rasmussen (b. 1959). Κολοιος, *koloiós*, is the Ancient Greek for jackdaw.

Description

Jackdaws are found across Europe, western Asia, and Africa. Like all the corvids, they are intelligent birds. They pair for life, but often live in groups, smaller than a rook colony, but larger than just one or two pairs and their young. They forage energetically for food, and have a habit that is very rarely seen in wild animals: they share food with each other on a regular basis, as chimpanzees do, and as humans do (at least sometimes).

General Attributes

Jackdaws are thieves and charming rascals in popular folklore. Gilbert White (1720–1793 CE) noted in his famous *The Natural History of Selborn* that jackdaws were nesting under the lintels of Stonehenge.[9] They are also reputed to nest in churches very frequently. Seeing a jackdaw on the way to a wedding as it leaves its steeple nest is considered a very fortunate omen for the happy couple. Like rooks, jackdaws forecast changes in the weather, and also sometimes foretell deaths.

The Jackdaw of Rheims

Perhaps the best-known tale about a jackdaw is *The Jackdaw of Rheims*, a humorous poem by Thomas Ingoldsby (real name the Reverend Richard Harris Barham, 1788–1845) in his collection *The Ingoldsby Legends*.

In the story, a bold jackdaw steals a ring from a cardinal's finger. The cardinal curses the jackdaw roundly, and the jackdaw begins to suffer remorse (and lose condition) quickly. He returns the ring and the tale ends happily and rather unexpectedly:

Then the great Lord Cardinal call'd for his book,
And off that terrible curse he took;
The mute expression
Served in lieu of confession,
And, being thus coupled with full restitution,
The Jackdaw got plenary absolution!
—When those words were heard,
That poor little bird
Was so changed in a moment, 'twas really absurd.
He grew sleek, and fat;
In addition to that,
A fresh crop of feathers came thick as a mat!
His tail waggled more
Even than before;
But no longer it wagg'd with an impudent air,
No longer he perch'd on the Cardinal's chair.
He hopp'd now about
With a gait devout;
At Matins, at Vespers, he never was out;
And, so far from any more pilfering deeds,
He always seem'd telling the Confessor's beads.
If any one lied,—or if any one swore,—
Or slumber'd in pray'r-time and happen'd to snore,
That good Jackdaw
Would give a great "Caw!"
As much as to say, "Don't do so any more!"
While many remark'd, as his manners they saw,
That they "never had known such a pious Jackdaw!"
He long lived the pride
Of that country side,
And at last in the odour of sanctity died;
When, as words were too faint
His merits to paint,
The Conclave determined to make him a Saint;
And on newly made Saints and Popes, as you know,
It's the custom, at Rome, new names to bestow,
So they canonized him by the name of Jim Crow![10]

Jay/Magpie (Several Species)

Phylum *Chordata*, Class *Aves*, Order *Passeriformes*, Superfamily *Corvoidea*, Family *Corvidae*, Genus (10 jays, 3 magpies), Species (at least 49 jays, at least 11 magpies)

Name

The original name for the magpie was simply pie, derived from Latin *pica*. Mag was a common diminutive for Margaret (like Meg, Peg or Peggy), and was often intended to mean a chatterer, someone who gossiped a lot. It was added to the front of pie to make magpie. Jay is derived from Old French *jai*, meaning merry or bright (cognate with the original meaning of English gay), referring to its bright plumage.

Description

Jays and magpies are both corvids, and are so similar in some respects that they are often confused. They are both extremely intelligent birds. Magpies recognize their own image in a mirror, as humans do. The Eurasian magpie is usually black and white, has a long tail, and is very talkative. The American jay is usually brightly colored and includes the well-known blue jay. It, too, is a noisy and very active bird.

General Attributes

Magpies and jays, like jackdaws, are considered lovable rogues. Both are reputed to steal objects, particularly if the objects are bright and shiny, although there is no actual evidence to show that brightness is a significant factor. Magpies and jays both appear commonly in folklore.

Whenever you see a magpie, you are supposed to say (no matter what time of day it is): "Good morning, Mr. Magpie—I hope you're well." If you are impolite enough to forget, you will have bad luck. (I learned this from my mother—I have no idea where it originated, although her heritage was Irish.)

The Jay and the Peacocks

This well-known Æsopic fable about vanity is found throughout the world:

A dull and dusty jay found some feathers that had fallen out of a peacock's tail. He picked them up admiringly. After first looking all around to check that nobody was watching, he began sticking the peacock feathers in among his own feathers. In a short while, he had a sort of peacock tail of his own, bright and shiny. He began to strut among his fellow jays. He lifted his beak high in the air and refused to speak to his old friends and companions. Now that he had a peacock's tail, ordinary jays were beneath his consideration.

Supremely pleased by his own beauty, he took a bold step further. He sought out a flock of peacocks and marched in among them, swaggering and grinning. As soon as they saw him, the peacocks leapt upon him and pulled out the peacock feathers, one by one, giving him many hard pecks as they did so. Finally, bedraggled, disheveled and feeling very sorry for himself, the jay managed to escape.

He went back to the other jays and told them the sad story of how the peacocks had beaten him up. But the other jays had no time for him. They remembered his arrogant strutting, and how he had ignored them previously. They gave him no sympathy at all, and he wandered off alone and dejected, having learned a hard lesson.

Moral: Happiness is not to be found in borrowed finery.[11]

Magpies in the Far East

Magpies are held in very high regard in the Far East. They represent good fortune, good health and prosperity. The magpie is a common subject in Chinese painting and sculpture, as well as in poetry.

The Qixi or Qiqiao Festival, sometimes called The Chinese St. Valentine's Day, is a famous Chinese folk event that commemorates a well-known mythological legend, which first appeared in writing over 2,600 years ago. The cowherd of the legend is the star Altair, and the weaver girl is the bright star Vega. (See Chapter 41.) They are not allowed to meet (they are on opposite sides of what the Chinese call the Silver River, but which we in the West call the Milky Way). However, on the seventh day of the seventh lunar month (*Qi* means seven and *xi* means day), a flock of magpies forms a bridge across the Silver River, and the cowherd and the weaver girl can cross and meet. This charming tradition, based on ancient astronomy, has been celebrated in China since the Han dynasty (206 BCE–220 CE).[12]

The Tanabata Festival in Japan and the Chilseok Festival in Korea are both based on Qixi. In Korea, the magpie is the national bird and emblem.

Chough (*Pyrrhocorax pyrrhocorax, Pyrrhocorax graculus*)

Phylum *Chordata*, Class *Aves*, Order *Passeriformes*, Superfamily *Corvoidea*, Family *Corvidae*, Genus *Pyrrhocorax*, Species *Pyrrhocorax pyrrhocorax, Pyrrhocorax graculus*

Name

The name chough comes from Old English *ceo*, and is pronounced to rhyme with rough or tough, rather than through or bough. *Pyrrhocorax* is derived from Ancient Greek πυρρος, *pyrrhos*, flame-colored, and κοραξ, *korax*, crow. (The bird itself is black, but the beak and feet are bright scarlet. The Alpine chough, *Pyrrhocorax graculus*, has a yellow-orange bill and feet.)

Description

Choughs live generally in the mountainous regions of southern Europe and North Africa. Some have settled further north, on the Atlantic seaboard.

General Attributes

Choughs have a very specific mythological significance in Celtic Druidism and the culture of Cornwall, Wales and Ireland. The chough is the symbol of Arthur, or King Arthur, and therefore of the resurgence and maintenance of Celtic national identity in the face of relentless domination by English culture and language.

In Cornwall

The chough appears on the Cornish coat of arms, and is recognized as an emblem of national identity. Its Cornish name is *palores*, although *choca*, back-formed from Old English *ceo*, is also found. One legend says that King Arthur did not die, but remains with his knights in a sacred chamber in the hills, waiting to return to rescue Britain in her hour of need. Another says that Arthur became a chough, and lives on the Cornish cliffs.

Daniel Defoe (1660–1731), author of *Robinson Crusoe*, first recorded the folk legend that choughs are fireraisers, stealing candles to set fire to haystacks and farm buildings. The red bill may account in part for this legend.

The French composer Olivier Messiaen (1908–1992) was fascinated by birdsong. He wrote a collection of piano pieces, *Catalogue d'oiseaux* (Bird Catalogue), based on the calls and songs of individual bird species, and the first of these is *Le chocard des Alpes* (The Alpine Chough), which captures the bird's complex chattering superbly.

23

Raptors (Several Orders and Families)

Hawk (Several Species)

Phylum *Chordata*, Class *Aves*, Order *Accipitriformes*, Family *Accipitridae*, Subfamily *Accipitrinae, Buteo,* Genus (4 or 5 *Accipitrinae*, 4 *Buteo*), Species (several)

Name

The common name, which was *heafoc* in Old English, is derived ultimately from a Proto-Indo-European root **kopugos*, related to Latin *capus*, bird of prey. The genus name *Accipitrinae* comes from Latin *accipiter*, seizer, which in turn was derived from Greek ωκυπτερος, *ōkypteros*, swift-winged. *Buteo* is the Latin name of the common buzzard.

Description

Hawks are medium-sized birds of prey. The subfamily *Accipitrinae* includes goshawks, sparrowhawks, and many other species, varying greatly in size and appearance. Members of the subfamily *Buteo* are also generally called hawks in America, while in Europe they are usually called buzzards.

General Attributes

The hawk can fly, and can see things from afar. Celtic druids dressed in cloaks of bird feathers for certain ceremonies, to allow their spirits to fly to other realms and to gain the sharp, clear, focused sight of the raptor. The hawk, large or small, is always a noble bird, fiercely independent, even haughty, but always worthy of respect.

Celtic Hawk Names

Gawain (also Gawan, Gawen) is one of King Arthur's knights. His name derives from Welsh *Gwalchmei Gwynn*, (Fair Hawk of May). Galahad, the son of Lancelot, who along with Perceval (also Percival, Parsifal) plays a principal role in the quest for the Holy Grail, is also called *Gwalch y Haf* (Hawk of Summer). Both names are perfectly suitable for someone on an important quest or search.

The Hawk of Achill

An ancient Irish folk tale is based on the frequent Celtic themes of truth telling and of which animals are the most ancient in the world. One freezing Beltane Eve (Beltane is the Celtic spring festival of Bel's Fire, celebrated on our about May 1), the Hawk of Achill took shelter in an eagle's nest, after killing and eating the chick that was in it. The eagle returned and said that she could never remember such a cold night. The hawk said he could remember a much colder one. The eagle, who still thought the hawk was her chick, only a month old, was disbelieving. The hawk told the eagle to ask the blackbird, the stag and the salmon whether he was speaking truth or not. The eagle flew off, and it was only when the wise old salmon said to her, "It was so cold that I was frozen into the ice of this pool, and the Hawk of Achill pecked out my eyes," that the truth dawned on her. She flew back, and found her nest empty.[1]

Amun-Ra

The god Amun (Invisible One) was so called because his presence was often known only by a fluttering of flags on a windless day or a sudden change in temperature within the temple. He was originally a minor deity, worshiped in a small temple at Karnak, but when the Theban princes became kings of Egypt, they combined Amun with the sun-god Ra to create a new divinity, Amun-Ra, who was called the god above all other gods, the supreme deity. He was usually depicted as a tall, handsome, bearded man, wearing a headdress of feathers colored red, green and blue. However, in later depictions associating the sun with the hawk, he has the head of a hawk, sometimes with the hawk's head encircled by a solar disk and a serpent.

Daedalion and Chione

In a Greek legend told in Ovid's *Metamorphoses* (book 11), Daedalion (Bright One) was a favorite of the gods Apollo and Hermes:

> Daedalion had a daughter called Chione, who was so beautiful that she was said to have a thousand men seeking to marry her. However, Apollo and Hermes, visiting their friend Daedalion, caught sight of his daughter and were instantly filled with insatiable lust for her.
> Apollo decided to wait until nightfall. Hermes took his chance, visited Chione during the day, hypnotized her, and then raped her. At nightfall, Apollo visited Chione, disguised as an old woman, but then revealed himself, and also raped her. As a result of that day's activities, Chione had twins nine months later.
> Chione was foolish enough to boast that she must be more beautiful than even the goddess Artemis, since both Apollo and Hermes loved her. In anger, Artemis killed Chione by shooting an arrow that pierced her tongue, the tongue that had done the boasting.
> Daedalion was distraught. At Chione's funeral, he tried three times to throw himself on her burning pyre, but friends held him back. Finally he ran all the way to the summit of Mount Parnassus and prepared to throw himself off. Just as he leaped, Apollo changed him into a hawk.[2]

Obumo

Obumo is the thunder-god of the Ibibio people of southern Nigeria. After creating the world, he grew tired of humankind, and went back to heaven. He orders the progression of the seasons, but otherwise he has very little to do with human affairs. He has a human wife, however, who is called Eka Abassi. Every year, at the beginning of the rainy season, he returns in the form of a hawk to spend some time with his wife on Earth.[3]

Falcon (Several Species)

Phylum *Chordata*, Class *Aves*, Order *Falconiformes*, Family *Falconidae*, Subfamily *Falconinae*, Genus *Falco*, Species (about 40)

Name

The common name and genus name come from Latin *falco*, falcon.

Description

There are about 40 species of falcon, spread across every continent of the world apart from Antarctica. Although they vary in size and appearance, they all have thin, very tapered wings and are fast, acrobatic fliers. Peregrine falcons have been observed diving at speeds of 200 miles per hour (320 kilometers per hour), and the fastest diving speed recorded was an astonishing 244 miles per hour, or 390 kilometers per hour, making the peregrine falcon easily the fastest animal on the planet.

General Attributes

Falcons have always been noble birds, used by royalty and aristocrats for hunting in many cultures. In mythology, they represent authority and nobility.

Horus

In the religion of ancient Egypt, Horus was perhaps the most important god of all. He was the national tutelary god of Egypt. He was worshiped without interruption from prehistoric times until the Roman occupation of Egypt, a period of about 3,500 years. The first inscribed depiction of him as a falcon dates from 3100 BCE.

Horus is usually depicted with a human body. In his left hand he carries the *ankh*, the symbol of eternal life. His head is that of a falcon, probably either a lanner falcon (*Falco biarmicus*) or peregrine falcon (*Falco peregrinus*). On top of the falcon head sits the *pschent*, the red-and-white crown that symbolizes the combined monarchy of Upper and Lower Egypt. The *pschent* was also called the *sekhemty* in ancient Egyptian, meaning literally the Two Powerful Ones.

In hieroglyphics, Horus' name was *hr.w*, or *haruw*, which meant falcon. It became 'Ώρος, *Hōros*, in Greek, then *Horus* in Latin. Initially, Horus was the brother of Isis, Osiris, Set, and Nephthys, but he later became thought of as the son of Isis and Osiris. Both Horus and Osiris became associated with the Pharaoh, hence with the empire of Egypt as a whole, but increasingly Osiris became the tutelary god of dead pharaohs and Horus the tutelary god of the living Pharaoh, so his rank and influence were of the highest order. Horus was also said to be the son of the great cow goddess Hathor (see Hathor, Chapter 7). Every evening he flew into Hathor's mouth, and night fell. Every morning he flew out again, and dawn broke.

The demonic Set killed Osiris, and Horus set out to avenge his father's death: that is the scenario that underpins a whole series of mythical battles between Horus and Set. In one of these, Set loses a testicle and Horus has his left eye damaged—but his right eye is the Sun and his left eye is the Moon, and thus the puzzling phases of the Moon were explained. The damaged eye was eventually healed by the god Thoth, and the icon of the restored eye, the Eye of Horus, became a powerful symbol of protection, which is still used to this day. The Egyptian word for the symbol was *w.jt* or *wedjat*, and it is still seen on amulets, rings and decorative boxes for small precious items, such as jewelry. It was common practice to paint the Eye of Horus on Egyptian and other Near Eastern boats to safeguard them against shipwreck.

Another battle between Set and Horus has a peculiar sexual aspect. Set attacks Horus, apparently trying to rape him, but Horus puts his hand between his own thighs and catches Set's semen, and then flings it off into the river. Horus then deliberately spreads his own semen on some lettuce, Set's favorite food, and Set eats it. When the two gods come before the other gods, each of them yet again trying to be confirmed as the most important god of all, the other gods first summon up Set's semen, but it answers from the distant river, and so is of no account. But when they summon up Horus' semen, it answers from inside Set's belly, thus confirming that Horus has the mastery and power over Set, not the other way round. Egyptologists have tried to connect the legendary battles between Set and Horus with either political or religious historical divisions between the Upper and Lower Kingdoms, or between the fertile land close to the Nile (Horus' portion) and the desert lands further away from the river (Set's portion), but there is no clear consensus on possible connections.

Horus later became amalgamated with Osiris. As Golden Horus-Osiris, he was lord of both the living and the dead. The Victorian poet, druid, spiritualist and amateur Egyptologist Gerald Massey (1828–1907) was convinced that Golden Horus-Osiris and Jesus Christ were the same person—he specifically identified Jesus with the Egyptian god Horus in his book *The Natural Genesis* (1883). Among other things, he noted that Horus had been born of a virgin on December 25, had raised the dead back to life, was crucified, and was resurrected three days later:

> Christian ignorance notwithstanding, the Gnostic Jesus is the Egyptian Horus who was continued by the various sects of Gnostics under both the names of Horus and of Jesus. In the Gnostic iconography of the Roman catacombs child-Horus reappears as the mummy-babe who wears the solar disc. The royal Horus is represented in the cloak of royalty, and the phallic emblem found there witnesses to Jesus being Horus of the resurrection.[4]

The Falcon and the Owls

In a story by the Persian Sufi mystic and poet Rumi (1207–1273) in the *Masnavi-ye-Ma'navi* (the Spiritual Couplets), the poet tells of a falcon that has lost its way and finds itself in a foul place occupied by owls, with pellets and bones scattered on the floor amongst the filthy droppings. The owls surround the falcon, accusing it of trying to invade their territory and steal one of their nests. The falcon tells the owls that he has no intention of living in such a foul place, nor of stealing a nest. He normally lives on the wrist of a king, he tells them. They mock him for his arrogance, arguing that a strange-looking bird like him could never consort with a king. The falcon tells them that the humble water and earth become part of the most beautiful and successful plants and flowers, and that even they, dusty owls, might become acceptable to a king if they were to copy the outward form and bearing that they see in him.[5]

Pariacaca

In the mythology of the Huarochiri Indians of western Peru, Pariacaca and his four brothers were the first men. After a great flood, five eggs were left on the heights of Mount Condorcoto. From these eggs were born five falcons, Pariacaca, the first-born, and his four brothers. They turned into men. Pariacaca, born of the flood, had wind and rain as his chief weapons. His rival, Hulallallo Caruincho, had fire as his. They fought many battles, several of them involving the wild animals of the forest. When the Inca came to Peru, they chose Pariacaca over Caruincho, and made him a god.[6]

Saint Bavon

In Christian legend, Saint Bavon (also called Allowin) of Belgium is the patron saint of falconers. A 7th-century nobleman, passionate falconer and widower of dissipated habits, he was converted to Christianity at the age of 50—a ripe old age in the 7th century. Mortified by his earlier dissolute personal history, he begged a former slave to beat him and throw him into prison. The slave obliged with the beating, but not the imprisonment. Bavon tried to live in a monastery in Ghent, but soon chose to live as a hermit deep in the forest instead. He is portrayed alternately as a rich nobleman or as a poor, humble hermit, but always with a falcon perched on his hand.[7]

Eagle (Several Species)

Phylum *Chordata*, Class *Aves*, Order *Accipitriformes*, Family *Accipitridae*, Genus (several), Species (60)

Name

The Normans brought the Old French name *aigle* with them to Britain. *Aigle* is derived from Latin *aquila*, eagle.

Description

The name eagle is used for many different kinds of large birds of prey. There are many genera and species. They are generally larger and stronger than other birds of prey, apart from vultures. They are widely distributed across the world.

General Attributes

The eagle is one of the most celebrated and valued sacred animals in the world. It is often described as King of the Birds in the same way as the lion is King of the Beasts. (But see also *wren* in Chapter 27.) It appears widely in heraldry, with outspread wings and talons, the epitome of strength and noble ferocity. It was associated with Zeus in classical mythology, and has always been thought royal, victorious, and justly proud.

The eagle was (and still is) venerated by almost every Native American nation. Eagle feathers were used by the Cree and others as a war flag. Stuffed and carved eagles were often displayed in council lodges. The Cherokees and the Dakotas awarded eagle headdresses only to those warriors who had killed enemies in battle. The Zuñi of New Mexico portrayed the four winds (i.e., the compass) with eagle feathers.[8]

The Eagle and the Arrow

An Æsopic folk tale describes a hunter seeing an eagle in the sky above him. He releases an arrow, which mortally wounds the eagle. As the eagle lands on the ground, dying, he looks closely at the arrow, and notices that it is fletched with one of his own feathers.

Moral: We often contribute to our own destruction.

Shape-Shifting

Celtic Druids reputedly shape-shifted into eagles to metaphorically climb into the sky (where the gods live) to look down on the world and gain a superior, clearer view of what was going on. Druids, kings and chieftains wore eagle feathers as a sign of their rank, as do powerful elders and leaders in Native American nations. Two druids are said to have permanently shape-shifted into eagles to guard King Arthur's secret burial place; they will wake him at the hour of Britain's greatest need. An annual gathering of druids at Beltane (on or about 1 May) on a small island in Loch Lomond was possible only because the sixty assembled druids flew to the island as eagles. There is an Irish legend that Adam and Eve did not die, but shape-shifted into the eagles that fly to this day in the wild mountains and over the lonely beaches of Galway. The eagle is the second oldest animal in the world, only the salmon being older and wiser.

Etana

In Babylonian mythology, the hero Etana flew to heaven on the back of an eagle. He flew up and up, past the chief gods Anu, Bel and Ea, until he reached the supreme height where the great goddess Ishtar lives. But here the strength of the eagle finally gave out, and he and Etana both fell back to their deaths on earth. Etana appears as Edinku in the Babylonian epic poem *Gilgamesh* (c. 2100 BCE).[9]

Garuda

In Hindu mythology, Garuda is an eagle god, the king of all birds and the enemy of all snakes. His mother was Vinata, who quarreled with Kadru, the mother of serpents, and was then imprisoned by her. Desperate to free his mother from Kadru, Garuda stole Amrita, the holy water of life, from the gods, thinking that only such an extraordinary ransom would persuade the evil snake-goddess. However, the great deity Indra, on behalf of all the gods, fought a battle with Garuda to have the Amrita returned. Indra won the battle, but at a cost—Garuda was so powerful that he destroyed Indra's thunderbolt.[10]

The Bird Augury Rite in Ancient Rome

In ancient Rome, *augur* was an official priestly status, and the work of augury, particularly bird augury, has given us two well-known religious words, temple and tabernacle (literally, tent or shed, but now used to indicate a wide range of religious structures or buildings). The mechanics of bird augury were set out in detail in books like the *Libri Augurales* and the *Commentarii Augurales*. Augury was not considered strange or esoteric—even magistrates used augury to help them decide cases.

At dawn, the augur—usually in the presence of the magistrate or client—began by climbing to a high spot and drawing with his staff in the ground a long line north to south, and another long line east to west crossing the first line. He then drew a large rectangle enclosing this cross and creating four internal rectangles. Each rectangle was called a *templum*, the origin of the word temple. Where the lines crossed, the augur erected a tent, called the *tabernaculum*, from which the word tabernacle is derived. The tent opened only on one side (facing north in the Greek tradition, south in the Roman). Any bird movement to the left, or east, was considered propitious. Any movement to the right, or west, was bad news. Crows, ravens and owls held special significance, but the most significant of all were vultures or eagles. Traditionally, the augur would report to the magistrate (or private person, usually rich and aristocratic), either, "The birds allow it," or "Another day," meaning delay or avoidance.[11]

Hino's Eagles

In the mythology of the Iroquois Indians of North America, Hino or Hinon the thunderer is a warrior-god. He is armed with a bow so huge and stiff that no human warrior could ever pull it. His arrows burst into flame as they leave the bow. He is accompanied by two eagles, Oshadagea, who carries a lake of fresh dew on his back, and Keneu, the golden eagle.[12]

The Bald Eagle and the United States

The United States of America adopted the bald eagle as their symbol on June 20, 1782, largely because of its ancient history as a symbol of the great Empire of Rome. It is both the national bird and the national animal of America, and appears on the Great Seal, although not every American agreed to its adoption at the time. Benjamin Franklin, in a letter to his daughter, said that the bald eagle was a cowardly, opportunistic bird, and that the humble turkey would make a much more suitable emblem for America.

Owl (Several Species)

Phylum *Chordata*, Class *Aves*, Clade *Afroaves*, Order *Strigiformes*, Family *Strigidae*, *Tytonidae*, Genus (26), Species (more than 225)

Name

The common name is Germanic: it was *oule* in Middle English and *ule*, pronounced *oo-la*, in Old English. The family name *Strigidae* is from Latin *strix*, owl, in turn from Greek στριγξ, *strinx*, screecher. *Tytonidae* is from Greek τυτω, *tutō*, probably an onomatopaeic name, like modern English *tu-whit, tu-whoo*.

Description

There are about 225 species of owl. They vary greatly in size and typical habitat, but they are generally solitary and nocturnal. They typically have round faces with forward-facing eyes, and have exceptional binocular vision and binaural hearing, both of which help them locate prey with great speed and accuracy.

General Attributes

The owl features in many religions and mythological traditions across the world, and in all of them she (symbolically the owl is almost always female, although real owls are obviously of both genders) is associated with wisdom, old age, and death. One of the many Gaelic names for owl is *Cailleach-oidhche* (Crone of Night), to which the adjective *gheal* (white) is sometimes added. Twilight, which is called the gloaming in Scotland, is also called "owl-light" in some places. In the Celtic quest for the world's oldest animals, which features in the Welsh tale *Culhwch and Olwen*, the owl is third oldest in the sequence (youngest to oldest) blackbird, stag, owl, eagle, salmon.

The Oracular Owl

In several traditions, the hooting of an owl signifies an impending death. The modern druid, teacher and author Ellen Evert Hopman (b. 1952) told me of one of her personal experiences:

> I had an owl perch on the roof above the kitchen where I was washing dishes and hoot and hoot without stopping. Finally I said out loud, "Okay, I hear you," and I knew someone had died. The owl stopped and the next morning I found out my mentor and teacher Druid Alexei Kondratiev had suddenly and tragically passed away on a sidewalk in New York.[13]

Athena

The great classical Greek goddess Athena had many other names and titles, including Athene, Pallas Athene, Athena Promachos (The Warrior) and Athena Parthenos (the

Virgin, the root of the name Parthenon for her famous ancient temple in Athens). She was a goddess of great importance, representing wisdom, arts and crafts, and warfare. The Romans later included her in their pantheon, changing her name to Minerva. She had many symbolic icons, especially owls, olive trees, snakes and the *gorgoneion* (the pictorial devices featuring the Gorgon's head that ancient Greeks used to protect their homes and belongings).[14] In statuary, she is often depicted with an owl perched on her finger. Through the influence of the Athena and Minerva mythology, which has been well known in Western culture for many centuries, Athena's totem animal, the owl, is now irrevocably connected with notions of wisdom, sagacity and mature judgment.

Blodeuwedd

The Welsh tale of *Math, Son of Mathonwy* is filled with ancient pagan themes, but ends with the character called Blodeuwedd being turned into an owl, who will never dare to face the light of day, and who will be shunned by all other birds. Since all the tales of the *Mabinogi* were written down by Christian scribes, it is difficult to know for certain whether this negative portrayal of the owl is part of the Celtic Druidic pagan original, or an addition by the scribe. The other elements of the story are so singularly and distinctively pagan Celtic, however, it seems likely that this negative description is original.

The goddess Arianrhod is the mother of the divine hero Lleu Llaw Gyffes (Lleu of the Steady Hand). She makes a *tynged* (a binding oath or spell) that Lleu will never take a human wife. However, Lleu and the magician (i.e., druidic god) Gwydion make a woman out of flowers, whom they name Blodeuwedd (Flower Face). She becomes Lleu's wife, but she falls in love with Gronw Pebr, and they conspire to murder Lleu. Lleu shape-shifts into the form of an eagle and flies to safety. Gwydion punishes Blodeuwedd by turning her into an owl. (See also *Lopamudra*, Chapter 40.)

Big Owl

In Apache Indian legend, Big Owl is a human cannibal who kills his victims by staring at them with huge, owl-like eyes. However, he is a creature of the day rather than of the night: his stare is said to be as fierce and blinding as looking directly at the Sun. Once mesmerized, his victims follow him home submissively, and meekly allow themselves to be killed and eaten.

For the Algonquins, the owl was the attendant of the Lord of the Dead. Cree medicine-men carried a stuffed owl-skin as the badge and emblem of their authority. The Cherokees placed a stuffed owl above the medicine stone in the council lodge.[15]

Screech Owls

In the mythology of the Mojave Indians of North America, the people were led by the culture hero Matowelia from the White Mountains to their homelands along the Colorado River. When they died, their bodies had to be burned, following the ritual prescribed by Matowelia, and their spirits would then return to the White Mountains. If anyone died without proper funerary rites, their spirit would turn into a screech owl (type species: *Strix acio*). A screech owl hooting was a restless ghost, complaining and longing to return to the sacred mountains.[16]

Uguku and Tskili

In the mythology of the Cherokee nation, Uguku and Tskili are respectively the hoot owl (*Strix varia*) and the horned owl or eagle owl (genus *Bubo*, several species). When the first fire burned in the world, caused by lightning striking a tree, they flew down to see what was going on (owls are curious animals). The tree stump burned so fiercely that smoke swirled all about them, nearly blinding them. That is why hoot owls and horned owls have white rings around their eyes.[17]

Mictlantecuhtli

In Aztec mythology, Mictlantecuhtli, Lord of the Dead, was represented as an owl, sometimes with a skull and bones beside him. Mictlan was the place of the dead, and Mictlantecuhtli was its *tecuhtli* or Lord and his wife Mictlantecihuatl was *tecihuatl* or Lady of the Kingdom of Death. He was associated with the north and with the color red, which is also the color of death in ancient Druidism.[18]

Langsuyar

In Malayan mythology, a woman who died in childbirth might come back to the world as a *langsuyar*, a child-killing owl. She would be easily recognized by her green robe, her long fingernails, and her jet-black hair, which reached to her ankles. The hair hid an owl's beak on the back of her neck, through which she would suck the blood of her victims. She could be tamed by cutting her nails and hair and stuffing them into the beak, to block it up. Even better was to prepare the corpse by putting glass beads in its mouth, a hen's egg under each armpit, and needles in the palms of the hands. The dead woman could then not open her mouth to shriek, wave her arms to fly, or open and shut her hands to turn them into wings.[19]

Vulture/Condor (Several Species)

Phylum *Chordata*, Class *Aves*, Family *Accipitridae, Cathartidae*, Genus (14), Species (27)

Name

The common name vulture is from Latin *vultur*. Condor is Spanish *cóndor*, derived from the South American native Quechua name *kuntur*. The family name *Cathartidae* for condors is from Greek καθαρτες, *kathartes*, purifier, referring to the cleansing of dead bodies.

Description

There are 16 species of Old World vultures and nine species of New World vultures, which are generally called condors. The largest of the vultures are the largest birds of prey. They are best known as scavengers, but they also hunt occasionally, and are very formidable.

General Attributes

Vultures are considered unclean and unhealthy because they spend so much time eating dead and decaying animal bodies. On the other hand, as the ancient Greek name *kathartes* suggests, they are the purifiers and cleaners of the natural world.

Nekhebet

In Egyptian mythology, Nekhebet was the vulture goddess of Upper Egypt. Despite the association between vultures and death or carrion, Nekhebet was a goddess of childbirth. She was portrayed as a vulture, or as a woman with a vulture's head. The Greeks took her into their pantheon, calling her Eileithyia.[20]

The Torment of Prometheus

In Greek legend, Prometheus (Forethought) was a Titan, one of the race of beings that preceded the classical Olympian gods. Prometheus angered Zeus by stealing fire and giving it as a free gift to humans. To punish Prometheus, Zeus chained him to a rock in the Caucasus Mountains where, every day, a vulture (in some versions, an eagle) would fly down and eat his liver. The liver would repair itself overnight so that the torture could continue again the following day.[21]

Dakhma Vultures and Sky Burial

In ancient Persian Zoroastrian funeral rites, a corpse was considered unclean because the *nasu daeva* (corpse demon) would rush into it and spread corruption and pollution as it began its work of dissolving the body and releasing the spirit. Cut hair and nail clippings were also unclean. The corpse could not be buried, because it would contaminate the earth, nor could it be burned, because it would pollute the fire, and the fire would spread the pollution (see *Other Guard Dogs*, Chapter Three).

For those reasons, a wooden platform called a *dakhma* was built above the ground. The body was laid out on top of the platform, and was eaten mostly by vultures. The practice of corpse exposure was first described in writing by the Greek historian Herodotus in the 5th century BCE, but the first documentary evidence of the platforms dates from the 9th century CE. In British colonial India in the early 19th century, a British government translator called Robert Murphy devised the term Tower of Silence for the *dakhma*, and that name is still occasionally used.[22]

A similar practice, still common in China, Tibet and Mongolia, is the practice called sky burial in English, where the corpse is left in an exposed place, usually a mountainside, again with the intention that vultures or other carrion-feeding birds and animals will clear the body away. In Buddhism, there is no resurrection in the body. A corpse is just something no longer of use, something that needs to be disposed of, as cleanly and conveniently as possible.

24

Freshwater Birds (Several Orders and Families)

Swan (Several Species)

Phylum *Chordata*, Class *Aves*, Order *Anseriformes*, Superfamily *Anatoidea*, Family *Anatidae*, Subfamily *Anserinae*, Genus *Cygnus*, Type species *Cygnus cygnus*, Species (6 or 7 extant)

Name

The name swan comes from Proto-Germanic **swanaz* and Proto-Indo-European **swen*, related to the Latin word *sonus*, sound, and Old English *geswin*, song. *Cygnus* is Latin for swan. (*Cycnus* or *Cygnus* was also Latin slang for a poet, which explains why William Shakespeare, 1564–1616, is sometimes referred to as "the Swan of Avon.") The family name *Anatidae* is from Latin *anas*, which means duck.

Description

Swans are the largest of the waterfowl family *Anatidae* and among the largest of all flying birds. They generally mate for life, and are usually seen in pairs. They tend to return to the same sites at different times every year. With their white coloring (there are also black swans in Australia), their large wings, and their long, slender necks, they are exceptionally beautiful and elegant birds.

General Attributes

One of the loveliest of birds, indeed of all animals, the swan symbolizes beauty and purity. Swans are powerful emblems of love, devotion, and marriage. In the Celtic tradition, they are also birds of death, but in the most beautiful and positive way—linked by golden chains, they carry gods and goddesses to and from the Otherworld, and mortals to Afalon and the blissful afterlife.

Tír na'n Óg

Tír na'n Óg (pronounced approximately *cheer-nan-awk*) is the Gaelic name for the land which the Brythons (Welsh, Cornish and Bretons) call Afalon or Avallen (the Apple

Orchard). It means Land of the (Ever) Young. Swans carry mortals to this holy place. In ancient Celtic art, swans were often depicted pulling funereal chariots. The crane, another very holy bird in Celtic tradition, also carries souls to the afterlife. Sometimes a swan depicts the soul itself, particularly of a woman, since the beauty and simple elegance of the bird reflect the gentle beauty of the soul.

Eala Bhàn

The Dream of Oengus is a complicated Celtic tale, which features swans. The god Oengus (the Irish name Oengus changes to Angus in Scotland) has a vision of the woman he must marry. Her name is Caer Ibormeith (Yew Berry—the yew in Celtic tradition is a tree of death and resurrection). Every Samhain (the main Autumn festival), Caer Ibormeith and 150 of her maiden companions shape-shift into swans. Oengus may only marry Caer if he recognizes her (even though they have not met, apart from in Oengus's dreams) among all the swans. Some years ago, I wrote a poem that tells the tale. The title, Eala Bhàn, means White (or Fair) Swan:

> When Oengus mac Oc first saw Caer,
> she swam as a beautiful swan
> with a hundred and fifty swan companions,
> and her name was Eala Bhàn.
>
> A silver chain connected them
> as they swam at Samhain-tide,
> but gold were the links at Caer's white throat
> and he wanted her for his bride.
>
> Ethel Anbual, father of Caer,
> forbade Oengus mac Oc
> from marrying his lovely daughter
> and sweeping her away in his cloak.
>
> The wind blew cold on the tarn's dark water
> in little rippling waves,
> and the swan feathers spun like snowflakes falling
> on the icy slab of a grave.
>
> Eala Bhàn looked to the sky,
> where the god shone like the sun,
> and she spoke not with her voice but her heart
> when she said, "You and I are one."
>
> Oengus mac Oc flew down to her then,
> shedding the robes he had on,
> and splashed in the cold water beside her
> in the princely form of a swan.
>
> Ethel Anbual mustered his men
> and rushed to the tarn's wild shore,
> bearing arms and uttering curses
> that Oengus would live no more.
>
> But the swan couple beat their beautiful wings
> and took to the golden air,
> and Caer's silver-linked swan maidens
> accompanied them there.

> Three times they flew around the tarn,
> its waters black and deep,
> until Ethel Anbual and his men
> fell into a charmèd sleep.
>
> Then Oengus mac Oc and Eala Bhàn
> flew to the god's own *sídh*,
> at Brugh na Bóinne where the river flows
> down to the western sea.
>
> "I love you, Eala Bhàn, my bride,
> and whatever you choose to be,
> I will shape myself to be with you
> for all eternity."

Echoes of this very ancient Celtic legend are found in many similar folklore stories, including the legends that were absorbed into Tchaikovsky's ballet *Swan Lake* (1876), which is still regularly performed throughout the world.

Lohengrin

Another Celtic swan legend that lives on through classical music is the story of Lohengrin, which Wagner used in his opera of the same name, first performed in 1848. The story appears in medieval German legend—which is where Wagner found it, in the *Parzifal* of Wolfram von Eschenbach (c. 1160–1220)—but the original, called *The Knight of the Swan* and other variants, is much older, and came into Teutonic folklore from the earlier Celtic tradition:

> Lohengrin, the Knight of the Swan, was the son of Perceval (Parzifal in German), the Keeper of the Holy Grail. Raised in the company of the holy knights, he was under a sacred oath that he must never reveal his name or origin until asked directly to do so, and then he must return immediately to the Grail Castle.
>
> At a certain time, Lohengrin was sent to defend an innocent woman who was being falsely accused with the murder of her brother. Her name was Else. Lohengrin traveled to Else's court in a magical boat drawn by white swans. When he reached her castle, he fought her accuser, Frederick, and won. Else then consented to become Lohengrin's wife without knowing his true name. They were married at Antwerp, with the Emperor in attendance at the celebrations.
>
> The marriage was happy, but Else could not resist finally asking her husband what his real name was. He brought her to the grand hall, where, before all the assembled knights, he said, "My name is Lohengrin, son of Perceval, Keeper of the Holy Grail." He embraced Else sorrowfully and added, "Love cannot live without faith. I must return to the Holy Mountain."
>
> He blew his horn, the magical swan boat sailed into view, he climbed aboard, and Else never saw him again.[1]

Leda and Zeus

In Greek mythology, Leda was an Aetolian princess, later famous as the mother of Clytemnestra, Helen, Castor and Polydeuces, and as Queen of Sparta. According to the legend, Zeus came to earth in the form of a swan to seduce Leda, who produced Helen and Polydeuces from an egg. The image of the beautiful maiden in the arms (or wings) of a powerful young swan has been irresistible for artists down through the ages, particularly during the Italian Renaissance. Some of the 16th- and 17th-century works were so explicitly erotic that they caused great controversy. Some modern versions have attracted similar outrage.

The Irish poet William Butler Yeats (1865–1939) wrote a poem on the theme:

> A sudden blow: the great wings beating still
> Above the staggering girl, her thighs caressed
> By the dark webs, her nape caught in his bill,
> He holds her helpless breast upon his breast.
>
> How can those terrified vague fingers push
> The feathered glory from her loosening thighs?
> And how can body, laid in that white rush,
> But feel the strange heart beating where it lies?
>
> A shudder in the loins engenders there
> The broken wall, the burning roof and tower
> And Agamemnon dead.
>
> Being so caught up,
> So mastered by the brute blood of the air,
> Did she put on his knowledge with his power
> Before the indifferent beak could let her drop?[2]

Phaethon

Phaethon, from Greek mythology, is the classical archetype of the boy trying to prove to his father that he is a man. He was the son of Apollo, the sun god. His childhood friends mocked him for always boasting about how the god Apollo was his father. He appealed to his father to be allowed to drive the chariot of the sun across the sky for just one day, so that his friends would know that he was telling the truth and would stop teasing him. Apollo consistently refused, saying it was too dangerous. Finally, however, he relented, and Phaethon was allowed to drive the chariot of the sun across the sky.

Within a short while, Phaethon lost control of the horses: the chariot was just too much for him to handle. He fell to earth, where his landing scorched the ground and created the Libyan desert. Zeus, impatient with the boy's foolish pride, killed Phaethon with a single thunderbolt. Phaethon fell into the Po River, where he was transformed into a swan. His sisters, the Heliades, came to mourn him. They were transformed into willow trees, and their tears fell as drops of amber.[3]

Goose (Several Species)

Phylum *Chordata*, Class *Aves*, Order *Anseriformes*, Superfamily *Anatoidea*, Family *Anatidae*, Genus *Anser, Chen, Branta*, Species (several)

Name

Goose comes from Proto-Germanic **gans*, related to Latin *anser*, goose, which is also one of the genus names.

Description

Geese are generally smaller than swans, but larger than ducks. Those of the *Anser* and *Chen* genera are usually a mix of white, pale brown and darker brown in color, with much variation between species. *Branta* geese, such as the Canada goose (*Branta canadensis*) are typically darker, often with a black neck.

General Attributes

The goose, even when domesticated, is the most aggressive of all poultry birds, but the aggression is not random: it is in defense of family and territory, so the goose symbolizes protection and guardianship. A metal sculpture of a goose—with wings akimbo and beak sticking forward aggressively—has been found on ancient Celtic war helmets. The Iron Age Celtic temple at Roquepertuse in France features a statue of a guardian goose. Like swans, many goose species mate for life, so they also symbolize happy and faithful marriage. Geese fly great distances to and from summer and winter homes, honking in the sky distinctively and unmistakably, and therefore symbolize seasonal and other changes, and the great annual cycle of nature.

Because they saved Rome (see *Juno's geese* below), geese were sacred to Juno, Mars and the fertility god Priapus. In Chinese mythology, the goose symbolizes the male principle, Yang. In Japan, the goose is associated with the autumn harvest and the harvest full moon. In Hindu mythology, Brahma is sometimes portrayed riding a gander.

Geb

In Egyptian mythology, Geb is a male god personifying the world's surface, or earth. The hieroglyph of his name was also the word for goose, so he was often portrayed as a man with a goose or goose crown on his head. According to the creation legend, Geb was married to his sister, the sky-goddess Nut (brother-sister marriages are common in Egyptian mythology). Shu, the god of the air, acting under orders from the sun god Ra, separated Geb and Nut. From that point onward, the sky and the earth were separate, different places. Geb was distraught at the loss of his sister-wife. He wept inconsolably, and thus created the oceans and seas of the world.

Juno's Geese

A flock of sacred geese was kept in the Temple of Juno in ancient Rome. According to Livy (Titus Livius Patavinus, 64 BCE—12 CE), it was a guardian flock of geese that sounded the alarm when a warrior band of Celtic Gauls attacked Rome by night in 390 BCE. Because they had saved the city, their descendants were entitled to permanent residence in Juno's temple.[4]

The Goose That Laid the Golden Egg

The old fairy tale of the goose that laid the golden egg may have its origins in real farming practice. Goose flesh is very fatty, but also very tasty, and goose preceded turkey in Europe as the traditional Christmas meat for some centuries. However, the ancient Celts rarely if ever ate goose flesh—there may have been a *geis* or taboo against doing so, since goose fat (which would therefore also have been quite rare) was highly valued as a salve and medication, especially for ulcers or other slow-healing wounds, such as burns. But the most likely explanation seems to be that the eggs were valued more highly for food than the meat, and killing the bird would end the supply of eggs, in the same way that killing the golden-egg laying goose would cut off the supply of gold.

The story of the goose and the golden eggs is widely known as a European folk tale, but there are also Chinese and Japanese versions. It also appears in the *Jakatas*, a series of tales about the early life of the Buddha, which date from the 4th century BCE, so it has been popular in many cultures for a very long time.

Barnacle Geese

Barnacle geese (*Branta leucopsis*) were thought in the Middle Ages to have been born not from eggs, but from barnacles, the small marine shellfish. That is the origin of their common name. The binomial is *Branta*, a New Latin coining from Old Norse *brandgás*, meaning "burned (i.e., black) goose" and *leucopsis*, from Greek λευκοσ, *leukos*, white, and οπσις, *opsis*, face. Several respected authorities swore that they had seen tiny young geese emerging from barnacles on boats or in rock pools close to beaches. (What they had probably seen were the delicate fronds, properly called *cirri*, with which barnacles sift for food through the water, which could easily be mistaken for tiny feathers underwater.) As a result, the flesh of the barnacle goose was deemed by the Catholic Church to be fish rather than fowl, and eating it was allowed on Fridays, when meat was forbidden.

In a related story, the German Bishop of Augsburg, Saint Ulrich, 890–973 CE, was dining with his friend Bishop Wolfgang one Thursday evening. They were eating goose. They ate and drank late into the night, enjoying each other's company and conversation. Shortly after midnight, a messenger from the Emperor arrived, came into the room, and saw the two bishops eating goose meat, which was strictly forbidden on a Friday—the German Emperor made no allowance for the legend of the barnacle goose. The messenger took a leg from the goose, put it in his pocket, and returned to the Emperor's palace to denounce the bishops. As he was explaining matters to the Emperor, the messenger reached into his pocket and brought out the goose leg as evidence—only to discover that it had miraculously turned itself into a fish.[5]

Cooking the Goose

A Swedish legend says that the phrase "cooking the goose," meaning to deal with something or put an end to something, arose when King Erik (most Swedish kings were called Erik for almost a thousand years—this is one of the early, legendary ones from the 10th century CE) approached an enemy city, and found a dead goose nailed to the city wall, a sign of their contempt for the king. As Erik torched the city and watched it crash down in flames, he laughed, "Their goose is cooked!"[6]

Stork (Several Species)

Phylum *Chordata*, Class *Aves*, Order *Ciconiiformes*, Family *Ciconiidae*, Genera (6), Species (19 extant)

Name

Stork was *storc* in Old English, derived from Proto-Germanic **sturkaz*. The family name *Ciconiidae* is from *ciconia*, Latin for stork.

Description

Storks are big wading birds with long, thin legs and long bills. They eat fish, but they tend to live in drier climates and environments than their close relatives, such as herons and ibises, so they also eat frogs, insects and even small mammals. They fly very efficiently, soaring on large wings like birds of prey. They range in size from the marabou stork (*Lepoptilos crumenifer*), which is 5 feet (152 centimeters) tall to the Abdim's stork (*Ciconia abdiminii*), which is 2 feet, 6 inches (75 centimeters) tall. They are found mostly in sub-Saharan Africa and tropical Asia, although some species migrate to European countries.

General Attributes

Storks appear in many European myths, but also in China, the Middle East, and Africa. The most common association is with prosperity and good fortune generally, and the bringing of babies in the spring more particularly.

Storks and Babies

One of the most common folklore stories in the USA and most of Europe is that of the stork either heralding the birth of a baby, or actually bringing a new baby to a household. The two most common euphemisms for being born are either "being found under a gooseberry bush" or "being brought by the stork." A suggested reason—at least for the European tales—is that the white stork (*Ciconia ciconia*), with its very distinctive large, white body and red legs, is often seen nesting on European rooftops after its migration in the spring. However, the same folk belief is found among the Sioux Indians of North America with the wood stork (*Mycteria americana*), but without any rooftops.

In Greek mythology, the stork was sacred to Hera, mother of the gods, and in Roman mythology to her equivalent, Juno. In Christian symbolism, the stork represents purity and is a messenger of good tidings, including the good news that spring is on its way. Aristotle began the common folklore belief that when storks grow old, their young provide them with food and fly alongside them to support their tired old wings with their own younger and stronger wings. In folklore, then, storks not only bring babies to humans, their own babies are very kind and thoughtful to them.

How the Stork Was Created

A Polish folk legend (also found in Romania) says that God grew tired of the vast numbers of frogs, toads, snakes and lizards in the world, so he put them all into a huge sack and gave the sack to a human to empty into the sea. The human, overwhelmed with curiosity (as humans sometimes are) opened the sack, and all the slimy creatures escaped back out into the world. God's response was to turn the unfortunate human into a stork and condemn him to a life of perpetually hunting and eating such creatures.[7]

Ibis (Several Species)

Phylum *Chordata*, Class *Aves*, Order *Pelecaniformes*, Family *Threskiornithidae*, Genera (13), Species (28 extant)

Name

The common name, the Latin name and the Greek name are all the same, *ibis*. They all derive from ancient Egyptian *hb* or *hib*, meaning very tall.

Description

There are 28 extant species of ibis. They are similar in appearance to mid-sized storks. They all have long, downward-curving bills. They can have white, black or scarlet plumage.

General Attributes

The most famous ibis deity is the Egyptian god Thoth (see below), represented by the sacred ibis, *Threskiornis aethiopicus*. The scientific name of this bird has gone through many changes, and is still disputed, although Birdlife International agreed *Threskiornis aethiopicus* in 2003. The name comes from Greek θρεσκος, *threskos*, religious, devout, sacred, and ορνις, *órnis*, bird, and New Latin *aethiopicus* for Ethiopian.

Thoth

In ancient Egyptian mythology, the ibis was the symbol of the god Thoth. His name (Θωθ, *Thōth*, in Greek) is derived from Egyptian *dhwtj*, *dihauti* or *jehuti* (He Is Like the Ibis). He is usually depicted with a human body and the head of an ibis, surmounted by a royal crown.

Thoth was a senior god, with many important roles. He and his wife Maat stood on either side of Ra's solar barge, or the Sun. He was the patron of writing, science, philosophy, religion and the magical arts. He was the scribe of the gods, a sort of deified secretary and bookkeeper, and he is said to have invented the Egyptian system of hieroglyphics. He later became associated with judging the dead. The Greeks absorbed much of Thoth into their god Hermes, and associated him in addition with astrology, astronomy, mathematics (including geometry, which was sacred), medicine, oratory and principles of government.

When Osiris had been killed and Isis was trying to resurrect him, it was Thoth who supplied the prayers needed to bring him back to life. When Horus, son of the restored Osiris and Isis, lost his left eye in battle with Set, it was Thoth who restored it to him, albeit it with the changes we see in the phases of the Moon. Thoth brought 365 days to the year. There were originally 360, but he gambled with the Moon for an extra five days, and won.

From the 3rd century CE all the way through to the Renaissance and beyond, there have been attempts to conflate Thoth, Hermes and Moses. An Egyptian Jew of the 2nd or 3rd century called Artapanus of Alexandria argued that Thoth and Moses were the same historical person. The Hermes Trismegistus (Three Times Master) of medieval alchemy and magical traditions was frequently associated with both Thoth and Moses. Aleister Crowley (1875–1947), the English occultist, magician and poet, set up a temple to the ancient Egyptian gods in Cairo in 1904, and called his Egyptian-style Tarot deck *The Book of Thoth*, in honor of the god.

Thoth's major temple in antiquity was at *hmnw xa manaw* (God called Khemenu), at the boundary between Lower and Upper Egypt, which was called by the Romans *Hermopolis Magna*, based on the associations between Thoth and the Greek and Roman god, Hermes or Mercury. The city was largely destroyed, but the remains lie close to the city now called el-Ashmanein in Egyptian Arabic.

Heron (Several Species)

Phylum *Chordata*, Class *Aves*, Order *Pelecaniformes*, Family *Ardeidae*, Genera (21), Species (64 extant)

Name

The common name heron is one of those interesting words that have changed significantly in sound and spelling in their long journey into Modern English. The assumed Proto-Indo-European root is **kreik* or **skreik*, meaning creak or screech (quite similar words). In Ancient Greek, this was κριζο, *krizo*. The Old English was *hragra*. The assumed Old Dutch was **heigero*, and Middle Dutch was *heiger*. However, the Anglo-Normans replaced *hragra* with their own version of the word, *heiron*, which came into Middle English as *heroun*, and finally into Modern English as heron.

Another early English name for the bird was *heronshaw* or *hernshaw*, from French *heronçeau*, which became corrupted in common speech to *handsaw*. When Hamlet says the apparently nonsensical "I am but mad north-north-west: when the wind is southerly I know a hawk from a handsaw" in Shakespeare's play (Act II, Sc. ii, 405), the "handsaw" means heron, which makes a lot more sense. The heron has also been nicknamed the shitepoke for its habit of defecating at the same time as it flies rapidly away when alarmed or disturbed.

Description

Herons are familiar long-legged wading birds of freshwater and seashore terrains. They stand either at the water's edge, or just into shallow water, as if they were statues, until a fish or other prey comes near enough, when they strike rapidly downwards with their long bills. They are carnivorous, eating a wide variety of aquatic and amphibious animals, and occasionally even birds, eggs and small land animals. They sometimes stir the water with their feet, or stalk slowly and stiffly along the water's edge, or hold their wings aloft over them, either to intimidate the fish or (more likely) to provide shade that might attract them. They are found on all continents except Antarctica, and in most landscapes except desert and very mountainous regions: anywhere where there is water.

General Attributes

Herons, like owls, are considered wise and venerable in much folklore, probably because of their ability to remain absolutely still for very long periods of time, which most humans find quite difficult.

Ba

In the ancient Egyptian religion, the *ba* was an individual person's soul. In *The Book of the Dead* there is a spell to raise the *ba* from death, but it comes back to the world as a heron, not as a human. It must wait patiently to see whether it will be granted another life as a human being. That is why herons stand so still in the water or by the water's edge—they are waiting and hoping to be shape-shifted back into humans.

Big Blue Heron and Old Gray Wolf

An ancient legend of the Algonquin peoples in North America tells the story of a meeting between Big Blue Heron and Old Gray Wolf.

> Blue Heron kindly carried two small weasels on his back across a rushing river. Old Gray Wolf saw him do it, and saw a chance to save himself a hard swim. He went up to Big Blue Heron and ordered the bird to carry him across, just as he had carried the weasels. Big Blue Heron took Old Gray Wolf on his back, but halfway across he said, "Phew! I'm not as strong as I thought I was." And with that, he flipped a wing, and Old Gray Wolf took an unwilling plunge into the swirling, icy torrent.[8]

Kingfisher (Several Species)

Phylum *Chordata*, Class *Aves*, Order *Coraciiformes*, Suborder *Alcedines*, Family *Alcedinidae*, Subfamilies *Alcedininae, Halcyoninae, Cerylinae*, Genus (several), Species (several)

Name

The common name is simply from king and fisher. It implies a high mythological status for the bird. The family and subfamily names come from the ancient Greek legend of Alcyone and Ceyx (see below). Halcyon is an alternative name for kingfisher. *Halcyon* is now the genus name of several species of African tree kingfishers, which are larger than European kingfishers and have larger, heavier bills.

Description

The kingfisher is a small, shy, brightly colored bird with a large head and sharp bill. It lives close to streams and rivers and darts into the water to catch fish. It is so shy, and moves so quickly, that very often all a human observer sees is a quick flash of bright blue disappearing into or emerging from the water at high speed and vanishing into the nearest foliage. Kingfishers of several different species are found everywhere in the world, in both temperate and tropical regions, apart from polar regions and deserts.

General Attributes

The kingfisher has been generally admired in many cultures (but see *In Borneo* below). It features in early Greek mythology and in folklore around the world. It is also revered in many Polynesian cultures, where it is reported to control the tides, evidence of its association with the Moon. Almost all kingfishers are brightly colored, usually blue, and strikingly beautiful. Modern photography has captured much of their beauty, which often moves too quickly for the human eye to follow.

Alcyone and Ceyx

Alcyone or Halcyone is a figure from Greek mythology, in one of its best-known legends:

> Alcyone was a princess of Thessaly. She later married Ceyx, the king of Trachis. Unlike many royal marriages in ancient Europe, where political and military factors determined who would marry whom, the marriage between Alcyone and Ceyx was a real marriage of love. They so treasured each other that they began jokingly referring to themselves as Zeus and Hera, because they thought themselves as happy as the king and queen of all the gods.
>
> Joke or not, daring to call themselves by the royal names Zeus and Hera was a sacrilege that could not go unpunished. When Ceyx went on a sea voyage to consult an oracle, Zeus sent down a thunderbolt to destroy his ship, and Ceyx drowned.
>
> The god of sleep and dreams, Morpheus, came to Alcyone in the form of Ceyx as she was sleeping in the palace at Thracis. The ghostly figure told Alcyone that he was now dead, that he still loved her, and he hoped that he might meet her again when her own time came to die. In horror and utter misery, Alcyone threw herself into the sea to join her dead husband.
>
> The other gods saw Alcyone's tears, and were greatly moved by her distress. Without Zeus' knowledge or permission, they turned Alcyone and Ceyx into brightly colored little birds, which they named "halcyon" or "kingfisher."[9]

Although the kingfisher is generally a freshwater bird, there was an ancient belief that they built their nests on the Aegean Sea, and that as long as they tended the nest, the sea would remain calm. For seven days before the midwinter solstice, and a further seven days afterwards, the sea and seashore had to remain quiet enough for the couple to build their nest and lay their eggs. Calm days were therefore referred to as "halcyon days." In modern common usage, "halcyon days" also means happy, carefree, easy times remembered from the past.

Robert Graves explains the symbolic significance of the Alcyone and Ceyx legend:

> The legend of the halcyon's, or kingfisher's, nest (which has no foundation in natural history, since the halcyon does not build any kind of nest, but lays eggs in holes by the waterside) can refer only to

the birth of the new sacred king at the winter solstice—after the queen who represents his mother, the Moon-goddess, has conveyed the old king's corpse to a sepulchral island. But because the winter solstice does not always coincide with the same phase of the moon, "every year" must be understood as "every Great Year," of one hundred lunations, in the last of which solar and lunar time were roughly synchronized, and the sacred king's term ended.... Pliny, who describes the halcyon's alleged nest in detail—apparently the zoophyte called *halcyoneum* by Linnaeus—reports that the halcyon is rarely seen, and then only at the two solstices and at the setting of the Pleiades. This proves her to have originally been a manifestation of the Moon-goddess, who was alternately the Goddess of Life-in-Death at the winter solstice, and of Death-in-Life at the summer solstice; and who, every Great Year, early in November, when the Pleiades set, sent the sacred king his death summons.[10]

In Borneo

Kingfishers are considered birds of omen in Borneo, sometimes good, sometimes bad. The Kadazan-Dusun people of the Malaysian state of Sabah of North Borneo will abandon a hunt if they catch sight of an Oriental dwarf kingfisher (*Ceyx erithaca*), believing that a hunter will be killed if they do not return home immediately.[11]

25

Sea Birds (Several Orders and Families)

Albatross (Several Species)

Phylum *Chordata*, Class *Aves*, Order *Procellariiformes*, Family *Diomedeiidae*, Genus (4), Species (22)

Name

The derivation of the common name is uncertain. The Spanish *alcatraz* means pelican, gannet or albatross (as well as being the name of the famous former prison on Alcatraz Island in California). It appears to derive either from Arabic *al-gattas* (the diver) or *al-gadus* (the water wheel bucket, referring to the pelican's pouch), with the intrusion of the letter b instead of g explained by confusion with Latin *albus*, white. Albatrosses have also been nicknamed gooneybirds and mollymawks.

The family name *Diomedeiidae* comes from the warrior god Diomedes in ancient Greek legend. He was a favorite of the goddess Athena, and played a major role in the Trojan War. According to one legend, he and his companions became either shearwaters or albatrosses after their deaths.

Description

Albatrosses are among the largest of sea birds. The wingspan of the genus of Great Albatrosses (*Diomedae*) can reach 12 feet (3.7 meters). They fly huge distances very efficiently, soaring closely over the waters of the Southern Ocean and the North Pacific, and nesting on small, remote islands. They live on krill, squid and fish.

General Attributes

The albatross is well known for its reputation of containing the soul of a drowned mariner (see *The Rime of the Ancient Mariner* below). In Japan, it is considered *aho-dori*, a clumsy idiot bird, an image which was continued in the 1977 Disney animation *The Rescuers*, where Orville the Albatross was a comically hopeless flier, in direct contrast to the reality of real albatross flight. In Hawaii and Polynesia, the albatross is a sacred bird. They are called *aumakua* in Hawaii, which means "sacred manifestations of the ancestors."

The Rime of the Ancient Mariner

Sailors have killed and eaten albatrosses for centuries. Nevertheless, a legend grew during the 18th and 19th centuries that albatrosses were holy birds, and that the souls of drowned sailors became albatrosses. As a result, more and more sailors, in particular those who made the famously dangerous passage around Cape Horn, began to refuse to kill the bird. Cape Horners (as those who had rounded the Horn called themselves) had once nicknamed themselves "albatrosses" as a sort of honorific, but the title fell into disuse as unease about killing or harming albatrosses increased.

The English poet Samuel Taylor Coleridge (1772–1834) captured the legend in his famous poem *The Rime of the Ancient Mariner*, first published in 1798. A ragged mariner stops a wedding guest on his way to a joyous event. The guest listens politely at first, then with exasperation, and finally with horror and sadness as the mariner finishes telling his story. The mariner describes how he unthinkingly shot an albatross, despite the legend that it would bring ill fortune on the ship. The ill fortune came rapidly. The ship was horribly becalmed:

> Day after day, day after day,
> We stuck, nor breath nor motion;
> As idle as a painted ship
> Upon a painted ocean.
>
> Water, water, every where,
> And all the boards did shrink;
> Water, water, every where,
> Nor any drop to drink.
>
> The very deep did rot—Oh Christ!
> That ever this should be.
> Yea, slimy things did crawl with legs,
> Upon the slimy sea.[1]

The other sailors tied the dead albatross around the Ancient Mariner's neck, a symbol of the dreadful evil he had brought about. Having "an albatross about your neck" has now become a common and powerful metaphor for suffering hardship, distress or frustration as a result of your own foolishness or wrongdoing.

All the other sailors died, one by one. The Ancient Mariner, brought close to death himself, lay helplessly in the boat as it drifted. The boat sank in a whirlpool, and the Ancient Mariner was rescued by a pilot boat.

> Oh! Dream of joy! Is this indeed
> The light-house top I see?
> Is this the hill? Is this the kirk?
> Is this mine own countree?
>
> We drifted o'er the harbour-bar,
> And I with sobs did pray—
> O let me be awake, my God!
> Or let me sleep alway.[2]

As penance for the crime of killing the albatross, the mariner must spend the rest of his days crossing the land, telling his story and expiating his sin. The wedding guest listens to the grim tale through to the end, finally leaving as "a sadder and a wiser man."

Petrel (Several Species)

Phylum *Chordata*, Class *Aves*, Order *Procellariiformes*, Family *Procellariidae*, Genus (several), Species (several)

Name

The derivation of the common name is uncertain. It may be a diminutive of Peter, referring to the Christian description of St. Peter walking on the water : "He [Jesus] said, 'Come.' So Peter got out of the boat, started walking on the water, and came towards Jesus."[3] Several petrels fly very low to the sea, their feet almost touching the waves.

The order name *Procellariiformes* and family name *Procellariidae* both mean "with tube-shaped noses," which is reflected in the alternative common name, tubenose. The order consists of albatrosses, shearwaters, petrels and storm petrels (sometimes called stormy petrels in Britain).

Description

Petrels are best known for the fact that they spend almost their entire lives at sea, returning to land only to breed. They are found almost exclusively in the Southern Ocean. Snow petrels, which are all white and very small (about the same size as a pigeon) endure almost unbelievable cold and harsh winds in the Antarctic in order to feed on krill and the other abundant food in the Southern Ocean.

General Attributes

Petrels are survivors. They overcome extremely harsh conditions in their chosen habitats. They hardly use their legs at all while they are at sea, so when they come to land to breed, they walk with great difficulty and are easily taken by predators, such as gulls, skuas, owls and falcons, or rats and cats where they have been introduced. As with albatrosses, petrels are thought to be or contain the souls of drowned sailors.

Mother Carey's Chicken

A common nickname for the storm petrel is Mother Carey's chicken, believed to be a corruption of the Latin name, *mater cara*, beloved mother, for the Virgin Mary, mother of Christ. This nickname suggests a special affection and reverence for the bird. Mother Carey appears as a character in other, later sources, including *The Water Babies* by Charles Kingsley (1819–1875).

Symbol of Revolution

The Russian name for the European storm petrel is Буревестник, *burevestnik*. In 1901, the Russian Soviet poet and revolutionary Maxim Gorky (1868–1936) published a poem called Песня о Буревестнике, *Pyesnya o Burevestnikye*, Song of the Storm Petrel. It achieved instant fame (or notoriety) as "the battle anthem of the revolution," and Gorky was nicknamed "the Storm Petrel of the Revolution."[4] The metaphor is still used to this day, and *Burevestnik* is an imprint and title still widely used by anarchist and revolutionary organizations.

Frigate Bird (Several Species)

Phylum *Chordata*, Class *Aves*, Order *Suliformes*, Family *Fregatidae*, Genus *Fregata*, Species (5)

Name

The genus name *Fregata* is a back-formation from the common name, frigate bird. The common name comes from French *frégate*, meaning frigate, a kind of fast warship. British sailors in the Caribbean used to call the bird a Man-of-War.

Description

Frigate birds are the tropical or subtropical equivalents of the albatrosses and petrels of colder waters. There are five extant species, all with predominantly black plumage. Males have a red throat pouch, which they inflate during mating season to attract females. Typical wingspan is up to 7 feet, 6 inches (about 2.3 meters), and frigate birds can soar for weeks on end, like their Southern Ocean counterparts.

General Attributes

Like the other ocean-soaring birds, frigate birds are generally respected and even venerated, especially in Polynesia and Micronesia.

Carrier Frigates

Frigate birds will reliably return to their home territories when released, in the same way that carrier pigeons will return to their lofts. The peoples of the Gilbert Islands and Tuvalu used this trait to their advantage, to send messages quickly from one island to another. Email and instagrams have probably replaced this custom now, or soon will.

Easter Island

The Rapa Nui people of Easter Island worshiped the frigate bird. As well as the famous giant carved heads, there was an annual ritual of great complexity, described in 1919 by Katherine Scoresby-Routledge. Contestants would swim to a nearby island, Motu Nui, to seek frigate bird eggs. Many were killed by sharks, or fell to their deaths from steep cliffs. The first to find an egg on Motu Nui would call across the sea to his patron or *ivi atua*, who immediately acquired *tapu* or sacred status, shaving his head and painting it white or red. For a full year, he lived a life of ease and privilege. The ancient ritual was suppressed by Christian missionaries in the 1860s.[5]

Fulmar (*Fulmarus glacialis* and *Fulmarus glacialoides*)

Phylum *Chordata*, Class *Aves*, Order *Procellariformes*, Family *Procellariidae*, Genus *Fulmarus*, Species *Fulmarus glacialis* (northern fulmar), *Fulmarus glacialoides* (southern fulmar)

Name

The common name fulmar is derived from Old Norse *fúll* (foul) and *már* (gull), in reference to the bird's habit of using foul-smelling projectile vomit as a deterrent to predators. The species names *glacialis* and *glacialoides* both mean icy or frozen, from Latin *glacialis*.

Description

Fulmars belong to the family Procelliariidae or tubenoses, like the albatrosses and shearwaters. They are much smaller than albatrosses, and can easily be mistaken for gulls. They can live for up to 40 years, an unusual age for any wild bird.

General Attributes

Fulmars are birds of the cold northern seas, but they have also spread southwards to more temperate zones, and the isolated Scottish island group of St. Kilda is famed for its fulmar populations, which were hunted in great numbers until humans abandoned the hard life on the isolated, often cold, wet and dreary main island of Hirta in 1930.

Sedna and the Fulmar

Sedna is the great Eskimo (Inuit) goddess of the sea. She was once human, but a male fulmar invited her to marry him and come and live with the wild birds. She accepted, but the fulmar treated her cruelly, and her father came in a small boat to rescue her. He killed the fulmar, and they fled across the waves. The other fulmars chased them and Sedna's father tried to distract them by cutting off his daughter's fingers and throwing them into the sea. But the fingers and nails became whales, whalebones and seals. When they reached land, Sedna took her revenge on her father by calling her dogs to gnaw off his feet and hands. Now Sedna rules as Queen of Adlivun, the land of the dead beneath the sea.[6]

Pelican (Several Species)

Phylum *Chordata*, Class *Aves*, Order *Pelecaniformes*, Family *Pelecanidae*, Genus *Pelecanus*, Type species *Pelecanus onocratulus*, Species (8)

Name

The name pelican is derived from Ancient Greek πελεκαν, *pelekán*, pelican, related to the word πελεκυς, *pélekus*, meaning hatchet, and Latin *pelecanus*, which is also the genus name.

Description

Pelicans are large, easily recognized water birds, with long beaks and large throat pouches. There are eight extant species, found in both subtropical and temperate zones, but not in the interior of South America, nor in the open ocean, but invariably close to seashores and marine islands close to the mainland.

General Attributes

To fishermen, the pelican is a competitor and a pest. Pelican populations have declined considerably in many areas through pollution, habitat destruction and disturbance.

The pelican has been an animal of special regard in several different cultures and mythologies. The ancient Egyptians associated it with death and the afterlife. In Judaism, its flesh was considered unclean. It was worshiped as a sacred animal by the Moche people of Peru. The prison island of Alcatraz near San Francisco was given its name because of the large number of brown pelicans that originally lived there (see **albatross**).

Christ the Pelican

In medieval Christianity, the pelican was strongly identified with Christ, after Saint Jerome wrote that the pelican shed its own blood to revive its young. (The belief comes from the biological fact that many bird species, including the pelican, pluck down from their own breasts to line the nest in which the young live, and sometimes they may bleed slightly from spots where they have plucked the down too vigorously.) Saint Thomas Aquinas made the same claim, and referred to Christ as "the loving, divine pelican." Queen Elizabeth I of England (1558–1603 CE) adopted the pelican as her personal symbol as Mother of the English Church.

In heraldry, the pelican was widely used as a symbol of saintly motherhood. A new word, "vulning," was coined from Latin *vulnere*, "to wound," as in "a pelican vulning," i.e., supposedly wounding herself to feed her blood to her offspring. Both Corpus Christi Colleges, at Oxford and at Cambridge, have the pelican in their coats of arms.

26

Chickens and Peafowl (*Galliformes*)

Chicken (*Gallus gallus domesticus*)

Phylum *Chordata*, Class *Aves*, Order *Galliformes*, Family *Phasianidae*, Genus *Gallus*, Species *Gallus gallus*, Subspecies *Gallus gallus domesticus*

Name

The ultimate derivation of the name chicken is uncertain, but it appears to be Germanic: the cognates in other Germanic languages are very similar—Frisian *schückling* and *sjuuken*, Dutch *kuiken*, German *Küken* and Old Norse *kjúklingr*. A male chicken is called either a cock, cockerel (if less than a year old), or rooster. Young females are called pullets. The genus and species name *gallus* is the Latin for cock or rooster.

Description

At approximately 20 billion in number, the chicken is the most populous bird in the world. Chickens were originally raised for cockfighting or for ceremonial purposes, and did not become commonly domesticated for meat and eggs until the Hellenistic period in Greece, i.e., approximately 400 to 200 BCE. Their existence in Egypt was first recorded in about 1500 BCE, when they were a source of wonder as "the bird that gives birth every day."

General Attributes

Chickens are very familiar everywhere. They can be excellent pets, and can be very affectionate, although they can also make a lot of mess digging and scratching and making themselves deep dust baths in the garden or pooping prodigiously in unacceptable places. Chickens appear in folklore and religion across the world.

Chickens in Religious or Mythological Legends

The male *Gallus gallus*, commonly called a cock or a rooster, features in several religions and legends. The ancient Greeks identified the cock with the sun-god Apollo and with the corn-goddess Demeter. In Aztec ceremonies, a cock was sometimes substituted for a human sacrifice (no doubt to the intended human victim's great relief). Romans sacrificed cocks to Mars, god of war, because they associated them with cock-fighting, a practice that is thousands of years old and that still takes place to this day, not only in wild places of the world but any place where people enjoy cruel bloodshed and rapid gambling. The cock was also sacred to Asklepios in Greece (Asclepius in Rome), the god of medicine—there may even be some connection with the ancient Jewish folk belief in the efficacy of chicken soup as the panacea for almost any disease.

In Christianity, Jesus tells Peter, his most faithful disciple, "Before the cock crow, thou shalt deny me thrice,"[1] but the cock is also a symbol of the Resurrection (because it proclaims the new dawn each day). In the 9th century, Pope Nicholas ordered that the figure of a rooster should be placed on top of every church steeple, a practice which has largely continued to this day.

Jesus even described himself as a mother hen in the Bible: "O Jerusalem, Jerusalem, you who kill the prophets and stone those sent to you, how often I have longed to gather your children together, as a hen gathers her chicks under her wings, but you were not willing."[2]

The Cock and the Pearl

According to a tale sometimes attributed to Æsop:

A rooster was strutting around the poultry yard, scratching and pecking for food. He saw something white, and scratched it out of the ground eagerly.

"Bah!" he said, as he rolled it over. "It's a pearl. It's no use to me. I thought it was a tasty grain of barley."

Moral: Precious things should only belong to those who know their value.

Alectryon

In Greek mythology, the god of war Ares was having an illicit affair with Aphrodite the goddess of beauty and love , wife of the sun-god Helios. Whenever Ares visited Aphrodite to make love to her, he posted a young soldier called Alectryon at the bedchamber door, to give warning if anyone were to come near.

One night, Alectryon fell asleep while he was on duty, and Helios came into Aphrodite's chamber to discover his wife sporting merrily with Ares. Helios was furious with Ares, but Ares was even more furious with Alectryon. He turned him into a rooster, and from that day to this, whenever Helios enters the room (i.e., when the sun rises), Alectryon cannot help but crow as loud as he can to announce the sun-god's imminent arrival.[3]

The Cock and Saint Vitus

Saint Vitus (died c. 300 CE) is a Christian saint who has several different jobs. He is the patron saint of dogs, of all domestic animals, of young people, of dancers, coppersmiths, actors and mummers. He is invoked against epilepsy, sleeplessness and snakebite. A constant involuntary movement of the limbs, chorea or Huntington Disease, is often called Saint Vitus' Dance after him.

Vitus was born into a pagan noble family in Sicily, but he was converted to Christianity first by his nurse and then by his foster-father, Modestus. His real father locked Vitus, now aged 12, in a cell to cure him of his obsession with Christianity, but was astonished to see seven angels in the cell with his son, dancing. Vitus and his foster-father escaped to mainland Italy, where Vitus healed the emperor, Diocletian, who nevertheless still insisted on Vitus worshiping pagan gods, which Vitus refused to do. Vitus miraculously survived several tortures and imprisonments before being brought to heaven by an angel.

Saint Vitus is patron of Sicily, Saxony and Prague. He is often depicted with a cock beside him, as in the cathedral at Prague. The cock, which had previously been a pagan symbol, was reassigned to Vitus, and offering a cock to the saint was still a regular practice in Prague until well into the 18th century.[4]

Chanticleer

Chanticleer (Clear Singer) is a clever rooster in medieval legend. He features in Chaucer's *The Nun's Priest's Tale*.

> The cunning fox, Dan Russell, comes to the poultry yard and tells Master Chanticleer what a magnificent, glorious singing voice he has. The rooster, immensely flattered, closes his eyes and begins to sing. The fox seizes the rooster by the neck, and runs for the fence.
>
> "I would recommend that you kill and eat me immediately," says Chanticleer calmly, "because I'm afraid I can hear your pursuers gaining ground on you very rapidly."
>
> Dan Russell opens his mouth to reply, and Chanticleer flies out and away to safety.[5]

Baba Yaga's Hut

In Russian folklore, Baba Yaga (Old Woman) is an evil ogress who kidnaps and then eats little children. Her hut is often surrounded by little human skulls on sticks. The chicken connection is peculiar: her hut, which can move magically from place to place, is depicted as standing on chickens' legs, yellow and scaly with big, sharp-clawed feet.

Baka

In Haitian voodoo, Baka or Babako is a dangerous and evil spirit of the dead. His malicious interference can only be prevented by sacrificing a black rooster to him. If a black rooster is not available, a black goat may be substituted.[6]

The Rooster and the Devil

In a medieval Christian legend, Saint Cuthman (died c. 900 CE) of Steyning in the English county of Sussex was walking on the South Downs when the Devil appeared beside him. The Devil told Cuthman, with malicious glee, that he was going to flood the land and destroy every Christian church and convent.

The saint went to see his sister Cecilia, who was mother superior of the convent that stood where Dyke's House now stands. Cuthman asked her to keep the convent lights burning all night and to have the Mass spoken over and over until daybreak.

At sunset, the Devil arrived with pickax, spade and shovel to dig the dyke that would let the sea in to drown every church and every convent. But the constant singing of the Mass buzzed in his head, and he found it very difficult to concentrate.

When the nuns lit all the candles in the convent, the roosters in every farm around thought it was dawn, and began their cock-a-doodle-doing in full voice. The Devil, who could only work at night, cursed the saint, the mother superior, and all the roosters, but his cause was hopeless. He fled in a cloud of evil-smelling smoke. The small hole he had made is still there to this day, and is called Devil's Dyke.[7]

The Evil Eater

In Indonesia, the chicken plays a vital role in the Hindu cremation ceremony. As the body is consumed by the fire, a chicken is tethered by the leg close by. Any evil spirits present will go into the chicken rather than into the family members and guests. After the cremation, the chicken is released and allowed to go back to its former status.

In a similar way, a chicken is sacrificed on the day before Yom Kippur in Judaism. The ritual, called *kapparos*, involves first cradling and massaging the bird, and then sacrificing it so that it will take into itself the sins of the person and allow atonement. Traditionally, a woman brings a hen to *kapparos*, while a man brings a rooster. The cooked flesh of the bird after the sacrifice is given to the poor.

Peafowl (Several Species)

Phylum *Chordata*, Class *Aves*, Order *Galliformes*, Family *Phasianidae*, Subfamily *Phasianinae*, Genus *Pavo*, *Afropavo*, Species (3)

Name

The genus name *Pavo* is Latin for peacock. (*Afroparvo* just means African peacock.) There are three indigenous species of peafowl, one in India (*Pavo cristatus*, crested peacock), one in southeast Asia (*Pavo muticus*, mute peacock), and one in Africa (*Afroparvo congensis*, African peacock of the Congo). The common name is pea (from *pavo*) plus fowl, just meaning bird. (The name has no connection with peas, the legumes.)

Description

Peafowl are native to three areas of the world, as just described, but they have been introduced to many other countries, not just in recent times but in ancient times as well. They were probably first brought to Greece from Persia by Alexander the Great (356–323 BCE).

Peafowl are exotic birds, recognized immediately by the male's extraordinarily complex and elaborate tail feathers, which have been highly prized for centuries, both as simple ornaments but also as religious symbols.

General Attributes

The peahen/peacock has symbolized different things in different cultures. In Greek mythology, Hera sent the hundred-eyed giant Argos to watch Io, one of Zeus's many mistresses. Zeus disguised himself as a woodpecker, and had Hermes kill Argos. Hera took the giant's hundred eyes and placed them in the tail of the peacock, an otherwise dull bird, which now became haughty and vain.

In the Far East, the peacock has far more positive attributes. In Buddhism, it represents compassion and watchfulness (see *Guanyin* below). In Chinese mythology, it represents rank, dignity and beauty—it was an emblem of the Ming Dynasty (1368–1644 CE).

Christian legend held that the flesh of a dead peacock never decayed (largely because peacock feathers retain their color for years). Saint Augustine is said to have experimented with dead peacocks and found no decay in them. Christianity has absorbed earlier Persian and Babylonian symbolism about the connection between peacocks and immortality and the Tree of Life. Paintings depicting peacocks drinking at a well or a vase are said to represent the faithful Christian drinking at the well of eternal life.

In Islamic folklore, the peacock was the original guardian of the Gates of Paradise, but it was persuaded by the Devil to assist in the fall of Adam and Eve. It now has a sort of dual citizenship: it represents beauty and glory, but also vanity and self-serving.

In Hinduism

The peacock is called *mayura* in Hindi. In Hindu mythology, the gods Brahma, Kama and Skanda all ride the peacock. It is often depicted killing a snake, i.e., defeating evil, but the snake also represents Time, and the killing of the snake then represents transcendence to a higher plane beyond time.

When the great god Indra was battling against the evil god Ravana, a peacock gave Indra shelter. The god repaid the kindness by placing "a thousand eyes" in the peacock's tail. Hindus use peacock tail feathers to clean holy statues and images, and generally keep them in the house for good luck, protection and prosperity.

Lord Krishna is often depicted with peacock feathers adorning his head. The peacock is associated with many Hindu deities, and particularly with the goddess Saraswati, who represents compassion, patience, sensitivity and wisdom.

Guanyin

The peacock is also associated with Guanyin, one of the most widely revered deities in the world (although she is scarcely known at all in the West). Guanyin has many versions of her name, including Gwanshiyin, Kwan Yin, Kwun Yam (Cantonese), Kannon or Kwanyon (Japanese—the company name Canon comes from this name), Gwan-eum (Korean), and Quán Thế Âm (Vietnamese). She is called Chenrézik in Tibet. Guanshiyin (Guanyin is a shortened version of this name) means literally "one who perceives the world's lamentations," and is a translation of the Sanskrit name Avalokiteśvara or Avalokiteshwara, a Buddhist *bodhisattva* (person on the path to becoming a Buddha) who was originally male.

As the many names indicate, Guanyin is worshiped very widely in China and all across the Far East, perhaps by more people than any other single deity. She is the goddess of mercy and compassion, protector of the poor, the young, the old, the infirm, the disabled, the dispossessed. She is worshiped not only by Mahayana Buddhists, but also by Taoists and in many rural folklore religions and traditions across China and Tibet. In the figure of Guanyin, the peacock symbol is always positive and powerful, by contrast to the ambivalence of the same symbol in the West, where vanity is always a negative presence. In Guanyin, the "thousand eyes" represent an ever-present watchfulness and caring love for the common people, which is why literally millions of people adore her.[8]

27

Perching Birds and Singing Birds (*Passeriformes*)

Blackbird (*Turdus merula*)

Phylum *Chordata*, Class *Aves*, Order *Passeriformes*, Family *Turdidae*, Genus *Turdus*, Species *Turdus merula*

Name

The common name is obvious. The genus name, *Turdus*, is Latin for thrush, the family to which the blackbird belongs. Several other birds, including the American robin, belong to this family. The species name, *merula*, is Latin for blackbird, and came into mediaeval French and English as *merle*, where, sometimes confusingly, it also meant thrush.

Description

Apart from the common blackbird (*Turdus merula*), there are also a Chinese blackbird (*Turdus mandarinus*), a gray-winged blackbird (*Turdus boulboul*), a white-collared blackbird (*Turdus albocinctus*), a Tibetan blackbird (*Turdus maximus*), and an Indian blackbird (*Turdus simillimus*). The common blackbird is found throughout temperate Europe and Asia and in North Africa, and has been introduced to Australia and New Zealand. Common blackbirds are widespread and abundant (estimated between 80 million and 160 million in Europe alone). They are omnivorous, medium-sized songbirds with sleek, black plumage, bright golden beaks and bright eyes. They often hop along the ground, or fly quickly low above the ground to seek cover in hedges or bushes.

General Attributes

The blackbird is best known for its song, which is exceptionally complex and musical. It is perceived as an oracular bird, favored by the gods. The blackbird is the national bird of Sweden, which has between one million and two million of them.[1]

The Druid Bird

One of the Gaelic names for the blackbird is *Druid Dubh*, meaning Black Druid. In both ancient and modern Celtic Druidism, the blackbird is a messenger between the mundane world and the Otherworld. A ninth-century Irish poem describes the blackbird's song as "a poem to the sun's first slender ray."

The blackbird's song is considered by many to be the most beautiful birdsong in the world. It is certainly very complex, with seemingly endless variations in rhythm and melody, and it is very easy to understand how the classical druids perceived it as language, as divine speech from another world. The rowan tree was (and still is) a sacred and magical tree in Druidic lore, its often brilliantly scarlet berries making it very recognizable; many birds eat rowan berries, but blackbirds are especially fond of them, and druids perceive the berries as magically giving blackbirds the power of oracular speech and song.

In the ancient Welsh tale *Branwen Daughter of Llyr*, the god Bendigeidfrân (Bran the Blessed) and his companions pass 72 years in a state of timeless enchantment, a foretaste of the eternal joys of Afalon. During their glimpse of the eternal afterlife, they are serenaded by the birds of the goddess Rhiannon, which are blackbirds. In another Welsh tale, *Culhwch and Olwen*, blackbirds are described as: "they that wake the dead and lull the living to sleep."

In that same tale, the hero is sent in search of the oldest animal in the world, to ask its advice as to the whereabouts of Mabon, the god of youth (in other words, eternal life). Culhwch and his companions talk to five animals in turn until they reach the oldest animal in the world. The animals are, in sequence: the blackbird, the stag, the owl, the eagle, and the salmon.

In Irish, *ghoba-dhu* means both blackbird and blacksmith. Smiths are associated with magical power in many cultures, but especially so in Druidism. Goibhniu is the Irish smith-god, and his Welsh equivalent is Gofannon. The blackbird is often described or depicted cracking open snails' shells on a stone, in the same way that the smith beats metal on an anvil.[2]

How the Blackbird Became Black

An old French legend describes how a white bird on a quest to find the priceless treasure of the Prince of Riches enters a mysterious cavern, following the advice of the wise magpie. He finds a huge pile of gold dust on the ground and stirs it with his beak. The gold dust clings to his beak and is reflected in his eyes. At the same moment, the demon guarding the treasure bursts in, trailing fire and smoke. The bird flies quickly from the cavern into the open air, and discovers that he is now deep black in color, with a golden beak and a bright gleam in his eye.

Colly Birds, Pie Meat and National Emblem

The English Christmas carol *The Twelve Days of Christmas* features "four calling birds" on the fourth day, but it is now thought that the word "calling" was originally "colly," meaning "coal-black," and indicating blackbirds. The nursery song *Sing a Song of Sixpence* describes "four-and-twenty blackbirds baked in a pie," but blackbirds are not generally eaten or known for their meat.

The Temptations of Saint Benedict

The Christian Saint Benedict from Spoleto in Italy lived from 480 to 543 CE, and is considered the father of Western monasticism. He was offended and disgusted by the debauchery he observed among the clergy when he went to study in Rome, and at the early age of 15 he escaped to the wilderness of Subiaco to live the life of a hermit. He underwent many temptations by the Devil, in one of which Satan appeared as a blackbird. Whether it was the bird's beautiful singing that distracted him, or whether he was just so hungry that he thought it might make a tasty meal, the saint resisted the temptation by making the sign of the cross, and the blackbird instantly disappeared. In some paintings, the bird is depicted as a raven, making it even more Satanic.[3]

Saint Kevin and the Blackbird

By contrast, the Christian fable of Saint Kevin and the blackbird is all sweetness and light. Kevin was abbot of Glendalough in County Wicklow, Ireland, in the 6th century CE. During Lent one year, he went to find an isolated place where he could contemplate without interruption. He chose a tiny hut on an uninhabited island. It was his habit to pray for many hours each day, with his hand stretched out through the window of the tiny hut. One day, a blackbird came down and began building a nest on the saint's outstretched hand. Not wishing to disrupt the bird, he left his hand extended. The blackbird built her nest, laid her eggs, sat on them, hatched her chicks, fed them until they were fledged, then finally flew away with them. Through all that long time, the saint kept his hand extended. Only when the blackbird and her new family had left at last did the saint bring his hand in from the window. Seumas Heaney wrote a poem about the legend in 1996.[4]

(Unfortunately, Kevin's sweet blackbird legend was marred by a slightly later event on the same island, when a woman named Kathleen came to the island and ruined the saint's solitude with her endless chattering. In rage, he threw her over a cliff to her death, and her ghost is said to haunt the island to this day. Presumably Kevin still made it into Heaven, otherwise he wouldn't be a saint.)

Robin (*Erithacus rubecula*)

Phylum *Chordata*, Class *Aves*, Order *Passeriformes*, Family *Muscicapidae*, Genus *Erithacus*, Species *Erithacus rubecula*, Subspecies (several)

Name

The common name was originally Robin Redbreast in full, the Robin being simply a diminutive of the name Robert. The species name *Erithacus rubecula* represents the European robin and means little red robin, from Greek εριθακος, *erithakos*, original attribution obscure but believed to mean robin, and Latin *ruber*, red. The American robin, *Turdus migratorius*, meaning migratory thrush, is a completely different genus and species, despite its similarities to the European robin in coloring; it is much larger, and different in physiology and behavior.

Description

The European robin is a small, active, often aggressive bird with a bright red breast. It hops from branch to branch and flies swiftly from cover to cover, like a sparrow or finch. It has a complex, richly melodious song, similar to that of the blackbird.

The American robin is also a beautiful bird. It is larger, looking exactly like a thrush, but with a red breast. It often hops or walks along the ground, something a European robin hardly ever does.

General Attributes

Robins are very popular birds, particularly in Britain and northern France, less so in other European countries. The robin has twice been unofficially voted Britain's National Bird in contest popularity polls. Through Christmas cards and other traditions, they have become associated in folklore with wintertime in general and Christmastide in particular.

Christ and the Robin

There are two legends that associate the robin with Jesus Christ.

In the first, the robin is present at the Crucifixion. Beset with unbearable sorrow and helplessness, the robin flies to Jesus on the cross, sits on his shoulder, and sings a long poem of lamentation and commiseration in his ear. As he does so, some of the blood from the crown of thorns drips onto the robin's breast, and its stain remains there to this day. Its presence reminds us of the compassion the robin showed to Jesus at his death.[5]

In the second legend, the robin is said to spend most of his waking hours delivering water to souls in Purgatory, a place that is neither Heaven nor Hell, but a waiting place in between. The red mark on the breast is said to represent singeing from flames, which somewhat confuses Purgatory with Hell, but the intention is obvious enough: the robin is again portrayed as compassionate to Christians.[6]

Other Legends

It was thought for a long time that the popularity of the robin on Christmas cards was based on the fact that Victorian postmen in Britain wore bright red jackets and were nicknamed Robins. However, robins appeared on Christmas cards long before the red jackets were introduced, so the connection is not proven.

In Norse mythology, the robin is attributed to Thor, presumably because of its aggressiveness: male robins are fiercely territorial and will attack other birds, even much larger ones, without hesitation.

In the ancient British folktale *Babes in the Wood*, the dead bodies of the murdered children are buried by robins.

Cock Robin

A folkloric British nursery rhyme and song of uncertain date (first printed in the 18th century, but possibly dating from much earlier) tells the story of the murder of Cock Robin:

Who Killed Cock Robin?

Who killed Cock Robin?
I, said the Sparrow,
with my bow and arrow,
I killed Cock Robin.

Who saw him die?
I, said the Fly,
with my little eye,
I saw him die.

Who caught his blood?
I, said the Fish,
with my little dish,
I caught his blood.

Who'll make the shroud?
I, said the Beetle,
with my thread and needle,
I'll make the shroud.

Who'll dig his grave?
I, said the Owl,
with my little trowel,
I'll dig his grave.

Who'll be the parson?
I, said the Rook,
with my little book,
I'll be the parson.

Who'll be the clerk?
I, said the Lark,
if it's not in the dark,
I'll be the clerk.

Who'll carry the link?
I, said the Linnet,
I'll fetch it in a minute,
I'll carry the link.

Who'll be chief mourner?
I, said the Dove,
I mourn for my love,
I'll be chief mourner.

Who'll carry the coffin?
I, said the Kite,
if it's not through the night,
I'll carry the coffin.

Who'll bear the pall?
We, said the Wren,
both the cock and the hen,
We'll bear the pall.

Who'll sing a psalm?
I, said the Thrush,
as she sat on a bush,
I'll sing a psalm.

Who'll toll the bell?
I, said the Bull*,
because I can pull,
I'll toll the bell.

All the birds of the air
fell a-sighing and a-sobbing,
when they heard the bell toll
for poor Cock Robin.[7]

* Probably the bullfinch.

Three historical or mythological events are suggested as possible sources for the rhyme: the undated death of a mythological figure, such as Balder in Norse mythology; the death of King William II of England, known as William Rufus (the Red), from an arrow in a hunting accident in 1100; and the fall of Robert Walpole's national government in 1742, shortly before the poem was first published.

Wren (Several Species)

Phylum *Chordata*, Class *Aves*, Order *Passeriformes*, Superfamily *Certhioidea*, Family *Troglodytidae*, Genera (about 19), Species (more than 84)

Name

Wren is an ancient Germanic word, written as *wrænna* or *werna* in Old English and *wrenne* or *wranna* in Middle English. The family name, *Troglodytidae*, literally means cave-dwellers, from Ancient Greek τρωγλε, *trōgle*, hole, and δυω, *duō*, "I get into." Wrens like exploring or hiding in rocky crevices.

Description

Wrens are medium-small to very small birds. There are 88 extant species, of which only one, the very small Eurasian wren, is native to Europe. All the rest are New World birds, their habitats ranging from Canada in the north to Argentina in the south. Wrens typically have drab coloring, sometimes with striping on the wings or body. The Eurasian wren is easily recognized by its very small, rounded body, its active, alert head and eyes, and its upright tail.

General Attributes

For such a tiny, often nondescript-looking bird, the wren has quite a reputation as a sacred animal. Perhaps starting with the story of Jupiter and the contest of the birds (see below), the wren features in a surprising number of religious and mythological traditions. It represents humility, because it's so small and ordinary, but also cunning, because of the Jupiter trick, and also divinity—in both Gaelic and Brythonic Celtic languages, the bird's name (variants of *dryw* or *drui*) also signifies druid, and the ancient Celtic druids considered it the most sacred of all birds. According to Breton druids, three birds brought fire into the world—first the wren, whose wings began to scorch, then the robin who took the fire from the wren but had to let go when its breast began to catch fire, and lastly the lark, who dropped quickly to earth and released the fire into the world.

The wren has a beautiful, complex song, as melodic and variegated as that of the blackbird, robin or nightingale. However, unlike the others, wrens also quite often sing in pairs, creating birdsong duets that are indescribably fascinating and intricate—but you will usually hear them rather than see them, because they like to hide in the bushes and lower branches, content to be heard but not seen.

Jupiter and the King of Birds

According to the classical Roman legend:

Jupiter, King of the Gods, decided to hold a contest to see which bird qualified as King of the Birds. The contest was very simple: whichever bird flew highest would win the crown. Jupiter naturally expected his own totem bird, the majestic eagle, to win. It appeared that the eagle would do exactly that, as it flapped its huge wings and rose rapidly towards the sun. When the eagle reached as high as it could go, way above the other birds, and it looked as though the contest was all over, the tiny wren emerged from its hiding place in the eagle's tail feathers, and flew just a little distance higher, singing lustily in her triumph. Jupiter had no option but to award the title—altered to Queen of the Birds—to the insignificant little wren.[8]

Hunting the Wren

In ancient Druidism, "hunting the wren" was a metaphor for seeking wisdom, for finding the eternal, often elusive and evanescent, in the mundane. The Native American vision quest and the Australian Aborigine walkabout are similar traditions. The acolyte would seek quiet places and "hunt" for the "wren," not literally but metaphorically, seeking divine inspiration from nature and the real world all around.[9]

However, Christianity turned this into a literal endeavor, perhaps as an attempt to drive out ancient pagan practices. On Boxing Day, or St. Stephen's Day, i.e., 26 December, boys and young men (always males—no females were allowed) in Britain and France would go hunting for wrens to capture and kill, usually by stoning them to death. They would process in the streets wearing outlandish costumes, sing loud and rough songs, and generally make merry in a laddish way. Versions of their songs, usually called *The Hunting of the Wren* or *Cutty Wren* ("cutty" means small or short, as in Cutty Sark, which means short shirt) have been noted all the way from the Orkneys in the north to Carcassonne in central France. One verse from an Irish wren hunt song runs:

> The wren, the wren, the king of all birds,
> On St Stephen's Day was caught in the furze;
> Although he was little, his honor is great,
> Jump up me lads and give him a treat.[10]

In Native American Mythologies

In most Native American cultures, wrens have little mythological importance. Like other small birds, they sometimes play the role of meek characters with more power than they appear to have at first glance. Among the Pueblo tribes, however, wrens are considered birds of war. Catching sight of a wren is believed to boost a person's courage, especially a warrior. The Hopi war spirit Tuposkwa is embodied by a canyon wren. In some Pueblo tribes, rock wrens are associated with madness and dangerous magic, and the people used to avoid touching one at any cost, though most modern Pueblo people consider this more of a superstition than a part of traditional Pueblo religion.[11]

Nightingale (*Luscidia megarhyncos*)

Phylum *Chordata*, Class *Aves*, Order *Passeriformes*, Family *Muscicapidae*, Genus *Luscidia*, Species *Luscidia megarhyncos*

Name

The common name is Germanic, from Old English *nihtegale*, literally night singer. The genus name *Luscinia* is Latin for nightingale, and the species name, *megarhyncos*, is from Greek, meaning large nose or bill.

Description

The nightingale is a small, plain bird, famous for its beautiful song. It is found in several European countries, but migrates to sub-Saharan Africa in the winter. It is not native to the New World.

General Attributes

The nightingale has been famed for its song since earliest times, and features in several European mythologies. It also became a symbol of the creative writer, especially the poet, often personified by the name Philomel, meaning lover of apples (not lover of song, as Ovid and several others mistakenly believed), after Philomela, a character in Greek mythology who is raped and has her tongue cut out (see below). She cannot speak the news of her tragedy, so she makes a tapestry and sings a wordless song of utter sorrow. She later became a symbol of poetic inspiration and creativity, and her feminine name Philomela became the masculinized Philomel for male poets. In *Sonnet 102*, Shakespeare compares himself to Philomel:

> Our love was new, and then but in the spring,
> When I was wont to greet it with my lays;
> As Philomel in summer's front doth sing,
> And stops his pipe in growth of riper days…[12]

Aëdon/Philomela

A somewhat peculiar and bloodthirsty—indeed, cannibalistic—Greek legend, in two versions, explains why the nightingale's beautiful song is so plaintive. In the earlier version, Aëdon is jealous because her sister-in-law, Niobe, has six fine sons. Aëdon tries to kill Niobe's eldest, but kills one of her own sons by mistake. Zeus transforms her into a nightingale, and she forever bewails her fate.

In the later, more complex version, Aëdon is happily married to Polytechnos. She foolishly boasts that they are a happier couple than even Hera and Zeus. Hera, infuriated, sends Eris (whose name means strife or trouble) to set up a wager between Aëdon and Polytechnos that whoever completes their piece of craft-work (he is making a chair, she is weaving a cloak), the other shall send them a slave as the prize for finishing first. Hera fixes the contest so that Aëdon wins.

In anger, Polytechnos sends for Aëdon's sister, Chelidonis, and disguises her as a slave. Aëdon, not recognizing her sister, plots with her to kill her own son, Itylus, cook him, and feed him to his father. When Polytechnos discovers the great sin that Aëdon and her sister have forced him to commit unknowingly, he cuts out Aëdon's tongue, and then pursues Chelidonis. However, at this point the gods, tired of the arguing and the bloodshed, turn them all into birds: Pandareos, Aëdon's father, into an osprey; Aëdon's mother into a kingfisher; Polytechnos into a pelican; Chelidonis into a swallow; and Aëdon into a nightingale.[13]

Virtually the same story is told as above in another version of the myth, except that Aëdon becomes Philomela and Polytechnos is replaced by King Tereus of Thrace. The ending is similar, with the chief protagonists being turned into various birds, but versions differ in the details.

"Ode to a Nightingale"

The poem "Ode to a Nightingale," written in 1819 by the English poet John Keats (1795–1821), is thought by many to be one of the finest poems ever written in the English language. He wrote it by hand one morning, "on a few scraps of paper" as he said himself, whilst sitting under a plum tree in his garden in Hampstead, London. The poem is too long to give in full here, but these are the first and last verses:

My heart aches, and a drowsy numbness pains
My sense, as though of hemlock I had drunk,
Or emptied some dull opiate to the drains
One minute past, and Lethe-wards had sunk:
'Tis not through envy of thy happy lot,
But being too happy in thine happiness,
That thou, light-winged Dryad of the trees,
   In some melodious plot
Of beechen green, and shadows numberless,
Singest of summer in full-throated ease…

…Forlorn! the very word is like a bell
To toll me back from thee to my sole self!
Adieu! the fancy cannot cheat so well
As she is famed to do, deceiving elf.
Adieu! adieu! thy plaintive anthem fades
Past the near meadows, over the still stream,
Up the hill-side; and now 'tis buried deep
   In the next valley-glades:
Was it a vision, or a waking dream?
Fled is that music:–do I wake or sleep?[14]

28

Cranes and Cuckoos (*Gruiformae, Otidimorphae*)

Crane (Several Species)

Phylum *Chordata*, Class *Aves*, Order *Gruiformes*, Superfamily *Gruoidea*, Family *Gruidae*, Genera (4), Species (15)

Name

The common name is Germanic, appearing as *cran* in both Old English and Middle English. The Dutch word is *kraan*, and the German word *Kran*. (The lifting machine takes its name from the bird.) The family name *Gruoidae* is from Greek γερανος, *geranos*, and Latin *grus*, both meaning crane. (The geranium flower takes its name from the Greek bird name. The flower is still sometimes called cranesbill.)

Description

There are 15 species of crane in four genera, with a cosmopolitan distribution (found in most parts of the world). They are large but graceful birds. They are easy to distinguish from herons in flight, because herons hold their heads up and their necks curved while cranes fly with their necks straight out in front of them.

General Attributes

The crane is an exceptionally beautiful and graceful bird, and features positively in many religious and mythological traditions. Its distinctive circular mating dance is recreated in several parts of the world. It represents grace, patience, trustworthiness, happiness and eternal youth, but also in some traditions, longevity, old age, death, and the transition to the afterlife.

Ogham

In the Celtic Druidic tradition, a sacred alphabet was used. It was called Ogham (pronounced approximately *ogum* in Old Irish, *owum* in modern Irish) after the god Ogmios or Ogma, who devised it. Ogmios is often depicted with golden chains coming from his mouth, representing the sanctity and importance of true and correct utterance. The swooping but still graceful flight of cranes in the sky reminded Druids of letters, so the term "crane knowledge" came to be used for familiarity or training in the secret Ogham alphabet, and then secret training in druidic lore of every kind. The nickname survived even into Christian times, when a particularly fluent or wise priest would be known as a "crane cleric."[1]

Three Cranes

In many legends, particularly Celtic ones, cranes appear in threes, possibly emblematic of the Triple Goddess, who is simultaneously young virgin, mature mother, and old crone, or in other traditions the Three Muses, the Three Fates or the Three Sisters of Wyrd (Destiny).[2] Three cranes guard the entrance to Annwn, the Celtic underworld. Tarvostrigaranus, depicted in stone sculptures in Paris and Trier, is a god of Gaul, depicted as a bull accompanied by three cranes (which is exactly what the name *Tarvos-Tri-Garanus* means). The bull symbolizes the male God, and the three cranes the Triple Goddess.

The Crane Bag

A bag made from the skin of a crane is traditionally the bag in which druids were reputed to carry their carved Ogham divination sticks. An Irish legend tells us that the sea god Manannán mac Lír carried a crane-skin bag that contained many wonderful magical relics and tools.

In Classical Mythology

Pliny the Elder (23–79 CE) wrote that cranes appoint one of their number to guard the rest of the flock at night, and the patient, dutiful crane holds a stone in one of its claws so that, if it falls asleep, the noise of the falling stone will wake it. The image of a crane with a heavy stone in its claw is still found in heraldry.

Aristotle describes the migration of cranes, but discounts the legend that cranes disgorge magical stones that can be used as touchstones to identify true gold. However, the notion of cranes ejecting small stones from their gizzards to replace them with newer stones is perfectly possible.

The Crane Dance

The crane's distinctive mating dance was associated in classical mythology with Apollo, the most beautiful of all the gods and the patron of art and music, and with Hephaestus, the god of fire, blacksmiths, carpenters and artisans generally, perhaps because Hephaestus was also associated with letters and sacred utterance—an invocation in his name is carved in the famous Linear B (Mycenaean Greek) inscription found at Knossos on Crete.

Ritual re-enactments of the crane dance are also found in India, Arabia, China, Korea, Japan and Native American nations. In Korea, a crane dance that was first performed at the

Tongdosa Temple in 646 CE is still enacted to this day.[3] Several styles of the oriental martial art of *kung fu* are modeled on and named after the graceful dance of the crane.

The Satanic Verses

In pre–Islamic Arabia, three goddesses of Mecca were depicted as cranes: they were called al-Lāt, al-'Uzzá and Manāt. They feature centrally in the novel *The Satanic Verses* by the British Indian writer Salman Rushdie (b. 1947), the meaning of their identities being central both to the plot and to the religious controversy on which it is based.

A passage in the Qur'an reads: "Have you thought of al-Lāt and al-'Uzzá and Manāt, the third, the other?"[4] While speaking this short text out loud, Muhammad added (in Arabic) the commentary: "These are the exalted *gharāniq*, whose intercession is hoped for." This sentence (which is merely six words in Arabic) represents "the Satanic verses" in their entirety, because Islamist authorities insist that they were spoken by the Prophet because they were forced into his mouth by Satan. Muhammad himself said that he had not intended to say those words, and that Satan had put them in his mouth, to appease the Meccans and create dissent and controversy among believers. The critical word is *gharāniq*, the meaning of which is unclear because it appears only once in the entire text, and therefore (like many words in the Bible) cannot be interpreted with absolute certainty because there are no other instances of the word to clarify or confirm its meaning. For a number of reasons (including its very close similarity to Greek γερανος, *geranos*) it is generally agreed by secular scholars to mean cranes, making the identification of al-Lāt, al-'Uzzá and Manāt as pagan animal goddesses explicit.

For non-believers, this is a trivial slip in which Muhammad momentarily either betrayed a personal belief in earlier pagan deities, or perhaps indeed tried to appease the Meccans. For devout Muslims, that very thought is a profound blasphemy and insupportable insult to the Prophet. For that reason, a *fatwa* (Islamic legal pronouncement) was issued by Ayatollah Ruhollah Khomeini, the Supreme Leader of Iran, on February 14, 1989, condemning Rushdie to death. This reaction led to intense (and often violent) disagreements about freedom of speech versus blasphemy, religious intolerance and racism. Many people were injured, and several killed, in protests and counter-protests that followed the controversy and Ayatollah Khomeini's *fatwa*. The British government put Rushdie under police protection, and he had to spend many years in hiding before moving to the United States. The controversy has still not entirely disappeared. In Islamic law, a *fatwa* can only be revoked by the authority who invoked it. Since Khomeini is now dead, the *fatwa* continues in effect.

Cuckoo (Several Species)

Phylum *Chordata*, Class *Aves*, Clade *Otidimorphae*, Order *Cuculiformes*, Family *Cuculidae*, Genera (about 32), Species (more than 144)

Name

The Middle English was *cokkou*, the Old French *cucu*, the Latin *cuculus*, and the Ancient Greek κοκκυξ, *kókkux*, all of them onomatopaeic. The word *cuculus* was also ancient Latin slang for an adulterer.

Description

The two most famous traits of the cuckoo are its unmistakable cry of *ku-ku, ku-ku* in the spring, and its habit of laying its eggs in the nests of other birds, saving itself the trouble of raising its young. Cuckoos are found all across the world.

General Attributes

In reality, the majority of cuckoo species raise their own young, so their reputation as a brood parasite is only partially deserved. They appear commonly in various mythologies, and are generally associated with spring and love. Lithuania and Russia have many cuckoo folklore legends and fairy tales.

The Cuckoo and the Turtledove

One of the best-known stories by the Russian satirical fabulist Ivan Krylov (1769–1844) is essentially a conversation between a female cuckoo and a turtledove, which reveals the cuckoo's insensitivity and selfishness:

> The cuckoo complains bitterly that her children neglect her, and that she is unloved. The turtledove is deeply sympathetic, and speaks with great warmth about how the love given to her by her own little dovelets sustains and rewards her. The cuckoo continues to grieve bitterly. The dove then asks how the cuckoo manages to build her nest so quickly and effortlessly.
> "Build a nest?" exclaims the cuckoo. "What a fool I would be to waste my time doing that! I always lay my eggs in the nests of other birds."
> From that point onward, the turtledove's sympathy for the cuckoo wanes rapidly.[5]

Cuckold

A cuckold is a man married to an unfaithful wife, especially one who is unaware of the wife's cheating. (There is a derived word, cuckquean, for a wife married to an unfaithful husband, but it is even more rare and archaic than cuckold.) The word was *cokewold* (various spellings) in Middle English, from Old French *cucuault*. In classical Latin, the slang *cuculus* or cuckoo meant adulterer, i.e., someone sleeping in someone else's nest or bed. The source for all these words is the cuckoo, which was associated with licentiousness and lasciviousness. The Greek god Zeus and the Hindu god Indra both turned themselves into cuckoos to seduce human maidens.

Kamadeva

Kamadeva is the Hindu god of love. His female counterpart is Rati. Kamadeva is the son of Lord Vishnu and the goddess Lakshmi. Like European Cupid, Kamadeva has a bow and arrows, and shoots arrows of desire: the bow is made of sugar cane and the arrows are decorated with five perfumed flowers, white lotus, blue lotus, ashoka tree, mango tree and jasmine. He rides a cuckoo, or sometimes a parrot, both of which are associated with spring, desire and love.[6]

Mr. Cuckoo

There is a very unpleasant modern urban legend in Korea about an insane man nicknamed Mr. Cuckoo, who attacks girls and young women at night in lonely places. Some say he carries a baseball bat, others an axe. He follows behind them, and says, "Cuckoo! Cuckoo!" until they turn around and take notice of him. At other times, he asks nonsensical questions, but always about cuckoos: "Is today a cuckoo day? Where is my cuckoo?"

Mr. Cuckoo was supposedly hospitalized with mental illness as a teenager, and received frequent beatings from female nurses. They called him cuckoo, because cuckoo, in Korean as in English, can also mean crazy. He escaped from the asylum he was sent to as an adult, and now prowls the streets of Seoul looking for revenge.[7]

Roadrunner (*Geococcyx californianus, Geococcyx velox*)

Phylum *Chordata*, Class *Aves*, Clade *Otidimorphae*, Order *Cuculiformes*, Family *Cuculidae*, Genus *Geococcyx*, Species *Geococcyx californianus, Geococcyx velox*

Name

Roadrunners are also called chaparral birds or chaparral cocks, chaparral meaning shrubland. *Geococcyx* is from Ancient Greek γεω-, *geō*-, earth, and κοκκυξ, *kókkux*, cuckoo. *Californianus* is obvious, and *velox* is Latin for quick.

Description

The roadrunner is a cuckoo of the southwestern United States, Mexico and Central America, mostly in desert regions, famed for running on the ground at very high speed, much of the fame arising from the Looney Tunes and Merrie Melodies cartoon series in which the roadrunner is the intended dinner of Wile E. Coyote, who always ends up going hungry.

The real roadrunner is considerably larger and leaner than most other cuckoos (22 to 24 inches, or 56 to 61 centimeters, from tail-tip to beak-tip), has much longer legs, and has been clocked at 20 miles per hour (32 kilometers per hour), which is indeed a pretty impressive speed for a medium-sized, ground-running bird.

General Attributes

The roadrunner features in the indigenous mythologies and folklore of the countries in which it is found. Its attributes are always positive: it is a medicine bird, and protector of humans, because evil spirits cannot capture or conquer it.

In Pueblo and Mexican Culture

The Pueblo Indians, which includes the Hopi, believe that the roadrunner is a medicine bird. Roadrunners leave a distinctive X-shaped claw print, which has become a sacred symbol in Pueblo culture. The natives paint, inscribe or carve the × in any place where they want to keep evil spirits at bay. The real bird's claw tracks give no indication of which direction the bird was traveling, and in the same way the X-shaped medicine symbols confuse evil-wishers.

For the same reason, roadrunner feathers are used to decorate cradleboards to protect babies. In some parts of Mexico, roadrunners were never eaten. In others, the meat was considered medicinal, and was traditionally given particularly to those who needed to gain weight, strength or greater mobility.

29

Hoopoes, Hummingbirds, Doves and Woodpeckers (Several Orders and Families)

Hoopoe (Several Species)

Phylum *Chordata*, Class *Aves*, Order *Bucerotiformes*, Family *Upupidae*, Genus *Upupa*, Species (3)

Name

The common name is derived from Greek εποψ, *épops*, and Latin *upupa*. The scientific name of the most common species, *Epops upupa*, therefore means hoopoe hoopoe.

Description

The hoopoe is a distinctive, colorful bird. It has a tall crest or crown of erect feathers on its head. It is indigenous to Africa and parts of Europe and Asia. *Upupa africana* lives mostly in sub-Saharan Africa, and *Upupa marginata* lives only on Madagascar. The African hoopoes do not migrate, but the Eurasian birds have been found migrating to several unexpected places, including one once in Alaska.

General Attributes

Hoopoes have figured in religion and mythology for millennia. They are disreputable thieves in most folklore, but can be aristocratic or even royal in mythology and legend. The hoopoe was chosen by Israel as its national bird in 2008.

In Ancient Egypt

Hoopoes were sacred in ancient Egypt. A symbolic representation of the hoopoe or hoopoe crest indicated the validity of legitimate royal succession. The hoopoe image confirmed the child as a true heir and successor.

In Greek Myth

Tereus is transformed into a hoopoe in the myth of Aëdon or Philomela (see **nightingale**, *Aëdon/Philomela* in Chapter 27). King Tereus is also a main character in Ορνιθες, *Órnithes*, *The Birds*, a famous comedy by Aristophanes (c. 446–c.386 BCE). This very clever and funny play is the source of the expression "Cloud-Cuckoo-Land," which is Νεφελοκοκκυλια, *Nephelokokkulía*, in the original Greek.

In Judaism and Christianity

We are told in the Old Testament that the hoopoe is a "detestable" bird:

> These you shall regard as detestable among the birds. They shall not be eaten; they are an abomination: the eagle, the vulture, the osprey, the buzzard, the kite of any kind; every raven of any kind; the ostrich, the nighthawk, the seagull, the hawk of any kind; the little owl, the cormorant, the great owl. the water-hen, the desert-owl, the carrion vulture, the stork, the heron of any kind, the hoopoe, and the bat.[8]

In Islam

The hoopoe, under the name *hudhud*, appears as a righteous bird in the Qur'an:

> And he took attendance of the birds and said, "Why do I not see the hoopoe—or is he among the absent? I will surely punish him with a severe punishment or slaughter him unless he brings me clear authorization." But the hoopoe stayed not long and said, "I have encompassed [in knowledge] that which you have not encompassed, and I have come to you from Sheba with certain news. Indeed, I found [there] a woman ruling them, and she has been given of all things, and she has a great throne. I found her and her people prostrating to the sun instead of Allah, and Satan has made their deeds pleasing to them and averted them from [His] way, so they are not guided."[9]

Hummingbird (several species)

Phylum *Chordata*, Class *Aves*, Order *Apodiformes*, Family *Trochilidae*, Genera (several), Species (several)

Name

The common name refers to the slight humming sound made by the bird's rapidly moving wings. The family name *Trochilidae* comes from Greek τρωγω, *trōgo*, meaning chew, gnaw or eat.

Description

Hummingbirds are tiny birds native to the Americas, best known for their precise hovering and darting flight as they move from flower to flower to feed. The bee hummingbird, at 2 inches (5 centimeters) in length, is the smallest bird in the world. One of their most unusual characteristics is their metabolic rate, which is one of the highest in any animal. At night, or when they need to recoup energy, they are able to almost hibernate for several hours, reducing their normal breathing and metabolic rate to 1/15th of the normal rate.

General Attributes

Hummingbirds were sacred in many parts of Central and South America. They are still respected and venerated by many Native American peoples.

Huitzilopochtli

In Aztec religion, Huitzilopochtli was a god of war, despite the fact that his name means Blue Hummingbird on the Left. He was the brother of Quetzalcoatl (Feathered Serpent), the god of wind, air and learning. The story of Huitzilopochtli's birth describes his nature:

> The goddess Coatlicue (Skirt of Snakes) found a bundle of bright feathers one day. She put them in her bosom, and miraculously became pregnant. Her family found out and decided to kill her. But the child, Huitzilopochtli, was born in the full accoutrements of a warrior. Instead of the family killing him or his mother, he killed them.[10]

Huitzilopochtli became a powerful Aztec god. After he returned to heaven, he left his skull on earth to be an oracle for the people. The English poet and novelist D.H. Lawrence (1885–1930) wrote in his novel *The Plumed Serpent* (1926) about ancient Aztec gods replacing Christianity in contemporary Mexico, and the book features a number of poems in honor of Huitzilopochtli.

Hummingbird Brings Tobacco Back to the People

A Cherokee legend describes how the Goose People (Dagul'ku) stole the very first tobacco plant, intending to keep it for their own use. The other animals lamented, even fell ill, because they had no tobacco. Several animals tried to steal the plant back from the Dagul'ku, but they all failed. Finally, Hummingbird volunteered, but the people all laughed, because he was so small and weak.

But Hummingbird showed them. Moving so fast that he was little more than a blur, Hummingbird flew to the tobacco plant and seized some flowers and seeds in his beak, then flew away again, without the Dagul'ku even knowing that he had been there. They suspected nothing. The people planted the seeds, the new plant grew miraculously, and the people had tobacco again.[11]

Dove/Pigeon (Several Species)

Phylum *Chordata*, Class *Aves*, Clade *Columbimorphae*, Order *Columbiformes*, Family *Columbidae*, Subfamilies *Columbinae*, *Raphinae*, Genera (about 42), Species (more than 300)

Name

The name dove, from Middle English *douve* and Old English *dufe*, is a Germanic word. The name pigeon came into English from Old French *pijon* or *pyjon*, which was derived from the accusative form *pipionem* of the Latin name *pipio*, which means chirping bird. The clade, order and family names are all based on *columba*, Latin for dove or pigeon, the same word also appearing in the famous Christian Saint Columba of Iona (521–597 CE), also called Colm Cille or Collum Keilley (Dove of the Church), in the explorer Christopher Columbus (1451–1506), and in the flower name columbine.

Description

In scientific classification, pigeons and doves are the same birds, although common English usage generally makes doves smaller than pigeons, and most often white in color as opposed to multi-colored, but common usage is not always consistent. Scientifically, they are just different subspecies of the same bird. Pigeon usually means the rock dove or rock pigeon (*Columba livia*), with the domestic pigeon, homing pigeon and feral pigeon all as one subspecies, *Columbia livia domestica*.

General Attributes

Dove also has more positive connotations than pigeon, although pigeon keepers, or "pigeon-fanciers" as they are generally known in Britain, might disagree. In common usage, the dove is a small, white, beautiful bird, representing peace and holiness, while the pigeon is a pest, an urban nuisance, a "flying rat," as some Londoners call them. There are a couple of good jokes about statues coming to life and strangling pigeons joyfully in revenge for the centuries of pigeon-poop they have had to endure.

Zhuge Liang

Zhuge (or Chu-ko) Liang (181–234 CE, called Komei in Japanese) was a genuine historical Chinese figure, although many of the tales about him now appear legendary—for example, he was supposed to be eight feet tall. He was a military general of great repute, and the chancellor and regent of the state of Shu Han during the 3rd century CE. He remains a highly respected figure in Chinese culture. He is said to have ended the practice of human sacrifices by substituting life-sized clay figures.

According to legend, when Zhuge Liang knew that he was dying, he asked that his body be placed on the battlefield with two pigeons sewn into his garments, one in each sleeve. His orders were followed. The advancing enemy knew that they had killed the general, but when they saw his body on the battlefield, his arms moving up and down and from side to side, they believed that he was coming back to life, and fled in terror. The tale is probably derived from a genuine strategic maneuver, involving messenger carrier pigeons, designed to capture arrows at the famous Battle of Red Cliff by setting up straw bales in which the enemy's arrows embedded themselves.[12] Historians have praised the arrow-capturing ruse, which probably really happened, but the folk tale of the moving sleeves has also been retold over and over as an exemplar of loyalty and endeavor even beyond death, and the name Zhuge Liang is still synonymous with heroism, self-sacrifice and outstanding public service.

The Peleiades of Dodona

In the north-west of ancient Greece, Dodona was the site of an oracle dedicated to Zeus, which may have dated back to the second millennium BCE. It is mentioned by Homer and Herodotus. The centerpiece of the oracle was an oak tree (or beech in some descriptions), which responded to supplicants' questions by rustling in a certain manner. (Some scholars have subsequently suggested that small bronze bells or similar objects were placed in the branches, like wind chimes.)

The priestesses who served at this oracular site were called the Peleiades, from Greek Πελειαδες, *Peleiádes*, Doves. The *pel-* part of the name means gray or black elsewhere, which may explain the legend re-told by the 5th-century BCE Greek historian Herodotus that the site was originally founded by a black dove, which modern scholars discount. Some people, understandably, confuse the Peleiades or Doves with the Pleiades, the star cluster in the constellation Taurus, supposedly named after the seven divine daughters of Pleione (see Chapter 41).

Aphrodite's Chariot

Eros and Aphrodite, the Greek god of love and desire and goddess of beauty respectively, held a friendly flower-picking contest. Eros was winning easily, picking the flowers far faster than Aphrodite, when two nymphs started helping the goddess. Angrily, Eros changed them into doves. Aphrodite then harnessed the doves to her chariot.

Astarte

Astarte, also called Astoreth and Ishtar, was worshiped in Syria and Canaan from some time in the 1st millennium BCE, although she may have been ultimately descended from the ancient Sumerian goddess Inanna of the 3rd millennium BCE. She is often depicted naked, sometimes with a crescent-moon crown. She is associated with several animals and symbols—the cow, the lion, the sphinx, the horse, and a circle with a star representing the planet Venus—but she also has a chariot pulled by doves, like Aphrodite (see above).

In the Bible

In the Old Testament story of Noah and the ark, Noah tests how far the waters of the great flood have subsided after forty days by first sending out a raven to look for land, then later a dove:

> Then he sent out the dove from him, to see if the waters had subsided from the face of the ground; but the dove found no place to set its foot, and it returned to him to the ark, for the waters were still on the face of the whole earth. So he put out his hand and took it and brought it into the ark with him. He waited another seven days, and again he sent out the dove from the ark; and the dove came

back to him in the evening, and there in its beak was a freshly plucked olive leaf; so Noah knew that the waters had subsided from the earth. Then he waited another seven days, and sent out the dove; and it did not return to him any more.[13]

The Babylonian epic of *Gilgamesh*, composed during the 2nd millennium BCE, includes a flood and ark story almost identical to the Biblical story, but preceding it by several centuries. Utnapishtim—the equivalent of Noah—is warned by the gods that the corrupt city of Shurippak is about to be destroyed by flood. He builds an ark and loads it with gold, silver, and animals of every kind. He sends first a dove, then a swallow, and finally a raven out to look for land—the reverse of the Biblical order. When the raven fails to return, Utnapishtim knows that land has emerged somewhere. When Utnapishtim lands, the gods relent and allow him, his family and all the animals to come out of the ark. The god Bel blesses Utnapishtim and his wife, and tells him that they will join the immortal gods.

Psalm 55 in the Bible, which laments the treachery of a friend, includes a dove metaphor which has become proverbial:

> My heart is in anguish within me,
> the terrors of death have fallen upon me.
> Fear and trembling come upon me,
> and horror overwhelms me.
> And I say, "O that I had wings like a dove!
> I would fly away and be at rest;
> truly I would flee far away;
> I would lodge in the wilderness;
> I would hurry to find a shelter for myself
> from the raging wind and tempest."[14]

In Matthew's account of Jesus's life in the New Testament, Jesus speaks to the twelve disciples about the persecutions they will face for following him, and again uses the dove as a symbol of purity and innocence:

> "See, I am sending you out like sheep into the midst of wolves; so be wise as serpents and innocent as doves.... They will hand you over to councils and flog you in their synagogues; and you will be dragged before governors and kings because of me, as a testimony to them and the Gentiles.... You will be hated by all because of my name. But the one who endures to the end will be saved."[15]

Joseph and Mary sacrificed a pair of turtledoves or pigeons when they brought the baby Jesus to Jerusalem after his circumcision.[16]

In medieval Christian iconography, depicting the Holy Trinity created an artistic problem: God the Father was a wise old man with a white beard, and God the Son was a handsome, young man with a brown beard and kind eyes, but the Holy Ghost or Holy Spirit was all together more difficult. The solution was to use the image of a dove, often hovering within a halo or circle of light above God and Jesus, or in the background, based on the depiction by Luke of the Holy Spirit appearing as a dove:

> Now when all the people were baptized, and when Jesus also had been baptized and was praying, the heaven was opened, and the Holy Spirit descended upon him in bodily form like a dove. And a voice came from heaven, "You are my Son, the Beloved; with you I am well pleased."[17]

Woodpecker (Several Species)

Phylum *Chordata*, Class *Aves*, Order *Piciformes*, Infraorder *Picides*, Family *Picidae*, Subfamilies (4), Genera (35), Species (about 240)

Name

The origin of the common name is obvious. In Middle English it was two separate words, *wod spek*. The order and family names are from the Latin name for the bird, *picus*, related to the name *pica*, for a jay or magpie.

Description

Woodpeckers range in size from tiny species (called piculets) no more than 2.8 inches (7 centimeters) long to the great slaty woodpecker (*Mulleripicus pulverulentus—pulverulentus* means full of dust or dusky) of India and southeastern Asia, which is almost 2 feet (60 centimeters) long and can weigh up to 20 ounces (570 grams). Not surprisingly from the name, what all woodpeckers have in common is that they peck wood: or rather, hammer vigorously and powerfully into trees to find insects, their main food. The skulls and musculature of woodpecker heads are adapted to withstand the tremendous forces generated by their pecking, and modern scientists have studied them in great depth to see whether any human benefit can be gained from these natural health and safety mechanisms.

General Attributes

In Greek mythology, the woodpecker was a prophetic bird of great power, sacred to both Zeus and Ares. Zeus transformed himself into a woodpecker for several sexual adventures, as did Indra in Hindu mythology. As a result, unsurprisingly, the woodpecker was considered evil and lascivious by early Christians.

Picus and Canens

In Roman mythology, Picus and Canens were a perfectly happy young couple. Picus was handsome, clever and thoughtful. Canens was a beautiful nymph who had a natural talent for sympathetic magic. She was the goddess of song. She charmed trees and rocks, she soothed wild beasts with her gentle voice, she even halted and diverted the flow of rivers.

Circe, a goddess of magic, was envious of Canens's skill and beauty. She made a play for Picus, hoping thereby to sow dissension between the happy couple. Picus refused her, so Circe turned him into a woodpecker. Ovid tells us (*Metamorphoses*, book 14) that Canens searched for her beloved Picus for six days, but, unable to find him, she pined away and vanished into thin air. (Or threw herself into the Tiber, in some versions of the legend.[18])

Woody Woodpecker

Woody Woodpecker, with his signature five-note giggle, was the hero of an animation series by the Walter Lantz Studio in the 1940s. Like Bugs Bunny and Daffy Duck, he is a screwball trickster who gets in and out of scrapes with a constant parade of impossible gymnastics and crazy comments.

Fish and Sea Animals
(Several Orders and Families)

30

Sea Fish (Several Orders and Families)

Fish

Fish appear in almost every major religion or mythological culture in the world. Mummies of fish from ancient Egypt have been found. There was a fish cult in the city of Oxyrhynchus in Middle Egypt, named by Alexander the Great in 332 BCE ('Οξυρρυνξου Πολις, *Hoxyrrynchou Pólis*, literally Town of the Sharp-Snouted Fish). In Greek mythology, the fish was sacred to Aphrodite, goddess of beauty, and, not surprisingly, to the sea-god Poseidon (Venus and Neptune in Roman mythology). In Norse mythology, fish were sacred to Frigga as goddess of fertility. In Hinduism, Vishnu is depicted as a fish in his role as savior of the world, as also is Jesus Christ in Christianity. The early Christians used the outline of a fish to show their religious allegiance, a practice still observed in modern car stickers and symbols. The initials of a Greek name of Christ, *Iesous Christos Theou Huios Soter* (Jesus Christ, Son of God, Savior) spell ιξθυς, *ichthys*, the Greek word for a fish.

Vaivasvata and the Flood

There are several Great Flood myths in different religions and cultures, enough to suggest that they represent a historical flood or series of rising sea levels sometime in the past. Hindu mythology has a flood myth similar to the Christian story of Noah and the Ark, except that the Hindu story has a great fish helping save humankind:

> There were fourteen people when the world began. Each was a Manu, or human being. They were destined to live for 4,320,000 years.
> The seventh Man was Vaivasvata. One day, while washing his hands in the river, he caught a fish. The fish begged to be released, saying that in return he would save Vaivasvata's life from the coming Great Flood. He asked Vaivasvata to keep him in an earthenware jar, and to keep replacing the jar with a larger one as he grew. The fish eventually became so huge that Vaivaswata had to release him into the ocean.
> The fish told Vaivasvata to build an ark, which he did. The Great Flood came, and Vaivasvata tied the ark to a magical horn on the fish's head.
> The fish pulled the ark safely over the drowned mountains.
> When the waters finally receded, Vaivasvata saw that all humankind had been destroyed. He prayed to the gods. A woman appeared from the ocean. She was his daughter, and she became his wife. From them, all humans are descended.[1]

Salmon (Several Species)

Phylum *Chordata*, Class *Actinopterygii*, Order *Salmoniformes*, Family *Salmonidae*, Subfamily *Salmoninae*, Genera *Salmo, Oncorhynchus*, Species (several, of which nine are commercially important)

Name

The common name comes from Old French *saumon*, derived from the Latin name, *salmo* (probably related to the verb *salire*, to leap), which is also the genus name of the North Atlantic salmon. The genus name of the Pacific Ocean salmon, *Oncorhyncus*, is derived from Greek ονκος, *ónkos* (hook) and ρυνξος, *rynkhos* (nose), in reference to the hooked jaws of males in the mating season.

Description

Salmon meat is as popular with humans as it is with bears and other carnivores. The North Atlantic salmon and the Pacific salmon are different genera, but they are both anadromous, which means that they migrate, beginning their lives in fresh water, moving great distances to the ocean, then returning to spawn to their original freshwater territory by an astonishing feat of navigation and memory. Another example of anadromous fish is the striped bass. (Eels are catadromous, meaning they migrate the other way around, living in fresh water but breeding in the ocean.) In modern times, salmon are farmed in large numbers, mostly in seashore or estuary locations. Salmon have also been introduced to non-native areas, such as the Great Lakes.

General Attributes

Atlantic salmon feature prominently in the Celtic mythology of Scotland, Ireland, Wales, Cornwall and Brittany. Pacific salmon feature in American Indian mythology, particularly in the many tribes of the Pacific Northwest of the United States and Canada. The attributions are always positive. Salmon meat (even farmed salmon) is healthy for the body, and salmon myths and sacred attributes are healthy for the soul.

The Celtic Salmon

According to Celtic Druidism, the salmon is the oldest and wisest of all animals. Its extremely complex life cycle, which includes traveling thousands of miles to return exactly to the place of its birth in order to mate, has inspired myths and legends in virtually every culture where it is known. Symbolically, it represents wisdom, inspiration, knowledge (especially esoteric sacred knowledge), rebirth and rejuvenation. In Celtic legends, cooked salmon brought to the table may speak, and will come to life again no matter how many times it is eaten.

Conla's Well

According to Irish legends, the oldest and wisest animal, Bradan the Salmon, lives in Conla's Well (also called the Well of Segais) at the source of the River Boyne. Bradan and his four companions feed on the sacred nuts of the nine hazel trees that guard the pool.

Finnegas and Fionn mac Cumhaill

This ancient Celtic tale is found, in slightly different versions, in Ireland, Scotland and Wales. The druid Finn Eces or Finnegas (White Wisdom) fishes for the great salmon of wisdom for seven years. He finally catches it and puts it in a cauldron to the fire to cook. A boy called Deimne (or the hero Fionn mac Cumhaill) comes seeking to learn the art of poetry. The druid sets the boy to mind the pot, but a splash of the sacred salmon broth splashes on the boy's thumb. He sucks his thumb, and thus instantly acquires all the salmon's knowledge and wisdom. In the Welsh version, Finnegas is replaced by the sow-goddess Cerridwen and Fionn by Gwion (actually the same name, meaning White or Fair One). After many shape-shifting chases and transformations, Gwion is re-born of Cerridwen, becoming the inspirational bard and druid Taliesin (Radiant Brow).

Some years ago, I wrote the Finnegas story as a poem:

> Finnegas the Druid stood three feet high,
> a leprechaun, goat-shaggy, nut-brown.
> Seven years he spent, patient and sly,
> feeding hazel nuts, big as his tiny, hairy fist,
>
> to the Salmon, wisest creature living, who down
> in the deep, dark pool of knowledge swished
> and thrashed, bright his staring eye.
>
> Finnegas caught him with a silver hook,
> heaved his shining, weighty shimmer
> into the bubbling cauldron to cook.
>
> Came that instant, from the forest glimmer,
> a boy, hair like frost, face like a berry,
> eyes blue as robin's eggs, his smile as merry
> as a gold sun rising on a green hill in spring.
> "Tend this, lad," said little Finnegas, knowing,
> as all good druids do, what next must come.
>
> The boy took the wooden spoon and stirred.
> A splash fell. He licked. Like a shot from a gun,
> all things past, present and future were upon him
> and in him and of him and never to be undone.
> "Fionn mac Cumhaill," said the broken-hearted druid.
> The little boy nodded and slowly sucked his thumb.

In Culhwch and Olwen

As mentioned elsewhere (e.g., see **blackbird** in Chapter 27), the salmon is the oldest and therefore wisest animal in the world. In the ancient Welsh tale of Culhwch (Pig Pen) and Olwen (White Track), King Arthur's knights Cai (Kay) and Bedwyr (Bedivere) have been sent to find Mabon ab Modron (Son son of Mother) a warrior-hero created from the earlier Romano-British god Maponus (Great Son). The salmon of Llyn Lliw (pronounced approximately *thlin-thlyoo*, the holy lake at the foot of Mount Snowdon) is the only animal that knows where Mabon ab Modron may be found. Cai and Bedwyr magically ride on the great salmon's back all the way up the Severn estuary to Gloucester, where Mabon has been imprisoned. The ancient myth clearly recognizes and uses the biological reality of the salmon's anadromous life cycle.

Thor and Loki

One of the central stories in Norse mythology is the accidental killing of the god Baldur (Radiant, Shining One) by the blind god Höðr. It was Höðr who fired the mistletoe arrow into Baldur, but it was the trickster-god Loki who guided his arm. Thor pursues Loki, but Loki changes himself into a salmon and dives into a fast-running stream to escape. Thor manages to grab him by the tail. According to *The Poetic Edda*, the distinctive narrowing of the salmon's tail towards its end is the mark of Thor's powerful grip.

The Proper Way to Eat Salmon

Salmon are an extremely important animal to both the lifestyle and the spirituality of many Native American cultures, especially the tribes of the Northwest Coast and the Columbia River. Like buffalo, salmon willingly give themselves up as food for humans in many Northwest Native American myths, and therefore these fish hold a special position of honor and respect. There are many taboos and other tribal rules regarding salmon, so as to avoid offending them, and special Salmon Dances and First Salmon Ceremonies are celebrated at the beginning of salmon fishing season throughout the Pacific Northwest region. In Native American artwork and literature, salmon are often used as a symbol of determination, renewal, and prosperity.

A Squamish legend, similar to several others, describes the proper way to eat salmon.

> The Chief of the Squamish and a group of warriors traveled west in search of the Salmon People, to ask that the salmon might come to them and help feed them. They knew that they had found the village of the Salmon People when they saw smoke coming from the chimneys in all the colors of the rainbow, like the colors that shine on salmon skin.
>
> Spring Salmon, the chief of the Salmon People, welcomed the visitors and later gave them a feast of four great salmon. But he made a special request: "Please keep and return all the bones at the end of the meal," he said. "We must return them to the waters where they belong."
>
> For three nights the visitors feasted, and each following morning Spring Salmon's four children came to the village and spoke with them in a friendly way. But on the fourth night, one of the visitors could not contain his curiosity. He kept a few bones and secretly hid them in his belt.
>
> The next morning, Spring Salmon's children came to the village, as usual, but one of them kept his hands over his face. When the visitors asked him what was wrong, he lowered his hands. He had no nose, no cheeks and no jaw.
>
> "Some bones went missing after last night's feast," said Spring Salmon.
>
> The Squamish warrior who had taken the bones hastily pulled them out from his belt. "I found these on the ground," he lied.
>
> Spring Salmon took the bones without a word. "Next year," he said, "I will send you salmon—Sockeye, Coho, Dog-Salmon and Humpback—but you must always keep the bones and return them to the water afterwards. Do you understand why?"

The visitors nodded, and that is how the salmon came to the Squamish people, and how they return every year.[2]

Tuna (Several Species)

Phylum *Chordata,* Class *Actinopterygii,* Order *Scombriformes,* Family *Scombridae,* Subfamily *Scombrinae,* Tribe *Thunnini,* Genera (5), Species (15)

Name

The common name and the tribe name are derived from Latin *thunnus,* which is derived from Ancient Greek θυννος, *thunnos,* tuna. *Thunnos* is related to the verb θυνω, *thunō,* which means to dart or rush. Tuna is also called tunny or tunny-fish.

Description

The bullet tuna (*Auxis rochei*) is about 1 foot, 7 inches (50 centimeters) long, while the Atlantic bluefin tuna can reach an astonishing 15 feet (4.6 meters) in length and over 1,500 pounds (680 kilograms) in weight. The yellowfin tuna (*Thunnus albacares*), a popular target of sporting fishermen, can swim in short bursts at an equally astonishing 47 miles per hour (75 kilometers per hour). Tuna are extensively fished commercially, and canned tuna is a regular commodity on supermarket shelves. However, although tuna species are distributed across the world's oceans, the distribution is often sparse. All five species of the bluefin group are either vulnerable, threatened or endangered. The southern bluefin tuna (*Thunnus maccoyii*) is critically endangered.

Dudugera

In Melanesian mythology, the Sun was called Dudugera in New Guinea. According to the legend, a woman was in the sea and rubbed her leg against a great fish, a tuna. The leg later began to swell enormously. When the medicine man cut it open, a baby emerged. His mother called him Dudugera. The boy hated living on the land, and was tormented by his playmates. His tuna-fish father came onto the land and took Dudugera back to the sea. But before Dudugera left and went back to the ocean, he told his mother and relatives to hide under a large rock, because he was going to climb into the sky and become the Sun.

Once beneath the waves, Dudugera found a great piece of seaweed and climbed up it into the sky. He took the place of the Sun, but his heat was so great that plants and animals on the earth began dying. His mother squeezed lime juice in his face, and the first clouds appeared, offering shade and relief on earth.[3]

Association with Dolphins

Many tuna species swim in company with dolphins, searching for the same food. As a result, dolphins used to be killed frequently as by-catch from commercial tuna fishing. Then tuna fishing industries yielded to public pressure and started guaranteeing that their product on the supermarket shelves was dolphin friendly. Unfortunately, the measures taken to protect the dolphins have made other species more likely to be part of the by-catch, particularly sharks, other ocean fish, and turtles. Attempts to farm tuna successfully are continuing, with Japan leading the way, since the Japanese eat more tuna per person than any other nation, particularly fresh bluefin tuna, which is considered a great delicacy. Tuna meat is high in protein, low in fat, has no carbohydrates, and is a rich source of phosphorous and vitamin D, but the American Medical Association has also raised concerns about the levels of mercury in tuna.[4]

Flying Fish (Several Species)

Phylum *Chordata*, Class *Actinopterygii*, Order *Beloniformes*, Suborder *Belonoidei*, Superfamily *Exocoetoidea*, Family *Exocoetoidae*, Genera (9), Species (about 64)

Name

The common name is obvious. The family name Exocoetoidae means literally sleeping outside, from Ancient Greek εξω-, *exō*, out, and κοιτος, *koitos*, bed. Ancient cultures believed that flying fish flew out of the water to sleep on land or in trees. The military Exocet missile takes its name from the same root, since it also skims along just above the waves before accelerating towards its target.

Description

Flying fish don't actually fly. They leap out of the water and use their long lateral fins like wings to glide above the surface. The flight is typically about 160 feet (about 50 meters), but flight lengths of an astonishing 1,300 feet (400 meters) have been recorded. They live in all the oceans, but are most commonly found in tropical or subtropical waters.

General Attributes

Flying fish are netted in Japan, China, Vietnam, Indonesia and India. They are said to taste like sardines. The Japanese use the roe to make a kind of *sushi* called *tabiko*. The Solomon Islanders hunt flying fish by outrigger canoe on moonless nights, using lanterns to attract them to fly into their aerial nets. In folk culture, flying fish are valued both for their food value and for their extraordinary flying ability.

The Flying Fish Wars

In Barbados, the flying fish is a national symbol, appearing in statues, coats of arms, and even in the Barbadian passport. After a deep-water harbor was completed in Bridgetown in 1961, the surrounding coral reefs died off, principally through pollution from shipping. The flying fish moved away, and at the time of writing (2019) are found only as far north as Tobago, over 120 nautical miles away from Barbados. Fishing boats from Barbados and from Trinidad and Tobago have pursued the flying fish across the same waters for decades, until in 2006 the council of the United Nations Convention on the Law of the Sea fixed a boundary between them and helped settle agreed fishing quotas, but Trinidad and Tobago claims that Barbadian vessels still pursue the fish south of the boundary.[5]

In Taiwan

Among the indigenous Yami people of Taiwan, the flying fish is sacred and is celebrated in a festival that lasts for nine months of the year. There are dozens of special events and rituals, all of which collectively add up to the ongoing Festival of the Flying Fish, which lasts from February until October each year. The rituals include blessing the fishing boats, a ceremony to celebrate and share the first catch of the season, and special rules and taboos about cooking and eating the fish. The fish must always be cooked whole, never cut into pieces before cooking. The first catch for any boat or even individual must be made wholesome by prayers of thanks: if the fish are eaten or even just tasted before the prayers of gratitude are spoken, the catcher will erupt in sores and boils. The exception is the fish's eyes, which must be eaten whole and raw before the cooking, otherwise the dead fish may come to life again and fly away.[6]

Sea Horse (Several Species)

Phylum *Chordata*, Class *Actinopterygii*, Order *Syngnathiformes*, Family *Syngnathidae*, Subfamily *Hippocampinae*, Genus *Hippocampus*, Type species *Hippocampus heptagonus*, Species (45)

Name

The common name is based on the animal's appearance, with the head and upright stance in particular being reminiscent of a horse. It is written as sea horse or seahorse.

The genus name *Hippocampus* is from Greek ἵππος, *hippos*, horse, and καμπος, *kámpos*, sea animal or sea monster. The species name *heptagonus* means seven-angled or seven-cornered, because of the very unusual structure of their tails and bodies, which are made up of square or many-angled segments, whereas the tail and body of every other animal in the world is generally either round or roundish in cross-section. They also have no ribs, but rather bony plates covered with skin, the number of sections varying from species to species.

Description

The sea horse is very unusual in several other respects. It is found in shallow temperate or tropical waters. The largest of the 45 species may reach 14 inches (36 centimeters) in length, but most are much smaller than that. They swim very slowly, and are often found with their square-sectioned or multi-sectioned tails wrapped firmly around vegetation or some other convenient anchor. Perhaps the best known and most unusual trait of seahorses is that it is the males that give birth. The female deposits her eggs in a special pouch in the male's belly, from which the young emerge between 9 and 45 days later, fully formed but very small, and very susceptible to predators.

General Attributes

Sea horses are generally tiny, slow, mysterious and fascinating creatures, grazing peacefully among the weeds of shallow waters. Perhaps surprisingly, they have extensive mythological status, in the form of the hippocamp or hippocampus, which takes the little sea horse into a realm of much larger dimensions.

In Ancient and Classical Cultures

The hippocamp or hippocampus is usually depicted as the front half of a horse attached to the body and tail of a large fish. It appears in Greek, Phoenician, Etruscan, Roman and Pictish art and mythology. Poseidon frequently appears in a chariot drawn by two-hoofed horses, i.e., hippocamps. The Trevi fountain in Rome, built in the 18th century and a popular tourist venue, depicts Poseidon with hippocamps. Hippocamps also appear frequently on the floor tiles of ancient Roman public baths. The Pictish carvings of hippocamps are similar in some ways to Roman carvings, but it seems very unlikely that the Romans actually had any input: they built Hadrian's Wall to keep the alien, barbarous Picts out of their way. Apart from Agricola's famous advance victory at Mons Graupius (now the Grampians) in 84 CE, the Romans kept away from what is now Scotland.

In Medieval and Modern Culture

Hippocamps were fashionable from the Renaissance onwards. They were used in art and in heraldry. As soon as emerging science identified the little sea horse, the real animal, the names began a reversal: hippocamp or hippocampus began to refer to the real animal, and sea horse or seahorse for the various mythical creatures. Nowadays, most people would probably recognize sea horse but not hippocamp. Usage seems to have settled down to sea horse or seahorse representing the real animal and sea-horse with a hyphen representing the mythical animals.

Air France have used a winged hippocampus logo since their incorporation in 1933. The image is still painted on the engine nacelles of Air France aircraft.

In 2013, a 14th moon was discovered orbiting the planet Neptune. It's the smallest moon yet discovered in the solar system, with a diameter of a mere 22 miles (34 kilometers). The discoverers called it Hippocamp.

Shark (Several Species)

Phylum *Chordata*, Class *Chondrichthyes*, Subclass *Elasmobranchii*, Infraclass *Euselachii*, Superorder *Selachimorpha*, Order (8 extant), Species (about 470 to 500)

Name

The derivation of the English name is unclear. It has been suggested that it might come from a Germanic word, which in turn was derived from the Latin word *carcharias*, which meant scoundrel or greedy man, but the evidence is flaky. Dutch has the word *schurk*, meaning scoundrel or villain, from which the name shark as in "card shark" may have come. In Middle English, the names used were either dogfish or haye, both of which are clearly not related to shark. Sailors and fishermen often called the fish a sea dog. The superorder name *Selachimorpha* means any cartilaginous fish, from Ancient Greek σελακος, *sélakhos*, cartilaginous fish, and μορφε, *morphe*, "in the shape of."

Description

Sharks have been in our oceans, more or less unchanged in appearance and behavior, for about 420 million years. There are eight extant orders and somewhere between 470 and 500 species of sharks. They have skeletons, but they are made of cartilage, which is softer, more flexible and much lighter than bone. Sharks have no ribs, so if they become stranded on land, they can be crushed to death by their own weight. A small number of shark species, called "obligate ram ventilators," have lost the ability to force water through their gills at rest, and have to continue swimming without stop for their entire lives: they continue to swim even when they are asleep, their spinal cord taking over while the brain is unconscious. A common misconception is that sharks are solitary killers, hard, cold and emotionless. In fact, most shark species are quite gregarious and have fairly complex social interactions.

General Attributes

Sharks are bad news in the West generally, whichever way you look at them. In reality, only four of the nearly 500 species have attacked or killed humans, but sharks of all species are thought to be dangerous. Another myth is that sharks never get cancer, and that their oil or body parts can cure cancer: neither statement is true. In the Pacific cultures, sharks have a much more realistic and positive status.

In Hawaii

In Hawaiian native religion, the *aumakua* are family gods. They are ancestors who have chosen a particular animal form to live in after their death. Sharks are a popular choice, because sharks can be powerful and protective animals. A shark *aumakua* is often thanked and blessed for driving fish into the waiting nets. The *kahuna* (wise man, priest) may even point to the markings on a particular shark and compare them to the clothing or other bodily attributes of the deceased ancestor.

There are shark-men (weresharks, you could say) who become sharks at certain times, and others who permanently have a full set of shark teeth on their backs. There are also several shark gods, of whom the greatest is Ka-moho-all'i, brother of Pele, the goddess of volcanoes who created Hawaii in the beginning. Ka-moho-all'i will guide ships to safety if they are lost at sea. He is paid in *kava*, an intoxicating drink made from the *kava* plant, *Piper methysticum* (drunk-making pepper).

31

Freshwater Fish (Several Orders and Families)

Fish Gods and Spirits

Atargatis is a Syrian mother goddess, associated with the moon and fertility, who has sometimes been called the mermaid-goddess, and who is strongly associated with fish and doves. She originates in classical antiquity, but as recently as 1936 Nelson Glueck observed that she was still being actively worshiped and priests were guarding fish sacred to her: "To this day there is a sacred fish-pond swarming with untouchable fish at Qubbet el-Baeddwī, a dervish monastery three kilometres east of Tripolis, Lebanon."[1] Atheh, a goddess worshiped at Taraus, depicted wearing a veil and seated on a lion, is said to be another version of Atargatis.

Al-Khadir (also Al-Khidr, El Khizr, meaning the Green One) is a saint from Islamic legend. He is said to appear in green robes to Muslims who are in distress or great need, the green representing eternal youth. He appears in *The Thousand and One Nights*, and is also mentioned in *surah* 18 of the Qur'an. Musa (the Arabic version of Moses) and his servant Joshua are sent by Allah in search of a prophet called Al-Khadir. Allah tells them to take a fish with them. They arrive at a rock "where two seas meet" and the fish vanishes. Suddenly, Al-Khadir appears. The prophet puts Musa to several tests of faith. Al-Khadir is sometimes identified with Khwadja Khidr, the guardian of the Fountain of Immortality in Indian Islamic belief. Khwadja Khidr is identified with a river god or the fish avatar of the god Vishnu, or with the Indus river, where he appears as an old man dressed in green clothes.[2]

Carp (*Cyprinus carpio*)

Phylum *Chordata*, Class *Actinopterygii*, Superorder *Ostariophysi*, Order *Cypriniformes*, Family *Cyprinidae*, Genus *Cyprinus*, Species *Cyprinus carpio*

Name

The common name and the species name are both from Latin *carpa*. The genus name is from Greek κυπρινος, *kuprinos*, also meaning carp.

Description

Carp are found all over the world, and there are many species, varying greatly in size and appearance. Large carp can grow to over 5 feet (150 centimeters) in length and over 100 pounds (50 kilograms) in weight. Even the tiny goldfish (*Carassius auratus*), a subspecies of carp that was originally bred in China as an ornamental garden fish, can grow to about 19 inches (48 centimeters) and weigh almost 2 pounds (1 kilogram).

General Attributes

Carp are liked and admired in their many varieties. They feature mostly in religions and mythologies of the East. Two fish (usually carp) swimming together is an almost universal symbol of happiness and prosperity in India and the Far East. The two fish originally represented the great holy rivers, Ganges and Yamuna, which brought water, food, trade and prosperity to the people.

In the Ashtamangala

The *Ashtamangala* are eight emblems or symbols found in Buddhism, Hinduism and Jainism. The name is variously translated as Eight Glorious Emblems, Eight Auspicious Signs, and similar alternatives. They are:

1. The conch (*Turbinella pyrum*), called the *sankha* in Sanskrit, which symbolizes the concept of *dharma* (cosmic law or right way of living—there is no simple English translation of this concept). The conch is a symbol of true and pure speech. William Golding uses it in his disturbing novel *Lord of the Flies* (1954) to represent order and civilized debate.
2. The endless knot (*srívasa* in Sanskrit), which symbolizes the intertwining of knowledge and compassion, of the ultimate unity of all things. In the *Svetambara* tradition of Jainism, the knot is replaced by a swastika, which was a religious symbol in Asia long before the Nazis appropriated and defiled it.
3. The pair of golden fish (see below).
4. The lotus flower (*padma* in Sanskrit), which symbolizes purity rising above attachment, like a pure flower floating above muddy water and sediment.
5. The jewelled parasol (*chatnaratna* in Sanskrit), which symbolizes protection from harm, the sky, and the unfolding of all space to the enlightened.
6. The vase of treasure, which symbolizes health, longevity, prosperity and wisdom. In Tibetan it is called *terchenpo'i bumpa*.
7. The Wheel of the Law (*dharmachakra* in Sanskrit), which represents Gautama Buddha and the teaching of eternal truths.
8. The victory flag or banner (*dhvaja* in Sanskrit), which symbolizes the Buddha's defeat of the four *māras* or obstacles on the path to enlightenment: pride, desire, emotion, and fear of death.

The pair of golden fish are carp. The carp has long been revered in China and elsewhere in Asia because of its beauty and its longevity. In the United States, carp have been considered a nuisance fish and invasive species, but attitudes are changing.

Chiang Shih

Chiang Shih or Kiang She is one of the *Erh-shih-ssu Hsiao* (24 Examples of Filial Piety) in Chinese folklore. He and his wife cared for his elderly mother throughout a long wasting sickness. Every day, Chiang Shih walked several miles to a river to fetch fresh water and fish for food. On the days when he caught no fish, he and his wife went without food so that his mother could have the small portion of rice that was all they could afford. One day, his loving care was rewarded with a miracle. A stream appeared right beside his humble cottage. The water was clean and clear, and every day, two large carp appeared and allowed themselves to be caught, allowing Chiang Shih to feed himself and his wife, and for his mother to eat and sleep and live out the rest of her days in comfort.[3]

The Dragon Gate

There are several places in China where a river passes through a narrow cleft or defile, creating a waterfall. Such a place is often known locally as the Dragon Gate. The most famous of these is at the border of the similarly named provinces of Shanxi and Shaanxi on the Yellow River in the Longmen Mountains. The cleft or pass here was supposedly cut by Emperor Yu the Great (c. 2123–2025 BCE), who did much to introduce flood control to China. Legend says that any carp that manages to leap the challenging falls is transformed into a dragon, hence the name Dragon Gate. The story is a very popular theme for Chinese artists and poets. It is also a metaphor for passing the rigorous examinations to become an employee in the Chinese civil service.[4]

The Goldfish

Carp have been farmed as food fish for thousands of years. The species farmed in China from ancient times, usually silver or gray in color, are collectively called Asian carp. Beginning with the Jin dynasty (265–420 CE), a few fish produced red, orange or yellow mutations. During the Tang Dynasty (618–907 CE), keeping these unusually golden-colored fish in ornamental ponds became popular. By the Song Dynasty (960–1279 CE), goldfish farming was firmly established. However, in 1162 the Song Empress declared that all golden or yellow goldfish belonged to her, since gold-yellow was the imperial color: the golden or yellow goldfish became sacred to the Empire. As a result, more red and orange goldfish were produced in home farms, even though they are more difficult to breed successfully. During the Ming Dynasty (1368–1644 CE), China began exporting these exotic fish, some with elaborate ornamental tails—they reached Europe beginning in the early 1600s, and the United States in 1850.[5]

Eel (Several Species)

Phylum *Chordata*, Class *Actinopterygii*, Superorder *Elopomorpha*, Order *Anguilliformes*, Suborders (4), Families (20), Genera (111), Species (about 800)

Name

Eel is a Germanic word. It was spelled *æl* in Old English and pronounced like the Al- in Alan, similar to Dutch *aal* and German *Aal*. The order name *Anguilliformes* means shaped like an eel, from Latin *anguilla*, eel. An ancient Latin proverb runs *anguilla est, elabitur*, literally "It is an eel, it slips away," i.e., "Don't expect to catch a slippery customer by the tail."

Description

There are about 800 species of eel, in 111 genera. They are all elongated ray-finned fish (*Actinopterygii*), and range in size from about 2 inches (5 centimeters) in the one-jawed eel (*Monognathus ahlstromi*) to the slender giant moray eel (*Strophidon sathete*), one specimen of which in Australia was measured at almost 13 feet (3.94 meters).

Eels are catadromous, meaning that they live in fresh water but breed in the ocean. (See also **salmon**, Chapter 30.) The life cycle is complex, the stages being named as larvae, glass eels, elvers, juveniles and finally adults.

Both freshwater and saltwater eels are eaten by humans, although uncooked eel blood contains toxins. Fried elvers, like oysters, used to be a cheap workingman's dish in Britain in Victorian times, the juvenile eels coming from the Thames estuary, but now (also like oysters) they are delicacies for a rich man, if you can find them at all. Jellied eels (adult eels skinned, cooked and cut into chunks preserved in their own congealed body liquid) are still popular, again especially in London, but they too are becoming harder to find. I have tried them myself, and can only describe them as being like pieces of a bicycle tire glued into salty fish jelly—not my favorite dish.

General Attributes

Eels are slippery customers, literally and metaphorically. They do feature in some mythology and folklore, but they are not generally admired or revered.

In European Culture

The Dutch city of Almere is built on the site of a former lake, also called Almere, which means Eel Lake. The annual journey of elvers up the Thames was called the "eel fare," and is probably the origin of the name elver. In Norway, eels are believed to eat the bodies of drowned humans, making the human consumption of eels akin to cannibalism. (The same could be said of worms on land.) In his 1959 novel *The Tin Drum*, Günter Grass (1927–2015) uses the human treatment of eels as a metaphor for the cruelty of the Nazi atrocities in Danzig before and during the Second World War, and the graphic scene in the 1979 movie of the book, where an eel slithers out of the eye socket of a horse's head, is one of the most iconic moments in cinema history.[6]

Maui and Tuna-Roa

There are eel legends in New Zealand, Hawaii, Samoa, Tonga, Tahiti and elsewhere, many of them very similar, with slight changes to the names of some of the main protagonists.

In Hawaii, Maui was an ancient chief, culture hero and demigod. He appears as a folklore hero across Polynesia, and his origins can be traced all the way to New Guinea in the west. The Hawaiian island of Maui is named after him. Maui brought new islands into being by fishing them from the bottom of the ocean with a magic hook. In the Maori legends of New Zealand, Maui hid in his brothers' *waka* or sea canoe after they had refused to take him fishing with them. When he revealed himself, they refused to share their bait with him, so he struck himself on the nose and used his own blood as bait. He hauled up a huge fish, which became North Island. The *waka* became South Island, and is still sometimes called *Te Waka a Maui*.

A Hawaiian and Maori legend tells how Maui went in search of a wife and ended up creating eels.

> Maui married Hina-a-te-lepo (Daughter of the Swamp), and they lived close by the river. One day, Hina was knocked off her feet while fetching water by Tuna-roa (Long Eel). She said nothing of this to Maui. But the next day, Tuna-roa did the same thing. Later, the eel killed two of Maui's children. Finally, Maui decided to catch the eel. He cut vines and timbers and placed them as stakes in the river bed. He prepared a strong net. Then he prayed for rain.
>
> The gods heard Maui's prayers, and sent a storm and flood, which flushed Tuna-roa into the eel trap. Maui chopped off Tuna-roa's head, and cut his body into pieces. The head and tail went out to sea. The head became fish and the tail became the great conger-eel. The parts that remained in the fresh water became eels. Maui taught the people how to catch them for food, flooding them into nets, just as he had caught Tuna-roa.[7]

Pike (*Esox lucius*)

Phylum *Chordata*, Class *Actinopterygii*, Order *Esociformes*, Family *Esocidae*, Genus *Esox*, Type species *Esox lucius*

Name

The common name is Germanic, related to the word pike meaning a spear or sharp-pointed stick, or pick- in the tool called a pickaxe. The fish has a long, pointed snout. The genus name *Esox* may be derived from Ancient Greek ισοξ, *ísox*, but that word is found only in a vocabulary list, so is not attested. It is possible that *esox* was derived from an ancient Celtic word: the salmon (meaning any large fish) is called *eó* in Old Irish and *ehawc* in Welsh (*eok* in Cornish).

Description

The pike is perhaps the most majestic of freshwater fish. They can grow to about 6 feet (1.8 meters) in length. They have razor-sharp teeth and are very efficient predators. Anglers who catch pike have to take great care of the strong jaws and sharp teeth, because the fish can still inflict serious wounds even when it is in its death throes.

General Attributes

In Russian folklore and Slavic mythology generally, the pike belongs to the class of водяной, *vadyanóy*, or evil water spirits. These creatures appear in many forms, including a full human body with webbed hands and a huge frog's head. The *vadyanóy* are malicious: they destroy mills and dams, they alter watercourses, they tear fishing nets to shreds, and they drown people and animals. In some areas, there are also good *vadyanóy* who try to prevent or repair the mischief and damage caused by the evil *vadyanóy*.

The pike appears quite frequently in medieval heraldry. In England, it was called a luce or lucy, in Scotland a ged.

Pike, like the royal sturgeon (see below), has often featured as a main dish at great banquets, but opinions differ as to how good a meal it makes. Good, bad or indifferent, it still contains hundreds of sharp, strong bones, so eating it requires some patience.

Ukko's Pike

In Finnish mythology, the pike played a special role (albeit unwillingly) in restoring fire to the world:

> An evil goddess called Louhi stole the Sun and Moon from the sky and fire from Earth, leaving the world in darkness. The god Ukko ("Old Man"), also called Pauanne ("Thunder"), was the only god who had the power to restore light to the world. He could send lightning down to the world, but unless it could be contained long enough to make fire, it would simply vanish into the earth in a flash, and would be useless. So Ukko had to find something cold and wet, but fiercely strong and determined, to hold the lightning in store. Ukko chose the pike. He sent a massive bolt of lightning down to earth, deep into Lake Alue. The lightning was swallowed by the pike. It burned and scalded his insides, but he never let anything go once his fierce jaws had clamped themselves over it, nor did he let go of the lightning. He thrashed and swam wildly around the lake, until eventually he was swallowed by a larger fish, which in turn was captured by the hero Vainamoinen. When Vainamoinen cut open the larger fish, he found the pike still alive inside, still thrashing wildly. Putting his hands on the pike's razor-sharp teeth with immense care, Vainamoinen managed to get the pike to open its mouth. Immediately, fire burst forth from its belly, and fire and light were restored to the world.[8]

Ukko has a hammer, *Ukonvasara*, which is very similar to Thor's *Mjölnir*. *Ukon vaaja* or Ukko's bolt was used to describe thunderbolts, as well as thunderstones—neolithic weapons or tools, such as stone axes, often placed in the foundations of buildings for spiritual protection.

Sturgeon (Several Species)

Phylum *Chordata*, Class *Actinopterygii*, Order *Acipenseriformes*, Family *Acipenseridae*, Subfamilies *Acipenserinae*, *Scaphyrhynchinae*, Genus (4), Species (about 23 extant)

Name

The origin of the common English name is unclear. It was *sturgiun* or *sturjoun* in Middle English, from Old French *estorjoun*, but the original root appears to be Germanic. *Acipenser* is Latin for sturgeon. The other subfamily name, *Scaphyrhynchinae*, comes from Greek words meaning literally boat snout. These species are also commonly called shovelnose sturgeon.

Description

There are 27 extant species of sturgeon. They have changed little since they first appeared in the Triassic period, some 240 million years ago. They can grow to 12 feet (3.5 meters) in length. They are smooth-skinned and have no scales, although they have a row of armor-like plates on each side and a vertical dorsal fin like that of a shark. The largest sturgeon ever captured was a Beluga female caught in the Volga River estuary in 1827, which weighed 3,463 pounds (1,571 kilograms) and was 24 feet (7.2 meters) long.

General Attributes

The roe of the sturgeon is called caviar, one of the most prized and expensive foods in the world. As a result, all sturgeon species have been overexploited, and are now endangered, some critically. In the 19th century, 90 percent of the world's caviar was produced by the USA and Canada, but sturgeon populations declined so rapidly that there is no longer a caviar fishing industry there: Russia is now the chief source and exporter. Caviar is so valuable that sturgeon poaching is still a major criminal activity.

In Judaism, sturgeon are not kosher as food because they do not have proper scales. In England, the sturgeon was declared a royal fish by King Edward II in 1324: all sturgeon (and whales, dolphins and swans) are the personal property of the reigning monarch, and may not be eaten by commoners.

The Convent of Schwartz-Rheindorf

A German folktale tells how the Convent of Schwartz-Rheindorf, founded in 1152, had important fishing rights:

> Every year, two great sturgeon would come up-river close to the convent, and their arrival heralded the beginning of a profitable fishing season. The fishermen would capture and eat the male sturgeon, but always released the female.
> One winter, however, the abbess insisted on both sturgeon being landed and prepared as food for the nuns and local gentry. The fishermen protested that this greed would bring bad luck, but the abbess insisted. When the guests were all assembled, servants brought in dozens of silver platters. The abbess said grace, then rang a little bell, and the servants removed the covers: but every single one of the platters was bare and empty. The abbess screamed at the servants, the cook, and whoever was standing close by, but when she screamed at the fishermen, they told her that it was her own fault, and that they would never see the great sturgeon again. And they never did, nor the shoals of fish that used to follow them.[9]

Mashenomak

A folk legend of the Menominee people of Wisconsin and Upper Michigan tells how the hero Manabush defeated the great sturgeon Mashenomak. He beat a drum and challenged the sturgeon to swallow him, and Mashenomak obliged. Manabush found other humans and many animals huddled in the huge sturgeon's stomach. Using his magic singing sticks and his sacred spear, Manabush killed Mashenomak from the inside and released all the trapped humans and animals.[10]

32

Crabs, Clams, Conches and Corals (*Crustacea, Mollusca, Cnidaria*)

Crab (Several Species)

Phylum *Euarthropoda*, Subphylum *Crustacea*, Class *Malacostraca*, Order *Decapoda*, Suborder *Pleocyemata*, Infraorder *Brachyura*, Families (93), Species (6,793 extinct and extant)

Name

The English name is Germanic, from a Proto-Indo-European root *grob- or *gereb, which meant to scratch or claw at (it is also related to the word carve.) There are many other similar Germanic words: *krab* (Dutch), *Krabb* (Low German) and *krabba* (Swedish) all mean crab; Frisian *krabbelje* and German *krabbeln* both mean creep or crawl; Dutch *krabbelen* means scratch. The class name *Malacostraca*, as mentioned in Chapter 2, is a misnomer: it means soft-shelled, whereas in fact almost all crabs are soft-shelled only when they are shedding an old shell and growing a new one. The order name *Decapoda* is from Greek, and means ten-footed.

Description

Crabs belong to the infraorder *Brachyura* (New Latin, from Greek βραξυς, *brachys*, short, and ουρα, *oura*, tail.) There are 6,793 species in 93 families. They are exoskeletal, i.e., they have a hard shell casing on the outside rather than a bone or cartilage skeleton on the inside. About 850 species live either in freshwater or on land, some even in trees. Many species are edible and fished commercially.

General Attributes

Crabs do not feature largely in religion or mythology, although the paragraphs below give some indication of their significance in different cultures around the world.

Batara Guru

Batara Guru (also Batara Siwa) is an alternative name of the Hindu god Siva or Shiva, which is commonly used in worship in Malaya, Bali, Java and Sumatra. The god is particularly associated with the sea-god Si-Ray or Madu-Ray, who lives in Pusat Tassek, a mysterious ocean region. Batara Guru is associated with several animals (he is sometimes depicted seated on a cow), but perhaps the strangest is the giant crab of Pusat Tassek, who accompanies Batara Guru or Si-Ray. The giant crab goes in search of food at regular times of the day and night, displacing thousands of tons of water as it moves: and that is why there are tides that ebb and flow.[1]

Ko Pala

Ko Pala is a mysterious figure in Burmese mythology. He was a crab. After the ruling king died without any successors, the priests brought Ko Pala into the palace in a basket and placed the basket on the empty throne. The people were mystified as to why a crab should be the next king, but they were so exhausted after months of arguing over who should succeed the dying king that they simply shrugged and accepted Ko Pala. After a while, however, having a crab for a king became laughable. Nobody dared kill Ko Pala, but they persuaded the priests to take him away so they could go back to arguing. The priests put Ko Pala on a deserted island, thinking he would starve to death. But there came a flood, which covered the entire land. Ko Pala floated away to safety and lived in the sea until the flood waters had abated. Then he went to Loi Pu Kao (Hill That the Crab Entered) and died.[2]

This very peculiar little tale seems to be about reincarnation. The priests obviously believed that Ko Pala was a royal person who had been reincarnated as a crab. Perhaps they expected him to die and reappear as a king.

Amphitrite

The ancient Greek sea goddess Amphitrite (She Who Encircles) was the wife of the sea god Poseidon, who saw her dancing with the Nereids on the island of Naxos and carried her off. She bore him five children. She was often depicted wearing a fish net over her hair, with a crown made of crab claws. Homer describes her making the waves crash against the rocks. The Romans named her Salacia (the Salty One).

Herakles and the Crab

In Greek mythology, the second of the twelve impossible labors set for Herakles by Hera is to kill the nine-headed monster, the Hydra of Lerna. The Hydra's greatest danger to any attacker is that, whenever one of its heads is cut off, it immediately grows two heads to replace the one that has gone. Herakles struggles with this problem for a while, then has the bright idea of cauterizing each wound with fire immediately after cutting off the head. He begins to make better headway (pun intended). Hera angrily sends a giant crab to slow Herakles down, but the hero crushes it with a single blow of his foot.[3] Hera sends the crab (Καρκινοσ, *Karkinos* in Greek, *Cancer* in Latin) into the sky as a constellation (see Chapter 41).

The Heike

In Japanese mythology, the Heike were a 12th-century warrior dynasty, who fought a great battle with their rivals, the family of the Genji. The Heike lost, and those who remained alive committed mass suicide by throwing themselves off a cliff into the sea. There they were turned into crabs (specifically the Japanese spider crab, *Macrocheira kaempferi*), and their anguished faces can still be seen on the backs of their shells.

Clam (Several Species)

Phylum *Mollusca*, Class *Bivalvia*, (several orders, families, genera and species)

Name

The common name is Germanic, from proto-Germanic **klam*, meaning press or squeeze. The class name *Bivalvia* means having two valves, i.e., two shell halves joined by a flexible hinge.

Description

In common usage, the name clam is used mostly for edible bivalve mollusks. Clams vary greatly in size, shape and age. Some have life cycles of just one year, while at least one giant clam has been estimated to be over 500 years old. Clams are very popular as food, either fried or chopped into a creamy soup called chowder.

General Attributes

Many cultures value clams as food. Middens of ancient clam shells found in the lands of the Chumash of California, the Nisqually of Washington State and the Tsawwassen of British Columbia show that clams have been an important food item for west-coast Native Americans for centuries. Clams feature in the cuisines of the USA, Canada, Japan, Italy, India and the West Indies.

Wampum

Clam shells became objects of value and power in some Native American nations. *Wampum* is usually translated as money, but it was far more than that. The Algonquian Indian nations of the American eastern seaboard made strings of sacred jewelry from whelk shells and the shells of the quahog, a hard-shelled clam. Before the Europeans came, the nations used *wampum* during sacred storytelling, as high-value gifts for special ceremonial occasions, and as honor gifts during the negotiation and making of treaties. It could also be used as a kind of currency for high-value transactions, but that was a secondary use: its main importance was as a sacred ceremonial tool. For a short while, Dutch colonists mass-produced their own *wampum*, using industrial techniques, but the use of *wampum* declined rapidly once European commodities and currencies, and American cash, became common.

Conch (Several Species)

Phylum *Mollusca*, Class *Gastropoda*, Family *Strombidae* and others, Genus *Strombus* and others, Species (several)

Name

The common name is derived from Latin *concha*, which comes from Greek κονξε, *konkhe*, shell or mussel. In both those languages, the final consonant sound was pronounced like an English k, i.e., like *konk*, and that pronunciation is still frequently heard, while others pronounce the final ch like the initial or final ch of church. The plural is usually written as conchs and pronounced either as *konks* or *konches*. The genus name *Strombus* is from Greek στρομβος, *strómbos*, which meant shell, conch, or snail.

Description

True conchs are medium to large sea snails in the *Strombus* genus, although there are several other similar marine animals that are also called conchs. They are found in most waters, but are most prolific in the West Indies. They are highly valued for food, and the empty shells are also objects of value in their own right.

General Attributes

Surprisingly for such humble animals, conchs feature in several religious and mythological traditions.

Musical Instruments

Conch shells have been used as musical instruments for centuries by many different cultures. Cutting a small hole in the narrow spiral end makes a mouthpiece, and the instrument is blown like a horn or bugle. A large conch can make a very loud sound. The pitch of the note can be changed by moving the hand inside the larger spiral of the shell, like using a mute on a trumpet. In Tamil Nadu in India, conchs are sounded at funerals to drive away evil spirits. In Grenada, fishermen blow conch shells when they come into port, announcing to the villagers or townspeople that they have fresh fish to sell.

Other Uses

Increasingly, conch shells are polished and sold to tourists for home decoration. Smaller conch shells and shell pearls are used for personal jewelry. The ancient Mayans made a kind of deadly boxing glove by inserting their hands into large conch shells with sharpened edges. Conch shells have been used as money. Bengalis in Bangla Desh and India always decorate the bride at a wedding with conch shells and coral bangles. Several Australian Aborigine tribes also use conchs as jewelry, some even for a kind of breastplate armor. In some Afro-Caribbean and African American communities, it is traditional to place at least one conch shell on the grave during a burial.

The Lord of the Flies

In William Golding's famous novel *The Lord of the Flies* (1954), a conch is used as a horn to summon all the castaway boys to a general meeting. They agree a rule that only the person holding the conch is allowed to speak, and each would-be speaker must wait his turn. The conch therefore becomes a symbol of courteous, civilized debate (as in many other cultures and circumstances). When the conch is smashed into pieces, it represents the dissolution of order and self-restraint and the beginning of a period of anarchy and primitive savagery.

Scallop (Several Species)

Phylum *Mollusca*, Class *Bivalvia*, Order *Pectenida*, Superfamily *Pectenoidea*, Family *Pectinidae*, Genera (disputed, perhaps about 50), Species (disputed, perhaps about 500)

Name

The name scallop is from Old French *escalope*, meaning shell. It can be pronounced as written, or as *scollop*. The order and family names are derived from Latin *pecten*, meaning comb.

Description

Scallops are very highly prized (and usually highly priced) seafood. The white meat shrinks and caramelizes when cooked, and has a very sweet flavor. The orange-colored roe, which is sometimes removed, is softer in texture and less sweet than the white meat, but still highly prized by many. Scallops are usually dredged up from the sea floor, a practice which causes considerable environmental damage. Hand-gathered scallops are much more expensive because of the high labor costs, but cause much less damage to the seabed. The Atlantic scallop (*Placopecten magellicanus*) is abundant, having recovered from overfishing, but other species in the world are declining.

General Attributes

Scallops feature in Christian symbolism, perhaps in association with older Celtic beliefs.

Saint James

The French name for scallops is *coquilles St. Jacques,* and the German is *Jakobsmuscheln,* both names including variants (*Jacques* and *Jakob*) for the English name James, representing Saint James the Great, one of the Twelve Apostles, supposedly the first apostle to be martyred (he died in 42 CE).

One of the legends of Saint James is that he rescued a knight who had fallen in the water and was smothered by scallops. After James had rescued the knight, he took the humble scallop shell as his symbol. In the Middle Ages, many pilgrims from all over Europe made the journey to Saint James's shrine at Compostela de Santiago in Galicia, in the northwest corner of the Iberian peninsula. (Santiago is Sant Iago, or Saint James.) To show that they had completed the journey, pilgrims were given scallop shells as a symbol of their pilgrimage and devotion to Saint James. Pilgrimages to Compostela continue to this day.

The scallop soon began to appear in heraldry, too. The coat of arms of the Spencer family, which included Winston Churchill and Princess Diana, has a scallop on it.

In the same way that many Christian churches were deliberately built on sites previously dedicated to pagan deities, it is possible that the Compostela de Santiago pilgrimage route follows an older, pre–Christian funereal pathway. We know that there were many such pathways in Neolithic and Bronze Age times, and that some of them have survived to this day: the Lyke Wake Walk in northern England is an example. It is possible that the original pathway to Compostela was made by druids from Gaul and northern Spain.

Saint Augustine

Saint Augustine of Hippo (354–440 CE) also used the scallop shell as an emblem. The legend is that he was walking on the beach one day, lost deep in thought about major theological questions, when he spotted a young boy using a scallop shell to take sea water from his bucket and pour it into a small hole that he had made in the sand.

"What are you doing?" asked the saint.

"I'm emptying the sea into this hole," replied the boy, continuing his laborious work.

The saint immediately realized that many truths were too big or too difficult for ordinary people to understand, including complicated notions like the Holy Spirit, and that Christian theologians and leaders needed to adjust their teaching accordingly.[4]

Coral (Several Species)

Phylum *Cnidaria,* Class *Anthozoa,* Subclasses *Hexacorallia, Octocorallia, Ceriantharia* (remainder of taxonomy disputed, several species)

Name

The common name is from Greek κοραλλιον, *korállion,* coral, via Latin *corallium.* The same root is found in the subclass names: *Hexacorallia* (six-sided corals) and *Octocorallia* (eight-sided corals). *Ceriantharia* is derived ultimately from Greek κερος, *keros,* meaning wax, and κεριον, *kerion,* meaning honeycomb, describing the physical structure of the coral reef.

Description

To somebody who doesn't know differently, a coral reef looks more like a group of plants than animals. Theophrastus (371–287 BCE) described coral as a plant. The Roman author Pliny the Elder (23–79 CE) said that corals were neither plants nor animals, but *tertius natura*, creatures of a third kind. Closer inspection shows that a coral reef consists of millions of tiny individual animals called polyps. Over time, these animals secrete calcium carbonate (or chalk), which forms a hard skeletal structure for the colony. Coral reefs are found in shallow waters around the world, where the sunlight can sustain them, but some species of corals are also found at much greater ocean depths. Coral reefs generally sustain huge populations of sea animals. Approximately 90 percent of all oceanic fish species live within the 10 percent of shallow waters near coastlines, where coral reefs typically grow. All coral reefs are under great stress now, mostly through human pollution and environmental damage. Coral reefs can take decades to re-grow.

General Attributes

Coral has traditionally been very highly valued for its beauty, and there is increasing recognition of its value in ecology. Coral is a very helpful indicator of changes in salinity and temperature in our seas, which themselves are strong indicators of climate change.

Jewelry

Red coral (which is what the Greeks usually meant by *korallion*) in particular has been used as jewelry since ancient times, but it is now so severely under threat that it is rarely if ever used. In China, coral was believed to have magical properties, and to bring prosperity and good fortune. Called *shan-hu* in Mandarin, it became reserved almost entirely for the Emperor and other very high-ranking persons, from the 17th century to the 20th century. Hongli, the Qianlong Emperor (1711–1799) promulgated strict rules concerning the use of coral for personal decoration.

In Ancient Medicine

Coral calx or chalk, called *Praval Bhasma* in Sanskrit, has been used extensively in traditional Indian medicine to overcome calcium deficiency. The Greek physician Dioscorides (40–90 CE) and Galen (129–c. 216 CE), a pioneering Greek physician in the Roman Empire, both prescribed crushed coral chalk as a remedy to calm stomach ulcers.[5]

Amphibians
(*Amphibia*)

33

Frogs, Toads, Salamanders and Newts (Several Orders and Families)

Frog/Toad (Several Species)

Phylum *Chordata*, Class *Amphibia*, Clade *Salientia*, Order *Anura*, Suborders (3), Families (33), Species (about 4,810)

Name

Frog is a Germanic word, ultimately derived from Proto-Indo-European **prew*, meaning jump or hop. Toad appears also to be Germanic—Middle English had several dialectal variations, including *tode, toode, tade* and *tadde* (the root of tadpole, meaning toad poll or toad head). Old English had two versions of the name, *taxe* and *tosca*. The order name *Anura* is from New Latin *an*, without, and Greek ουρα, *oura*, tail.

Description

In scientific taxonomy, there is no difference between a toad and a frog. The name toad is typically used for larger frogs with drier, more leathery skins, and warts or bumps covering the parotoid glands. (Parotoid glands are similar to the parotid glands that secrete saliva in the mouths of mammals, including humans; they secrete alkaloid substances on the frog or toad's skin, depending on the species, many of which are poisonous to deter predators, and are therefore known as bufotoxins.)

General Attributes

The frog or toad symbolizes magical change in many traditions. It is active but cold-blooded, a creature of water and land. Its thin, sensitive skin is considered magical by shamans in several cultures. It is not surprising that the most familiar western folkloric image of the frog is found in the fairy tale of a prince being changed into a frog (usually by a witch) or being changed from a frog back into a prince. Next to the black cat and the crow or raven, the frog or toad is the animal most likely to be identified as a witch's or wizard's familiar.

The Frog Prince Story

There are several variants of the Frog Prince story, especially in Celtic culture. A story found in Wales, Scotland and Brittany is typical, and runs as follows:

> The queen was ill, and sent her three daughters, one by one, to the magical well to bring back healing water. Each princess returned saying that she had been confronted by a hideously ugly frog, which demanded that she should marry him. The youngest (and loveliest) daughter was the only one to agree to the frog's request. She was given access to the well.
>
> The frog turned up at the palace later that evening. The youngest princess let him in, but left him on the floor. When he complained, she trapped him under a cup. When he continued to complain, she made him a tiny bed of straw by the fireside. Still he complained, begging to be allowed into her soft bed with its fine, silken sheets. The princess could not bear that, no matter how piteously the frog begged her to keep her promise.
>
> Finally, the frog insisted that she put him out of his misery by chopping off his head. The princess made to do so, but the instant she struck him he turned into a handsome young prince. The two were married and lived happily ever after.

A variant of the tale has the young princess playing with a golden ball in the palace garden. The ball runs into an ornamental pond and disappears among the reeds. The frog brings the ball to the surface and negotiates his terms for its return.

Wowta

The Warau people of the Guianas in South America have a variant of the Frog Prince story, which features a mythological hero called Abore. The witch Wowta captured Abore when he was a young boy and used him as a slave. As the boy grew, the ugly Wowta began to lust after him. Abore lured Wowta to a tree, in which he had hidden a pot of honey, the witch's favorite food. She climbed up into the tree, but got stuck, allowing Abore to make his escape. Wowta struggled and struggled, but could not free herself. Eventually, she turned herself into a small, green tree frog, the form in which she still appears to this day.[1]

Dzelarhons

The American Indian tribes of the Pacific Northwest have a legend, said to have originated with the Haida, that involves an unusual combination of the bear, the salmon and the frog. Dzelarhons or Dzalarhons was originally a mortal woman whose husband began abusing her physically and mentally soon after their marriage. She escaped by becoming a goddess and protector of animals. When her family came looking for her, all they found was a stone statue of her holding a burning staff.

One version of the legend has her coming to the deep forest of the Olympic Peninsula to marry the bear-god Kaiti, chief of the Grizzlies. Kaiti mistreats her. Her uncle, Githawn, a shaman whose totem animal is the salmon (his name means Salmon Eater), comes in search of her but finds only the statue.

Dzelarhons is called Copper Woman, Volcano Woman, Frog Woman, or Copper Frog. The Dzalarhons Mons, a volcano on the planet Venus, is named after her.[2]

The Stone of Power

Philip Carr-Gomm describes the Stone of Power associated with frogs and toads:

The frog or toad carrying a secret within is the possessor of a power object—a dark gray or light brown stone said to be found in the heads of very old specimens. This mythological object has been known by many names, including Crepandia, Borax, Stelon, and Bufonite. The frog or toad, adder, otter, and fox are all carriers of these secret, invisible power objects. The otter and fox carry magical pearls, the adder leaves a serpent stone, and the toad or frog when old carries the stone of magical properties in its head. These objects, at one level, represent a crossing-over from the animal to the mineral realm—rendering the transient life of the animal eternally cast within a stone. By carrying such a stone, and using it magically, the Druid or shaman would be able to contact his ally, the animal spirit.[3]

Borax is a real chemical, a salt of boric acid with many industrial applications, but also sometimes used in artisanal gold mining. The mythical bufonite is from Latin *bufo*, meaning toad. If from the head of a frog, it was called batrachite. Both, commonly known as toadstones, were reputedly effective antidotes to all known poisons, and to epileptic attacks and to kidney disease—stone against stone. Alchemists were reputed to lay by stocks of bufonite and batrachite in case they accidentally ingested poisons during their experiments. In reality, the stones commonly called toad stones were the fossilized teeth of an extinct fish called *Lepidotes*, usually no larger than a small fingernail, ranging in color from pale brown or pale green through to black, and exceptionally round and smooth, like small buttons. They were frequently set into jewelry, and were deemed effective only when held against the skin.

The Frog and the Ox

A well-known European folk tale, sometimes attributed to Æsop, describes some young frogs rushing home in a panic:

"Father, Father!" they croaked. "We have seen the most gigantic, terrible monster! It had great horns, a shaggy fur coat, huge feet and a big, swishing tail."

"Bah!" croaked the father frog. "That was merely an ox. Nothing to be afraid of. Why, I could make myself as big as an ox quite easily."

And the father frog puffed himself up and gave a very loud croak, just to prove that what he said was true.

"Oh no," croaked the little frogs, "he was much, much bigger than that."

So the father frog huffed and puffed and blew himself up like a round ball.

"Oh no," croaked the little frogs again, "he was even bigger than that."

So the father frog huffed and puffed and blew himself up again, as big as a basket.

"No, no, father" croaked the little frogs again, "even bigger than that."

So the father frog huffed and puffed and blew himself up again, until he exploded with a loud pop, and was no more.

Moral: Conceit leads to self-destruction.[4]

Liu Haichan/Gama Sennin

In Chinese and Japanese legend, a poor old man (or alchemist) was transformed into an immortal god when the three-legged frog or toad of perfection came into his life.

In Chinese, he was called Liu Hai or Liu Haichan (Master Sea-Toad), said to have lived some during the 10th or 11th century CE. He is sometimes depicted as a wealthy young man with a fringe or bangs—*liúhǎi* is the modern Mandarin word for bangs—but also as an old man scratching his head as he searches for wisdom. Presuming there was a historical Liu Hai behind the legend, he was a Taoist, and practiced alchemy, and probably died before 1050 CE. His many other names include Liu Chánchú (Liu of the Moon-Toad), Xuanying (Mysterious Blossom), Guangyang Xiansheng (Sir Guangyang) and Guangyang Liu Zhenren (Liu the Perfected Person from Guangyang). The three-legged toad is a symbol of the Moon, of prosperity and good fortune, and of the Taoist concept of perfection or transition from ordinary mortality to immortality. (The three-legged crow was a symbol of the Sun, the *yang* to the toad's *yin*.)

In Japan, the same Taoist immortal is called Gama Sennin (Immortal Toad). His three-legged companion is called Seiajin (Frog God). In the Japanese folk tales, Gama Sennin makes a drug that allows him to live to be 270 years old, is followed whilst bathing by a man called Bagen who transforms himself into a frog to remain undetected, and later sells a magical pill to Bagen to allow him also to live an extraordinarily long life. In art, this scene is portrayed as an old man giving a magical pill to a frog.[5]

Salamander (Several species)

Phylum *Chordata*, Class *Amphibia*, Order *Urodela*, Suborders *Salamandroidea*, *Cryptobrachoidia*, *Sirenoidea*, Families (10), Genera (disputed, several), Species (disputed, several)

Name

The common name and suborder name are from Ancient Greek σαλαμανδρα, *salamándra*. *Cryptobrachoidea* means "the order of animals with hidden arms or legs."

Description

Salamanders are lizard-like, with four short limbs. They are found in temperate and tropical regions. Some species have no back limbs (hence *Cryptobrachoidea*). Like newts (see below) they can regenerate not only lost limbs or tails, but also eyes, spinal cords, hearts, intestines, and upper and lower jaws, a process of great interest to medical researchers, because the same ability, if it could be reproduced in humans, would obviously be of immense benefit to humankind.

Most lizards and some salamanders can move very quickly over short distances to escape predators, but most salamander species, like some toads, defend themselves by excreting a powerful poison called tetrodotoxin or TTX: these salamanders are usually slow-moving and brightly colored, to warn predators that they are poisonous. TTX is so toxic, it has been estimated that the poison from just one salamander or newt (see below) could kill 25,000 mice.[6]

General Attributes

Salamanders are surprisingly widely present in various religious and mythological traditions. The distinction between salamanders (which are amphibious) and lizards has not been clear until relatively recently in science, but some of the ancients seem to have been aware of it. Pliny the Elder (23–79 CE) described the salamander as "like a lizard in shape" but recognized that it was not a lizard. He did also say that the coolness of its body could extinguish fire, which is demonstrably not true.

Almost all salamanders secrete toxic liquid on their skin when attacked, but their toxicity was greatly exaggerated in classical times. They were reputed to be able to poison a whole well, or make the fruit of a whole tree deadly for humans to eat—again, demonstrably not true. The fire salamander (*Salamandra salamandra*) can actually project the liquid poison a distance of almost 80 centimeters (31 inches) in a fine stream from a ridge on its back, and modern scientists are still studying the relative toxicity of different species.

In Classical Mythology

The classical antidote to salamander poisoning was to drink boiled stinging nettles in a broth of tortoise stew. Many salamanders nest in rotting logs. If those logs are put on a fire, the salamander will suddenly appear and dart off for safety, leading to a common belief in the ancient world that salamanders are born from fire. The ancient belief that salamander vomit or saliva could put out fire, but also removed human hair and caused skin discoloration, continued into Judaism and early Christian mythology.

In Judaism and Christianity

In the Talmud, the salamander was said to have been created by fire, and anyone who smeared his body with salamander blood would never be harmed by fire. This belief came from Greek and Roman traditions.

Following a similar theme, medieval Christian commentators saw the salamander as a symbol of the cool spirit quenching the hot, flame-filled lusts and desires of the flesh. Saint Augustine of Hippo (354–430 CE), believing that salamanders could live in fire, argued that they provided proof of the existence of Purgatory, where souls lived in flames but were not consumed. (He also gave volcanoes as an example of living fire.)

King Francis I of France (1494–1547) chose the salamander as his royal emblem, with the legend *nutrisco et extinguo* ("I nourish and I extinguish"). The famous (or infamous) Swiss astrologer and magician Paracelsus, real name Philippus Aureolus Theophrastus Bombastus von Hohenheim, whose dates 1493 to 1541 are contemporaneous with King Francis, is said to have provided an illustration of a salamander with a Pope's miter in an anti-papal tract written in 1527, but the historical truth is not proven: Paracelsus would have put his life in jeopardy if he had admitted drawing the cartoon. From roughly the same period, Leonardo da Vinci (1452–1519) wrote that salamanders eat fire rather than ordinary food.

Newt (Several Species)

Phylum *Chordata*, Class *Amphibia*, Order *Urodela*, Family *Salamandridae*, Subfamily *Pleurodelinae*, Genera (14 to 17 extant), Species (about 100)

Name

The common name in Middle English was *ewte* (various spellings), from Old English *eft* or *efete*, a Germanic word. As happened with many other English words, e.g., norange (a norange > an orange), napron (a napron > an apron), nadder (a nadder > an adder), the n of "an" either disappeared or was added, so Middle English "an ewte" became modern English "a newt." Terrestrial juveniles are still called efts. The etymology of the subfamily name *Pleurodelinae* is uncertain. *Pleuro-* indicates lungs, from Greek πλευρα, *pleura*, rib, side or flank (the same root as in pleurisy, which means "inflammation of the lining of the lungs"). *-delinae* may be from Latin *delenio*, which means smooth down or soothe.

Description

Newts, like salamanders, have four limbs and a tail. They are smaller than salamanders, generally have rougher or more knobbly skins, and are semi-aquatic, beginning their lives as water larvae and returning to water to breed as adults. They are widely distributed in North America, Europe, North Africa and Asia.

General Attributes

In the grand scheme of things, newts are very ordinary, little animals, although they are often kept in home aquaria as interesting pets, especially in China and elsewhere in the Far East. Nevertheless, they do feature in folklore in several cultures, mostly because of their extraordinary regenerative powers.

As Bioindicators

Newts are of great interest to modern ecological scientists. They have thin, very sensitive skins, which are permeable to water, and through which they absorb oxygen. They react very quickly and sensitively to changes in water acidity or pH levels. The condition and behavior of newts in water environments gives scientists many useful and immediate clues about the ecological condition of the water.

In Witchcraft

In medieval Europe, newts were associated with witchcraft. In Shakespeare's *Macbeth* (Act IV, Sc. 1), the three witches throw "eye of newt and toe of frog" into their magical cauldron. Newts were considered evil, and deadly poisonous (their toxin is not actually fatal to humans).

In Modern Medicine

Between 1994 and 2010, a team from the University of Dayton tested the limits of the regenerative power of newts. Over those 16 years, half a dozen Japanese newts (*Cynops pyrrhogaster*) had their eye lenses surgically removed 18 times apiece. Not only did new lenses appear after every single extraction, but the replacements functioned just as well as the originals had.

According to Panagiotis Tsonis, who headed up the experiment, the discovery could have enormous medical implications: "We are still a long way from relating this to humans," he told *Wired UK*, "but what this shows is that the newt is an excellent source for finding answers to regeneration."[7]

(The newt species *Pleurodeles waltl* has been sent into space six times, to study how the weightless environment affects their ability to regenerate body parts. The regeneration slowed down while they were in space, but then accelerated to faster than normal levels when they returned to earth. Since rapid growth in human cancers and rapid regeneration of body parts in newts seem to have some kind of connection, this is an area of intense interest for medical researchers.)

Insects and Other Creepy-Crawlies (*Insecta, Arachnidae* and *Gastropoda*)

34

Flying Insects (*Insecta*, Several Orders and Families)

Flying Insects (Several Species)

Hotaru Hime

A Japanese legend involves several different flying insects:

Hi O was the king of the fireflies. He had a beautiful daughter, Hotaru Hime, who was courted by many suitors, but she was haughty and difficult to please. For each suitor, she set the same task to prove their love and their worth: they had to bring her fire.

The golden beetle, the black bug, the scarlet dragonfly and the hawk moth were the main contenders. The first three all attempted to fetch fire from a lamp, and each was singed and finally burnt to death. Only the cunning hawk moth stood a chance. He crawled inside the paper wick of a candle, and, fortunately for him, the candle was snuffed before he reached the flame. At least he escaped with his life.

Finally, along came a successful suitor. It was Hi Maro, the firefly prince, who carried his own flame with him. Hi Maro and Hotaru Hime were married, to Hi O's delight. To this day, however, when dead insects are seen around temple lamps in Japan, worshipers say, "Princess Hotaru Hime has had many lovers tonight."[1]

Bee (Several Species)

Phylum *Euarthropoda*, Class *Insecta*, Order *Hymenoptera*, Suborder *Apocrita*, Superfamily *Apoidea*, Families (7), Genus (several), Species (about 20,000)

Name

The common name is Germanic. The Old English was *beo*, as in the name of the famous Old English poem about the hero Beowulf (Bee-Wolf). The suborder and superfamily names come from *apis*, Latin for bee. The Greek name was μελισσα, *melissa*, which is a female personal name today, and is the root of many *mel-* words in different languages relating to honey and sweetness.

Description

Bees are closely related to wasps and ants. There are over 16,000 species, found on every continent except Antarctica. The western honey bee (*Apis mellifera*) is the best-known species, both for its honey and for beeswax, which have been used by many cultures for thousands of years.

General Attributes

The bee is, almost by definition, the epitome of industriousness and purpose. "As busy as a bee" is a very common expression. The bee also symbolizes community, fellowship and mutual organization, because of its complex societal behaviors. The central role of the Queen Bee reflects the views of the many pagans who celebrate the supreme deity as the Goddess or Great Goddess, rather than as a male God. Honey can survive without any preservation for literally centuries—it is the only natural food in the world that never needs preserving—and it is therefore widely associated with good health and long life. Mead, fermented from honey, has been a treasured beverage in several cultures in Europe, Asia and Africa, notably that of the ancient Celts. Honey and beeswax are highly valued products across the world to this day.

Telipinu

In Hittite mythology, Telipinu (Exalted Son) was the patron god of farming:

Telipinu created the world, but soon grew tired of the Earth and humans, and went off by himself to leave humans to get on with things by themselves. It was a disaster. Crops failed, herds disintegrated, even logs on the fire would not burn. The gods took turns in trying to persuade Telipinu to return, but he shrugged them all away. He had had enough.

Finally, the great Mother Goddess Hannahanna sent a bee after him. The bee found Telipinu asleep and stung him to wake him. Not surprisingly, Telipinu woke in pain and in great anger. He returned to the world, but before he could put matters to rights, a place had to be found for his anger. Kamrushepa, the goddess of magic, took his anger and gave it to the gatekeeper of the Underworld, from which there was no escape. Once rid of his anger, Telipinu returned to his duties, and fertility returned to the world.[2]

The Bee and the Mantis

According to the legends of the San people (or Bush People) of the Kalahari Desert in Africa, the first bee helped the first mantis by carrying it across a wide river. The bee was so exhausted by its efforts, that it died, but it laid the mantis carefully on a floating flower, and as it was dying it laid a seed in between the mantis's legs. From that seed, the first human was born.[3]

Parvati

In Hindu mythology, the gods summoned the goddess Parvati and ordered her to kill the demon Arunasura, who had taken over the universe under the name Bhramari Devi or

Great God. Parvati stung Arunasura to death, with thousands of black bees emerging from her body, and power was restored to the gods.[4]

The Bee Dance and Bee Laws

In the Celtic Druidic society of ancient Ireland, law was the province of specialist priests called *brehons*, and the remnants of their wisdom, which date back many centuries, are now commonly known as the Brehon Laws. We know that there were several Brehon laws designed to preserve bees and hives. On the Isle of Man it was a capital offense to steal bees.[5] The bee dance, in which bees return to the hive and communicate with the other bees by wiggling and turning themselves repeatedly, is now understood to be a sophisticated geometrical semaphore that indicates the distance and direction towards food very precisely by describing angles between plants and the sun, but the ancient Celts knew about it, too, describing it as a sun-dance in honor of the Goddess.

Kvasir

In Norse mythology, Kvasir was a divine being formed from the sacred saliva of the Æsir and Vanir combined (the name means saliva or spittle). His blood was the source of the Mead of Poetry. Whoever drank it immediately became either a poet or a scholar.[6] Mead wine averages only 3.5 percent or so alcohol-by-volume (ABV), but mead liqueur can reach 20 percent ABV, and a drink of that strength might well lead the imbiber to believe they had acquired new powers of eloquence. (The name may be related to *kvass* or *kvas*, the low-alcohol fermented rye bread beer found widely across Eastern Europe and Asia, including China.)

According to a rather convoluted tale in the *Prose Edda*, Kvasir may also have invented (or recovered) the fishing net. The mischievous god Loki was in hiding from the other gods, having killed the beloved god Baldr. Loki hid in the waterfall of Frangangsfors in the form of a salmon. Kvasir discovered his hiding place, and watched from behind a tree on the riverbank one evening when Loki weaved the first ever fishing net, seated beside a small fire. Loki heard the other gods approaching and threw the net into the fire, then ran and dived into Frangangsfors to resume his form as a salmon, but the clever Kvasir was able to reconstruct the fishing net by carefully observing the patterns of the ashes in the fire, and thus made an invaluable tool for all humankind to use subsequently.

Saint Ambrose and Aristaeus

In Christian legend, Saint Ambrose (339–397 CE) is the patron saint of beekeepers and wax refiners. As an infant, he was said to have allowed a swarm of bees to settle in and around his mouth, and not one of them stung him. (The same story is told of Plato and several other Christian saints, including Saint Bernard of Clairvaux—the bees are thought to represent profound or sacred utterance, or, more simply, persuasive sweetness in preaching. An alternative legend has the Virgin Mary appearing to Saint Bernard and moistening his lips with her breast milk.)

The counterpart of Ambrose and Bernard in ancient Greek mythology is Aristaeus, who was the god of beekeeping and the protector of fruit trees. He was born of the god Apollo, a half-brother to Orpheus. Although he was married, he fell desperately in love with Eurydice. In pursuing her too ardently, he accidentally poisoned her, and the gods punished him by killing all his bees. On the advice of his mother, Cyrene, he sacrificed a number of cattle to placate the gods. Nine days later, swarms of bees emerged from the bodies of the cattle, and he was back in the beekeeping business, greatly relieved.[7]

Other Classical References

In Greek mythology, Zeus was sometimes called Μελισσαιος, *Melissaios* (Bee Man) because he had a son by a nymph and secretly sent him food (so that his wife, Hera, would not find out), using bees as his carriers to the baby's hiding place in the forest. The bee was sacred to Artemis, and associated with the Greek goddess Demeter and the Roman goddess Cybele. In all three associations, the prevalent themes were fertility and fecundity, and the sacred rituals involved orgiastic practices. According to Homer, Apollo received the gift of prophecy from three bee-goddesses.

In Hinduism

The gods Vishnu, Krishna and Indra are all occasionally referred to as *Madhava*, which means "born of nectar," and clearly implies the bee, since the most common pictorial depiction is always a bee resting on a lotus flower. The Hindu god of love, Kama, has a magical bow (like Cupid), and the bowstring is made of live bees.

Kintu, Nambi and the Friendly Bee

A charming little episode in the creation myth of the Buganda people in Uganda, Africa illustrates how helpful and friendly bees can be:

> Kintu and Nambi were the first man and woman. To begin with, Kintu lived alone with his cow. Nambi met him for the first time, and fell in love with him. Unfortunately, Nambi's father, the sky-god Gulu, disliked Kintu and did everything he could to make life difficult for him. He stole Kintu's cow and took her up to Heaven, so Kintu had no more milk to drink. Gulu set Kintu several challenges, all of which he managed to pass.
> Finally, after some years, Gulu set Kintu one final test. He brought him up to Heaven and showed him his heavenly cattle, three massive herds of them. Kintu could return to Earth and live in peace with Nambi, but only if he could identify his own original cow from the thousands before him.
> Kintu thought that he was defeated, and he put his hands over his head in sorrow. But a bee flew close to his ear. The bee not only told Kintu which cow was his, but even showed him which calves she had given birth to whilst in Heaven. Kintu returned to Earth with Nambi, the cow, and her calves, and from that day forward he was a wealthy and respected man, thanks to the friendly bee.[8]

In Folklore

Aristotle and Virgil both said that bees are born from the decaying corpses of cattle. There may be some truth behind the belief, since a cow's or ox's rib cage makes a perfect natural frame for bees to use to build a hive. Medieval German Christians believed that God created bees specifically to provide wax for church candles.[9] A Breton legend says that bees were first formed from the tears of Christ on the cross, which explains why honey is so sweet and never needs any kind of preservative—mead wine and liqueur are still very popular in both Brittany and Cornwall. (A similar legend in ancient Egypt says that the tears of the supreme sun-god Ra were made of honey.) A very common beekeeper's legend is that if a beekeeper dies, the bees must be informed the same day, or they will stop work and die.

Wasp (Several Species)

Phylum *Euarthropoda*, Class *Insecta*, Order *Hymenoptera*, Suborder *Apocrita*, Species (tens of thousands)

Name

Wasp was *wæsp* in Old English, and *vespa* (pronounced *wespa*) in Latin, from Proto-Indo-European **wobhseh*, related to the word weave. Yellowjackets and hornets are also species of wasps. In modern American-English slang, WASP stands for White Anglo-Saxon Protestants, i.e., wealthy white Americans of British descent, or sometimes just for middle-class white people more generally. (The term is also used in a similar way in Australia, New Zealand and Canada.) The suborder name *Apocrita* is from Greek απokριτος, *apókritos*, separated or chosen.

Description

Wasp species number into the tens of thousands. They are distributed all across the world, apart from the polar regions.

General Attributes

Wasps have appeared in many cultures since ancient times. An example is the well-known Greek comedy Σφεκες, *Sphékes*, *The Wasps*, by Aristophenes (446–386 BCE). Wasps are often more aggressive than bees, and are considered dangerous pests in many cultures. Wasp nests, particularly if they are very densely populated, and particularly in the autumn when wasps are more likely to sting, can present real difficulties. Wasp stings are not usually fatal, although there have been several cases of humans dying of anaphylactic shock after receiving multiple stings.

The Mason Wasp

According to the mythology of the Ila people of Zambia in Africa, the mason wasp or potter wasp (Family: *Vespidae*, Subfamily: *Eumeninae*, about 200 genera and about 3,000 species) found the world too cold. It volunteered to go to Heaven to ask God for fire. Three birds went along, too, but the three birds all died because the journey was so long and arduous. Only the mason wasp reached God. God saw how hard the wasp had worked, and granted his wish. The mason wasp brought fire back to Earth, and thus blessed all humankind, because they could now cook their food and keep themselves warm.

A Navajo Creation Myth

Wasps appear in a poetic Navajo creation myth. The First Man and the First Woman appear on a tiny island with just one pine tree, born of elemental mists and lights. Gradually the world expands and fills up around them, and new people arrive, including the Tsts'na or Wasp People, the Naazo'zi or Spider Ants, the Wolazhi'ni or Black Ants, and finally the Wolazhi'ni-nlchu-nigi or Stinking People. At each stage, the world becomes a less innocent and a more aggravating place.[10]

In Military Names

The ability of many wasps to repeatedly deliver powerful and painful stings has led to use of the name for military purposes. Since 1775, eleven ships of the U.S. Navy have been called USS *Wasp*. The *Westland Wasp* was a British helicopter. A flame-thrower developed from the Bren Gun Carrier was also called the Wasp.[11]

Fly (Several Species)

Phylum *Euarthropoda*, Class *Insecta*, Order *Diptera*, Families (110), Species (about 1,000,000)

Name

The common name in Middle English was *flye* or *flie*, and in Old English *flyge* or *fleoge*, derived from Proto-Indo-European *plewk*, to fly. The order name *Diptera* is from Greek δι, *di*, two, and πτερον, *pterón*, wing.

Description

There may be a million species of flies: nobody knows for certain. Flies have two sets of wings, the first for moving forward, and a second pair, called *halteres*, at the back for balance and stability. Although several other species are called fly (including the butterfly), they are not true flies or Dipterans. Flies have mobile heads, complex eyes and mouths shaped for piercing and sucking for food. (Mosquitoes are flies.) Flies are found all over the world. They are important pollinators, but they also carry many diseases infectious to humans, including major diseases like malaria.

General Attributes

Nobody likes flies. They are invariably at best a nuisance and at worst downright evil in almost all cultures and mythologies.

Prometheus

In Προμεθευς Δεσπωτες, *Prometheus Despōtes* (*Prometheus Bound*), commonly attributed to the tragic playwright Æschylus (525–455 BCE), the Titan Prometheus gives fire to humankind, in defiance of the gods. As punishment, he is chained by the smith-god Hephaestus to a mountain in the Caucasus. One of his visitors is Io, a human maiden who has been plagued by unwanted sexual interest from Zeus, father of the gods. Zeus turns Io into a cow, and Hera, Zeus's wife, sends a gadfly to torment her. The torture is obviously based on close observation of the wretched discomfort experienced by cattle, horses and other animals that are plagued by flies.

Beelzebub/Beelzebul

In Christianity, Beelzebub is a demon sometimes associated directly with Satan or Lucifer. The alternative name Beelzebul is thought to have been originally Ba'al Zebûl, meaning Lord of the (Heavenly) Dwelling, but it is thought that the Hebrews deliberately mocked the name by changing it to the very similar Ba'al Zebûb, which means Lord of the Flies. In the *Septuagint*, the first Greek translation of the Hebrew Bible, the name appears both as Βααλζεβουβ, *Baalzeboúb*, and as Βααλ μυιαν, *Baal muian*, Lord of Flies. In the New Testament, Jesus mentions Beelzebul by name when the Pharisees accuse him of having cured a blind and mute man by using Beelzebul's powers: "If I cast out demons by Beelezebul, by whom do your own exorcists cast them out? Therefore they will be your judges. But if it is by the Spirit of God that I cast out demons, then the kingdom of God has come to you."[12]

William Golding's famous novel *The Lord of the Flies* (1954), mentioned in an earlier chapter, tells of a group of schoolboys marooned on an island who rapidly degenerate into savages as the conventions of life quickly fade from their memories. A pig's head stuck on a stick, surrounded by buzzing flies, symbolizes the blood lust and dangerous wildness that overtakes them once they start hunting for fresh meat.

Brok and Loki

In Norse mythology, Brok or Brokk was a hunchback dwarf who had a very important job. The dwarf sons of Sindri were the makers of gold, and in order to do their work successfully, they relied on Brok to pump the bellows that heated the fire that melted the precious metal out of the ore. Brok, like all dwarfs, was not a cheerful or particularly sociable character, but he was very conscientious, and kept his bellows pumping day and night. Also, like all dwarfs, he was protected by many secret enchantments.

The god Loki, always looking for mischief and resentful of Brok's dependable character and devotion to his job, sought ways to torment the dwarf, but Brok's protective spells were too strong for him to come to any harm. However, Loki finally worked out the most subtle and invincible torment. He turned himself into a fly and buzzed about Brok's sweaty head and face. No matter how much the dwarf shook his head, puffed his cheeks and blew, or took a hand off the bellows and waved it about his face and long beard, Loki continued to buzz and spin all about him, until he was almost insane with exasperation. The tale is told in the Norse *Prose Edda*.[13]

Mosquito (Several Species)

Phylum *Euarthropoda*, Class *Insecta*, Order *Diptera*, Superfamily *Culicoidea*, Family *Culicidae*, Subfamilies *Culicinae, Anophelinae*, Genera (41), Species (about 3,500)

Name

Mosquito is a Spanish word, meaning little fly, from Latin *musca*, fly. The family name *Culicidae* is from Latin *culex*, genitive *culicis*, meaning gnat or small fly.

Description

There are about 3,500 species of mosquitoes. They diverged from other insects about 226 million years ago, and fossilized specimens from about 100 million years ago have been found. Females pierce the skin of animals, including humans, with a special proboscis or tube, and feed on their blood. The common term is a mosquito "bite," but mosquito "suck" would be more accurate. (Male mosquitoes do not bite.) The pierced skin can become extremely irritated and itchy, as anybody who has experienced mosquito bites will readily attest. The bites also act as a conduit for several diseases, including malaria, West Nile virus, yellow fever, dengue fever, and more. In terms of human fatalities and sickness, the mosquito is the most dangerous animal in the world. Research has shown that some people are genetically more predisposed to be targets of mosquito bites than others. In general, mosquitoes will seek out people with type O blood, people who breathe heavily, people with abundant bacteria on their skin, people with high body heat, and pregnant women.[14]

General Attributes

Like flies in general, mosquitoes are not popular. They do appear in mythology and folklore, usually in a negative way.

The Elephant and the Mosquito

This tale appears in many forms in many ancient cultures around the world, always with the same message. (The elephant is sometimes a bull or a horse.)

> An elephant (or any other large animal) was crossing a river (or a bridge, or any other sizeable obstacle). A mosquito hopped on its back.

310 Insects and Other Creepy-Crawlies (*Insecta, Arachnidae* and *Gastropoda*)

"What a fine morning for a crossing!" said the mosquito.
The elephant said nothing, but continued walking.
"Be careful just here," said the mosquito. "It gets a little tricky just here."
The elephant said nothing, but continued walking.
"I'm sure you're very relieved that I'm here to help you and guide you," said the mosquito. "Without me, you might well have stumbled and come to grief."
The elephant said nothing, but continued walking.
"Here we are at last," said the mosquito, "safe and sound. Thank you for the ride. I'm glad that we were able to cooperate and help each other across. Perhaps we can do this again some day. Goodbye!"
The elephant said nothing, but continued walking.

Moral: Sometimes vanity makes us think that we are changing the world, when all we are really doing is making a little buzzing noise in the wind that nobody hears or cares about.

Butterfly (Several Species)

Phylum *Euarthropoda*, Class *Insecta*, Order *Lepidoptera*, Suborder *Rhopalocera*, Families (several), Species (about 20,000)

Name

Butterfly (which children sometimes jumble as "flutterby") is a Germanic word, found in Old English as *buterfleoge*. It is assumed that the name comes from folk belief that butterflies either eat butter or produce butter. The German cognate *Schmetterling* comes from *Schmetten*, cream. An alternative German nickname is *Molkendieb*, literally "whey thief." The order name *Lepidoptera* is from Greek λεπις, *lepís*, scale, and πτερον, *pterón*, wing.

Description

Butterflies (which includes moths) have four-part wings covered with tiny scales, which is what the order name *Lepidoptera* means. They are distributed in about 18,500 species across almost the whole world, apart from the polar regions. Butterflies are generally more brightly colored than moths, and several species use their coloring as camouflage against predators. Butterflies are mostly diurnal, moths mostly nocturnal.

General Attributes

Many butterflies are extremely beautiful. Butterflies have appeared in art, folklore and mythology for millennia.

Zhuang Zhou's Paradox

One of the most famous and oldest quotations about butterflies is from the Chinese Taoist philosopher Zhuang Zhou (Master Zhuang), also called Zhuangzi, Chuang Tzu, and other variants, who lived in the 4th century BCE. Zhuang dreamed one night that he was a butterfly, flying around happily in a garden. The next morning, when he awoke drowsily, he asked himself, "Was I Zhuang last night, dreaming that I was a happy butterfly, or am I a butterfly today, dreaming that I am Zhuang Zhou?"

Zhuang Zhou was said to have been offered the position of chief minister in the court of King Wei of Chu, with a huge salary and every comfort. His reply to the king's messengers was that he would rather be a happy beggar in a filthy ditch than a miserable chief minister in a rich palace. He wrote about the connectedness of all living things, to the extent that some have interpreted his ideas as a precursor of Darwin's theories on natural selection and evolution.

Leippya

In Burmese mythology, the name *leippya* (literally butterfly) is given to the soul materializing as a butterfly when it leaves the body. Sickness is often interpreted as a restless *leippya* trying to leave the body to go on adventures. The *leippya* can be trapped and preserved: for example, the soul of King Mindon Min, who died in 1878, was preserved in a small, heart-shaped piece of gold suspended above his body while it was on public display, then buried with the body in due course.[15] When a body remains in the family home, it is customary to leave all doors and windows open to allow the *leippya* to fly out.

Ciuateteo

In Aztec mythology, the Ciuateteo were the anguished ghosts of women who had died in childbirth. They lived in Tamoanchan, the Aztec version of heaven, but on certain days of the year they returned to the world to bring disease to children, because of their never-ending grief and anger. On those days, Aztec parents did not allow their children to play outdoors. They built temporary temples, especially at crossroads, and placed offerings to the Ciuateteo on them. The offerings were of bread baked in the shape of butterflies, because the bread would appease the terrible hunger of the Ciuateteo and the butterfly shapes would remind them of all the beauty and goodness that is in the world, and bring them a measure of peace.[16]

In Christianity

In medieval Christian symbolism, the butterfly was not only an example in and of itself of the beauty of God's creation, but also a symbol of resurrection, from the humble first life as a caterpillar, through the death-like entombment in a chrysalis, to the final release of the soul into eternity as a beautiful butterfly. The Gnostics, however, portrayed it as a symbol of physical death and corruption. In Slavic Christian legend, a demon or witch could be recognized if butterflies emerged from his or her mouth: they were trapped souls trying to fly back to God, or to enter another human body.

35

Creeping, Crawling Animals (*Insecta, Arachnidae, Gastropoda,* Several Orders and Families)

Beetle (Several Species)

Phylum *Euarthropoda*, Class *Insecta*, Order *Coleoptera*, Suborders (4 extant), Species (about 400,000)

Name

Beetle is a Germanic word, ultimately from Proto-Germanic **bitulaz*, biter. The order name, *Coleoptera*, is from Greek κολεος, *koleós*, sheath, and πτερον, *pterón*, wing.

Description

There are over 400,000 known species of beetle in the world, with perhaps as many unknown species again yet to be discovered. Whereas flies and butterflies have four wings, in beetles the front wings have hardened to become wing sheaths, which is what the order name *Coleoptera* means. Beetles are found everywhere except in polar regions.

General Attributes

Beetles are generally industrious and resourceful. A humble dung beetle, the scarab (see below) has been historically one of the most sacred animals in the world.

Scarab

The best-known sacred beetle is the scarab of ancient Egypt. The species name is *Scarabaeus sacer*, which literally means "sacred scarab." It is a dung beetle, its only distinguishing feature being that it has six little projections on its head, and four more on each front leg. Its habitat is coastal dunes and marshes in southern Europe and northern Africa. It rolls dung into a ball, pushes the dung down a hole, then eats it. So how did such a humble, undistinguished insect acquire such a powerful reputation as a sacred symbol, so powerful that even Linnaeus in 1758 felt compelled to officially name it as *sacer*, or sacred?

The answer lies in the ancient Egyptian belief that Khepri or Khepera, a manifestation of the god Ra (later Amun-Ra) began each day by rolling the sun out of the darkness of night and up into the sky. They saw the scarab as imitating the action of the god, as it rolled its dung ball laboriously across the sand. Furthermore, they noticed that young scarabs emerged from the hole where the dung ball had been deposited (always by a male, as they thought), and they connected that observation with their belief that Ra was so powerful that he could father children without any goddess or woman being involved, a belief later repeated by the Roman author Plutarch. The name Khepri is derived from hieroglyphs that in English represent the sound of the letters *xpr* or *hpr*. As an Egyptian word, this means "to come into being," "to transform" or "to become."

Khepri was said to have been born of his own substance. He copulated with his own shadow to produce Shu (Air) and Tefnut (Moisture). Shu and Tefnut produced Geb (Earth) and Nut (Sky), and these two produced Osiris, Isis, Set and Nephthys. These primal gods are often referred to as the Egyptian Ennead or Company of Nine Gods. Khepri was portrayed as a beetle-headed man, or simply as a beetle. Ordinary Egyptians had such belief in the powerful and protective scarab image that even the occupying Roman troops in the colony established after the Egyptian wars wore scarab finger rings and brought them back in significant numbers to Rome, where they were hugely popular. They were said to guarantee a successful transition to the Elysian Fields, the Roman Paradise.

As a result, over centuries of use, the humble dung beetle *Scarabaeus sacer* became a widely recognized symbol of resurrection and rebirth. Scarab carvings, often of glass, jade or other green stone (green symbolizing living plants) were placed over the chests of corpses before mummification or burial, to protect the heart and make sure that it came back to life in good condition during resurrection. Scarab motifs appeared on jewelry (as they still do to this day), and the little beetle became a significant character in Egyptian, Greek and Roman mythology (there is even an Æsop fable about the eagle and the scarab).

Dayunsi

The Cherokee nation of North America celebrate a little water beetle called Dayunsi as part of their creation myth. The whole world was once Galunlati, a place of nothing but water, but the animals were all very crowded and complained. Someone had to go down through the water to see what else might be found. All the animals were afraid, except for little Dayunsi. He darted about on the surface of the water, but found no place to rest. Then he dived, down and down and down. When he came back, he brought with him some soft mud. The mud began to grow and spread, until it became the whole Earth, which the animals tied to the sky with four strong ropes. Now they had sky, land and water to move and live in, and they honored the little water beetle for his bravery.[1]

As Food

Beetles and their grubs are an important part of human diets around the world. In Southeast Asia, grubs of the Red Palm Weevil (*Rhynchophorus ferrugineus*) and Asiatic Rhinoceros Beetle (*Oryctes rhinoceros*) are roasted and eaten as delicacies. The Chinese collect giant water scavengers (*Hydrophilidae*) and remove the head and appendages before frying them in oil or soaking them in brine. The Aborigines of Australia collect large, nut-flavored longhorn (*Cerambycidae*) larvae (witchetty grubs) from rotten logs and roast them.[2]

Ant (Several Species)

Phylum *Euarthropoda*, Class *Insecta*, Order *Hymenoptera*, Superfamily *Formicoidea*, Family *Formicidae*, Subfamilies (16), Species (estimated 22,000)

Name

The common name is found in Middle English as *ampte* or *emete* (various spellings), cognate with the Scots dialect name *emmot* and the Cornish dialect name *emmet*. It means biting thing or cutter. The family name *Formicidae* (from which the chemical name "formic acid" is derived) comes from Latin *formica*, ant.

Description

There are more than 12,500 species of ants. They are eusocial, which means that their social organization is unusually complex and sophisticated: they cooperate in care of the young, working collectively; different generations all live together in the same colonies; work is distributed fairly between reproductive and non-reproductive individuals; specialized groups adapt to perform specific tasks, and are not expected to do anything else.

General Attributes

The ant is generally considered the representative of industry in some parts of the world, and of spite and malice elsewhere. The Bible invites us to learn from the ant's willingness to get on with the job in hand: "Go to the ant, thou sluggard, consider her ways, and be wise."[3] Æsop similarly recommends the ant for her hard work (see below). The Japanese word for ant combines the word for insect with characters representing unselfishness, justice and courtesy. The Pueblo Indians of North America, however, consider the ant to be vindictive and the cause of disease. In West Africa, ant nests are places where evil spirits and demons live. In Hinduism, ants signify the pettiness of all things and the futility of earthly pursuits.[4]

The Ant and the Grasshopper

A tale attributed to Æsop, although it was written down in the Middle Ages by Phaedrus, tells of a meeting between an ant and a grasshopper:

> One frosty autumn day an ant was busily storing away some of the kernels of wheat he had gathered during the summer to eat throughout the coming winter.
> A grasshopper, half perishing from hunger, came limping by. Seeing what the industrious ant was doing, he asked for a morsel from the ant's store to save his life.

"What were you doing all during the summer while I was busy harvesting?" inquired the ant.

"Oh," replied the grasshopper, "I was not idle. I was singing and chirping all day long."

"Well," said the ant, smiling grimly as he locked his granary door, "it looks as though you will have to dance all winter."

Moral: It is thrifty to prepare today for the wants of tomorrow.

There is an old Cornish proverb: *Yn Hav, por' ko' Gwav*—"In summer, remember winter."

Aba and the Ants

The Choctaw Indian nation call the Creator Aba (The One Above). The first place on Earth was Nane Chaha (High Hill), which had a passageway leading down to subterranean caverns. The first Choctaws emerged from these caverns, pursued by enemies from other tribes. When the Choctaws reached the surface, they called on Aba to help them. Aba sealed the entrance to the underworld, locking in the enemy tribes, and then Aba turned the enemies into ants—that is why ants sting and bite.[5]

Myrmidons

There are several versions of the ancient Greek legend of the Myrmidons, but the Roman poet Ovid's version, in Book 7 of his *Metamorphoses* (8 CE), runs as follows:

> Hera, Queen of the Greek gods, was furious because her husband, Zeus, had named an island after his mistress, the nymph Aegina. She sent down a plague, which killed all the island's inhabitants. Aeacus, King of the Aeginans, begged Zeus to intercede and repopulate the island. Zeus sent down a lightning bolt, to confirm that he had heard the prayer. Aeacus saw a tree covered with ants, and asked Zeus for as many people as there were ants. Aeacus slept, and in his dreams, the ants fell from the tree and became people. When he awoke, his dream had come true. In gratitude, he called the people Myrmidons (from Greek μυρμεξ, *myrmex*, meaning "ant").[6]

In return for Aeacus's humanity and strong faith, Zeus later appointed him one of the judges of the dead.

Spider (Several Species)

Phylum *Arthropoda*, Subphylum *Chelicerata*, Class *Arachnida*, Order *Araneae*, Suborders *Mesothelae, Opisthothelae*, Families (113), Species (about 46,000)

Name

Spider is a Germanic word meaning spinner, ultimately derived from Proto-Indo-European **(s)pen* or **(s)pend*, meaning spin or weave. The class name is taken from a story in Greek mythology. Arachne, daughter of the famed cloth dyer Idmon, challenged the goddess Athena to a weaving contest. Arachne wove a scatological tapestry depicting various sexual activities of the gods. Deeply offended, Athena destroyed the tapestry. Arachne hanged herself, but Athena took her body down from the noose and shape-shifted her into a spider, after which all spiders belong to the class *Arachnida*.

Description

Spiders, like insects, are joint-legged invertebrates or arthropods, but all arachnids have eight legs rather than six. Scorpions, ticks, and mites are also arachnids.

General Attributes

The arachnids feature in some myths and legends, but not usually in sacred traditions. With a few exceptions, they are not well liked—indeed, arachnophobia, or fear of spiders, is a fairly well known phenomenon. Scorpions, ticks and mites are not everybody's favorite animals, either.

However, spiders are associated with the unraveling of fate (probably because of the imagery of spider webs) in ancient Greek mythology (the Fates and the Moirae), in Norse mythology (Holda and the Norns) and in Near Eastern mythology (Ishtar and Agatatis). The Chibcha Indians of Colombia believe that the dead cross the lake of death on boats made of spiderwebs, and will therefore never kill or even harm a spider. In the mythology of the Yoruba people of western Africa, the spider-god Yiyi brought fire from heaven to help humankind.

Ariadne

In the legend of the Minotaur of Crete (see Chapter 39), Ariadne (The Most Pure) was a Cretan princess who helped the hero Theseus to destroy the monster. She gave him a sword (fairly ordinary), but also a huge ball of string (not so ordinary). Theseus let the string unwind as he moved further and further into the Labyrinth in search of the Minotaur. Once he had killed the beast (no mean feat), he used Ariadne's thread to retrace his steps and find his way out again.[7] There are many complicated variants of the legend, but the central device of the string is reminiscent of a spider's thread, so Ariadne is sometimes compared to Arachne (see above).

Jorōgumo

Jorōgumo or Jorō Kumo is a spider goddess who appears in several Japanese folkloric tales. Her name means woman spider. (The large, yellow-and-black golden orb-web spider *Nephila clavata*, common in Japan, China and Korea, is called the Jorō or Jorōgumo spider.)

In one story, a beautiful, young, pregnant woman presented herself before a young warrior. "There," she said to the child inside her, "is your father. Present yourself to him and prepare to be embraced." But the young warrior was not fooled. He struck the woman with his sword and she fled to the attic. Next day, he found a huge, dead Jorō spider in the attic along with the remains of several of its human victims.

In another tale, Magoroku was dozing on his verandah. A woman in her 50s approached and told Magoroku that her daughter had taken a fancy to him. He visited the woman's estate and met her young daughter, who boldly asked the older man to marry her. He declined, because he was already married, but the young woman persisted. She claimed that Magoroku had almost killed her mother two days earlier, so she surely deserved some consideration. In confusion, Magoroku stumbled back home. The next thing he knew, his wife was shaking his shoulder. She told him that he had been asleep on the verandah all this time. With relief, he looked up to the eaves and saw the fresh web of a small Jorō spider, and remembered that he had driven away a much larger Jorō spider just two days earlier.[8]

There are several variations of a legend that always has at least four components: a Jorōgumo spider that appears as a young woman; a mystical waterfall; a woodcutter; and a tree stump. In most of them the woman-spider is trying to drag the woodcutter to his death in the waterfall, but is tricked or manipulated into attaching her silken thread to the tree-stump instead.

Kananesky Amaiyehi

In the creation myth of the Cherokee nation of North America, Kananesky Amaiyehi, the water spider, brought fire to the world. In the beginning there was no fire, and the Earth was cold. The Thunderers sent down lightning, which put fire into the bottom of a sycamore tree, but no animals could get near it. The water spider made many attempts, but the problem was always how to carry the fire away. Finally, she spun a thread from her body and twisted it round and round until it became a small bowl. She swam over to the island where the sycamore tree was burning. She put one little ember of fire in her the bowl on her back and swam safely back across to land. From that single ember, all the fire of the world was made.[9]

Spider Grandmother

The Spider Grandmother is a main character in the complex creation myth of the Hopi Indians of the southwestern United States. As in several other indigenous creation myths from around the world, humans are very slow to catch on to the purpose of creation and are generally a disappointment to the gods.

> Taiowa the Sun Spirit asked Kohyangwuti (Spider Grandmother) to go down to the world to explain the meaning of life to the creatures who lived there. Kohyangwuti taught the insects, the animals, and finally the people. But the people chose *powaka*, or false prophets. With the help of the birds, Kohyangwuti cut a hole in the sky, and brought all of Creation into the upper world, but they found Masuwu (Death) there, and some of the *powaka* managed to follow them: and that is why there is death and false witness among the nations.[10]

Iktomi

In the mythology of the Oglala Lakota, Iktomi (Spider) is a culture hero and trickster spirit whose totem is the spider. In tribal names he is also variously called Unktomé, Ikto, Ictcinike and Iktinike. He was the second manifestation (Hindus would say avatar) of the god Ksa, who invented language, names, stories and games, but Iktomi played so many mischievous tricks that he was no longer an immortal god, merely a mortal hero. He is used as an exemplar to young people of how folly leads to pain whereas wisdom leads to maturity and happiness.

Nevertheless, although he often comes to grief through some kind of foolishness, he is also associated with magical power. The dreamcatcher, a hoop of willow or other wood covered with a net and beads or feathers, is well known in the West. Many non-indigenous people put dreamcatchers in their windows. The dreamcatcher is associated with Iktomi, because it is a magical web: it catches good vibrations, happy dreams and prosperity and keeps them in the home, while keeping out bad dreams, poverty and failure, and Iktomi is the spirit who builds and maintains the magical web.[11] Because he is the spirit of language, communications and webs, he is associated in modern Oglala mythology with social media, telecommunications and the internet.

Ancient Spider and Nareau

In Micronesian mythology, two spider gods, Ancient Spider and Young Spider, played important roles in the creation of the world. Ancient Spider was born of Te Bo Ma (Darkness) and Te Maki (Cleaving Together). Ancient Spider made Heaven and Earth from a shell. He ordered the sand and the sea to mate, and they produced Nakika, the octopus, Riiki, the eel, and Nareau, or Young Spider.

Nareau's job was to transform fools and mutes into normal human beings. He loosened their limbs and tongues and opened their ears and eyes. Then he told them to lift the sky, but the task was too great for them. Nareau asked Nakika and Riiki to help, and they managed to get the sky up into position. Riiki was so exhausted by the work, however, that he died and became the Milky Way. Ancient Spider became the Sun and Moon. His brains became stars, trees and rocks, and human beings came from the rest of his body.[12]

Anansi, Miss Nancy

Anansi is a West African god, a trickster and sometimes malevolent spirit, who frequently shape-shifts into a large spider. He is also called Gizo and Kwaku Ananse. Tales of his mischief traveled with the slave trade to the West Indies, where the name became Miss Nancy and the god became a female spirit.[13]

King Robert and the Spider's Web

One of the best-known historical legends concerning the spider is that of Robert de Brus, or The Bruce (1274–1329), who claimed the throne of Scotland in 1306, despite vigorous opposition from the English and from other Scottish contenders. At one point, according to the legend, Robert's fortunes were so low that he was forced to hide in a sea cave on the tiny island of Rathlin. Cold, hungry, exhausted and deeply dispirited, he lay on the cave floor. As he looked up, he caught sight of a spider spinning her web in a dark corner. Time after time, a sudden gust of wind would catch the web and destroy it before the spider could complete it. Nevertheless, the spider persisted, never giving up, and finally she completed her web. Encouraged by the spider's patience and persistence, Robert left the island in 1307, landed at Carrick, subsequently drove the English back home by winning a completely unexpected Scottish victory against Edward II at the Battle of Bannockburn in 1314, and in 1320 was acknowledged rightful King of Scotland in the Declaration of Arbroath sent to Pope John XXII.

Although there has been much discussion about whether the Bruce's spider was real or just a fiction (and much exploration of where exactly his cave may have been—there are many claimants in addition to Rathlin), the main theme of the legend is a variation on a story that is thousands of years old. In the Judeo-Christian tradition, King David hid in a cave from pursuit by King Saul. A spider spun a web over the mouth of the cave while David was hiding inside. King Saul's men decided the cave wasn't worth searching, since if David had entered, the web would have been broken. Similarly, an Islamic legend says that Muhammad and his companion Abu Bakr were being pursued by soldiers, and they took refuge in the Cave of Thawr. Muhammad commanded a spider to build a web across the entrance, and, as in the story of King David and King Saul, the pursuers passed by the cave without bothering to search it.

Scorpion (Several Species)

Phylum *Arthropoda*, Subphylum *Chelicerata*, Class *Arachnida*, Order *Scorpiones*, Superfamilies (6), Families (13), Species (about 1,750)

Name

Scorpion comes from Greek σκορπιος, *skorpíos*, via Latin *scorpio* (which is also the name of an astrological sign of the Western zodiac). The order name comes from the same root.

Description

Scorpions are small, but considered deadly. As with tarantulas, their reputation is not entirely deserved. Of the approximately 1,750 species, only 25 carry enough venom to kill a human. Most scorpion stings do not need medical treatment, although it is true that in certain areas, particularly remote areas where medical treatment of any kind is not available, human fatalities do occur on a regular basis.

General Attributes

The ancient Egyptians greatly admired scorpions (see below). Increasingly, scorpions are being found in crowded urban environments (e.g., São Paulo in Brazil).

In 2018, 140,000 people were stung by scorpions in Brazil.[14]

Companions of Isis

In Egyptian mythology, Isis was the sister-wife of Osiris. Osiris was killed by the evil god Set (also Isis' brother), and his body parts scattered across the whole of Egypt. Isis patiently gathered all the parts and reassembled them, bringing Osiris back to life. Set subsequently imprisoned Isis, who at this time was pregnant with Osiris' son, the great hawk-headed god Horus.

Thoth, god of law and justice (among many other things), came to Isis' rescue. He visited her and suggested how she might escape. Isis had seven handmaidens, who were scorpion goddesses. Their names were Tefen, Befen, Mestet, Mestetef, Petet, Thetet and Maatet (-en and -et were common feminine endings in ancient Egyptian names). The scorpions forced open the cell door and led Isis in the dead of night across the dangerous papyrus swamps to a village.

Isis knocked on the door of a rich woman, but the woman refused to give her shelter. Tefen slipped under the door, stung the woman's child to death, and then knocked over a lamp to burn the house down. Isis took pity on the woman despite her callousness, restored the child to life and called down a heavy shower of rain to put out the fire.

Next, the goddess went to the home of a poor woman. The peasant woman welcomed the goddess without a moment's hesitation and fed her what little she had. Isis rewarded her with good health and great prosperity, and her rich neighbor suffered agonies of remorse when she later realized the mistake she had made.

On the journey, Isis gave birth to her son Horus in the papyrus swamps. She needed to keep the baby hidden from her brother Set, so she kept him covered by the long reeds, with her scorpion companions guarding him.

One day, Isis went to the nearby city of Am, to get provisions. When she returned, she found the baby Horus lying dead, with foam on his lips. He had obviously been stung by a scorpion. After questioning her seven companions and reassuring herself that none of them would ever harm her baby, she realized that the cunning Set must have disguised himself as a scorpion to pass among the others without notice, and had thus managed to come close enough to sting Horus to death.

Isis cried for help, and Ra, the god of the Sun, heard her weeping. He stopped still in the heavens. Ra became Thoth, and came down to Isis. He taught her a resurrection prayer, and when Isis carefully repeated the sacred words, Horus came back to life.

Worship of Isis spread all across Egypt and beyond, and it extended in time as well as in space. In Greek mythology, Isis became associated with the legends of Athena, Persephone and Tethys. In Rome, she was called Isis Campensis, and Apuleius in the 2nd century CE still referred to her as *regina coeli*, "Queen of Heaven," the same title given to Mary, mother of Jesus. Among modern pagans, Isis is still a very powerful and important goddess.[15]

Serket

Another of Isis' scorpion companions became an Egyptian goddess in her own right. She was called Serket (also Serqet, Selket and Selcis) and became a significant goddess of fertility, animals, magic and medicine, particularly healing the bites and stings of poisonous animals. Her name has been interpreted as "she who allows the throat to breathe," which would be very fitting for recovery from the paralysis of venomous bites or stings. She was often depicted with outstretched wings in a gesture of protection. She was believed to have special power to protect the entrails of the deceased. Those who gave due worship to Isis and Serket were said to be immune to scorpion stings.[16]

Snail/Slug (Several Species)

Phylum *Mollusca*, Class *Gastropoda*, (several orders, families, genera and species)

Name

The common name snail is Germanic, from proto-Germanic **snagilaz*, snail. The name slug was *slugge* in Middle English, and referred to a slow, lazy person. The same meaning is given for the dialectal Norwegian word *sluggje*. The order name *Gastropoda* is from Greek, and literally means stomach foot.

Description

The *Gastropoda* or gastropods, more commonly known as snails and slugs, are a very large class (somewhere between 65,000 and 80,000 species) within the phylum *Mollusca*. The class includes not only land snails and slugs but also many marine animals, including whelks, periwinkles, and others. Some of these appear in sacred traditions.

Snails of various kinds are found on land, in freshwater, and in the sea. Most can fit entirely inside their spiral shells—the common metaphor is that they are "carrying their house" on their backs. Snails without shells are called slugs. Some species are "semi-slugs," having shells too small for the whole body to fit into.

General Attributes

Snails are about the lowest of the low on the sacred animal totem pole. They are very slow, easy food for predators and humans alike, and considered by many to be outstandingly uninteresting at best, and slimy and repellent at worst. Nevertheless, even humble snails and slugs do feature in some mythology and folklore.

As Pests

Snails and slugs munch their way slowly but deliberately through thousands of tons of growing produce across the world, so that farmers and gardeners are always trying to find more effective ways of deterring them. Gritty sand, salt and eggshells are commonly used as protective borders. Commercial snail and slug repellents are usually based on toxic chemicals. Copper is an expensive barrier, but apparently quite effective. There are plenty of other animals that steal or contaminate food, but there is something especially repellent about tucking into a fresh salad and discovering a slow, slimy slug on a lettuce leaf.

As Food and Dye-Providers

However, snails are eaten in many parts of the world, most famously (or notoriously) in France, where they are known as *escargots*. In fact, they are also eaten generally in Europe, North Africa, India and the Far East. In countries that produce and export bananas, land snails are useful because they eat the discarded shed leaves, and can then themselves be eaten as food.

Snails can be useful in other ways. The *Muricidae* family of rock snails produce a rich, purple-red dye. Extracting the dye was so labor-intensive in classical times that the color was reserved only for the highest nobility in ancient Rome, and purple or dark maroon have been considered royal or aristocratic colors ever since.

In Divination and Mythology

The Greek poet Hesiod described how farmers carefully watched for snails climbing plant stalks, as indicators of propitious times for planting. A complex Javanese myth features Princess Dewi Sekartaji being transformed into a snail to entice the Prince Panji Asmoro Bangun. The island of Kauai in Hawaii is said to have taken its unusual shape after it was attacked by a giant snail. In Japanese mythology, the edible snail *sazai-oni* (very popular in Japanese cuisine) can sometimes become angry and resentful at being eaten all the time: if and when it reaches 30 years of age (some say 100), it will suddenly become gigantic in size, grow human hands, and attack any humans nearby. The Aztecs believed that the snail was a moon god, and that the spirals in its shell were related to the lunar cycle. The modern psychologist Carl Jung (1875–1961) often used the snail as a metaphor for the human mind: the outer shell is the conscious mind, the self that we display to the world, while the soft body inside is the subconscious mind, alive and active, but protected from the onslaughts of the world by the shell of conscious thought.

The Love Dart

Most snails are hermaphrodite, i.e., both male and female simultaneously. A very unusual feature of the mating of these animals is the so-called "love dart," which is not a penis, but rather a body part used exclusively in mating. Each of the prospective mating pair produces a long, thin appendage, often very large in relation to their bodies, which looks just like an arrow. When the pair pierce each other with their love darts, no semen is delivered (the darts serve no actual significant biological purpose in the mating sequence), but a hormone is introduced which makes it more likely that the mating will be fertile and productive. Professor Ronald Chase of McGill University in Montreal has suggested that the snail's love dart, specifically of the species *Helix aspersa* or common garden snail, may be the origin of the classical myth of Cupid shooting his arrows of love into prospective partners.[17]

Sea Snails

Whelks (usually *Buccinum undatum*) and periwinkles (*Littorina littoria*) are popular seafoods. Various species of whelk or wilk are eaten in the USA, the West Indies, Britain, Ireland, Scotland, the Netherlands, Belgium, Japan, Vietnam, Korea, Australia and New Zealand. Periwinkles (or just winkles) are smaller and darker than whelks, but have been a cheap and fairly nutritious food source for working-class people in Britain for centuries (millennia, if you include their almost certain use for food by pre-historic peoples). A

Sunday afternoon tea of freshly brewed tea, and whelks, winkles, cockles, or small brown prawns and bread and butter was a standard weekly meal for many working-class families, including my own when I was a child.

Worm (Several Species)

Phylum *Annelida* (Worms used to be considered as reptiles, but they are now divided into three phyla *Platyhelminthes* includes flukes, flatworms and tapeworms; *Nematoda* includes hookworms, threadworms and roundworms; *Annelida* includes the segmented worms, such as the earthworm and several sea worms.)

Name

Worm is a Germanic word, written *wyrm* in Old English, but obviously from the same Indo-European root as Greek ʽρομος, *hrrómos* and Latin *vermis* (pronounced *wair-mis*). The three phylum names, *Platyhelminthes*, *Nematoda* and *Annelida* are New Latin words from Greek roots meaning flat worms, thread-shaped and little ring-shaped respectively.

Description

Some marine worms are over 3.3 feet (1 meter) in length, while others are so small that you need a microscope to see them. The largest recorded land-based worm is the African giant earthworm (*Mirochaetus rappi*) at 22 feet (6.7 meters),[18] and the largest recorded marine worm is the nemertean or bootlace worm (*Lineus longissimus*) at 190 feet (58 meters).[19] (We know so little about the deep ocean that there may well be marine worms that are even longer.)

An obsolete taxon *Vermes* (from the Latin name *vermis*) was coined by Linnaeus, but it has become obvious that the many creatures called worm in common parlance are far too diverse to belong to a single group. When most people talk about worms, they usually have one of two kinds of animal in mind: earthworms, i.e., worms that live in the soil and perform the important task of decomposition, or parasitic worms that live inside humans and other animals, usually causing disease or death. A third kind of worm is the monstrous or gigantic worm of mythology.

General Attributes

Worms, usually of the giant or monstrous kind, occur in various mythologies, usually as evil creatures that must be destroyed by a hero. The distinction between worm and snake or dragon becomes blurred in many of these tales (see Chapter 38). (The name wyvern usually means a giant worm-like creature with wings like a dragon, but it does not breathe fire.)

Worms of Scotland, England and Wales

Tales of the Linton Worm date back to the 12th century CE. Linton Hill is in Roxburghshire on the Scottish borders. According to the legend, the worm was big enough to eat both livestock and humans. William (or John) de Sommerville went to nearby Jedburgh and saw the worm for himself. He noticed that if the worm was confronted by anything too big to swallow immediately, it stood in a kind of stupor with its mouth wide open. Accordingly, he prepared a bolus of twigs and hay soaked in pitch, set fire to it on the end of a lance, rode his horse up to the worm's face, and thrust the flaming bolus into the worm's mouth. The worm's agonized thrashing as it died is said to be the cause of the unusual ripples in the topography around Linton Hill.

The worm or wyvern of Sockburn near Durham in northern England dates from the 14th century. Lewis Carroll (1832–1898) is said to have heard the tale of the Sockburn Wyrm from the local people, and to have incorporated some features of it in his well-known fantasy poem, *Jabberwocky*, which includes the famous lines:

> One, two! One, two! And through and through
> The vorpal blade went snicker-snack!
> He left it dead, and with its head
> He went galumphing back.[20]

The Sockburn Wyrm is said to have been slaughtered by one John Conyers with his "falchion" or sabre. By tradition, every newly appointed Bishop of Durham was presented with this blade and the accompanying speech:

> My Lord Bishop, I hereby present you with the falchion wherewith the champion Conyers slew the worm, dragon or fiery flying serpent which destroyed man, woman and child; in memory of which the king then reigning gave him the manor of Sockburn, to hold by this tenure, that upon the first entrance of every bishop into the county the falchion should be presented.[21]

Perhaps the most famous of the northern English worms is the Lambton Worm, celebrated in folk song for centuries, which also hails from County Durham. The Lambton Worm started life as a water dragon in the River Wear, but the rebellious John Lambton, who used to skip church on Sundays to go fishing instead, caught it as an eel or lamprey, only 3 feet (1 meter) or so in length, although it did have nine holes on each side and some peculiar markings. Out of curiosity, Lambton kept it and foolishly threw it into a well, where it grew to a monstrous size while Lambton was away fighting in the Crusades. When Lambton returned, the worm (i.e., dragon) was merrily feasting on sheep, lambs, calves and children. Lambton hacked it to death. The chorus of the folk song runs:

> Whisht, lads, ha'd yer gobs (hold your tongues)
> I'll tell yez aal an awfu' story,
> Whisht, lads, ha'd yer gobs,
> I'll tell yez 'bout the Worm![22]

In west Wales, not far from Swansea, the most westerly point on the Gower Peninsula is Worm's Head, a tiny almost-island of rock connected to the headland by a rocky causeway. Worm's Head and nearby Rhossili were favorite walking places of the famous Welsh poet Dylan Thomas (1914–1953). This is the only part of Wales that the Vikings invaded successfully. Worm's Head was named by them, since it is shaped like the head of a great worm or dragon, an effect enhanced in strong weather by the thudding, booming and hissing that emerges from a blowhole near its summit.

Adu Ogyinae

In the mythology of the Ashanti people of Ghana, Africa, the first man was called Adu Ogyinae. On Monday night he came to the surface of the earth through bore holes made by a giant earthworm. He led a group of seven men, eight women, a dog, and a leopard, all of whom were terrified by everything they saw. On Tuesday, Adu Ogyinae showed the world to them, and they calmed down. On Wednesday, they built the first homes, but the leopard went off by herself. While they were building, a tree fell on Adu Ogyinae and killed him. On Thursday, they sent the dog into the forest, and he came back with fire, a smoldering branch in his teeth. On Friday, they fed meat to the dog, and when he showed no signs of sickness, they ate the meat themselves. Every year, the Ashanti hold ceremonies in the forest to celebrate the great earthworm, Adu Ogyinae and the first people.[23]

Leech (Several species)

Phylum *Anellida*, Class *Clitellata*, Subclass *Hirudinea*, Infraclass *Euhirudinea*, Species (about 700)

Name

Leech is a Germanic word (cf. modern Dutch *laak*). In Middle English it was *leche*, and in Old English *læce* (pronounced *lak-uh*). Leech came also to mean doctor or surgeon, particularly in the 18th and 19th centuries (see below). The subclass and infraclass names *Hirudinea* and *Euhirudinea* come from *hirudo*, the Latin for leech.

Description

Leeches, of which there are about 700 species, are parasitic worms, mostly found in freshwater. The medicinal leech, *Hirudo medicinalis*, feeds on blood, first secreting a peptin called hirudin, which prevents the blood from clotting.

Leech bites in the wild are generally more uncomfortable than dangerous, although some people do experience anaphylactic shock after bites, and some people find the bites more painful than others. Leeches can carry viruses and bacteria in their guts for several months, so rapidly brushing or knocking a leech off the skin is not a good idea: the leech may regurgitate some of the blood it has eaten into the wound it has created, and thus present an infection risk. Peeling the leech off carefully and slowly, mouth end first, is the recommended protocol.

General Attributes

The only attribute for which the leech has ever been highly regarded is its ability to suck blood. It would be wrong to say that any culture has thought of it as sacred, or magical, or even pleasant, but its ability to assist in healing has been known and respected in many cultures for thousands of years.

In Ancient Medicine

Ancient Indian Ayurvedic texts recommend leeches for a variety of ailments. In the 5th century BCE, the Greek natural philosopher Alcmaeon of Croton (c. 540–500 BCE) described the human system as being composed of four elements or "humors" which needed to be kept in balance: blood, phlegm, black bile, yellow bile. A surfeit of blood was considered dangerous for many reasons, so bloodletting was a highly valued treatment, a belief which persisted into the 19th century CE, and is still considered valid in many ways to this day by some. Pliny the Elder (23–79 CE) tells us that leeches were often used to relieve gout in ancient Rome, and that patients became addicted to their use because they were so effective. He also describes elephants being driven to dangerous frenzy by the torment of leeches attaching themselves to the insides of their trunks.[24]

In Modern Medicine

Leeches are still in use in medicine today, and not just in undeveloped countries. Modern surgeons use leeches to clean and drain wounds, particularly since the advent of microsurgery in the 1980s. They are especially helpful in restoring circulation during microsurgery to reattach severed body parts.

Reptiles
(*Reptilia*)

36

Snakes and Lizards (*Squamata*)

Snake (Several Species)

Phylum *Chordata*, Class *Reptilia*, Order *Squamata*, Suborder *Serpentes*, Infraorders *Alethinophidia*, *Scolecophidia*, Genera (several), Species (several)

Name

The English word snake comes from Old English *snaca*, and ultimately from Proto-Indo-European **sneg*, meaning crawl or creep. The order name *Squamata* is from Latin *squamatus*, "having scales," from *squama*, scale. The suborder name *Serpentes* obviously means serpents—it comes from Latin *serpens*, which itself comes from Greek ἑρπειν, *hérpein*, crawl (the same root gives the disease name *herpes*). The infraorder name *Alethinophidia* is from Greek αλεθοφινος, *alethophinós*, true or genuine, and οφις, *óphis*, snake, and *Scolecophidia* is from σκωλεξ, *skōlex*, earthworm, and οφις, *óphis*, snake.

Description

Snakes are long-bodied, legless, carnivorous reptiles. They are found on every continent except Antarctica, and in almost every country of the world, with some exceptions (notably Ireland, where Saint Padraig or Patrick is said to have banished them). They kill their prey either with venom, or by crushing them: the crushing snakes are generally called constrictors.

General Attributes

Snakes—especially the venomous ones—can kill humans, so they are generally feared and respected. In many religions, especially Hinduism, they are believed to be sacred and very powerful (see below).

Australian Aboriginal Snakes

In Australian aboriginal mythology, there are two great snakes connected with death. The first is the wombat snake, called Biggarro, who gently leads souls to the spirit land. The other is Goonnear, an evil carpet python, who does everything he can to prevent the dead from entering the spirit land. Ironically, the carpet python (*Morelia spilota variegata*), while impressively large at over 6 feet (2 meters) and patterned in many colors, is completely harmless to humans—it is not venomous, and lives on birds and small mammals that it kills by constriction.

The most widespread Aborigine mythological snake, however, is the Rainbow Snake, which is called by a bewildering variety of names and has a wide range of attributes. Among the Wikmunkan people it is called Taipan, and is associated with healing, the circulation of the blood and female menstruation. Thunder, lightning and severe rain, against which background the Rainbow Serpent often appears, are expressions of anger by Taipan at human failure to follow the rules of appropriate sexual conduct. Called Julunggul by the people of the eastern Arnhem Land, the Rainbow Snake is believed to swallow up young boys and vomit them out as young men, symbolic of initiation into adulthood. The Rainbow Snake can be portrayed as male or female, or as male with female breasts. Other names for it include Kunmangurr, Galeru, Ungur, Wonungur, Worombi, Wonambi, Wollunqua, Yurlunggur, Langal, Muit and Yero.[1]

Wollonqua

The Warramunga Aborigines also have a great snake god, called Wollonqua, which rose out of the Thapauerlu, a vast water hole in the Murchison Ranges. Even though Wollonqua journeyed many miles from the water hole, he was so gigantic that his tail never left it. He had a human companion, Mumumanugara, who once tried to force Wollonqua back into his water hole, but the snake coiled itself around Mumumanugara. In drawings and in stylized dances, the Warramunga still celebrate the exploits of Wollonqua and pay homage to the god.[2]

The Ouroboros

The Ouroboros is a very ancient symbol, first seen in Egyptian art, passed on to the Greeks, thence to the medieval Gnostics and Hermeticists, and finally into alchemy. It is a world serpent, so big that it encompasses the entire world, and with its tail in its mouth, as if eating itself. The name comes from Greek ουρα, *oura*, tail, and βορα, *bora*, food. An image probably originally dating to the third century CE has the Greek words 'εν το παν, *hen to pan*, "one is all," written within the snake circle, suggesting that it symbolizes the eternal cycle of birth, life, death and rebirth. For the Gnostics, the Ouroboros symbolized eternity.

Extraordinarily, the image was involved in the modern discovery of the chemical formula for benzine by August Kekulé in 1865, as he described himself after seeing a mental image of the Ouroboros while he was working on the formula:

> I was sitting, writing at my text-book; but the work did not progress; my thoughts were elsewhere. I turned my chair to the fire and dozed. Again the atoms were gamboling before my eyes. This time the smaller groups kept modestly in the background. My mental eye, rendered more acute by the repeated visions of the kind, could now distinguish larger structures of manifold conformation: long rows, sometimes more closely fitted together; all twining and twisting in snake-like motion. But look! What was that? One of the snakes had seized hold of its own tail, and the form whirled mockingly before my eyes. As if by a flash of lightning I awoke; and this time also I spent the rest of the night in working out the consequences of the hypothesis.[3]

Naga/Sarpá

Snakes play a very important role in Hinduism. The Sanskrit word *naga* means snake or serpent, but also more specifically the genus of cobras, which is named in scientific classification as *Naja* (see below). The same word is also used in Jainism and Buddhism. The Sanskrit word *sarpá* is also used for a wide variety of snakes. So, the words *naga* and *sarpá* can be used in these three religions to refer to many different kinds of animals, just as snake and serpent do in English.

However, the eastern terms also refer to divine, semi-divine or supernatural beings. They may be wholly human, or part-snake, part-human. A female *naga* is called a *nagi* or *nagini*. A king of snakes is called a *nagaraja* or *rajanaga*. *Nagas* live in an enchanted underworld, where they guard a great treasure, called *Naga-loka* or *Patala-loka*. They are proud, brave, admirable creatures, not to be trifled with. Vasuki is a *nagaraja* who lives coiled around the neck of the god Shiva. Vishnu and other gods are often depicted reclining, as if on a couch, on the great body of Sheshanaga, the *rajanaga* of all *rajanagas*.

A story from Buddhist mythology tells how the Buddha was meditating in a forest shortly after his enlightenment. A great, threatening storm arose. Immediately, the *nagaraja* Mucalinda extended his seven serpent heads over the Buddha to protect him from the storm. When the storm was over, Mucalinda shape-shifted into human form and worshiped at the Buddha's feet.

Other *nagas* and *nagarajas* of note are: Naga Seri Gumum of Malaysia, who, like the Loch Ness Monster, lives in a deep lake and appears infrequently; Bakunawa, a Philippine serpent-dragon who causes eclipses and earthquakes; Karkotaka, an Indian *nagaraja* who also controls weather; Manasa, a Hindu goddess of *nagas* who cures snake bites; Padmavati, a *shasana devï* or goddess of protection; Paravataksha, whose sword rattling causes thunder; Takshaka, a tribal *nagaraja* who features in the epic poem *The Mahabharata*; and Yulong, a Chinese dragon king who became a *naga* after completing his journey from China to India in the 7th century CE with the Buddhist monk, traveler and translator Xuanzang.[4]

Cassandra

Cassandra the prophetess, daughter of King Priam and Queen Hecuba, is well known in Greek legend. Perhaps not so well known are the stories of how she acquired her prophetic skill. According to the first, she and her twin, Helenus, went as small children with their parents to the temple of Apollo, but, as small children do, they fell asleep during the sacred rites. While they slept, the temple snakes licked the ears of the sleeping children. Hecuba screamed when she saw the snakes, and they fled, but both children had been given the power of prophecy.

The second variant legend, perhaps better known, is that Apollo fell in love with Cassandra and promised that he would give her the gift of prophecy. Cassandra agreed to marry Apollo, but then capriciously changed her mind. Apollo could not withdraw the gift of prophecy, but added a curse: no matter what Cassandra prophesied, nobody would believe her. And so it was. She warned the Trojans about the Wooden Horse, but was ignored. She warned Agamemnon that he would be killed by his wife, Clytemnestra, but he refused to believe her. Eventually, Clytemnestra killed not only Agamemnon, but also Cassandra herself.[5]

Orpheus and Eurydice

In the well-known classical legend, Orpheus's wife Eurydice (Wide Justice) was killed by a snakebite. Orpheus begged Hades to be allowed to enter the Underworld and bring Eurydice back to the land of the living. Because he was famed for his enchanting singing, and because he was the son of the muse Calliope and the god Apollo, Orpheus, a mortal, was allowed to descend into the Underworld, but on one condition: he must walk out in front of Eurydice, and must never look back for her. He almost made it back to the living world, but at the last moment, no longer hearing Eurydice's footsteps, and fearing that Hades had tricked him, he glanced backwards. Instantly, Eurydice returned to the Stygian depths, and Orpheus had to return to the world alone.[6]

Tiresias

In many cultures, snakes represent esoteric knowledge. In Greek legend, the blind prophet Tiresias, who appears in the works of many classical writers, saw two snakes mating. He killed the female snake, and was immediately transformed from a man into a woman. Seven years later, s/he again saw two snakes mating, but this time killed the male snake, and was transformed immediately back into a man. Zeus and Hera later argued about who gained the greatest pleasure from lovemaking, the man or the woman. They asked Tiresias, who answered that it was the woman. Hera was so angry with his reply (she was trying to get Zeus to admit the wrongness of his philandering ways) that she struck Tiresias blind. Zeus could not reverse Hera's curse, but he blessed Tiresias with the ability to see the future and with a long life.[7]

Adam and Eve

The serpent plays a major role in the legend of Adam and Eve, found in the three Abrahamic religions. In Christianity (but not in Judaism or Islam), the legend supports the doctrine of original sin.

In the first chapter of Genesis in the Bible, God creates humans *en masse*: "So God created humankind in his image, in the image of God he created them; male and female he created them. God blessed them, and God said to them, 'Be fruitful and multiply, and fill the earth and subdue it….'"[8] From this passage arose two strange folkloric or mythical legends: the first, that the first humans were hermaphrodites ("male and female he created them"), the second that Adam's first wife was Lilith, who later became a she-demon. However, in the next chapter, God creates the first man from "the dust of the ground, and breathed into his nostrils the breath of life," and also "planted a garden in Eden, in the east."[9] He gives the first man (as yet still unnamed) strict instructions about a certain tree : "You may freely eat of every tree of the garden; but of the tree of the knowledge of good and evil you shall not eat, for in the day that you eat of it you shall die."[10] By tradition, the fruit is an apple, but it is never actually named as such in the Bible. Some have suggested that a fig would have been more likely, since the Bible does say that what Adam and Eve used to cover their nakedness was fig-leaves.

The evil serpent, "more crafty than any other wild animal that the LORD God had made,"[11] persuades the first woman (also still unnamed) to try the forbidden fruit. She does so, and then persuades the first man to try the fruit too. As soon as they have tasted it, "Then the eyes of both were opened, and they knew that they were naked…."[12] God curses the man to a lifetime of hard labor followed by death, the woman to pain in childbirth and subordination to her husband through her lust ("Yet your desire shall be for your husband, and he shall rule over you"[13]), and the serpent to a life crawling on its belly ("and dust you shall eat all the days of your life"[14]).

Abuk

In the mythology of the Dinka people of Eastern Sudan in Africa, the snake-goddess Abuk is the patron of all women and the goddess of plenty, of produce, grains and gardens. She and her consort Garang were the first woman and man, made by the Great Being from clay. As they grew larger, Abuk became greedy, and demanded more than the allotted one grain of corn each per day. The sky was offended, which is why it still tries to destroy crops with its heat, and the reason that snakes fear and hide from the sky, but it was through Abuk that farming began and the people could live from generation to generation.[15]

Herakles

In Greek mythology, Amphitryon, King of Tiryns, was the husband of the beautiful Queen Alcmena. While Amphitryon was away at war, Zeus came down and assumed Amphitryon's shape, so that he could sleep with Alcmena. Later the same night, the real Amphitryon returned, and also slept with Alcmena. Two boys were born of that night's lovemaking, Herakles (Hercules) and Iphikles. Amphitryon was told by a priest what Zeus had done, and he accepted both babies as his sons. However, out of curiosity, he put two harmless snakes into their crib. Iphikles ignored them, but Herakles seized both snakes and killed them instantly. Then, Amphitryon knew that Iphikles was his own son, and Herakles was the son of Zeus.[16]

Laocoön

The classical story of Laocoön is actually only a small sub-plot in the far better known story of the Wooden Horse that the Greeks used to trick their way into Troy, but several classical statues were made depicting Laocoön's death, his story features in Virgil's *Aeneid*, and there have been many other depictions and retellings throughout history.

The story is simply told. The Greeks built a large wooden horse, filled it with armed warriors, and brought it to the gates of Troy. They sent their spy, Sinon, into the city to help persuade the Trojans that this was a magnificent gift, and that they should wheel it in through the city gates. Only the Trojan priest, Laocoön, had doubts about the horse. He said (in Virgil's Latin version), "*Timeo Danaos et dona ferentes,*" literally, "I fear the Greeks when they bring gifts." He begged his fellow Trojans to burn the wooden horse.

According to Virgil, Minerva sent two great sea serpents to kill Laocoön and his two sons (Quintus Smyrnaeus says it was Athena, who is actually the same goddess as Minerva, and Apollodorus says it was Apollo). Whoever sent them, the massive serpents did their job, squeezing and strangling the Trojan priest and his sons to death.[17] The gruesome scene has appealed to painters and sculptors for many centuries.

(To complete the Wooden Horse story, in case anyone doesn't already know the ending, the foolish Trojans wheeled the horse into the city, the Greek warriors climbed out of it during the night, and the Greeks captured Troy.)

Asklepios or Aesculapius

The association of snakes with healing and medicine has a very long history, but is perhaps best illustrated in the legend of the god Ασκλεπιος, Asklepios, as the Greeks called him. His mother was Coronis, and his father was the god Apollo. Coronis was sentenced to death by burning by Artemis, for unfaithfulness to Apollo. As the pregnant Coronis was burning on the pyre, Apollo snatched the baby from her womb and gave him to the wise centaur Chiron to raise. Chiron raised the baby, originally called Hepios, and taught him everything he knew about medicine and healing.

Eventually, Hepios knew more about healing than either Chiron or Apollo. He was reputed to have even brought the dead back to life. He healed King Askles of Epidaurus of a supposedly incurable eye disease, and in acknowledgment of this great feat was thereafter known as Asklepios (He Who Cured Askles). He took as his totem animal the snake of healing. He is often depicted in Greek statuary as a bearded man with a stout staff, with a serpent entwined about the staff. This was called the Rod of Asklepios. Zeus eventually killed Asklepios with a thunderbolt, either from jealousy of his healing power, or because he feared that Asklepios would soon conquer death all together and humans would live eternally, like the gods. (Hades, the god of death, is said to have complained about Asklepios's activities.)[18]

The Romans adopted Asklepios into their pantheon, changing his name slightly to Aesculapius, after a plague of 293 BCE almost destroyed the city. Temples dedicated to Aesculapius kept snakes, which were sacred to the god, and his cult became widespread.

In the late 19th century and early 20th century, various medical bodies—including the U.S. Army Medical Corps in 1902—mistakenly confused the original Rod of Asklepios (unadorned, with a single serpent) with the *caduceus*, or rod of Hermes/Mercury (adorned with wings, with two serpents intertwined), and it is now a commonplace to see the *caduceus* as a symbol of medicine, in advertising, logos, letterheads, etc., when in fact Hermes/Mercury had nothing to do with healing. It would be good to see the true Rod of Asklepios with its single serpent restored as the international symbol of medicine, but the *caduceus* appears to have won that particular iconography battle.

Asklepios had five daughters. Three of them are not well remembered, but the other two had names which have come to live permanently in the English language: Hygieia, the goddess of cleanliness in healing (something the ancient Greeks understood better than many other Europeans in later ages) gave us the word hygiene, and Panacea, the goddess of universal remedy or healing (from παν, *pan*, all, and ακος, *ákos*, cure), gave us the word panacea.

The Woodman and the Serpent

Snakes do not often appear in Æsopic fables, but one well-known tale also involves a woodman, or in some versions a poor old woman living in the forest:

A woodman was returning to his cottage after a hard day's work in the winter forest. As he crossed a stream, he saw a snake lying frozen stiff in the grass. Taking pity on the creature, he brought it home and set it close to the fire to warm up. No sooner had the snake revived, however, than it lunged with fangs bared at the woodman's young daughter, terrifying the child and coming very close to killing her. The woodman grabbed his axe and without any hesitation chopped off the snake's head.

Moral: Don't expect gratitude from the inherently evil.

Ahriman

In Zoroastrianism, Ahriman, who is often depicted with a snake-skin hood and is reputed to have created demons, snakes and all things evil, is the spirit of badness opposed to Ahura Mazda, the spirit of goodness. The two were brothers, born of the great god Zurvan. At the time of their conception, Zurvan told their mother that whichever brother was born first would become king. As the time of their birth approached, Ahriman ripped open his mother's womb and thus claimed his primogeniture and right to the throne. Zurvan kept his word, but Ahura Mazda finally triumphed over Ahriman after nine thousand years. An early Persian sculpture depicts Ahura Mazda riding a horse, which is trampling Ahriman's snake-covered head.[19]

Hiawatha and Atotarho

The name Hiawatha is well known mostly because of the popularity of the poem purportedly about him, *The Song of Hiawatha* by Henry Wadsworth Longfellow, published in 1855, immensely popular with the Victorians, but less so since. Longfellow claimed, quite rightly, that the poem was inspired by genuine Indian legends, but he was wrong to call the hero Hiawatha—the legendary material he gathered from genuine Indian sources, including the Ojibwe chief Kahgegabowh and Black Hawk of the Sauk people, was in fact about a trickster deity called Manabozho.

The historical Hiawatha was an Iroquois chief, Haien'wa'tha in Onondaga, who was a leader of the Onondaga people and a highly skilled politician. He founded the first *Haudenosaunee* or five-nation Confederacy of the Iroquoian People. His mentor and guide had been the Huron prophet and medicine man Deganawida (Great Peacemaker), who had a severe speech impediment and could not make speeches as effectively as Hiawatha. In 1722, the Tuscarora people joined the Onondagas, Senecas, Cayugas, Oneidas and Mohawks to complete the six-nation Iroquois Confederacy.

The Hiawatha of the animal legend has a similar aim to unite the various tribes, but is opposed by the war-chief Atotarho, whose head is covered with snakes instead of hair. Atotarho uses magic to bring down a huge white bird from the sky, which kills Hiawatha's beloved daughter. Hiawatha is sorely tempted to attack and kill Atotarho in revenge. But he remembers his higher purpose, and instead, showing great resolve and self-control, continues to persuade the war-chief to support his idea of unification. Finally Atotarho agrees. Hiawatha combs the snakes out of Atotarho's hair, symbolizing his conversion from evil to good.

Animals and birds other than snakes also feature strongly in Longfellow's poem, "The Song of Hiawatha." In the introduction, he demonstrates how integral animal lore is to Native American culture, as well as to his poem:

> Should you ask me, whence these stories?
> Whence these legends and traditions,
> I should answer, I should tell you,
> "From the forests and the prairies,
> From the great lakes of the Northland,
> From the land of the Ojibways,
> From the land of the Dacotahs,
> From the mountains, moors, and fenlands,
> Where the heron, the Shuh-shuh-gah,
> Feeds among the reeds and rushes.
> I repeat them as I heard them
> From the lips of Nawadaha,
> The musician, the sweet singer."
>
> Should you ask where Nawadaha
> Found these songs, so wild and wayward,
> Found these legends and traditions,
> I should answer, I should tell you,
> "In the bird's-nests of the forest,
> In the lodges of the beaver,
> In the hoof-prints of the bison,
> In the eyry of the eagle!
> All the wild-fowl sang them to him,
> In the moorlands and the fenlands,
> In the melancholy marshes;
> Chetowaik, the plover, sang them,
> Mahng, the loon, the wild goose, Wawa,
> The blue heron, the Shuh-shuh-gah,
> And the grouse, the Mushkodasa!"[20]

Although some modern critics deride the poem for its rigid rhythm scheme, its anthropomorphism and its sentimentality (there have been many parodies), it was, in 1855, one of the earliest positive descriptions of Native American culture, and, in my view, made a significant contribution to the general greater appreciation of Indian society that is still slowly creeping its way forward to this day.

Ukuhi

In the mythology of the Cherokee Indian nation, Ukuhi is the name of the black racer snake (*Coluber constrictor*). Ukuhi went in search of fire, but when he found it he was scorched black. Ever since, he wriggles and darts about on the ground as if seeking to escape from flames.[21]

Quetzalcoatl

Quetzalcoatl was a major god in Aztec mythology, and the name was also used by a later culture-hero. It means plumed or feathered (*quetzal*) serpent (*coatl*). The first images of an unnamed feathered-serpent god are dated as early as c. 900 BCE, but the cult of Quetzalcoatl flourished much later throughout central Mexico, from about 600 CE onwards. The name was later used as a military title by the Toltecs (c. 900–1168 CE).

Quetzalcoatl was above all a god of the wind, storms, hurricanes, waterspouts and tornados. Several times he destroyed life on earth, once leaving only monkeys behind, on another occasion only fish. He had three brothers, two called Texcatlipoca (one red, one black), and the fourth Huitzilopochtli. Quetzalcoatl drove Tlaloc, the rain god, from the sky, and placed the goddess Chalchiutlicue, Tlaloc's wife, to rule as the Sun, but she drowned in a great flood. Eventually, Quetzalcoatl threw his own son into a great fire to become the Sun, and Tlaloc threw his son into the same fire to become the Moon. The gods decreed that there must be war on Earth so that they would always have human victims for blood sacrifice.

When Hernando Cortéz and the Spanish Conquistadors came to Central America in the 16th century, the Aztecs believed that they were their own gods finally returned to them, and their willingness to yield up their gold, their other treasures and their temples and palaces contributed to the downfall of Aztec civilization.[22]

Bachúe

In the mythology of the Chibcha people of Colombia, Bachúe (Large Breasted), also called Fura-chogue (Generous Woman), is a creation myth goddess frequently depicted as a snake. The supreme god Chiminigagua created the sky. Bachúe then emerged as a serpent from a lake, bringing a three-year-old child (not her own) with her. She changed into human shape. She raised the child until he was of age, and then had six children by him, who were the first humans, and populated the land. After staying on a while longer to ensure that all the crops of the world were safely started, she became a snake again and returned to her sacred lake.[23]

Gagavitz

In the mythology of the Mayan Indians, Gagavitz (Hill of Fire) was a creator god and hero. He was helped by a human, Zakitzunún (White Sparrow), to bring fire to the world. He descended into the volcano Gagxanul while Zakitzunún threw water and stems of green corn into the mouth of the volcano to keep it calm. After a long while, Gagavitz emerged carrying fire, which he gave to Zakitzanún to share with the rest of humanity. When Gagavitz finally died, he resumed his real shape: he became a huge serpent and slithered back into the earth.[24]

Benzaiten

Benzaiten or Benten is a Japanese Shinto-Buddhist goddess, a version of the Hindu goddess Saraswati, the goddess of love, beauty and the arts. She is one of the Shichi Fukujin (Gods of Fortune). She is frequently portrayed with a white serpent, and is often referred to as the White Snake Lady. Her two main temples are on the sacred island of Enoshima, not far from Tokyo, and at Miyajima on the island of Itsukushima near Hiroshima. Like many Hindu deities, she has four or eight hands, symbolizing the extent of her reach into human affairs. Each hand holds a different tool or symbol. She wears a crown, sometimes with a phoenix resting on it, sometimes with her white serpent coiled about it. The serpent often has the face of an old man. She is a goddess of wisdom as well as protection. In Shinto, she is a *kami* (ancestor or elemental presence or spirit) and has many Shinto shrines as well as Buddhist temples dedicated to her.[25]

The Midgard Serpent

In Norse mythology, a great serpent encircles the whole earth. Sometimes called the Midgard Serpent, it was fathered by Loki, the god of harm and mischief. Its Norse name is Jörmungandr (Wolf Serpent). It bites its own tail and causes storms and shipwrecks. Thor struck it with his magical hammer Mjölnir, but the serpent survived and remains a present danger. (See Chapter 38.)

The Head and the Tail

A whimsical Jewish fable in the *Talmud* (central text of Rabbinic Judaism) runs as follows:

> The tail of a snake once said to its head, "Don't you get tired of being in front all the time? How much longer are you going to stay in front and make me go wherever you want to go, dragging me behind you? Let me lead for a change, and you follow."
>
> "Fine," said the head. "You go first. I don't care."
>
> So the tail led, and the head followed. First the tail fell into a ditch filled with water, and the head naturally fell in too. Then the tail led the head into a thorn bush, and they both got scratched and wounded.
>
> The moral of the story is a question: Which was the bigger fool, the tail for asking to lead, or the head for agreeing to be led?[26]

Cobra (Several Species)

Phylum *Chordata*, Class *Reptilia*, Order *Squamata*, Suborder *Serpentes*, Family *Elapidae*, Genus mostly *Naga*, Species (9)

Name

The English name cobra was borrowed directly from Portuguese, which in turn took it from Latin *colubra*, snake. The family name *Elapidae* is from Greek ελαπς, *élaps*, venomous snake.

Description

Cobras are deadly, and therefore to be treated with great respect. All of the known cobras have hoods, all are capable of rearing up and striking very quickly, and all are venomous and potentially fatal to humans.

General Attributes

Cobras have been venerated for millennia. They symbolize death, and the ability to deliver death quickly, and therefore terrestrial and political as well as spiritual power.

The Uraeus

The *uraeus* is an image or sculpture of the head of a cobra rearing to strike, used widely in Egyptian art to indicate divinity, royalty or authority. The name is Latin, from Greek ουραιοσ, *ouraïos*, "on its tail," from Egyptian hieroglyphs *j'r.t*, *iaret*, "rearing cobra." It appears in many depictions of pharaohs and deities, almost always prominently on the headdress immediately above the forehead and eyes.

The first *uraeus* is said to have been made by the goddess Isis, from dust and the spittle of the sun-god Ra. The *uraeus* became the symbol of Lower Egypt, and the vulture Nekhebet as the totem of Upper Egypt. A carved wooden *uraeus*, covered in gold leaf, was found among the tomb goods of Tutankhamun. In several depictions, cobras spitting fire guard the gates of the underworld.[27]

Adder/Asp/Viper (*Vipera berus*)

Phylum *Chordata*, Class *Reptilia*, Order *Squamata*, Suborder *Serpentes*, Family *Viperidae*, Genus *Vipera*, Species *Vipera berus*, Subspecies (3), Related species (3 closely related within *Viperidae*)

Name

Adder is one of several words in English where the letter n of the indefinite article "an" has been either added or removed through mishearing or misinterpreting the letter combination. "An adder" was originally "a nadder." The Old English word was *nædre* (cf. German *Natter*, Welsh *neidr* and Latin *natrix*, water snake). Asp is from Greek ασπις, *aspis*, shield, via Latin *aspis*. Viper is from Latin *vipera*, which is also the genus name. The root of *vipera* itself may be *vivus*, alive, and *parere*, to give birth, since giving live birth is common in vipers but not in other snakes.

Description

The adder is the only venomous snake in the British Isles. Various species of adder, asp or viper are found throughout the world, except the polar regions, Australia, New Zealand, Hawaii, Madagascar and some other islands or island groups.

General Attributes

In the Celtic tradition, the adder represents healing and transition, including transition from death to life. She is sacred to the Goddess of Earth, where humans live, and to the kingdom of the sky, where the gods live. As in other snake traditions, the adder is associated with secrecy and esoteric rituals, and with fertility.

The Serpent's Egg

The adder delivers its young by aplacental viviparity, which sounds complicated but is actually easily explained. Snakes are not mammals, so they do not have a placenta to nourish the young growing inside them—they are aplacental. Viviparity means giving birth to live young, which is what the adder does. The young, who are inside membrane-covered eggs, live off the nutrients inside the egg, then, when they are ready to be born, they hatch out inside the mother and only then emerge from her as live offspring. Hence, aplacental viviparity.

However, in the Celtic Druidic tradition, there is an object of great magical power that is known as the Serpent's Egg, and in Britain that can only be the adder's egg, which biologically doesn't exist. In Welsh it was called *glain neidre* (the adder's stone). Pliny, the classical Roman author, described it as being red and very shiny, but nobody has yet successfully explained what it actually was. It may have been an object made of glass, it may have been some kind of fossil. The archaeologist Stuart Piggott suggested that it might be the cast-off egg case of the common whelk (*Buccinum undatum*) that is often found lying on the sea shore, but it is difficult to see how such a common object (dull and black, not red and shiny) could be valued so highly as powerful and sacred.

In Christian Iconography

Christians traditionally believe that the adder is deaf. The Bible says, "Their poison is like the poison of a serpent: they are like the deaf adder that stoppeth her ear."[28] The deafness symbolizes those who are unwilling to listen to the Christian gospel. Philippe de Thaon wrote in a 12th-century bestiary that the adder is "sly and aware of evil: when it perceives people who want to enchant it and capture it, it will stop up its ears."[29]

The Ark of the Covenant, which is an important item in both Judaism and Christianity, was a chest made of acacia wood and overlaid with gold.[30] It was placed in the Holy of Holies in the temple, and is said to have held the original Ten Commandments given to Moses by God on Mount Sinai. It later disappeared, perhaps stolen, perhaps destroyed. The search for it is the main theme of the film *Raiders of the Lost Ark* (1981). In medieval Christian exegesis, the Ark came to represent Mary, mother of Jesus, who bore and sheltered him as the Ark sheltered its treasure. It is thought by some that the original Ark may have housed a live snake-god.[31]

Rattlesnake (Several Species)

Phylum *Chordata*, Class *Reptilia*, Order *Squamata*, Suborder *Serpentes*, Family *Viperidae*, Subfamily *Crotalinae*, Genus *Crotalus, Sistrurus*, Species (36), Subspecies (about 70)

Name

Rattlesnakes (or rattlers) have a rattle at the end of their tails, which makes a buzzing or rattling noise to deter predators. (Young rattlesnakes in particular are common prey for eagles, hawks, weasels, and even other snakes.) The genus names are based on the rattle. *Crotalus* is from Greek κροταλον, *krótalon*, which means castanet. *Sistrurus* is from Greek σειστρουρος, *seistrouros*, rattle-tail, related to the name of the sistrum or rattling drum found in Egypt and several other African countries.

Description

Rattlers are predatory snakes found throughout the Americas, from Canada to Argentina. There are 36 known species and about 70 subspecies. If antivenom is given within six hours to someone bitten by a rattler, the chances of recovery are 99 percent, but the venom can be fatal, and early treatment is essential. People eat rattlesnake meat, the journalist Alistair Cooke describing the taste as "like chicken, but tougher."[32]

General Attributes

Rattlesnakes are feared and respected. They feature in several American religions and mythologies.

In South and Central America

Rattlesnakes were sacred to the Aztecs and to the Mayans. Aztec paintings, temples and burial mounds were frequently decorated with rattlesnake images or motifs. The Maya saw the rattlesnake as a vision serpent with direct access to the underworld.

The Rattlesnake Husband—A Peoria Indian Legend

> A woman left her village to fetch firewood. A stranger, whistling a merry tune, came and asked her to go away with him for three days. She agreed. They walked many miles and came at last to a cave.
> The three days turned out to be three years. During all that time, the woman's family searched for her. At last they found her in the cave. She told them that her husband, as she called the man, had been good to her, bringing plenty of meat and skins.
> The husband returned and saw the woman's relatives. "You have found me," he said. "This is who I am."
> With that, he dropped to the floor and his body returned to its real form as a rattlesnake. The relatives sped the woman out of the cave to safety, warning her never to pay heed to a whistling man again.[33]

Count Zindendorf and the Rattlesnake

Count Nikolaus Zindendorf (1700–1760) was an early Christian missionary among Native Americans. He once visited the Shawnees in the Wyoming Valley. He had badly misjudged the mood of the tribe. He was welcomed politely, and given a tepee in which to spend the night, but the council met and decided that a small group of warriors would go to the tepee and kill him. When they opened the tepee flap, they saw the Count seated by a small fire, reading the Bible. As they watched, a rattlesnake slithered into the tent, crawled over the Count's crossed knees without striking him, and curled itself up to sleep by the fire. This was enough to persuade the Shawnee warriors that this white man had the *manitou* or *wakan*, the medicine, within him, and that he was not to be harmed.[34]

In American Christianity

A small number of evangelical Christian sects in Appalachia and the American Southeast, especially Alabama, Mississippi, Georgia, Kentucky, North and South Carolina, Tennessee and West Virginia, have included rattlesnake handling sessions in their church activities, following a literal interpretation of a passage in the New Testament, which reads:

> And these signs will accompany those who believe: by using my name they will cast out demons; they will speak in new tongues; they will pick up snakes in their hands, and if they drink any deadly thing, it will not hurt them; they will lay their hands on the sick, and they will recover.[35]

Following several deaths and injuries (the exact numbers are unclear), many states have outlawed snake handling in church ceremonies, but the practice continues to this day.

Python (Several Species)

Phylum *Chordata*, Class *Reptilia*, Order *Squamata*, Suborder *Serpentes*, Family *Boidae*, Subfamily *Boinae*, Genus *Python*, Species (8)

Name

Πυθων, *Puthón*, Python, was the name of the mythical great snake killed by Apollo at the oracle of Delphi, the name being related to πυθω, *puthō*, meaning rot or decay. The family and subfamily names *Boidae* and *Boinae* are from Latin *boa*, just meaning large snake, as in *Boa constrictor*.

Description

Pythons are large, nonvenomous snakes found in Africa, India, the Far East and Australia. A group of Burmese pythons (*Python milurus bivittatus*) was introduced to the Everglades in the USA in the 1990s and have now become an invasive species.

General Attributes

Pythons are cautious ambush predators. They very rarely attack humans. They are hunted for their meat. They carry several diseases harmful to humans, including salmonella, chlamydia, and leptospirosis. They feature in several mythologies and folklores, often in folk medicine.

In Africa

Zulu healers wear python skin as an emblem of their power with folk medicines. Python body fat is rubbed on joints to ease arthritis and rheumatism, and on the temples to ease distress, anxiety, depression and other mental illnesses. Patients drink python blood as a source of iron to combat anemia, and as a general tonic and restorative for the weak. The Sukumu tribe of Tanzania put python feces on the back to ease back pain.[36] In Nigeria, python gallbladders and livers are used as an antidote to venomous snakebites.[37] In the folklore of Ghana, it is unlucky to harm or kill a python, and the meat is *tabu*: according to folk legend, the python anciently rescued the people from danger by becoming a bridge over a fast-flowing river. Similarly, the San people of Botswana believe that Python created all the riverbeds at the beginning of the world.

Lizard (Several Species)

Phylum *Chordata*, Class *Reptilia*, Superorder *Lepidosauria*, Order *Squamata*, Families (many), Species (more than 6,000)

Name

The general name for a newt or lizard in Middle English was *ask* or *aske*, which still survives as a dialect word, but it was replaced in the 11th century by Norman-French *lusard*, from Latin *lacertus*, lizard.

Description

There are at least 6,000 lizard species spread across the whole world apart from Antarctica, and no doubt there are more species yet to be discovered. The largest is the Komodo dragon (*Varanus komodoensis*), which can reach 10 feet (3 meters) in length and is strong enough to injure or even kill humans, although attacks are very rare. Komodo dragons have been observed killing and eating mammals as large as water buffalo. Most lizards are much smaller, many of them ambush predators living mostly on insects. They often escape predators by darting into narrow cracks between rocks or stones.

General Attributes

Lizards are generally humble animals, but they appear in folklore and mythology around the world.

Adno-artina and Tarrotarro

In Australian Aboriginal mythology, Adno-artina is the gecko lizard that fought the dog Marindi, whose blood dyed rocks red. (See **dingo**, Chapter 4.) Tarrotarro, a lizard creation god, first divided people into men and women, and first taught people how to find materials and make paintings on rocks.

Aunyain-á

In the mythology of the Tupi people of Brazil, iguanas and lizards were created from the body of an evil god called Aunyain-á. He had tusks like those of a boar, and ate children. The people climbed a vine, knowing that Aunyain-á would follow, which he did. The clever parrot then flew above Aunyain-á and bit through the vine. When the god reached the broken part, he fell to his death on the jungle floor below. His arms and legs became caymans and iguanas. His fingers and toes became smaller lizards. Vultures ate the rest of his body.[38] (In many legends of the Amazon Basin, the lizard, not the lion, is the King of the Beasts or King of the Jungle.)

Chameleon (Several Species)

Phylum *Chordata*, Class *Reptilia*, Order *Squamata*, Suborder *Iguania*, Clade *Acrodonta*, Family *Chamaeleonidae*, Genera (12), Species (203)

Name

The common name and the scientific family name both come from Ancient Greek ξαμαι, *chamaí*, meaning "on the ground," and λεων, *leōn*, lion.

Description

Chameleons are small to medium-sized lizards, best known for their ability to change their skin color to camouflage themselves (but not all chameleon species actually do this). The color changing not only deters or baffles predators, it is also used to communicate with other chameleons. The physical mechanism is based on guanine nanocrystals, which lie just beneath the chameleon's skin. By altering the distance between the crystals, the chameleon changes the wavelength of the light reflected from the skin, and hence changes the color. Blue and green represent low temperature and calm mood, while excitement and heat generate yellow, orange and red.

General Attributes

Chameleon fossils date from well over 60 million years ago, so chameleons have been around for a long time. They feature in many African traditions, including those of the Bantu people. In Malawi, chameleons are considered evil.[39]

Ilé-Ifé

Ilé-Ifé is the name of the place of creation, according to the mythology of the Yoruba people of southwestern Nigeria in Africa. When God created the Earth, he sent a chameleon to check it out. The chameleon came back and said that there was plenty of room—it was wide enough—but he would like it if the Earth was a little bit hotter and a little bit more dry. God listened to the chameleon, and called the Earth Ifé, meaning wide. He made it a little hotter and a little drier, which is why it can be uncomfortably hot and dry sometimes for humans (but chameleons love it). Once everybody was settled, God added the word Ilé, meaning house, so that everyone would know that this was the place where all creation came from, Ilé-Ifé, "the wide house."[40]

37

Crocodiles and Turtles (*Crocodylia, Testudines*)

Crocodile (*Crocodylus niloticus*)

Phylum *Chordata*, Class *Reptilia*, Order *Crocodilia*, Family *Crocodylidae*, Subfamily *Crocodylinae*, Genera (two extant, *Crocodylus* and *Osteolaemus*, and one proposed, *Mecistops*), Type species *Crocodylus niloticus*

Name

Crocodile was written and pronounced *cocodrill* in Middle English, but in the 16th century was deliberately returned to the original sound order in Greek κροκοδειλος, *krokódeilos* and Latin *crocodilus*. *Niloticus* means of the River Nile.

Description

Crocodiles are large, semi-aquatic tropical reptiles. They are found in Africa, Asia, the Americas and Australia.

General Attributes

The crocodile has a well-deserved reputation as an atavistic, ruthless killer. It floats, barely visible with most or all of its body underwater, then suddenly leaps up and snatches its intended prey in its huge jaws. It is a shocking predator, with a scaly, primitive body clearly designed a very long time ago. It is naturally considered evil and demonic in many mythologies.

Nevertheless, it has also been seen as beneficent, and has been widely worshiped. It was sacred to Set, Horus and Sebek in Egypt, where priests fed crocodiles with cakes, milk and honey. Some Arab countries in the Middle Ages had a rite of judgment similar to the witch's stool in Europe: they would throw suspected unbelievers and idolaters into crocodile-infested waters—the guilty got eaten, the innocent swam out untouched. In Hinduism, crocodiles are the reincarnations of murdered Brahmins.

In European folklore, crocodile tears are false or hypocritical expressions of sorrow or regret. Crocodiles do, in fact, shed tears, usually to keep their eyes protected while they are out of the water, but the tears may also be triggered as a reflex when eating, suggesting that the crocodile is filled with sorrow as well as meat, hence the metaphor.

Nuga

In Melanesian mythology, Nuga was the first of the crocodile men, from whom the Kiwaians of New Guinea are descended. Nuga was first made of wood, carved by a man named Ipila. He put some sago milk on the carving, and it came to life as Nuga. Nuga then asked Ipila to make three more people, so that he would not be lonely.

Ipila made the other three, but they wanted more to eat than just sago milk, so they began killing animals for food. At first, they were only half-crocodiles, and they produced only male children, but from them were descended the Kiaiwans. Ipila was so displeased with his creation that he forced Nuga to hold the Earth on his shoulders forever.[1]

Sebek

In Egyptian mythology, Sebek was a crocodile god. Called Σουξος, *Souchos*, by the Greeks, and *Suchus* in Latin, he is depicted either just as a crocodile, or as a man with a crocodile's head. In a composite form with the sun-god Ra, sometimes called Sebek-Ra, he also has a solar disk encircled by a *uraeus* or a pair of horns surmounted by a disk and plumed feathers. He remained in the Egyptian pantheon all the way through from the Old Kingdom (c. 2686–2181 BCE) through to the Roman occupation (c. 30–350 CE), so his longevity alone suggests that he was important. The meaning of his name is disputed: it could mean either "he who impregnates" or "he who unites." His strength and ferocity were invoked for protection against evil. Modern Falyum, approximately 60 miles (100 km) south-west of Cairo, was called Κροκοδειλοπολις, *Krokodeilópolis*, Crocodile City, by the Greeks: crocodiles sacred to Sebek were raised in temples there, and mummified after their deaths.[2]

Alligator (*Alligator mississippiensis*)

Phylum *Chordata*, Class *Reptilia*, Order *Crocodilia*, Family *Alligatoridae*, Subfamily *Alligatorinae*, Genus *Alligator*, Type species *Alligator mississippiensis*, Other species *Alligator sinensis*

Name

The Latin word *lacertus* meant lizard. It came into Spanish as *el lagarto*, the lizard, and from there into English as alligator. *Mississippiensis* means of Mississippi, and *sinensis* means of China.

Description

Although both animals are very similar, alligators differ from crocodiles in several respects: they are less aggressive; they are found in the southeastern states of the USA or

China only; they can tolerate lower temperatures than crocodiles; they have wider, flatter snouts than crocodiles; their teeth are completely hidden when their mouths are closed.

Alligator meat was formally declared acceptable for Roman Catholics to eat on Fridays (i.e., as "fish") by the Archbishop of New Orleans in 2010.[3] The commonplace description is that it "tastes like chicken."

General Attributes

Alligators are not quite as intimidating as crocodiles, but they have a remarkable turn of speed in short bursts on land as well as in the water.

The Alligator and the Hunter

An elegant story of the American Indian Choctaw nation expresses a philosophy of hunting which is found in many indigenous cultures, and, one would hope, in all true hunters.

> A hunter who always had bad luck went deep into the forest in an attempt to improve his chances of success. He found an alligator dying of thirst in a dried-up water hole. The alligator begged the hunter for water. Very cautiously, the hunter picked up the alligator and carried him to a pool, where the alligator swam and drank to his heart's content. In gratitude, the alligator gave the hunter some advice:
>
> "When you find a small doe who has not yet borne children, do not kill her, but pass her by. Greet her, praise her, and move on. When you meet a young buck who has not yet sired a family, pass him by. Greet him, praise him, and move on. When you meet an old buck, larger than any you have ever met, he will offer himself to you. Greet him, praise him, and kill him with one clean shot from your bow. Thank him for giving himself to you."
>
> The hunter followed the alligator's advice, and brought back to the village on his shoulders the biggest buck they had ever seen. The elders heard his story and agreed that the alligator's advice had been wise. From that day, the Choctaws became great hunters.[4]

Two-Toed Tom

In American folklore, Two-Toed Tom was a 14-foot (4.5 m) alligator, which lived in marshy country near Montgomery, Alabama. He got his name from having all but two of his toes snapped off by a steel trap. He killed animals and humans alike, and nobody could catch him. Eventually, Pap Haines dynamited him out of his pond, but he escaped through an underground tunnel. He took his revenge by killing and eating Haines's 12-year-old daughter. Tracks of a massive alligator with only two toes were observed as recently as the 1980s.[5]

Sewer Alligators

The modern urban myth, that the sewers of New York and other cities are populated by alligators descended from pet alligators, mostly bought in Florida novelty shops, that were flushed down toilets when they became too large for comfort, began as early as the 1920s and 1930s, and still has street credibility among some people a century later. Using undeniable logic, the legend has expanded to suggest that generations of crocodiles and alligators living on rats and refuse in the sewer system will have become blind, albino giants.

The closest reality to the urban legend is that alligators have indeed been found in sewers and storm drains in Florida, but these connect to swamp lands where alligators live, and their taking shelter in convenient man-made shelters is not surprising. A two-foot (97 centimeters) alligator was found in a New York sewer near a Chinese restaurant in Queens in 2010, but winter temperatures are far too cold in New York to sustain an alligator population, even underground.[6]

Caiman/Cayman (*Caiman latirostris*)

Phylum *Chordata*, Class *Reptilia*, Order *Crocodilia*, Family *Alligatoridae*, Subfamily *Caimaninae*, Type species *Caiman latirostris*

Name

The name caiman or cayman came into English from Spanish or Portuguese, but the original root is thought to be the Carib native word for the animal, *acayouman*.

Description

Caimans are considerably smaller than crocodiles or alligators. They have a more scaly skin (which is therefore of less commercial value). They are found in Central and South America, and in the Caribbean.

General Attributes

Caimans are opportunistic predators, just like crocodiles and alligators, although caimans tend to be more nocturnal. They do not often appear in mythology or folklore.

Maconaura and Anuanaitu

In the creation myth of the Carib Indians of the Orinoco region of South America, the god Adaheli made the first humans. From them was born Maconaura, a handsome young man who was a fisherman, and lived with his mother. One day he found his basket net torn apart and his fish stolen. After watching the river carefully, he discovered that a caiman had stolen his catch. He shot an arrow between the beast's eyes, and it sank beneath the water. Shortly afterwards, a beautiful young maiden, Anuanaitu, stepped out of the water. She was weeping bitterly. Maconaura took her home. When she became old enough, he married her. They lived happily for a while, but then one day Anuanaitu killed Maconaura and his mother. The caiman which Maconauru had killed was her brother, and now she had her revenge. She changed back into caiman form and returned to the river.[7]

Turtle/Terrapin/Tortoise (Several Species)

Turtle, Phylum *Chordata*, Class *Reptilia*, Clade *Testudinata*, Order *Testudines*, Subgroups *Cryptodira*, *Pleurodira*, Families (14 extant), Species (356)

Tortoise, Phylum *Chordata*, Class *Reptilia*, Clade *Testudinata*, Order *Testudines*, Family *Testudinae*, Type species *Testudo graeca*

Name

There is a great deal of confusion about the names of these animals. Turtle is scientifically the broadest term, covering the greatest number of species. In American English, a tortoise is a turtle, because turtle is generally any member of the order *Testudines*, whether water-based or land-based. However, in British English, the word turtle is used only for those *Testudines* that live in water—the land-based animal is always called a tortoise, and never a turtle. And a terrapin is also a turtle, in both American and British English, but the name is usually used only for smaller members of the order. In Spanish, the word *tortuga* is used for all three animals, turtle, terrapin and tortoise. Scientists tend to use the term Chelonian for all members of the superorder *Chelonia*, which is based on Greek ξελωνε, *chelóne*, turtle, and ξελυς, *chelys*, tortoise. Turtle and tortoise (and Spanish *tortuga*) are from Medieval Latin *tortuca*. Terrapin, which looks as though it might be from the same root, is actually from an Algonquin Indian word, *torope*, little turtle.

The Latin word *testudo*, the root of *Testudines*, means shell, and was the nickname of a military maneuver in which advancing infantry lifted and locked their shields over their heads to protect themselves from incoming spears or arrows, making the whole troop look like a slowly advancing turtle.

Description

Turtles are found across the world. What they have in common is that they all have hard shell bodies. The largest is the leatherback sea turtle (*Dermochelys coriacea*), which can reach a length of 6.6 feet (2 meters) and weigh over 2,000 pounds (900 kilograms). The smallest is the speckled padloper tortoise (*Chersobius signatus*) of South Africa, which measures just over 3 inches (8 centimeters) in length.

General Attributes

Turtles and tortoises carry their own homes on their backs. They are slow and wrinkly, so they look old even when they are young. In many cultures, they are associated with innocence and wisdom.

Creation Turtles

The turtle (sometimes the tortoise) is depicted as carrying the world on its back in many different and widely separated cultures, especially Hinduism, Chinese mythology, various indigenous mythologies of Polynesia and South America, and even in modern Scientology. There must be some characteristic of the animal which has promoted the appearance of these legends in so many different places over many centuries, but it is difficult to say what that characteristic might be. It may have something to with the fact that turtles swim on the surface (in the air, so to speak), where the gods live, but also in the ocean, where human souls live after death. More likely is that in trying to find an explanation for the turtle's hard shell, early humans decided that it must have been intended to carry something very heavy—perhaps the entire planet.

In Siberian mythology, the two creator gods, Chagan-Shukuty and Otshirvani, come down from heaven one day. They watch a turtle repeatedly diving into the depths of the ocean and returning to the surface. Otshirvani sits on the creature's stomach to prevent it from diving again, and asks Chagan-Shukuty to go down and see what the turtle was looking for in the depths. On his first attempt, Chagan-Shukuty finds nothing. On his second attempt, he brings up a handful of dirt, which he sprinkles on to the turtle's stomach. Both gods now sit on the turtle, but the animal sinks out of sight, leaving only the soil. The Devil comes along, intending to drown the two gods, but when the Devil grabs the soil he finds that he can no longer see the water, because the Earth has grown so rapidly. He grabs the two gods and puts one under each arm, then runs to find the edge of the Earth so that he can drown them, but the faster and farther he runs, the faster and farther the land extends in front of him. He drops the gods and leaves them to their fate, but by this time the Earth as we now know it has been created.[8]

In Hinduism, Akupera, also called Chukwa, is the turtle or tortoise on which the entire Earth is carried. (In most versions, an elephant stands on the turtle, and the Earth stands on the elephant.) The British philosopher John Locke mentions this in his *An Essay Concerning Human Understanding* (1689), as an example of how beliefs can continue even without any supporting evidence.

In Chinese mythology, the creator goddess Nuwa seizes the giant sea turtle Ao and cuts its legs off. She places the Earth on the turtle's body and uses its legs to prop up the sky.

In Micronesian mythology, the god of fertility in the Caroline Islands is called Nanimulap. His sacred animal is the turtle, which may be eaten only by chiefs.

Several North American and Canadian Indian nations, including the Lenape and the Iroquois, have creation myths involving the turtle. When a Jesuit missionary was trying to explain earthquakes to a group of Wyandot natives in Ontario, they are reported to have explained to him that what he was describing was the world turtle shifting its position to relieve cramp in its muscles.

The Chibcha Indians of Colombia have a similar legend: their god of laborers and traders, Chibcachum, accused them of laziness and sent a great flood to punish them. They appealed to their sun-god, Pochica, who drove Chibcachum underground, to support the Earth on his back. Whenever there is an earthquake, it is Chibcachum shifting his burden from one shoulder to the other.

In the *Discworld* series of fantasy novels by Terry Pratchett (1948–2015), the eponymous Disc is carried on the backs of four elephants, which, in turn, are carried by the turtle Great A'Tuin.

Kana

In Polynesian mythology, Kana is a trickster god, rather like the Norse god Loki, who can do evil deeds or good deeds, depending on his whim. In one legend where he is trying to do good, he attempts to rescue a girl who has been abducted and imprisoned on a tiny island. Each time he stretches out to reach her, the hill on which she is standing grows, and she moves further away. After several attempts, Kana has stretched himself so thin that he goes to his grandmother, Uli. She feeds him, and explains that the island is really a giant turtle. After eating and regaining his strength, Kana returns, breaks off the giant turtle's flippers, and rescues the maiden.[9]

Mythical Animals, Hybrids and Animal Gods

38

Dragons

Types of Dragons

Dragons are mythical creatures, but they appear in sacred mythologies all across the world in many different forms. The earliest dragons, and the dragons of the Far East, are essentially huge snakes, wingless, but with four legs. Unlike lizards, they are serpentine in shape. In the West, early medieval dragons began acquiring wings and the ability to breathe fire. They became more dangerously beast-like, more ferocious and less intelligent (Chinese and other Eastern dragons are always highly intelligent). Christian saints (and some pagan heroes) often made their reputations by killing dragons that had been ravaging or threatening helpless communities. Dragons also began to be seen as guardians of hidden treasure, usually in dark, dangerous places. In many traditions, the dragon guards a source of water, which, as a precious and scarce commodity in some cultures, is a treasure of a different kind. It has been suggested that the earliest dragons represented human fear of snakes, which often hide in secret crannies or in cool, damp places.

General Attributes

Dragons have appeared in many cultures across the world, but their perceived or imagined nature varies according to where and when. They were present in the mythologies of the ancient Middle East and ancient Mesopotamia, and they still appear regularly in modern literature and film.

The *mushussu* or *mush-khush-shu* of Mesopotamia was a scaly dragon dating from the 6th century BCE. Apep (Greek form Apophis) was the ancient Egyptian god of chaos and misrule (see *Apophis*, Chapter 39). Vrirtra appears in the Rig Veda, one of the sacred texts of ancient Hinduism; he is a dragon who brought drought to the world, until the great god Indra defeated him and restored the rivers, lakes and seas. Leviathan (Livyatan in Hebrew) is the great sea monster or dragon of the early Judaic and Christian traditions; he is mentioned in the Book of Job, Psalms, the Book of Isaiah, and the Book of Amos. Jörmungandr is also a sea monster, born of the giantess Angrboða (She Who Brings Sorrow) and the mischievous god Loki; he encircles Midgard (i.e., our world) holding his tail in his mouth, and when he releases it, Ragnarök will begin and the world will end.

Celtic Elemental Dragons

In British Celtic mythology, different types of dragon have been associated with the four ancient elements, water, earth, air, and fire. Ley lines, the supposed lines of power connecting sacred or magical places, so named by the English folklorist and antiquarian Alfred Watkins (1855–1935), are also called dragon lines.

The water dragon is a dragon that lives either at sea or in fresh water. The most famous is Nessie, or the monster of Loch Ness in Scotland. According to Christian legend (specifically Adomnán's *Life of Saint Columba* written in 565 CE), Saint Columba saw the dragon or monster about to eat a friend who was swimming in the River Ness. Columba called out, "Go thou no further, nor touch the man, go back at once," and the monster promptly obeyed.

The earth dragon is often a guardian of a great treasure. It lies with its tail coiled around the precious items, and is associated with spirals and mazes. It avoids contact with humans, if at all possible. The many burial barrows in England, several of them close to Stonehenge, are reputed to be guarded by earth dragons. The places filled with treasure are well-known, and can be named without fear, because nobody has ever been able to penetrate the dragon defenses: they are Old Field Barrows in Shropshire; the Drakelow Barrows in Derbyshire and Worcestershire; the Drake Howe Barrow in Yorkshire; Wormelow Tump in Herefordshire; Money Hill on Gunnarton Fell in Northumberland; Cissbury Hillfort in Sussex; Bignor Hill in Sussex; Glastonbury Tor in Somerset; the maze at Hollywood in Ireland; and the near-island of Tintagel Head in Cornwall.[1]

The air dragon flies from mountain-top to mountain-top, and is often associated with the British god Bel or Beli Mawr (Great Bel). Air dragons may be quite small by comparison with water or earth dragons. An air dragon supposedly sighted at Henham in Essex was estimated to be just eight or nine feet (2.5 to 3 m) in length, with very small wings.[2] Several air dragon sightings have been attributed to unusual atmospheric conditions and events, including tornados, whirlwinds, the Northern Lights, and fast-moving clouds, especially when lit by a rising or setting sun.

The fire dragon is the most active and in some ways the most powerful of the Celtic elemental dragons. According to the legend, it was the sight of a fire dragon in the sky that led King Uther, father of Arthur, to take on the honorific title Pendragon, meaning Head Dragon or Chief Dragon. Arthur, whose totem animal is the bear (see **bear**, Chapter 10), is sometimes described as wearing a helmet with a golden dragon (i.e., fire dragon) emblazoned on it.

When King Vortigern dies in the Arthurian legend, it is by fire. Vortigern is a title rather than a name. It means Over-King or High King. The Ancient Celtic version of the name is Gwrtheyrn, and in the Welsh Triads he is called Gwrtheyrn Tenau (the Thin). He was alleged to have married the daughter of the Roman general Magnus Maximus (called Macsen Wledig in Welsh), by whom he had a son and later heir, Vortimer (Gwerfethyr). In Geoffrey of Monmouth's version of events, Vortimer overthrew Vortigern after the latter had disastrously invited the mercenaries Hengist and Horsa into Britain. There certainly were English incursions from early on in the fifth century, and the suggestion that some of these were federates, i.e., mercenaries given land in return for military service, is historically very likely. The death of Vortigern in a tower of fire is a symbol of the fire dragon, Uther Pendragon, taking over control of the kingdom.

The Dragon-Slayer

The dragon is so universally recognized as a mythical animal that the dragon-slayer, the hero who kills the troublesome monster, also appears in many cultures.

Saint George, patron saint of England, actually lived in Cappadocia (modern Turkey) in the 3rd century CE and never visited England. According to his legend, a local dragon insisted on eating a young man or young woman every so often to satisfy its appetite. Lots were cast to choose the victim, and on one occasion the lot fell to the king's daughter. The king naturally tried to stall the sacrifice, but the people insisted, and the princess went forward to suffer her fate. Just as the dragon was about to seize her, Saint George rode in on his white charger, made the sign of the cross, drew his sword, and attacked the dragon. The dragon quickly succumbed and fell to the ground, but George did not give it the death blow. Instead, he took the girdle from about the princess's waist and tied it around the dragon's neck as a collar. From that moment onward, the dragon followed George around as tamely as any puppy, and never again demanded human meat.

Siegfried (Victory Joy) or Sigurd (Victory Protection) is a dragon-slayer from Norse/Germanic mythology. There has been speculation among modern scholars that Siegfried represents a historical victory by Germanic tribes over the Roman imperial army or even by a specific Germanic leader, but the evidence is disputed. In legend, Siegfried/Sigurd slew a dragon and was later murdered. Siegfried is a major character in Wagner's 19th-century *Ring Cycle*, particularly in the operas *Siegfried* (1876) and *Götterdämmerung* (*Twilight of the Gods*, also 1876), but he is also a major figure in several earlier legends and texts, including the *Nibelunglied* (c. 1200 CE), the *Völsunga Saga* (13th century CE) and the Norse *Poetic Edda* (12th or 13th century CE).

Among Siegfried's battle powers are a cloak of invisibility and skin which cannot be punctured by any weapon because it has been sealed by dragon's blood. In the Old Norse legends, he eats some of the dragon's flesh (or puts a bloodied finger in his mouth) and acquires the ability to speak with birds. The Siegfried/Sigurd legend has appeared over many centuries, in many languages and many geographical locations all across Northern Europe, and has persisted into modern literature in different forms, including William Morris's poem *Sigurd the Volsung* (1876), Fritz Lang's film *Die Neibelungen* (1924) and J.R.R. Tolkien's poem *The Legend of Sigurd and Gudrún*, written about 1930 and published by his son Christopher in 2009.

Ladon

Ladon was a hundred-headed dragon in Greek mythology. It was his job to guard the golden apples of the Hesperides. He is commonly depicted in Greek sculpture and vase paintings coiled around the sacred tree. He was killed by Herakles.

Alkha

In Siberian mythology, Alkha is a dragon used to explain eclipses of the Sun and Moon. There are several eclipse myths that depend on some beast or monster devouring the Sun or Moon, but Alkha is unusual in that every variant of his story involves his body being cut in two, so that the Sun or Moon emerges from where his back half would be if he still had it.

In the earliest version, Alkha swallows both Sun and Moon, leaving the Earth in complete darkness. The gods cut him in half, one part remaining in the sky, the other falling and being destroyed. Thus, whenever Alkha tries to eat Sun or Moon again, the heavenly body eventually re-emerges.

In a variant version told by the Buriat people, Alkha is called Arakho, and he keeps eating the hair off human bodies. The gods are angry, because they gave hair to humans to protect them from the cold, so they chop Arakho in half. In a variation on the variation, Arakho steals a cup made by the Sun and Moon that contains the Water of Life. Because he has dirtied and spoiled the holy cup, God cuts him in two.[3]

Kiyohime

Japanese *Noh* musical dance drama has been performed since the 14th century CE and is the oldest style of continuously performed theater in the world. One of the plays features the old legend of Kiyohime.

> When Kiyohime was a little girl, the daughter of a rich village headsman, a priest called Anchin often visited their house while making pilgrimage journeys. He played with Kiyohime and told her funny stories. When Kiyohime grew up, she became obsessively infatuated with Anchin, and followed the priest everywhere. Finally, in an act of desperation, he hid himself under a temple bell. Kiyohine transformed into a fire dragon and blasted the bell with her breath. The bell melted, and all that was left of Anchin was a pile of white ash.[4]

Níðhöggr

In Norse mythology, the great world tree is an ash tree called Yggdrasill. It extends through all things, and coiled about its roots is the dragon Níðhöggr or Nidhogg, which gnaws away constantly at the roots in an effort to bring on Ragnarök, the end of the world. It also drinks the blood of those who have died ignominiously, such as murderers, adulterers and oath-breakers.

Chinese Dragons

In China, dragons are associated with high status (including imperial rank or authority), high intelligence, power and prosperity. Liu Bang, who reigned as Gaozu of Han, the first emperor of the Han dynasty from 202 to 195 BCE, claimed that he was conceived after his mother dreamed about a dragon. In the Yuan, Ming and Qing dynasties, the five-clawed dragon was reserved strictly as an imperial emblem. Many Chinese think of the dragon as a national symbol, but are cautious about using it internationally because of its association with aggression and monstrous violence in the West.

A number of fossilized dinosaur remains found in China have been called *Mei long*, which means sleeping dragon in Mandarin. In the popular imagination, dragons are mythical and magical, but were (and perhaps still are) real animals, too.

Chinese dragon culture is itself very old: a dragon statue discovered in Henan in 1987 has been dated to the fifth millennium BCE.[5]

Like mythical beasts in many other cultures, Chinese dragons have attributes from several different animals, e.g., the head of a camel, the neck of a snake, the feet of a tiger, and so on. In some areas, these attributes are specifically from the other 11 animals in the Chinese zodiac (see Chapter 41), such as the whiskers of the rat, the legs of the horse, the cleverness of the monkey, the horns of the ox, etc.

Chinese dragons rule the weather, and therefore the seas. They cause not only great storms, but also mists and fog, because they are fond of disappearing or hiding themselves. They may be associated with any of the four classical elements (or indeed with the fifth element, pure spirit), but their special province is water, which has particular significance in Chinese culture through the influence of Taoism. Water is humble, because it always falls to the lowest level available; it is passive, accepting change as it happens, literally going with the flow; it is pure and innocent; but it also accumulates tremendous weight and power. The main Taoist sacred text, the *Tao Te Ching* or *Dao De Jing* (*The Book of the Way of Virtue*, 6th century BCE) pays a lot of attention to the religious symbolism of water. There are four Dragon Kings for the four Chinese oceans, north, south, east and west (Lake Baikal, the South China Sea, the East China Sea and Qinghai Lake). In modern Communist China, flood prevention and control fall within the remit of the State, but in popular culture it is the cardinal dragons that are summoned as well as the comrade technicians and civil engineers.

The Dragon God is especially venerated on the 13th day of the sixth lunar month of every year, but there are many other dragon-related festivals on other days too. Dragon rituals during the fifth and sixth moons include sacrificial offerings and ceremonial processions. The linguist Michael Carr has analyzed over 100 dragon names, showing how extensive and systematized dragon worship is in China. They include: Tianlong (heavenly dragon that guards palaces, also tutelary god of the constellation Draco); Shenlong (thunder god); Fuzanlong (hidden treasure dragon); Dilong (earth dragon, controller of rivers and seas); Yinglong (dragon of rain and floods); Jialong (crocodile dragon).[6]

During the Ming dynasty (1368–1644 CE, the one from which all the really expensive vases come), several lists of the Nine Offspring of the Dragon were written. These are represented in many aspects of Chinese design and architecture. They are: *pú lao* (small, screaming dragons, appearing most often as handles for ceremonial bells); *qiú niú* (decorations on other musical instruments); *chi wen* (swallowing dragons, put on roof ridge poles to swallow evil); *cháo feng* (dragons of adventure and enterprise, typically put on the four corners of a roof); *yá zi* (killing dragons, engraved on sword blades); *xi xi* (found on the sides of gravestones and monuments); *bì àn* (guardian dragons carved or sculpted on prison gates); *suan ní* (dragons that lie curled at the feet of the Buddha); *bì xì* (tortoise dragons supporting heavy objects, especially large grave monuments). In 2012 (the Year of the Dragon in the Chinese calendar—see Chapter 41), the Chinese government issued commemorative coins designated by the names of the nine Sons of the Dragon King, along with a tenth denomination for the Dragon King himself.[7]

39

Animal Hybrids and Monsters

Animal Hybrids

In many mythologies, monsters are created or assembled from different elements of real animals. Most of them are intended to inspire awe (e.g., with parts of eagle, lion, horse or bear) or terror (e.g., with parts of snake, bat, wolf or crocodile). Some of these hybrids are benevolent, but most are unpleasant at best and abominable at worst.

Enki/Ea/Hea

Enki (Lord of the World) was a Sumerian creator god, later called Ea (also Hea or Hoa) in Akkadian and Babylonian mythology. Despite his monstrous appearance (he had the body of a fish and the head of either a ram or a goat), he was a benevolent and civilizing god, who taught humans how to build houses, collect food, and make laws. He sometimes appears as a full human, often with a spiked crown, or as a merman, half-man, half-fish. His chief site of worship was Eridu in the Persian Gulf. Excavations have shown the temple site to have been established about 4500 BCE. Thousands of carp bones have been discovered at several of his temple sites, suggesting that the fish was sacred to him. Ea was later associated with the constellation now named after the classical winged horse, Pegasus (see Chapter 41).

Enki features in several ancient legends, and is associated with many sites of importance. Dilmun, the Sumerian paradise to which Enki first brought water, is identified with modern Bahrain, which means "Two Seas" in Arabic—it is where the fresh water of the Arabian aquifer meets the salt waters of the Arabian Gulf. This mingling of waters was called Nammu in Sumerian, which is also the name of Enki's mother. It has been suggested that the Christian tradition of the baptismal font has its earliest origins in the myth of Enki as the king of Apsu, the watery abyss believed to be at the core of the earth.[1]

Humbaba

In the Babylonian epic *Gilgamesh*, Humbaba or Kumbaba is the evil spirit who guards the sacred Cedar Tree. He is portrayed in many different ways, but the most striking aspect of his many images is that he has a long beard made of the still-writhing entrails of the animals he has killed and eaten. He is eventually killed by Gilgamesh and Enkidu.

Makara

In Hindu mythology, Makara is the mount of the ocean god Varuna. He is also called Jala-rupa (Water Foam) and Asita-danshtra (Black Teeth). He has the head and forelegs of an antelope, but the body and tail of a fish. His depiction frequently appears on the flag of Kama, the god of love. Makara is the equivalent of Capricorn in the Hindu zodiac (see Chapter 41).

The Unicorn

The unicorn, known the whole world over, is the opposite of a monster. It is a shy, gentle creature, almost entirely a small and beautiful horse, except that it has a single horn (which is what the word unicorn means) in the middle of its forehead.

It has been suggested that the unicorn came into being as a result of mistranslation. When the Bible was being translated from Hebrew to Greek, the Hebrew word *re'em*, possibly meaning ox, was translated as μονοκερως, *monókerōs*, meaning "one-horned." The Revised Standard Version of the Bible has "God, who brings them out of Egypt, is like the horns of a wild ox for them," whereas the earlier 1604 King James Version has "God brought them out of Egypt; he hath as it were the strength of an unicorn."[2]

But the unicorn has been described and depicted in religions and mythologies much older than even Judaism and Christianity. It was depicted in the Indus Valley Civilization (c. 3300–1300 BCE) and mentioned by several ancient Greek writers, including Aristotle and Strabo (not in mythological stories, but in works of natural history).

Probably sometime during the Middle Ages, the legend arose that unicorns were very timid animals, likely to keep themselves hidden from humans, but that they were especially attracted to virgin maidens: they thus acquired a reputation for purity, chastity and goodness. More specifically, the unicorn became associated with the Virgin Mary, Christ's mother. The legend also developed that a unicorn could not be hunted or caught by any man—it would simply disappear into the mist—but that it would willingly seek out a chaste maiden, come to her, and lay its head (i.e., horn) in her lap, an obvious symbol of wild masculinity willingly yielding to feminine purity and chastity. Setting a virgin as bait in a trap was even considered a way to hunt the unicorn. Leonardo da Vinci wrote in one of his notebooks:

> The unicorn, through its intemperance and not knowing how to control itself, for the love it bears to fair maidens forgets its ferocity and wildness; and laying aside all fear it will go up to a seated damsel and go to sleep in her lap, and thus the hunters take it.[3]

The unicorn appears very frequently in medieval art, especially tapestries, and in heraldry. It is the symbolic animal of Scotland, and appears on royal coats-of-arms down through the ages.

K'ilin

In Chinese mythology, the *k'ilin* or *chi-len* is a gentle, unicorn-like creature that represents goodness and love. It walks so quietly that nobody can hear its footfalls. Its breath smells of rose petals. According to legend, a *k'ilin* appeared at the birth of Kong Fuzi or Confucius (551–479 BCE), and again at his death. The name is a fusion of *k'i*, indicating male, and *lin*, indicating female. The animal was said to have the body of a deer, the legs and hooves of a horse, the head of a dragon (dragons are sensitive, intelligent and spiritual in Chinese traditions), the tail of a lion, and a single horn.

Lei Kung

In Chinese mythology, Lei Kung is a thunder god. He is a large bat, but with clawed feet, a monkey's head, and an eagle's beak. He destroys buildings with a hammer and chisel.

The Chimaera

In Greek mythology, the Chimaera (She-Goat) was a fire-breathing monster with the head of a lion, the body of a nanny goat, and the tail of a serpent or dragon. It appears in Greek in Homer's *Iliad* (book 6), in Latin in Virgil's *Aeneid* (book 6) and in Ovid's *Metamorphoses* (book 9), and in English in Spenser's *Faerie Queen* (book 6) and Milton's *Paradise Lost* (book 2). The hero Bellerophon killed the Chimaera by riding his flying-horse Pegasus close to the monster and shooting it with his arrows.

Amphisbaena

Amphisbaena, from ancient Greek, means "going in both directions." It was the name given to a mythical snake that had two heads, one at each end of its body. Although it was called a snake, it also had legs. It could put one head inside the mouth of the other, tuck in its legs, and then roll in either direction—hence the name. In Aeschylus's play *Agamemnon*, the king's wife and murderer, Clytemnestra, is called Amphisbaena, implying "two-faced snake." In medieval Christian bestiaries, the two-headed serpent is a symbol of the Devil.

Scylla and Charybdis

In Greek mythology, Scylla was originally a beautiful sea nymph who was poisoned by Circe and became a terrible sea monster with six dog-like heads, who lurked in the straits of Messina between Italy and Sicily. She dragged ships and men to their deaths. Opposite Scylla was Charybdis, also once a beautiful maiden, but who was then transformed into another monstrous sea beast which constantly swallowed vast amounts of sea water and then spewed the water out in a raging torrent. Sailors passing through the dangerous straits had to avoid Scylla on the one hand and Charybdis on the other, so the saying "between Scylla and Charybdis" came to mean between two difficult or dangerous places or choices, like the more modern "between the Devil and the deep blue sea" or "between a rock and a hard place."

The Hydra

The Hydra was a Greek serpent monster with not just two heads but many heads. If one head was cut off, two new heads would grow in its place. It lived in Lake Lerna in Argolis. Its venom and blood were poisonous, and even its scent could kill humans. Herakles' second labor was to kill the Hydra, which he achieved with the assistance of his cousin

Iolaus. Every time Herakles cut off a head, Iolaus cauterized the wound with a flaming torch so that the two new heads could not grow.

Hydra is the name given to a fictional, Nazi-inspired, secret terrorist organization in contemporary Marvel comics and movies. "Hail Hydra!" is its password and motto.

Apollyon

Apollyon (the name is obviously very similar to that of Apollo, a major god in the Greek and Roman pantheons) is described in the New Testament as a monster, the "angel of the bottomless pit."[4] The Greek name is based on Abaddon in the Old Testament, a poetic name for the land of the dead. Apollyon appears in John Bunyan's *Pilgrim's Progress*, where Pilgrim battles against the monster, which is described as having fish scales, a dragon's wings, a bear's feet and a lion's mouth.

Apophis

Apophis is the Greek form of the Egyptian name Apep, which was a giant serpent. Every night, Apophis fought with the sun-god, Ra. A Greek translation of an Egyptian ritual manual tells us that Apophis was a central feature of morning prayers. Before each dawn, the priests of Ra's temple were required to recite all the wounds that Ra was about to inflict on the monster: it would be speared and gashed; each of its bones would be broken; it would be seared and roasted until its entire body had been consumed by fire; its demon assistants, Sebau and Nak, would also be destroyed. Only when all the ritual prayers had been recited could Ra rise from the night and bring the Sun back into the world.[5]

Basilisk/Cockatrice

The basilisk (Greek for little king) was a half-rooster, half-lizard (or half-snake) creature, known since classical times (Pliny describes it in his *Historia Naturalis*), which was believed to be able to kill a human either just by its stare (like the Medusa) or by its poisonous breath. It is often equated with the cockatrice. Pliny says that it was born from the egg laid by a toad or a rooster. Pliny also suggests that it should be destroyed by letting a weasel chase it, although the weasel will also die. (Some commentators have suggested that this refers to a cobra being killed by a mongoose.)

The basilisk appears in the Bible and in Shakespeare. The Latin Vulgate version of the Bible uses the word basilisk (*basiliscum*), but the King James version translates *basiliscum* as "dragon" and modern versions read "serpent." In Shakespeare's *Richard III* (Act 1, Sc. 2), when Richard praises the beautiful eyes of Ann, King Edward's widow, she replies bitterly, "Would they were basilisks to strike you dead."

The Phoenix/Firebird

In Chinese mythology, the mythical phoenix is called Feng-Huang, meaning respectively "male," "female," because it is neither one nor the other, but rather represents faithfulness between man and woman. The classical phoenix takes its name from Greek φοινιξ, *phoinix*, which was associated with the region called Phoenicia (modern Lebanon) after a purple-red dye made there from conch shells, although modern research suggests that the names come from different roots.

The phoenix is famous in the West as the bird that dies in self-generated flames every five hundred years and is then spontaneously re-born from its own funeral pyre. Herodotus, Pliny, Solinus, Philostratus and Tacitus all describe the phoenix as brightly colored, usually red or gold, and similar to an eagle in appearance. In the 9th century, the phoenix became a metaphor for Christ's resurrection and a Christian symbol. The English poet and novelist D.H. Lawrence (1885–1930) often used the phoenix as a symbol of spiritual and emotional rebirth. A phoenix called Fawkes appears in J.K. Rowling's *Harry Potter* novels, where its tears are able to heal poisoning, injuries and sickness.

The Russian Firebird, which appears in many folk tales, has been compared to the phoenix. In one version, Prince Ivan is journeying in search of the mythical firebird, having previously seized one of its feathers. Ivan is helped by a gray wolf, and the wolf also leads Ivan to fall in love with a beautiful maiden called Yelena. Ivan is killed by his two jealous brothers, and Yelena is taken captive. The gray wolf revives Ivan with holy water, and Ivan rescues and later marries Yelena. Stravinsky's well-known ballet *L'Oiseau de Feu* (*The Firebird*) is based on this old folk tale.

Kappa

Animals don't have to be huge to be terrifying. The Japanese *kappa* is small. He has the body of a tortoise, the limbs of a frog, and the head of a monkey. His head is dish-shaped on the top, and contains a fluid that keeps him strong. He lives in the water, and he eats only blood, either from horses, cattle or humans. He sucks the blood from his victim's anus, causing them intense pain. There is only one way to deal with a *kappa*. With great politeness, you must bow deeply before him. Because this is Japan, politeness must always be matched with politeness. The *kappa* bows deeply in return, his life fluid flows out of the bowl in his head, and you are safe.

Al Jassasa

In the Qur'an, Al Jassasa (The Spy) is named in *surah* 27 as the apocalyptic beast that will appear at the Last Judgment. He, she or it (it is described as all three) has the head of a bull, the eyes of a pig, the ears of an elephant, the horns of a stag, the neck of an ostrich, the breasts of a lioness, the color of a tiger, a back like a cat, the legs of a camel, the voice of an ass, and the tail of a ram. The monster's task is to indicate those humans who are to be saved and those who are to be damned.[6]

The Dendan

The *dendan* is a monstrous fish that appears in Arabic legend, and specifically in a tale from *The Thousand and One Nights*, which involves two friends, both called Abdallah. Abdallah the Fisherman spreads the fat from a *dendan* over his body. This allows him to live underwater, and visit his friend, Abdallah the Merman. Whilst the two Abdallahs are chatting with each other beneath the waves, a black *dendan*, bigger than a camel, approaches menacingly. Abdallah the Fisherman shouts at the monstrous fish, which promptly dies, unable to bear the sound of a human voice.

The Kraken

The Kraken is also a monstrous sea creature, variously described as a sea snake, giant squid or octopus, or underwater dragon. The Scandinavian name is related to the words crooked and crank in English. It was described by Erik Pontoppidan, Bishop of Bergen, as being a mile and a half wide, with huge tentacles big enough to pull a full-sized man-o'-war under water. Giant squids can grow to 13–15 meters (40–50 feet) in length, so there may be some real basis for the legendary animal. Linnaeus included it in his 1735 catalogue as a real animal, but later withdrew the name from the list. Alfred Lord Tennyson's poem about the kraken appeared in 1830:

> Below the thunders of the upper deep;
> Far far beneath in the abysmal sea,
> His ancient, dreamless, uninvaded sleep
> The Kraken sleepeth: faintest sunlights flee
> About his shadowy sides; above him swell
> Huge sponges of millennial growth and height;
> And far away into the sickly light,
> From many a wondrous grot and secret cell
> Unnumber'd and enormous polypi
> Winnow with giant arms the slumbering green.
> There hath he lain for ages, and will lie
> Battening upon huge seaworms in his sleep,
> Until the latter fire shall heat the deep;
> Then once by man and angels to be seen,
> In roaring he shall rise and on the surface die.[7]

The Griffin

In European and Near Eastern folklore and mythology, the griffin was a fantastic composite animal with the head and wings of an eagle, the body of a lion, and the tail of a serpent. Griffins drew the chariots of Zeus, Apollo and Nemesis, the goddess of retribution. The name comes from Middle English *griffoun*, in turn from Old French *griffon*, in turn from Latin *gryps* or *gryphus*, in turn from Greek γρυψ, *grúps*, griffin.

In medieval Christianity, griffin claws were said to have several magical properties, the most useful being that they would change color if they came into contact with any poison. Griffin-claw cups (probably made from antelope horns) became very popular among the rich and powerful who might fear being poisoned.

Despite its long pagan history, the griffin also became a symbol of Christ—a lion, because he was a king, and an eagle, because he rose to heaven after his resurrection.

The Hippogriff

The hippogriff (from Greek ἱππο, *hippo*, horse, and γρυψ, *grúps*, griffin) was a Renaissance monster created by Ariosto of Italy in his epic poem *Orlando Furioso* (1516). (The hero

Orlando became Roland in the 11th-century Old French *Chanson de Roland*, and it was the name Roland that came into English rather than Orlando.) The hippogriff was sired by a griffin, but its mother was a mare. The beast had its father's wings, feathers, forelegs, head and vicious beak and claws, but the rest of its body was that of a horse.

The Questing Beast

The Questing Beast appears in the medieval legends of King Arthur. It has the head of a serpent, the buttocks of a lion, the body of a leopard and the feet of a deer. It makes a sound like thirty hounds baying. According to the legends, the beast was hunted by King Pellinore.

The Guallipen

The *guallipen* or *huallepen* is a legendary monster of the Araucanian Indians in Peru. It has the head of a calf, the body of a sheep, but it is also amphibious and can breathe under water. If a pregnant woman comes into contact with a *guallipen*, or even dreams of one, her child may be born deformed.

The Doodang

The doodang appears in Joel Chandler Harris's richly amusing *The Complete Tales of Uncle Remus* (1881). The poor doodang is a combination of the alligator, the rhinoceros and the elephant. He is as confused and as unhappy as his mixed parentage suggests. First he wants to swim, and then he wants to fly. When he finally gets his wings, the combination is just too much to be workable. He tries to fly, fails, and dies.

40

Human-Animal Hybrids

Human-Animal Hybrids

Human-animal hybrids occur in many traditions and cultures. The most common combination is a single human body with a single animal head, but there are all sorts of variations, for example the Japanese Hotai, which is a creature with a monkey's body but a human head with long hair. The Egyptian Sphinx is also an animal with a human head.

Sometimes, the hybridization is metaphorical rather than actual. For example, the Greek legend of Adrastus, King of Argos, includes a prophecy that he will marry his daughters, Argeia and Deipyle, to a lion and a boar. One day, two strangers, Polynices and Tydeus, arrive in Adrastus's court seeking lodging, but begin arguing and fighting loudly. Polynices is wearing a lion-skin cloak, and Tydeus a boar-skin cloak. Adrastus comes to see what the noise is about, sees the men's cloaks, and takes their arrival as the fulfillment of the prophecy.[1]

In the extremely complex Hindu pantheon, the hybridization may be between two humans, rather than a human and an animal. For example, Ardhananari is an epithet, meaning half-man, and refers to an androgynous composite of Lord Siva or Shiva, the male element, and his wife, Parvati. Ardhananari is able to see things from a man's point of view and a woman's point of view simultaneously, surely a very useful attribute at any time. By contrast, another Hindu legend has Asanga, reputedly the author of some of the hymns of the *Rig-Veda*, being changed from a man to a woman as a curse from the gods, then being returned to male form after repenting.

Another figure who changes from a woman to a man, this time in classical Greek mythology, is Caeneus, who was called Caenis at birth, because she was a girl, daughter of Elatus and Hippea, the king and queen of Thessaly. Caenis was exceedingly beautiful, and as she grew she attracted the attention of the sea-god Poseidon, who eventually came to Thessaly and raped her. By way of apology, the god granted her any wish. She asked to be turned into a man, so that she would never be raped again, and Poseidon granted the wish. Caeneus, whose name means "renewed," now became leader of the Lapiths, a tribe of great warriors and horsemen. The Lapiths fought a famous battle with the Centaurs (see below). In his *Metamorphoses* (book 12), the Roman poet Ovid says that Caeneus was eventually changed by Zeus into a bird.[2]

Also in Greek mythology, the god/goddess Ἑρμαφρόδιτος, *Hermaphróditos*, in later Latin *Hermaphroditus*, was simultaneously male and female, giving us the English word hermaphrodite. S/he was given that name because s/he was the son/daughter of Hermes and Aphrodite. S/he was also called Atlantius/Atlantiades because s/he and her/his father Hermes were both descendants of Atlas. (It is worth noting that while complete physical hermaphroditism is very rarely found in humans, there are many organisms and animals in the world—for example, snails, slugs, earthworms and several species of fish—that do not have separate sexes and in which hermaphroditism is the norm, not the exception.)

In the mythology of the Cherokee Nation of North America, Asgaya Gigagei, who is invoked by the medicine man to cure sickness, is either the Red Woman or the Red Man, depending on the gender of the patient. Many Native American nations are reputed to have recognized up to seven different human genders, acknowledging that a wide range of what the West today would generally call sexual orientations or gender preferences are present as normal and natural situations in human development.

The "human with two heads" is an amusing figure in Islamic folklore. Palis was a demon who specialized in sucking the blood of travelers in the desert. He would suck the blood out through the soles of their feet while they were sleeping. Two camel-drivers, knowing how Palis operated, lay down foot-to-foot on the ground and covered themselves to sleep. When Palis arrived, he circled around and around, but eventually he gave up, crying, "I have traveled a thousand valleys and thirty-three, but never before did I meet a man with two heads!"[3]

Beauty and the Beast

The archetypal folklore tale of a human-animal hybrid is the story of *Beauty and the Beast* (*La Belle et la Bête* in the French original), which never loses its charm, nor its message about truth being more important than appearances, from generation to generation. The original, written by Gabrielle-Suzanne Barbot de Villeneuve, was first published in 1740. Since then, many other versions have appeared, in books, in television, and in films. Villeneuve's story, greatly simplified, runs as follows:

> A rich merchant had twelve children, the youngest of them a sweet, kind girl called Belle ("Beauty or Beautiful"). Her elder siblings were more mercenary and selfish than she was. The merchant was setting out on a journey to the harbor to meet an incoming cargo, and asked his children what gifts they would like him to bring back for them. They all made extravagant requests, apart from Belle, who at first asked for nothing, then finally agreed that a single rose would be perfect.
>
> The merchant discovered that his ship had foundered, his cargo was lost, and his assets had been seized. The family was reduced to living in a humble cottage in the forest. The father could bring no gifts home. On his journey, however, he discovered a strange château. A meal appeared to be prepared for him, so he ate it, but nobody appeared. He went out into the garden, ready to leave. The sight of some beautiful roses reminded him of Belle's request, so he picked one.
>
> Immediately, the Beast appeared. He had a normal body, but the head of some kind of wild beast, part lion, part ape, part bear, but all of it hideous and terrifying. Roaring and threatening, he demanded to know of the merchant by what right he had stolen one of his precious roses. The merchant explained his recent troubles and his promise to his youngest daughter. The Beast said that the merchant might take the rose, if he promised that one of his children would come to stay with the Beast in return. The merchant agreed, and went home laden with gifts and treasure, as well as Belle's rose.
>
> Belle was the only one of the children who was brave enough to return to the Beast's château. At first, she was revolted and terrified by the Beast's hideous appearance and animalistic habits, but she gradually came to recognize that there was goodness in him. She imagined him as a handsome young man, and this image grew stronger every day she knew him. She was surrounded by every luxury, and experienced magical events and enchantments in many rooms of the château. Her pleasure was very gratifying to the hideous Beast. Eventually, however, she grew worried about her father and her family, and the Beast allowed her to return home, after promising that she would return within two months.

As the two months came to a close, her concerns reversed: she saw that her family was well, but had a premonition that all was not well with the Beast. She hurried back to the château and found her suspicions confirmed: the hideous Beast was on his deathbed. Closing her eyes and listening instead to her heart, she told the Beast that she loved him, and that she hoped he would marry her. Immediately, the Beast not only recovered, but transformed himself into a handsome young prince. He explained the wicked spells that had made him a Beast, and that only the love of a good woman, who could love him no matter how ugly his outward appearance was, could break the enchantment. The couple married and lived happily ever after.[4]

The tale is found with many variations throughout Europe and parts of Asia. Jean Cocteau made a film of the story in 1946. Since then, there have been many movie versions, the best known being: *Beauty and the Beast*, 1962, starring Joyce Taylor and Mark Damon; a memorable 1976 made-for-television film, starring George C. Scott and Trish van Devere; *Beauty and the Beast*, 1991, a commercially successful Disney animation; and *Beauty and the Beast*, 2017, a live-action adaptation of the 1991 Disney animation, starring Emma Watson and Dan Stevens.

Baginis

The Australian Aborigines believe in half-woman, half-animal creatures called Baginis. They have beautiful faces, but vicious claws instead of toes and fingers. They capture men and rape them, but usually set them free once they are satisfied. The worst thing a man can do is to resist the rape: he will surely be torn to pieces.

Ba

In Egyptian mythology, the soul was called the *ba*. Humans had three vital components: the *ba*, the *ka* (a person's double or alternate body), and the *ib* (the heart, which was incorruptible). In the pyramids of Meroë, tiny openings were left in the stone covering the apex so that the *ba* might enter.[5] The *ba* was usually represented as the head of the deceased person on the body of a bird. The heron was also a symbol of the *ba* (see **heron**, Chapter 24).

In later Islamic folklore, the *ka* or body double is called the *badal*. When a saint or holy man dies, he may leave his double or *badal* behind to take his place. Only Allah knows whether a person is real, or a *badal*.

The Sphinx

The Egyptian Sphinx is perhaps the best-known animal-human hybrid in the world. The name appears to mean "Throttler," or "One Who Squeezes," because she squeezes the life out of her victims. She has the body of a lion and the face of a beautiful woman, although most of the Egyptian myths treat her as a male god, an aspect of the god Horus. (This male god is sometimes called an *androsphinx*, from Greek Ανδροσφινξ, Man Sphinx.)

The Sphinx asked every visitor a simple, famous riddle: "What is it that has one voice, but is four-legged in the morning, two-legged at midday, and three-legged in the evening?" The answer is a human, because humans crawl on all fours as babies, walk on two legs as adults, but require a stick (the third leg) when they are old and infirm. If the visitor could not give the correct answer, they were killed and eaten by the Sphinx.

The Great Sphinx of Giza, which is now an icon and national symbol of Egypt, probably dates from the reign of the pharaoh Khafre (c. 2558–2532 BCE), although the reign of Khafre's father, Khufu (known to the Greeks as Cheops), has also been suggested, in which case the dates would be earlier, 2589–2566 BCE. The face has been severely affected by weathering, but the missing chin is assumed to have once worn a beard, an important symbol of power in ancient Egypt. Even female pharaohs (there were a few) put on false beards for public appearances. There are other sphinxes in Egypt, and they all appear to be male.

The psychologist Carl Jung (1875–1961) suggested that the Sphinx represents the ancient Great Mother Goddess who was destroyed by the greater force of male-dominated pantheons, as represented by the god Osiris. The ambivalent gender of the Sphinx complicates this theory.

It was Oedipus who answered the Sphinx's riddle correctly. In despair, she threw herself from a rock and died, and Oedipus became King of Thebes.

Vishnu

In Hindu mythology, Vishnu, originally a comparatively minor deity, grew in popularity over many centuries and has achieved similar status to Brahma and Shiva. Vishnu is famous for his many well-known reincarnations or avatars, the best-known being Rama, the seventh, and Krishna, the eighth. However, Vishnu is also a good example of the very frequent hybridization between human and animal forms which occurs in the Hindu pantheon. He has literally dozens of alternative names, e.g., Ananta-sayana (He Who Sleeps on the Waters), Lakshmipati (Lord or Husband of Lakshmi), Pitam-bara (Clothed in Yellow Garments), etc., and he appears as a dwarf, as the Buddha, as a man with an ax, etc., but his four main animal avatars are: the fish Matsya, who saved humans from the great flood, like Noah; the tortoise or turtle Kurma, who helped the other gods to find Amrita, the water of life, after the great flood; the sacred boar Varaha, who fought the demon Hiranyaksha for a thousand years before killing him; and the man-lion Nara-sinha, who cleansed the world of the demon Hiranya-kasipu for a million years.

Rakshasas

In Hindu mythology, Rakshasas are demons which live in the Lanka (Sri Lanka), where Ravana is the demon king. In the epic poem *The Ramayana*, the monkey god Hanuman enters the kingdom and meets the Rakshasas. Some are divinely beautiful (but deadly), while others have crooked teeth or breasts hanging down to their ankles, or are obscenely fat or skeletally thin. The ugliest have serpent heads, or the heads of donkeys, horses or elephants.

Lopamudra

In the Hindu epic poem *The Mahabharata*, Agastya (Mountain Thrower) is a great sage who lives in a hermitage on Mount Kunjara. He is a friend and adviser to the divine couple, Rama and his wife Sita. One day, Agastya has a terrible vision: he sees his ancestors in a pit, tied up by their heels. He realizes that he must have children, but he is not married, he has no mistress, and he has become permanently settled into the quiet life of a hermit and cannot bear the thought of all the tedious socializing he would have to endure in order to find a wife. He fashions himself a human wife from the most beautiful parts of the most beautiful animals (in the same way that Blodeuwedd is fashioned from beautiful flowers in the Celtic tradition—see **owl**, *Blodeuwedd*, Chapter 23), and calls her Lopamudra. Her name means loss (*lopa*) of beauties (*mudra*), meaning the different beautiful aspects that all the animals contributed to her creation. The creation of an artificial woman to be a spouse or partner to a lonely man also occurs in Finnish mythology, more precisely the epic *Kalevala*, where the magical smith Ilmarinen creates a wife out of gold and silver, but, no matter how stunningly beautiful she is, she remains cold, and Ilmarinen gets no comfort from her.

There may well have been a historical Lopamudra, a philosopher in her own right and author of many of the hymns written some time during the Rigvedic period (1950–1100 BCE). Agastya is widely revered in all the Hindu traditions, and many sacred and poetic texts are also ascribed to him. The Hindu name for the star Canopus, which is the second brightest star in the southern sky after Sirius, is Agastya (see Chapter 41).

Ashur

Ashur was an Assyrian god, husband of the great goddess Ishtar. He was a warrior god, patron of the military city named after him that he built by the River Tigris. He is often depicted with a winged disc about his head, which is portrayed as the head of an eagle. As is typical of war gods, he was also associated with the ox, the bull and the lion.

Pan

The Greek god Pan was human from the waist up (except for his horns), but had the lower body of a goat, although he stood erect. He was called Faunus by the Romans. He had a reed pipe called the syrinx after the nymph, Syrinx, whom he had tried to rape; the pipe or flute is also sometimes called Pan pipes in his honor. He was an important god of fertility, shepherds, forests and wild animals. Christians later identified him with Satan, and his name is said to be the root of the word panic.

Satyrs were half-human, half-animal (usually goat legs and horns), looking very similar to Pan. They were followers of Dionysus and Pan, and loved wine and women above all things. A famous painting by Peter Paul Reubens (1577–1640) called *Nymphs and Satyrs* captures them in all their debauchery.

Harpies

In Greek mythology, harpies (from Greek ἁρπυια, *harpuia*, snatchers) were winged monsters with the face of a woman and the body of a vulture. They are named in Greek by Hesiod, Homer and Aeschylus, and in Latin by Virgil. Although their faces were beautiful, they had disgusting breath and razor-sharp claws like vultures. They were used as agents of punishment by the gods, who sent them to snatch wrongdoers and carry them away to oblivion.

According to legend, Zeus gave King Phynias of Thrace the gift of prophecy, but Phynias earned the god's disfavor by revealing his secret plans. Zeus punished Phynias by blinding him and then exiling him to a tiny island, where a buffet of delicious food was permanently laid out, but, before Phynias could locate it, the harpies would come and eat it, or defecate all over it and make it inedible.

The epithet harpy has come to mean any shrill, cruel, petty, vindictive woman in modern parlance. (In American slang of the 1940s and 1950s, it also meant prostitute.) Virginia Woolf (1882–1941) called the main character of her novel *Mrs. Dalloway* (1925) "a leering, sneering obscene little harpy."

Valkyrjr

The Valkyrjr or Valkyries of Norse mythology are as fierce and ruthless as the ancient Greek Harpies, but are considered welcome and beneficent because they come to Earth not to condemn the wicked and foolish to death, but to bring heroes and great men to Valhalla, the hall of the slain, where they may spend eternity in glory, eating and carousing. The name means "Choosers of Those to Be Slain." They are daughters of the Allfather, Odin. Of those killed honorably on the battlefield, half go with the Valkyrjr to Valhalla, and the other half go with the goddess Freyja to Fólkvangr, the summer meadow of the afterlife, where they are equally cosseted, feasted and celebrated. The Valkyrjr usually appear as wild, flying women of terrible strength and beauty, but they can also appear in the form of any of the widely recognized death animals, ravens, swans, horses or wolves.

The Valkyrjr are named in various texts. They include Skuld (Shield), Skögul (Shaker), Gunnr (War), Hildr (Battle), Göndul (Wand Wielder), Geirskögul (Spear Shaker), Hrist (Shaker), Mist (Cloud), Skeggjöld (Ax Age), Þrúðr (Power), Hlökk (Noise), Herfjötur (Host Fetter), Göll (Tumult), Geirahöð (Spear Fight), Randgríð (Shield Truce), Ráðgríð (Council Truce) and Reginleif (Power Truce).

The Valkyrjr legends and themes continued from Germanic and Nordic origins into Old English, and most modern English speakers would still recognize the name and be able to give at least a rough description of their nature and purpose. Richard Wagner (1813–1883) wrote the *Ride of the Valkyries* as part of his Ring Cycle opera *Die Walküre*, and it remains one of the best known and easily recognized pieces in classical music.

Azhi Dahaka

In the mythology of Persia, Azhi Dahaka was an archdemon with three heads and six eyes. He was a servant of the supreme god of evil, Ahriman. When the hero Traetona plunged his sword into Azhi Dahaka, a slimy tangle of ugly animals fell out of his chest: snakes, toads, scorpions, lizards and frogs. Traetona imprisoned the monster inside Mount Demavend, where he still resides, awaiting the end of the world, when the hero Keresapa will finally kill him.

Benini

In Babylonian mythology, Benini was a monster with a human body but the head of a bird, usually a raven. He and his mother, Melinni, attacked the city of Babylon, but were defeated by prayers and sacrifices to the gods.

The Minotaur

The Minotaur is one of the best-known human-animal hybrids. He was part man and part bull (usually depicted as the head). The name is from Greek Μινωταυρος, *Minōtauros*, from Μινως, *Minōs*, a king's name, and ταυρος, *tauros*, bull, the whole meaning "Minos's bull." This is the Minotaur story:

> Minos was the king of Crete. When Minos became king, he prayed to Poseidon, god of the sea, for a white bull, to show the people that he had the god's support. Poseidon sent the bull, which Minos was supposed to sacrifice, but the bull was so beautiful that Minos decided to keep it. Insulted, Poseidon retaliated by making Minos's wife, Pasiphaë, fall deeply in love with the bull. She persuaded Minos's great magician and craftsman, Daedalus, to make a hollow wooden cow, in which she hid and mated with the great white bull.
>
> The offspring was the Minotaur. Pasiphaë tried to suckle the monster, but, to her horror, it demanded human flesh. Eventually, Minos had Daedalus and Icarus construct a vast maze, called the Labyrinth (possibly from an ancient Cretan word *labrys*, meaning "double axe"), to contain the monster.
>
> Minos's son was Androgeos, whose name means "Man or Son of the Earth." Prince Androgeos was a great athlete. He went to the first celebration of the Panathenaea (games in honor of the goddess Athena) and won almost every contest. King Aegeus of Athens, humiliated that a Cretan foreigner had beaten all the Athenian athletes, sent Androgeos to fight the bull of Marathon. The bull killed Androgeos. In revenge, Minos demanded a tribute of seven young men and seven young women every nine years to be fed to the Minotaur. Eventually, with the assistance of Ariadne [see **spider**, Chapter 35], the hero Theseus came to the Palace of Knossos and killed the monster.[6]

Medusa

In Greek mythology, a Gorgon (from γοργος, *gorgós*, dreadful) was one of three monster sisters, each of which had a mass of writhing snakes instead of hair. Two of them, Stheno and Euryale, were immortal, but the third, Medusa, was killed by the hero and demigod Perseus. The Gorgons feature in very early Greek art, and may date back as far as 6000 BCE, according to Marija Gimbutas.[7] The legend of Perseus slaying Medusa, briefly summarized, runs as follows:

> The evil King Polydectes lusted after Perseus's mother, Danaë. He sent Perseus to slay the Medusa in the hope that the Medusa would kill Perseus and get him out of the way. Perseus had to use several devices to conquer the Medusa, since one of the Gorgons' main strengths was that mere sight of their snaky heads would turn any attacker to stone. The god Hermes gave Perseus a scythe (no sword could harm the Medusa) and the goddess Athena gave him a mirror (so that he would not have to look directly at the monster). Perseus struck off the Medusa's head and returned to Polydectes's palace. When the king, astonished to see Perseus return, asked whether the hero had killed the monster, Perseus held up the Medusa's head, and Polydectes was turned to stone—his just desserts.[8]

There are many variant versions of the legend, which has remained popular for centuries. In one of them, the winged horse Pegasus (see Chapter 11) is born out of the ocean from drops of blood falling from the Medusa's severed head. In another, the severed head is used to turn the god Atlas, who carried the sky on his shoulders, into stone, specifically the Atlas Mountains of Morocco, Algeria and Tunisia in North Africa.

On ancient Greek buildings, a γοργονειον, *gorgoneion*, was any sculpture or engraving of a Gorgon's head to protect the occupants from harm. It was also used on battle armor.

Hypnos

The Greek god Hypnos (Greek Ὕπνος, *Hypnos*, Sleep) gives his name to hypnotism. By day he was a handsome youth, but by night he became a bird. He sent people to sleep by touching them with a feather or one of his wings, or (according to Virgil) with a magical tree branch.

Chiron and the Centaurs

A centaur, from Greek κενταυρος, *kéntauros*, "(strong as) a hundred bulls," was a mythical creature with the upper body, head and arms of a human, but the lower body and four legs of a horse. Centaurs have been familiar in classical mythology for centuries, but recognition of them has been made easier for modern readers and audiences by their inclusion in J.K. Rowlings' *Harry Potter* books and films.

The earliest legends portray centaurs as wild, drunken, lascivious beasts, an image which persisted into medieval Christian iconography, where they represent humankind's most basic instincts. Centaurs were invited to the wedding of Hippodameia and Pirithous, king of the Lapiths, but they ruined the celebration by attempting to rape the women and kill the men. War between the Centaurs and the Lapiths began, and stories of that conflict appear in Virgil (*The Aeneid*, book 6) and Ovid (*The Metamorphoses*, book 12). The famous poem *The Faerie Queen* by Edmund Spenser (1552–1599) describes the Centaurs fighting against the Lapiths and against Herakles.

But Chiron (from Greek ξειρων, *kheirōn*, hand), the most famous of the centaurs, was an altogether more civilized being (which is why the *Harry Potter* centaurs, despite being rough, dangerous and intimidating, are essentially good rather than evil characters). He was the son of Kronos or Chronos, one of the Titans who preceded the gods, and the Father of Time (hence "chronology"). But Chiron was foster-fathered by the god Apollo, who taught him music, archery, hunting, prophesy, astrology and many other skills, but, most of all, medicine. Chiron in his turn became a great teacher of medicine and herbalism. To indicate that he was more civilized than your average centaur, he was often depicted with human front legs rather than horse legs. As an archer, he is commemorated in the constellation of Sagittarius the Archer (see Chapter 41), which Zeus granted to him on his death from a poisoned arrow (the legend of Chiron, the great physician and healer struggling with his own death but unable to find the antidote to the poison which is slowly killing him, is a major piece of Greek mythology all by itself). As a guide, teacher and tutor, he profoundly influenced many of Greece's most treasured mythological heroes. He was also revered as a judge, and many acts and sayings of great wisdom are attributed to him.

Cecrops

Cecrops, or Κεκροψ, *Kekrops* in the original Greek spelling, was a legendary king, the first King of Athens. The historian Strabo (63 BCE–24 CE) believed that the name Cecrops was not of Greek origin, but others have argued that it signified Face-Tail, since Cecrops is universally depicted as half-man (the top half) and half-serpent. The region in which Athens stands was originally called Acte or Attica after its first king, Actaeus, but was later called Kekropia or Cecropia after Kekrops. When the goddess Athena and the sea-god Poseidon were disputing who had authority over this region, Kekrops had to decide whom to support. To show his power, Poseidon struck the rock of the Acropolis with his trident, and a white horse (in some versions, a wave of sea water) came from the rock. In response, Athena quietly planted the first olive tree. Kekrops, anticipating how important the sacred olive would always be to Greece, and recognizing it also as a symbol of peace, gave Athena his allegiance, and the capital of Attica, and of Greece, has been called Athens ever since. Kekrops also banned human sacrifice, introduced reading and writing, instituted marriage, and devised proper funerary rites.

Abraxas

Abraxas is a pagan god, called a demon by the Abrahamic religions, who appears in Gnostic texts and in alchemy. His name has been found inscribed on jewelry of the 2nd century CE. He has a human body, but the head of either a cock or a lion, and his feet terminate in scorpions. According to early alchemists, the spell word *abracadabra* derives from his name.[9]

Adrammelech, Moloch

Adrammelech is an archdemon in Christian mythology. He and his fellow demon Anammelech are named in the Bible: "The Sepharvites burnt their children in fire to Adrammelech and Anammelech, the gods of Sepharvaim."[10] Adrammelech was said to appear as a peacock, a mule, a horse, or a lion, or any combination of those with human parts. The name also appears as Adramelek, Adramelos and Ardumuzan. It may be a variant of Moloch or Molech, the Canaanite god also associated with child sacrifice by fire, who was famously worshipped as an idol with human hands and a bull's head. The Biblical injunction never to sacrifice children to the fire of Moloch or Molech is repeated several times. Typical is : "Again, thou shalt say to the children of Israel, 'Whosoever he be of the children of Israel, or of the strangers that sojourn in Israel, that giveth any of his seed unto Molech; he shall surely be put to death: the people of the land shall stone him with stones.'"[11]

Baphomet

In medieval Christianity, Baphomet was a demon said to have been worshiped secretly by the Knights Templar. She/he was depicted in 1856 by Eliphas Levi as having the body of a large-breasted woman, but with the legs, head and horns of a monstrous goat, plus large wings like those of an angel. Earlier descriptions mention several heads. The name is assumed to be a corruption of the Islamic Mahomet or Muhammad. Baphomet came to general recognition through the Crusades, but the critical event was the inquisition of the Knights Templar begun in 1307 by King Philip IV of France, who accused them of homosexuality, heresy and spitting on the cross, among other sins. Over a hundred knights confessed under torture. Whether any of them was actually guilty or not remains a matter of conjecture. One plausible defense given by many of them was that they had been trained to confess "with their tongues and minds, but not with their hearts" in the case of capture and torture by the Saracens, and that spitting on the cross was part of that training.

Asmodeus

Asmodeus or Ashmedai is another demon from Judeo-Christian-Islamic mythology. He is the main character in the *Book of Tobit* from the Biblical Apocrypha. He also appears in several Talmudic legends. Tobias kills Sarah's previous seven husbands one by one in order to marry her, aided by Asmodeus. The archangel Raphael intervenes and drives Asmodeus away by burning the heart and liver of a fish on an open fire: Asmodeus cannot bear the smell, and flees to Egypt.

In another tale, Asmodeus steals a ring from King Solomon, and throws it into the sea. By prayer, Solomon finds the ring in the belly of a fish (a common folklore story theme), and Asmodeus and his fellow demons are captured and imprisoned in a large jar.

According to the *Lemegeton*, a 17th-century manual of ceremonial magic, Asmodeus is a prince of lust, not just of Hell. He rides a dragon, carries a spear, and has two additional animal heads as well as his own: a ram's, and a bull's, both symbolic of his lechery.

The Manticore

The manticore (the name means "man eater," from Early Middle Persian *Merthykhuwar*) was a medieval Christian fabulous beast with a human head, the body of a lion, and the tail of a scorpion. It was developed from a Persian version of the Egyptian Sphinx, to which it is similar. It was known by the Greeks and Romans, but only became prominent when medieval Christians developed legends about its ferocity. It was reputed to have three rows of teeth and to devour humans whole, bones and all. Through a linguistic mistake, it is sometimes confused with the mantyger or man-tiger.

Azrael

Azrael is yet another demon, this time from Jewish and Islamic mythology. He has 70,000 feet, 4,000 wings, four faces and more eyes and tongues than there are people in the world. He keeps a scroll with the name of every person born in the world. Allah tells him which humans are due to die by letting fall a leaf, on which the person's name is written. If the person is a true believer, he sees the leaf and accepts his fate without complaint. If he hesitates, Allah sends him an apple with his sacred name of compassion written on it, and the person yields to death. If the person is an unbeliever, or struggles, Azrael tears his soul roughly from his body, the gate of Heaven closes, and the unbeliever's soul is flung into Hell.

Borak

Also from Islamic mythology, Borak is the legendary animal that carried the prophet Muhammad to Heaven. *Surah* 17 of the Qur'an mentions the prophet's vision of his journey, but neither names nor describes the animal. However, legend describes Borak as something between an ass and a mule, but with tail and hoofs like those of a cow, and a human face. In art, Borak is sometimes depicted with the head of a woman, her face veiled, and the tail of a peacock.

Grendel and Grendel's Dam

In early English medieval legend, the feats of an Anglo-Saxon hero are celebrated in an epic poem in Old English called *Beowulf*, written by an unnamed monk of Northumbria in the early 700s CE. The hero's name means Bee-Wolf. This is a summary of the poem:

> Beowulf came with his band of warriors to the feasting hall of King Hrothgar of the Danes. Beowulf and his men were Geats, foreigners (from Sweden or Jutland), looking for adventures, challenges and plunder.
>
> Hrothgar greeted the visitors cordially and told them of a monster that had been plaguing his people: it was a giant, misshapen, half-human creature, hideous to behold, called Grendel. Beowulf and his men waited in the hall that night. When Grendel arrived and ate one of the Geats in a single gulp, Beowulf pulled off the monster's arm. Grendel, mortally wounded, ran off to his cavern under the lake to die.
>
> The Danes and Geats celebrated their victory with much food and beer, and Beowulf was showered with gifts and praises. But Beowulf's triumph was short-lived. The following night, Grendel's dam (mother) came to avenge the death of her son. She could take human form, like her son, but she also appeared as a giant monster, hideously ugly. She seized and ate one of Hrothgar's men, who was still sleeping off the celebration of the night before. His screams woke the hall.
>
> Beowulf pursued the monster to the lake and dived in after her. After a desperate underwater struggle, during which Beowulf lost his sword and found another magical sword hidden in Grendel's cavern, the hero finally killed Grendel's dam and peace returned to Denmark. Beowulf became King of Geatland, and ruled for fifty years before being killed fighting a dragon.

Mermaids and Mermen

There are countless legends of mermaids (half-woman, half-fish) and mermen (half-man, half-fish) in different cultures all across the world. The earliest recorded legend comes from Assyria and dates from about 1000 BCE, whilst the most recent are contemporary—mermaid sightings are still occasionally reported.

The Assyrian goddess Atagartis, mother of Queen Semiramis, loved a human shepherd, but accidentally killed him. In shame, she threw herself into a lake to drown, but the water of the lake refused to kill her or completely disguise her beauty. She became a fish from the waist down, but a beautiful woman with large breasts and long hair from the waist up—the archetypal mermaid. The Greeks adopted this mermaid goddess under the name Δερκετο, Derketo.

The Greek natural philosopher Anaximander argued that humankind was descended from mermaids, or from some large aquatic mammal. His reasoning was that only water could provide sufficient shelter and support for the unusually long period of time that human babies require to reach maturity.

A famous and charming ancient Greek legend says that Thessalonike, the sister of Alexander the Great, was turned into a mermaid after her death. (The Greek word is γοργον, *gorgón*, which we have already met in the story of Medusa above, but she is clearly a mermaid in this story.) She confronted Greek ships with the following question: "Ζει ο Βασιλευς Αλεξανδρος?," *"Zei o Basileus Alexandros?"* ("Does King Alexander live?") If the captain refused to reply, or gave the wrong answer, Thessalonike would whip up an instant storm and capsize the ship. In order to keep the sea calm, the captain was required to answer precisely: "Ζει και βασιλευει και τον κοσμον κυριευει," *"Zei kai basileúei kai ton kósmon kurieúei"* ("He lives and reigns and rules the world.")

The Roman natural philosopher and historian Pliny the Elder (23–79 CE) reported sightings of mermaids washed up on the beaches of Gaul (modern France). The 2nd-century Syrian writer Lucian of Samosata reported images of mermaids in the temples of Derketo.

In the Cornish village of Zennor, a bench in the parish church is carved with the image of a mermaid, said to be at least six centuries old. The local legend is that Matthi or Matthew Trewhella was a tenor in the church choir, who sang so sweetly and loudly (Cornish choirs admire volume—they have a saying, "Sweeter I've heard, but louder never") that the mermaid fell in love with him, and enticed him to come and live with her beneath the waves. Cornish fishermen still say that they sometimes hear Matthi and his family singing deep in the ocean.

The Bretons call mermen *lutins* (imps or elves of the sea). The fishermen of Saint-Brieuc still claim that if their nets become tangled, it is the work of Nicole (Nicholas), their local *lutin*, whom they curse by name for his mischief. Breton fishermen also call mermaids by the name Mari Morgan (Mary, Song of the Sea).

One legend re-told in Breton by François-Marie Luzel (1821–1895), a folklorist and poet better known by his Breton name Fañch an Uhel (the Tall), is *The Hawk and the Siren*. It is typical of many mermaid stories:

> A fisherman caught a mermaid in his net. She begged the fisherman to release her back into the sea, and offered him a magical gold coin. If he left the coin untouched in a safe place, it would grow into a great treasure. All she asked in addition was that the fisherman would also bring his new-born son to the shore, so that she might kiss the baby—kissing a human baby would bring good fortune to her, in return for the good fortune she was offering with the gold coin.
>
> The fisherman agreed. He accepted the gold coin, released the mermaid, and brought his baby son to the beach the following day. The mermaid smiled, took the baby to kiss it, but then dived back into the sea with the baby still in her arms. The fisherman was brave enough and angry enough to dive right in after her. He wrestled with her, and finally brought the baby back to the shore.
>
> Despite the friction caused by the baby snatching incident, the fisherman put the gold coin away, and it performed as promised, doubling every month until a considerable fortune accrued. The fisherman and his wife named their son Fañch and were able to raise him in unusual wealth and luxury for a fishing family.
>
> As the years rolled by, they forgot about the mermaid. Fañch grew into a man, but he was so well educated, well spoken and well dressed that he wasn't sure whether the life of a fisherman was really the life for him. He was walking on the beach very early one morning, thinking on these matters deeply, when a beautiful girl suddenly appeared before him. He was astonished to see such a gorgeous stranger so early, dressed magnificently, in such an unusual place. She laughed and joked with him, her smile and bright eyes beguiling Fañch completely. She suggested they paddle in the gentle waves on the shore.
>
> The second they touched the water, the woman changed into her real form: she was the mermaid who had tried to snatch Fañch as a baby, and who had spent all these intervening years (merpeople do not age as humans do) waiting patiently to complete her intended kidnapping. She dragged Fañch beneath the waves, towards her *houle* (sea-cave home). What the mermaid did not know was that part of Fañch's expensive education had been coaching in the magical arts. He wrestled himself free of her, and as she went to grab him again, he changed himself into a hawk, pulled himself to the surface, then flew over the waves back to freedom.[12]

The Scottish legend of the Blue Men of Siant paints an even starker and weirder picture of mermaid/merman cruelty. Siant (pronounced *shant*) is a small group of isolated and unspoiled islands lying between the Scottish mainland and the Isle of Lewis, the largest island in the Outer Hebrides. The Blue Men of Siant live in ocean caves (like the Breton *houles*), but they feast on human flesh whenever they can: it is their favorite meat. As their name suggests, their skin is dark blue in color, and they have razor-sharp, pointed teeth. Whenever a ship passes above them, they rise to the surface, looking to feast on the corpses of the sailors or fishermen they will drown by whipping up an instant storm.

However, they play fair by offering the humans the opportunity to pass by unharmed. They recite poetry, which they improvise. The human crew must respond accurately (as the Greeks had to, for Thessalonike), following the given theme sensibly, but also—this is most important—in verse that rhymes, matching the rhyme scheme of the mermen's poem exactly. Nobody knows how this very peculiar legend originated, but even today Scottish sailors approach the tricky waters of the Siant passage with great caution, and perhaps with a bard on board, just in case they meet the Blue Men.

It is highly likely that several of the reported sightings of mermaids, ancient and modern, are in fact sightings of the sea animals collectively known as sirens, particularly the dugong and manatee (see Chapter 21).

Adaros

In Melanesian mythology, *adaros* are sun spirits that move from place to place in waterspouts. They are part-fish, part-human. They fire flying fish as weapons, and if a human is hit, prayers and special invocations to Nyorieru, chief of the *adaros*, must be made while the victim is unconscious, otherwise he or she will die.

Erzulie

Erzulie is a mermaid in Haitian voodoo, married to the sea god Agwé. She is also called, in Haitian French, *La Sirène* (the Siren). She lives with Agwé on the *zilet en bas de l'eau*, the "island below the sea," which is where the souls of the dead live.

Azeto

Also found in Haitian voodoo is Azeto, who is an evil spirit of the dead, appearing either as male or female. He or she appears mostly as a werewolf, but also as a vampire.

Akkruva, Cacce-jielle and Cacce-jienne

Akkruva is a mermaid fish-goddess traditionally worshipped in Lapland. She has the typical mermaid combination of a lower body covered in scales and ending in a fish tail, but the upper body of a beautiful maiden with long, golden hair that she combs incessantly. Finnish fishermen are still known to invoke her by name in the hopes of bringing home a big haul of fish.

Cacce-jielle and Cacce-jienne are respectively a male and a female water-god also found in Lapp mythology. Cacce-jielle appears as a white-haired old man, while Cacce-jienne can appear either as a mermaid like Akkruva, combing her long tresses and tempting sailors to dive into the ocean, or as a naked child, or as a fish.

Domovoi/Dobby

Either knowingly or unwittingly by the author, J.K. Rowling's elf character Dobby in the *Harry Potter* series of novels is very similar to Domovoi, a character in Slavic folklore. Domovoi is a house spirit, sometimes called grandfather or master of the house. When God created the world, some spirits rebelled against him, and he cast them out from Heaven. Those who landed in wild places remained rebellious and evil. Those who landed on houses or in gardens became tamed by contact with humans, and even became servants to them, but they are smaller than humans, with long, pointed noses and big ears and eyes. Domovoi, the male spirit (like Dobby), enjoyed staying close to the stove. His wife, Domovikha or Kikimora (there is no equivalent character in *Harry Potter*), preferred to hide down in the basement.

The Krampus and Other Christmas Monsters

The Krampus is a relatively modern (probably 16th-century) monster found in Germany, the Netherlands and parts of eastern Europe around Christmastime. Part human, part devil, part goat, with horns, fangs and clawed hands, the Krampus is definitely not a child-friendly creature, especially during the Christmas festivities. On *Krampusnacht* (German for Krampus Night, December 6), the season of festive giving begins, and the Krampus seeks out those children who deserve a beating rather than a gift. Bad-mannered children can expect the Krampus to leave a switch of birch twigs for their parents to use on them.

Jacob Grimm's *Deutsche Mythologie* of 1835 also describes Perchta or Bertha, an old witch who punishers spinners who leave their work incomplete. She punishes over-indulgers by cutting open their stomachs and stuffing them with straw before sewing them closed again with a ploughshare for a needle and an iron chain for a thread.[13]

Iceland has Gryla, a hoofed and horned ogress who punishes naughty children at Christmas-time by throwing them in a sack and carrying them back to her mountain lair to eat them. The *Jólasveinarnir* (Yule Lads) bring pleasant gifts to good children and vile, putrid things to bad children.

The Abominable Snowman

The high mountains of our planet are still sufficiently wild and remote for notions to persist of an abominable (i.e., terrible or terrifying) snowman (also called a yeti, from Tibetan *gya-dred*, rock bear). This legendary man-like or ape-like creature of the Himalayas is also called *metkokhangmi* in Tibetan, meaning "evil-smelling man of the snows."

41

Animals in the Sky

Zodiacs

The Sun appears to travel across the sky from east to west. (In reality, the spinning of the Earth creates this illusion.) The arc or line along which it appears to travel is called the ecliptic. At night, varying from season to season, different constellations appear to follow this same line. In addition, our moon and the other planets in the solar system also travel along the ecliptic, within eight degrees either side. The circle of constellations (360°) was anciently divided into twelve sections (called houses) of 30° each, with each section named after the dominant constellation. In about 400 BCE, when the Babylonians first devised this system, there were in fact 13 prominent constellations, but they ignored one of them (Ophiuchus, the snake-holder) and kept the division to twelve, which made measurement and calculation much easier. Several of these constellations are named after animals, and/or have animal legends associated with them, with which most if not all readers will already be familiar. The twelve constellations are: *Aries* the ram, *Taurus* the bull, *Gemini* the twins, *Cancer* the crab, *Leo* the lion, *Virgo* the virgin, *Libra* the scales, *Scorpio* the scorpion, *Sagittarius* the archer or centaur, *Capricorn* the goat, *Aquarius* the water carrier, and *Pisces* the fishes.

The Greeks and Romans (who took astronomy/astrology very seriously) took the Babylonian system on board. The Greco-Roman mathematician and astronomer Ptolemy (c. 90–168 CE) wrote an astronomical text called *The Almagest*, in which (among other things) he set our planet, the Earth, as the center of the universe. This idea persisted for many centuries until it was challenged by Nicolaus Copernicus (1473–1543) and Galileo Galilei (1564–1642).

In early Judaism and Christianity, the four great beasts of the cosmos, the lion, the bull, the man and the eagle, corresponding with the four evangelists Matthew, Mark, Luke and John, were believed to also correspond respectively with the zodiac constellations Leo, Taurus, Aquarius and Scorpio.

The Hindu zodiac is based on the sidereal coordinates system, which calculates the movements of the planets against the fixed stars. The constellation names are quite different to the ones we use in the West, but the symbols are almost identical:

Sanskrit Name	Animal	Western Equivalent
Mesha	ram	Aries
Vrshabha	bull	Taurus
Mithuna	twins	Gemini

Sanskrit Name	Animal	Western Equivalent
Karka	crab	Cancer
Simha	lion	Leo
Kanya	virgin	Virgo
Tula	scales	Libra
Vrshcika	scorpion	Scorpio
Dhanusha	bow and arrow	Sagittarius
Makara	sea monster	Capricorn
Kumbha	water-pourer	Aquarius
Mina	fishes	Pisces[1]

The Chinese zodiac is based on a different scheme entirely. It assigns twelve animals to succeeding years, the whole cycle beginning again in the thirteenth year:

Animal (female/male)	Element	Yin/Yang	Years
rat	water	Yang	1937, 1949, 1961, 1973, 1985, 1997…
ox	earth	Yin	1938, 1950, 1962, 1974, 1986, 1998…
tiger	wood	Yang	1939, 1951, 1963, 1975, 1987, 1999…
rabbit	wood	Yin	1940, 1952, 1964, 1976, 1988, 2000…
dragon	earth	Yang	1941, 1953, 1965, 1977, 1989, 2011…
snake	fire	Yin	1942, 1954, 1966, 1978, 1990, 2012…
horse	fire	Yang	1943, 1955, 1967, 1979, 1991, 2013…
goat	earth	Yin	1944, 1956, 1968, 1980, 1992, 2014…
monkey	metal	Yang	1945, 1957, 1969, 1981, 1993, 2015…
rooster	metal	Yin	1946, 1958, 1970, 1982, 1994, 2016…
dog	earth	Yang	1947, 1959, 1971, 1983, 1995, 2017…
pig	water	Yin	1948, 1960, 1972, 1984, 1996, 2018…[2]

The birth-year animal represents only one astral influence, signifying how you present yourself to the world. In addition to the birth-year, animals are assigned by month ("inner animals"), by day ("true animals"), and by hours ("secret animals"). So, your birth-year might make you a rat, but your inner animal could be a rooster, your day animal a dragon, and your secret animal a monkey, making your composite self complex enough for anybody.

Constellations

Constellations, from Latin *con-* (with) and *stella* (star), are groups of stars that appear to form a connected shape. "Appear" is a critical word, because the fact that stars appear close to other stars takes no account at all of how far away they actually are from us or from each other, so what appears to be a pattern in the almost two dimensions of the night sky has no bearing on what relationship they might or might not actually have in three dimensions.

Constellations Named After Animals

There are 88 constellations recognized by the International Astronomical Union, of which 42 are named after animals:

Apus: bird of paradise. *Apus* is a small constellation in the southern sky. It represents the bird of paradise, which is the origin of its Greek name, meaning without feet, because the ancient belief was that birds of paradise had no feet.

Aquila: eagle. *Aquila* is a constellation on the celestial equator, so it is surrounded by the Milky Way. Several nebulae and star clusters lie within its area, although they are faint.

Aries: ram. *Aries*, the ram (not to be confused with Ares, Greek god of war), is a northern constellation, which lies between Pisces to the west and Taurus to the east. In ancient Egypt, it was associated with the supreme god Amon-Ra, before the Greeks and Romans demoted it to the ram. It is a faint constellation, with only four reasonably bright stars, so its shape has been interpreted differently by different cultures—the Chinese call part of it by a name that means "two land inspectors," Messrs. Zuogeng (marshes and ponds) and Yeou-kang (pastures).

Camelopardalis: giraffe. *Camelopardalis* is a large but faint northern constellation. It was not included in Ptolemy's *Almagest*, but was added by Petrus Plancius (1552–1622) in 1613.[3]

Cancer: crab. *Cancer* is a faint, medium-sized constellation between *Gemini* and *Leo*. Its classical legend is that, when Herakles was trying to complete his Twelve Labors or impossible tasks, the goddess Hera sent a giant crab to impede him. When the crab bit Herakles on the ankle, he crushed it with his foot and Hera set it in the sky to commemorate its sacrifice (see **crab**, Chapter 32).

Canes Venatici: hunting dogs. *Canes Venatici* is a small northern constellation named by the Polish astronomer Johannes Hevelius (1611–1687). The dogs are the working dogs of Boötes the Herdsman (or ox-driver, from Greek βους, *bous*, ox).

The star Izar, or ε (*epsilon*) *Bootis*, is popular with amateur astronomers because it is a binary system (two stars circling around each other) that can be resolved with a reasonably powerful telescope (aperture 3 inches or 77 millimeters). The most noticeable star in the constellation, however, is the orange-red giant Arcturus, α *Boötis*, the brightest star in the northern celestial hemisphere and the fourth-brightest in the whole night sky.

Canis Major, Canis Minor: big dog, little dog. *Canis Major* is the big dog and *Canis Minor* is the little dog. Both southern constellations follow the easily recognized constellation of Orion the Hunter across the sky. The bright star below Orion's right heel, Sirius or α (*alpha*) *Canis Majoris*, is the brightest star in the night sky. Its name comes from Greek Σειριος, *Seírios*, meaning scorching. In ancient Mesopotamia, Sirius was characterized as an arrow, with other stars making up the bow, which was said to be wielded by the great goddess Ishtar. For the Greeks and Romans, the constellation was *Canis* (the dog), but there are several candidates for which dog precisely was meant: Laelaps, a dog which never failed to catch whatever it was hunting, given by Zeus to Europa; alternatively, Custos Europae (Guardian of Europa), the dog retained to keep Zeus away from Europa; the unnamed hunting dog of Procris, a nymph of Diana, one of many poor maidens in mythology and folklore accidentally mistaken for a wild animal and killed during the hunt; or one of Orion's hunting dogs, pursuing either *Lepus* the hare or *Taurus* the bull.

The Arabian astronomers called the constellation *al-Kalb al-Akbar* (the Greater Dog.) In Chinese astronomy, *Canis Major* forms part of a larger constellation called *Nán Fāng Zhu Qué* (the Vermilion Bird). The brightest star in *Canis Minor* is Procyon or α *Canis Minoris*, its name coming from Greek προκυων, *prokuōn*, meaning "before the dog."

Capricornus: goat. Capricornus or Capricorn, the horned goat, is the smallest constellation in the zodiac; it is also very faint. Called Makara or the sea-monster in the Hindu zodiac, the goat is the legendary sea-goat, the top half a goat and the bottom half a fish. (Presumably flocks of them live with mermen and mermaids.)

Centaurus: centaur. Centaurus is the mythological centaur, the most famous of whom was Chiron (see Chapter 40). The constellation is bright and large in the southern sky. *Proxima Centauri* ("nearest star of Centaurus") is the nearest star to us (apart from our own Sun) at 4.244 light years (the distance covered by light traveling at 186,000 miles or 297,600 km per second for 4.244 years).

Cetus: whale. Cetus lies close to the ecliptic, but it is not included in any zodiac. The star *Mira* (Wonderful) or ω (*omicron*) *Ceti* is famous because it was the first variable star ever discovered. Over a period of 322 days, ω Ceti changes in magnitude from -3 (easily visible to the naked eye) to 10 (invisible), so the star is a "wonder" because it vanishes and then reappears.

(In one sense, all stars, including our Sun, are variable, because their magnitude fluctuates by certain amounts, usually very small. Stars officially designated as variable are either intrinsic, i.e., they do actually increase or decrease in brightness, or extrinsic, i.e., some other object, usually another companion star in a binary or multiple system, passes in front of the star and obscures some of its light.)

Chamaeleon: chameleon. Chamaeleon is a small constellation of the southern sky, first designated by Petrus Plancius in 1597. In Chinese astronomy, the same constellation is called the Little Dipper, which is one of the asterisms (common or familiar star or star group names) for *Ursa Minor* (see below) in Western astronomy.

Columba: dove. Columba, a small and faint constellation just south of *Canis Major*, was originally named *Columba Noachi* (Noah's Dove) by Petrus Plancius, clearly referencing the Christian story of the dove that returned to the Ark with an olive branch in its beak to show that the flood waters had receded and land was near.

Corvus: crow. Corvus, a small southern constellation, was listed by Ptolemy. It perches, so to speak, on the back of the water-snake, *Hydra* (see below). It was called by a name meaning raven in the Babylonian catalogs dating from c. 1100 BCE—it was sacred to Adad, the god of storms.

In classical mythology, *Corvus* was associated with Apollo:

> *Corvus* is associated with the myth of Apollo and his lover Coronis the Lapith. Coronis had been unfaithful to Apollo; when he learned this information from a pure white crow, he turned its feathers black in a fit of rage. Another legend associated with *Corvus* is that a crow stopped on his way to fetch water for Apollo, to eat figs. Instead of telling the truth to Apollo, he lied and said that a snake, Hydra, kept him from the water, while holding a snake in his talons as proof. Apollo, realizing this was a lie, flung the crow (*Corvus*), cup (*Crater*), and snake (*Hydra*) into the sky. He further punished the wayward bird by ensuring it would forever be thirsty, both in real life and in the heavens, where the Cup is just out of reach.[4]

Cygnus: swan. Cygnus is a prominent and easily recognized northern constellation, sometimes called The Northern Cross. Its brightest star, Deneb, α *Cygni*, takes its name from *deneb*, Arabic for tail. In classical mythology, the swan may be any of six candidates: the swan that Zeus turned himself into in order to seduce Leda (see Chapter 24); the bard Orpheus, placed in the sky next to his lyre (*Lyra*); King Cycnus or Cygnus; Cygnus, brother of Phaethon, whose pathetic attempts to find his brother's bones after he had plummeted to earth excited the compassion of the gods; a young suicide called Tempe, whose sad story is told by Ovid; or a son of Neptune who is defeated by Achilles in the Trojan War and set in the sky by his father.

In Hinduism, a day is divided into thirty equal periods of 48 minutes, each called a *muhurta*. The most auspicious and productive *muhurta* of the day is (in Western time) between 4:24 and 5:12 a.m. This *muhurta*, called *Brahma Muhurta* or "the time of the universe," is associated with the swan and with the constellation *Cygnus*.

Delphinus: dolphin. Delphinus is a small constellation lying just above the celestial equator. γ (*gamma*) *Delphini* is another popular star with amateur astronomers: it is a binary system of a large orange-gold star of magnitude 4.3 and a smaller yellow star of 5.1, the two being easily resolved in a small telescope or even binoculars. There are two major classical legends relating to the constellation (see **dolphin**, Chapter 21).

Dorado: swordfish. Dorado, the dolphinfish, swordfish or goldfish (*dorado* is Portuguese, rather than Greek), is a southern constellation. It contains most of the Large Magellanic Cloud, an object of interest because it is one of the closest galaxies outside our own Milky Way galaxy—it is expected that the Milky Way and the Large Magellanic Cloud will collide into each other in about 2.4 billion years, when neither you nor I will be here to see or experience the collision, we hope.

Draco: dragon. Draco was listed by Ptolemy. It is a circumpolar northern constellation, meaning that it can be seen all year round in the northern hemisphere—it is "the dragon that sits in the top of the sky," so to speak. *Thuban* or α *Draconis* was the Pole Star from c. 3924 BCE to 1793 BCE: the Egyptians oriented the pyramids to *Thuban* as they built them.

Another object of interest in this constellation is Q1634+706, a quasar (quasi-stellar object, usually a black hole surrounded by a massive, extremely bright halo of energized gases), which is said to be the most distant object that an amateur astronomer can see. It is 12.9 billion light years away, and it can be seen in most amateur telescopes.[5]

In traditional Arabic astronomy, the constellation is called *al'awa'id* (the Mother Camels.) It depicts a group of camels protecting one of their young from an attack by two jackals or wolves.

Equuleus: little horse. Equuleus, the little horse, pony, or colt, is stabled in the northern sky. It is very small and its stars are very faint. It may be associated with the foal Celeris (Swift One), the brother (son, in some versions) of Pegasus, the winged horse (see Chapter 11).

Grus: crane. Grus is a southern constellation. In Chinese astronomy (not all of *Grus* is visible from China), it forms part of the constellation *Bei Fang Xhán Wu* (Black Tortoise of the North).

Hydra, Hydrus: water snake. Hydra, the female water snake or sea serpent, was recognized by Ptolemy and is the largest of the 88 modern constellations, sprawling at length (over 100 degrees) just below the celestial equator. It was also a serpent in Babylonian astronomy. The rather faint star σ (*sigma*) *Hydrae* (magnitude 4.5) has the asterism *Minchir*, from the Arabic for snake's nose.

The much smaller *Hydrus* is the male water snake or sea serpent. It lies deep in the southern sky, close to the southern celestial pole. Herman Melville (1819–1891) alludes to the constellation in *Moby Dick*, confirming his genuine knowledge of southern oceans.

Lacerta: lizard. Lacerta forms a W shape in the northern celestial hemisphere somewhat like that of the larger constellation Cassiopeia, and is sometimes called the Little Cassiopeia for that reason.

Leo, Leo Minor: lion, little lion. Leo, the lion, is a constellation of the zodiac, lying between *Cancer* to the west and *Virgo* to the east. To the Greeks and Romans it symbolized the Nemean lion killed by Herakles or Hercules. The mane and shoulders, shaped like a question mark written backwards, are sometimes known separately by the asterism The Sickle.

Leo Minor (The Little Lion) lies to the north of Big Leo. Ptolemy saw no distinct pattern in this part of the sky, so it fell to Johannes Hevelius to name *Leo Minor* in 1687. The Little Lion has a little meteor shower of its own every October 18–29, but little else of interest. Ptolemy may have been right to include it among his αμορφοται, *amorphotai* or amorphous star clusters.

Lepus: hare. Lepus crouches in the long grass just south of Orion the Hunter and east of *Canes Venatici*, the hunting dogs. One of the Arabic asterisms for this group of stars is *al-Nihal* (the Camels Drinking).

Lupus: wolf. Lupus has had a number of name changes. The Babylonians called it *Ur Idim* (Mad Dog). Hipparchus of Bythnia (2nd century BCE) called it Qerion or Therion (Beast). Ptolemy did not recognize it as a constellation, but included the star group within *Centaurus*. Eventually, the Greek of Ptolemy's *Almagest* was translated into Latin, and it became a beast again, but this time specifically *lupus*, a wolf.

Lynx: lynx. Lynx is a faint northern constellation, named by Johannes Hevelius in 1687. Hevelius was making his own small joke: the constellation is so faint that only those with exceptionally keen eyesight (like a lynx) will be able to find it in the sky.

Monoceros: unicorn. Monoceros is also very faint and difficult to find with the naked eye, although it lies on the celestial equator. The triple star system β (*beta*) *Monocerotis* was discovered in 1781 by the German-born British astronomer William Herschel (1738–1822), who described it as, "one of the most beautiful sights in the heavens."

Musca: fly. Musca was also called *Apis* (Latin for bee). It lies deep in the southern hemisphere, below the horizon for most observers in the northern hemisphere. The constellation *Chamaeleon* lies close by, perhaps trying to catch the fly with its quick, long tongue.

Ophiuchus: serpent grasper. Ophiuchus means "the snake grabber" or "the serpent grasper," the person or god who grasps *Serpens*, from Greek Οφιουξος, *Ophioukhos*. It has also been called by the Latin names *Serpentarius* and *Anguitenens*, both of which have the same meaning as *Ophioukhos*. All three names almost certainly refer to Asklepios or Aesculapius, the ancient Greek god of medicine (see **Asklepios**, Chapter 36). The constellation, which straddles the equator, was listed by Ptolemy.

Pavo: peacock. Pavo is a southern constellation. It was originally named Argos, after the builder of the ship Argo. Juno changed Argos into a peacock and set him with his ship in the night sky.

Pegasus: (flying) horse. Pegasus is named after the famous flying horse of the Greek hero Bellerophon (see Chapter 11). Its three brightest stars, plus the brightest star of adjacent *Andromeda*, form an easily located rectangle called *The Square of Pegasus*. In Hindu astronomy, *Pegasus* covers the 26th and 27th lunar mansions, the place where the Moon goes to sleep. The Babylonians called the constellation Iku (Field), and in Greek it was called simply 'ιππο, *Hippo* (Horse) before it was called *Pegasus*.

Phoenix: phoenix. Phoenix is a small constellation in the southern sky, one of the four Southern Birds, i.e., *Grus, Pavo, Phoenix* and *Tucana* (see below). Arab astronomers called the constellation either *al-Ri'al* (the Young Ostriches) or *al-Zaurak*, (the Boat).

Pisces: fishes. Pisces is a constellation of the zodiac, with Aquarius lying to the west and Aries to the east. They represent the Greek gods Aphrodite and Eros, who escaped from the monster Typhon by leaping into the sea and changing themselves into fish; in the later Roman version of the legend, they are Venus and Cupid.

Piscis Austrinus: southern fish. Piscis Austrinus is a small and faint southern constellation. It had been called *Mul Ku* (the Fish) by the Babylonians. In Egyptian mythology, this was the great fish that saved the life of the goddess Isis. For the Greeks, it was the fish that swam in the stream of water poured by Aquarius, the water-carrier. It was the mother of the two fishes called Pisces (see above).

Scorpius: scorpion. Scorpius is another constellation of the zodiac. In Greek mythology, the hunter Orion boasted that he would hunt and kill every living creature on Earth. Artemis and her mother Leto sent a scorpion to kill Orion. Zeus set the scorpion in the sky, to commemorate the feat, and Orion as a warning to hunters (and humans in general) not to be boastful or proud. Every winter, huge Orion crosses the sky with his sword and famous belt, followed by the dog-star, Sirius, both of them pursued by the little, deadly scorpion.

Serpens: serpent. Serpens is divided into two parts (the only constellation so divided), with *Serpens Caput* (Head of the Serpent) to the west and *Serpens Cauda* (Tail of the Serpent) to the east of *Ophiuchus*, or Asklepios the serpent-bearer (see above). *Serpens Cauda* crosses the galactic plane of the Milky Way, so it is filled with objects of great astronomical interest, including the spectacular Pillars of Creation, three huge galactic dust clouds photographed by the Hubble Space Telescope and widely circulated and admired.

Taurus: bull. Taurus is a large and prominent constellation of the zodiac. It is easily recognized by the horn-tips, of which the brighter is Elnath or β *Tauri*, and the bright red eye of the bull, the red giant Aldebaran or α *Tauri*. A cave painting in Lascaux, France, which dates from about 15000 BCE, appears to be a depiction of the bull of the constellation, with the star-cluster called the *Pleiades* included. In the Old Babylonian epic *Gilgamesh*, the goddess Ishtar sends Taurus the bull to kill Gilgamesh. The Egyptians and Greeks interpreted the spatial relationships of the constellation's stars differently, but they both saw it as a great and sacred bull: the Greeks specifically identified the constellation with Zeus. The ancient Celtic Druids also paid special homage to *Taurus*, assigning it to the spring god Bel, Belinus or Beli Mawr (Great Bel), and (after the Roman occupation) to the many Celtic gods associated with the Roman god of war, Mars. The Inuit of the arctic regions see Aldebaran as a polar bear, the stars of the Hyades being dogs who have cornered the bear menacingly.[6]

Tucana: toucan. Tucana is a faint southern constellation, named after the South American bird. One of its stars, ζ (zeta) *Tucanae*, is very similar to our own Sun, so it has attracted interest as a possible solar system with a planet similar to our own, although none has yet been found.

Ursa Major, Ursa Minor: big bear, little bear. These well-known constellations are associated mainly with the Greek legend of Callisto. Callisto (Most Beautiful) was a nymph in Greek mythology, who attracted the attentions of Zeus. Callisto worshiped the goddess Artemis (whose totem was the bear), and had taken a vow of chastity. Zeus therefore used cunning as well as force to rape her. He appeared first in the form of Artemis and began caressing her, which Callisto found both pleasing and confusing, then shifted back to his own form to complete the assault.

There are three different versions of how Callisto became a bear: Zeus transformed her, to hide her from his wife, Hera; Artemis transformed her, to protect her faithful follower from further predations by Zeus; Hera transformed her to punish Zeus for his philandering. There are also several different endings to the story, but they all agree that Callisto bore a son, called Arcas.

Zeus placed Callisto in the sky as the constellation Arctos, with Arcas beside her as the constellation Arctophylax (Bear Watcher). The Romans later called these constellations Ursa Major (Great Bear) and Ursa Minor (Little Bear).

Hera was unhappy to see Callisto and Arcas honored by being made constellations.

She appealed to her former nurse, the sea-goddess Tethys, and to Tethys's husband, the god Oceanus, begging them never to allow Callisto and Arcas to enter their realm. That is why these constellations circle endlessly around Polaris, the northern Pole Star.

Ursa Major also has the asterisms The Plough, The Big Dipper, The Wagon and Charles's Wain. It was recorded by Ptolemy in the 2nd century CE, but was known long before then. In Indo-Chinese-Vietnamese mythology, it represents Van Xuong, the god of literature, and is visualized as an old man holding a pen in his hand. It is the third largest of the modern constellations.

Volans: flying (fish). *Volans*, originally *Piscis Volans*, flying fish, is a small southern constellation. For the Greeks, it represented a flying fish accompanying the nearby ship *Argo*, pursued by the adjoining constellation *Dorado*, the dolphinfish or swordfish (see above).

Although *Volans* itself is not very distinctive, it contains many interesting astronomical objects, including a galaxy known as *The Lindsay-Shapley Ring* after its discoverers. Ring- or doughnut-shaped galaxies are very rare: this one, bright blue in color and 150,000 light years in diameter, was formed by a galactic collision of literally astronomical proportions.[7]

Vulpecula: little fox. *Vulpecula* means little fox, from Latin *vulpes*, fox. This northern constellation is faint, but is easily found because it lies just below (i.e., south of) *Cygnus* the swan, and was no doubt visualized as creeping cautiously towards the swan in hopes of an early dinner, although it was also called *Vulpecula cum ansere*, "the little fox with a goose (in its mouth)."

Stars Named After Animals

There are about 10,000 visible stars in the night sky, but only a few hundred of them have names. Very often they are named by asterisms, which, as we have already seen, are popular names given to a group of stars or individual stars. So, for example, the star cluster in the constellation *Taurus* officially called the *Pleiades* is more popularly known as the Seven Sisters. If a star is part of a well-known constellation, it may be called by a name connected to the asterism. For example, Phecda in the constellation *Ursa Major* has an official star designation (see paragraph below) but is also known by a common or popular name derived from Arabic *fakhth al-dubb* (Thigh of the Bear). Many star names are derived from Arabic, since the Islamic Golden Age from the 9th to the 13th centuries saw significant advances in Arab astronomy while the West remained relatively inactive and ignorant. Names other than in Arabic are generally either Greek or Latin.

The official designation of a star, as opposed to its popular name, follows a regular pattern, originally devised by the German astronomer Johann Bayer in 1603. The first part of the name is a Greek letter, which often (but not always) tells us how bright the star is by comparison with other stars in the same constellation or group. In most cases, α (alpha) is the brightest, followed by β (beta), γ (gamma), δ (delta), ε (epsilon), ζ (zeta), η (eta), and so on. When the 24 Greek letters ran out, Bayer continued with Latin letters, first capitals, then lower case. However, Bayer was judging apparent brightness (also called magnitude) by eye, so the brightest star by modern measurement is not always designated α or alpha. Since he could see only some of the southern constellations from Germany, several other designations have since been added to his system. The classification devised later by the English astronomer and first Astronomer Royal John Flamsteed (1646–1719) uses numbers rather than Greek and Roman letters, so Chalawan or 47 *Ursae Majoris* (see below) is 47th in the long list of stars in that constellation.

The second part of the designation (either Bayer or Flamsteed) is the name of the constellation in Latin, but in the genitive case or form, showing possession, i.e., "of" or "belonging to." So, Phecda in the previous paragraph is designated γ *Ursae Majoris* or *gamma Ursae Majoris*, meaning "*gamma* (or the third brightest star) of *Ursa Major*."

Modern star names are listed by the International Astronomical Union. The following are some of the more notable stars that are named after animals or have a connection with animal mythology:

Acrab	β *Scorpii*	The Scorpion	From Arabic *al-aqrab*, the scorpion.
Acubens	α *Cancri*	The Claws	From Arabic *al-zubanah*, the claws, referring to the claws of *Cancer*, the crab.
Adhafera	ζ *Leonis*	The Braid	From Arabic *al-dafirah*, braid or curl, here meaning "strand of the lion's mane."
Aladfar	η *Lyrae*	The Talons	From Arabic *al-uzfur*, the talons (of the swooping eagle).
Alchiba	α *Corvi*	The Tent	From Arabic *al-xiba*, the tent. Also called *Rostrum Corvi* (Beak of the Crow) in Latin.
Alcyone	η *Tauri*	Alcyone	From Alcyone in Greek mythology (who also gave her name to the halcyon or kingfisher), one of the Pleiades, the seven daughters of the god Atlas. The *Pleiades* is a star-cluster in *Taurus*.
Aldebaran	α *Tauri*	The Follower	From Arabic *al-dabaran*, follower (of the Pleiades), also called by the asterism The Eye of the Bull.
Aldhanab	γ *Gruis*	The Tail	From Arabic *al-danab*, the tail. Although the star is in *Grus*, the crane, the name refers to the tail of *Piscis Austrinus*, the Southern Fish.
Aldhibah	ζ *Draconis*	The Hyenas	From Arabic *al-diba*, the hyenas.
Algorab	δ *Corvi*	The Crow	From Arabic *al-ghurab*, the crow.
Altair	α *Aquilae*	The Flying (Eagle)	From Arabic (*al-nasr*) *al-ta'ir*, the flying (eagle).
Anser	α *Vulpeculae*	The Goose	From Latin *anser*, goose. The goose is held in the jaws of Vulpecula, the little fox.
Arcturus	α *Boötis*	Of the North	After Arcas, King of Arcadia and son of Zeus and Callisto—he watches over his mother, whom Zeus turned into the Great Bear.
Arneb	α *Leporis*	The Hare	From Arabic *ar-nab*, the hare.
Azelfafage	π *Cygni*	(meaning uncertain, see right)	Possibly from Arabic *al-sulahfah*, turtle, or *al-tilf al-faras*, horse track, or *al-azal al-dajajah*, the tail of the hen (see **Deneb** below).

Azha	η *Eridani*	Nest	From Arabic *azha*, nest (of the ostrich).
Betelgeuse	α *Orionis*	(meaning unclear, see right)	From Arabic, either *ibt-al-jauza*, armpit of the hunter, or *yad-al-jauza*, hand of the hunter. Pronounced several different ways, including Beetle-Juice.
Canopus	α *Carinae*	Canopus	After Canopus in Greek mythology. The brightest star in the constellation *Carina*, and the second-brightest star in the southern sky after Sirius, from Greek Κανωβος, *Kanōbos*, Latinized as Canopus. The constellation is called Agastya in Hindu astronomy, after Agastya who fashioned a wife, Lopamudra, from animal parts (see Chapter 40). Canopus was the mythical navigator for Menelaus, King of Sparta. He died from a serpent bite. The name of the constellation *Carina* means keel, and refers to the ship *Argo*.
Capella	α *Aurigae*	The Little Nanny Goat	From Latin *capra*, goat. In classical mythology, the goat-goddess Amalthea (Gentle Goddess) suckled Zeus.
Chalawan	47 *Ursae Majoris*	Chalawan	An unusual star name, derived from Chalawan, a crocodile king in Thai mythology.
Deneb	α *Cygni*	The Tail of the Hen	A very bright and easily found star, the "head" of the Northern Cross. The less bright star **Azelfafage** or π *Cygni* (see above) may take its name from *al-azal al-dajajah*, the tail of the hen, but *al-dhanab al-dajajah*, also meaning the tail of the hen, is given as the most likely derivation for Deneb.
Dziban	ψ *Draconis*	The Two Wolves/Jackals	From Arabic *al-dhi'ban*, meaning either the two wolves or the two jackals. Actually a triple star system, but close enough (about 75 light years) for the two brightest component stars to be seen separately, hence the Arabic dual name.
Elnath	β *Tauri*	The Butting	From Arabic *al-nath*, the butting (of the bull's horns).
Eltanin	γ *Draconis*	The Great Serpent or The Five Camels	From Arabic *al-tinnin*, the great serpent, but also called *al-'awaid*, the five (Dromedary) camels, or *Quinque Dromedarii* in Latin.
Fafnir	42 *Draconis*	Fafnir	After Fafnir the dwarf in Norse mythology, whose greed led him to shape-shift into a treasure-guarding dragon.

Fomalhaut	α *Piscis Austrini*	Mouth of the Fish	From Arabic *fum al-haut*, mouth of the fish. It was also called *al-difdi al-'awwal*, the first frog. This very bright star was designated "royal" by ancient Persian astrologers. It was called *os piscis meridionalis* or "mouth of the southern fish" in Latin. In 1980, astronomer Jack Robinson proposed that Native Americans had aligned cairns to Fomalhaut at the Bighorn Medicine Wheel in Wyoming, USA, and the Moose Mountain Medicine Wheel in Saskatchewan, Canada.[8]
Hamal	α *Arietis*	Head of the Ram	From Arabic *ras al-hamal*, head of the ram. This star was anciently high in the sky at the time of the vernal equinox, and so has become associated with spring planting.
Menkar	α *Ceti*	Nostril (of the Whale)	Either from Arabic *manhar*, nostril, or *al-minhar*, the nose.
Peacock	α *Pavonis*	Peacock	A rare English name among star names, in the constellation *Pavo*, which is Latin for peacock. The designation was made by the British Nautical Almanac Office in the 1930s.
Prima Hyadum	γ *Tauri*	First Hyad	Latin for "the first hyad" (rain-making nymph). The Hyades is a star-cluster within *Taurus*.
Procyon	α *Canis minoris*	Before the Dog	From Greek προκυον, *prokúon*, preceding the dog, i.e., the dog-star or Sirius (see below). Procyon is a binary star system just 11.46 light years from Earth (that's still a very long way, but it's a near neighbor in astronomical terms). The Babylonians called the star Nangar (the Carpenter). In Hawaiian mythology, Procyon was a prominent navigational guide, part of the star group they call *Ke ka o Makali'i*, the canoe bailer of Makali'i. The Tahitians call it *Anâ-tahu'a-vahine-o-toa-te-manava* (Star the Priestess of Brave Heart).[9] The Inuit call the star Sikuliarsiujuittuq, which means "the one who never goes out on the newly-formed sea ice." The legend behind the name describes a fat man who stole food from his neighbors because he was too fat and lazy to hunt for himself. The other hunters forced him out onto the new sea ice. He fell through into the sea and tried to climb out, but the hunters cut him with their harpoons and knives until he vanished beneath the ice, leaving behind blood stains the same red color as the star Sikuliarsiujuittuq when it rises above the waves during the Arctic winter.[10]

Rigil Kentaurus	α *Centauri*	Foot of the Centaur	From Arabic *rijl qanturis*, foot of the centaur.
Sirius	α *Canis majoris*	Scorching	From Greek Σειριος, *Seirios*, glowing or scorching. The brightest star in the sky. Originally a faithful dog named Μερα, Mera (Shining) in Greek mythology, later called Sirius. The star has over 50 other names from different languages and traditions. In Sanskrit it was Mrgavyadha, deer hunter. In Scandinavia it has been called Lokabrenna, Loki's burning. In ancient Persian Zoroastrianism, it was Tishtrya, the rain-god. In several Native American mythologies, Sirius plays a major role and is often characterized as either a dog or a wolf. The star is even mentioned in the Qur'an, where it is called *ash-shirah*, the leader.
Toliman	α *Centauri*	The Two Ostriches	From Arabic *zaliman*, two (male) ostriches.
Unukalhai	α *Serpentis*	Neck of the Serpent	From Arabic *unuk al-hayyati*, neck of the serpent, which was later Latinized as *Cor Serpentis*, heart of the serpent.
Vega	α *Lyrae*	Landing Vulture	From Arabic *al-nasr al-waqi*, the alighting vulture, Latinized as *Vulture Cadens*, falling vulture. Vega was the northern Pole Star about 14,000 years ago, and it will be again in the year 13727, for those of us who can wait that long. In Polynesia, it is called *whetu o te tau*, star of the year.

Glossary

(This glossary includes the main Greek- and Latin-based names and name-parts used in scientific animal classification that appear in this book. Animal scientific names that can be easily recognized and understood, e.g., *Alligator mississippiensis*, are omitted. Greek means Ancient Greek throughout.)

abaton   An isolated sleeping chamber in a temple or religious site, where visitors would seek inspiration or healing through dreams. (Greek, literally "Do not tread.")

Accipitrinae   Hawks. (Latin *accipiter*, seizer, from Greek ωκυπτερος, *ōkypteros*, swift-winged.)

Acinonyx jubatus   Cheetah. (Greek ακινετος, *akínetos*, motionless, and ονυξ, *onyx*, claw, and Latin *jubatus*, maned.)

Acipenserinae   Sturgeon. (Latin *acipenser*, sturgeon.)

Acoelomorpha   Flatworms. (Greek α-, *a-*, not + κοιλος, *koilos*, coiled or hollow + μορφη, *morphé*, shape.)

Actinopterygia   Ray-finned fishes (about 99 percent of all known fish). (New Latin *actino-*, having rays + Greek πτερυξ, *ptérux*, wing.)

ahimsa   The doctrine that all life is sacred, found mostly in Hinduism, Buddhism and Jainism, which many people follow by eating vegetarian or vegan diets. Jains are known for wearing face masks and sweeping the ground they are about to walk on to avoid killing even the smallest insect. (Sanskrit *ahimsa*, no harm.)

Ailuropoda melanoleuca   Panda. (Greek αιλουρος, *aïlouros*, domestic cat, and ποδα, *poda*, foot, so "cat-footed." The species name *melanoleuca* is New Latin for "black and white.")

Ailurus fulgens   Red panda. (Greek αιλουρος, *aïlouros*, domestic cat and Latin *fulgens*, shining.)

Alces alces   Moose. (Greek αλκε, *álke* and Latin *alces*, possibly borrowed from very early Germanic loanwords.)

Ammonoidea   Ammonites, a fossilized species of cephalopods. (Latin *Ammonis cornu*, "horn of Ammon," an ancient Middle Eastern region where the city Amman in Jordan now stands.)

Amphibia/us   Amphibious, of land and water. (Greek αμφι, *amphi*, both, + βιος, *bíos*, life.)

anadromous   Living in salt water, but migrating to freshwater to breed, like salmon and striped bass. (See also **catadromous** below.)

Anatidae   Ducks, swans and geese. (Latin *anas*, duck.)

Anguilliformes   Eels. (Latin *anguilla*, eel, + *formes*, shaped.)

anima   Breath, physical life. (Latin.)

animism   The belief that all things are alive, and have a spirit or soul. (Latin *animus*, spirit or soul.)

animus   Spirit, soul. (Latin.)

ankh   The ancient Egyptian symbol of eternal life, often reproduced in jewelry to this day. It is a cross with a loop instead of the top arm.

Annelida   Segmented worms. (Latin *annellus*, little ring.)

Annwn   The Celtic Underworld. (Welsh.)

Anserinae   Geese. (Latin *anser*, goose.)

Anura   Frogs and toads. (New Latin *an*, without, + Greek ουρα, *oura*, tail.)

Apocrita   Wasps. (Greek αποκριτος, *apókritos*, separated or chosen.)

Apodemus   Genus of field mice. (Greek, απο, *apo*, away from, and δεμος, *demos*, house or home.)

Apoidea   Bees. (Latin *apis*, bee.)

Arachnida   Spiders, scorpions, ticks and mites. (The Greek goddess Arachne.)

arhat   In Buddhism, a person who has achieved **nirvana** or perfection. (Sanskrit, enlightened.)

artio-   Even in number, as in **artiodactyla** (see below). (Greek αρτιο, *ártio*, even.)

artiodactyla   Having an even number of toes. (Greek αρτιο, *ártio*, even, and δακτυλοσ, *daktylos*, finger.)

Aves   Birds. (Latin, plural of *avis*, bird.)

ba   In ancient Egypt, the *ba* was a person's eternal soul.

Balaenoptera musculus   Blue whale, largest animal ever known to have existed. (Latin *balæna*, baleen, + *musculus*, muscular.)

BCE   Before the Common Era. (Replaces the outdated B.C., Before Christ)

Belemnoidea   Belemnites, a fossilized species of cephalopods. (Greek βελεμνον, *bélemnon*, dart or javelin.)

Bison bison   American bison. (Latin, wild ox.)

Bison bonasus   European bison. (Latin, *bison*, wild ox, and Greek βονασος, *bonásos*, also meaning bison.)

Bos taurus   Cow or bull. (Latin, *bos*, cattle, and *taurus*, bull.)

Bovidae   Cattle, oxen. (Greek βους, *bous* and Latin *bos*, cattle.)

Brachyura   Crabs. (New Latin, from Greek βραξυς, *brachys*, short, and ουρα, *oura*, tail.)

Branta   Canada goose. (Old Norse *brandgás*, burned black.)

Branta leucopsis   Barnacle goose. (Old Norse *brandgás*, burned black + Greek λευκοσ, *leukos*, white and οπσισ, *opsis*, face.)

Bubalus arnee   Wild water buffalo. (Greek βουβαλος, *boúbalos*, buffalo, and Hindi *arni* or *arnee*, the female variant of *arna*, water buffalo.)

Bubalus bubalis   Domesticated water buffalo. (Greek βουβαλος, *boúbalos*, buffalo.)

Bubalus mindorensis   Dwarf buffalo of the Philippines. (Greek βουβαλος, *boúbalos*, buffalo, and Mindoro, Philippine place-name.)

Buteo   Buzzard. (Latin.)

Camelus   Bactrian camel (two humps). (Latin *camelus* + Bactria, place- **bactrianus** name.)

Camelus dromedarius   Dromedary camel (one hump). (Latin *camelus* + Greek δρομας, *dromas*, running.)

Camelus ferus   Wild camel. (Latin, *camelus*, camel, + *ferus*, wild.)

Canidae   Dogs. (Plural of Latin *canis*, dog.)

canis   Dog. (Latin.) (Since dogs are descended from wolves, the name **canis lupus**, dog wolf, is also used, for both dogs and wolves.)

Canis adustus   Jackal. (Latin, scorched, i.e., striped dog.)

Canis aureus   Golden jackal. (Latin, golden dog.)

Canis latrans Coyote. (Latin, barking dog.)

Canis lupus dingo Dingo, wild dog native to Australia. (Latin and Australian Aboriginal language Dharug, *dingu*, wild dog.)

Canis lupus lupus The Eurasian wolf. (Latin, dog, wolf, wolf.)

Canis lupus lycaon The American timber wolf. (Latin and Greek, dog, wolf, wolf.)

Canis lupus occidentalis The northwestern American timber wolf. (Latin, dog, wolf, western.)

Canis mesomelas Jackal. (Latin, black-backed dog.)

Capra aegagrus hircus Goat. (Latin *capra*, she-goat or smell of the armpits, *aegagrus,* of Persia/Iran, and *hircus* smelly he-goat or filthy person.)

Capra ibex The Alpine ibex. (Latin, *capra*, she-goat, and *ibex*, ibex.)

Caprinae Sheep and goats, a subfamily of the family *Bovinae*. (Latin *capra*, female goat.)

caribou (See **Rangifer tarandus** below.)

Carnivora, carnivores Meat eaters. (Latin *carnis*, meat.)

Castor Canadian beaver. (Latin, *castor*, beaver.)

Castor fiber Beaver. (Latin *castor* and *fiber*, both words meaning beaver.)

catadromous Living in fresh water, but migrating to breed in salt water, like eels. (See also **anadromous** above.)

Cathartidae Vultures or condors. (Greek καθαρτες, *kathartes*, purifier.)

CE Of the Common Era. (Replaces the outdated A.D., *Anno Domini*, In the Year of the Lord.)

Cephalopoda Squid, cuttlefish and octopuses. (Greek κεφαλόποδα, *kephalópoda*, head-feet.)

Cercopithecoidea Old World monkeys. (Greek κερκος, *kérkos*, tail, + πιθεκος, *pithekos*, monkey.)

Cervus canadensis Elk or wapiti. (Latin *cervus*, deer, and New Latin *canadensis*, Canadian. Wapiti is from Shawnee and Cree *wapiiti*, white rump.)

Cervus elaphus Red deer. (Latin *cervus*, deer, and Greek ελαφος, *élaphos,* also meaning deer.)

Cetacea Whales. (From Greek κετος, *ketos*, great fish, which became *cetus* in Latin.)

chevrotain African mouse deer. (French, little goat.)

Chiroptera Bats. (Greek, ξειρ, *khéir*, hand, + πτερον, *pterón*, wing.)

Chondrichthyes Cartilaginous fishes, including sharks, rays, skates, and sawfish. (Greek ξονδρος, *khóndros*, grain, corn or cartilage, + ιξθυς, *ikhthús*, fish.)

Chordata Animals which have a backbone or spine. (Latin.)

Ciconia Stork (Latin.)

clade A group of animals sharing a common ancestry. (Greek κλαδος, *klados*, branch.)

cladogram A chart or diagram showing how individual species are related to each other. (Greek κλαδος, *klados*, branch and γραφειν, *gráphein*, to write.)

Cnidaria Jellyfish, corals and anemones. (Greek κνιδη, *knide*, nettle.)

Coleoptera Beetles. (Greek κολεος, *koleós*, sheath, and πτερον, *pterón*, wing.)

Coloeus monedula Jackdaw. (Greek κολοιος, *koloiós*, jackdaw, + Latin *moneta*, money.)

Columba Dove or pigeon. (Latin.)

Corvidae Crows. (Latin, *corvus*, crow or raven.)

Corvus frugilegus Rook. (Latin, *corvus*, crow or raven, + *frugilegus*, grain- gathering.)

Crocuta crocuta Spotted or laughing hyena. (Greek κροκοττας, *krokóttas*, which originally signified the golden jackal, now called **Canis aureus**.)

Crustacea Animals with shells. (Latin *crusta*, shell.)

Cuculidae Cuckoos. (Greek κοκκυξ, *kókkux*, and Latin *cuculus*, cuckoo.)

Culicidae Mosquitoes. (Latin *culex*, genitive *culicis*, gnat.)

Cygnus cygnus Swan. (Latin.)

Cyprinus carpio Carp. (Greek κυπρινος, *kuprinos*, carp, + Latin *carpa*, also carp.)

-dactyla -toed, as in **artiodactyla** (see above) and **perissodactyla** (see below). (Greek δακτυλοσ, *daktylos*, finger.)

Dama dama Fallow deer. (Latin, *dama* or *damma*, deer or venison.)

Desmodus rotundus Mouse-sized common vampire bat of Central and South America. (Greek δεσμος, *desmós*, fetter, + Latin *rotundus*, round.)

dharma Truth, doctrine, or cosmic law and order, or the teachings of the Buddha, found in Hinduism, Buddhism, Jainism and Sikhism. (Sanskrit.)

Diaemus youngi White-winged vampire bat. (Genus name *Diaemus* devised by Gerrit S. Miller in 1906, species name *youngi* given in honor of Dr. Charles Grove Young, 1849–1934.)

Diomedae Great albatrosses. (From Greek warrior god Diomedes.)

Diphylla ecaudata Hairy-legged vampire bat. (Latin *dis*, double, and *phyllon*, leaf, + *e*, without and *cauda*, tail.)

Diptera Flies. (Greek δι, *di*, two, and πτερον, *pterón*, wing.)

diurnal Active by day, opposite of **nocturnal**. (Latin *dies*, day.)

dokhma Death tower used by ancient Zoroastrians where bodies decomposed naturally. (Persian.)

domestica/us Domesticated. (Latin.)

-donta -toothed, as in **loxodonta** (see below). (Greek οδουσ, *odoús*, stem *odont-*, tooth.)

Echinodermata Starfish and sea urchins. (Greek εξινος, *ekhinos*, hedgehog, + δερμα, *dérma*, skin.)

Edda (See **Poetic Edda** and **Prose Edda** below.)

Elephas maximus Indian elephant. (Greek ελεφα⍵, *elephas*, elephant, + Latin *maximus*, very big.)

elk (See **Cervus canadensis** above.)

endoskeletal Having a bony skeleton on the inside. (Greek, ενδον-, *endón-*, within, and σκελετοσ, *skeletós*, skeleton.)

entheogen Any substance used to promote or enhance spiritual experiences, e.g., alcohol or psychotropic drugs. (Greek, literally *en-*, in, + *theos*, god, + *-gen*, maker.)

Epic of Gilgamesh Major religious/mythological text of ancient Mesopotamia (parts of modern Iraq, Kuwait, Saudi Arabia, Turkey and Iran) written sometime between 2800 and 2500 BCE.

Equidae Horses. (Latin.)

Equus africanus asinus Ass or donkey. (Latin, *equus*, horse, + *africanus*, African, + *asinus*, ass.)

Equus ferus caballus Horse. (Latin, *equus*, horse, + *ferus*, wild, + *caballus*, also horse.)

Equus hemionus Onager or wild ass. (Latin *equus*, horse, + *hemionus*, part load-bearing.)

Erethizontidae New World porcupines. (Greek ερεθιζειν, *erethizein*, irritate.)

Erinaceidae Family of hedgehogs. (Latin *erinaceus*, hedgehog.)

Erithacus rubecula European robin. (Greek εριθακος, *erithakos*, robin, + Latin *ruber*, red.)

Esox lucius Pike. (Etymology uncertain.)

eukaryota/es Organisms whose cells have a nucleus (includes all plants and animals). (Greek ευ, *eu*, well or true, and καρυον, *karyon*, nut or kernel.)

Eulipotyphla Order of small mammals including hedgehogs, moles and shrews. (Greek ευ, *eu*, truly, + λιπος, *lipos*, fat, + τυφλος, *tuphlós*, blind or short-sighted.)

Exocoetoidae Flying fish. (Greek εξω-, *exō*, out, and κοιτος, *koitos*, bed.)

exoskeletal Having a hard, shell-like body-supporting system on the outside, rather than a bony skeleton on the inside. Insects are exoskeletal, for example. (Greek, εξο-, *exo-*, outside, and σκελετοσ, *skeletós*, skeleton.)

familiaris Familiar, common. (Latin.)

Feliformes/ia Cat-shaped animals. (Latin *felis*, cat.)

felis Cat. (Latin.)

Felis catus Domestic cat. (Latin *felis*, cat, and New Latin, *catus*, backformed from English cat.)

Felis lybica African wildcat. (Latin and New Latin, cat of Libya.)

Felis lybica ornata The spotted Asian wildcat. (Latin and New Latin, spotted cat of Libya.)

Felis sylvestris Wildcat. (Latin, cat of the woods.)

Formicidae Ants. (Latin *formica*, ant.)

Gallus gallus Chicken. (Latin, rooster.)

Gastropoda The class that includes snails and slugs. (New Latin, from Greek γαστηρ, *gaster*, stomach, + πους, *poús*, foot.)

geis Religious command or taboo (sometimes fate) in Celtic Druidism. (Brythonic Celtic.)

genus The classification level just above species. (Latin, meaning type, group or race.)

Geococcyx californianus, Geococcyx velox Roadrunner. (Greek, γεω, *geō*, earth, and κοκκυξ, *kókkux*, cuckoo, + New Latin *californianus*, Californian, or Latin *velox*, speedy.)

Gilgamesh (See **Epic of Gilgamesh** above.)

Giraffa camelopardalis Giraffe. (Arabic *zarāfa*, giraffe, + Latin *camelus*, camel, + *pardalis*, female panther or leopard.)

Gruoidae Cranes. (Greek γερανος, *geranos*, and Latin *grus*, both meaning crane.)

Haplorhini Suborder of Primates, monkeys without a **rhinarium** (raised area around the nostrils, usually moist). (Greek 'απλος, *haplos*, simple, + 'ρινος, *hrinos*, nose.)

Herbivora, herbivores Animals that eat only plants. (Latin *herba*, vegetation.)

Herpestes Type genus name for mongooses. (New Latin, coined from ancient Greek 'ερπεστες, *herpestes*, creeping.)

Hippocampus heptagonus Sea horse. (Greek 'ιππος, *hippos*, horse, and καμπος, *kámpos*, sea animal or sea monster, + Latin *heptagonus*, seven-angled.)

Hippopotamus amphibius The hippopotamus. (Greek 'ιππο, *hippo*, horse, +ποταμι, *potámi*, river, and Latin *amphibius*, of land and water.)

Hominoidea Apes, Old World tailless simians. (Latin, *homo*, man or humankind.)

Hylobates Genus of gibbons. (Greek 'υλος, *hylos*, creature, and βατος, *batos*, bush.)

Hystricidae Old World porcupines. (Latin, *hystrix*, porcupine.)

Jatakas Major collection of early Buddhist folk stories, also called *Birth-Stories of the Former Lives of the Buddha*, dating from the 4th century BCE. (Sanskrit, commentaries.)

Kalevala Epic poem containing major Finnish mythology, written in the 19th century.

karma An Eastern doctrine, which says that every action or word is a cause, that every cause has an effect, and that every effect returns to the originator of the cause.

Lagomorpha Order of lagomorphs, i.e., hares, rabbits and pikas. (Greek λαγος, *lagos*, hare, and μορφε, *morphé*, shape.)

Lama glama Llama. (New Latin, both words from Peruvian Chechua, *lama*.)

leo Lion. (Latin.)

Lepidoptera Butterflies and moths. (Greek λεπις, *lepís*, scale, and πτερον, *pterón*, wing.)

Leporidae Hares and rabbits. (Latin *lepus*, hare.)

Lepus timidus Hare. (Latin, *lepus*, hare, + *timidus*, timid.)

Lissamphibia Subclass of amphibia that includes frogs, toads, salamanders, newts and caecilians. (Greek λισσος, *lissós*, smooth, + αμφι, *amphi*, both, + βιος, *bíos*, life.)

loxo- Slanting, as in **loxodonta** (see below). (Greek λοξοσ, *loxós*, slanting.)

loxodonta Having tusks. (Greek λοξοσ, *loxós*, slanting, and οδουσ, *odoús*, stem *odont-*, tooth.)

Loxodonta africana African bush elephant. (See **Elephas maximus** and **loxodonta** above.)

Loxodonta cyclotis African forest elephant. (See **loxodonta** above. *Cyclotis* is New Latin for round-eared.)

lupus Wolf. (Latin.) See **canis** above.

Luscidia megarhyncos Nightingale. (Latin, *luscidia*, nightingale, + Greek, μεγα, *mega*, large, and ῾ρυνκος, *hrunkós*, bill.)

Lutra Genus name of otters. (Latin *lutra*, otter.)

Lynx canadiensis Canadian lynx. (Greek *lynx* and New Latin *canadiensis*, Canadian.)

Lynx lynx Lynx. (Greek, possibly meaning bright-eyed.)

Lynx pardinus Iberian lynx. (Greek *lynx* and Latin *pardinus*, little panther.)

Lynx rufus Bobcat. (Greek *lynx* and Latin *rufus*, red.)

Mabinogi(on) Major text in Celtic mythology. (Welsh.)

Macropus Genus name of kangaroos. (Latin, large foot.)

Mahabharata Major Sanskrit epic text of Indian Hinduism, probably begun in the 8th or 9th century BCE, but first appearing in complete written form about 400 BCE.

Malacostraca Largest class of crustaceans, includes crabs, lobsters, crayfish, shrimp, krill, wood-lice and others, a misnomer by French zoologist Pierre André Latreille in 1802, since most of the approximately 40,000 extant species are in fact hard-shelled. (New Latin, from Greek μαλακος, *malakós*, soft, + οστρακον, *ostrakon*, shell.)

Marmota monax Marmot, groundhog or woodchuck. (From Latin, *mus monti*, mountain mouse, + Algonquin *móonack*, digger.)

Mergini Sea ducks. (Name devised by zoologist Constantine Rafinesque in 1815.)

merula Blackbird. (Latin.)

Metamorphoses Major Latin text about mythological stories involving change, written by Roman poet Ovid (43 BCE–18 CE). (Greek, changes.)

Mollusca The phylum of molluscs, including snails and several species of shelled sea animals. (Latin *mollusca/us*, from *mollis*, soft.)

Monodon, monoceros Narwhal. (Greek, one tooth one horn.)

Mus musculus Mouse. (Latin *mus*, mouse or rat, + *musculus*, little mouse—also used for sea mussel.)

Mustela Genus of weasels. (Latin mustella, weasel.)

Mustela putorius furo Ferret or polecat. (Latin *mustella*, weasel, + *putorius*, stinking, + *furo*, thief.)

myrmex Ant. (Greek.)

Myrmidon Ant-Man. (Greek μυρμεξ, *myrmex*, ant.)

Mysticeti Baleen whales, including blue whales, right whales, bowhead whales and gray whales. (Etymology uncertain.)

naga Sanskrit for snake, found in many names of deities. *Nagi* or *nagini* means female snake and *nagaraja* or *rajanaga* means king snake.

New Latin Latin words created during the Renaissance and beyond to describe new scientific ideas and subjects.

nirvana Liberation from the cycle of birth, life and death, found in Buddhism, Hinduism and Jainism. (Sanskrit, literally blown out or extinguished.)

nocturnal Active by night, opposite of **diurnal**. (Latin *nox*, night.)

Odobenus rosmarus Walrus. (Greek οδους, *odous*, tooth, and βαινω, *bainō*, walk, + *rosmarus*, Old Norse, horse of the sea.)

Odontoceti Toothed whales, including dolphins, orca, porpoises, beluga whales, narwhals, sperm whales and beaked whales. (Greek, οδους, *odóus*, tooth, + κετος, *ketos*, sea monster.)

Ogham A secret, sacred alphabet of the Celtic Druidic tradition.

Okapia johnstoni Okapi. (Mvuba language of Uganda, *o'api* + Johnston, explorer's name.)

Omnivora, omnivores Animals that eat both meat and vegetation. (Latin *omnes*, all.)

Oncorhyncus Pacific salmon. (Greek ονκος, *ónkos*, hook, and ρυνξος, *rynkhos*, nose.)

Ornithorhynchus anatinus Duck-billed platypus. (New Latin coined in 1800 by Johann Blumenbach, 1752–1840, *Ornithorhynchus* meaning bird snout, and *anatinus* meaning duck-like.)

Orycteropus afer Aardvark. (Greek ορυκτος, *oruktós*, dug out, and πους, *pous*, foot, + Latin *afer*, African.)

Oryctolagus cuniculus European rabbit. (*Oryct-* is Greek for digging up, and *lagos* is Greek for hare, so the New Latin coining *Oryctolagus* means "hare-like digging animal." The species name *cuniculus* means burrow or small conduit.)

Otariidae Sea lions. (Greek 'ωταριον, *hótarion*, little ears.)

Ovis aries Domestic sheep, ram. (Latin *ovis*, sheep, and Greek εριφος, *ériphos*, domestic animal.)

Pan paniscus Pygmy chimpanzee or bonobo. (From the Greek god Pan, + Latin *paniscus*, a little Pan.)

Panthera Big cats, such as the lion, tiger, jaguar, etc. (Latin.)

Panthera leo Lion. (Latin, big-cat lion.)

Panthera onca Jaguar/panther. (Latin *panthera*, big cat, and *lyncea*, lynx.)

Panthera pardus Leopard. (Greek λεοπαρδος, *leópardos*, from λεων, *léōn*, lion, and παρδος, *párdos*, pard or male panther.)

Panthera tigris Tiger. (Latin, big-cat tiger.)

Pan troglodytes Common chimpanzee. (From the Greek god Pan, + Latin *troglodyta*, cave-dwelling people.)

Pavo Peacock, peahen. (Latin.)

perisso- Odd in number, as in **perissodactyla** (see below). (Greek περισσο, *perisso*, uneven.)

perissodactyla Having an odd number of toes. When animals have an odd number of toes, the middle toe may develop differently to the others, and the outside toes may become smaller or redundant. (Greek περισσο, *perisso*, uneven, and δακτυλοσ, *daktylos*, finger.)

Phocidae Seals. (Latin, *phoca*, seal.)

phylum A broad level of classification, determined by similarities in shape or ancestry. (Greek φυλον, *phylon*, race or stock.)

Picus Woodpecker. (Latin.)

Pinnipedia Clade name for seals, sea lions and walruses. (Latin, *pinna*, fin, + *pes*, foot.)

Pisces Fish. (Plural of Latin *piscis*, fish.)

Platyrrhini   New World monkeys. (Greek πλατυς, *platus*, flat, + ῥινος, *hrinos*, nose.)

Poetic Edda   Major Icelandic poetry text in Old Norse, 13th century. (Etymology uncertain.)

Pongo abelii   Orangutan. (Named after zoologist Othenio Abel, 1875–1946.)

Pongo pygmaeus   Borneo pygmy orangutan. (New Latin *pongo*, from Kongo *mpungu*, orangutan, + *pygmaeus*, pygmy.)

Pongo tapanuliensis   Sumatran orangutan. (New Latin *pongo*, from Kongo *mpungu*, orangutan, + *tapanuliensis*, "from South Tapanuli on the island of Sumatra.")

Porifera   Sponges. (Latin *porus*, pore, + *fera*, bearing.)

Primate   Order which includes apes and monkeys. (Latin, *primus*, first or excellent.)

Procellariidae   Albatrosses, shearwaters, petrels and storm petrels. (Latin, "with tube-shaped noses.")

Procyon lotor   Raccoon. (New Latin, *procyon*, from Greek προ, *pró*, "in place of" and κυων, *kuōn*, dog, and *lotor*, New Latin, laundryman or "one who washes things.")

Prose Edda   Major Icelandic prose text in Old Norse, 13th century. (Etymology uncertain.)

Proteles cristata   Aardwolf, South African hyena. (Greek προτος, *protos*, and τελεος, *teleos*, collectively meaning "complete in front" and Latin *cristata*, crested.)

Proto-Indo-European   The scientifically reconstructed basis from which many Indian and European words may have been derived. Since the words or word-parts have never been attested in text, they are usually written preceded by an asterisk, to show that they are constructs, e.g., **sneg*, the reconstructed possible origin of the English word snake.

psychopomp   A god or spirit who leads the dead into the Underworld. (Greek, ψυξη, *psyche*, soul, + πομπος, *pompós*, leader.)

Puma concolor   Cougar, puma or mountain lion. (Chechua, *puma*, powerful, and Latin, *concolor*, "of the same color.")

quadripedal   Four legged. (Latin.)

Qur'an   The main scriptural text of Islam. (Arabic, "act of reciting.")

Ramayana   Major Hindu text in Sanskrit written sometime between the 7th century and 4th century BCE, relating the exploits of Lord Rama and his wife Sita. There are also Buddhist, Jain and Sikh adaptations, as well as many translations into other languages.

Rangifer tarandus   Caribou or reindeer. (Latin *rangifer*, reindeer, and Greek ταρανδος, *tárandos*, also meaning reindeer.)

reindeer   (See **Rangifer tarandus** above.)

Reptilia   Reptiles, a class that includes turtles, crocodiles and alligators, and lizards, as well as snakes. (Latin *reptilis*, creeping.)

rhinarium   Raised area around the nostrils, usually moist, found in most mammals. (Greek ῥινος, *hrinos*, nose.)

Rodentia   Rodents. (Latin.)

ruminant   Animal that has a specialized stomach to ferment and pre-digest plant foods with low food value, such as grass. (Latin *ruminor*, "chew the cud.")

sag-did   Zoroastrian funerary ritual in which a dog confirms that the person is dead, and keeps evil spirits away. (Also found among Parsees in India.) (Persian.)

Sarcopterygii   Lobed-fin fish. (Greek σαρξ, *sarx*, flesh, + πτερυξ, *ptéryx*, wing.)

Sciuridae   Squirrels. (Latin *sciurulus*, little squirrel.)

Selachimorpha   Sharks and rays. (Greek σελακος, *sélakhos*, cartilaginous fish, and μορφε, *morphe*, "in the shape of.")

shaman   A human priest or celebrant, male or female, whose main function is to enter the world of spirits on behalf of individuals or the community. (*Manchu-Tungus* or Siberian, "one who knows.")

sídhe   Pronounced *shee-uh*, "the fairy folk" in Celtic mythology. (Irish Gaelic.)

Simia belzebul   Howler monkey. (Beelzebub monkey, from Latin *simia*, monkey, and Beelzebub, the name of a Philistine god, and major demon in Judaism, Christianity and Islam.)

Simiiformes   Monkeys and animals similar to monkeys. (Latin, *simia*, monkey.)

sistrum   A West African musical instrument often used in sacred rituals. (Ancient Egyptian *sekhem* and Greek σειστρον, *seïstron*.)

skin-walker   In American Indian traditions, particularly that of the Navajo, an evil being that can shape-shift between human and animal form to confuse and trick people. (American English.)

Squamata   Animals with scales, such as snakes. (Latin *squama*, scale.)

Strigidae   Owls. (Latin *strix*, from Greek στρινξ, *strinx*, screecher.)

Suidae   Pigs. (Latin.)

surah   A section or chapter of the Islamic main scriptural text, the Qur'an. (Arabic.)

Sus scrofa domesticus   Domestic pig. (Latin *sus*, swine, and *scrofa*, sow, +*domesticus*, domestic.)

Sus scrofa sylvestris   Wild pig or boar, not domesticated. (Latin *sylvestris* means "of the woods.")

Syncerus caffer   African or Cape buffalo. (New Latin, Sparrman 1779, African buffalo.)

Tachyglossa   Family of echidnas or spiny anteaters. (New Latin, from Greek ταξυς, *tachys*, quick, and γλωσσα, *glōssa*, tongue.)

tarbhfess   Ancient Celtic Druidic ritual to choose a successor king or queen. (Gaelic, bull sleep.)

taxon   A level of organization in a taxonomy. (Back formation from taxonomy.)

taxonomy   A system for grouping things by common attributes. (Greek ταξις, *taxis*, order or arrangement, see **taxon** above.)

Testudinae   Turtles and tortoises. (Latin *testudo*, shell.)

Thunnus   Tuna. (Latin.)

Troglodytidae   Wren family. (Greek τρωγλε, *trōgle*, hole, and δυω, *duō*, "I get into.")

Turdus merula   Blackbird. (Latin *turdus*, thrush, and *merula*, blackbird.)

Turdus migratorius   American robin. (Latin *turdus*, thrush, and *migratorius*, migratory.)

ungulate   Hoofed animal. (Latin *ungula*, hoof.)

uraeus   The head of a cobra rearing to strike, used widely in Egyptian art to indicate divinity, royalty or authority. (Latin, from Greek ουραιοσ, *ouraïos*, "on its tail," from Egyptian hieroglyphs j'r.t, *iaret*, rearing cobra.)

Ursus americanus   American black bear. (Latin *ursus*, bear, and New Latin *americanus*, American.)

Ursus arctos   Brown bear. (Latin *ursus*, bear, and Greek αρκτος, *arktós*, also meaning bear.)

Ursus lotor   (See **Procyon lotor** above.)

Ursus maritimus   Polar bear. (Latin *ursus*, bear, and *maritimus*, "by or on the sea.")

Ursus thibetanus   Asian black bear or moon bear. (Latin *ursus*, bear, and New Latin *thibetanus*, of Tibet.)

Vicugna pacos   Alpaca. (Etymology uncertain.)

Vicugna vicugna   Vicuña. (Etymology uncertain.)

Vipera   Vipers, adders, or asps. (Probably Latin *vivus*, alive, and *parere*, "to give birth," since giving live birth is common in vipers but not in other snakes.)

Viverroidea   Infraorder name for mongooses, civets, genets and similar animals. (Latin *viverra*, ferret.)

Vulpes vulpes   Fox. (Latin.)

Vulpes zerda   Zennec fox of northern Africa. (Latin *vulpes*, fox, and Greek ξερος, *xeros*, dry place.)

wampum   Hand-crafted items, often from shells or stones, used by several Native American nations during sacred storytelling, as high-value gifts for special ceremonial occasions, and as honor gifts during the negotiation and making of treaties, also used as a kind of currency for high-value transactions.

wapiti   (See **Cervus canadensis** above.)

Whippomorpha   Clade (q.v.) containing whales, dolphins and hippopotamuses. (From English wh[ale] + hippo[potamus] + Greek μορφη, *morphe*, shape.)

Appendix: World Religions and Mythologies

There are many difficulties associated with the paradigm of world religions. Judaism, for example, is always included in the top five of major world religions because of its great influence on Christianity and Islam, but in contemporary demographic terms it is much smaller than either of those two religions. The inclusion of Christianity, which is demographically much larger, is criticized on different grounds, namely that the title now generally signifies Protestant Christianity, which, in the totality of its various forms, has many more followers than Roman Catholicism—in other words, a semantic assumption is tolerated.

Mythological cultures are not the same as religions, but for the purposes of this book they can be included in the same list. Mythologies tend to be more associated with specific geographical areas, and typically arise from oral traditions.

The notes below are intended only as a very simple guide to the major historical and contemporary religions and world mythologies. They are listed in alphabetical order since even approximate chronological order is disputable in some instances.

Abrahamic Religions

The three religions Judaism, Christianity and Islam, so called because the patriarch Abraham figures in all of them. Historically, they arose in the same chronological order as listed above. (See separate entries below.)

Australian Aboriginal Religion and Mythology

Often referred to as the Dreamtime, Dreaming Stories, or Songlines. Similar myths and beliefs are found in several different aboriginal languages. Many involve specific geographical locations and features, similar to First Nations and Native American religion and mythology. Shape-shifting and human-animal hybrids are common themes. Dreamtime is very old—estimates vary from 62,000 to 75,000 years. There are about 900 distinct aboriginal groups, making a total population of about 760,000, but many of these have been converted to Christianity, so the actual number of traditional followers is difficult to determine.

Principal deities: Many aboriginal groups, with different languages and traditions, so there are many deities. The Rainbow Serpent is the most common sacred animal. Captain Cook is a generalized mythical villain, based on the historical explorer James Cook (1728–1789).

Major sacred texts: No written texts (oral tradition, first recorded by European settlers).

Bahá'i

Bahá'i is a world faith established by Bahá'u'lláh in Persia (modern Iran) in 1863. It combines elements from the Abrahamic religions (see above) and believes that all world religions deserve respect and understanding. Its following is now world-wide, with estimates of its followers varying from five million to eight million. It is too modern to have a long or deep tradition of sacred or mythological animals, but its literature does sometimes refer to symbolic animals found in Judaic, Christian and Islamic texts.

Principal deities: One God, who reveals Himself in different manifestations, including Buddha, Jesus and Muhammad.

Prophets: Bahá'u'lláh (1817–1892), leadership continued by his son Abdu'l-Bahá (1844–1921) and his grandson Shoghi Effendi (1897–1957).

Major sacred texts: *The Kitáb-i-Íqán* (*Book of Certitude*), *The Seven Valleys* and *The Four Valleys*.

Buddhism

Buddhism has over 520 million followers, and is the world's fourth-largest religion. It began in ancient India in the 6th century BCE. There are two main branches, *Theravada* (from Pali, School of the Elders) and *Mahayana* (from Sanskrit, The Great Vehicle). *Vajrayana* is a subdivision of *Mahayana* based on the teachings of adepts in India, and Tibetan Buddhism is an important subdivision of *Vajrayana*. The Buddha, or Siddharta Gautama, lived from c. 563 to c. 483 BCE, although the exact dates are disputed. Buddhism focuses on the cycle of life, death and rebirth, and the achievement of *nirvana* or release from that cycle. The Three Refuges (often called The Three Jewels) of Buddhism are: the Gautama Buddha, the historical Buddha; the Dharma, law or way of life which includes the Eightfold Path towards enlightenment; and the Sangha, the community of Buddhist monks worldwide. Animals feature widely in Buddhist teachings, often as symbols of religious ideas.

Principal deity/prophet/teacher: The Buddha, but also many minor deities and icons in different regions.

Major sacred texts: Canon varies from country to country, but is vast. Main texts are: *Vinaya Pitaka*, *Sutta Pitaka* and *Abhidhamma Pitaka* (*The Three Baskets*); *Visuddhimagga* (5th century CE); *Mahayana sutras* (China and Tibet).

Celtic Druidism

The ancient Celts of Europe wove religion into their daily lives, as attested by several classical authors, especially Julius Caesar, who described the beliefs and organization of the Druids of Gaul in some detail. Celtic Druidism was essentially animist, believing that everything has spirit or soul (*anam*, to use the ancient Irish name). The priests of ancient Celtic culture were the Druids. From the 18th century CE onwards, various modern versions of Druidism have come into being, some of them taking an intuitive, nature-led path, some based on scholarly study of ancient Celtic mythology, and some combining both approaches. Animals feature very strongly in Celtic Druidism.

Principal deities: Many hundreds of deities, including: mother goddesses, e.g., Dôn, Madron, Rhiannon, Danu, Macha; healing deities, e.g., Bel or Belenos, Brighid; deities of sacred waters or rivers, e.g., Sequana (Seine), Boanna (Boyne), Sinann (Shannon); solar or warrior gods, e.g., Lugh, Lenus; horse goddesses, e.g., Epona; horned gods, e.g., Cernunnos; divine couples, e.g., Nantosuelta and Sucellos, Sirona and Grannus, Damona and Borvo.

Major sacred texts: No ancient written texts (oral tradition, not captured in writing until the Middle Ages).

Chinese Mythology

China is a vast and ancient country with a huge population, so there are many religious and mythological traditions to be found there. The Han Chinese people make up about 92 percent of the mainland Chinese population, but there are geographical and cultural variations even within the Han community. Animals feature very significantly in Chinese mythology and folklore, as deities, as mythological figures, and as symbols of religious or philosophical ideas.

Principal deities: Many indigenous deities, plus many others imported from Hinduism, Buddhism, Taoism and other sources. Main indigenous deities include: Yùhuáng (The Jade Emperor);

He Xian'gu, Cao Guojiu, Li Tieguai, Lan Caihe, Lü Dongbin, Han Xiangzi, Zhang Guolao and Han Zhongli (The Eight Immortals); Guanyin or Kuan Yin (The Goddess of Mercy, possibly the deity worshiped by the greatest number of humans on the planet); the Laughing Buddha; Zhong Kui (destroyer of evil beings); Chang 'e (The Moon); Xi Wangmu (Queen Mother of the West).

Major sacred texts: Very wide mixture of oral and written traditions, many of them continuing in Chinese media and popular culture.

Christianity

Christianity has well over two billion followers worldwide. Christianity uses animals as symbols, but denies that animals have souls or spirits: the Bible specifically states that God included animals in the Creation for humankind's use.

Principal deity: One God, who manifests in three forms or names: God the Father, Jesus Christ or the Son of God, and the Holy Spirit, known collectively as the Holy Trinity.

Major sacred text: The Bible, which is in two parts, the Old Testament and the New Testament. The first five books of the Old Testament, called the Pentateuch, are also part of the Judaic canon. The New Testament contains several books, but mainly features the accounts written by the four evangelists, Matthew, Mark, Luke and John, of the life, teachings, death, and resurrection of Jesus Christ.

Confucianism

Confucianism is based on the teachings of the Chinese philosopher Confucius or Kong Fuzi (Master Kong, 551–479 BCE). It transcends the division between religion and humanism, and many of its followers would describe it as simply a way of life. It believes that humans are fundamentally good, and can be taught to be even better. Animals are treated with compassion and respect.

Principal deities: Kong Fuzi was not a god, but a teacher. Some Confucian rituals have sacred liturgies: the gods are worshiped because they represent the *zhèngtong* or ideal praxis of moral behavior.

Major sacred texts: *The Five Classics*, which consist of: *The I Ching* (*Book of Changes*), with which many Westerners will be familiar as a book of divination and prognostication; *The Book of Songs*, an anthology of ancient sacred, moral and philosophical Chinese poetry; *The Book of History*, a collection of historical speeches; *The Book of Rites,* a manual for all formal protocols and procedures; and *The Spring and Autumn Annals*, which examine the period 771–476 BCE in detail, drawing lessons for future living and governance.

The Egyptian Pantheon

Ancient Egyptian religion flourished from c. 3000 BCE to the 1st century CE, when Roman occupation brought their classical gods to Egypt. The pantheon is extremely complex, and animals are very much part of the overall picture—several gods are depicted as human-animal hybrids. The principal deities also feature in the complex Osiris myth. From hieroglyphs carved in stone to sophisticated commentary by Greek and Roman authors, we have a huge amount of information about ancient Egyptian religion. As a result, many modern pagans still worship Egyptian deities, in a variety of geographical and cultural settings.

Principal deities: The pantheon is vast. The major deities include: Nun (chaos); Geb (the Earth); Nut (the sky); Ra (the Sun); Thoth (ibis-headed); Horus (falcon-headed sky god); Osiris (god of the underworld and rebirth); Set or Seth (god of chaos); Isis (goddess of healing and the afterlife, sister and wife of Osiris); Anubis (jackal-headed god of death and mummification).

Major sacred texts: First hieroglyphs and inscriptions date from 3100 to 2686 BCE. *The Pyramid Texts* (funerary incantations) date from the 24th century BCE. *The Book of the Dead* (often called *The Egyptian Book of the Dead* to distinguish it from *The Tibetan Book of the Dead*) dates from the 6th century BCE.

First Nations and Native American Religions and Mythology

The various waves of colonization and settlement in North and South America pushed native indigenous cultures to the fringes, often into complete obscurity, from the 16th to the 20th century CE. However, during the 20th and now into the 21st century, greater respect has been shown to these ancient native cultures. The traditions are very rich and varied. They are mostly animist, but many of them also recognize a universal Creator, called by many names. Many indigenous nations are now fighting back against the destruction and dissolution of their ancient cultures and languages.

Principal deities: Names for the Great Creator include: Gitche Manitou (Great Spirit, Algonquian); Nanook (Master of Bears, Inuit); Coyote (Trickster, Navajo); and Atabey (Mother, Tainó). There are hundreds—perhaps thousands—of other Native American names for gods and mythological beings.

Major sacred texts: No written texts (oral tradition).

The Greek Pantheon

The ancient Greeks introduced many important ideas and beliefs to world culture. They built an important tradition of pure philosophy and science, with particular emphasis on mathematics (especially geometry). They also had a large and complex pantheon of deities and heroes, making classical Greek mythology one of the most widely studied fields in human culture. Animals feature very strongly in Greek mythology, particularly as exemplified in the *Metamorphoses* (Changes or Transformations) of the poet Ovid (43 BCE–18 CE), where changing from human to animal form is the major theme of every story.

Principal deities: Zeus (father of the gods); Hera (wife of Zeus); Apollo (sun god); Aphrodite (goddess of love and beauty); Ares (god of war); Artemis (goddess of the Moon); Athena (goddess of wisdom, the arts and military strategy); Dionysus (god of wine and pleasure); Gaia (Mother Earth); Dis (king of the underworld or Hades); Hermes (psychopomp and messenger of the gods); Nike (goddess of victory); Pan (god of woods and wild animals); Poseidon (god of the sea); Selene (the Moon).

Major texts: The ancient Greek legends are found in a large number of poets and other writers. The following are the best known: Aeschylus (525–455 BCE); Æsop (c. 620–564 BCE); Diodorus Siculus (1st century BCE); Herodotus (484–425 BCE, often called "the father of history"); Homer (dates unknown); Sophocles (496–405 BCE).

Hinduism

Hinduism is probably the most complex of the world's religions, at least in the size and scope of its huge pantheon of deities and avatars (material manifestations of a deity in another form or life). Hinduism began in India sometime between 500 and 300 BCE. It is a religion, but also a *dharma*, which means "way of life" but also rules or duties. The mythology of Hinduism is vast. Many Hindu gods are portrayed as animals or human-animal hybrids, and a Hindu tradition is that most deities ride a particular animal as their mount or spiritual companion.

Principal deities: The pantheon is extremely large and very complex. The three main gods are Brahma (the Creator), Vishnu (the Preserver) and Siva or Shiva (the Destroyer). They have wives, respectively Saraswati (goddess of knowledge and learning), Lakshmi (goddess of wealth and prosperity) and Parvati (goddess of fertility, love and beauty). These deities appear in several subsequent incarnations, or as avatars. The best known are Rama (the seventh avatar of the god Vishnu) and Krishna (the eighth). The other best known Hindu gods or avatars are: Ganesh or Ganesha (the elephant god of wisdom, remover of all obstacles) and Hanuman (the monkey god and devotee of Rama).

Major sacred texts: The main scriptures are the *Vedas* (the oldest scriptures), the *Upanishads* (also called the *Vedanta*, or interpretation of the *Vedas*), the *Bhagavad Gita* (part of the epic poem the *Mahabharata*), and the *Ramayana* (the life of the deity Rama).

Islam

Islam has about 1.8 billion followers across the world. The name means submission (to the will of God). Islam is based on the teaching of the prophet Muhammad, who lived from c. 570–632 CE. Islam incorporates elements from Judaism and Christianity. As in those other Abrahamic religions, animals have no souls and cannot be deities. Nevertheless, Islamic commentary and literature includes several references to animals and animal stories.

Principal deity: One God, called Allah, and the prophet Muhammad (various spellings) as the messenger of God. Islam recognizes Jesus of Nazareth as a holy prophet.

Major sacred texts: The main scripture is the Qur'an or Koran (various spellings, transliterations of the Arabic name), which is divided into sections called *surahs*.

Jainism

Jainism or *Jain Dharma* ("Way of Life of the Victor") is simultaneously a religion, a philosophy and a way of life (one of the meanings of *dharma*). In the same way that Buddhists seek *nirvana*, Jainists seek *Kevala Jnana* ("knowledge of all things"), through a program of asceticism and meditation. One of their main principles is *ahimsa* (non-violence). Jains are vegans who go to great lengths to avoid harming any living creature, including insects. They may sweep the ground before them so that no life will be injured or killed by their walking, they may refuse to go outside in the rain for fear that their heavy wet robes will hurt or kill insects, they may even wear face masks so that they do not accidentally breathe in small insects. Jainism has about five million followers, mostly in India.

Principal deities: Jains worship 24 *tirthankaras* (teachers who have successfully crossed the bridge from the material world to the world of pure spirit). The first of these is Rishabhanatha, who, according to Jains, lived millions of years ago. The twenty-third *tirthankara* was Partshvanatha, who lived around 900 BCE, and was succeeded by the twenty-fourth *tirthankara*, the Mahavira, in about 500 BCE.

Major sacred texts: Jainism is very ancient, and its first texts were written down thousands of years after their oral traditions began. There are two major sects of Jainism, the Digambara and the Svetambara, and they do not agree on which texts are canonical.

Japanese Mythology

Japanese mythology and native religion encompasses a very wide range of themes and legends, several of them combining elements from Shinto (see below), Buddhism (see above) and indigenous folklore. The word *kami* in Japanese can mean gods or spirits, or the god or the spirit inside every person. (Japanese words can be either singular or plural, depending on the context.) *Kami* features both in Japanese mythology and in formal Shinto. Animals and human-animal hybrids appear very frequently in Japanese mythology.

Principal deities or mythological beings: The *Kamiumi* or gods of the Creation were Izanagi no Mikoto (Exalted Lord) and Izanami no Mikoto (Exalted Lady). Their eight children were the first islands of Japan: Awaji, Iyo (later Shikoku), Oki, Tsukushi (later Kyushu), Iki, Tsushima, Sado and Yamato (later Honshu). (Hokkaido, Chishima and Okinawa were not included.) Amaterasu is a powerful sun goddess. Susanoo is a great dragon-slayer. Several early emperors also reappear as gods or divine heroes.

Major sacred texts: No written texts (oral tradition).

Judaism

Judaism is the most ancient of the three Abrahamic religions. There are approximately 17 million followers of Judaism in the world, most of them Jews by birth. Various interpretations of Jewish scripture and law have led to modern Judaism dividing into three groups: Orthodox, Conservative and Reform. Animals do not have souls and cannot be deities in Judaism, but they do appear in Judaic folklore and literature.

Principal deity: There is one God. The speaking of God's name has been forbidden since at least the 3rd century BCE. The Tetragrammaton (Four Letters) refers to the written form of the name, namely YHWH (Hebrew writes consonants, but not vowels). This has been anglicized as Yahweh and Jehovah, but generally both the Bible and Jewish religious texts use "the Lord" ("Adonai" in Hebrew). Some orthodox Jews consider even this euphemism too sacred to be spoken or printed, and so use HaShem (The Name).

Sacred texts: *The Torah* (also called *The Pentateuch* or *The Five Books of Moses*); *The Mishna* (which combines the Torah with subsequent oral traditions); *The Midrash* (a collection of ancient Biblical exegesis); and *The Talmud* (the central text of Rabbinic Judaism and the primary source of Judaic religious law and theology).

Korean Myths

Korean mythology is based on a very long oral tradition, which goes back to shamanism and animism before Buddhist, Confucian and Taoist ideas came to Korea. There is a large pantheon of deities, most of their names not even recognized in the West. Korean mythology is rich in animal legends, featuring dragons, the nine-tailed fox, a winged horse called Chollima, several three-legged animals, and a host of others.

Principal deities: Cheonjiwang Bonpuri (King of the Gods); Bagiwang (Queen of the Earth); Grandmother Mago (who made the rocks of Earth from her urine and excrement); Dangun Wanggeom (founder and first king of Korea); Namu Doryeong (who survived the Great Flood, like Noah in Christianity); Gangrim Doryeong (the god of death).

Major sacred texts: No written texts (oral tradition).

Maori Myths

The Maori of New Zealand have an ancient culture, which was heavily suppressed by Christian missionaries in the 18th and 19th centuries, but which has been undergoing a strong revival in more recent times. There is a rich pantheon of deities. Maori mythology and folklore contain many references to animals, mostly of the sea.

Principal deities: Ranginui (the Sky father); Papatuanaku (the Earth mother); their children Tumatauenga (god of war), Tawhirimatea (god of weather), Tanemahuta (god of forests and birds), and Tangaroa (god of the sea).

Major sacred texts: No written texts (oral tradition).

The Norse Pantheon

Norse mythology is vast in range and scope. It incorporates deities and traditions from Scandinavia, Germany and other parts of northern Europe. Animals feature strongly in Norse mythology.

Principal deities: The principal deities are generally well known: Odin (King of the Gods); Frigg (Odin's queen); Thor (god of thunder, Odin's son); Loki (Thor's brother, god of mischief); Freyja (goddess of beauty); Baldr (the shining god); Heimdall (guardian of the Rainbow Bridge that connects Asgard, home of the gods, to the other worlds).

Major sacred/mythological texts: A long and ancient oral tradition, but two Icelandic texts are very important: *The Prose Edda*, composed in the 13th century by Snorri Sturluson, and *The Poetic Edda*, a collection of earlier anonymous poems, compiled in the 13th century.

The Roman Pantheon

The Roman pantheon is essentially the Greek pantheon renamed, with some additional material. In ancient Rome, Latin was the everyday language of commerce, politics and ordinary living, but Greek was the language of high literature. Through the expansion of the Roman Empire, many classical myths and legends reached across the world. Animals feature in many of them.

Principal deities: Iuppiter or Jupiter (father of the gods); Juno (wife of Jupiter); Apollo (sun god); Venus (goddess of love and beauty); Mars (god of war); Diana (goddess of the Moon); Minerva (goddess of wisdom, the arts and military strategy); Bacchus (god of wine and pleasure); Terra (Mother Earth); Pluto (king of the underworld or Hades); Mercury (psychopomp and messenger of the gods); Victoria (goddess of victory); Faunus or Silvanus (god of woods and wild animals); Neptune (god of the sea); Luna (the Moon).

Major texts: The ancient Roman legends are found in a number of writers, of whom the best known are: Ammianus Marcellinus (c. 330–c. 391 CE); Julius Caesar (100–44 BCE); Livy (Titus Livius Patavinus, 64 BCE–12 CE); Lucan (Marcus Annaeus Lucanus, 39–65 CE); Ovid (Publius Ovidius Naso, 43 BCE–18 CE), particularly the *Metamorphoses*; Pliny the Elder (Gaius Plinius Secundus, 23–79 CE); Tacitus (56–120 CE); and Virgil (Publius Virgilius Maro, 70–19 BCE).

Shinto

Shinto is the traditional folk religion of Japan. Its first texts were recorded in the 8th century CE. Originally Jindo or Shindo, it took its name from Chinese *Shen Tao* or *Shendao*, meaning "Way of the Spirits" or "Way of the Gods." Part of Shinto is respect for the past and for family ancestors, and respect and compassion are also extended to animals and animal spirits, which feature widely in Japanese religion and folklore.

Principal deities: Amenominakanushi ("Heavenly Ancestral God of the Originating Heart of the Universe"); Amaterasu (goddess of the Sun); Sarutahiko Okami (god of strength and martial arts); Ame no Ozume no Mikato (wife of Sarutahiko Okami, goddess of dawn, mirth and revelry); Inari (god of foxes, swordsmiths, fertility, rice, tea and saké wine); Tsukuyomi (god of the Moon).

Major sacred texts: There are no canonical texts as such, but three ancient texts are very important: *Kojiki* (a collection of early myths) and *Nihon Shoki* ("*The Chronicles of Japan*"), both written in the 8th century; and *Engishiki* (a full catalog of Shinto rituals, which are very complex).

Sikhism

Sikhism, from Sikh, meaning disciple, student or follower, is one of the world's newest religions, based on the teachings of Guru Nanak Dev (1469–1539). It is monotheistic, and envisages two co-existent realms, Miri (the temporal world) and Piri (the spiritual world). There are perhaps 25 million Sikhs in the world, most of them living in the Punjab. Sikhism describes ego, anger, greed, attachment and lust as the "five thieves" which take humankind further from the eternal spirit. Sikhs are prohibited from eating *halal* or *kutha* meat, and many avoid beef, or are vegetarians or vegans. Sikh literature makes frequent reference to Hindu traditions, but animals do not feature very strongly.

Principal deity: There is one God.

Major sacred texts: *Guru Granth Sahib*, written by the ten Gurus of Sikhism, of whom Guru Nanak Dev was the first, and believed by Sikhs to be itself a living teacher and guide to the faithful—it is placed reverently in the *gurdwara* or temple and all prostrate themselves before the text on entering.

Taoism

Tao or *Dao* means "Way" or "The Way." Taoism is a philosophy and religion of the East, dating from at least the 4th century BCE. It was influenced by the *I Ching* of Confucianism, but its main text is the *Tao Te Ching* or *Dao De Jing* written by Lao Tzu or Laozi (dates unknown, possibly contemporary with Confucius in the 6th century BCE, possibly 4th century BCE). Taoism emphasizes the principle of *wu wei*, literally "action without intention." Believers are encouraged to detach themselves from emotional states, and to behave like water, flowing with life, not resisting. Animal metaphors and images do not feature in early Taoism, but modern Taoism has imported a lot of legends, superstitions and protocols designed to bring good luck or avert paranormal influences, and some of this material does include animals.

Principal deities: None in early Taoism, but many spirits, ghosts and monsters in subsequent developments.

Sacred text: *The Tao Te Ching* or *Dao De Jing*. *Tao* means way. *Te* means virtue, truth or integrity. *Ching* means great book. "The Great Book of the Virtuous Way" is one of many possible translations.

Wicca

Wicca is a modern restoration of traditional witchcraft, based largely on the writing and teaching of the British occultist Gerald Gardner (1884–1964). Traditional witchcraft was closely connected to folklore about animals, but modern Wicca is very vague about animals and animal traditions. Its central moral precept is, "An (if) it harm none, do as thou wilt," or, in more colloquial modern English, "Do what you like, as long as nobody gets hurt."

Principal deities: The Lord or Horned God; the Lady or Moon Goddess.

Major sacred texts: No major traditional written texts (oral tradition), but plenty of modern books, varying greatly in quality.

Zoroastrianism

Zoroastrianism is one of the world's oldest religions, and it is still practiced to this day. It was the religion of ancient Persia (modern Iran). The prophet Zoroaster or Zarathustra (Zardosht in Persian) probably lived sometime between 2000 and 1000 BCE, but nobody knows for certain. He described the god of wisdom, Ahura Mazda (Wise Lord) as the supreme (and only) deity of the universe (Zoroastrianism was originally monotheistic). Several concepts in Zoroastrianism, such as free will, judgment after death, heaven and hell, and the coming of a Messiah, found their way into early Judaism, Buddhism, Christianity and Islam. Animals do feature in ancient Persian folklore, but very little in Zoroastrianism *per se*.

Principal deities: Ahura Mazda (Wise Lord); Angra Mainyu (Angry Spirit), originally a human characteristic, became personified as Ahriman, a precursor of the Devil.

Major sacred text: *The Avesta*, now largely lost, the most recent fragment dating from 1288 CE. Several Persian texts written during the 10th and 11th centuries CE have had a strong influence on contemporary Zoroastrianism, but are considered commentary rather than canonical texts.

Chapter Notes

Preface

1. "Animals in Jannah?" Muftisays.com (Islamic Forum), http://muftisays.com/qa/question/2325/animals-in-jannah.html, accessed 12/21/2018.

Chapter 1

1. Ansari, 2006, p. 24.
2. *Ibid.*, p. 37.
3. Baldick, 2000, p. 167.
4. Hoppál, Mihály, 1994. "Sámánok, lelkek és jelképek" (in Hungarian, "Shamans, Souls and Symbols"). *Helikon Kiadó*. Budapest, p. 62. Taiwan: National Dong Hwa University. cis.ndhu.edu.tw/ezfiles/16/1016/attach/63/pta_4889_2122681_80852.pdf, accessed 12/31/2018.
5. Carr-Gomm, 1994, p. 11.

Chapter 2

1. Burnie, 2010, p. 28.
2. *Ibid.*, p. 31.

Chapter 3

1. "Where Does the Word Dog Come From?," English Language and Usage Stack Exchange, https://english.stackexchange.com/questions/16377/where-does-the-word-dog-come-from., accessed 12/18/2018.
2. "How Many Breeds of Dogs Are There in the World?," *Psychology Today UK*, May 2013, https://www.psychologytoday.com/us/blog/canine-corner/201305/how-many-breeds-dogs-are-there-in-the-world, accessed 12/18/2018.
3. Yang, Lihui, et al., 2005, pp. 47–52.
4. Mercatante, 1988, p. 149.
5. Author's retelling, based on Mercatante, 1988, p. 627.
6. *Ibid.*, p. 15.
7. Author's retelling, based on Graves, 1995, p. 732.
8. Author's retelling, based on Graves, pp. 514–517.
9. All stories of Æsop are retellings by the author, unless otherwise noted.
10. Jones and Jones, 1949, p. 97.
11. Salaperäinen, 2016, p. 52.
12. Mercatante, 1988, p. 54.
13. Metzger et al., 2007; 1 Kings 21:23.
14. Salaperäinen, 2016, pp. 52–54.

Chapter 4

1. Hendrickson, 1997, p. 684.
2. Mech, L. David, 1999. "Alpha Status, Dominance, and Division of Labor in Wolf Packs," *Canadian Journal of Zoology* 77 (8): 1196–1203, www.wolf.org/wp-content/uploads/2013/09/267alphastatus_english.pdf., accessed 5/3/2019.
3. Carleton, 1983, p. 66.
4. Metzger et al., 2007; Matthew 7:15.
5. Mercatante 1988, p. 103.
6. Author's retelling, based on Mercatante, 1988, p. 469.
7. Metzger et al., 2007, Lamentations 4:3, 8.
8. Metzger et al., 2007, Nehemiah 2:13, 9.
9. Metzger et al., 2007, Job 30:29.
10. Mercatante, 1988, p. 22.
11. Carr-Gomm, 1994, p. 36.
12. Author's retelling, based on Mercatante, 1988, p. 328.
13. Author's retelling, based on Mercatante, 1988, p. 464.
14. Mercatante, 1988, p. 3.

Chapter 5

1. Wade, N., 2007. "Study Traces Cat's Ancestry to Middle East," *New York Times*, https://www.nytimes.com/2007/06/29/health/29iht-29cat.6404420.html, accessed 5/6/2019.
2. Quirke, 1992, p. 165.
3. Metzger et al., 2007, Ezekiel 30:17.
4. "Kilkenny Cats," http://catquotes.com/kilkennycats.htm, accessed 5/6/2019.
5. "Pangur Bán," Poetry Foundation https://www.poetryfoundation.org/poetrymagazine/poems/48267/pangur-ban, accessed 5/6/2019.
6. "14 Legends About Cats from Around the World," Mental Floss (Minutemedia.com), http://mentalfloss.com/article/83422/14-legends-about-cats-around-world, accessed 5/6/2019.
7. Carr-Gomm, 1994, p. 55.

Chapter 6

1. Brakefield, T., 1993. *Big Cats: Kingdom of Might*, pp. 50–67. London: Voyageur Press.
2. Mercatante, 1988, p. 53.
3. Metzger et al., 2007, Genesis 49:9.
4. Metzger et al., 2007, Daniel 2:14.
5. Metzger et al., 2007, Isaiah 29:1–2.
6. Metzger et al., 2007, Daniel 6:1–28.
7. Metzger et al., 2007, Revelation 4:6–7.
8. Metzger et al., 2007, Revelation 4:8.
9. Anderson, Kenneth, 1954. *Nine Man-Eaters and One Rogue*, p. 47. London: Allen & Unwin.
10. "Jaguar Conservation Units," https://databasin.org/datasets/b530e75d0b464cf59a04a5da69b59735, accessed 3/27/201.
11. "Chibcha Language," *Online Spanish-. Muysccubun Dictionary*. University of Bergen, 2009, https://www.secret-bases.co.uk/wiki/Chibcha_language, accessed 3/26/2019.
12. Durant, S.; Mitchell, N.; Ipavec, A.; & Groom, R., 2015. "*Acinonyx jubatus*: The IUCN Red List of Threatened Species," *International Union for Conservation of Nature*, https://www.discovery.ucl.ac.uk/1529368, accessed 3/26/2019.
13. Author's retelling, based on Graves 1955, pp. 89–96.
14. "True Tiger," Native American Languages Net, http://www.native-languages.org/true-tiger.htm, accessed 3/27/2019.
15. "Accademia Nazionale dei Lincei," https://www.interacademies.org/12929/Accademia-Nazionale-dei-Lincei, accessed 3/27/2019.

Chapter 7

1. Author's retelling based on Mercatante, 1988, pp. 276–277.
2. Author's retelling based on Cowell, E.B., translated by W.H.D. Rouse, "The Jataka," Volume II, 1895, https://sacred-texts.com/bud/j2/j2139.htm, accessed 4/1/2019.
3. Graves, 1955, pp. 478–481.
4. Mercatante, 1988, pp. 7–8.
5. Graves, 1955, pp. 190–193.
6. *Ibid.*, pp. 716–731.
7. Metzger et al., 2007, Judges 2:11–13.
8. Metzger et al., 2007, 2 Kings 23:13.
9. Mercatante, 1988, p. 87.
10. Carr-Gomm, 1994, p. 119.
11. *Ibid.*, p. 121.
12. Author's retelling, based on "Biróg," http://dictionary.sensagent.com/Biróg/en-en/, accessed 4/1/2019.
13. Rees and Rees, 1961, pp. 57–61.
14. Metzger et al., 2007, Exodus 32:1.
15. Metzger et al., 2007, Exodus 32:26–28.
16. "Heiti-eibib," https://www.godchecker.com/african-mythology/HEITSI-EIBIB/, accessed 4/1/2019.
17. Mercatante, 1988, p. 95.
18. Robinson, F.N. (ed.). 1974. *The Complete Works of Geoffrey Chaucer*, p. 114. Lines 1183–1188, *The Tale of the Clerk of Oxenford, The Canterbury Tales*. Oxford: Oxford University Press.
19. Rothwell, C., 1995. *Around Garstang*, p. 102. Stroud, UK: Alan Sutton Publishing.
20. Mercatante, 1988, p. 97.
21. "About Head-Smashed-In Buffalo Jump World Heritage Site," https://headsmashedin.ca/about-head-smashed-buffalo-jump-world-heritage-site, accessed 4/1/2019.
22. Lightning Medicine Cloud, http://lightningmedicinecloud.com/legend.html, accessed 4/1/2019.
23. Lewis, 2013, p. 226.
24. "Kannon Notebook," https://www.onmarkproductions.com/html/kannon.shtml, accessed 4/1/2019.
25. "Hippopotamus Attack Kills 13 People, Including 12 Children, in Boat Near Niger's Capital Niamey," Australian Broadcasting Corporation, November 20, 2014, https://www.abc.net.au/news/2014-11-20/hippopotamus-attack-kills-13-in-boat-in-niger, accessed 2/24/2019.
26. Metzger et al., 2007, Job 40:15–23.
27. "San Mythology," https://occult-world.com/african-mythology/san-mythology, accessed 4/1/2019.
28. "Wawere Goddess, Egyptian Hippo Goddess," http://www.secretsofancientegypt.com/2010/01/hippopotamus-goddesses.html, accessed 4/1/2019.

Chapter 8

1. Carr-Gomm, 1994, p. 101.
2. Metzger et al., 2007, John 1:29.
3. Metzger et al., 2007, Revelation 7:9–17.
4. Black, Jeremy A.; George, Andrew; Postgate, J.N., 2000. *A Concise Dictionary of Akkadian*. Wiesbaden, Germany: Otto Harrassowitz Verlag and London: School of Oriental and African Studies, University of London, https://www.soas.ac.uk/cda-archive, accessed 1/22/2019.
5. Graves, 1955, p. 56.
6. Mercatante, 1988, pp. 26–27.
7. *Ibid.*, pp. 197–198.
8. Metzger et al., 2007, Leviticus 16:7–10.
9. Metzger et al., 2007, Matthew 23:31–46.
10. Mercatante, 1988, p. 230.
11. *Ibid.*, pp. 305–306.
12. "Fainting Goats," https://www.petworlds.net/fainting-goats/, accessed 4/1/2019.
13. Dežman, Karel (Karl Deschmann), in *Laibacher Zeitung*, no. 43, February 21, 1868, reproduced in *Europa 1997—Tales and Legends, Post of Slovenia* (via InterPlanetary File System), https://ipfs.io/ipfs/QmXoypizjW3WknFiJnKLwHCnL72vedxjQkDDP1mXWo6uco/wiki/Zlatorog/html, accessed 4/2/2019.

Chapter 9

1. Gantz, 1981, p. 47.
2. Carr-Gomm, 1994, p. 23.
3. *Ibid.*, p. 27.

4. "Weeks 4–6: The Language of Seduction, Comments," https://lit-desirethree2018.blogspot.com/2018/03/weeks-4-6-language-of-seduction.html, accessed 4/2/2019.
5. Graves, 1948, p. 51.
6. Mercatante, 1988, p. 126.
7. "Eikthyrnir," http://www.ancientpages.com/2019/02/11/eikthyrnir-mythical-male-deer-and-heidrun-she-goat-stand-on-the-top-of-valhalla/, accessed 4/2/2019.
8. Handford, 1951, p. 154.
9. *Natural History*, Book 8, Chapter 16, 77 CE, www.perseus.tufts.edu/hopper/text?doc=Perseus:text:1999.02.0137:book=8: chapter=31, accessed 4/3/2019.

Chapter 10

1. Carr-Gomm, 1994, p. 32.
2. Graves, 1955, p. 84*h*.
3. *Ibid.*, p. 264*c*.
4. Carr-Gomm, 1994, p. 31.
5. Shepard and Sanders, 1992, pp. 115–117.
6. Jones & Pennick, 1997, pp. 154–156.
7. Metzger et al., 2007, Daniel 7:17–18.
8. "Jambavantha Race of Ramayana Were Not Bears," https://www.sanskritimagazine.com/indian religions/hinduism/jambavantha-race-ramayana-bears/, accessed 4/3/2019.
9. Knight, C., 2008. "The Moon Bear as a Symbol of Yama: Its Significance in the Folklore and Upland Hunting in Japan," *Asian Ethnology*. 67 (1): 79–101, https://www.researchgate.net/publication/287821999_The_Moon_Bear_as_a_Symbol_of_Yama, accessed 1/12/2019.

Chapter 11

1. "Digital Report: FAO Statistics—Live Animals." Food and Agriculture Organization of the United Nations. December 16, 2009, www.fao.org/statistics, accessed 1/23/2019.
2. Metzger et al., 2007, Revelation 6:8.
3. Metzger et al., 2007, Revelation 19:11–14.
4. "What Is the Significance of Ashwamedha Yagna?," https://hinduism.stackexchange.com/questions/619/what-is-the-significance-of-ashwamedha-yagna, accessed 1/23/2019.
5. "Legendary Uchchaihshravas," http://www.ancientpages.com/2017/05/01/legendary-uchchaihshravas-divine-seven-headed-flying-horse-of-god-indra/, accessed 1/23/2019.
6. Mercatante, 1988, p. 85.
7. "Tištrya," http://www.iranicaonline.org/articles/tistrya-2, accessed 1/23/2019.
8. Mercatante, 1988, p. 3.
9. Graves, 1955, pp. 253*c*, 255(3).
10. *Ibid.*, p. 158*c*.
11. "Bucephalus," https://www.ancient.eu/Bucephalus, accessed 1/23/2019.
12. Graves, 1955, pp. 486–491.
13. *Ibid.*, pp. 356–358.
14. "Saint Hippolytus," http://www.catholic-saints.info/patron-saints/saint-hippolytus.htm, accessed 1/23/2019.
15. "Dharmapala," http://www.chinabuddhismencyclopedia.com/en/index.php/Dharmapala, accessed 1/23/2019.
16. Green, 1992, pp. 90–92.
17. Crofton, 2016, pp. 270–271.
18. King, 1998, pp. 131–133.
19. Mercatante, 1988, p. 114.
20. *Ibid.*, p. 235.
21. *Ibid.*, p. 419.
22. *Ibid.*, pp. 596–597.
23. Medcalf, Stephen (ed.), 1994. *Poems For All Purposes, the selected poems of G.K. Chesterton*, p. 35. London: Pimlico (Random House).
24. Metzger et al., 2007, Numbers 22:22–34.
25. Mercatante, 1988, p. 86.
26. *Ibid.*, pp. 86–87.
27. *Ibid.*, pp. 105–106.
28. "Has Demand for Rhino Horn Truly Dropped in Vietnam?,". November 3, 2014, National Geographic, https://blog.nationalgeographic.org/2014/11/03/has-demand-for-rhino-horn-truly-dropped-in-vietnam, accessed 4/4/2019.
29. Tuite, Tom. "Dublin Zoo Pleads Guilty to Safety Breach in Tapir Attack on Child," *The Irish Times*, October 14, 2014, https://www.irishtimes.com/news/crime-and-law/courts/dublin-zoo-pleads-guilty-to-safety-breach-in-tapir-attack-on-child-Dublin-Zoo, accessed 4/4/2019.

Chapter 12

1. Metzger et al., 2007, Matthew 19:23–24.
2. "Rabi'a al-Basri," http://www.deeptrancenow.com/rabia.htm, accessed 4/4/2019.
3. "Urcuchillay: God That Watched Over Animals," http://www.thewhitegoddess.co.uk/divinity_of_the_day/inca/urcuchillay.asp, accessed 4/4/2019.
4. "The World's Largest Rock Art Petroglyph," www.bradshawfoundation.com/giraffe/index.php, accessed 4/4/2019.
5. "Elite of Ancient Pompeii Dined on Sea Urchin, Giraffe," Live Science, http://www.livescience.com/42309-food-eaten-by-pompeii-residents.html, accessed 8/4/2019.
6. "10 Beasts That Used to Be Mythical," Listverse, http://listverse.com/2010/04/16/10-beasts-that-used-to-be-mythical, accessed 8/4/2019.

Chapter 13

1. Carr-Gomm, 1994, p. 41.
2. Author's retelling, based on Graves, 1955, pp. 263–267.
3. Graves, 1955, pp. 475–478.
4. *Ibid.*, pp. 105*f*.
5. Mercatante, 1988, pp. 263–264.
6. *Ibid.*, pp. 567.
7. Carr-Gomm, 1994, p. 88.
8. Mercatante, 1988, p. 589.

9. Metzger et al., 2007, Luke 8:26–34.
10. Qumsiyeh, Mazin B., 1996. *Mammals of the Holy Land*, p. 64. Lubbock, TX: Texas Tech University Press.
11. Burn, A.R., 1984. *Persia and the Greeks*, p. 353. Stanford, CA: Stanford University Press.

Chapter 14

1. "Ganesha," http://www.religionfacts.com/ganesha, accessed 4/8/2019
2. Mercatante, 1988, p. 32.
3. *Ibid.*, pp. 340–341.
4. "Story of Aṣṭadiggajas," https://www.wisdomlib.org/hinduism/compilation/puranic-encyclopaedia/d/doc241415.html, accessed 4/8/2019.
5. "Maya (Mother of Buddha)," http://dictionary.sensagent.com/Maya%20(mother%20of%20Buddha)/en-en/, accessed 4/9/2019.
6. "African Myths: Legends About Elephants," Africa Road Travel, https://africaroadtravel.com/2011/05/05/african-myths-legends-about-elephants/, accessed 4/9/2019.
7. "Blind Men and the Elephant," https://www.allaboutphilosophy.org/blind-men-and-the-elephant.htm, accessed 1/12/2020.
8. "The Dwarf Elephant of Malta; Origin of the Cyclops Myth?," https://ccccomedy.wordpress.com/2015/01/27/the-dwarf-elephant-of-malta-origin-of-the-cyclops-myth/, accessed 4/9/2019.
9. "Surah 105: The Elephant," http://www.wrighthouse.com/religions/islam/Quran/105-elephant.php, accessed 1/12/2020.

Chapter 15

1. Mercatante, 1988, p. 65.
2. Lutgendorf, Philip, 2007. *Hanuman's Tale: The Messages of a Divine Monkey*, pp. 26–32, 116, 257–259, 388–391. Oxford: Oxford University Press.
3. Ohnuki-Tierney, Emiko, 1987. *The Monkey as Mirror: Symbolic Transformations in Japanese History and Ritual*, pp. 42–43. Princeton, NJ: Princeton University Press.
4. "Mizaru, Kikazaru & Iwazaru," http://www.oldtokyo.com/mizaru-kikizaru-iwazaru-c-1910/, accessed 4/9/2019.
5. "The Monkey's Paw," https://americanliterature.com/author/w-w-jacobs/short-story/the-monkeys-paw, accessed 4/9/2019.
6. Orangutan Foundation, https://orangutan.org, accessed 4/9/2019.
7. "The Woman Who Gave Her Life to Save the Gorillas," http://www.bbc.com/earth/story/20151226-the-woman-who-gave-her-life-to-save-the-gorillas, accessed 4/9/2019.
8. "11 Legendary Monsters of Africa," Mental Floss, https://mentalfloss.com/article/12818/11-legendary-monsters-africa, accessed 4/10/2019.
9. Merriam-Webster Dictionary, 2002, p. 311. Springfield MA: Merriam-Webster Incorporated.
10. Smith, 1855, p. 506.

11. Werness, Hope, B., 2007. *The Continuum Encyclopedia of Animal Symbolism in World Art*, p. 86. London: Continuum.
12. "Online Extra: Frodo @ *National Geographic* Magazine," National Geographic, May 15, 2002, http://ngm.nationalgeographic.com, accessed 4/10/2019.

Chapter 16

1. Lewis, 2013, pp. 51–52.
2. Mercatante, 1988, pp. 429.
3. "Wenet the Swift One," https://mirrorofisis.freeyellow.com/id599.html, accessed 4/10/2019.
4. Mercatante, 1988, pp. 29–30.
5. Woods, W. David; MacTaggart, Kenneth D.; O'Brien, Frank, 1969. "NASA Transcripts Day 5: Preparations for Landing," *The Apollo 11 Flight Journal*, p. 179. Washington, D.C.: National Aeronautics and Space Administration, https://history.nasa.gov/afj/ap11fj/26day9-reentry.html, accessed 4/12/2019.
6. Author's retelling, based on Mercatante, 1988, p. 142.

Chapter 17

1. Mercatante, 1988, p. 452.
2. *Ibid.*, p. 443.
3. Gill, Victoria. "South Georgia Rat Eradication Mission Sets Sail," British Broadcasting Corporation, January 23, 2015, https://www.bbc.com/news/science-environment-30922255, accessed 4/16/2019.
4. Mercatante, 1988, p. 300.
5. *Ibid.*, p. 527.
6. *Ibid.*, p. 527.
7. Lewis, 2013, pp. 112–115.

Chapter 18

1. Metzger et al., 2007, Isaiah 2:20.
2. "Camazotz: 'Death Bat' Vampire God in Ancient Maya Beleifs," http://www.ancientpages.com/2017/06/08/camazotz-death-bat-vampire-god-ancient-maya-beliefs/, accessed 4/16/2019.
3. Mercatante, 1988, pp. 329–330.
4. *Ibid.*, p. 221.
5. Fletcher, Martin. "The World's Most-Trafficked Mammal—And the Scaliest," British Broadcasting Corporation, May 2, 2015, https://www.bbc.co.uk/bbc-three/clip/9ab955e9-1a63-4029-8649-4476f4ac90f4, accessed 4/22/2019.
6. *Ibid.*
7. Mercatante, 1988, p. 217.
8. Author's retelling, based on Peck, C.W. *Australian Legends: The First Kangaroo*, Internet Sacred Text Archive, http://www.sacred-texts.com/aus/peck/peck13.htm, accessed 4/23/2019.
9. "How the Kangaroo Got Its Pouch," East of England Broadcast Network, http://myths.e2bn.org/mythsandlegends/userstory22096-how-the-kangaroo-got-its-pouch.html, accessed 4/23/2019.
10. "The Great Fight," Internet Sacred Text Archive,

http://www.sacred-texts.com/aus/mla/mla06.html, accessed 4/23/2019.

Chapter 19

1. Author's retelling, based on Graves, 1955, p. 449g.
2. Mercatante, 1988, p. 104.
3. "Deganawidah," https://www.encyclopedia.com/people/literature-and-arts/european-art-1599-biographies/deganawidah, accessed 4/22/2019.
4. Mercatante, 1988, p. 56.
5. "Cuthbert and the Otters," https://englishlanguageandhistory.com/?id=cuthbert-otters, accessed 4/22/2019
6. Mercante, 1988, p. 226.

Chapter 20

1. Carr-Gomm, 1994, p. 147.
2. Árnason, Jón, 1866. *Icelandic Legends Collected by Jón Árnason* (George E.J. Powell and Eiríkr Magnússon, translators), pp. xliii–xliv. London: Longman, Green, and Co., https://archive.org/details/icelandiclegend00powegoog, accessed 4/26/2019.
3. Hayward, Andrea. "Monster Sea Lion Likely to Be 'Playing' with Teen," news.com.au, April 15, 2007. https://ipfs.io/ipfs/QmXoypizjW3WknFiJnKLwHCnL72vedxjQkDDP1mXWo6uco/wiki/Sea_lions.html, accessed 4/26/2019.
4. "The Goddess of the Sea: The Story of Sedna," Native American Languages Net, http://www.native-languages.org/sedna.html, accessed 4/26/2019.
5. "Natsilane," https://www.firstpeople.us/FP-Html-Legends/Natsilane-Tlingit.html, accessed 4/26/2019.
6. Carroll, Lewis, "The Walrus and the Carpenter," https://www.poetryfoundation.org/poems/43914/the-walrus-and-the-carpenter-56d222cbc80a9, accessed 4/26/2019.

Chapter 21

1. Metzger et al., 2007, Jonah 2:10.
2. Metzger et al., Matthew 12:38–40.
3. "The Story of Paikea and Ruatapu," http://teaohou.natlib.govt.nz/journals/teaohou/issue/Mao-40TeA/c5.html, accessed 4/27/2019.
4. "Legendary Native American Figures: Glooskap (Glooscap)," http://www.native-languages.org/glooskap.htm, accessed 4/27/2019.
5. "Legendary Native American Figures: Moshup (Maushop)," http://www.native-languages.org/moshup.htm, accessed 4/27/2019.
6. "How Raven Killed the Whale," Alaska Native Knowledge Network, University of Alaska Fairbanks, http://www.ankn.uaf.edu/NPE/CulturalAtlases/Yupiaq/Marshall/raven/HowRavenKilledWhale.html, accessed 4/27/2019.
7. "Bizarre Whale Treatment for Rheumatism Revealed," *The Sydney Morning Herald*, March 30, 2014, https://www.smh.com.au/environment/conservation/bizarre-whale-treatment-for-rheumatism-revealed, accessed 4/27/2019.
8. Lilley, Ray. "Dolphin Saves Stuck Whales, Guides Them Back to Sea," National Geographic Society, March 12, 2008, news.bbc.co.uk/2/hi/asia-pacific/7291501.stm, accessed 4/28/2019.
9. Graves, 1955, p. 106*h*.
10. "Herodotus, Arion and the Dolphin," https://www.storynory.com/2-herodotus-arion-dolphin/, accessed 4/28/2019.
11. "Dolphins in Mythology," Dolphins-World, https://www.dolphins-world.com/dolphins-in-mythology, accessed 4/28/2019.
12. "Killer Whale," Native American Languages Net, http://www.native-languages.org/killer-whale.html, accessed 4/29/2019.
13. Author's retelling, based on Mercatante, 1988, p. 517.
14. Melville, Herman, 1851. *Moby-Dick; or, The Whale*, p. 246 (Footnote, Chapter 32—Cetology). New York: Richard Bentley.

Chapter 22

1. "Karshipta," https://dictionary.babylon-software.com/karshipta/, accessed 4/29/2019.
2. Mercatante, 1988, p. 335.
3. Carr-Gomm, 1994, p. 68.
4. *Ibid.*, p. 69.
5. Metzger et al., Matthew 3:17.
6. "Chiminigagua Explained," https://everything.explained.today/Chiminigagua/, accessed 4/2/9/2019.
7. "*Corvus frugilegus* (The Rook)," Corvid Corner, http://corvidcorner.com/wordpress/category/rook, accessed 4/29/2019.
8. "Nottingham—Citylife—Ghosts and Legends," British Broadcasting Corporation, http://www.bbc.co.uk/nottingham/citylife/ghostsandlegends/therooks.shtml, accessed 4/29/2019.
9. White, Gilbert, 1833. *The Natural History of Selborne*, p. 163. London: Hailes.
10. Richard Harris Barham, "The Jackdaw of Rheims," All Poetry Online, https://allpoetry.com/The-Jackdaw-Of-Rheims, accessed 4/29/2019.
11. Author's retelling, based on Mercatante, 1998, p. 357.
12. "How to Celebrate the Qixi Fesitval," http://www.chineseamericanfamily.com/qixi-festival/, accessed 4/29/2019.

Chapter 23

1. Author's retelling, based on Carr-Gomm, 1994, pp. 44–45.
2. Author's retelling, based on "Chione," https://www.greekmythology.com/Other_Gods/Minor_Gods/Chione/chione.html, accessed 4/29/2019.
3. Mercatante, 1988, p. 488.
4. Massey, Gerald, 1883 (republished 1998). *The Natural Genesis*, p. 752. Baltimore, MD: Black Classic Press.
5. "Stories in the Rumi's Masnavi English

Translations by Nicholson (1925–1940) & Whinfield (1898)," https://hojja-nusreddin.livejournal.com/2986386.html, accessed 4/29/2019.
 6. Mercatante, 1988, pp. 510–511.
 7. *Ibid*., p. 114.
 8. Lewis, 2013, p. 44.
 9. "The Legend of Etana," https://ezine.mythicscribes.com/issues/issue-3/the-legend-of-etana/, accessed 4/29/2019.
 10. "Garuda," https://www.britannica.com/topic/Garuda, accessed 4/29/2019.
 11. Mercatante, 1988, pp. 95–96.
 12. "Legendary Native American Figures: Hinon (Hinun, Hinu, Hino')," http://www.native-languages.org/morelegends/hinon.htm, accessed 4/29/2019.
 13. Email correspondence to the author, May 22, 2017.
 14. Mercatante, 1988, pp. 91–93.
 15. Lewis, 2013, p. 44.
 16. Mercatante, 1988, p. 440.
 17. "How Grandmother Spider Brought Fire to the People," https://earthengirl.wordpress.com/2013/07/03/grandmother-spider-steals-the-sun-a-cherokee-legend/, accessed 4/30/2019.
 18. "Mictlantecuhtli," https://www.britannica.com/topic/Mictlantecuhtli, accessed 4/30/2019.
 19. "Langsuyar," https://encyclopedia2.thefreedictionary.com/Langsuyar, accessed 4/30/2019.
 20. "Nekhbet," https://ancientegyptonline.co.uk/nekhbet/, accessed 4/30/2019.
 21. Graves, 1955, pp. 144*e*–145*j*.
 22. "Dakhma," https://www.britannica.com/topic/dakhma, accessed 4/30/2019.

Chapter 24

 1. Author's retelling, based in part on Mercatante, 1988, p. 415.
 2. W.B. Yeats, "Leda and the Swan," Academy of American Poets, https://www.poets.org/poetsorg/poem/leda-and-swan, accessed 4/30/2019.
 3. Graves, 1955, p. 156*d*.
 4. "How Holy Geese Saved the Republic During the First Sack of Rome (390 BCE)," https://www.warhistoryonline.com/ancient-history/how-holy-geese-saved-the-republic-in-390-bce-during-the-first-sack-of-rome.html, accessed 4/30/2019.
 5. "St. Ulrich of Augsburg," https://www.christianiconography.info/2018various/ulrichLeftSide.html, accessed 4/30/2019.
 6. Mercatante, 1988, p. 283.
 7. "Storks in Mythology and Literature," Polish Culture Website, http://culture.polishsite.us/articles/art350.html, accessed 5/2/2019.
 8. Author's retelling, based on "Honeyed Words Can't Sweeten Evil—An Algonquin Legend," First People of North America and Canada, https://www.firstpeople.us/FP-Html-Legends/HoneyedWordsCantSweetenEvil-Algonquin.html, accessed 5/2/2019.
 9. Author's retelling, based on Graves, 1955, pp. 163*a*–164*c*.
 10. Graves, 1955, pp. 164.1–165.3.
 11. Woodall, Peter, 2001, *Family Alcedinidae (Kingfishers)*, in del Hoyo, Josep; Elliott, Andrew; Sargatal, Jordi (eds.), *Handbook of the Birds of the World, Volume 6, Mousebirds to Hornbills*, pp. 103–187. Barcelona, Spain: Lynx Edicions, https://www.lynxeds.com/product/handbook-of-the-birds-of-the-world-volume-6, accessed 5/2/2019.

Chapter 25

 1. Coleridge, Samuel Taylor, *The Rime of the Ancient Mariner* (1798), in Morgan, Edwin (ed.), 1963, *Collins Albatross Book of Longer Poems*, p. 429, lines 115-126.
 2. *Ibid*., p. 439, lines 464–471.
 3. Metzger et al., 2007, Matthew 14:29.
 4. Mironov, Boris Nikolaevich, 2012. *The Standard of Living and Revolutions in Imperial Russia, 1700–1917*, p. 461. London: Routledge.
 5. Scoresby-Routledge, Katherine, 1919, *The Mystery of Easter Island*, p. 312. London: Hazell, Watson & Viney.
 6. Mercatante, 1988, p. 578.

Chapter 26

 1. Metzger et al, 2007, Matthew 26:75.
 2. Metzger et al, 2007, Matthew 23:27.
 3. Mercatante, 1988, p. 26.
 4. *Ibid*., p. 663.
 5. Author's retelling, based on Chaucer, Geoffrey, *The Nun's Priest's Tale*, 1393?–1400?, in Robinson, F.N. (ed.) 1974, *The Complete Works of Geoffrey Chaucer, Second Edition*, , pp. 199–205, Oxford: Oxford University Press.
 6. Mercatante, 1988, p. 104.
 7. *Ibid*., pp. 192–193.
 8. "Guan Yin," https://www.nationsonline.org/oneworld/Chinese_Customs/Guan_Yin.htm, accessed 5/2/2019.

Chapter 27

 1. Snow and Perrins, 1998, p. 1215.
 2. Carr-Gomm, 1994, p. 21.
 3. "Saint Benedict Tempted in the Wilderness," https://artsandculture.google.com/asset/saint-benedict-tempted-in-the-wilderness/hgGqNXLOD-SL3BQ, accessed 5/2/2019.
 4. Heaney, Seamus, "St Kevin and the Blackbird," http://www.poetrybyheart.org.uk/poems/st-kevin-and-the-blackbird/, accessed 5/2/2019.
 5. "The Fabled Folklore of Robin Redbreast," https://from-bedroom-to-study.blogspot.com/2012/12/the-fabled-folklore-of-robin-redbreast.html, accessed 5/2/2019.
 6. "Explore Bird Superstitions and Myths," https://exemplore.com/legends/birds-myths-superstitions-about-birds, accessed 5/2/2019.
 7. "Who Killed Cock Robin,?" https://allnurseryrhymes.com/cock-robin, accessed 5/2/2019.
 8. Author's retelling, based on "How the Wren

Became the King of the Birds," http://littlebrownwren.com/2015/11/24/how-the-wren-became-the-king-of-the-birds, accessed 5/2/2019.

    9. Carr-Gomm, 1994, pp. 128–129.

    10. "Wren Song," http://www.musicanet.org/robokopp/scottish/thewren.htm, accessed 5/2/2019.

    11. "Animal Stories About Wrens," Native American Languages Net, http://www.native-languages.org/legends-wren.html, accessed 5/4/2019.

    12. Shakespeare, William, *Sonnet 102*, lines 5–8.

    13. Mercatante, 1988, p. 16.

    14. Cerf, Bennet A.; Klopper, Donald S; & Haas, Robert K. (eds.). 1966. *The Complete Poems of Keats and Shelley*, pp. 183–185. New York: The Modern Library, Random House.

Chapter 28

    1. Carr-Gomm, 1994, p. 60.

    2. *Ibid.*, p. 60.

    3. Archibald & Forshaw, 1991, pp. 95–96.

    4. *The Qur'an*, surah 53:19–20, https://quran.com, accessed 5/4/2019.

    5. Author's retelling, based on Mercatante, 1988, p. 192.

    6. "Kamadeva," https://sacred-texts.com/hin/hmvp/hmvp32.htm, accessed 5/5/2019.

    7. "Scary Urban Legends," Quotev.com, https://www.quotev.com/story/9037386/Scary-Urban-Legends/69, accessed 5/5/2019

Chapter 29

    8. Metzger et al., 2007, Leviticus 11:13–19.

    9. *The Qur'an*, Al-Nami, surah 27:20-24, https://quran.com, accessed 5/5/2019.

    10. Author's retelling, based on Mercatante, 1988, p. 329.

    11. Author's retelling, based on "Hummingbird Brings Back Tobacco," First People of North America and Canada, https://www.firstpeople.us/FP-Html-Legends/HummingbirdBringsBackTobacco-Cherokee.html, accessed 5/6/2019.

    12. "Three Kingdoms: Capturing Arrows with Boats of Straw," https://www.shenyunperformingarts.org/explore/view/article/e/-iFdXfJV1Es/romance-of-the-three-kingdoms-zhuge-liang-capturing-arrows, accessed 5/6.

    13. Metzger et al., 2007, Genesis 8:8–12.

    14. Metzger et al., 2007, Psalms 55:4–8.

    15. Metzger et al., 2007, Matthew 10:16–22.

    16. Metzger et al., 2007, Luke 2:22–24.

    17. Metzger et al., 2007, Luke 3: 21–22.

    18. Graves, 1955, pp. 192–193.

Chapter 30

    1. Author's retelling, based on "Vaivasvata Manu," http://blavatsky.net/Wisdomworld/additional/ListOfCollatedArticles/VaivasvataManu.html, accessed 5/7/2019.

    2. "Why the Salmon Come to the Squamish Waters," First People of North America and Canada, https://www.firstpeople.us/FP-Html-Legends/Why-The-Salmon-Come-To-The-Squamish-Waters-Squamish.html, accessed 5/7/2019.

    3. Mercatante, 1988, p. 224.

    4. Roe, Sam, and Hawthorne, Michael. "*How Safe Is Tuna?*" *Chicago Tribune*, December 13, 2005, https://www.chicagotribune.com/news/ct-xpm-2005-12-13-chi-0512130114dec13-story.html, accessed 5/7/2019.

    5. "Claims of Caribbean Piracy as National Symbol Takes Flight," *Sydney Morning Herald*, December 18, 2004, https://www.smh.com.au/world/claims-of-caribbean-piracy-as-national-symbol-takes-flight, accessed 5/7/2019.

    6. "Aboriginal Ceremonies," Tourism Bureau, Republic of China (Taiwan), 2008, https://eng.taiwan.net.tw/m1.aspx?sNo=0002016&id=R2, accessed 7/5/2019.

Chapter 31

    1. Glueck, Nelson, 1937. "A Newly Discovered Nabataean Temple of Atargatis and 41.3 Hadad at Khirbet Et-Tannur, Transjordania," *American Journal of Archaeology*, July 1937, pp. 361–376, https://www.ajaonline.org/toc/413, accessed 5/8/2019.

    2. Mercatante, 1988, pp. 40–41.

    3. *Ibid.*, 1988, p. 240.

    4. Christie, 1968, pp. 65, 74.

    5. "The History of Goldfish," https://www.itsafishthing.com/the-history-of-goldfish/, accessed 5/8/2019.

    6. "Tin Drum, the Review," https://www.empireonline.com/movies/reviews/tin-drum-review/, accessed 5/8/2019.

    7. Author's retelling, based on Westervelt, W.D., 1910. *Legends of Maui: A Demi-God of Polynesia*, Internet Sacred Text Archive, http://www.sacred-texts.com/pac/maui/maui10.html. accessed 5/8/2019.

    8. Author's retelling, based on Mercatante, 1988, p. 639.

    9. "The Sturgeon," Fairytalez.com, https://fairytalez.com/the-sturgeon, accessed 5/13/2019.

    10. "Mashenomak, the Fish Monster," First People of North America and Canada, https://www.firstpeople.us/FP-Html-Legends/MashenomakTheFishMonster-Menomini.html, accessed 5/13/2019.

Chapter 32

    1. Mercatante, 1988, p. 113.

    2. *Ibid.*, p. 387.

    3. Graves, 1955, p. 470*e*.

    4. Willard, Barbara, and Owens, Mary B., 1997. *Augustine Came to Kent*, p. 68. Warsaw, ND: Bethlehem Books.

    5. "Pedanius Dioscorides—Der Wiener Dioskurides," *Codex medicus Graecus 1 der Österreichischen Nationalbibliothek*. Graz: Akademische Druck- und Verlagsanstalt 1998, fol. 391, verso (Band 2), Kommentar S., 47 und 52. Zentrales Verzeichnis Antiquarischer Bücher (zvab.com), https://www.zvab.

com/buch-suchen/titel/der-wiener-dioskurides-codex, accessed 5/13/2019.

Chapter 33

1. Mercatante, 1988, p. 4.
2. *Ibid.*, p. 226.
3. Carr-Gomm, 1994, p. 65.
4. Author's retelling, based on Mercatante, 1988, p. 266.
5. *Ibid.*, p. 414.
6. "10 Neat Facts About Newts," Mental Floss, http://mentalfloss.com/article/70471/10-neat-facts-about-newts, accessed 5/15/2019.
7. "Overturning 250 Years of Scientific Theory," https://phys.org/news/2011-07-overturning-years-scientific-theory-age.html, accessed 5/15/2019.

Chapter 34

1. Author's retelling, based on Mercatante, 1988, p. 327.
2. Author's retelling, based on "Telipinu," https://oxfordindex.oup.com/view/10.1093/oi/authority.20110803102938491, accessed 5/15/2019.
3. "The First Bushman," Gateway Africa, www.gateway-africa.com/stories/The_First_Bushman_San.html, accessed 5/15/2019.
4. *The Devi Bhagavatam: The Tenth Book: Chapter 13*. Internet Sacred Text Archive, www.sacred-texts.com/hin/db/bk10ch13.htm, accessed 5/15/2019.
5. Carr-Gomm, 1994, p. 113.
6. "Kvasir," https://www.britannica.com/topic/Kvasir, accessed 5/15/2019.
7. Graves, 1955, p. 278*i*.
8. Author's retelling, based on Mercatante, 1988, p. 385.
9. *Ibid.*, p. 117.
10. "The First World," First People of North America and Canada, https://www.firstpeople.us/FP-Html-Legends/TheFirstWorld-Navajo.html, accessed 5/15/2019.
11. Bishop, Chris, 2002. *The Encyclopedia of Weapons of World War II*, p. 272. New York: Sterling.
12. Metzger et al., 2007, Matthew 12:27–28.
13. Mercatante, 1988, p. 144.
14. Shirai Y.; Funada H.; Seki T.; Morohashi M.; & Kamimura K. July 2004. "Landing Preference of *Aedes albopictus (Diptera: Culicidae)* on Human Skin Among ABO Blood Groups, Secretors or Nonsecretors, and ABH Antigens," *Journal of Medical Entomology* 41(4): 796–9, https://www.ncbi.nlm.nih.gov/pubmed/15311477, accessed 5/15/2019.
15. Mercatante, 1988, p. 406.
16. "Cihuateteo," https://www.azteccalendar.com/god/Cihuateteo.html, accessed 5/15/2019.

Chapter 35

1. "Cherokee Legend: How the World Was Made," https://www.legendsofamerica.com/na-cherokeecreation/, accessed 5/16/2019.
2. "Beetles in Art, Myths and Society," Mother Earth News, https://www.motherearthnews.com/nature-and-environment/wildlife/beetles-in-art-ze0z1502zdeh, accessed 5/16/2019.
3. Metzger et al., 20007, Proverbs 6:6.
4. Mercatante, 1988, p. 60.
5. *Ibid.*, p. 2.
6. Author's retelling, based on Graves, 1955, p. 213*g*.
7. Graves, 1955, p. 339*k*.
8. "Jorōgumo," http://yokai.com/jorougumo/, accessed 5/16/2019.
9. Mercatante, 1988, p. 379.
10. Author's retelling, based on Brockman, 2000, pp. 221–239.
11. "Iktomi," http://www.native-languages.org/iktomi.htm, accessed 5/16/2019.
12. "Nareau," https://pantheon.org/articles/n/nareau.html, accessed 5/16/2019.
13. Mercatante, 1988, pp. 52–53.
14. "Venomous Yellow Scorpions Are Moving Into Brazil's Big Cities—And the Infestation May Be Unstoppable," Theconversation.com, https://www.theconversation.com/venomous-yellow-scorpions-are-moving-into-brazils-big-cities-and-the-infestation-may-be-unstoppable, accessed 5/16/2019.
15. Mercatante, 1988, pp. 346–348.
16. "Serqet," https://ancientegyptonline.co.uk/serqet/, accessed 5/16/2019.
17. Mayell, Hillary. February 13, 2004, "Lovebirds and Love Darts: The Wild World of Mating," *National Geographic Magazine*, www.edwardbetts.com/find_link/Darts, accessed 5/16/2019.
18. Parrack, Keely. June 21, 2005, "Worm Digest," *The Christian Science Monitor*, https://www.questia.com/newspaper/1P2-32616744/the-mighty-worm, accessed 5/18/2019.
19. Carwardine, Mark, 1995. *The Guinness Book of Animal Records*, p. 232. Dublin: Guinness Publishing.
20. Carroll, Lewis, 1872, *Jabberwocky*, from *Through the Looking-Glass and What Alice Found There*, http://www.jabberwocky.com/carroll/jabber/jabberwocky.html, accessed 5/18/2019.
21. "The Sockburn Worm," http://www.oldcorpseroad.co.uk/folklore/legendary-creatures/the-sockburn-worm, accessed 5/18/2019.
22. "Lambton Worm," http://www.traditional-music.co.uk/folk-song-lyrics/Lambton_Worm.htm, accessed 1/16/2020.
23. Mercatante, 1988, p. 15.
24. Marren, Peter, and Mabey, Richard, 2010. *Bugs Britannica*, pp. 45–48. London: Chatto & Windus.

Chapter 36

1. Mercatante, 1988, p. 546.
2. *Ibid.*, p. 677.
3. Read, John, 1957 (corrected and reprinted 1961). *From Alchemy to Chemistry*. London: Bell & Sons. Dover republication, 1995, pp. 179–180.
4. "Naga," https://www.britannica.com/topic/naga-Hindu-mythology, accessed 5/18/2019.
5. Graves, 1955, pp. 414h–416*l*.

6. Ibid., p. 112c.
7. "Tiresias," https://pantheon.org/articles/t/tiresias.html, accessed 5/18/2019.
8. Metzger et al., 2007, Genesis 1:27–28.
9. Metzger et al., 2007, Genesis 2:7–9.
10. Metzger et al., 2007, Genesis 2:15–17.
11. Metzger et al., 2007, Genesis 3:1.
12. Metzger et al., 2007, Genesis 3:7.
13. Metzger et al., 2007, Genesis 3:16.
14. Metzger et al., 2007, Genesis 3:14.
15. Mercatante, 1988, p. 6.
16. Graves, 1955, pp. 447c–448d.
17. Ibid., pp. 692–696.
18. Ibid., pp. 173–175.
19. Mercatante, 1988, pp. 28–29.
20. Longfellow, Henry, 1855, "The Song of Hiawatha, Introduction," https://www.hwlongfellow.org/poems_poem.php?pid=62, accessed 5/18/2019.
21. Mercatante, 1988, pp. 639.
22. "The 'Myth' of the Plumed Serpent: Revealing the Real Message Behind the Feathered Snake," https://www.ancient-origins.net/ancient-places-americas/myth-plumed-serpent-revealing-real-message-behind-feathered-snake-009200, accessed 5/18/2019.
23. Mercatante, 1988, p. 103.
24. Ibid., p. 268.
25. Bocking, 1997, p. 239.
26. Author's retelling, based on *The Talmud*, http://www.bialystoker.org/talmud.htm., accessed 5/18/2019.
27. "Ancient Egypt: The Mythology," Egyptianmyths.net, http://www.egyptianmyths.net/cobra.html, accessed 5/18/2019.
28. Metzger et al., 2007, Psalm 58:4–5.
29. Mercatante, 1988, p. 13.
30. Metzger et al., 2007, Exodus 25: 10–22.
31. Mercatante, 1988, pp. 77–78.
32. Cooke, Alistair, 1980. *The Americans: Fifty Talks on Our Life and times*, p. 183. New York: Knopf.
33. "The Snake Husband," Illinois State Museum, www.museum.state.il.us/muslink/nat_amer/post/htmls/popups/be_snake.html, accessed 5/19/2019.
34. Lewis, 2013, p. 47.
35. Metzger et al., 2007, Mark 16:17–18.
36. Vats, R. and Thomas, S. May 2015 "A Study on Use of Animals as Traditional Medicine by Sukuma Tribe of Busega District in North-Western Tanzania," *Journal of Ethnobiology and Ethnomedicine* 11(1): 38, https://ethnobiomed.biomedcentral.com/articles/10.1186/s13002-015-0001-y, Vats accessed 5/19/2019.
37. Soewu, D.A. June 2008. "Wild Animals in Ethnozoological Practices Among the Yorubas of Southwestern Nigeria and the Implications for Biodiversity Conservation," *African Journal of Agricultural Research* 3(6): 421–7, https://unaab.edu.ng/, accessed 5/19/2019.
38. Mercatante, 1988, p. 97.
39. "Chameleon Myths/Legends," Chameleonforums.com, https://www.chameleonforums.com/threads/chameleon-myths-legends-etc.11569/, accessed 5/19/2019.
40. Mercatante, 1988, p. 336.

Chapter 37

1. Mercatante, 1988, p. 485.
2. "Sobek," https://ancientegyptonline.co.uk/sobek/, accessed 5/21/2019.
3. *The Tablet (UK)*, March 22, 2014, p. 15, https://www.thetablet.co.uk, accessed 5/21/2019.
4. Author's retelling, based on "The Alligator and the Hunter—A Choctaw Legend," First People of North America and Canada, https://www.firstpeople.us/FP-Html-Legends/TheAlligatorandtheHunter-Choctaw.html, accessed 5/21/2019.
5. Mercatante, 1988, p. 637.
6. Emery, David. "Alligators in the Sewers of New York: Is It True That Giant Albino Alligators Inhabit the SEWERS of New York City?" May 5, 2017, https://www.thoughtco.com, accessed 5/21/2019.
7. Mercatante, 1988, p. 423.
8. Ibid., p. 169.
9. Ibid., p. 379.

Chapter 38

1. Carr-Gomm, 1994, pp. 136–137.
2. Ibid., p. 139.
3. Mercatante, 1988, p. 40.
4. Author's retelling, based on Mercatante, 1988, p. 386.
5. Giskin and Walsh, 2001, p. 126.
6. Carr, Michael, 1990. "Chinese Dragon Names," *Linguistics of the Tibeto-Burman Area* 13(2): 87–189, http://sealang.net/sala/archives/pdf4/carr1990chinese.pdf, accessed 7/2/2019.
7. de Visser, Marinus Villem, 1913. *Dragon in China and Japan*, p. 116. Biodiversity Heritage Library, https://www.biodiversitylibrary.org/page/38191817#page/116/mode/1up, accessed 7/2/2019.

Chapter 39

1. Bottero, Jean, 1995. *Mesopotamia: Writing, Reasoning, and the Gods*, p. 486. Chicago: University of Chicago Press.
2. Metzger et al., 2007, Numbers 23:22.
3. Leonardo da Vinci. c. 1478. *Young Woman Seated in a Landscape with a Unicorn*. Oxford: Ashmolean Museum (ashmolean.org), https://www.freewebs.com/fantasyandfable/theunicorn.html, accessed 7/2/2019.
4. Metzger et al., 2007, Revelation 9:11.
5. Mercatante, 1988, p. 70.
6. Ibid., p. 40.
7. Tennyson, Alfred Lord, "The Kraken," https://poets.org/poem/kraken, accessed 3/18/2019.

Chapter 40

1. Mercatante, 1988, p. 15.
2. Graves, 1955, pp. 260–262.
3. Mercatante, 1988, pp. 508.
4. Author's retelling, based on two online versions

of "Beauty and the Beast," https://shortstoriesshort.com/story/beauty-and-the-beast/, and "https://www.pookpress.co.uk/project/beauty-and-the-beast-history/, both accessed 5/23/2019.

5. Mercatante, 1988, p. 101.
6. Author's retelling, based on Graves, 1955, pp. 337–340.
7. Gimbutas, 2001, p. 25.
8. Author's retelling, based on Graves, 1955, pp. 238d–240i.
9. Mercatante, 1988, p. 5.
10. Metzger et al., 2007, 2 Kings 17:31.
11. Metzger et al., 2007, Leviticus 20:2.
12. Author's retelling, based on Mewes, Wendy, 2014. *Brittany, A Cultural History* (*Landscapes of the Imagination* series), pp. 92–93. Oxford: Signal Books.
13. Salaperäinen, 2016, p. 58.

Chapter 41

1. "Hindu Astrology," https://cultureastrology.com/hindu-astrology/, accessed 5/28/2019.
2. "Chinese Zodiac," https://www.chinahighlights.com/travelguide/chinese-zodiac/, accessed 5/28/2019.
3. Ridpath and Tirion, 2001, pp. 92–93.
4. Author's retelling, based on Ridpath and Tirion, 2001, pp. 128–130.
5. French, Sue. July 2012. "By Draco's Scaly Folds," *Sky & Telescope* 124(1), https://www.skyandtelescope.com/sky-and-telescope-magazine/sky-telescope-july-2012-2, accessed 5/28/2019.
6. Penprase, Bryan E., 2010. *The Power of Stars: How Celestial Observations Have Shaped Civilization*, p. 43. Berlin, Germany: Springer Science & Business Media.
7. Wilkins, Jamie and Dunn, Robert, 2006. *300 Astronomical Objects: A Visual Reference to the Universe*, p. 234. Richmond Hill, Ontario, Canada: Firefly Books.
8. Robinson, J.H. September 1980. "Fomalhaut and Cairn D at the Big Horn and Moose Mountain Medicine Wheels," *Bulletin of the Astronomical Society* 12: 887, adsabs.harvard.edu/abs/1980BAAS, accessed 5/28/2019.
9. Henry, Teuira, 1907. "Tahitian Astronomy: Birth of Heavenly Bodies," *The Journal of the Polynesian Society* 16(2): 101–04, jps.auckland.ac.nz/document/Volume_16_1907/Volume_16,_No._2, accessed 5/28/2019.
10. MacDonald, John, 1998. *The Arctic Sky: Inuit Astronomy, Star Lore, and Legend*, pp. 72, 231–233. Toronto: NWT: Royal Ontario Museum/Nunavut Research Institute.

Bibliography

Adkins, Lesley, and Adkins, Roy A. 1996. *Dictionary of Roman Religion*. New York: Facts on File.
Andersen, Hans Christian (translator Dulcken, H.W.). 1889 as *Stories for the Household*. Reprinted facsimile 1983 as *The Complete Illustrated Stories of Hans Andersen*. London: Chancellor Press.
Ansari, Zafar Ishaq (translator). 2006. *Tafhīm Al-Qurʾān (Towards Understanding the Qurʾan)* by Mawlānā Sayyid Abu'l A'Lā Mawdūdī. Leicester, UK: The Islamic Foundation.
Archibald, George W., and Forshaw, Joseph, eds. 1991. *Encyclopaedia of Animals: Birds*. London: Merehurst Press.
Árnason, Jón, 1866. *Icelandic Legends Collected by Jón Árnason* (George E.J. Powell and Eiríkr Magnússon, translators), London: Longman, Green and Co.
Attenborough, David. 1979. *Life on Earth*. London: David Attenborough Productions Limited.
Baldick, Julian. 2000. *Animal and Shaman: Ancient Religions of Central Asia*. New York: New York University Press.
Benyus, Janine M. 2014. *The Secret Language of Animals*. New York: Black Dog & Leventhal.
Beolens, Bo, and Watkins, Michael. 2003. *Whose Bird?* London: Christopher Helm.
Berresford Ellis, Peter. 1987. *A Dictionary of Irish Mythology*. London: Routledge & Kegan Paul.
Black, Jeremy A.; George, Andrew; Postgate, J.N., 2000. *A Concise Dictionary of Akkadian, Wiesbaden*, Germany: Otto Harrassowitz Verlag and London: School of Oriental and African Studies, University of London.
Bocking, Brian. 1997. *A Popular Dictionary of Shinto*. London: Routledge.
Bord, Janet, and Colin. 1978. *A Guide to Ancient Sites in Britain*. London: Latimer.
Bottero, Jean, 1995. *Mesopotamia: Writing, Reasoning, and the Gods, Chicago*: University of Chicago Press.
Bouquet, A.C. 1954. *Sacred Books of the World*. London: Penguin.
Brakefield, T., 1993. *Big Cats: Kingdom of Might*, London: Voyageur Press.
Branston, Brian. 1957. *The Lost Gods of England*. London: Thames and Hudson.
Brockman, Robin. 2000. *Myths and Legends from Around the World*. London: Arcturus Publishing.
Burland, Cottie. 1965. *North American Indian Mythology*. London: Hamlyn.
Burnie, David (consultant editor). 2010. *The Natural History Book*. London: Dorling Kindersley (DK).
Campbell, Joseph. 1949, Pantheon, New York, 3d ed. 2008. *The Hero with a Thousand Faces*. Novato, CA: New World Library.
Carleton, James Henry. 1983. *The Prairie Logbooks*. Lincoln: University of Nebraska Press.
Carr-Gomm, Philip. 1993 and 2006. *The Druid Way*. London: Element Books (1993), and London: Thoth Publications (2006).
____, with Stephanie Carr-Gomm. 1994 and 1996. *The Druid Animal Oracle*. New York: Simon & Schuster (1994), and London: Connections Publishing (1996).
Castleden, Rodney. 2012. *The Element Encyclopedia of the Celts*. London: HarperCollins.
Cavendish, Richard (ed.). 1982. *Legends of the World*. London: Orbis.
Christie, Anthony. 1968. *Chinese Mythology*. London: Hamlyn Publishing.
Clouter, Gregory A. 2003. *The Lost Zodiac of the Druids*. London: Vega.
Conze, Edward (ed. and translator). 1959. *Buddhist Scriptures*. Baltimore: Penguin.
Cooper, J.C. 1992. *Symbolic and Mythological Animals*. London: Aquarian Press.
Cotterell, Arthur. 1979. *A Dictionary of World Mythology*. New York: Perigee Books.
____.1996. *The Encyclopedia of Mythology*. London: Anness Publishing.
Crofton, Ian. 2016. *A Dictionary of Scottish Phrase and Fable*. Edinburgh: Birlinn.
Cross, F.L. (ed.). 1957. *The Oxford Dictionary of the Christian Church*. Oxford: Oxford University Press.
Crossley-Holland, Kevin. 1980. *The Norse Myths*. London: Andre Deutsch.
Cunliffe, Barry. 1979. *The Celtic World*. London: The Bodley Head.
____. 1997. *The Ancient Celts*. Oxford: Oxford University Press.
____; Bartlett, Robert; Morrill, John; Briggs, Asa; Bourke, Joanna. 2001. *The Penguin Atlas of British & Irish History*. London: Penguin.

Davidson, H.R. Ellis. 1964. *Gods and Myths of Northern Europe*. Baltimore: Penguin.
Delin, Håkan, and Svensson, Lars. 2002. *Photographic Guide to the Birds of Britain and Europe*. London: Chancellor Press.
Dell, Christopher. 2010. *Monsters, a Bestiary of Devils, Demons, Vampires, Werewolves and Other Magical Creatures*. Rochester, VT: Inner Traditions.
Dorje, Gyurme (translator). 2006. *The Tibetan Book of the Dead*. London: Penguin.
Drake-Carnell, F.J. 1938. *Old English Customs and Ceremonies*. London: Batsford.
Fleming, Fergus, and Lothian, Alan. 1997. *The Way to Eternity: Egyptian Myth*. London: Duncan Baird Publishers.
Forty, J. 2001. *Mythology: A Visual Encyclopedia*. New York: Sterling Publishing Co.
Gantz, Jeffrey (translator). 1981. *Early Irish Myths and Sagas*. London: Penguin.
_____. 1995. *Tales of Cú Chulaind, Irish Heroic Myths*. London: Penguin.
Gimbutas, Marija. 1974 and 1982. *The Goddesses and Gods of Old Europe*. Berkeley, (1974): University of California Press, and London (1982): Thames & Hudson.
_____. 2001. *The Living Goddesses*. Berkeley: University of California Press,
Giskin, Howard, and Walsh, Bettye S. 2001. *An Introduction to Chinese Culture Through the Family*. New York: SUNY Press.
Grant, Michael (translator). 1956. *Tacitus: The Annals of Imperial Rome*. London: Penguin.
_____. 1992. *Readings in the Classical Historians*. New York: Charles Scribner's & Sons.
Graves, Robert. 1948. *The White Goddess*. London: Faber & Faber.
_____. 1955 and 1960. *The Greek Myths*. New York (1955): George Braziller, and London (1960): Penguin.
Green, Miranda J. 1992. *Dictionary of Celtic Myth and Legend*. London: Thames & Hudson.
_____. 1995 and 1996. *Celtic Goddesses*. London (1995): British Museum Press, and New York (1996): George Braziller.
Hadingham, E. 1983. *Early Man and the Cosmos*. London: Heinemann.
Hall, Derek; Beer, Amy-Jane; Gilpin, Daniel. 2017. *The World Encyclopedia of Fish & Shellfish and Other Aquatic Creatures*. London: Lorenz Books, Anness Publishing.
Handford, S.A. (translator). 1951. *Caesar: The Conquest of Gaul*. London: Penguin.
Harbison, Peter. 1988. *Pre-Christian Ireland*. London: Thames & Hudson.
Hendrickson, Robert. 1997. *QPB Encyclopedia of Word and Phrase Origins*. New York: Fact on File.
Heselton, Philip. 2000. *Wiccan Roots*. Chievely, Berkshire, UK: Capall Bann.
Hinnells, John R. 1973. *Persian Mythology*. London: Hamlyn.
_____. (ed.). 1984. *The Facts on File Dictionary of Religions*. New York: Facts on File.
Hole, C. 1940. *English Folklore*. London: Batsford.
_____. 1965. *Saints in Folklore*. New York: Barrows.
_____. 1976. *A Dictionary of British Folk Customs*. London: Granada.
Ions, Veronica. 1967. *Indian Mythology*. London: Paul Hamlyn.
James, T.G.H. 1969. *Myths and Legends of Ancient Egypt*. New York: Gosset & Dunlap.
Jones, Gwyn, and Jones, Thomas (eds.). 1949 and 1974. *The Mabinogion*. London (1949): Everyman's Library, and London (1974): J.M. Dent & Sons.
Jones, Prudence, and Pennick, Nigel. 1997. *Late Germanic Religion: A History of Pagan Europe*. London: Routledge.
King, John. 1994. *The Celtic Druids' Year*. London: Blandford.
_____. 1998. *Kingdoms of the Celts*. London: Blandford.
Kinsella, Thomas. 1969. *The Táin*. Dublin: Oxford University Press.
Lavers, Chris. 2000. *Why Elephants Have Big Ears: Nature's Engines and the Order of Life*. London: Victor Gollancz.
Leach, Amy. 2013. *Things That Are: Encounters with Plants, Stars and Animals*. Edinburgh: Canongate.
Lempriere, J. (n.d.) *Lempriere's Classical Dictionary*. London: Routledge and Sons.
Lewis, Jon E. (editor). 2013. *Native American Myths & Legends*. Philadelphia, PA: Constable & Robinson. (A reworking of: Spence, Lewis. 1914. *Myths and Legends of the North American Indians*. London: Harrap.)
Lubbock, John. 2005. *The Origin of Civilisation and the Primitive Condition of Man*. Whitefish, MT: Kessinger Publishing Company.
Lum, Peter. 1951. *Fabulous Beasts*. New York: Pantheon Books.
Lutgendorf, Philip, 2007. *Hanuman's Tale: The Messages of a Divine Monkey*, Oxford: Oxford University Press.
MacCana, Proinsias. 1970. *Celtic Mythology*. London: Hamlyn.
MacDonald, John, 1998. *The Arctic Sky: Inuit Astronomy, Star Lore, and Legend*, Toronto: NWT: Royal Ontario Museum/Nunavut Research Institute.
Margul, Tadeusz. 1968. *Present-Day Worship of the Cow in India*. Crowthorne, Berkshire, UK: Numen.
Marren, Peter, and Mabey, Richard, 2010. *Bugs Britannica*, London: Chatto & Windus.
Massey, Gerald, 1883 (republished 1998). *The Natural Genesis*, Baltimore, MD: Black Classic Press.
McEwan, Graham J. 1986. *Mystery Animals of Britain and Ireland*. London: Robert Hale Ltd.
Mattingly, H. (translator). 1948. (Translation revised by Handford, S.A., 1970). *Tacitus: The Agricola and the Germania*. London: Penguin.

McMaster, Gerald, and Trafzer, Clifford E. (eds.). 2004. *Native Universe: Voices of Indian America*. Washington D.C.: National Geographic/Smithsonian Institution, National Museum of the American Indian.
Melville, Herman, 1851. *Moby-Dick; or, The Whale*, New York: Richard Bentley.
Mercatante, Anthony S. 1974. *Zoo of the Gods: Animals in Myth, Legend, and Fable*. New York: Harper & Row.
_____. 1978(a). *Good and Evil: Mythology and Folklore*. New York: Harper & Row.
_____. 1978(b). *Who's Who in Egyptian Mythology*. New York: Clarkson N. Potter.
_____. 1988. *The Facts on File Encyclopedia of World Mythology and Legend*. New York: Facts on File.
Merriam-Webster (contributors and editors unnamed). 2002. *Webster's New Encyclopedic Dictionary*. Springfield, MA: Merriam-Webster.
Metzger, Bruce M. (on behalf of the committee of translators). 2007. *Holy Bible, New Revised Standard Edition*. London: HarperCollins.
Mewes, Wendy, 2014. *Brittany, A Cultural History (Landscapes of the Imagination* series), Oxford: Signal Books.
Michell, John. 1977. *A Little History of Astro-Archaeology*. London: Thames & Hudson.
More, Brookes (translator). 1978. *Ovid's Metamorphoses*. Francestown, NH: Marshall Jones Company.
Morwood, James, and Taylor, John. 2002. *The Pocket Oxford Classical Greek Dictionary*. Oxford: Oxford University Press.
Ohnuki-Tierney, Emiko, 1987. *The Monkey as Mirror: Symbolic Transformations in Japanese History and Ritual*, pp. 42–43. Princeton, NJ: Princeton University Press.
O'Rahilly, Thomas F. 1946. *Early Irish History and Mythology*. Dublin: University College.
Penprase, Bryan E., 2010. *The Power of Stars: How Celestial Observations Have Shaped Civilization*, Berlin, Germany: Springer Science & Business Media.
Piggott, Juliet. 1969. *Japanese Mythology*. London: Paul Hamlyn.
Piggott, Stuart. 1968(a). *Ancient Europe*. Chicago: Aldine Publishing Company.
_____. 1968(b). *The Druids*. London: Thames and Hudson.
Poignant, Roslyn. 1970. *Myths and Legends of the South Seas*. London: Hamlyn.
Porter, J.R., and Russell, W.M.S. (editors). 1978. *Animals in Folklore*. Ipswich: D.S. Brewer, Ltd., and Totowa NJ: Rowman & Littlefield, for The Folklore Society.
Powell, T.G.E. 1958. *The Celts*. London: Thames and Hudson.
Quirke, Stephen. 1992. *Ancient Egyptian Religion*. London: British Museum Press.
Read, John, 1957 (corrected and reprinted 1961). *From Alchemy to Chemistry*, London: Bell & Sons. Dover republication, 1995.
Rees, Alwyn, and Rees, Brinley. 1961. *Celtic Heritage*. London: Thames & Hudson.
Richmond, Ian. 1947 and 1987. *Roman Britain*. London: Bracken Books.
_____, and Tirion, Wil. 2001. *Stars and Planets Guide*. Princeton, NJ: Princeton University Press.
Ross, Anne. 1970. *Everyday Life of the Pagan Celts*. London: Batsford.
Rothwell, C., 1995. *Around Garstang*, Stroud, UK: Alan Sutton Publishing.
Salaperäinen, Olento. 2016. *A Field Guide to Fantastical Beasts*. London: Apple Press.
Scoresby-Routledge, Katherine, 1919, *The Mystery of Easter Island*, London: Hazell, Watson & Viney.
Scullard, H.H. 1979. *Roman Britain*. London: Thames and Hudson.
Shepard, Paul, and Sanders, Barry. 1992. *The Sacred Paw: The Bear in Nature, Myth, and Literature*. London: Arkana, Penguin.
Smith, William. 1855 (reprinted 1947). *A Smaller Latin-English Dictionary*. London: John Murray.
Snow, David, and Perrins, Christopher M., eds. 1998. *The Birds of the Western Palearctic, Concise Edition*. Oxford: Oxford University Press.
Soper, Tony. 1989. *A Companion to British Wildlife*. London: Marshall Cavendish Books Ltd.
Sterry, Paul. 1997. *Collins Complete British Wildlife Photo Guide*. London: HarperCollins.
Waring, P. 1978. *A Dictionary of Omens and Superstitions*. London: Souvenir Press.
White, Gilbert, 1833. *The Natural History of Selborne*, London: Hailes.
Wilkins, Jamie and Dunn, Robert, 2006. *300 Astronomical Objects: A Visual Reference to the Universe*, Richmond Hill, Ontario, Canada: Fire¬fly Books.
Yang, Lihui. 2005. *Handbook of Chinese Mythology*. Oxford: Oxford University Press.

Index

Entries in **bold** indicate main entries

aardvark 167-168
aardwolf see hyena
Aaron 69, 82
Aba 315
abaton 23, 391
Abderus 109
Abe no Seimei 37
Abe no Yasuna 37
Abenaki 105, 187
Abigail 78-79
abominable snowman/yeti 377
Abore 295
Aborigines/Australian Aborigines 7, 29-30, 172, 195, 249, 289, 314, 329, 366; *see also* Australia/Australasia
Abrahamic religions 1, 4, 39, 142, 331, 372, 401, 405
Abraxas 372
Abstemius 27
Abuk 332
Accademia dei Lincei 58
Achelous 65
Achilles 129, 382
Acoelomorpha/flatworms 12, 391
Acrab 386
Actinopterygii/ray-finned fishes 13, 269, 272, 273, 274, 278, 280, 281, 282, 283
Acubens 386
Adaheli 347
Adam and Eve 19, 213, 242, 331-332
Adaros 376
adder/asp/viper 338-339
Adhafera 386
Adlivun 236
Admetus 129
Adno-artina 17, 342
Adrammelech 372
Adu Ogyinae 20, 324-325
Aëdon 251, 260
aegis/aigis 80
Aegisthus 80
Aeolus, King 109-110
Aeschylus 80, 308, 359, 368, 404

Aesclepius/Asklepios 239, 333, 383, 384
Æsir 29, 198, 304
Æsop/Æsopic tales 21, 26, 27, 33, 34-36, 40, 116, 152, 157, 158, 205, 213, 239, 296, 313, 314, 333, 404
Æthelwulf 26
Aetolia 129, 222
Afagddu 132; *see also* Cerridwen
Afghanistan 120
Africa/African 2, 6, 14, 17, 20, 32, 34, 38, 44, 47, 51, 52, 53, 54, 55, 60, 64, 69, 71, 73, 75, 89, 90, 110, 114, 118, 120, 124, 125, 126, 128, 133, 135, 136, 138, 147, 148, 149, 154, 167, 168, 194, 195, 203, 206, 226, 229, 241, 244, 250, 259, 289, 299, 303, 305, 306, 312, 314, 316, 318, 322, 323, 324, 332, 339, 341, 343, 344, 370, 393, 394, 395, 396, 397, 398, 399, 400; *see also* South Africa
Afrikaans 59
Agamemnon 80, 223, 330, 359
Agave 129
agave 158
Agni/Chagaratha 81
Agnus Dei 79
Ah Puch 19
ahimsa 7, 391, 405
Ahriman 334
Ahura Mazda 65, 109, 134, 198, 334, 408
AIDS (Auto-Immune Deficiency Syndrome) 149
aikido 144
Ailill 68
Aïluros see Bastet
Aino 153-154
Ainu 95, 97
Air France 275
Aisoyimstan 108
Ajax 129
Akaiyan 164, 182
Akela 25

Akkruva 376
Akshobhya 137
Akupera/Chukwa 349
Aladfar 386
Alaska/Alaskan 94, 95, 99, 159, 259
Alba Longa 28
albatross 232-233, 234, 235, 236, 394, 398
Alberta 72
albinism 49
Al-Buraq 108
Alchiba 386
Alcmena 174
alcohol 6, 98, 304, 394
Alcyone 230-231; star 386
Aldebaran 386
Aldhanab 386
Aldhiba 386
Alectryon 239
Alexander the Great 110, 241, 268, 374
Alfadir/Allfather *see* Odin
Algonquian/Algonquin 56, 58, 91, 152, 162, 163-164, 182, 216, 229, 287, 348, 396, 404
Algorab 386
Al Jassasa 361
Allah 4, 260, 278, 366, 373, 405
alligator 14, **345-347**, 363, 391, 398
alpaca 123, 399
alpha-male 26
Alphaeus, River 65
Altair 386
Amaguq 7
Amalthea 80, 81, 387
Amanita muscaria (fly agaric mushroom) 6
Amazon, River/Basin 188, 194, 343
Amazons (female warriors) 110
Ambrose, Saint 304-305
Amenhotep 46
Amergin/Amergin Glúingel 87
America/American 6, 18, 26, 31,

423

44, 53, 55, 70, 71, 83, 85, 90, 93, 95, 101, 105, 107, 123, 126, 127, 133, 151, 154, 162, 163, 164, 169, 173, 176, 179, 180, 181, 188, 202, 203, 205, 208, 214, 244, 246-247, 260, 273, 288, 299, 306, 340, 341, 346, 348, 369, 392, 393, 399; American eagle emblem 214; *see also* Central America; South America
American Indian *see* Native American
American jackal *see* coyote
American timber wolf *see* wolf
Ammonoidea/ammonites 13, 391
Amphibia/Lissamphibia/amphibians 14, 294, 297, 298, 391, 396
Amphion 7
Amphisbaena 359
Amphitrite 286
Amphitryon 174
Amulius 28
Amun-Ra 209
An Sionnach see Ua Leochann
Ananda 65
Anansi 318
Anath 47
Andarta 97
Anderson, Kenneth 52
Andes 55, 122
Andhrimnir 130
Andrew, Saint 22
Androcles 47-48
Andvari 176-177
Angles 97, 112
Anglo-Saxon *see* Saxon
Angurboda 28
anima 4, 391
animism 6, 7, 391, 406
animus 4, 391
Annelida/segmented worms 12, 323, 392
Anselm, Saint 79
Anser 386
ant 7, **314-315**
Antaea 109
antelope 71, **73-74**, 358, 362
Anthea 129
Antiope 7
Anu 63
Anuanaitu 347
Anubis 32-33, 74, 403
Apache 56, 216
Apaosha 109
Aphrodite 42, 58, 151, 189, 239, 263, 268, 364, 383, 404
Apis/Hapi 63
Apocalypse 107
Apollo 66, 80, 129, 155, 189-190, 209, 223, 238, 254, 305, 330, 331, 332, 333, 341, 360, 362, 371, 381, 404
Apollo Cunomaglus 23
Apollo 11 Moon landing 155

Apollyon 360
Apophis 360
Apuleius 66-67, 320
Apus 380
Aquila 380
Arachnidae/arachnids 13
Aramipinchiwa 58
Arawn Pen Annwn 22
Arcadia 27, 96, 129, 386
Archilocus 134
Arcturus 386
Ardehe 97
Ardennes 7, 130
Arduinna 7, 130; *Arduenna Silva* 130
Aredvi Sura Anahita 107
Ares 27-28, 239, 265, 380, 404; *see also* Mars
Argentina 52, 83, 90, 166, 188, 249, 340
Argos (dog) 20
Argos (giant) 242
Argos (place) 7, 364
Argos (shipbuilder) 383
arhat 50, 392
Ariadne 316, 370
Arianrhod 216
Ariel 48
Aries 380
Arioch 48
Arion 189-190
Aristaeus 304-305
Aristophanes 260
Aristotle 50, 226, 254, 305, 358
armadillo 2
Arne 109-110
Arneb 386
Artemis 78, 86, 96, 110, 129, 209, 305, 333, 384, 404
arthropods 12-13, 285, 302, 306, 307, 309, 310, 312, 314, 315-316, 319
Arthur/King Arthur 23, 97, 111-112, 200, 206, 208, 213, 270, 353, 363
Artio 7, 97
artiodactyl 62, 71, 73, 74, 75, 77, 79, 83, 85, 88, 89, 90, 91, 93, 106, 120, 122, 124, 125, 127, 130, 191, 192, 193, 392
Arunasura 303-304
Asgard 21, 82, 198, 406
Ashab-e-Kahaf 1
Ashanti 20, 51, 138, 324-325
Ashmedai *see* Asmodeus
Ashtamangala 279
Ashtoreth *see* Astarte
Ashur 368
Ashvamedha 107, 108
Ashwins/Aswins 108
Asia/Asian 6, 32, 44, 49, 51, 52, 53, 54, 55, 56, 80, 85, 89, 90, 95, 99, 100, 101, 118, 119, 120, 127, 133, 136, 149, 162, 163, 168-

169, 203, 226, 241, 244, 259, 265, 279, 280, 299, 303, 304, 313, 344, 366, 395, 399; *see also* Eurasian; Far East
Asian black bear *see* black bear
Asikni 81
Asklepios *see* Aesculpius
Asmodeus/Ashmedai 67, 373
asp *see* adder
ass/donkey/mule/onager 70, 74, 111, **114-117**, 122, 123, 126, 167, 367, 372, 373, 394
The Assembly of the Wondrous Head 200
Astaroth *see* Astarte
Astarte/Ashtoreth/Astaroth/Ishtar 63, 66-67, 263; *see also* Asmodeus
Atalanta 96-97; *Atalanta in Calydon* 129
Athebaskan 187
Athena 20, 80, 215-216, 232, 315-316, 320, 332, 370, 371-372, 404; *see also* Minerva
Atotarho 334
Atreus 78
Audhumla 69
Augeas/Augean Stables 65
Augustine, Saint 242
Augustine of Hippo, Saint 290
Aunyain-á 342-343
Auriga 81, 387
aurochs 70, 71
Australia/Australasia 7, 29, 30, 107, 128, 133, 169, 170, 171, 181, 188, 194, 220, 244, 281, 306, 322, 338, 341, 344, 393, 401
Autolycus 26
Autonoe 129
Avalokiteshvara 74
Aventine Hill 28
Aves see birds
Ayyappan 50
Azazel 82
Azebam 105
Azelfafage 386
Azeto 376
Azha 387
Azhi Dahaka 369
Azrael 373
Aztec/Nahuatal 2, 31, 53, 104, 106, 158, 217, 239, 261, 311, 322, 335-336, 340

ba 78, 229, 366
Baal/Ba'al 47, 66, 308
Baba Yaga 240
Babako/Baka 240
Babe the Blue Ox 70
Babi 7
baboon 7, 142, 143
Babylon/Babylonian 61, 213, 242, 264, 357, 369, 378, 381, 382, 383, 384, 388

The Bacchae 81, 129-130
Bacchus *see* Dionysus
Bachúe 336
Bactria/Bactrian 120-121, 392; *see also* camel
badger 38, 173, **177-178**
Bagadjimbiri 30
Baginis 366
Baha'i/ Bahá'u'lláh 121-122, 176, 401-402
Baile Cronin 67
Bajang 175
Balaam 115-116
Balarama 116-117
Balder/Baldr/Baldur 91, 248, 271, 304, 406
Bali 108, 136, 286
Balor 68
Ba-neb-jet 78
Banghaisgidheach 42
Bangladesh 49, 136; *see also* Bengal/Bengali
Banks, Sir Joseph 171
Baphomet 372
Barham, the Reverend Richard Harris 203-204
Barnum, P.T. 141
basilisk/cockatrice 360
Bastet/*Ailuros*/Baast/Bast/Bsst/ Oubaste/Pasht 39-40, 47
bat 12, **165-167**, 260, 357, 359, 393, 394; bumblebee bat 12
Batara Guru/Batara Siwa 286
Bato Kanzeon/Kannon Bosatsu 74
Bavon, Saint 212
Bayard 112
bear 7, 10, 26, 37, **95-102**, 104, 179, 269, 295, 353, 357, 360, 365, 377, 384-385, 386, 399; black 99-102; brown 95-98; grizzly 95; Kodiak 95; polar 98-99, 384; Smokey the Bear 102; teddy bear 18, 102
Beauty and the Beast 365-366
beaver 38, **162-164**, 170, 182, 335, 393
Beddgelert 24
bee/bumblebee/honeybee 13, 91, **302-306**, 383, 392
Beelzebub 150, 308, 399
beetle 170, 248, 302, **312-314**, 393; scarab 312-313
Beg-Ts'e 111
Behemoth 75
Bel/Beli/Beli Mawr 23, 67; Beltan/Beltane 67, 209
Belemnoidea/belemnites 13
Belgium 130, 154, 212, 322
Bellerophon 109, 359, 383
Benedict, Saint 246
Bengal/Bengali 49, 289
Benini 369
Benzaiten 336-337

Beornwulf 26
Bern 97
Berserkr/Berserker 98
Besla 69
Betelgeuse 387
Beth-Luis-Nion/tree-alphabet 87-88
bhakti 143
Bharata, King 88
The Bible 5, 22, 33, 39, 48, 59, 69, 74, 78-79, 82, 98, 107, 115, 121, 132, 186, 239, 255, 263-264, 308, 314, 331, 339, 340, 358, 360, 372, 403; King James (Authorized) Bible 59
Bicorn 69-70
Bifröst 21
The Big Bad Wolf 26-27
The Bili Ape 147; *see also* chimpanzee
bioindicator 299
birds 5, 6, 12, 14, 19, 21, 28, 36, 45, 59, 108, 132, 140, 152, 159, 161, 170, 172, 198-207, 307, 317, 329, 334, 335, 354, 364, 366, 369, 371, 380, 381, 383, 392; bird augury 5, 28, 214; birdsong 5; freshwater 220-231; passerines 244-252; raptors 208-219; sea birds 232-237
The Birds (play by Aristophanes) 260
Biróg 68
birth-brick 64
bison/buffalo 71-73, 271, 335, 342, 392; buffalo fish 71; buffalo jumps 72; White Buffalo Calf Woman 72-73; *see also* Ptesánwin
Black Shuck 22
blackbird 5, 161, 209, 215, **244-246**, 249, 396, 399
Blackfoot/Blackfeet 72, 91, 108
Blake, William 49
Blodeuwedd 216
Blodighofi 130
The Blue Men of Siant 375-376
Blumenbach, Johann 170
Bo, Empress Dowager 103
boar 7, 42, 87, 97, 98, **127-130**, 131, 133, 342, 364, 367, 399; *see also* Calydonian boar hunt
Bodhisattva 74, 242
Boeotia/Boeotian 5, 110
Boeotus 110
Bok, Gordon 180-181
bonobo 147, 148, 397
The Book of Revelation 48, 79, 107-108
Bor 69
Borak 373
Borneo 145, 146, 230, 231, 398
Boudicca/Boadicea/Buddug 153
Bovidae 62, 71, 73, 77, 79, 83, 392

The Boy Who Cried Wolf 26-27
Brahma 81, 100, 224, 242, 367, 382, 404
Bran (nephew of Fionn mac Cúmhaill) 23
Brân/ Bendigeidfrân/Brân Fendigaidd 200, 245
Brazil 118, 319, 342
brehons/Brehon Laws 304
Br'er Fox *see* fox
Br'er Rabbit *see* rabbit
Brid/Bride/Bridget/Brighid 40
Bright Heart 105
Brising 41
Brisson, Mathurin 182
Bristol 70
Britannia 112
Brittany 67, 269, 295, 306
Brok 308-309
Bubastis 39
bucca 79
Bucephalus 110, 411
Buckingham Palace 98
Buddha/Gautama Buddha 44, 50, 65, 107, 110, 116, 137, 138, 140, 225, 242, 244, 279, 330, 356, 367, 394, 395, 402; *see also* Jatakas; Siddharta
Buddhism/Buddhist mythology 7, 44, 48, 50, 51, 61, 74, 107, 110, 131, 136, 137, 219, 242, 279, 330, 391, 392, 394, 397, 402; Mahayana 110, 131, 137; Tibetan 117, 131
buffalo *see* bison
Buganda people *see* Uganda
bull 7, 36, **62-63**, 65, 66, 68-69, 110, 254, 309, 361, 368, 370, 371, 372, 373, 378, 381, 384, 386, 387, 392, 399; *see also* cattle; cow; ox
bumblebee bat *see* bat
Bunyan, Paul 70
Bur 69
Buriat/Buryat 19, 113, 355
Burkhan 19
Burma 136, 140
butterfly 307, **310-311**
Byama 172

Caball/Cavall 23
Cacce-jielle and Cacce-jienne 376
caecilian 14, 396
Caer Ibormeith 221-222
Caesar, Julius 92, 125, 402
Cailleach Beinn a' Bhric, Cailleach Mhòr Chlibric, Cailleach Mhòr nam Fiadh 86
caiman/cayman 347
Cairbar cinn Chait 45
California 31, 104, 181, 232, 257, 287, 395
Callisto 96, 384-385, 386

Calydonian boar hunt 97, 129
Camalotz/Camazotz 166
Cambodia 140, 144
camel/camelid 1, 12, **120-122**, 124, 126, 361, 362, 365, 382, 383, 387, 392
Camelopardalis 380
Cameroon 149
Canaan/Canaanite 47, 64, 66, 263, 372
Canada 55, 56, 71, 72, 83, 90, 92, 93, 94, 95, 128, 191, 224, 269, 284, 287, 306, 340, 388; Canadian goose *see* goose
Cancer 381
Canens 265
Canes Venatici 381
Canis Major, Canis Minor 380-381
cannibalism 28, 60, 78, 178, 216, 251, 281
Canopus 387
The Canterbury Tales 70
Canti 112
Capella 81, 387
Capricornus/Capricorn 380
Care Bears 105
caribou/reindeer 17, 26, **93-94**, 191, 393, 398; Caribou Inuit 94; Taimur herd 93
carp 71, **278-280**, 357, 394; goldfish 280
Carr-Gomm, Philip 2, 8, 128, 296
Carroll, Lewis 183-184
Cassandra 330
Castor (beaver genus) 162-164, 393; castoreum 163
Castor (Greek hero) 129
cat/*Felis*/*Felidae* 4, 5, 7, 8, 9, 10, 11, 12, 30, 34, 37, **38-45**, 47, 50, 54, 59, 60, 80, 102; guard 40-41; Kilkenny 42; lucky 41; roasting 40; Scottish clan 45; troll 45; wildcat 44-45
catamount *see* cougar
Cathbad 23
cattle/oxen 12, 16, 26, **62-63**, 65, 66, 67, 68, 71, 73, 77, 121, 305, 308, 361, 392; fairy cattle *see* bull; cow; deer; ox
Cayuga 26, 334
Cecrops 371-372
Celtic Druidism 4, 5, 7, 22, 23, 30, 36, 39, 66, 67, 68-69, 78, 86, 87-88, 107, 111, 128, 130, 131, 132, 151, 176, 180, 199, 200, 206, 208, 211, 213, 215, 216, 217, 245, 249, 253-254, 269, 270, 290, 296, 304, 339, 384, 395, 397, 399, 402
centaur 97, 110, 129, 333, 364, 371, 378, 380, 383, 389; *see also* Chiron

Centaurus 380
Central America 31, 52, 56, 150, 166, 257, 336, 340
Cephalopodia/cephalopods 13, 391, 392, 393
Cerberus *see* Kerberos
ceremony of throwing the ball *see* Tapa Wanka Yap
Cernunnos/Kernunnos 7, 78, 402
Cerridwen 132, 270
Cesi, Federico 58
Cetacea 185, 188, 393
Cetus 380
Ceyx 230-231
Chagan-Shukuty 349
Chagaratha *see* Agni
Chalawan 387
Chamaeleon (constellation) 380
chameleon 343
Chan, Jackie 169
Chandra 74
Chang Kuo-Lao 117
Chang'e 155
channúnpa/peace pipe 73
Chanticleer 240
charango 2
Charlecote Park 89
Charlemagne 112
Charybdis *see* Scylla
Chaucer, Geoffrey 70, 240
Chauvet 46
Chavin culture 53
cheetah 54-55, 391
Chelidonis 251
Ch'en Nan 18
Cherokee 56, 213, 216, 217, 261, 313, 317, 335, 365
Chesterton, G.K. 114-115
chevrotain 89
Chi Chi 102
Chiang Shih/Kiang She 280
Chibcha 201
Chichevache 69-70
chicken 71, 174, **238-241**, 346, 395
Chimaera 109, 359
Chiminigagua 201
chimpanzee 146, **148-149**, 203, 397; Nim Chimpsky 149
China/Chinese 14, 17, 44, 55, 74, 92, 95, 102, 103, 118, 119, 137, 143, 149, 178, 188, 226, 244, 273, 279, 299, 304, 316, 345-346, 347
Chinese astrology/astronomy 18, 49, 206, 379-382, 385
Chinese folklore/mythology 5, 18, 36-37, 41, 48, 49-50, 51, 74, 119, 144, 149-150, 151-152, 155, 165, 169, 195, 205-206, 218, 224-225, 226, 242-243, 254, 262-263, 279, 280, 291, 296-297, 310-311, 313-314, 330, 348-349, 352, 355-356, 358-359, 360-361, 379, 402-403; *see also* Taoism
Chinook 31, 32, 181
Chinvat Bridge 21
Chione 209
Chiron 110, 129, 333, 371, 380
chitin 13
Chomsky, Noam 149
Chondrichthyes/cartilaginous fishes 13, 276, 393
chough 199, 200, **206-207**
Christ *see* Jesus
Christian/Christianity 1, 4, 6, 7, 8, 19, 22, 40, 44, 48, 59, 60, 67, 74, 79, 82, 91, 98, 110-111, 114, 115-116, 121, 130, 131, 143, 150, 152, 167, 177, 195, 199, 200, 201, 202, 211, 212, 216, 226, 234, 236, 237, 239-240, 242, 246, 247, 249-250, 254, 260, 261, 262, 264, 265, 268, 289-290, 298, 304, 306, 308, 311, 319, 331, 339, 340, 341, 352, 353, 357, 358, 359, 361, 362, 368, 371, 372, 373, 378, 381, 399, 401, 402, 403; *see also The Bible*
Chukchi 99, 182
Chukwa *see* Akupera
Chumash 287
Churchill, Winston 22
Cicero 148
Circe 265, 359
circumcision 30
Circus Maximus 125
Ciuateteo 311
Ckírihki Kuuruúriki see Skidi/Skiri Federation
clade 1, 10, 11, 165, 168, 179, 181, 182, 185, 188, 215, 255, 257, 261, 262, 294, 348, 393
cladogram 10
clam 287-288
class 9
classical Greek mythology/pantheon 2, 7, 13, 27, 63, 65, 80-81, 86, 96-97, 107, 109, 110, 115, 129, 169, 189, 194, 222, 223, 226, 230, 239, 242, 251, 260, 265, 268, 286, 298, 304-305, 315, 316, 320, 332, 354, 359, 364, 368, 370, 373, 379, 380, 381, 382, 384, 386, 387, 389, 403, 404
classical Roman mythology/pantheon 7, 57, 66, 74, 86, 96-97, 125, 226, 228, 239, 249, 265, 268, 271, 275, 286, 291, 298, 305, 313, 315, 333, 339, 345, 360, 364, 368, 373, 375, 378, 380, 381, 382, 383, 384, 396, 403, 406-407
classification 9-14, 32, 44, 60, 73, 75, 100, 101, 135, 148, 199, 262, 330, 385, 391, 395, 397

Clavijero, Francisco Javier 31
Clotaire, King 113
Clytemnestra 80, 222, 330, 359
Cnidaria/jellyfish/anemones 12, 285, 290, 393
cobra 61, 78, 30, **337-338**, 360, 399
cockatrice *see* basilisk
Coleridge, Samuel Taylor 233
Colombia 53, 201, 316, 336, 349
Columba (constellation) 381
Columba/Colom/Colomcille, Saint 262, 353, 381, 393
Commentarii de Bello Gallico 92
conch 14, 136, 279, 285, **288-289**, 361
condor *see* vulture
Confucius/Kong Fuzi/Confucianism 144, 158, 403, 407
Congo 60, 75, 125-126, 147, 148, 241
Conla's Well 270
Connacht 68
Con-tici/Kon-tiki 56
Convention on International Trade in Endangered Species (CITES) 118
Cooley, Cattle Raid of *see Táin Bó Cúailnge*
coquilles St. Jacques see scallop
coral 12, 273, 285, 289, **290-291**, 393
cornucopia 81, 111
Cornwall 22, 24, 111, 200, 206, 269, 306, 353
Cortéz, Hernando 336
Corvus 381
cougar/mountain lion/puma 10, 51, **55-56**, 398
cow 4, 12, 45, 62, **63-64**, 66, 68, 69, 70, 75, 127, 131, 205-206, 211, 263, 286, 305, 308, 370, 373, 392; *see also* bull; cattle; ox
coyote/Coyote/American jackal/little wolf/prairie wolf **30-32**, 72, 257, 393
crab 14, **285-287**, 378, 379, 381, 386, 392
crane 27, 221, **253-255**, 382, 386, 395; crane bag 254; crane cleric 254; crane dance 254-255
crayfish 14, 104, 396
Cree 58, 90, 91, 152, 162, 213, 216
Crete 81, 140, 189, 254, 316, 370
crocodile 14, 146, **344-345**, 346, 347, 356, 357, 387, 398
Cronos 115
Crouching Tiger, Hidden Dragon 50
crow 4, 5, 7, 35, 132, 161, **199-207**, 214, 294, 297, 381, 386, 393; Morfran 132
Crowshoot, Joe 72

Crustacea/crustaceans 13-14, 393
Cú Chúlainn 23, 68
cuckold *see* cuckoo
cuckoo 253, **255-257**, 260, 394, 395; Cloud-Cuckoo-Land 260; cuckold 256; Mr. Cuckoo 257
Culhwch and Olwen 128, 215, 245, 270-271
Cunobelinus/Cunobelinn/Cymbeline 23
Cunoglasus 23
Cusco/Cuzco 56, 123
Custer, Lt. George Armstrong 73
Cuthbert, Saint 70, 177
Cuthman, Saint 240-241
cuttlefish 13
Cwn Annwn/hounds of Annwn 24
Cyclops 140
Cygnus 381-382
Cyhiraeth 34
Cynewulf 26
Cyprus 38

Daedalion 209
Daedalus 370
Dagobert, King 113
Dagr 113
Dagul'ku 261
Daire, King 86
Dajoji 53
dakhma 218-219
Dakota Sioux *see* Sioux
Daksha 81-82
Danaë 7, 370
Dangun 97
Daniel 48, 98
Dante 21
Darius the Mede 48
Dark Horse Records 108
Darwin, Charles 142
David, King 78-79, 319
Dayunsi 313
deer 45, 51, 57, 67, 74, **85-94**, 358, 363, 389, 393; fairy cattle 86; fallow 88-89; mouse 89-90; red 85-88
Deert 30
Defoe, Daniel 206-207
Deganawidah/Dekanawida 176
Delaware 25
Delphinus 382
Demeter 57, 239, 305
The Dendan 362-362
Dendera 64
Deneb 387
Denmark 24, 78, 98, 374
Desmotes 110
Devi *see* Kali
Devil's Dandy Dogs 24
Devil's Hole 178
Dežman, Karel 83-84
dharma 110, 279, 394; *dharmachakra* 279; Dharmapala 110

Dharu 29
Dhenuka 116-117
Di Ku 18
Diana, Princess 290
Diana (Roman goddess) 86, 96, 110, 130, 381, 407
Diggajas/Dikpala 137-138
Dilga 30
dingo **29-30**, 393
dinosaur 14
Diodorus Siculus 1, 61
Diomedes 109, 232, 394
Dionysus/Bacchus 81, 115, 129-130, 189, 368, 404
Dioscorides 291
Disney, Walt 105
The Divine Comedy 21
Djanbun 170
Djauan 30
Dodona 65, 263
dog 1, 5, 7, 8, 10, 12, **16-24**, 26, 29, 30, 31, 34, 38, 40, 48, 55, 59, 60, 85, 86, 104, 106, 113, 133, 142, 147, 157, 159, 172, 177, 236, 239, 325, 342, 359, 379, 380, 381, 383, 384, 388, 389, 392; black dogs/Black Dog 22; dog 16; ghost 22; guard 21
Dogedoi 113
dokhma 21, 394
dolphin 75, **188-191**, 192, 193, 194, 272-273, 284, 382, 397; bycatch (tuna, dolphin) 272-273
domain 9
Domovoi 377
donkey *see* ass
Donn 68
doodang 363
Dorado 382
dormouse 11
Douglas, Archibald 157
dove/pigeon 5, 7, 178, 201, 248, 256, **261-264**, 278, 381, 393; turtledove 256
Drachenloch 96
Draco 382
Dracula 167
dragon 2, 18, 49, 50, 58, 161, 167, 280, 323, 324, 330, **352-356**, 359, 360, 362, 373, 374, 379, 382, 387, 405, 406; air 353; Chinese 355-356; dragon gate 280; dragon slayer 354; earth dragon 353; fire dragon 49, 353; Komodo dragon *see* lizard; water dragon 58, 324, 353
The Dream of Oengus 221-222
Dreamtime mythology 30, 171, 195, 401; *see also* Aborigines/Australian Aborigines
Dromi 29
druid/Druid/Druidism/modern Druidism *see* Celtic Druidism

Duat 64
Dublin Zoo 119
duck-billed platypus *see* platypus
Dudugera 272
dugong 194-195
Duhalar 94
The Dun Cow 70; Dun Cow Rib Farm 70
Dun Holm 70
Dunsmore Heath 70
Durga *see* Kali
Durham Cathedral 70
Dutch 59
Dyfed 22
Dzalarhons/Dzelarhons 295
Dziban 387
Dzoavits 178

Ea *see* Enki
eagle 6, 12, 48, 98, 161, 178, 198, 209, **212-214**, 216, 218, 245, 249, 260, 313, 335, 339, 357, 359, 361, 362, 368, 378, 380, 386; bald eagle 214
Eala Bhàn 221-222
East *see* Far East; Middle East
Easter Bunny *see* hare
Easter Island 235-236
echidna/spiny anteater 169
Echinodermata/starfish/sea urchins 12, 394
eclipse 18, 176, 330, 354
Edda see *Poetic Edda and Prose Edda*
Edfu 64
Edji 19-20
eel 280-282
Egil 82
Egypt 66, 80, 114, 339, 358, 373; *see also* Kemet; Mesr
Egyptian pantheon/mythology 7, 32, 39-40, 46-47, 54-55, 61, 63-65, 74, 75, 76, 78, 91, 115, 124, 133, 142, 143, 153, 157, 158, 209, 210, 211, 218, 224, 227-228, 229, 237, 238, 259, 268, 306, 312-313, 319-320, 338, 344, 345, 352, 360, 364, 366-367, 373, 380, 382, 384, 391, 392, 399, 403
Eikthyrnir 88
Eilythia 174, 218; *see also* Nekhebet
Eithne 68
Elbis 82
Eldhrimir 130
elephant 1, 7, 12, 102, 121, **135-141**, 158, 191, 309-310, 326, 349, 361, 363, 367, 394, 396, 404; Mahmud 140; white elephant 140-141; *see also* Ganesh/Ganesha
Eleusinian Mysteries 20

Eliot, T.S. 78
elk/wapiti 85, **90-91**, 92, 93, 393; Benevolent and Protective Order of Elks 91; Hiisi Elk 91
Ellis, Steven 125
Elnath 387
Eloy, Saint 112-113
Eltanin 387
Enki/Ea/Hea 357
Enkidu 63
entheogen 6, 394
Epaphus 66
Epiphi 64
Epona 7, 107, 111, 402
Equuleus 382
Erik, King of Sweden 225
Erinaceidae 11
Erlang 18
Eros 151, 189, 263, 383
Erymanthus, Mount 129; Erymanthian boar 129
Erzulie 376
Estonia 92
Etain 111
Etana 213
Ethiopia 48, 75
Eulipotyphla 11
Eurasian 25, 32, 56, 57, 92, 163, 205, 249, 259, 393
Euripides 81, 129, 140, 381
Europa 7, 381
Europe/European 4, 7, 17, 23-24, 26, 32, 34, 44, 47, 48, 51, 57, 69, 71, 78, 80, 83, 85, 89, 90, 91, 92, 93, 95, 97, 111, 113, 126, 127, 133, 142, 151, 154, 156, 157, 160, 162, 170, 175, 177, 179, 191, 193, 203, 206, 208, 224, 225, 226, 229, 230, 234, 244, 246, 247, 249, 250, 256, 259, 280, 281, 287, 288, 290, 296, 299, 303, 304, 312, 333, 344, 354, 362, 366, 377, 392, 394, 397, 398, 401, 402, 406; *see also* Proto-Indo-European
Eurydice 331
Eurymedousa 7
Eurystheus/Eurystheus of Tiryns 20, 129
Eustathius of Antioch 73
Exodus, Book of 82, 116
exoskeleton 12-13

Fafnir 387
fainting goats *see* goat
falcon 198, **210-212**, 234, 403
The Fantastic Mr. Fox 37
Far East 48, 108, 118, 119, 137, 144, 164, 205-206, 242, 279, 299, 322, 341, 352
Faunus *see* Pan
Feast of Fools 116
februum 28
Feliformes/Feliformia 9, 59, 60, 395

Felis/Felidae see cat
fennec fox *see* fox
Fenrir 28-29
Fergus 67
ferret/polecat 173, **174-175**, 396, 400
Festa Stultorum 116
Festival of Drunkenness 64
Festival of the Beautiful Reunion 64
Fianna 86-87
Findbennach 68
Finland 91, 92, 93
Finnegas 270
Finno-Ugric mythology 94, 113
Fionn mac Cúmhaill/Finn McCool 23, 86, 270
firebird *see* phoenix
fish 7, 13, 33, 71, 76, 104, 114, 122, 132, 154, 175, 176, 177, 180, 181, 185, 186, 191, 192, 193, 225, 226, 228-229, 230, 232, 248, **268-277, 278-284**, 286, 288, 291, 296, 336, 346, 347, 357, 358, 360, 361-362, 365, 367, 373, 374, 376, 378, 379, 380, 383-384, 385, 386, 388, 391, 393, 395, 398; flying fish 273-274
Flidais 67
Flood/Great Flood 5, 21, 31, 87, 212, 263-264, 268, 286, 336, 349, 367, 381, 406
fly 307-309, 383
fly agaric mushroom (*Amanita muscaria*) 6
Fomalhaut 388
Fomorians 68, 200
Foo/Fu Dogs 18
The Forty-Seven Ronin 37
Fossey, Dian 147
fox 7, 10, 11, 26, **33-37**, 38, 116, 134, 155, 174, 240, 296, 385, 386, 400; Br'er Fox 37, 155; *Fantastic Mr. Fox* 37; fennec fox 34; fox hunting 34; nine-tailed fox 36-37; Reynard the fox 37
France 40, 46, 67, 69, 78, 96, 97, 112, 113, 130, 188, 200, 224, 247, 250, 275, 298, 321, 372, 375, 384
Freemasonry 116
freshwater birds *see* birds
Frey 42, 130
Freya/Freyja 41-42, 58, 98, 369, 406
frigate bird 235-236
Frigg/Frigga 42, 268, 406
frog/toad 14, 71, 104, 155, 175, 226, 283, **294-297**, 299, 361, 369, 388, 392; frog prince 295; stone of power 296
fulmar 236

Gabriel's Hounds 24
gadfly 109, 308
Gagavitz 336
Galanthis 174
Galdikas, Birutè 146-147
Galen 291
Galileo Galilei 58
Gama Sennin 297
Gandalf 113
Ganesh/Ganesha 7, 136-137, 404
Ganga/Ganges 190
Garm/Garmr 21
Garuda 213-214
Gastropoda/gastropods 14
gato monte *see* cougar
Gaul/Gaulish/Gauls 36, 78, 111, 130, 199, 224, 254, 290, 375, 402
Gaunab 69
Gautama *see* Buddha
Gavaevodata 64-65
Gavida 68
Gawain/Gawan/Gawen 208-209
Geb 78, 224, 313, 403
gecko 17, 342
Ged 78
Gelert 24
Georgics see Virgil
Ghana 20, 51, 138, 324, 342
Giambattista della Porta 58
gibbon 149-150, 395
Gilgamesh 63, 213, 264, 357, 384, 394
Gio 148
giraffe 124-125, 126, 380, 395
Gleipnir 29
Glires 11
Glooskap 187
Gnipahellir 21
goat 7, 12, 26, 35, 41, 73, **79-83**, 89, 131, 240, 270, 357, 359, 368, 372, 377, 378, 379, 380, 387, 393; fainting goats 83
The Golden Ass 66-67
The Golden Calf 69, 116
The Golden Fleece 78
goldfish *see* carp
Goldhorn 83-84
Golding, William 130, 279, 289, 308
Gollum 177
Goodall, Jane 147
goose 223-225, 261, 335, 385, 386, 392; Canada goose 249, 392; golden egg 224-225
Gorgon 13, 80, 109, 216, 370, 374
gorgoneion 370
gorilla 145, **146-147**, 148; *Gorillas in the Mist* 147; King Kong 147
Gorky, Maxim 234-235
Graves, Robert 2, 80, 230
gray wolf *see* wolf
Great Lakes 105, 152, 269, 335

Greek mythology/pantheon *see* classical Greek mythology/pantheon
Grendel/Grendel's Dam 374
griffin 362
Grimm, Jacob 24, 377
Griselda 70
groundhog/Groundhog Day *see* marmot
Grus 382
Gryla 377
guallipen 363
Guanyin/Guan Yin *see* Kuan Yin
Guardians of the Galaxy 105
Guatemala 71, 150, 166
Guðmundsson, Jón 180
Gullinbursti 130
Gundestrup Cauldron 78
Gur Aryeh 48
Guy of Warwick 70
Gwich'in 94
Gwion/Gwion Bach 132, 270
Gwydion 216
Gwynn ap Nudd 24

Hades 20, 200, 331, 333, 404, 407
Hadhrat Ismael 1
Hadhrat Saleh 1
Hadhrat Uzair 1
Haile Selassie 48
Haitsi-aibed 69
halal 6, 121, 407
Hamal 388
Han 94
Hanblecheyapi see vision quest
Hand Looks for Buffalo, Floyd 72
Hannahanna 303
Hanno 146
hantu 90
Hanuman 142-143
hare 5, 9, 11, 132, **151-154**, 161, 381, 383, 386, 395; Easter Bunny 153; *see also* rabbit
Harimau Kramat 50
harpies 368-369
Harris, Joel Chandler 37, 155
Harris, Richard 72
Harrison, George 108
Harry Potter 360, 371, 377
Hathor 63-65, 211
Hati 29
Hatshepsut 54
Hattara Aonja 50
Hatto, Archbishop 159-160
Hausa 168
Hawaii/Hawaiian mythology 7, 160, 232, 276-277, 281-282, 322, 338, 388
hawk 6, 63-64, 87, 132, **208-210**, 228, 260, 320, 339, 375, 391; The Hawk of Achill 209

Hayagriva 111
Hea *see* Enki
Head-Smashed-In Buffalo Jump *see* bison
Heaney, Seumas 42-43, 246
Hebrew 39, 59, 66, 116, 308, 352, 358, 406
hedgehog 11, 35, 38, 61, **133-134**, 169, 394
Heidrun/Heithron 83
Heike 287
Heimdal/Heimdall 21, 406
Heimskringla 28
Helgakviða Hjörvarðssonar 130
Helheim 21
Helicon, Mount 109
Helios 65, 239
Hembe 148
Hengist and Horsa 111-112
Hephaestus 80
Hera 42, 65-66, 81, 174, 226, 230, 242, 251, 286, 305, 308, 315, 331, 381, 384, 404
Herakles/Hercules 18, 20, 27, 65, 109, 110, 129, 174, 286, 332, 354, 359-360, 371, 381, 383
heraldry 51, 74, 213, 237, 254, 275, 283, 290, 358
hermaphroditism 60, 322, 331, 364, 365
Hermes 20, 78, 109, 209, 227-228, 242, 333, 364, 370, 404
Herodotus 40, 75, 107, 190, 218, 263, 361, 404
heron 226, **228-229**, 253, 260, 335, 366
Her-tchema *see* Horus
Hesiod 322
Heyerdahl, Thor 56
Hiawatha/Haien'wa'tha 176, 334-335
hibernation 96
Hido *see* Sido
High King of Ireland 68-69
Hildisvíni 98
Himalayas 100, 143, 377
hind 86
Hinduism/Hindu pantheon 7, 21, 32, 33, 48, 50, 61, 63, 65, 74, 81, 86, 88, 100, 107, 108, 111, 116, 136-137, 143-144, 190, 213, 224, 241, 242, 256, 265, 268, 279, 286, 303-304, 305, 314, 317, 328, 330, 336, 344, 348, 349, 352, 358, 364, 367-368, 378-379, 380, 382, 383, 387, 391, 394, 396, 397, 398, 402, 404
Hinny/Jenny 117
Hino/Hinon 214
Hippocrene 109
hippogriff 362-363
Hippolyta/Hippolyte/Hippoltus 110

hippopotamus 11, **74-76**, 395
Höðr 271
hog *see* pig
Hokkaido 95
Homer 20, 66, 263, 286, 305, 359, 368, 404
honey-badger 61
hoopoe 259-260
Hopi 250
horse 5, 7, 8, 12, 22, 36, 72, 74, 80, **106-113**, 114, 117, 119, 123, 126, 130, 137, 182, 223, 263, 275, 281, 308, 309, 324, 334, 356, 357, 358, 359, 361, 362, 364, 367, 369, 370, 371, 372, 379, 382, 383, 386, 394, 402, 406; pantomime 111; white 107-108, 372; Wooden Horse of Troy 330, 332-333
Horus/Her-tchema 63-64, 74, 75, 210-211, 227, 320, 344, 366, 403
Hotaru Hime 302
howler monkey *see* monkey
Hrímfaxi 113
Hualapai/Walapai 56
Huarochiri/Warachiri 36
Huathiacuri 36
Huehuecóyotl 32, 78
Huginn and Muninn 161, 199, 200-201
Huitzilopochtli 261, 336
Humbaba 357
hummingbird 12, **260-261**
Hunahpú 166
Hunkpapa Lakota *see* Sioux
Hunkpapi/relative ceremony 73
Hvergelmir 88
hybrids, animal-human 364-365
Hydaspes, Battle of 110
Hydra 359-360
Hydra, Hydrus (constellations) 382
hyena/*aardwolf* **58-60**, 386, 393, 398
Hypnos 371

ibex 83-84, 393
ibis 226, **227-228**, 403
Iceland 45, 180, 182, 377, 398, 406
Iduna 198
Ihy 64
Ikanam 32
Iko *see* Sido
Iktomi 317-318
Ilé-Ifé 343
Illini 58
Imbolc/Oimelc/Oimelg 67
immrama 41
Inachus 66
Inari 37
Inca 7, 56, 122-123, 212
India/Indian folklore 5, 11, 19, 21, 25, 26, 27, 44, 49, 51, 52, 55, 60-61, 74, 108, 116, 135, 136-137, 138, 140-141, 143-144, 149, 156, 157, 158, 161, 188, 199, 218, 241, 244, 254, 255, 265, 273, 278, 279, 287, 288, 289, 291, 322, 325, 330, 394, 396, 398, 402, 404, 405
Indian/American Indian *see* Native American
Indra 33, 107, 108, 137, 143, 214, 242, 256, 265, 305, 352
Inipi 73
Ino 129
insects 4, 5, 7, 12-13, 18, 32, 71, 167, 169, 226, 265, **301-311**, **312-315**, 342, 391, 395, 405
Inuit/Eskimo 6, 7, 94, 99, 183, 193, 236, 384, 388, 404; Caribou Inuit 94
Inupiat 94
Inuvialuit 94
Io 65-66
Iran 54, 63, 79, 98, 255, 393
Iraq 63, 394
Ireland 36, 45, 67, 68, 86, 111, 180-181, 202, 206, 246, 269, 270, 304, 322, 328, 353
Iroquois 26, 53, 176, 214, 334, 349; Iroquois Confederacy 26, 176, 334
Irving, Washington 202
Isaiah 48, 352
Ishnata Awicalowan see womanhood ceremony
Ishtar *see* Astarte
Isis 64, 211, 227, 313, 319-320, 338, 384, 403
Islam 1, 4, 6, 7, 41, 82, 108, 121, 122, 131, 140, 143, 150, 199-200, 242, 255, 260, 278, 319, 331, 365, 366, 372, 373, 385, 398, 399, 401, 402, 405
Israelites 66, 69
Italapas 32
Italy 17, 65, 125, 129, 240, 246, 287, 359, 362

jackal 31, **32-33**, 59, 382, 387, 392
jackdaw 199, **203-204**, 393; *The Jackdaw of Rheims* 203-204
Jacob 48
Jackson, Peter 50
Jacobs, W.W. 145
Jacobson's organ 38
jaguar 51, **52-53**, 397; Jaguar Knights 53
Jain/Jainism 7, 136, 144, 279, 330, 391, 394, 397, 398, 405
Jambavantha/Jambavat 100
James, Saint 290
Japan 95, 97, 104, 273, 287, 322
Japanese mythology 18, 36-37, 41, 48, 50, 74, 95, 97, 100, 105, 117, 119, 137, 143-144, 150, 151, 165, 174, 178, 195, 199, 206, 224, 225, 232, 242, 254, 262, 273, 287, 296, 297, 299-300, 302, 314, 316, 322, 336, 355, 361, 364, 405
Jason 129
The Jatakas 65, 116, 395
jay/magpie 204-206
Jehovah 406
Jeremiah 59
Jerusalem 33, 48, 66, 108, 114, 116, 121, 239, 264
Jesuits 116
Jesus/Jesus Christ/Christ 48, 72, 79, 82, 107-108, 114, 116, 121, 122, 132-133, 186, 211, 234, 239, 247, 264, 268, 308, 320, 339, 401-402, 403; *see also* Christianity
Jewish/Judaic folklore/Judaism 1, 4, 6, 7, 21, 82, 116, 121, 143, 239, 337, 373, 405-406
Jezebel 22
jinn/djinn 60
John 48, 79
Johor 50
Johnston, Henry Hamilton 125-126
Jólakötturinn 45
Jólasveinarnir/Yule Lads 377
Jonah 186
Jorōgumo/Joro Kumo 316-317
Judah 48
Judaism *see* Jewish
Judas 91
Juksakka 94
Jung, Carl 367
The Jungle Book 25, 61
Juno 42, 224, 226, 383, 407; *see also* Hera
Jupiter/Iuppiter/Juppiter 66, 249, 407; *see also* Zeus
Jutes 112
Juutas 91

kaftar 60
Kaguru 60
The Kalevala 91, 153-154, 368, 395
Kali/Kalika/Devi/Durga/Mahadeve/Mahakali/Parvati 32-33, 50, 303-304
Kalki 107
Kama 305
Kamadeva 256
Kamadhenu 65
kami 100, 144, 337, 405, 407
Kamohoalii/Ka'moho-all'i 7, 277
Kamrushepa 303
Kana 349-350
Kanaloa 7
Kananesky Amaiyehi 317

kangaroo 170-172, 396
Kannon Bosatsu *see* Bato Kanzeon
Kanthaka 107
kappa 361
kapparos 241
Karadjeri 30
Karashishi 48
karma 7, 395
Karma (Hindu god) 305
Karshipta 198
Keats, John 251-252
Kekulé, August 329
kelpie 111
Kemet/Kumat 80
Kentucky 104
keratin 118, 132, 168
Kerberos/Cerberus 20
Kevin, Saint 246
Khafre 367
Khepri 313
Khnum 78
Khomenei, Ayatollah 255
Kiffian culture 124
K'ilin 358-359
Kilkenny cat *see* cat
Kimat 19
King Arthur *see* Arthur
King James (Authorized) Bible *see* Bible
King Kong *see* gorilla
The King of the Cats 43
King of the Jungle 47
kingdom 9
kingfisher 229-231, 251, 386
Kinsella, Thomas 68
Kintu 305
Kipling, Rudyard 25, 61
The Kitáb-i-Íqán 122, 402
Kitsune 37
Kivalliq 94
Kiwaian 132
Kiyohime 355
Ko Pala 286
koala 171
Koeda /Kuda/Sembrani 109
Kohyangwuti/Spider Grandmother 317
Komodo dragon *see* lizard
Kon-tiki *see* Con-tici
Kong Fuzi *see* Confucius
Kootenai 91
Korea 17, 95, 322
Korean mythology 37, 49, 50, 51, 97, 119, 206, 242, 254, 257, 316, 406
kosher 6
The Kraken 13, 362
The Krampus 377
krill 14
Krishna 100, 116-117, 242, 305, 367, 404
Kuan Yin/Guanyin/Guan Yin 74, 242-243

Kubera 61
Kublai Khan 159
Kujamaat 60
Kuwait 63
Kuzunoha 37
Kvasir 304
Kwakiutl 192

Lacerta 382
Laerath 83
Lagomorpha 11
Lakedaimonia 7
Lakota Sioux *see* Sioux
Lakshmana 143-144
Lakshmi 108, 256, 367, 404
lamb 78; Lamb of God 4, 79
Landseer, Edward 86
langsuyar 217
langur 143
Laocoön 332-333
Laos 140
Laotho 27
Lapp/Saami/Sámi 7, 93, 97, 154-155
Lascaux 46, 96
Latvia 92
Laughead, William B. 70
Lawrence, D.H. 261, 361
Lawrence, Saint 110
Lebanon 47
Leda 7, 222-223, 381
leech 325-326
Lei Kung 359
Leib-olmai 97
leippya 311
Lemminkainen 91
lemur 11
Lenape 164
Leo, Leo Minor 382-383
leopard 20, 46, **51-52**, 53, 54, 55, 98, 103, 124, 146, 325, 363, 395, 397
Leporidae 9
Lepus 383
Levi/Levites 69
Lewis, C.S. 80
Leyding 29
Lha-Mo 111
Li 18
Li Shizen 103
Liberia 148
Libya 110, 223, 395
The Life of Pi 100
Liguria 57
Linnaeus/Carl von Linné 11, 203, 231, 313, 323, 362
lion 9, 10, 18, 20, 27, 35-36, 37, 39, 41, 42, **46-48**, 50, 51, 53, 54, 59, 66, 74, 88, 98, 100, 116, 124, 137, 153, 158, 213, 263, 278, 343, 357, 359, 360, 361, 362, 363, 364, 365, 366, 367, 368, 372, 373, 378, 379, 382-383, 386, 396; guardian lions 48;

The Lion, the Witch and the Wardrobe 80; mountain lion *see* cougar
Little Bighorn, Battle of the 73
Little Red Riding Hood 27
Liu Hai/Liu Haichan 296-297; *see also* Gamma Sennin
Liu Heng 103
Livingstone, David 126
lizard 14, 17, 226, 297-298, **342-343**, 345, 352, 360, 369, 382; Komodo dragon 342
llama 7, 36, **122-123**, 396
Lleu Llaw Gyffes 216
Llyn Lliw 271
Llywelyn 24
lobster 14, 396
Loch Ericht 86
Lohengrin 222
Loki 82, 176, 198, 271, 304, 308-309, 337, 349, 352, 389, 406
London Zoo 102
Lopamudra 367-368
Lord of the Flies 130, 279, 289, 308
The Lord of the Rings 113, 177
Louernius 36
Loups *see* Skidi/Skiri Federation
Lourdes 97
Lucifer 57, 82; *see also* Satan
Lud 113
Lugaid 86
Lugh 68, 200, 402
Lukaon/Lycaon 27-28
Luke 48, 264, 378, 403
Lungu 60
Luperca/Lupercal/*Lupercalia* 28
Lupus 383
Lusifee 57
Luxembourg 130
Luxor 64
Lycaeus *see* Zeus Lycaeus
lycanthrope 25
Lydney Park 23
Lyncus 57
lynx 11, 41, 52, **56-58**, 383, 396
Lynx (constellation) 383

Mabinogi/Mabinogion 21, 128, 216, 396
Mabon ap Modron 270-271
Mac Cinnfhaelaidh/McKinley 68
Macedonia 57, 173
Macha 111
Maconaura 347
Madderakka 94
Madhava 305
Maeve *see* Medb
Mafdet 47
Magia Naturalis 58
Magnesia 109
Magoroku 316-317
magpie *see* jay

The Mahabharata 100, 108, 136, 143, 330, 367, 396, 404
Mahadeve *see* Kali
Mahakali *see* Kali
Mahmud *see* elephant
Maidu 31
Makara 358
Malacca *see* Princess of Malacca
Malacostraca/crabs 13-14, 285-287, 396
Malawi 147, 343
Malaya/Malaysia 49, 50, 194
Malayan mythology 49, 50, 51, 90, 109, 145, 168, 175, 193, 194-195, 217, 231, 286, 330
Mallochio 17
Mammalia/mammals 9, 12
mammoth 1, 72
A Man Called Horse 72
Manabozho 152-153
Manabush 284
Managarm 28-29
manatee 194-195
Maneki-Neko 41
The Manticore 373
Maori 7, 186-187, 282, 406
Marathi 60
Mari Lwyd 111
Marindi 17, 342
Mark 48, 378
marmot 162
Mars 28, 224, 239, 384, 407; *see also* Ares
marsupial 171
Martel, Yann 100
Marut 74
Marvel 105
Mashenomak 284
Masr/Mesr/Misr 80
Massey, Gerald 211
Matchi-Manitou 58
Math, Son of Mathonwy 216
Matthew 48, 264, 378, 403
Maui 281-282
Maya (mother of Buddha) 138, 140
Mayan (Mesoamerican) mythology 19, 53, 150, 166-167, 336, 340
Mayauel 158-159
McKinley *see* Mac Cinnfhaelaidh
mead 83, 303, 304, 306
Mecca 108, 121, 140, 255
Medb/Maeve 68, 161
medicine (healing)/folk medicine 90, 100, 103, 118, 163, 195, 227, 239, 291, 299-300, 320, 325-326, 333, 341, 371, 383
medicine (magical or spiritual power)/medicine-man/medicine-woman 72, 73, 152-153, 163-164, 182, 193, 216, 257, 258, 272, 320, 334, 340, 365, 388

Medina 121
Medusa 80, 109, 360, 370, 374; *see also* Gorgon
Meeko 105
Melanippe 109
Meleager 129
Melissa 81
Melville, Herman 195, 382
The Men Who Stare at Goats 83
menet 64
Menkar 388
Menominee 58, 284
Mergini 6
mermaids/mermen 374-376
mescaline 6
Mesoamerican *see* Central America
Mesopotamia 21, 49, 61, 63, 66, 114, 352, 380, 394
Messiaen, Olivier 5, 206
Metamorphoses/Ovid 28, 57, 129, 174, 209, 265, 315, 359, 364, 371, 396, 404
Mexico 31, 52-53, 71, 151, 166, 194, 257, 258, 261, 335
Mi-Ki 41
Miami 58
Miao 18
Michabo 152
Michigan 101, 284
Michtom, Morris 102
Mictlantecuhtli and Mictlantecihuatl 217
Middle East 32, 47, 60, 61, 66, 120, 133, 226, 352, 391
Midewiwin 152-153
Mi'kmaq 93
Milne, A.A. 101
Milton, John 66
Minerva 74, 80, 216, 332, 407; *see also* Athena
Ming 103, 242, 356
The Minotaur 316, 370
Moan 19
Moby Dick 195, 382
Moche/Mochica culture 53, 56, 123, 237
Mohawk 26, 164, 176
Mohegan 164, 187
Mollusca/molluscs 14
Moloch 372
Mongolia/Mongolian folklore/mythology 92, 94, 111, 113, 218-219
mongoose 60-61, 360, 395
monkey 41, 51, 90, **142-145**, 148, 149, 150, 336, 356, 359, 361, 364, 367, 379, 393, 395, 398, 399, 404; Beelzebub 150; howler 150; *The Monkey's Paw* 145; three wise monkeys 144-145
Monoceros 383
Montespan, Madame de 67

Montezuma 31
moon bear *see* black bear
moose 90, **91-93**, 391
Morfran *see* crow
Morrígan 7, 68, 200
Moses 4, 69, 228, 278, 339, 406
mosquito 309-310
Mother Carey's chicken *see* petrel
Motu Nui 235-236
Mount Olympus 109
Mount Sinai 69, 339
mountain lion *see* cougar **mouse** 11, 40, 42-43, 61, 137, **156-159**, 173, 174, 396; field 157-159; house 156-157; *The Town Mouse and Country Mouse* 157
Mozart, Wolfgang 26
Mu-monto 36
Muhammad 41, 108, 121-122, 140, 255, 319, 372, 373, 402, 405
mule *see* ass
Musca 383
Muse 109
Mustelidae/mustelids 60, 173-177
Mut 64
Muthappan 19
Mvuba 125
Mycenae 78
myotonia congenita 83
Myrmidon 7, 315, 396

Nabal 78-79
Nag/Naga/Nagaina 61, 330; *see also* snake
Nahuatl *see* Aztec
Najara 30
Nakhoda Ragam 50
Nakota Sioux *see* Sioux
Nambi 305
naming animals 10-11
Nanvut 94
Naples 125
Naraka 21
Nareau 318
narwhal 70, **193-194**
Nasu 21
National Wildlife Federation 105
Native American/American Indian mythology/religion/culture 2, 7, 31-32, 72-73, 91, 101-102, 104, 105, 152, 163-164, 181, 187, 192, 195, 213, 249, 250, 254, 261, 271, 287-288, 334-335, 340, 365, 388, 389, 400, 401, 404; Plains Indians 71-72; *see also* Abenaki; Algonquin; Apache; Athebaskan; Aztec; Blackfoot; Cayuga; Cherokee; Chibcha; Chinook; Chukchi; Chumash; Cree; Hopi; Hualapai/Walapai; Illini; Inca; Inuit; Iroquois; Kootenai; Kwakiutl; Lenape; Maya;

Menominee; Miami; Mi'kmaq; Moche; Mohawk; Mohegan; Navaho; Nisqually; Nootka; Oglala; Ojibwe; Olmec; Oneida; Onondaga; Ottawa; Pawnee; Penobscot; Pequot; Piikani; Potawatomi; Ptuksit; Pueblo; Seneca; Shawnee; Sioux; Squamish; Tlingit; Tohono O'odham; Tsawwassen; Tuscarora; Ute; Wabanaki; Wampanoag; Warau; Zuñi
Natsilane 182
The Natural History of Selborne 203
Naturalis Historia 75
Navaho 31, 101, 307, 399, 404
Nazis 137
Neanderthal 96
Nebuchadnezzar 48
Nekhebet 218
Nemequene 53
Nenet 99
Nepal 102, 136, 138
Nettleton Shrub 23
New Guinea 132, 169, 272, 282, 345
New Mexico 104, 213
New Zealand 7, 89, 90, 133, 159, 181, 186, 189, 190, 244, 281-282, 306, 322, 338, 406
newt 14, 297, **298-300**, 342, 396
Newton, Isaac 107
Nganasan 6
Ngariman 30
Níðhöggr 161, 355
Niflheim 21
Niger 75, 168
Nigeria 17, 168, 210, 342, 343
nightingale 5, 249, **250-252**, 396; *Ode to a Nightingale* 251-252
Nile, River 39, 40, 64, 76, 211, 344
Nile virus 309
Nim Chimpsky *see* chimpanzee
nine-tailed fox *see* fox
Ninisina/Nintinugga 21
Ninkillim 61
Nisqually 287
Nivkh 97
Noah 263-264
Nodens 23
Nootka 181
Nordic/Norse pantheon/mythology 2, 7, 19, 21, 28, 39, 41, 42, 57, 58, 62, 69, 82-83, 88, 91, 93, 107, 113, 130, 161, 176, 182, 193, 198, 199, 200-201, 225, 236, 238, 247, 248, 268, 271, 304, 308, 309, 316, 337, 349-350, 354, 355, 369, 387, 392, 397, 398, 406
North America *see* America

Norway 92, 93, 188, 281
Nótt 113
Nuadu Argat Lámh 23
Nuga 345
Numitor 28
Nut 224

'Obby 'Oss 111
Obumo 210
O'Caharney/O'Kearney 36
Ocru Male 17
octopus 7, 13, 318, 362, 393
Ode to a Nightingale see nightingale
Odin/Woden/Wotan 24, 28-29, 42, 69, 161, 199, 200, 369, 406
Odysseus/*The Odyssey* 20, 66, 190
Oeneus, King 129
Oestre 153
Ogham/Ogma/Ogmios 253-254
Oglala 72, 317-318
Ogun Onire 17
Ohnuki-Tierney, Emiko 144
Oimelc/Oimelg *see* Imbolc
Ojibwe 56, 58, 91, 152, 162, 334
Okami 144, 407
okapi 125-126
Oken, Lorenz 148
Olmec 53
Olwen 128
Olympian gods 1, 218
Olympic Peninsula 295
onager *see* ass
Oneida 26, 334
O'Neill, Eugene 78
Onondaga 26, 334
Ophiucus 383
opossum 171
Opus 109
oracular animals 5-6, 161, 162, 199, 215, 244, 245, 263
orangutan 145-146, 147, 148, 398
orca 182, 185, 189, **191-192**, 397
order (taxonomy) 9
Oresteia 80
Orinoco Basin 6
Orkney 180
Orpheus 331
Orthus 21
Oscines 5
Osiris 33, 74, 78, 91, 153, 211, 227, 313, 319-320, 367, 403
Otshirvani 349
Ottawa (people) 58
otter 132, 170, 173, **175-177**, 296, 396
Oubaste *see* Bastet
Ouroboros 329
Ovid *see* Metamorphoses
owl 12, 19, 33, 211-212, 214, **215-217**, 229, 234, 245, 248, 260, 399; screech 216-217

ox/oxen 48, **62-73**; *see also* bull; cattle; cow

Pa-Hsien 117
Padstow 111
Paikea 186-187
Pak Belang 50
Pakistan 120
Palatine Hill 28
Palden Lhamo 117
Pan/Faunus/Silvanus 80, 148, 368
Panar 52
The Panchatantra 116
panda 101, **102-103**, 104, 179, 391; Quinling 102; red 102
pangolin 168-169
Pangur Bán 42-43
Panhu 18
panther 27, 42, 51, **53-55**, 58, 395, 396, 397; *see also* jaguar; leopard
Panthera 9, 46, 49
Panthera leo see lion
Panthera tigris see tiger
Paora 6
Paracelsus 298
Paradise Lost 66
Paraguay 52
Parassinikkiadavu 19
Pariacaca 36, 212
parrot/parrakeet 5, 59, 256, 342-343
Parsees 21, 398
Parthenon 216
Parvati *see* Kali
Pasht *see* Bastet
passerines *see* birds
patera 111
Pavati 137
Pavo 383
Pawang Pukat 193
Pawnee 26, 31, 91, 164
peace pipe *see* channúnpa
peacock 137, 205, **241-243**, 372, 373, 383, 388, 397; peafowl 241; peahen 242, 397
Peacock (star name) 388
Pegasus 107, 109, 357, 359, 370, 382, 383
Pegasus (constellation) 383
Pelasgus 27, 109
Pele 277
Peleiades of Dodona 263
Peleus 129
pelican 232, **237**, 251
Pelorus Jack 190-191
Penelope 20
Peneus, River 65
Penobscot 187
pentagram 82
Pentheus 129-130
Pequot 187
perissodactyl 106, 117, 119, 397

periwinkle/winkle 14, 321, 322
Perrault, Charles 27
Perseus 7, 109, 370
Persia/Persian 21, 32, 51, 60, 64, 79, 98, 107, 109, 124, 134, 211, 218, 241, 242, 334, 357, 369, 373, 388, 389, 393, 394, 398, 401, 408
Peru 14, 36, 52, 53, 56, 122, 123, 212, 237, 363, 396
Peter, Saint 234, 239
petrel/stormy petrel 234-235, 398; Mother Carey's chicken 234
peyote 6
Phaedra 110
Phaethon 223
pharaoh 46, 54, 63-64, 211, 338, 367; *see also* Amenhotep; Hatshepsut; Khafre
Philip of Macedon 110
Philippines 19, 71, 194, 392
Philomela 251, 260; *see also* Aëdon
Phoenicia 66, 135, 275, 361
Phoenix (constellation) 383
phoenix/firebird 336, 360-361, 383
phylum 9
Pi-beseth *see* Bubastis
Picus 265
The Pied Piper of Hamelin 160
pig/hog 27, 61, 65, 119, **127-128**, **130-133**, 164, 192, 195, 270, 308, 361, 379, 399; Three Little Pigs 27; *see also* boar
pigeon *see* dove
Piikani 72
pika 11
pike 282-283
Pikoi 160
Pisces 383
Piscis Austrinus 383-384
Pithia 7
Plains Indians *see* Native Americans
platypus 12, 169, **170**, 397
Pliny the Elder 57, 75, 93, 191, 231, 254, 291, 298, 326, 339, 360, 361, 375, 407
Plutarch 110, 313
Pochantas 105
Poetic Edda 28, 130, 201, 271, 354, 398
Pogo 105
Pohjola, Maiden of 91
polecat *see* ferret
polydactyl 44
Polydeuces/Pollux 129, 222
Polytechnos 251
Pompeii 125
Pongo 145
porcupine 164
Porifera/sponges

porpoise 75, 185, 188, **192-193**, 397
Portia Stabia 125
Poseidon 28, 109, 110, 189, 190, 268, 275, 286, 364, 370, 372, 404
Potawatomi 152
potlatch 181-182
Powhatan 104
Prasutagus 153
Priam 28, 330
Priapus 115
Prima Hyadum 388
Princess of Malacca 50
Procyon 104, 381, 388; star name 388
Prometheus 218, 308
Prose Edda 28, 29, 83, 304, 309, 398
Proteus 109
Proto-Indo-European 20, 25, 34, 56, 71, 106, 127, 175, 185, 208, 220, 228, 285, 294, 306, 307, 315, 328
Prydain 112
psychopomp 24, 33, 398
Ptah of Memphis 63
Ptesánwin 73
Ptuksit 25
Pueblo 250, 258, 314
pulche 158-159
Pulimau Harimau 50
puma *see* cougar
pussy willow 41
Pwyll Prince of Dyfed 21-22
Pyesnya o Burevestnikye 234-235
Pygmy 126
Pyrenees 97
python 341-342

Les Quatre Fils Aymon 112
Quechua 55, 122, 217
The Questing Beast 363
Quetzalcoatl 335-336
Qiqiao/Qixi Festival 205-206
quipu 123
Quiracus, Saint 22-23
The Qur'an 4, 121-122, 140, 186, 255, 260, 278, 361, 373, 389, 398, 399, 405

Ra 64, 78
rabbit 9, 11, 38, 45, 151, 153, **154-155**, 174, 379, 395; Br'er Rabbit 155
Rabi'a al-'Adawiya 122
raccoon 104-105, 179, 398; Rackety Coon Chile 105
Ragnarök 21, 28-29, 352, 355
Rakshasas 367
ram 1, 77-78, 81, 137; *see also* sheep
Rama 100, 116, 143-144, 161, 367, 398, 404

The Ramayana 143-144, 161, 367, 398, 404
Ranger Rick 105
raptors *see* birds
Rastafarianism 48
rat 11, **159-160**, 356, 379, 396; Ratatoskr 161
rattlesnake 339-341; handling 341
raven 4, 5, 68, 161, 183, 187, 199, **200-201**, 202, 214, 246, 260, 263, 264, 294, 369, 381, 393; *see also* crow
Ravgga 7
ray 13
red panda *see* panda
Redcoat, Big and Little 65
reindeer *see* caribou
relative ceremony *see* Hunkpapi
Reptilia/reptiles 14
Revelation, The Book of 48, 79, 107-108
Reynard the fox *see* fox
Rhea Silvia 28
Rhiannon 107, 111, 245, 402
rhinoceros 117-118, 119, 363
Rhodes 65, 89
The Rig-Veda 74, 364
Rigil Kentaurus 389
Rikki-Tikki-Tavi 61
Rime of the Ancient Mariner 233
roach 164
roadrunner 257-258, 395
Robert the Bruce, King 318-319
robin 5, 244, **246-248**, 249, 270, 394, 399; Cock Robin 247-248
Rocket Raccoon 105
Rodentia/rodents 11
Roman mythology/pantheon *see* classical Roman mythology/pantheon
Romania 57, 167, 226
Romany 133
Romulus and Remus 28
rook 5, 199-200, **201-202**, 248, 393; *see also* crow
Roosevelt, President Theodore (Teddy) 18, 102
Roskova 82
Rowling, J.K. 360, 371, 377
Rudraprayag 52
Rumi 211-212
ruminant 62, 77, 85, 89, 398
runes 5
Rushdie, Salman 255
Russia 92, 93, 95, 97, 188, 234-235, 240, 256, 282, 284, 361

Saami/Sámi *see* Lapp
Saan/San 76
Saehrimnir 130
sag-did 21, 398
Sahara/sub-Sahara 124, 226, 250, 259

Sakhalin 97
salamander 14, **297-298**, 396
Saleh 121-122
salmon 13, 87, 95, 209, 213, 215, 245, **269-272**, 282, 295, 304, 391, 397
Samhain 67, 221
Samoyed 6
samudra manthana 108
San Gun 51
Sanskrit 54, 136, 137, 143, 242, 279, 291, 330, 378-379, 389, 391, 392, 394, 395, 396, 397, 398, 402
Santa Claus 94
Sarakka 94
Saranyu 108
Sarasuati 86
Sarcopterygii/lobe-finned fishes 13
Sarutahiko 144, 407
Satan 57, 82, 246, 255, 260, 308, 368; *The Satanic Verses* 255; *see also* Lucifer
Saturnalia 116
satyr 7, 80
Saudi Arabia 63, 122, 394
Saul, King 78, 319
sawfish 13
Saxe, John Godfrey 138-139
Saxon/Saxons/Anglo-Saxon 97, 112, 127, 153, 201, 306, 374
Saxony 240
scallop **289-290**; *coquilles St. Jacques* 290
scapegoat 82
scarab *see* beetle
Sceolang 23
Schwartz-Rheindorf, Convent of 284
Scoresby-Routledge, Katherine 235
scorpion/Scorpio/Scorpius 13, 316, **319-320**, 369, 372, 373, 378, 379, 384, 386, 392
Scorpius (constellation) 384
Scotland/Scottish folklore/mythology 36, 40, 45, 67, 86, 111, 112, 114, 157, 180, 183, 215, 221, 236, 269, 270, 275, 283, 295, 314, 318-319, 322, 323-324, 353, 358, 375-376
Scylla and Charybdis 359
Scythia 57
sea birds *see* birds
sea horse **274-275**; *see also* hippocampus
sea lion 10, **181-182**, 191
seal 10, 98, 154, **179-181**, 191, 236, 397; selkie 180-181
Sebek 345
The Secret of Roan Innish 181
Sedna 183, 236
seïstron see sistrum

sekhem see sistrum
Sekhmet 39, 47
selkie *see* seal
Selkups 6
Semele 81
Seneca (people) 26, 176, 334
Senegal 60
Serapeum 63
Serket 320
Serpens 384
serpent *see* snake
Set 74, 75, 115, 211, 227, 313, 319-320, 344, 403
Setanta *see* Cú Chúlainn
Seventh-Day Adventists 131
Shadowfax 113
Shaka Zulu *see* Zulu
Shakespeare, William 23, 26, 89
Shakti/*shakti* 33, 143
shaman 1, 6, 7, 53, 201, 294, 295, 296, 399
shape-shifting 1, 22, 30, 51, 65, 68, 75, 78, 86, 97, 98, 99, 112, 117, 132, 151, 154, 167, 174, 183, 199, 200, 213, 216, 221-222, 229, 270, 316, 318, 330, 332, 336, 387
Shapiro, Gary L. 146
shark 7, 13, 236, 273, **276-277**, 284, 393
Shawnee 58, 90, 340
She (people) 18
sheep 7, 12, 17, 26, 27, 35, 65, 73, **77-79**, 80, 82, 123, 127, 131, 264, 324, 363, 393
Shetland 180
Shinto 143, 144, 336-337, 405, 407
Shiva/Siva 19, 33, 50, 74, 81-82, 137, 286, 330, 364, 367, 404
shrimp 14, 396
Shu 78, 224, 313
Shulman 19
Siant, The Blue Men of 375-376
Siberia/Siberian mythology 6, 19, 36, 49, 92, 93, 99, 113, 191-192, 349, 354, 399
Sichuan 18, 103
Sicily 65, 140, 190, 240, 359
sídh/sídhe 67, 222, 399
Sido/Hido/Iko 132
Siguniang 103
Sikh/Sikhism 144, 394, 398, 407
silkworm 13
Silvanus *see* Pan
Sinai *see* Mount Sinai
Sioux Nation: Hunkpapa Lakota 73; Sioux, Dakota 72-73, 226; Sioux, Lakota 9, 72-73, 91, 105, 226; Sioux, Nakota 72-73 226
Sirius 107, 109, 368, 380, 384, 387, 388, 389; star name 389
sistrum/sekhem/seïstron 64, 339, 399
Sita 100, 143-144, 161, 367, 398

Sitting Bull 73
skate 13
Skennenrahawi 176
Skidi/Skiri Federation 26
Skinfaxi 113
Sköll 29
Slav 97
Sleeping Bear Dunes National Lakeshore 101
Slieve nam Bán 87
Slovenia 83
slug 14, 134, **321-323**, 365, 395
snail 14, 245, 288, **321-323**, 365, 395
snake/serpent 14, 19-20, 30, 33, 36, 44, 61, 65, 78, 79, 89, 117, 137, 139, 169, 189, 213-214, 216, 226, 239, 242, 261, 323, **328-342**, 352, 356, 357, 359, 360, 362, 369, 370, 378, 379, 381, 382, 383, 397, 398; The Midgard Serpent 337; ram-headed serpent 78; the serpent's egg *see* adder
Solobong Yubin 113
Solomon 66
Soma 74
Sonargöltr 130
Song of the Sea 181
South Africa 52, 76, 138, 348, 398
South America 52, 55, 89, 119, 123, 128, 167, 181, 188, 194, 217, 237, 261, 295, 340, 347, 349, 384, 404
South Dakota 72
species 9
The Sphinx 366-367
spider 2, 4, 13, 152, 287, 307, **315-319**, 392; Spider Grandmother *see* Kohyangwuti
spiny anteater *see* echidna
Squamish 271-272
squid 13, 232, 362, 393
squirrel 38, **160-161**, 162, 398
Sri Lanka 52, 136, 143, 161, 367
Stanley, Henry Morton 126
stink eye 17-18
Stoker, Bram 167
stone of power *see* frog
stork **225-227**, 260, 393
storm/stormy petrel *see* petrel
sturgeon **283-284**
Sturluson, Snorri 28, 406
Sumatra 145, 286, 398
Sumeria 63, 263, 357
sun dance ritual/*Wiwanyag Wachipi* 72-73
Surabhi 65
surah 399
Surya 107, 108, 143
Svartálfaheimr 29
Svastika/swastika 137
swan 5, 7, 12, **220-223**, 224, 284, 369, 381, 382, 385, 391, 394

sweat lodge ceremony see *Inipi*
Sweden 92, 93, 98, 244, 374
Swinburne, Algernon Charles 129
Switzerland 96, 97
Syria 64, 263, 278, 375

Tadaklan/Kadaklan 19
Taghairm nan Cath 40
Taimur herd see caribou
Táin Bó Cúailnge 67, 68
Táin Bó Flidhais 67
Taiwan 102, 274
Taliesin 132, 199, 270
Talmud 121, 298, 337, 373, 406
Tamamo no Maye 37
Tamil Nadu 288
Tanuki Bozo 178
Tanzania 6, 126, 138, 342
Taoism 117, 149-150, 310-311, 402
Tapa Wanka Yap/ceremony of throwing the ball 73
tapir 118-119
Tara 68-69
tarbhfess 68-69
Tarrotarro 342
Tarvostrigaranus 254
Tasmanian devil 171
Tasmanian wolf see wolf
Taurt/Taweret/Thoueris 76
Taurus 384
Taweret see Taurt
taxon/taxonomy 9-14; wastebasket taxon 73
Tefnut 47, 313
Telamon 129
Telemachus 190
Telipinu 303
The Ten Commandments 69
Tennessee 83, 341
Teotuihacan 31
Tereus 251
terrapin see turtle
Texas 104
Tezcatlipoca 53
Thailand 136, 140, 144
Thamud 121-122
Thathanka Iyotake see Sitting Bull
Thea 109
Thebes 110, 129, 367
Theodoric the Great 24
Theophrastus 57
Theseus 110, 129, 316, 370
Thialfi 82
Thomas, Doubting 116
Thor 19, 41, 82, 247, 271, 283, 337, 406
Thorkook 172
Thoth 47, 64, 142, 211, 227-228, 320, 403
Thoueris see Taurt
Thrace 109, 251, 369
three wise monkeys see monkey

Thrinicia 66
Through the Looking Glass 183
Thviti 29
Tiberinus 28
Tibet/Tibetan folklore/mythology 18, 27, 61, 99-100, 102, 117, 122, 131, 218-219, 242, 244, 279, 377, 399, 402, 403
Tierra del Fuego 16
tiger 9, 10, **48-51**, 52, 53, 146, 356, 361, 373, 379, 397; white tiger 49-50
Tigris, River 49, 368
timber wolf see wolf
tingo 29
Tinguian Islands 19
Tír na'n Óg 220-221
Tiresias 331
Tishtrya 107, 109
Titans 1, 65, 115, 218, 308, 371
Tlingit 182, 192
toad see frog
Toba, Emperor 37
tobacco 6, 164, 187, 192, 261
Tohono O'odham 31
Tolkein, J.R.R. 113, 177, 354
Toliman 389
Torah 115, 406
Torongoi 19-20
Torslunda 98
tortoise see turtle
Tory Island 68
totem animals 4, 7, 23, 25, 26, 45, 47, 53, 74, 85, 97, 115, 161, 182, 192, 216, 249, 295, 317, 321, 333, 338, 353, 384
Tower of London 200
trafficking animals 168-169
tree-alphabet see Beth Luis-Nion
Trinity 264, 403
Triptolemus 57
troll cat see cat
Troy 28
Ts'angs-pa Dkar-po 111
Tsawwassen 287
Tskili 217
Tsonis, Panagiotis 300
Tuatha Dé Danann 68
Tucana 384
Tumnus 80
tuna 272-273, 399; by-catch (tuna, dolphin) 272-273
Tuna-Roa 281-282
Tupi 52, 55, 118, 342
Tuposkwa 250
Turen 23
Turkey 63, 354
turtle/tortoise/terrapin 14, 137, 273, **348-350**, 367, 386, 398, 399
turtledove see dove
Tuscarora 105, 334
Tutchone 94

tuxedo 25
Twain, Mark 151
Two-Toed Tom 346
Twrch Trwyth 128
Typhon 115
Tyr 21, 29

Ua Leochann/*An Sionnach* 36
Uchchaihshravas 107, 108
Uffington 107
Uganda 125, 126, 305, 397; Buganda people 305
Uguku 217
Ukko 283
Uksakka 94
Ukuhi 335
Úlfheðnar 98
Ulrich, Saint 225
Ulster 67, 68
Ulster Cycle 68
Uncle Remus: His Songs and His Sayings 37, 155
Underworld 20, 21-22, 24, 56, 64, 91, 166, 191, 254, 303, 315, 330, 331, 338, 340, 392
Ungnyeo 97
ungulate 62, 73, 117, 119, 120, 399
unicorn 358
United States of America see America
University of Cincinatti 125
Unukalhai 389
uraeus 78, 338, 345, 399
Urcuchillay 7, 123
Ursa Major, Ursa Minor 96, 380, 384-385
Uruk 63
Ushas 108
Ute 31
Uther Pendragon 111-112

Vainamoinen 153-154
Vaishravana 61
Vaivasvata 268
Vajravarahi/Vajrayogini 131
Valdemar Atterdag 24
Valhalla 83, 130, 369
Valkyrjr/Valkyries 369
Ve 69
Vega 389
Venezuela 6
Venice 84
venison 86, 89
Venus 40, 42, 58, 113, 263, 268, 295, 383, 407
Vesuvius 125
Vexillum 79
Victoria, Queen 18
vicuña 123
Vietnam/Vietnamese 17, 118, 164, 169, 242, 273, 322, 385
Viking 98, 324
Vili 69
viper see adder

Viracocha *see* Con-tici
Virgil 28, 80, 305, 332, 359, 368, 371, 407
Vishnu 19, 88, 107, 116-117, 256, 268, 278, 305, 330, 367, 404
vision quest ritual/*Hanblecheyapi* 72-73, 249
Vitus, Saint 239-240
Vivaswat 108
Viverroidea/Viverrids 60
Volans 385
von Linné, Carl *see* Linnaeus
von Middendorff, Alexander 95
voodoo 240, 376
Vortigern 111-112
The Voyage of Maelduin 41
Vulpecula 385
vulture/condor 212, 214, **217-219**, 260, 338, 343, 368, 389, 393

Wabanaki 57
Wachaga 138
Wagner, Richard 176-177, 222, 354, 369
Wakan Tanka 73
Walapai *see* Hualapai
Wales 111
wallaby *see* kangaroo
wallaroo *see* kangaroo
walrus 10, 179, **182-184**, 191, 397
Wampanoag 187
wampum 287-288
Warau 295
wasp 303, **306-307**, 392
wastebasket taxon *see* taxon
water dragon *see* dragon
weasel 45, 60, **173-174**, 179, 229, 360, 396
Wenen/Wenenut 153
werehyena 60
weretiger 51
werewolf 8, 25, 51, 376
whale 12, 70, 75, 182, 183, **185-188**, 192, 193, 194, 195, 236, 284, 380, 388, 392, 393, 397, 400; *The Whale Rider* 186-187
whelk 14, 287, 321, **322-323**, 339

whistle-pig *see* marmot
White, Gilbert 203
White Buffalo Calf Woman *see* bison
white tiger *see* tiger
Wild Hunt 23-24
wildcat *see* cat
winkle *see* periwinkle
Winnie-the-Pooh 102
A Winter's Tale 26
Wisht Hounds 24
Wiwanyag Wachipi see sun dance ritual
Woden/Wotan *see* Odin
wolf 7, 16, 24, **25-29**, 30, 31, 32, 36, 68, 72, 77, 98, 152, 229, 302, 337, 357, 361, 374, 383, 389, 392, 393, 396; little wolf *see* coyote; prairie wolf *see* coyote; in sheep's clothing 27; Tasmanian wolf 30; *see also Úlfheðnar;* werewolf
Wolf Pawnee *see* Skidi/Skiri Federation
Wolfgang, Bishop 225
Wollonqua 329
womanhood ceremony/*Ishnata Awicalowan* 73
wombat 171
woodchuck *see* marmot
woodlice 14
woodpecker 242, **264-265**, 397; Woody Woodpecker 265
worigal 29
World Wildlife Fund 102
worm 12, 20, 63, 167, 281, **323-325**, 328, 365, 391, 392
Wowta 295
wren 213, **248-250**, 399; hunting the 249-250
Wulfilaich/Wolfroy, Saint 130

Xbalanqúe 166
Xerxes 107
Xī Fāng Bái Hǔ 50

Yahweh 66, 406; *see also* Jehovah

Yama 21
Yamaotoko 100
Yami 274
Yao 18
Yeats, William Butler 223
The Yellow Book of Lecan 45
Yeruba/Yoruba 17, 75
yeti *see* abominable snowman
Yggdrasill 88, 161, 355
Yi 155
Ymir 69
Yom Kippur 241
Yoruba *see* Yeruba
Ysbaddaden Pencawr 128
Ysgithyrwyn 128
Yuan 150
Yukon 55, 94
Yule Lads *see* Jólasveinarnir
Yum Cimil 19
Yupik 99

Zagazig 39
Zambia 60, 306
Zethos 7
Zeus 5, 7, 19, 28, 65-66, 81, 109, 115, 129, 174, 213, 218, 222, 223, 230, 242, 251, 256, 263, 265, 305, 308, 315, 331, 332, 333, 362, 364, 369, 371, 381, 384, 386, 387, 404; Zeus Lycaeus 28; Zeus Melissaios 305; *see also* Jupiter
Zhuang Zhou 310-311
Zhuge/Chu-ko Liang/Komei 262-263
Zhurong/ Ch'ih Ti/Chu Jung 49
Zimbabwe 118
Zindendorf, Count Nikolaus 340
zodiac 18; Chinese 18, 81, 379; Hindu 378-379, 380; Persian 109
Zoroastrianism 21, 63, 64-65, 107, 109, 134, 198, 218, 334, 389, 395, 398, 408
Zulu 75, 138, 341-342; Shaka Zulu 138
Zuñi 213

www.ingramcontent.com/pod-product-compliance
Ingram Content Group UK Ltd.
Pitfield, Milton Keynes, MK11 3LW, UK
UKHW051851210426
5322IPUK00025B/661